BLACKNESS IN LATIN AMERICA
AND THE CARIBBEAN

Social Dynamics and Cultural Transformations

VOLUME II
Eastern South America
and the Caribbean

Compiled, edited, and with a general introduction by
Arlene Torres and Norman E. Whitten, Jr.

INDIANA UNIVERSITY PRESS
Bloomington and Indianapolis

This book is a publication of
Indiana University Press
601 North Morton Street
Bloomington, Indiana 47404-3797 USA

www.indiana.edu/~iupress

Telephone orders 800-842-6796
Fax orders 812-855-7931
Orders by e-mail iuporder@indiana.edu

The paper used in this publication meets the minimum
requirements of American National Standard for Information
Sciences—Permanence of Paper for Printed Library
Materials, ANSI Z39.48-1984.

Manufactured in the United States of America

Library of Congress Cataloging-in-Publication Data

Blackness in Latin America and the Caribbean : social dynamics and
  cultural transformations / compiled, edited, and with a general
  introduction by Norman E. Whitten, Jr. and Arlene Torres.
      p.   cm. — (Blacks in the diaspora)
    Contents: v. 1. Central America and Northern and Western South
  America — v. 2. Eastern South America and the Caribbean.
    ISBN 0-253-33404-7 (v. 1 : cl : alk. paper). — ISBN 0-253-21193-X
  (v. 1 : pa : alk. paper). — ISBN 0-253-33406-3 (v. 2 : cl : alk.
  paper). — ISBN 0-253-21194-8 (v. 2 : pa : alk. paper)
    1. Blacks—Latin America—History. 2. Blacks—Caribbean Area—
  History. 3. Latin America—Race relations. 4. Caribbean Area—
  Race relations. 5. Blacks—Race identity. 6. Social change.
  7. Functionalism (Social sciences). I. Whitten, Norman E.
  II. Torres, Arlene. III. Series.
  F1419.N4B53 1998
  305.89608—dc21   97-44093
  1 2 3 4 5   03 02 01 00 99 98

CONTENTS

PREFACE

The *longue durée* involved in publication of this work has puzzled many of our colleagues, including those who anonymously reviewed various drafts in various stages or who tried to purchase the work over the past four years. Accordingly, we feel it necessary to give a history of the project leading to these two volumes and to explain the initial and eventual focus.

During the summer of 1990, Howard Doddson, chief of the Schomburg Center for Research in Black Culture at the New York Public Library, wrote to invite Norman Whitten to prepare an edited volume on the subject of comparative black settlements and community patterns. The compilation, with a significant introduction, was to be part of an ambitious and important series, the Schomburg Library of the Black Experience in the Western Hemisphere, 1492–1992. In August 1990, Whitten invited Arlene Torres to participate with him in this project. The two of us then asked Doddson to expand the project to two volumes; to limit the region covered to Central America, South America, and the Caribbean; and to allow us up to 100 pages for our introduction to each volume. We completed the project for the Schomburg Library series in early February 1991 on the schedule set by Schomburg.

By midwinter 1992, serious doubts were cast on the fate of the Schomburg series, which was to have numbered between thirty-five and sixty-five volumes. Because we wanted our volumes to appear in 1992, the year of the quincentennial celebration of the European conquest, we agreed to publish independently with Carlson, the publisher-designate of the Schomburg series. It was hoped that if a series did materialize, our tomes would be reincorporated therein.

In November 1993 we talked to Joan Catapano of Indiana University Press about publishing a paperback comprising selections from the larger work. Then, as it became increasingly apparent that the work would not appear with Carlson, Indiana University Press set to the process of anonymous peer review, followed by a marketing survey to see if the Press could pull the project out of the fire, so to speak, and publish the two volumes. In the fall of 1996 Indiana agreed to bring this work out.

Originally we were charged with pulling together previously published materials on comparative black settlements and community patterns in English, Spanish, French, and Portuguese. This we did. Because we were restricted to pre-published articles and chapters, we could not commission any articles or include articles in preparation but not yet accepted for publication. In the contract we signed with Indiana University Press, we agreed to select only publications in English or to provide translations but were free to select a limited number of new contributions to Afro–Latin American or Afro-Caribbean systems of community, culture, and communication.

The agreement with Indiana University Press allowed us to do what we originally wanted to do—to provide readers with a set of chapters that range from early groundbreaking pieces to exemplars of contemporary Afro-Americanist scholarship of the late 1990s. Selections such as those of Roy Simon Bryce-Laporte on Panama, Nina S. de Friedemann on Colombia, Madeline Barbara Léons on Bolivia, Florestan Fernandes on Brazil, B. Edward Pierce on Suriname, Leo A. Despres on Guyana, and M. G. Smith on Carriacou are heavily and, for the time, appropriately "social scientific" and analytical of plural systems of social relationships. Serious ethnography of complex social processes set in nation-state contexts of inclusion and exclusion—the hallmark of later "ethnicity studies"—are the strengths of these pieces, as is serious attention to kinship and family systems unfamiliar to anthropological and sociological specialists in this panhuman domain.

Such groundbreaking and enduring presentations are complemented by many "intermediate" pieces ranging from Virginia Kerns's on Belize through those by Michael Taussig on Colombia, Kathleen Klumpp and Norman Whitten on Ecuador, Lee Drummond on Guyana, Sally Price on Suriname, Douglas Midgett on Grenada, John Stewart on Trinidad, and Frank E. Manning on Bermuda. These essays represent an interesting and creative merging of social science rigor with humanistic skills; each is grounded both in the harsh realities of being black in plural systems and in the creative adjustments and accomplishments of actors in such systems. Blackness in these "middle" articles begins to emerge as a creative force as the authors tease out the symbolic dimensions of cultural phenomena, with careful attention to social relations, including gendered interaction and symbolism, community formations, and regional and national systems. In most of the latest contributions we find a definite swing into the cultural creativity of blackness together with metaphors and movements of cultural transformation and resistance by people forging anew their positions in dynamic local, regional, national, and global dimensions. In short, this work has benefited by the four "lost" years. We hope that its readers will appreciate the mix of older, middle, recent, and brand new that these two volumes provide.

The general introduction to these volumes, "To Forge the Future in the Fires of the Past: An Interpretive Essay on Racism, Domination, Resistance, and Liberation," was prepared in 1991. It was designed and written to provide a broad framework for our selection of articles and chapters in the two volumes. The introductory chapters designed specifically for volumes I and II set forth discursive accounts of the contents of the volumes within the framework established in the general introduction. Since we were forced by circumstances of length and style to eliminate several pieces originally selected, in the introductory chapters we indicate other works, especially in Spanish and French, which should be used, when possible, to supplement these volumes. Both introductory chapters are designed to pick up and in some instances elaborate on the themes of the general introduction. The reader may want to read all three as an extended essay on blackness in Latin America and the Caribbean.

In these three introductions we try to give breadth and depth to our subject matter by understanding "blackness" and "illumination" as together constituting a dynamic, international aesthetic pattern across space and through time. We also want to help readers to rethink some deeply held but illusory notions about Latin America and the Caribbean and about the subject of blackness there. To do this we chose an essay format for all of the introductions. By use of this format we draw attention to history and geography to show how the focus on blackness among human beings transcends the boundaries imposed through nearly 500 years of cultural transformations and across some of the least known topographical spaces for most North Americans and Europeans.

We seek to challenge readers to think more about the issues raised in the introductions and thereby to appreciate more thoroughly the strengths of the varied articles and chapters that are reprinted and the three printed here for the first time. We also take readers into quotidian and ritual life, and where possible we draw attention to cosmological features of cultural significance. To do so we weave in and out of meaning in vernacular and written Spanish, as do many of the authors, to allow readers to consider seriously the nature of speech, talk, discourse, writing, and all other systems of human communication as they condition humanity's view of humanity. Inasmuch as viewpoints are also conditioned by systems of domination and hegemony in active interaction with processes of resistance and creativity, we indicate something of the local, regional, national, and international situations affecting blackness and illumination.

During 1992–93, with the celebration of European conquest and of whiteness, a veritable deluge of publications emerged on imagery and imaginations and on histories and reinterpretations of the European New World of 1492 and the shattered yet enduring indigenous worlds of 1492–1992. We have been able to incorporate but a handful of these references into this work. We hope nonetheless that our endeavors will place something of a corrective on the polarized European–Indian theme and lead those not specializing in Afro-Americana to understand that within *la leyenda negra* of indigenous destruction and black slavery is the illumination of transformed Africanity in the Americas and the creativity of freedom seized. We seek to portray the image of blackness as something not bound to skin color or stereotypes of complexion.

The subject of blackness in the Americas was given short shrift during the celebrations and lamentations of 1992, and accordingly the literature presented here did not find its way into the references and discussions of that brief period. What we offer is a critical review of blackness in systems dominated by whiteness; we argue that such domination and polarization emerged in their powerful racist dimensions sometime before 1502 and that the issues we address and which are now being addressed by more and more scholars require the sustained attention recently given to Europeans and Native American systems of response to the European conquest and colonization of the Americas.

The year 1992 did witness an upswing of serious research and publication on the subject of these volumes, though nothing came forth compared to the foci on Europeans and "disappearing Indians." An important complement to these volumes is the slim but powerful publication of the North American Congress on Latin America, *The Black Americas 1492–1992*. Also, the editors of the *Encyclopedia of World Cultures* commissioned a few chapters on blackness in the Americas, including Venezuela, Colombia, Ecuador, Bolivia, and Brazil, for its volume on South America. Nonetheless, on the volume's thirteen maps of culture areas with 456 peoples of South America presented, the only black people listed are the Saramaka of Suriname. Not a single other African American culture, community, or ethnic group is mentioned in the legends or placed on the maps. *Negreado* is the Spanish term for this common phenomenon of leaving cultures of black Americans off maps and out of history. It is a phenomenon receiving considerable attention among peoples of color in Latin America.

A serious historic complement to our work is found in *Race, Discourse, and the Origin of the Americas*, published in 1995 by the Smithsonian Institution Press. Although the book was part of the Smithsonian's program to commemorate 1492 and the voyages of the Admiral of the Ocean Sea, and although it is rich in literature on African-European and African American experiences and histories, the foreword by Robert McCormick Adams, distinguished anthropologist and director of the Smithsonian Institution, fails to mention Africans or African Americans. Also in 1995 the Minority Rights Group in London brought forth *No Longer Invisible: Afro-Latin Americans Today*, with commissioned essays on all nation-states of Latin America. Reading this work, one is struck by the lack of attention in its chapters to contemporary people of African American descent, as well as the failure to comprehend self-liberation as a dramatic and enduring Afro-American enactment throughout the Americas.

As we complete our writing, we continue to review exciting papers on blackness in Latin American and Caribbean regions by scholars submitting their works to professional academic journals. We hope that our compilation and interpretation of materials in these volumes ignites even more attention to this critical area of African diaspora studies.

This endeavor could not have been carried out over the initial five-month period of selection, research, interpretation, and writing without significant support from the University of Illinois at Urbana-Champaign. The Research Board of this university provided assistance on two previous projects that established the foundation upon which this present project was conceptualized and carried to completion. The previous grants allowed Norman Whitten, with the support of two research assistants, Isabel Pérez and Diego Quiroga, to build a database on black, indigenous, and "mixed" people in northern South America and Central America vis-à-vis nationalist and ethnic-bloc formations and their motivating symbolic agencies. Arlene Torres also participated in this research, with the support of an Illinois Consortium for Educational Opportunity Fellowship.

In October 1990, the Department of Anthropology of the UIUC provided initial funding for copying materials. Subsequently, the Office of the Vice-Chancellor for Academic Affairs provided a shoestring grant for part-time research assistance in fall 1990 and for additional copying. We are grateful to both sources for the necessary funding.

The faculty and staff of the Afro-American Studies and Research Program at the UIUC provided valuable assistance, including reference materials, computer facilities, and technical support. Rosemary M. Stevenson and Vera Mitchell at the Afro-American and Africana Library enthusiastically furnished us with needed reference materials, particularly those pertaining to the life and work of the late Arthur Alfonso Schomburg.

Ingrid Offenbacher, a sophomore in the Campus Honors Program (in 1990), volunteered to work for us without pay as our first assistant. Soon thereafter we employed José Antonio Ruíz, a research assistant in Library Science; later, Jeffrey Vanderziel and Ricardo Herrera provided necessary technical support and assistance. As our work progressed, various colleagues submitted suggestions and recommendations for book selections or for our own reading, and we wish to thank each: Alice A. Deck, Virginia Kerns, Jill Leonard, Consuelo López Springfield, and Inga Treitler. We also thank an anonymous reviewer for Carlson Publishing, Inc., for many helpful suggestions on our introductory essay and several anonymous reviewers for Indiana University Press for valuable suggestions and for the moral encouragement to keep the project alive and to strive to publish the results.

Marvin A. Lewis helped this project in many ways over many years, and his comparative studies of Afro-Hispanic literature offer a parallel view to what we are attempting here in cultural anthropology and critical thought. In 1992, in excerpting a small part of the general introduction for publication in *The Black Americas 1492–1992*, the NACLA Report on the Americas, Mark Fried gave sustained and needed encouragement with regard to directions in analysis and presentation. As the project entered its penultimate phase in 1994, Harriet Stockanes demonstrated her remarkable talents in securing permissions from contributors. The last stage, from 1994 through January 1997, was set by Joan Catapano, with whose guidance and creative encouragement this project is now carried through to completion.

We greatly appreciate the critical readings by Pedro M. Hernández, Jill Leonard, Alejandro Lugo, Marvette Pérez, Diego Quiroga, Dorothea Scott (Sibby) Whitten,

Kevin A. Yelvington, and Marta Zambrano in the preparation of our introductions and the collegial support provided by each of them during various segments of research, writing, and editing.

Finally, we wish to express our deepest gratitude to internationally renowned Puerto Rican artist Arnaldo Roche Rabell for permission to reproduce his painting *Azabache*. In our view, *Azabache* embodies what we have tried to convey ethnographically, the power (*ase*) of blackness in the African diaspora.

Urbana, Illinois
January 1997

PART ONE

THE BLACK AMERICAS
AND THE AFRICAN DIASPORA
IN THE LATE TWENTIETH CENTURY

GENERAL INTRODUCTION

TO FORGE THE FUTURE IN
THE FIRES OF THE PAST

An Interpretive Essay on Racism, Domination, Resistance, and Liberation

Arlene Torres and Norman E. Whitten, Jr.

Soy de carbón
y mis pies zapatean por liberarse de la candela de una rumba
soy de carbón
y el fósforo del bombo enciende mi cintura.

I am of charcoal
and my feet tap to liberate them from the fire of a rhumba.
I am of charcoal
and the match of the drum ignites my waist.

—Antonio Preciado Bedoya, *Jolgorio: Poemas* (1961);
translation by Marvin Lewis (1983:121)

Blackness, Culture, Communities, and Regions

The two volumes introduced here present essays on the social systems and dynamics of communities and regions from areas of Latin America and the Caribbean where blackness is significant in human social relations and historical and contemporary discourse. The term *black*, according to Webster, is an adjective derived from Latin constructs meaning, in a literal sense, "sooted, smoke black from flame." Its first meaning in the twentieth century is "opposite to white." The "sooted" (darkened, blackened) concept derives in an earlier (or deeper) etymology from the Latin *flagrare*, "flame," "burn" with a transformation to "flagrant." The concept of blackness, as it is explored in these two volumes, reflects again and again on the ironies of its origins. A theme running through these books is the dialectic between the darkening influences of white domination in the African diaspora and the enlightened cultural, social, and economic creativity produced and reproduced in the eternal fires of black rebellion.

These volumes deal with black culture. But that is to say, at one and the same time, too much and too little. *Culture* is an ambiguous but important term. In Spanish, the feminine article *la*, as in *la cultura*, elevates a concept to something refined, European, civilized. When one goes to an expensive opera in Bogotá, Colombia, for example, wearing "fine" clothes and speaking in a "refined manner," one is participating in *la cultura* and one is *muy culto*, very civilized. Today, in most Latin American societies, to affix *cultura* to blackness without the article *la* is to demean traditions and lifeways to something "vernacular," worthy of study by folklorists but insignificant in the processes leading to higher and higher levels of Latin American civilization.

Still worse, *cultura negra* or *una cultura negra* is something to be viewed as unrefined, inchoate, confused, fragmented, stagnant, and static. One studies *una cultura negra* (a black culture) to find "Africanisms" as scattered traits, retentions, reinterpretations, or syncretisms (e.g., Herskovits 1945, 1948, 1956) that suggest a bit of Africa retained and an enormous amount of culture lost. At the First Congress of Black Culture in the Americas held in Cali, Colombia, in 1977, black people, well aware of these stereotypes and the power of racist symbols, insisted on the article *la*, as *La Cultura Negra*, for black cultures: black, sophisticated, existential, experiential, and adaptable—entwined processes of tradition, history, and modernity moving toward higher and higher levels of black civilization in the Americas. And many (but not all) white scholars there vociferously resisted incorporation of the Spanish article that changes the culture signified from low to high.

Important developments in anthropological, historical, and literary theory in the late twentieth century with regard to the concepts of culture, according to the distinguished historian Daniel J. Boorstin (1983), resonate well with the insistence of Latin American black spokesmen and spokeswomen for *La Cultura Negra*. " 'Culture' (from Latin *cultus* for 'worship') originally meant reverential homage. Then it came to describe the practices of cultivating the soil, and later it was extended to the cultivating and refinement of mind and manners. Finally, by the nineteenth century 'culture' had become a name for the intellectual and aesthetic side of civilization" (Boorstin 1983:647).

Black culture, as used in this general introduction, is that which is worthy of reverential homage by black people within their communities, regions, and nation-states; it is also the means by which the cultivation and refinement of mind and manners has been nurtured, developed, and adapted in the African diaspora of the Americas for over 500 years. Survival itself, as in the cultivation of the soil, figuratively and literally, is a critical concept contributing to the sense and reference of "black culture." Black culture is that which is illuminating to black people, and through them to others who will read, reflect, and think about blackness in settings of white domination. It is also reflected in, and contributes to, subsistence and commercial survival strategies and is adaptive to a myriad of structures of domination encountered and overcome in the African diaspora.

To discuss "communities," "regions," or "societies" in the Americas, where blackness is an important criterion for social categorization and interaction, is to plunge into contradictory ideologies of "races" to chart the currents of histories, stereotypes of moral (and immoral) topographies, and deeply held religious and aesthetic feelings. It is to delve into questions of racial separation, racial mixture, and the combined results—in structures of power and domination—of separation and mixture. This process of immersion is a richly rewarding one, as it reveals increasingly insightful and illuminating cultural experiences. These experiences became increasingly expansive, insightful, and revelatory in the wake of the European conquest's quincentennial celebration of 1992.

> *Barrio de los negros*
> *de calles oscuras*
> *preñadas de espantos,*
> *que llevan, que asustan,*
> *que paran los pelos*
> *en noches sin luna*
>
> *Barrio encendido,*
> *de noche y de día,*
> *infierno moreno,*
> *envuelto en las llamas*
> *de son y alegría.*
>
> Barrio of blacks
> of dark streets
> bursting with spooks
> that carry off, that frighten,
> that make hairs stand
> on moonless nights
>
> Inflamed barrio
> by night and by day,
> black hell
> enveloped in the flames
> of rhythm and happiness.
>
> —Preciado Bedoya, *Jolgorio: Poemas* (1961);
> translation by Lewis (1983:121–122)

Community was a key term in the original charge to develop these volumes. As nearly as we can see, every sociologist and anthropologist using the term has eschewed definitions offered by others and has developed his or her own definition and perspective according to the nature of the work at hand. The verb *com-*

mune, as "the action of communing," and the noun *community*, as "those . . .
practicing community together," are here used in their processual and dynamic
senses, as defined by the *Oxford English Dictionary*. The word *commune* stresses
"to talk together, converse; . . . to hold intimate (mental or spiritual) intercourse"
(see for elaboration Desan 1989 and Honigmann 1959:136–155). A community
may, as in the case of the Pacific Lowlands of Colombia, be a regional culture
self-aware of its ethnic status, or it may be an interaction group participating as
actors and audience in a stick fight outside a bar in Trinidad. The former community may be relatively self-contained in its internal discourses, while the latter
may commune in its collective interest in jazz from the United States and drum
rhythms from Africa.

The purpose of this general introduction is to set forth features that lead to
commonalities and broad divergences of black people in selected regions of the
Western Hemisphere. We seek to present illustrative material on the vitality of
black people in their varied social and cultural settings. The regions to which we
direct our attention share a history. They were first affected by conflict-ridden
Iberian discovery and the initiation of conquest. By the early sixteenth century,
subjugation of the Western Hemisphere had been undertaken by the rapidly
expanding colonial forces of the Spanish, Portuguese, French, Dutch, and English conquerors.

Eventually colonial rule gave way to national forces, but at that point North
America began to impose its economic and cultural will on the area. As a result of
this history, these areas are today characterized by external European and North
American domination and rampant internal underdevelopment. To allow the
reader to appreciate the selection of chapters published in these two volumes, we
first consider key concepts and then present facets of the emergence of the power
potential within what Roger Bastide (1967) referred to as *les amériques noires* and
what Stokely Carmichael (1967) called "the black Americas."

After the editors' introductory chapters, the first volume, which focuses on
Central America and Northern and Western South America, opens with a chapter by Norman E. Whitten, Jr., and Diego Quiroga about black culture of the
West Coast of Colombia and Ecuador. The second volume, on Eastern South
America and the Caribbean, closes with a chapter by Michel S. Laguerre on the
Vodún religion of Haiti and its dual role as an egalitarian liberation ideology for
its practitioners and a hierarchical organization of political control wielded by
the elite. The beginning and end of these books establish a contrast that we see
running through the history of black people with diverse lifeways in the Americas
since the time 500 years ago when the first black-Hispanic slave fled to the interior of the island of Hispaniola to live there with native Taíno Arawakans.

Those two chapters explore in complementary ways the key features that guide
the presentation of materials in the two volumes: blackness, culture, social relations, cultural continuity, radical change, structures of domination, religion, ideology, resistance, and creativity. Significantly, all the authors presented here must

somehow cope with powerful ideologies of "race" in modern, underdeveloping nation-states and with the inner essence of "being black" within aggregates of New World peoples who may be classed as Negro, mulatto, *negro, zambo, moreno, trigueño, mulato, pardo, negre, preto, cafuço, noire,* or *nengre,* or who self-identify by these or cognate terms.

Nationalism, Ethnic-Bloc Formation, and Ideologies of Racial Cultures

In our exploration, let us begin with the crucial concept of *nationalism.* This word refers to the identity of the majority of people within a nation-state with the republic, nation, or national society as the primary reference group. A nation-state must, above all else, retain all power of sovereignty and all power of territoriality. Ideologies of nationalism are located within the cultural space of nation-state control. In Spanish-speaking, Portuguese-speaking, and French-speaking republics in the 1990s we find two complementary and one competing nationalist ideology of racial culture, often denoted by one of these symbols: racial mixture, Indianism, or blackness. We present each of them briefly, by reference to the terms in the language with which they are most commonly associated.

Mestizaje, the ideology of racial intermingling, is an explicit master symbol in all Latin American countries. Perhaps ironically, we take the concept of *Indianism* to be a nationalist dimension of *mestizaje. Indigenismo* is a dual concept reflecting, on the one hand, a search for the creative dimensions of nationalism through the symbolism of an indigenous past and, on the other hand, a social-political-literary symbol that conveys the mood of remorse over the living conditions of contemporary "acculturated Indians." The ideology of *mestizaje* embraces both senses of *indigenismo* (e.g., Bourricaud 1962; Pitt-Rivers 1967, 1973; Tomoeda and Millones 1992). Indeed, *indigenismo* may be thought of as a key support for the exclusion of contemporary native peoples from nation-state affairs. A third component of *mestizaje* is *blanqueamiento,* which means "whitening." We discuss this later because it is not usually an explicit component of nationalist ideology.

At the other end of the spectrum is *négritude,* a concept that denotes the positive features of blackness among people classed as, or self-identifying as, "black." This term was brought into French literary being in 1947 by the black Martiniquan poet Aimé Césaire (Coulthard 1962:58). It provides a single term by which to assert the positive power inherent in, and the positive aesthetic forces of, "blackness," leaving many avenues open for the definition of what and who is, and what and who is not, to be considered "black." Within the Americas, only Haiti has adopted an explicit nationalist ideology of *négritude,* and the literary and artistic roots of this concept provide the basis for Césaire's (and for others', such as Frantz Fanon's) literary and political creativity (Coulthard 1962:58–70).

Nationalist ideologies develop not only symbols of internal "oneness" based on concepts of "racial classification," but also ideas of oppositions using the criterion of "cultural exaggeration" as discussed by James Boon (1982). We submit that throughout the New World, the *mestizaje–négritude* contrast represents a symbolic opposition reflecting cultural exaggeration of ideologically conjoined social constructs of race, civilization, nationalist patrimony, and social movement. We develop and illustrate this argument throughout this general introduction.

Thus far we have been discussing nationalism and the dominant racialist ideological contrasts that obtain during processes of nationalist consolidation. A nation-state is also often characterized during the consolidation of its developing nationalism by what Clifford Geertz (1973:234–310) calls *ethnic-bloc formation*. An ethnic bloc constitutes a conscious reference group for those who share recurrent processes of self-identification. Ethnic blocs may be based on criteria such as common residence, language, tradition, and custom. Indeed, the bases for bloc identity may slip and slide around the criteria themselves, as the bloc itself becomes increasingly strong.

The concept *bloc* is taken from politics (as in a political bloc); whatever its bases, the power of identity and the power of representation are crucial. Such powers come into being when ethnic exclusion takes place, as when indigenous people or black people are ethnically disfranchised from full participation in the dominant society.

Other powers within ethnic blocs derive from a collective, inner sense of a oneness of a people, in contradistinction to nationalist racialist hegemony. The powers are related, but the nature of such a dynamic relationship requires careful empirical study. Whitten (1985), following Geertz (1973) and Stutzman (1981), has argued that ethnic-bloc formation is a process of contra-nationalism and that the symbolic processes of ethnic-bloc formation are similar to, or the same as, those identified in processes of nationalist consolidation. Ethnic exclusion from nationalist consolidation and ethnic perspectives and contra-nationalism from ethnic and nationalist perspectives are related in multiple manners, which are quite specific in numerous instances. But the relationships in all cases ramify through the political-economic fabric of any social order. Ethnic-bloc formation, in other words, is as international in scope as it is local in origin.

In Hispanic-American, Gallic-American, Luso-American, Anglo-American, and Creole-American communities and regions, we anticipate that black-based ethnic-bloc formations will use the ideology of *négritude* and, in so doing, will be perceived as a threat to nationalist sovereignty and nationalist territoriality.

In the processes of ethnic-bloc formation in the Americas, we can identify three master symbols of ideology, the latter two of which are potentially complementary: phenotypical, cultural, or ethnic lightening (or whitening); black liberation; and indigenous autodetermination. Again, as in nationalist ideology, we discuss these in the language in which each is most commonly associated.

Blanqueamiento refers to the processes of becoming increasingly acceptable to those classified and self-identified as "white." This is an ethnic movement—coterminous with socioeconomic advancement governed by the ideology of "development"—that depends upon socioeconomic and political assistance and loans from the developed (i.e., highly industrialized, highly energy-dependent) countries. Although not often recognized as such, the ideology of "whitening" is an unconscious psychological process accompanying the economic state of underdevelopment in the twentieth century. *Blanqueamiento* essentially accepts the implicit hegemonic rhetoric of the United States with regard to "white supremacy" and often blames those people classed as black and indigenous for the worsening state of the nation.

Ethnic or cultural "lightening" may occur as an ideological feature among people self-identifying as "black." One example would be nineteenth-century Haitian literary circles wherein the positive attributes of blackness (via Egypt and the Sudan) were juxtaposed to French civilization. *Blanqueamiento*, an enduring ethnic-bloc complement to the nationalist ideology of *mestizaje*, is an ephemeral feature of enduring *négritude*. To the extent that people in the Americas accept, however implicitly, northern Anglo-American standards of whiteness as attached to "developmental potential," the phenomenon of hegemony may be said to exist.

Négritude (*négritud* in Spanish) may express the same sets of meanings in ethnic-bloc rhetoric that it does in nationalist rhetoric. Indeed, the Haitian ethnologist Jean Price-Mars, during the United States occupation of Haiti from 1915 to 1934, conscientiously turned to the voices of Haitians for concepts of blackness, Africanness, and being Haitian. He published the results of his extended ethnographic studies in 1928 as *Ainsi parla l'oncle*. Price-Mars sought to liberate nationalist ideology from its European francophonic bases in "whitening," where the powerful, literate elite of Haiti saw themselves as mulatto (somewhat analogous to *mestizo*). It is worth pausing here to reflect on the vision of Price-Mars as described by G. R. Coulthard (1962:64):

> Price-Mars urged his compatriots to look into their folklore—into the stories, legends, proverbs, religious practices, music and dancing of the Haitian people which had been ignored or scorned during the "French" nineteenth century. He recommends the study of African civilizations and of African elements in Haitian folklore, pointing out that the mystique of Africa is still very much alive in Haitian folklore, full of reference to "Guinée." He lashes out savagely at the racial prejudices of the Haitian *élite*, its snobbish worship of everything French or foreign, its attempts at racial and cultural dissociation from the people.

From the writing of Price-Mars onward, *négritude* and its implicit and explicit cognates must be considered to have two senses: in their nationalist sense they may or may not reflect a process of "lightening," but in their ethnic-bloc sense they are profoundly populist and rejecting of nonblackness as a criterion for sophisticated self-awareness (see especially Trouillot 1990:124–136).

Autodeterminación indígena is the assertion that indigenous people who were

deposed and disfranchised by the European conquest of the Americas must speak
to New World nation-states in modern, indigenous ways which they themselves
will determine. It is a proclamation of indigenous sovereignty and territoriality.
This symbol of liberation specifically looks to contemporary indigenous cultures
in multiple communities and societies across the Americas. It rejects the literary-
based ideological component of *indigenismo* just as early twentieth century ethnographers such as Price-Mars in Haiti and Fernando Ortiz in Cuba turned away
from elite academician definitions of national culture and sought out the voices
of the culturally rich black poor in both urban and rural areas. Today indigenous
self-determination is appealing to black people in many areas. It would seem
that *négritude* and *autodeterminación indígena* are complementary constructs of
ethnic-bloc ideology, both of which are contrary to *mestizaje* as nationalist ideology and ethnic-bloc ideology.

In the first chapter of the first volume and the last chapter of the second volume, the authors address the issues of blackness within three nation-states characterized by dominant, articulate ideologies of "race": *mestizaje* in Ecuador and
négritude in Haiti. In the nonanglophonic world today, Ecuador and Haiti constitute polar nationalist opposites. In the former, the colonial dream of overcoming the barriers of racial classification linked to economic opportunities became
transformed into a nationalist, democratic ideology of "racial mixture." In the
latter, blackness inundated a formative New World gene pool to create the first
self-liberated democratic island republic in the Americas with collective, self-
conscious roots in its African and European past.

Moral Ordering of Racialist Topography

Let us explore for a moment how these nationalist and ethnic-bloc ideologies
play out in the Caribbean, Central America, and northern and western South
America. We begin with one country in which *négritude* is explicitly nationalist.

Haiti has its sovereign locus on the western portion of the island of Hispaniola
(named Española in 1492 by Columbus). Hispaniola is the island where Columbus established his first colony to carry on the work of the Kingdom of Castile.
The island at that time was inhabited by indigenous Arawakan-speaking people,
the Taíno, but became increasingly black in the interior and western region and
"mixed" on the east coast as self-liberated Africans and Spaniards and their mixed
progenies mingled genetically with one another and with indigenous people
(Moya Pons 1986a, 1986b; Price 1979:419). Haiti is a black republic that
achieved its formal independence from France in 1804. Its name was immediately changed from that of the slaveholders, Saint Domingue, to the Arawakan
word for "mountains" (*haiti*), home of the native Taíno before 1492 and haven
of indigenous, black, and "mixed" maroons thereafter. (Maroons were people
who had escaped from the domination of European colonizers.) The eastern portion of Hispaniola became the nation of the Dominican Republic.

Blackness in Haitian ideology constitutes the sovereign and territorial locus of the inner power of its nationalism. That contrasts with the *mestizaje* ideology of the liberated lands of the northern Andes and the Spanish Main, Gran Colombia (which became Ecuador, Colombia [which included Panama until 1903], and Venezuela in 1830).

Black Haiti, the nation, looks out toward Cuba's Oriente region across the Windward Passage to the west. It was in this black region of Cuba where Fidel Castro began to form his revolutionary movement and from which he launched it in 1956 in the Sierra Maestra mountains. On March 25, 1959, Castro announced that "racial discrimination in Cuba was 'possibly the most difficult of all the problems that we have to confront' " (Rout 1976:308).

Adjoining Haiti on the east is the Dominican Republic. Santo Domingo, the first Spanish settlement in the Americas, is its capital. This section of Hispaniola did not achieve independence until 1844.

> The 1844 independence movement stressed the European, Catholic, "civilized" culture of the Dominicans over against the African and "barbarous" Haitians, and on these grounds appealed for sympathy and support to the United States and to European nations. Racialism has, in fact, played a significant part in relations between the two countries, as many Dominican historians acknowledge. (Collier, Blackmore, and Skidmore 1985:284)

Four hundred miles south of Haiti lie Venezuela and Colombia, lands also governed by *mestizaje* ideology. But in the coastal areas of Colombia and Venezuela the people are predominantly black. In the wars of liberation against European colonialism (between 1813 and 1822) led by Simón Bolívar, a Venezuelan, black troops from Haiti were used in the overthrow of colonial governments in Venezuela, Colombia, and Ecuador. As the creole nationalist spirits rose, so too did ethnic-bloc unity among black aggregates who rebelled against masters and oppressors, marched with Bolívar, then continued their struggles internally in these three nations (Guss and Waxer 1994).

Racialist ideologies influencing the complementary processes of nationalism and ethnic-bloc formation became intertwined historically in what was once the Republic of Gran Colombia, constituted of territory from the Orinoco River to the Pacific coast, and from what is now northern Peru to Panama. In literary and historical treatises on Simón Bolívar, his possible black ancestry as evidenced by his "mulatto blood" is mentioned from time to time. Whereas in Haiti this was and is viewed as a positive trait, it became a negative one in Gran Colombia.

One senses an uneasiness of white and mestizo biographers about the relationship of a mulatto as descendant of blackness and *mestizaje* as legitimate "mixture." There is an anticipated paradox to this unease, because Bolívar himself feared the worst for elite whites and mixed creoles if the energies residing in black cultures were unleashed (Wright 1990:27–29). Indeed, when black soldiers of liberation began to rally around one of his black Haitian generals, he allegedly had the general shot.

Cuba has long been the setting for dynamic African American ethnic-bloc solidarity based upon extant social relationships symbolized by African languages (especially Lucumí [Yoruba]) and religious brotherhoods such as Santería (see, e.g. Ortiz 1975b, 1975c, 1986; Cabrera 1969a, 1969b, 1970b; Brandon 1993). We are not clear on such relationships in the 1990s (compare, e.g., Moore 1988 with Pérez Sarduy 1990; Brandon 1993).

We know that black ethnic blocs in many parts of Venezuela, Colombia, and Ecuador are taking on the powerful rhetoric of *négritud* in opposition to that of nationalist *mestizaje*. In some areas of Colombia (e.g., the Department [state] of Chocó) and Ecuador (e.g., in Esmeraldas and Carchi Provinces), those developing an ethnic-bloc ideology of *négritud* and those developing an ethnic-bloc ideology of *autodeterminación indígena* are discussing alliances between black and indigenous people in opposition to the *mestizaje-blanco* barrier found in political-economic affairs. And the Chocó state formally petitioned the government of Colombia in 1989 to grant it the legal status of an "indigenous region" (*comunidad indígena*).

In Central America, especially Honduras and Nicaragua, one finds the phenomenon of the merger of indigenous and black ethnic populations. People such as the Garífuna, for example, who speak creolized Arawakan (the language of ancient Hispaniola, the Greater Antilles, and parts of the Guianas), Spanish, and English, are usually identified as Afro-American. For another example, the Miskito (from the English word *musket*) of Nicaragua and Honduras may fiercely identify as indigenous people seeking indigenous self-determination, but they are classed in Nicaragua as "indigenous" when they appear "Indian" to the nationalists and "ethnic" when they resemble the Anglo-Caribbean-Nicaraguan black people in the eyes of the dominant classifiers.

Négritude is not generally respected in images held of Haiti by white and *mestizo* people living in the Spanish Caribbean and the adjacent Spanish Main and down the Andes in Ecuador, Peru, and Bolivia. We must stress that the negative racialist image of Haiti is confined to those self-identifying in a nationalist manner with various doctrines of *mestizaje* that have the implicit or explicit facet of *blanqueamiento*. Nor does the image of Haiti enjoy a positive ideological image in the dominant sectors of Anglo-Caribbean politics.

The concept of Haiti as a nation within the popular culture of these regions by those self-identifying as "white" or "light" includes the idea of impoverishment to the point of creating an island of infrahumans. It also contains the imagery of revolts out of control, of a revolution not completed that could someday overwhelm the democracies of mainland South America. The imagery of black Haiti held by mainland South American whites (*mestizos*) suggests an undesirable power of blackness within *mestizaje* that is to be feared and controlled. It suggests a racialist revulsion and spiritual awe of latent and nascent power that survived the transformation from distinct gene pools into a *mestizo* "cosmic race" (*raza cósmica* Vasconcelos 1925).

Phenotypical and cultural categories within Haiti—the nation-state constituted ethnically by an ideology of descent from Africans who undertook the first act of self-liberation by active black-nationalist revolution in the Americas—are also prey to the ideological specter of "lightening" in a political-economic sense. According to Laguerre (e.g., 1976, 1982a), such lightening in stereotypic features has combined with political-economic power in a modern system where sets of urban mulatto elite have separated themselves from the rural black masses of poor people. Moreover, in downtown Port-au-Prince, capital of the Republic of Haiti, a "black ghetto" (Belair) has come into being through the historical processes of flow of power away from the black poor.

> The term ghetto refers to a sociological and economic phenomenon. Ghetto designates an urban district within which residents socially bound to each other are kept as a group in a marginal political, economic, and sometimes geographic position. I see the evolution of Belair as a satellite community tied to and largely dependent upon the development of the city itself, which, in turn, was a satellite of France during the colonial period (1625–1791) and is now more or less a satellite of the United States. (Laguerre 1976:26; for excellent discussions of the light elite–black yeoman distinctions in Haiti, see, e.g., Price-Mars 1928, Leyburn 1941, Coulthard 1962, and Mintz 1966)

The phenomenon of "lightening" is well known in Venezuela, Colombia, and Ecuador, where it is called *blanqueamiento*, or "whitening." Those pursuing a course of becoming "whiter" (people classed as *mestizo*, mixed, usually refer to themselves as *blanco*, white) refer to their "whiteness" in "cultural" terms as becoming more civilized and "conscious" than their "darker" black and indigenous national congeners. They classify some individuals, groups, and aggregates as *negro* (black), or *negreado* (darkened, blackened), implying lack of civilization and lack of culture—people without consciousness (*a los que les falta conciencia*) and hence unself-reflective and stupid. Those classed as *indio* (Indian) are regarded in the same manner.

Processes of pernicious pluralism activate and perpetuate the clash of three dynamic, paradigmatic symbols of nationalism as manifest in *mestizaje, indigenismo*, and *blanqueamiento*, on one side of the nationalist–ethnic-bloc ideological polarity. The same processes animate two vehicles of ethnic-bloc liberation—*négritud[e]* and *autodeterminación indígena*—on the other side. By "paradigmatic" here we mean that the entire complex is evoked—however implicit the evocation may be in a given text or discourse—when any one of these master symbols on either side of the nationalist–ethnic-bloc polarity is brought into discursive consciousness.

Mestizaje is a powerful force of exclusion of both black and indigenous aggregates in the Americas in the late twentieth century (see, e.g., Rout 1976; Stutzman 1981; Whitten 1985, 1986a; Friedemann 1984; Wade 1993). This exclusion mechanism is likely to continue to generate its polar opposite: black and indigenous awareness of exclusion and a continuous struggle for ethnic powers.

These processes are especially evident in the United States territory of Puerto Rico, an island just east of the Dominican Republic. This island is the last vestige of United States colonialism in the Caribbean. Spain ceded Puerto Rico, as well as the Philippines and Guam, to the United States at the Treaty of Paris on December 10, 1898, following the Spanish-American War (waged by the United States against the Spanish in Cuba and Puerto Rico in the Caribbean). In this same treaty Cuba gained its status as an independent nation-state.

In the fall of 1993 the residents of Puerto Rico voted in a nonbinding plebiscite to maintain the island's commonwealth status. On the island itself, *puertorriqueños* clearly regard their territory as a *nación* and they are as "nationalist" about their identity as are Colombians, Ecuadorians, Venezuelans, Jamaicans, Cubans, or Haitians.

Historically, the emergence of nationalist Puerto Rico as a creole colony under Spanish rule embraced the ideology of *mestizaje*. Within this ideology the *jíbaro* came to symbolize the Puerto Rican peasant, the bearer of a nascent Puerto Rican identity and culture that emphasizes a primary Spanish-indigenous heritage. In this mixture the sense of rural Spanish is privileged over indigenous descent. Although, in many areas, *jíbaros* vary in phenotype from brown to black, there is little if any "national" emphasis on the African component of Puerto Rican heritage in the conceptualization of the rural population or its significant black population.

The 1898 invasion of Puerto Rico by U.S. troops and the events thereafter give impetus there to the nationalist ideology of *mestizaje* and especially to the dimension of *blanqueamiento*. This ideology was further reinforced by the view that the paternalist social order of the plantation contributed to the social integration of racial aggregates (Quintero-Rivera 1987). More than a hundred years later these ideological and literary interpretations of Puerto Rico's ethnic past and present heritage are being challenged by black urban and rural Puerto Ricans who have, since the formation of maroon groupings on the island, maintained their autonomy. It is clear that Puerto Rico, while not a nation-state, is nonetheless characterized by a nationalist ideology of *mestizaje*, on the one hand, and the formation of black ethnic blocs, on the other.

Historically, social unities have developed in Puerto Rico between rural maroons and the urban mulatto populations. This has resulted in the creation of black ethnic blocs that have constantly redefined the Puerto Rican national identity by invoking series of ascriptions attached to "blackness." Spokesmen and spokeswomen for these blocs draw on dimensions of *mestizaje* or *négritud* (or both) depending upon the social context of racialist discourse. Today, Puerto Rican migration to the mainland United States and return migration from the mainland to the island have intensified the multifaceted discourse as features of the categorization of Puerto Ricans as "minorities" and as "people of color" enter the *mestizaje–négritud* dialogue.

The African Diaspora

The sociologist Ruth Simms Hamilton and her associates at Michigan State University, who have initiated long-range, sustained research on the African diaspora with funding from the Ford Foundation, define this subject as follows:

> the African diaspora represents a type of social grouping characterized by a histori-
> cal patterning of particular social relationships and experiences. As a social forma-
> tion, it is conceptualized as a global aggregate of actors and subpopulations, dif-
> ferentiated in social and geographical space, yet exhibiting a commonality based
> on historical factors, conditioned by and within the world ordering system. Among
> characteristics that distinguished the diaspora as a global formation from other
> socially differentiated groups are the following shared historical experiences: *Mi-*
> *gration and Geo-Social Displacement: The Circularity of a People;* . . . *Social Op-*
> *pression: Relationships of Domination and Subordination;* . . . *Endurance, Resis-*
> *tance, and Struggle: Cultural and Political Action.* (Simms Hamilton 1990:18)

There is a myth, widely held in the United States and widely printed in history books, about the progress of the African diaspora in the New World. According to this myth, Africans were first brought to the southern United States as slaves. There they lived in submission for a long time, until they were eventually liber-ated by white people of the North. In this myth the U.S. congressional enactment of the Fugitive Slave Law of 1850 is never mentioned.

The transformation of this myth into historical fact is well illustrated in the words of Lerone Bennett, Jr. (1987 [1962]:30): "The captain [of the Dutch slave ship] 'ptended,' John Rolfe noted, that he was in great need of food; he offered to exchange his human cargo for 'victualle.' The deal was arranged. Antony, Isabella, Pedro, and 17 other Africans stepped ashore in August 1619. *The history of the Negro in America began*" (emphasis added). The fact is that self-liberation by black people began 117 years prior to the day when that Dutch slaver brought twenty "negars" to Jamestown, Virginia. Over a century of black freedom had expanded the African diaspora throughout the Caribbean and Latin America (in-cluding the Pacific regions) and into what is now the continental United States before the date inscribed in this racialist American legend of origin. We turn now to blackness at earlier dates to understand more of the African diaspora in the Americas.

Whether black Africans or black Iberians reached the New World with Colum-bus on either of his first two voyages is not clear; they probably did not (Schom-burg 1928:93, Alegría 1985:59). Nor is it clear whether Africans reached the New

World prior to Columbus. We do know, however, that when serious European settlement began on the island of Hispaniola, African diaspora relations began in an immediate moment of self-liberation:

> With the fleet of Governor Ovando, bound for Hispaniola in 1502 to reinvigorate the faltering colony that Columbus had left behind the previous year, sailed "a few Negroes . . . brought out by their masters." (Parry and Sherlock 1965:16)

> Among them was the first Afro-American maroon, an anonymous slave who "escaped to the Indians" [Taíno Arawakans] in the mountainous interior soon after setting foot in the New World. (Guillot 1961:77, from R. Price 1979:1)

In western Hispaniola, where the French established colonial Saint Domingue, and in the interior of the Spanish territory that eventually became the Dominican Republic, *marronage* sustained a liberation atmosphere: "From the first years of slavery on the Island, Indians and [black] slaves had run away to inaccessible mountains, and throughout the colonial period, every mountain in Haiti was used at one time or another by fugitive slaves" (Laguerre 1989:41).

The Puerto Rican historian Jalil Sued Badillo (Sued Badillo and López Cantos 1986:175–189) documents the processes of slavery, self-liberation (*cimarronaje*), and indigenous and black rebellion and the consequences for people in Europe, Africa, and the New World in meticulous detail in *Puerto Rico Negro* (Black Puerto Rico). He documents the first active indigenous and black revolution in 1514 on the island of Puerto Rico. In this revolt two Taíno Arawakan chiefs (*caciques*) and their people allied with black (*ladino*) rebels to fight actively against the governmental representatives of the Spanish Crown. This was the beginning of the maroon in Puerto Rico.

Sued Badillo also documents a second major uprising in 1531 involving the enslaved black population. This represented a greater threat to the colonizers because the number of "blacks" had increased, while the "white" population had decreased. He argues (Sued Badillo and López Cantos 1986:187) that relatively little attention has been paid to these initial uprisings because the Spanish conquerors publicly supported the capture of "cannibals" (including Arawakans) as substitutes for costly African slaves. The "Caribs" were regarded as captives of "just wars" (Palencia-Roth 1993), whereas black slaves were regarded as "inferior beings." In retaliation for black Puerto Rican uprisings, the Church and Crown accused freed and enslaved black men and women of sorcery and witchcraft. In 1591 four enslaved women were hanged and burned in the outskirts of San Juan (Sued Badillo and López Cantos 1986: 151–154).

In 1522, black people revolted in Santo Domingo, the major city of Hispaniola: "Some forty slaves working at the sugar mill on the plantation of the governor, Admiral Diego Columbus (a son of the explorer), conspired with other blacks working on nearby establishments" (Rout 1976:104; see also 21 ff.). Thereafter, revolt was ubiquitous in the Caribbean and mainland South and Central America.

Wherever slavery existed, self-liberation began, and in many areas ethnic blocs of rebellious black people maintained their own sovereignty and territoriality for a century or more (see Barnet 1966; Baralt et al. 1990; R. Price 1979, 1983, 1990; Pérez de la Riva 1946, 1952, 1979; Whitten 1986 [1974]; Friedemann and Arocha 1986; Carvalho Neto 1965; Kent 1979).

Writing about Haiti, Laguerre (1989:39–40) says:

> Marronage was a central fact in the life of the colony, not only because of maroon military power and the number of slaves who constantly joined them, but also because of the danger inherent in expeditions to destroy revolutionary centers of these fugitive slaves. Any study centered upon the slaves must also consider this phenomenon of marronage; for wherever there were slaves, there were also maroons. . . . Living in free camps or on the fringes of port cities, they were a model for the slaves to imitate, embodying the desires of most of the slaves. What the slaves used to say in *sotto voce* on the plantations, they were able to say aloud in the maroon settlements.

Most of the prominent black areas of eastern and northern South America, Central America, and the Caribbean derive directly from creative processes of rebellion, self-liberation, and sovereign territoriality that were initiated and sustained by African American people. And these areas are many. They include various regions of Brazil; the *yungas* of Bolivia; the northwest coast of Ecuador; the Pacific and Atlantic coasts and Cauca Valley of Colombia; the Venezuelan *llanos* (plains) and northern coastal crescent; the interior of the Guianas; the Darién, coasts, and interior of Panama; the Mosquitia of Honduras and Nicaragua; the west coast of Guatemala, Belize, Honduras, and Nicaragua; the mountains of Haiti and the Dominican Republic; the Jamaican Blue Mountains and Red Hills regions; the Cuban Oriente region. This list is by no means exhaustive. The people of these areas have, over the years, affected the dominant colonial, republican, and nation-state systems in a variety of ways.

Although few scholars in the twentieth century have taken time to document such information (notable exceptions include Baralt et al. 1990, Cabrera 1970a, Arrázola 1970, Friedemann and Cross 1979, Ortiz 1986, R. Price 1983), self-liberation — with its awful manifestations of war, pestilence, and death — are thoroughly embedded in the dynamic historicities of African American people hemisphere-wide.

Among the Saramaka people of Suriname, for example, this information is part of a historical complex called First-Time (R. Price 1983). First-Time (*fési-tén*), refers to the time when the ancestors heard the guns of war. Saramakan speaker Tebíni, in 1976, told the ethnographer-historian Richard Price:

> Those people who didn't live to see the Peace, they must not be jealous. Their hearts must not be angry. There is no help for it. When the time is right, we shall get still more freedom. Let them not look at what they have missed. Let us and

them be on one side together, those First-Time people! It is to them we are speaking. (R. Price 1983: epigraph)

According to R. Price (1983:epigraph), who has done extensive historical work in European and other archives, Tebíni was quoting words "first spoken in 1762."

But the African diaspora did not, as so many suppose, originate in the New World; it began in North Africa and the circum-Mediterranean, in Europe, and in Asia. We do not know how long black people had been traveling there or when the first slaves were brought there. We do know that in 711, as the Muslim conquest of Iberia began, black soldiers were present in the Islamic forces. Farther north, according to the historian Folarin Shyllon (1982:171), "Irish records suggest that during a Viking raid on Spain and North Africa in 862, a number of Africans were captured and some carried to Dublin, where they were known as 'blue men.' " In the tenth century, black African fighters were a significant part of the conquering army of North African Moors.

By the eleventh and twelfth centuries (and on into the sixteenth), images of black Africans were to be found in monumental art and architecture, Christian iconography, heraldic shields, and other aesthetic forms throughout Western Europe (Devisse and Mollat 1979, Devisse 1979). Indeed, imagery of Africans is pervasive in Europe between the fourth and fourteenth centuries (Devisse 1979:35; Courtés 1979). Representations of Africans in many postures and guises occur in connection with religious ideology involving the land of Ethiopia, the coming of the Magi, the realm and person of Prester John, the Queen of Sheba, Saint Maurice, and the meaning of Old Testament legendary histories and prophecies about darkness and light.

By the middle to late fifteenth century, the religious imagery of blacks in Europe acquiesces to the power politics of the Iberian kingdoms. The African American historian Leslie Rout is quite clear about the European correspondences that developed as Iberians recognized an inversion of imagery—black African warriors to be feared, on the one side, and black Africans as beings to be conquered and enslaved, on the other:

> During the centuries of bitter struggle, the black African had become known to the Christians essentially as a soldier fighting for the Moors or as a slave laborer. The Portuguese, therefore, looked upon blacks as the logical answer to their problems of a cheap source of labor after 1250, and as early as 1258 Moorish traders appeared at fairs at Guimaraes (Northern Portugal) offering sub-Saharan Africans for sale. (Rout 1976:4)

Rout is also clear about Hispanic views of black people during the period of the Christian reconquest of Iberian territory and the subsequent expulsion of Moors, Jews, and non-Christian blacks, which was completed between 1492 and 1502: "Ultimately, to the white Christians of Spain, the captive from Negrería and/or his *ladino* descendant were believed to be loyal, superstitious, lighthearted, of low mentality, and distinctly in need of white supervision" (Rout 1976:21–22). Rout defines *Negrería* as "the totality of western Africa occupied by black people" (335, note 80).

With the perfection of the lateen sail and other innovations such as the single rudder and caravel-designed vessel, movement farther and farther down the coast of Africa (and eventually around the Cape; see, e.g., Boorstin 1983:221) and back was made possible for Iberian (mostly Portuguese) explorers and traders.

As soon as Europeans were able to travel back to Iberia with relative ease from their ventures to the west coast ports of black Africa, the Atlantic traffic in African slavery (the ships bringing slaves were called *negreros*, "black bringers") began in earnest and the African diaspora expanded exponentially. "Between 1441 and 1550, more than half of the slaves extracted from the coast of West Africa were destined for the labor market in Europe, particularly the Iberian peninsula, or for use in the emergent plantation economies of the Atlantic islands" (Collier, Blackmore, and Skidmore 1985:138; see also Terborg-Penn 1986, Forbes 1993, Russell-Wood 1995; and see Alegría 1985:62 for an illustration of a sixteenth-century lateen-rigged slave ship in the Caribbean).

The same innovations—nurtured by the Portuguese planner known as Prince Henry the Navigator—that allowed the small, sturdy caravels to return to Iberia from West Africa also helped ships to return to Europe after traversing the Atlantic (using especially the remarkable route discovered and charted by Columbus), and, more important, to tack through islands and river channels and around reefs in Europe's New World. The African diaspora of this New World is a circum-Atlantic phenomenon that rapidly reached the Pacific region of northern South America, Central America, and Mexico.

The first slaves of Europeans in the Americas were not black people of African descent but native Americans, definitely Arawakan and possibly Cariban. Columbus brought them to Iberia on his first two voyages, and by his order many were sold into slavery. The fate of at least some of these native Americans was to become enslaved on the Canary Islands, where sugar was rapidly becoming a cash crop and where the reconquest by Iberian Christianity was nearing completion.

Two key Old World words have a great significance in the African diaspora of the circum-Atlantic as manifest in Spanish classificatory power: *ladino* and *bozal*. A *ladino* in the sixteenth century was someone not originally Christian (e.g., Jewish-Hispanic, indigenous-Hispanic), and/or non-Moorish Hispanic but not white. Black *ladinos* were Africans or African-descended people who became Hispanicized and accepted (or paid lip service to) Christianity. Also known as *negros latinos* or *negros Castilla* (Alegría 1985:60), they could be free or slave, rich or poor, but they were bound to serve whites. *Bozales* were blacks "fresh from Africa." They were slaves in the sense of being "muzzled," or tethered by a "halter." From the concept of the *ladino/bozal* opposition came the opposition of "mulatto/slave," which continues to permeate the literature in Brazil, Cuba, and

Haiti, and elsewhere. "Mulatto" may often be read as "free black" as well as "lightened black." In some areas of Latin America and the Caribbean, however, it may mean "darkened white" or just plain "darkened."

Mulatto (French *mulâtre*) comes from the Spanish and Portuguese *mulato*, which itself comes from "mule," progeny "mixed" by the crossing of a horse and a donkey. According to the *Oxford Universal Dictionary*, the highly uncomplimentary definition is this: "One who is the offspring of a European and a Negro; hence any half-breed resembling a mulatto." With the abolishment of slavery in the middle to late nineteenth century, the terminology transformed to "mulatto/black" in black regions, and "white/mulatto" in regions dominated by lighter phenotypes. This transformation was facilitated in several areas (e.g., Nicaragua, Haiti, and Puerto Rico) by extended occupation by United States troops.

A popular saying of white-*mestizo* intellects in categorizing the masses of their nations in Ecuador and Peru is this: "Quien no tiene de inga, tiene de mandinga (whoever is not of [the] Inca is of [the] Mandinga)." A variant of this is "Lo que no tiene de inga tiene de mandinga (that which is not of [the] Inca is of [the] Mandinga)." The latter refers to that which is in the blood (e.g., Hurtado 1980:325). Such figures of speech—and there are many more—"halfbreedize" in a pejorative manner the darkening of national histories. For but one salient example, in the Hispanic Caribbean the word *dinga* (for Dinka) is substituted for the Andean *inga*. Isabelo Zenón Cruz (1975:256) offers the phrase "el que no tiene dinga, tiene de mandinga" as one of many that assert a universal "black blood" for people of color. Another phrase loaded with stigma is "¿y tu abuela dónde está? (and your grandmother, where is she?)," which means "you may not look black, but [the speaker knows] you descend from blackness." Arlene Torres pursues the meanings of this and cognate tropes in volume II. Writing of this process in the Chincha and Cañete valleys of Peru, the French historian and sociologist Denys Cuche (1981) has a section of his chapter on "métissage et discrimination raciale" (miscegenation and racial discrimination) on the subject of the "métis négroïde" (the black-like mixed person).

From the beginning of the African diaspora in Europe and the Americas, "whitening" and "darkening" have been dual symbolic processes of classification and identity. Dominant though it may be in nationalist rhetoric in Hispanic nation-states, *mestizaje* is not a positive ideological feature in communities and regions where people classed as *negro* (black) reside. In such communities, from a nationalist (but not ethnic-bloc) perspective, lightness as superior to darkness is the general classificatory feature, however complex the issues of lightness and darkness may be. In fact, in many regions and communities inhabited by black people, the word *mestizo* may refer to "black blood" (meaning "darkened"—*negreado*) with none of the connotations of "lightening" implied. This, by the way, is the meaning of the Portuguese term *mestiço* ("darkening" or "darkened") in many parts of Brazil and the French *métissage* in parts of the francophonic

Caribbean. The process of darkening is called *mulatización* ("mulattoization") in Cuban communities in Cuba and Miami.

Historically, a key feature in the development of African diaspora awareness in the Americas has been self-liberation, called *cimarronaje* (run-awayism) in Spanish, *marronage* (same meaning) in French. These concepts come from the New World Spanish word *cimarrón*, influenced by Arawakan (Price and Price 1993), which is also the derivation of the English term *maroon* and the French term *marrón*. Self-liberation brings with it a sense of belonging, of New World identity (e.g., Mintz and Price 1976, Price 1983, Laguerre 1989). It may or may not include a sense of being African; histories and historicities of black people in the Americas vary considerably with regard to a sense of dispersal from a common African homeland.

Today, from their own perspectives over at least the past two centuries, the self-identifying term for a full participant in black culture in the Department of Chocó, Colombia, is *libre* (free). Farther south, in the Pacific Lowlands of Colombia and Ecuador, black people regard the coastal and riverine sectors of this tropical rain forest as their original homeland. There, they say, their ancestors seized their freedom, asserted their culture, and made the productive land "theirs." Africa and the "congos," they say, are far to the north—"down the coast"—beyond the Panamanian Darién, in an undesirable location. Until very recently, black people, who constitute 90 percent or more of the population of the Pacific Lowlands of Panama, Colombia, and Ecuador, have emphatically denied an African diaspora. They have actively rejected concepts that suggest that they are lost souls separated from a distant homeland. They have insisted, and most still insist, that they are possessors of their own homeland. Like the maroons in the interior of Suriname and French Guiana, their self-conscious historicity is alive with events establishing their own communities, called *palenques*, in their own territory by their own creative volitions.

In 1990, Cuban nationalist rhetoric drew fresh allusions from the metaphor of "darkened." According to Marifeli Pérez-Stable, Cuba's political consciousness ("*consciencia*" as defined by the late Ernesto [Che] Guevara) of its nationalism is manifest in the symbol of maroon liberation.

"The future of our homeland will be an eternal Baraguá!" Raúl Castro proclaimed on March 15 in Santiago de Cuba. To announce next year's Communist Party congress, Fidel's younger brother read a text steeped with historical allusion. Baraguá was where mulatto independence leader Gen. Antonio Maceo met with his Spanish adversary in 1878 to discuss the Pact of Zanjón, a compromise negotiated by the civilian, mostly propertied wing of the separatist movement to end the Ten Years' War (1868–1878). Maceo and his *mambises*—the guerrillas of the Ejército Libertador (Liberation Army)—refused peace without independence. . . . (Pérez-Stable 1990:32)

He argues that Maceo's protest in the name of maroon (*mambises*) liberation was "an early expression of Cuban radical nationalism, one of the principal ideologies of the island's politics, which would later inspire the 1959 revolution" (32). By this argument we can see initial Cuban regional ethnic-bloc black liberation as transforming into movements of nationalist liberation and the allusion to the dark origins of the *Movimiento veinte y seis de julio* as being sparked again in the 1990s (for background, see Ibarra 1972).

The play on themes from the various discourses and practices of "white culture" and "darkened people" took on myriad dimensions, only a couple of which we mention here. Columbus was struck by one feature of the Taíno Arawakan indigenous people he encountered: they did not wear clothes. Rather, they presented their sense of individual and collective selfhoods by such means as body and face painting, hair dressing, stone adornments in lips and cheeks, nasal and ear adornments of precious metals (gold and *guanín*). One code of the Old World immediately promulgated on the New World was to "clothe" the subjugated Native Americans in appropriate (i.e., inferior) European garb. Significantly, then, in Dutch Guiana, which was to become Suriname, one of the first things that self-liberated slaves did was to shed their European clothes. Equally appropriate, perhaps, is the call of dark people in the Caribbean, as elsewhere, when beginning the English game of cricket: "put on your whites!"

Structures of Domination

The sociologist Max Weber (e.g., 1958, 1964), who has had far greater influence on modern symbolic and political anthropology and on neo-Marxism than many are willing to admit, argued strongly for a social-research methodology that involves three dimensions.

The first dimension of systematic research is what he calls "objective." It consists of measuring the relations of class by reference to people aggregated in society vis-à-vis their relations to the market. If poor people in a given community or region cannot afford to purchase the adequate carbohydrates and proteins while another aggregate of people in the same community or region purchases basic foodstuffs and special foods, pays for the education of its children, and builds up a stock of reserve funds, we can measure the relationships of the two aggregates to the market and state the results in terms of a "lower class" and a "middle class." If we find, as is usually the case, that a small interlocking group of people controls the local and regional markets that contribute to their superior wealth, then we can speak of an "upper class," or local or regional elite, and we can measure the economic power of this class and compare it objectively by the use of statistics to the others.

The second dimension of Weber's research strategy is to seek out the "subjective" aspects of a given community or region (or nation-state). Subjectivity refers to "status" as clearly differentiated from "class." Status is the shared style of life,

determined by the amount of social honor people have within the subjective social order. In the understanding of status one must understand classificatory
schemes that people in varied walks of life use to order the people around them,
to keep people away from them, to establish interactional bases that transcend
market forces, and to categorize people whom they know, whom they have been
told about, and whom they imagine. Matters of status are categorical and stereotypical. Ethnicity and "race relations" fall into the dimension of subjective, categorical, and stereotypical social relations.

Weber's third research method of social analysis was to see how, in the development of public policy, struggles for dominance crystallized in political arenas.
Such dominance crystallization constitutes the forces that initially shape the
structure of power.

One important dimension of power is what Weber called *Macht*, the ability to
force one's will upon others against resistance (Weber 1964:152). When one party
achieves dominance over another, it may influence the acquiescing party to
accept, however implicitly, the symbols of domination; such acceptance is the
essence of hegemony. Power always involves struggle, and the struggle is categorized by cultural conventions, motivated and shaped by magico-ideological constructs, and supported by political-economic resources.

When issues of class and status are dictated by questions of "race" or ethnic
representations, structures of domination are in evidence.

One would like to think, and many would have us believe, that in Latin America and the Caribbean there is substantial fluidity in class, ethnic, and power relationships. Such is not the case. Almost everywhere, serious research turns up a
pyramidal class structure, cut variously by ethnic lines, but with a local, regional,
and nation-state elite characterized as "white." And white rules over color within
the same class; those who are lighter have differential access to some dimensions
of the market. This is one significant manifestation of enduring structures of
domination. When a majority of black people constitutes the entire urban and
rural lower class of a region, this is another dimension of the structure of domination. Any combination of features that results in the perpetuation of lightness
as superior to darkness adds to the features of a racialist structure of domination,
with clear international repercussions.

Structures of domination appear strikingly in the structure of language; they
intensify culturally by simple rhetorical devices.

The first of these is *simile*. When a person says, "s/he sure doesn't look like a
Negro," or "el [ella] no parece como negroide[a]," a powerful statement has been
made that some other people will "look like" someone who "is" black. The "like"
(*como*), in other words, signals a conscious or unconscious awareness that there
are agreed-upon commonalities or properties that attach to persons of color. In
fact, the use in "science" or "social science" of the English suffix "oid" (which
means "like, as") is nothing more than rhetorical deployment of simile to reflect
the enduring imagery of a symbolic formation that stems from the fifteenth cen-

tury. For example, "Negroes" come from Africa and "Negroids" live in New Guinea. Although *negroide* and *négroïde* (negroid) are very common terms in New World and Old World Spanish and French discourse about "race" and even "culture," nowhere in the Spanish-speaking world does one ever encounter *blancoide* (Caucasoid, "like white"; Lewis 1983).

Metaphor is the second rhetorical strategy in maintaining structures of domination. When someone says "s/he is black," "s/he is descended from blacks," "s/he is part black," a metaphor is deployed. With metaphor the person, class, aggregate, group, community, or region is tagged with the cognitive and symbolic associations of a category of "darkened." These associations constitute properties of blackness that convey meaning, as though physical features, genealogy, or heritage have some real correspondences among people and categories. People of color, in other words, are signified by qualities and resemblances that belong to signifiers that stem from racialist and racist cultural constructs. Whereas, for example, black Panamanians think of themselves as *gente*, people, and black English speakers in Panama think of themselves as "people," both are tagged *negro* in Spanish and "black" in English. The properties of the signification "blackness" attached to certain Panamanians and Anglo-Caribbeans in Panama lump very different people, traditions, and customs, and garb them with attributes of convergent but false resemblance.

Structures of domination are given form, meaning, and power of repression by the rhetorical strategy of *reification*, regarding an abstraction or mental construction as though it were a real thing in the world. Reification occurs when people consciously read symbolic, religious, moral, or ideological properties into categorical social relationships, as though these properties actually "existed." In a chapter on "Humanity and Animality," the British structuralist Edmund Leach (1982:107) says, "The naming of relationships marks the beginnings of moral sanctions." This is the process of signification wherein meaning is constructed by strengthening the relationship between the signified (individuals, aggregates, groups, or categories of people) and the signifier (cognitive and symbolic associations and labels that constitute the properties of categories). When nationalist ontology and ideology reify racial mixture not only as an ideal but also as a "reality," they create objectifications of "outsidership" among indigenous and black populations of modern nation-states. People in communities and regions so objectified and morally sanctioned by undesirable attributes self-consciously reflect on such reifications and attempt to overcome the barriers imposed by racialist structures of domination. This involves symbolic as well as practical dimensions of actions of moral inversion in society. The invariable result is a reordering of visions that people hold of humanity and spirituality in the world perceived and the world imagined. When such actions spark movements of self liberation they may be said to become "flagrant." Dolgin, Kemnitzer, and Schneider (1977: 37) write: "Each action situation is the locus of such reification; and because such reification is the practical key and the ontological root of domination, every action situation is the site of negotiation for, or struggle against, domination." These authors (1977:3) open their book with a phrase from Karl Marx: "As people express their lives, so they are . . . " This is an intriguing figure of speech because it begins with a simile ("As") and it ends with a representational metaphor ("they are"). One need but classify the "they" in ethnic or "racial" terms to have a powerful reification. In circumstances where people come to express their lives in a manner corresponding with the structure of domination, the phenomenon of hegemony occurs.

Finally, in the process of formation and strengthening of structures of domination and the inevitable forces of resistance to them, we must consider the phenomenon of *hypostasis*. This word, which entered the English language by 1529, literally means "that which stands under"; i.e., a support or foundation (for other concepts). *Hypostatize*, according to Webster, means "1. to make into or consider as distinct substance; attribute substantial or personal existence to, 2. to regard as a reality; assume to be actual." A structure is a set of relatively invariant reference points that remain after a series of transformations has occurred. Hypostatized structures are those that are taken to be enduring realities. They are structures with deep historical underpinnings and supports that unite concepts of humanity and divinity and separate both from animality (see, e.g., Leach 1982).

In the ethnic formation of the circum-Atlantic structure of European domination, three relatively invariant reference points were the categories of the white (European) in superior relationship over the black (African) and the native ("Indian"). Such a categorical hypostasis established by phenotype and pigmentation constitutes, as an undergirding foundation, a multitude of ethereal and even fantastic classifications that people took to be "real" 500 years ago and still take to be "real." During the colonial, republican, and modern eras of Latin American and creole transformations, these were complemented, as we have seen, by reference to *mestizaje*, *blanqueamiento*, and *indigenismo* in Spanish, denoted by other cognate concepts in English, French, Portuguese, and Dutch.

This structure of domination manifests a pyramidal class structure with white people on top, masses of pluralized mestizo, mulatto, and white people in the middle, and poor, pluralized black, mestizo, and indigenous people on the bottom. It is assumed to be an unchanging, static reality by people at the pinnacle and middle of the structure. The full power of bureaucracy is wielded to solve the "black problem," find new ways to overcome the "Indian problem," and accelerate the processes of *mestizaje*. While such solutions to hypostatized problems are being sought, national, regional, and local resources flow to the top, are partially redistributed in the middle, and deprive those on the bottom of the class-ethnic hierarchy. This is a process of reproduction of underdevelopment of Fourth World people in underdeveloping Third World nations and the production of increased distance between Third World poverty and First World wealth (see, e.g. Worsley 1984).

Within any given structure of domination, we expect to find that those in power strive to maintain hegemony over those immediately below them by blaming those on the bottom (especially ethnically distinct indigenous and black people) for the "undeveloped" condition of regions and communities where they are designated by reification. The hypostatized "reality" is often inscribed in developmental reports, plans, and educational materials and in scholarly publications. At the same time, this symbolic but negatively concretized "reality" is challenged by powerful, dynamic counterideologies. The rhetoric of such counterideologies seeks to spark recognition of the falsity of the static ideological structures with their locus in white-supremacy doctrines.

Ethnic-bloc formation undertaken under the ideological aegis of *négritud* and/ or *autodeterminación indígena* strongly illustrates the challenges mounted in the late twentieth century to false yet hypostatized "reality" that has been with the New World since 1492. No wonder, then, that during the conquest quincentennial celebration many black (and mestizo) people in Latin America joined their indigenous fellow citizens in the cry "¡Despues de 500 años de dominación, autodeterminación en 1992! (After 500 years of domination, self-determination in 1992!)."

Processes of Liberation

Understanding processes of liberation involves us at still greater depth with the elements of dominance crystallization that constitute structures of power. Structures of domination and the ways in which blocs coalesce, change, and are expressed, maintained, and transformed are highly dynamic and volatile. While hegemony may come into being, it never lasts, for people are conscious actors attuned to their life situations. Dolgin and colleagues (1977:44) summarize as follows:

> People act on the basis of belief. To study belief in action . . . is to examine the possibilities of freedom, and the roots of oppression and alienation. But these can be studied only in the context of a *practical* commitment to freedom and a determination to overcome that which stands in its way. People made it, is the principal lesson of modern anthropology; people can remake it, must become the principal lesson of our work in the future.

When discussing structures of domination we introduced briefly the idea that people are signified by signifiers as they become parts of categorical webs of signification in modern nations. The signifier *negro* (black), when wielded by whites and mestizos in the Cauca Valley of Colombia to represent people of dark complexion, expresses a series of attributes that includes laziness, danger, and "migrating" to "work" for wages from a "jungle" littered with African "superstitions." People categorized as "black" in the Cauca Valley are looked upon as morally "darkened" by history, geography, and descent. The history of the Cauca Valley is one of increasing white wealth, oppression of black yeomanry, and destruction of indigenous people.

Such white categorization stems from the conjoined legacies of slavery and self-liberation of black people, and later the white tradition of this region of importing black laborers from the adjacent Pacific Lowlands. It also stems from a deep-seated nonblack fear of free black people who have long resided there. This is a region where self-liberation came early to black slaves, and by the late eighteenth century both white-owned plantations and black *palenques* were developing not only in competition with one another but at times in collaboration (Taussig 1980). Writing of the descendants of the self-liberated black *cimarrones* there in the 1880s, Michael Taussig says:

> these black peasants were outlaws—free peasants and foresters who lived by their wits and weapons rather than by legal guarantees to land and citizenship. The fearful specter of a black state was not lost on some observers. "In the woods that enclose the Cauca Valley," wrote the German traveler Freidrich von Schenk in 1880, "vegetate many blacks whom one could equate with the maroons of the West Indies." They sought solitude in the woods, "where they regress once again slowly to the custom of their African birthplace as one commonly sees in the interior of Haiti. . . . These people are tremendously dangerous, especially in times of revolution when they get together in gangs and enter the struggle as valiant fighters in the service of whatever hero of liberty promises them booty." (Taussig 1980:58)

Being "signified" or "represented" as "black" in a white-dominated world is to be stigmatized to a position of ethnic disadvantage in a discourse of racial asymmetry. This does not mean, however, that people so stigmatized will accept a position of disadvantage or elect to describe their situation through the dominant discourse. Indeed, the black narrative modes that are all too often strung together and published as "folklore" constitute, as Price-Mars (1928), Ortiz (1975c, 1986), R. Price (1983, 1990), Taussig (1980), and Friedemann and Cross (1979) have shown, a rich embodiment of enlightened and insightful black representation of the entwined histories, presents, and futures of conquest, domination, and self-liberation. As Taussig (1987:135) puts it, "From the represented shall come that which overturns the representation." This statement relates directly to the idea of people remaking the world and being in a world refashioned from the conquered one.

For one example taken from the power of language to reformulate perspectives of being in the world, let us return to two illustrations previously presented and see them in a dialogical or confrontational manner. Black people from Ecuador who attended the First Congress of Black Culture in the Americas in 1977 were well aware of the phrase "Lo que no tiene de inga tiene de mandinga." They resented immensely its introduction as a way of asserting the *mestizo* character of

Ecuadorian "popular" or "vernacular" culture by a prominent Ecuadorian folk-lorist who was invited there to present a formal paper based on his extensive re-search on Afro-Ecuadorian "beliefs and superstitions." They immediately pointed out that the lack of the Spanish article *la* (the) before both Inca and Mandinga relegated indigenous cultures of the Americas (bound up in the word *inga*) and indigenous cultures of Africa (bound up in the word *mandinga*) to something unrefined and static. The scholar responded forcefully that this was part of "Ecuadorian folklore" and should be presented as collected among "the poor and the backward" (*los pobres y los atrasados*). Black people publicly argued back against the scholar's flawed rhetoric, and a clear insistence on the phrase *La Cultura Negra* came forth. Blackness of the past and present and toward the future was what the conference was all about. Blackness in all its flagrant dimensions is to be cultivated and understood, not "studied" as a set of scattered artifacts, they asserted. Having stressed the positive value of blackness in Ecuadorian, Colombian, and Peruvian cultures and traditions, black delegates and others called the distinguished scholar *un mestizo*, a halfbreed. This, still in confrontational context, was also significant, because the man clearly self-identified as *blanco*, white, while proclaiming the nation of Ecuador to be *mestizo*.

Blackness at the 1977 congress referred (and continues to refer) to that epitomizing referent worthy of a macro-identity to which communities, regions, even nations could aspire. Such a referent is transcendental; it comes from black people in black communities, but it is the polar opposite of "popular culture." In the United States and elsewhere in the Americas and the Atlantic rim, the epitomizing symbol of blackness in its transcendental character is expressed as "soul" (in volume II, see especially the chapters by Mitchell on Brazil and Laguerre on Haiti). This is an aesthetic quality that people self-identifying with human blackness and/or black cultures find and appreciate across the boundaries of specific communities, regions, nations, or traditions.

Let us now consider *travel*, for through this mechanism the circum-Atlantic cultural system of inter-regions and inter-traditions came into existence, and through this mechanism its collective vitality in remarkable diversity is constantly enriched. According to Daniel J. Boorstin (1983), Mary W. Helms (1988), and Mary B. Campbell (1988), a universal in culture is the inextricable relationship between travel and power.

The European "discovery" of America in 1492 and the rapidly ensuing conquest expanded structures of domination exponentially. Domination was the European ideological and practical issue in 1492 (as it still is) by those representing struggling kingdoms. Columbus sailed for the king and queen of Castile. His motivation was to discover a cheaper and safer route to the East Indies (all land from India eastward through Asia and the Pacific islands) and to find ways to make huge profits there. He claimed that he had done so (and that he had discovered the location of paradise) and announced his greatness to the literate world in a public "letter to a prince" in 1493.

In addition to his self-designation as "bearer of Christ," Columbus demanded and was granted the secular tide of "Admiral of the Ocean Sea." He (in error) also named the inhabitants of an entire continent of diverse native people as *indio* (of the "Indies," from which come the French *Indiens*, the German *Indianer*, and the English *Indian*), the most common representation used today in most of the world for the Native Americans burdened by the crushing weight of Old World expansionist hegemony.

Columbus clearly "marked the beginning of moral sanctions" (Leach 1982) with his designation *indio*. Not long after, Bartolomé de las Casas defended the "humanity" of the *indios* and in so doing recommended the massive importation of black Africans (*negros de Africa*) to take over the animal tasks heretofore relegated to the native inhabitants of the New World. The hegemonic morality of white power and *indio*/black forced subservience to the Church, State, and secular holders of land and people was established in the early sixteenth century in Europe and the Americas.

But there were many—including black people of many origins—who traveled far and wide in the New World. We quote here from a piece of fiction based upon archival documents (e.g., Cabeza de Vaca 1542a, 1993) to allow the reader to capture something of the flavor of such ventures in the early exploration and conquest of the Americas.

> I am Estevân, a black man from Azemmour, in Morocco. . . . After completing necessary preparations, on the seventeenth day of June, 1527, a Friday, we departed Spain in five ships—six hundred we were, a few more or less—and, except for the score or two who fell sick with the vomits and one lost in the sea, it was a fair and easy voyage to the Island of Santo Domingo, where we rested forty-five days procuring provisions and horses. (Panger 1982:34)

Estevân, a *ladino* slave, also classed as a Moor, then traveled by ship and on foot around the New World with Alvar Núñez Cabeza de Vaca, during which time he was granted his freedom. The novel *Black Ulysses* (1982), from which we quote, is based on a translation of a sixteenth-century journal (Cabeza de Vaca 1542b). This travel took place more than ninety years before the "negars" were brought by the Dutch slaver to Jamestown. The journal describes in detail the first European-African expedition to explore the southern part of what is now the United States and northern Mexico. In terms of present regions, the travelers went from Santo Domingo (Hispaniola) to Trinidad, then Cuba, on to Florida, up the west coast of the Gulf of Mexico, across the northern shores of that gulf, down to Corpus Christi, Texas, into the interior of Mexico, back up to El Paso and down to Culiacán on the west coast of Mexico. Insights brought out by the eight-year chronicle suggest relationships more than 450 years ago that might have existed beyond the pale of Spanish conquest society. The fictionalized Estevân says:

> With these Indians [of west Mexico, near the Gulf of California] with whom I dwelt for many months, I was not a slave, and because I came to them as a trader I was permitted to go from one tribe to another, a thing forbidden to all except this one class of beings. Because of the color of my skin and because of my profession as a trader—one who brings both commodities and messages which to these Indians is of the highest importance—I was treated with great honor while amongst these Charrucos, as I was by every nation to which I traveled as far distant as fifty leagues north and even a greater distance south. (Panger 1982:363)

For individuals to venture out beyond the realm of the known and to return with new information of great worth to those who sent them creates an increasing "fund of power" for the travelers (Helms 1988: 169). Black people from black Africa had long been going out and coming back to increase funds of power for states and empires developing in Central and West Africa.

The possibility of journeys by Africans to the New World and back to the Old is occasionally debated by a handful of scholars (e.g., Jeffreys 1971). For our purposes we can state with confidence that African-diaspora social relations began to appear in Hispaniola at least by 1502 and soon thereafter throughout the New World from Florida to Argentina. From that time on, activities of African-Americans were to be partially, sometimes inextricably, bound to the upper realms of wealth and power in New World colonies, republics, and eventually modern nation-states.

This does not mean that freedom could not be seized. Such freedom is evident in the sustained movements of black self-liberation found throughout the Americas. As Richard Price has written,

> For more than four centuries, the communities formed by such runaways dotted the fringes of plantation America, from Brazil to the southeastern United States, from Peru to the American Southwest. Known variously as *palenques, quilombos, mocombos, cumbes, ladeiras,* or *mambises,* these new societies ranged from tiny bands that survived less than a year to powerful states encompassing thousands of members and surviving for generations or even centuries. Today their descendants still form semi-independent enclaves in several parts of the hemisphere, remaining fiercely proud of their maroon origins and, in some cases at least, faithful to unique cultural traditions that were forged during the earliest days of Afro-American history. (Price 1979:1; see also Thoden van Velzen and van Wetering 1988; Friedemann and Cross 1979)

Even in the myriad fortified black, indigenous, and black-indigenous territories, however, a close connection with structures of domination was maintained by war, by trade, and by the creation of many mechanisms of "distance" (see, e.g., Taussig 1986, S. Price 1983, R. Price 1990, Thoden van Velzen and van Wetering 1988). Estevan, for example, may have thought about remaining with Native Americans near the coast of California (where, perhaps, a *palenque* could be developed), but instead he pressed on southward with Cabeza de Vaca, to unite with Hernán Cortés.

> Accompanied by scores of Christians met along the way and hundreds of Indians, we entered Mexico City July 25, 1536, eight years, two months and twenty five days from our landing on the coast of Florida. . . . Viceroy Mendoza came up and, after presenting me with a likeness of Christ's Mother, Mary, done in gold and jewels, declared that he was claiming me for his household. Although I forced my face to give no sign, within my heart turned to ice. Nothing Alvar Nuñez [or the others with whom he had traveled] could say altered the Viceroy's determination. Thus despite the silks I now wore, the gold and silver coins that filled my pockets, I was again a slave. (Panger 1982:400–401)

We stated that black Americans who escaped slavery in the New World were nonetheless partially bound because of the necessary links to dominant colonial, republican, and nation-state societies. This does not mean that black people were powerless because of these links. There are other dimensions of power that shape and communicate ethnic and cultural forces. As William Arens and Ivan Karp (1989:xii) put it, "The concept of 'power' as it is used by all peoples encodes ideas about the nature of the world, social relations, and the effects of actions in and on the world and the entities that inhabit it." These sources of power in the African diaspora constantly give rise to meaningful resistance, to revelation of structures of oppression, to insight into the nature of political-economic barriers, and to a sense of worth of human congeners struggling together against forces of repression. It is in these struggles that the sense of community is found.

Anthropological understanding of black cultures and traditions in the New World has often bogged down in debates about how to scale Africanisms in the aesthetics, ritual, play, theater, folklore, cosmology, music, dance, religion, and ideology of black aggregates against Europeanisms in black cultures. Some scholars have even stewed about relationships of Native American cultures and African American cultures, and learned conferences have been held on the past, present, and future of "black Indians." Our position is that the elements and themes of cultural traditions may come from any source. Traditions are not static, and they may change radically for a variety of reasons (e.g., Shils 1981, Hobsbawn and Ranger 1983). The white Mississippians' taste for okra, which blacks brought to the Americas from Africa, is no less "theirs" in the late twentieth century than is the black Bermudans' fondness for English cricket. Emergent patterns, with very shallow time depths, nonetheless suggest relationships to the past and trajectories toward the future. Sahlins (e.g., 1981:7), as well as Kuper (1988), correctly locates *transformation* as a means of understanding traditions.

Consider human beings interacting in myriad aggregations around the globe. Now, zoom down on the circum-Atlantic as a culture region of intersystems. It is immediately apparent that the elements, complexes, and themes that compose traditions are spread and sorted variously by ongoing transactions within actual groups, communities, and regions. Cultures, we could say, embrace diversities of traditions while at the same time scrutinizing their arbitrary nature (e.g., Babcock 1978:29).

Traditional African American arts and rituals, for example, exist as objects (sculpture, carving, painting, quilting, weaving, pottery) or stylistic renditions (storytelling, joking, poetry, mythmaking, historic narrative, worship, dance, mime, music, theater) that particular people take to be part of their own past, present, and unfolding future heritage. They may also exist in the living memory of people who no longer perform the rituals or craft the arts. Absence of ongoing practice is not necessarily evidence of culture loss or "acculturation," for talk about objects, past activities, and events is a powerful mechanism of culturally sustained ability, of creativity, of power. Put differently, the discourses about past practices may be taken as a model of cultural continuity and a model for transformations in present ideology and cosmology. And such discourses may reveal far more about black or indigenous historical dynamics than reified inscriptions in learned volumes about the so-called "genuine but 'disappearing' Africans and Indians in the New World."

Let us again turn to the Saramaka of the interior of Suriname. In the 1970s people there cautiously told Richard and Sally Price about customs they no longer practice except in times of collective crisis, because they were associated with First-Time, a real, historic time-space of war and rebellion which, if discussed, would "kill people." Using many techniques of sophisticated communication, Saramaka speakers told of battles, of rituals, and of powerful artifacts while at the same time keeping the bulk of their specific knowledge diffuse and protected (Price and Price 1980). In Richard Price's *Alabi's World* (1990), there is moving testimony to the strength of this tradition as maintained through the Saramakans' historical lore, and we learn about the continuing struggle against domination in the late twentieth century.

> In 1978, the Saramaka elder Peléki voiced the greatest fear of all Maroons, prophesying that those times—the days of war and slavery—shall come again. In 1986, after two centuries of peace, they did. Great war *óbias* that had lain dormant since the eighteenth century were dug from the earth and revivified. The blood of hundreds of Maroons—men, women, and children—as well as that of other Surinamers has once again stained the ground. And as this book goes to press, the end is not in sight. (Price 1990:epigraph)

In a review of Richard Price's *First-Time* (1983), Whitten (1986b) argues that "the creative act of territorial and societal formation at the frontier of colonial-state or nation-state places cultures so formed (maroon cultures) in continuous jeopardy of reconquest. The jeopardy lurking in the present and future, in turn, motivates continuous reproduction of poignant and accurate images of the past."

The creativity of African American ethnogenesis that led to the emergence of six nations (not nation-states) of self-liberated black people in the interior of Suriname and French Guiana is an example of what we call ethnic-bloc formation. These people self-identify as Saramaka, Matawai, Kwinti, Djuka, Paramaka, and Aluku. They are collectively called *bushenenge*, "forest blacks," by Dutch-speaking outsiders and "bush Negroes" by English speakers searching for "lost Africans." Each of these peoples fought for more than a hundred years against the Dutch and the French, and they won their independence. Then, in the late twentieth century, as Suriname entered a phase of nation-state socialist nationalism, the sheer existence of peaceful black people in a "plural" nation seemed to threaten the sovereignty and territoriality of an increasingly bloodthirsty and oppressive military state. The consequence was a civil war waged in Suriname, news of which scarcely reached the metropolitan news services of industrial nations. Ethnicity emerges in sharp relief within nation-states undergoing intensive movements of nationalist selfconsciousness, where "ethnic" comes to mean something other than what nationalist ideologues proclaim is "traditional" to an "authentic past" of the nation. "*Ethnicity* labels the visibility of that aspect of the identity formation process that is produced by and subordinated to nationalist programs and plans—plans intent on creating putative homogeneity out of heterogeneity through the appropriative processes of a transformist hegemony" (Williams 1989:439).

As for ethnic power, Arens and Karp (1989), writing about black Africa, state: "Underlying much of the ritual and cosmology is a sense of power derived from different capacities and uses to act on the world." In a survey of symbolism and language of power in African societies and cultures, they find that indigenous concepts of power in Africa refer to ability or capacity, as contrasted with physical strength. They state that "there is no word for authority and duly constituted government authorities are referred to by some of the words for control" (xx), adding:

> Once we incorporate semantics, cosmology, and action, power can be understood as something significantly more subtle and meaningful than sovereignty of domination isolated at one single point in time or place. Rather, it is recognized as a pervasive social resource, which provides the ideological bases for various domestic and public relationships in Africa and elsewhere. (xx–xxi)

INTRODUCTION TO VOLUME II

EASTERN SOUTH AMERICA

AND THE CARIBBEAN

Arlene Torres and Norman E. Whitten, Jr.

In late August 1996 the Afro–Latin American Research Association (ALARA) held its First International Conference in Salvador-Bahia, Brazil. Panelists in the opening session echoed the sentiments of the Afro-Colombian spokeswoman, Zulia Mena, and the Afro-Bolivian spokeswoman, Fortunata Medina Pinedo de Pérez, as cited in our introduction to volume I of this work. Gabriel Marques, an Afro-Brazilian scholar, and Michael Mitchell, a North American scholar and contributor to this volume, challenged the view of Brazil as a racial democracy. In his opening remarks Marques stated that of the 80 million people of African descent living in Brazil, few hold political and economic power. People of African descent in Brazil, he said, "constituen, na verdade, uma grande massa de 'escluidos sociais' (constitute the masses of people who are socially excluded)."

Michael Mitchell stressed the significance of "race" as a critical component of human rights violations in Brazil. He stated that Brazil is at a turning point in its racial character in terms of its political economy. Afro-Brazilians are participating in national and international movements to ensure their human rights and by doing so they are challenging the so-called vitality of Brazilian democracy.

Following these contemporary authors and analysts and in concert with the materials we have culled and presented in this volume, we contend that analyses of ethnic cleavages and competition in eastern South America generally and in Brazil, Guyana, and Suriname in particular set the stage for an understanding of the ways by which black people of this vast region, as elsewhere in Latin America and the Caribbean, continually struggle to retain their land and property rights and to reaffirm what, taking our clue from the Saramaka people of Suriname, we might call their First-Time ideology.

We noted in the general introduction that one area of neglect in African American Studies results from the failure of scholars to adequately take into account self-liberation and the maintenance of freedom in societies grounded in slavery. We also noted that one strong exception to this generalization is the work of Richard Price. More than a decade ago Price brought forth a work sketching the historical complex of First-Time (R. Price 1983). According to one Saramakan speaker, Tebíni, who tells of words "first spoken in 1762," First-Time (*fési-tèn*) for the Saramaka nation of African American people in the interior of the nation-state of Suriname refers to the time when the ancestors "heard the guns of war." Price was able to determine the Western chronological dates of Tebíni's gnosis by serious and extended research in Dutch archives, wherein the records of European wars to subdue the self-liberated African American Surinamers people are deposited.

Price continued his ethnographic and historical work with the Saramaka, including gathering and analyzing information garnered during the recent nationalist war waged by the army of Suriname against its citizens. Recently, in putting together the material for a war-crimes inquiry into Suriname's nationalist genocide, he again discussed the Saramaka historicity of First-Time. His information came from Saramakan and Ndjukan war refugees from Suriname now living in Guyane, which was previously called French Guiana and which still is, like Martinique in the Caribbean, a territory of France:

> If the Maroons' greatest fear, as expressed to me during the 1960s, was that "those times [the days of slavery and the struggle for freedom] shall come again," then the New Year's Eve killings of 1987 may stand, emblematically, for the ways that specific continuities of "othering" have produced, and continue to reproduce in Suriname, precisely those conditions that make such fears well grounded. (R. Price 1995:440)

Price goes on to explain that following the ratification of a new constitution and general elections in Suriname, Maroons were brutally tortured and killed by members of the Suriname military as they returned from the nation-state capital of Paramaribo, where they had gone to purchase food and other supplies. As a result of investigations and lengthy court proceedings by the Inter-American Court of Human Rights, compensatory damages were distributed to some but not all of the family members of the deceased (R. Price 1995:462).

These atrocities consistently reinforced Maroon views that non-Maroon Afro-Surinamers and other outsiders seek to destroy what they and their ancestors fought to retain over centuries—their freedom and their cultural autonomy. In the midst of a civil war that began in May 1986 and ended in August 1992, between the national army of Suriname and the Ndjukan and some Saramakan Maroons, Maroons were forced to leave their land and their homes to seek shelter in the refugee camps located westward across the border in Guyane.

As the Maroon chiefs reluctantly signed a treaty to end the civil war in August 1992, they later asked that provisions contained in the document regarding land rights and titles be clarified. Songo Aboikono, a Saramaka chief, raised the serious issue for all people of African American descent when he stated and queried: "from Mawasi Creek on up, all of the forest is ours. Do we have to fight our ancestors' war all over again?" The government representative, District Commissioner Libretto, failed to respond (R. Price 1995:459). The silence was revealing. Price (467 n.29) noted that the peace treaty clearly indicates that rights to land, minerals, and resources are "unambiguously claimed by the state." In 1994 the government of Suriname entered into negotiations with an Indonesian multinational corporation to exploit 30 million acres of land in the Suriname interior.

The Guianas are constituted by Guyana (once British Guiana, which abuts Venezuela to the west), Suriname (once Dutch Guiana) in the middle, and Guyane (once French Guiana), which is the easternmost region of this colonially ravaged, sugar-rich land historically based on massive slave-labor imports and wealth-producing exports. All of the Guianas abut Brazil's northern boundary. Brazil figured prominently in colonial history of the Guianas, as did the Guianas, especially Suriname, in Brazilian history. Here native people and those of African descent fought for freedom in the interiors, as Spanish, English, Dutch, and French battled along the coasts and major rivers (such as the Orinoco) for control of the burgeoning sugar industry. This is the land of the mythologized and dread "Carib," or "Caribee," from which comes both the name of the Caribbean Sea and also the ideas held firmly by white Europeans of indigenous cannibalism: "as late as the 18th century, the Spanish were still chronicling the appearance of Carib armadas, involving perhaps over 200 warriors, on the Orinoco" (Whitehead 1988:1). Below the Guianas, on the coast, lie the Brazilian shores, and in Brazil's vast interior, called Amazonia after the mighty Amazon which drains the area for 4,000 miles, is a Portuguese-speaking area the size of the United States. Here the native peoples encountered by Europeans belong to the Tupi, or Tupi-Guaraní, family of languages, whose people also mustered armies in the thousands to travel from central Amazonas thence to various interiors and the coast. Until the past century, and in some places more recently, Tupi, often called Nheengatú, not Portuguese, was the lingua franca of Brazil's Amazonian interior.

The history of early Brazil, like that of the Guianas, is one of warfare, exploitation, destruction of the native populations, and importation of vast numbers of slaves fresh from Africa. The most prominent entrepôt of African slaves was Bahia-Salvador, the site of the ALARA meeting mentioned at the outset of this introductory chapter. Brazilian slavery remained legal until 1888, making this the last modern nation-state in the Americas to undertake formal manumission. According to R. K. Kent (1979), writing about the African state of Palmares in colonial Brazil, African slaves were first documented as imported to this Portuguese colony in 1552, and "in 1580, five years after the founding of Loanda and on the eve of Brazil's sugar boom, there were no fewer than 10,000 Africans in Brazil" (Kent 1979:170).

For their part, the Dutch expanded avariciously out of their holdings in Suriname and laid claim to Brazil between 1630 and 1654, when the Portuguese, with the help of the Afro-Portuguese Black Regiment of Henrique Dias (Kent 1979:170–71), finally defeated them and drove them northward into the Guianas. By this time there were free societies of African-Brazilians, many speaking Tupi, scattered throughout the interior of Brazil. These Quilombos, as they were (and are) called, soon made themselves known:

Slaves who freed themselves by escaping into the bush became something of a problem several decades before the Dutch took Pernambuco. In 1597, a Jesuit Father, Pedro Rodrigues, was able to write that the "foremost enemies of the colonizer are revolted Negroes from Guiné in some mountain areas, from where they raid and give much trouble, and the time may come when they will dare to attack and destroy farms as their relatives do on the Island of São Thóme." (Kent 1979:174)

The most famous of the Quilombos is that of Palmares, the "Black Republic," which emerged sometime in the late sixteenth or early seventeenth century, was acknowledged in Brazilian writings to be in Pernambuco in 1640 (the heart of what was Dutch-controlled territory), and maintained its statehood until 1694, when its legions were eventually defeated by the Brazilian colonial army. According to Kent (1979:188),

> the most apparent significance of Palmares to African history is that an African political system could be transferred to a different continent; that it could come to govern not only individuals from a variety of ethnic groups in Africa but also those born in Brazil, pitch black or almost white, latinized or close to Amerindian roots; and that it could endure for almost a full century against two European powers, Holland and Portugal. And this is no small tribute to the vitality of the traditional African art in governing men.

On the "art of governing" we come not only to social relations, politics, and power but also to the world of deities and spirits. With the spiritual we transcend the world of long-dead heroes and move to contemporary times, when African American people of Brazil gather to revere their ancestry, seen in its ethnic diversity as well as its American Africanity. We seek here images that stand emblematically for endurance, continuity, change, and creativity. The stage is set as Afro-Brazilians of the late 1990s invoke the powers of Òguń.

As a participant in the ALARA Conference in Bahia, Torres, together with others there, was recently introduced to the dances which characterize Òguń as they were performed for and consumed by tourists and Western scholars alike in a popular restaurant and in a small Candomblé house in the Marechal Rondon district of Salvador-Bahia. Òguń, the aggressive warrior, delighted the spectators at the restaurant and challenged all to explore the meaning of these performances in the socioeconomically impoverished Afro-Brasilian communities throughout Bahia and elsewhere. Margaret Thompson Drewal's comparative analysis of dances for Òguń in Yorubaland and Bahia eloquently demonstrates the latent power embodied in these performances. As devotees of Candomblé, they honor and summon the gods. Òguń, the god of iron and of war, comes first. He clears the way for other deities with a steel cutlass in his hand, subtly engaging in movements in a performance that "offers a gross understatement of underlying warlike

intent" (Thompson Drewal 1989:228) that culminates in a trance and in the ultimate expression of power and force.

In this second volume we seek to demonstrate to readers how the forces of
history synergize with the powers of the present and recent past to form a system
of blackness transcending cultural color coding, and how such systems transcend
the barriers of racial and racialist oppression. This volume opens with eight chapters on Eastern South America. We begin and end this part with Brazil, with three
chapters on Guyana and two on Suriname in between. The flow is from recent
movements of Black Power in Brazil to structures of domination that have long
characterized this Third World development-oriented nation-state that is the size
of the United States. We then explore such structures vis-à-vis political resistance
and socioracial pluralism, moving to black ethnic, religious, and ceremonial
power and symbolic insurgence.

In "Blacks and the *Abertura Democrática*," the opening essay in this part, the
political scientist Michael Mitchell analyzes what happened when the authoritarianism of the Brazilian power structure tried to "open" democratically and was
confronted with organized black protest in the *sociedade do clases*. The contemporary Black Power movement in Brazil has two "high points," according to the
author: "One is the development of the cultural phenomenon known as Black
Soul and the other is the creation of the Movimento Negro Unificado contra
Discriminacão Racial [Black Unified Movement against Racial Discrimination]."

"Brazil is a society of classes" is a common observation, reflecting an important facet of Brazilian ideology. According to the prominent Brazilian sociologist
Florestan Fernandes, this ideology serves to cloak a system of antiblack racism
with a mantle of nationalist racial mixture and cultural syncretism. In a long essay
presented here, Fernandes's important argument is this: "As long as color prejudice operates predominantly under cover of clearly defined class situations, its
victims ordinarily have to contend with insuperable difficulties, and it is often
impossible for them to defend their social interests through the social techniques,
forms of behavior, and controls consecrated and guaranteed by the competitive
social order." And he goes on to document this generalization by saying, "color
operates as a dual frame of reference: it inseparably links race and social position,
socially stigmatizing an entire racial category [that of darkened, or black]."

We follow these two expositions of Brazilian oppression and black sociopolitical resistance with three complementary views of Guyana. To visualize the plural
structure of this nation-state, think of a horizontal bar over several vertical bars.
The horizontal bar is the white, foreign, colonial elite. The vertical bars represent
separated racial populations, especially black, East Indian, and indigenous American. When the top bar is removed in the transformation from foreign colony to
nation-state, those in the successful, upwardly mobile middle class assume power.
This gives a radically transformed plural character to the new elite, who coexist
with the old white (and lightened) elite. The Guyanese sociologist Ralph C.
Gomes, in his chapter, writes about this new elite from the standpoint of an "in-

sider," indicating present and future dynamics of continuing ethnic conflict that characterize the breaking down of hegemonic relations of color. Next, Leo A. Despres discusses the nature of resource competition and the ethnogenesis of color coding in Guyana at many class levels, and Lee Drummond offers a theory of intersystems drawn from Creole linguistics to understand Guyanese ethnic relationships far from the centers of power and wealth. Both Despres and Drummond review the concept of "ethnicity" from various standpoints. These reviews, together with the analysis of Gomes, should give the reader an excellent orientation to the issues that saturate the literature on blackness and other racialist characteristics throughout the Caribbean and Central and South America in the twentieth century.

In the next two chapters, by B. Edward Pierce and Sally Price respectively, blackness in two regions of Suriname is examined, and we see different processes of oppression at work. The first focuses on black (*nengre*) kinship and residence in Paramaribo, the nation-state's capital, and the second on enduring social relations among the Saramaka Maroons of Suriname's interior. In Paramaribo, as noted in volume I among the Garífuna and in western Colombia and Ecuador, great flexibility of family structure allows black urbanites to undergo transformations while maintaining certain reference points—especially male mobility and female-focused nuclearity—over several centuries.

In the interior of Suriname, Price demonstrates the very important roles of women's activities in art and song in the social construction of a distinctive Maroon reality. She further demonstrates the need for cosmopolitan knowledge and orientation to be held simultaneously with a local, specifically Maroon, awareness:

> Whether in the streets of Paramaribo, the construction sites at Afobaka [missile-launch site in French Guiana], the Djuka villages in eastern Suriname, the towns of French Guiana, or the diamond-mining camps of Brazil, Saramaka men must know how to converse in foreign languages, deal with people from other ethnic backgrounds, hold down a job, and make wise purchases for the return home.

Women, by contrast, are seen by men, and by themselves, as tied to house and garden. Price carefully alerts us to the fact that though the configuration of woman-at-home-and-garden, man-out-in-the-world may appear functional from some structural perspectives, the women themselves are fundamentally dissatisfied with their contemporary lot: "The strong sexual asymmetries of Maroon life—material, social, and conceptual—are deeply embedded in the arts as they are in subsistence practices, in marriage patterns, or in religious beliefs. Each Maroon woman's life experience represents, in part, a response to the attitudes and institutions that define her as a woman."

The final chapter in this part deals with Brazil. In "Dancing for Ògún in Yorubaland and in Brazil," Thompson Drewal explores the commonality of Brazilian and Nigerian (specifically Yoruban) communal rituals by a focus on dance. She defines dance itself as "a poetic, non-verbal expression continually created and recreated by countless performer/interpreters over generations." Through dance, participants commune with one another and with the spirits: "ritual dance is an unspoken essay on the nature and quality of metaphysical power. . . . [it] is a metaphysical force actualized in the phenomenal world."

Appropriately, the author begins her description and analysis in Africa and moves to Brazil to demonstrate remarkable communal features of ritual activity in two key sectors of the circum-Atlantic culture area. She focuses on Ògún, the powerful deity whose embodiment is iron and who transforms concepts into actions that often reflect violence.

This chapter deals especially with the power of verbal utterances and documents the commonalities of the use of rhetoric in Candomblé ritual in Bahia (Salvador) and Brazil (where Yoruba slaves were brought as late as the 1800s and where slavery was not formally abolished until nearly the twentieth century) and in Yoruba ritual in Nigeria. A significant feature in the Brazilian Candomblé is that the person taking the role of Ògún in ritual activity slashes with a sword, symbolic of active fighting and resistance to domination, whereas in Yorubaland, tales are told of Ògún-out-of-control with a sword, but no ritual enactment symbolizing combat takes place.

Thompson Drewal, following the Brazilian writer Filho (1888), suggests that Ògún's warrior stance in Brazilian Candomblé developed from an earlier black performance in which people called Congos fought ritually with people called Quilombos. In such activity the Congos represented slaves fresh from Africa (*bozales* in Spanish), and the Quilombos were black Maroon people from fortified villages created through self-liberation. The fusion of Ògún (as iron) and Shangó (as lightning) in Brazil, as elsewhere in the Americas, unites the features of blackness and fire in ritual activity around the African American Atlantic-rim culture region.

Power (*ase* in Yoruba), as a key concept in understanding human communities from Africa to the Americas, is again underscored by the presentation of data and sophisticated analysis in this essay.

> We can go beyond the creative/destructive dichotomy and examine the wellspring of power that underlies both creation and destruction: Ògún àse. The dynamic configurations expressed in Ògún's dances and verbal arts serve as models of and for humans so that . . . they may cope with the environment. Through ritual performance, people tap and use the power that is appropriate for meeting life's demands.

The final part of this second volume deals with the Caribbean. In writings on this region, three perspectives predominate. There is American historicism, wherein cultural traits, complexes, themes, foci, and syncretisms (e.g., Herskovits

1958) are examined for their resemblance to European, Native American, *or* (the everlasting polarity) African correspondences. There is European-American structural-functionalism, especially as manifest in the work of the Harvard sociologist Talcott Parsons and the British anthropologists Meyer Fortes and Raymond T. Smith. And there is pluralism.

Before moving into chapters that may be understood by one or another of these models, we present a recent study undertaken by Arlene Torres in Puerto Rico, one of the last vestiges of U.S. colonial domination in the Americas. This is the world of islands south of Florida, east of Central America, and north of the Spanish Main, the northeastern sector of South America. Here, in the Bahamas, Columbus made landfall on October 12, 1492, to initiate the processes of war, conquest, and enslavement that became the legacy of the *leyenda negra*. We focus on Puerto Rico as a microcosm of domination and resistance in the Greater Antilles (Cuba, Haiti–Dominican Republic, and Jamaica as well as Puerto Rico) because this area was the awful crucible of the first wave of the Spanish Conquest. The dates and events given here are used to present a sketch of a microcosm of Antillean cultural transformation and to present the context for Torres's chapter.

Puerto Rican historiographers generally have argued that black slavery in Puerto Rico was not significant as compared with the rest of the Spanish-speaking Caribbean. Scholars who compared the racial-color continuum in Latin America and the Caribbean have also argued that in Puerto Rico the Iberian variant of race relations dominated (Hoetink 1967, Mintz 1974, Carrión 1993). As Puerto Ricans commemorated the 122nd anniversary of the abolition of slavery, Peggy Ann Bliss (1995:30) summarized the views of the linguist Manuel Alvarez Nazario:

> the African influence in Puerto Rico can be seen most in music, dance and popular customs, where they left "significant traces." The "successful Hispanization" of blacks led to the loss of the most socio-cultural traces of Africa, especially in beliefs and religious rites, customs, dress and food, he said.

Ironically, Alvarez Nazario has written one of the few scholarly works on African influences in Puerto Rican language and speech patterns. Similar views were expressed by the historian Luis Díaz Soler and the anthropologist Ricardo Alegría, their own historical and ethnographic work notwithstanding.

Using Puerto Rico as our microcosm, we turn to the early history of the European conquest of the Caribbean to appreciate the depth of violence that spawned the history of blackness in the Caribbean. The initial period of the Spanish conquest of the Americas was marked by the subordination of indigenous and black peoples and their concomitant resistance to the oppressive Spanish militia in Puerto Rico and Hispaniola (present-day Haiti and the Dominican Republic). Juan Ponce de León and his fellow explorers did not hesitate to engage in fierce attacks against the natives, wherein trained war dogs as well as firepower were actively deployed. Varner and Varner (1983:27) point out that the use of dogs in Puerto Rico is not as extensively chronicled when compared with other areas of the Americas. However, there are accounts of two dogs, Becerillo (Little Calf) and Leoncico (Little Lion), that were used to subjugate, maime, and kill large numbers of men, women, and children of the native population. Becerillo viciously attacked the Arawak people who conspired to rid themselves of the colonists. As the "Indians" invaded the village of Aguada in response to orders from the *cacique* (chief) Agüeybana, the Spanish defended themselves with their firearms and Becerillo. Men quickly moved to secure the capital at Caparra as the indigenous population waged a massive attack. Once again, Becerillo was unleashed.

> Not far from Juan Ponce's capital at Caparra, Becerillo had helped the Spaniards, under the capitancy of Salazar, to subjugate a group of Indians. Once the struggle was over, the Christians, plagued with ennui, were awaiting the arrival of the governor, who was not far distant. To relieve his men from tedium, Capitán Salazar summoned an old Indian woman and placed a fragment of paper in her hands, ordering her, under threat of being cast to the dogs, to carry the paper to the governor. Reasoning that such an errand might provide a means of escape for her people, the woman readily set out on her mission. When she had proceeded but a short distance, the amused soldiers unleashed Becerillo, and crying *tómala* (take her), sent the dog in swift pursuit. They assumed, of course, that the animal would overtake her, tear her to pieces, and devour her on the spot. (Varner and Varner 1983:24–26)

Ponce de León's declaration of war against the "Indians" in 1511 prompted Sancho de Arango, among others, to raid indigenous settlements. He had captured "twenty-five slaves or prisoners, the majority women and children, and war booty" (Murga Sanz 1959:65). The indigenous people retaliated. Three years later, there was an attempt to destroy the estate of Capitán Sancho de Arango. As the "Caribs" invaded, Becerillo was unleashed. This time he was killed with a poisonous arrow by a warring "Carib" (Varner & Varner 1983:24).

As early as 1512 the southern region of Puerto Rico was being sacked and pillaged by the Spaniards in search of indigenous slaves, who were captured and later sold in Caparra, in the northern part of the island. The Spaniards organized *cabalgadas*, which were military raids to acquire indigenous slaves and their possessions (Alegría 1985:69). On June 15, 1512, it was reported that Alvaro de Saavedra conducted a *cabalgada* in the land of the *cacique* of Guayama (Murga Sanz 1959:65, Sued Badillo 1983:22). Murga Sanz (1960:329) also confirms that the expeditions were carried out to capture indigenous slaves in the interior as well as in neighboring islands. Documents of the Real Hacienda of 1515 report the capturing of two indigenous women of the *cacique* of Guayama who were sold as slaves for twenty-eight and ten *pesos de oro*, respectively.

As the decade progressed, colonizers settled in the southern region. *Estancias,* small farms, developed as men in search of fortune engaged in the hunting of wild animals and clandestine operations to capture indigenous slaves. With the capital they acquired from their expeditions in the area and the support of prominent colonizers in Hispaniola and Puerto Rico, they financed maritime activity to the coast of Venezuela in search of pearls and slaves.

In 1537, a Spanish conqueror, Gerónimo de Ortal, was anchored in the port of Guayama preparing for his departure to Cubagua. Based on the licenses granted to transport goods in caravelles, they were required to make a stop in Hispaniola or Puerto Rico (Otte 1963:230–31). In 1527, one year after the order to cease the exportation of indigenous slaves from Puerto Rico to the pearl beds of Cubagua, Diego Cavallero, a *vecino* in Hispaniola, requested and was granted a license to bring two caravelles from Seville directly to Cubagua loaded with supplies and twelve *esclavos negros*, black slaves, from Cape Verde or Guinea. These black slaves were to furnish the deadly labor heretofore performed by native people, diving for pearls (Otte 1963:231). Shortly thereafter (1528), a license was granted to import 4,000 black slaves, at least one third of whom were women, to be distributed in Hispaniola, San Juan (Puerto Rico), and Tierra Firme (Venezuela).

As the *cabalgadas* engaged in horrific activities to capture indigenous slaves, they obtained the necessary labor to extract pearls from the islands of Cubagua and Margarita off the coast of Venezuela. The members of the *cabalgadas* did not recognize a 1518 decree ordering Spaniards to return the "Indians" captured in the pearl coasts to their native lands (Otte 1963:105).

The island of Cubagua anchored vessels from Puerto Rico and Hispaniola. Licenses were granted to *vecinos* and *pobladores* to acquire pearls and slaves "wherever they may be found" (Otte 1963:60). One of the first colonists to settle in the valley of Guayama was Francisco Juancho de Luyando. He had joined Ponce de León in 1508 on his expedition to Puerto Rico (Murga Sanz 1959:35). He is recognized along with Diego Ramos for waging war against the "Caribs," who invaded Caparra from the southeast in 1513. Juancho de Luyando and Ramos were authorized by the Crown to actively engage in the search for and capture of "runaway and rebellious blacks and Indians." Juancho possessed haciendas and *granjerías* and supported the expeditions to Cubagua and Margarita by providing the *cabalgadas* with food in exchange for slaves, gold, and salt (Sued Badillo 1983:27). Even though the population at Cubagua and Margarita had been declared non-Carib, with pressure from the colonists in Puerto Rico and Hispaniola, the coast was later declared "Carib," which allowed for the enslavement of the indigenous population (Otte 1977:356, cited in Whitehead 1988:11, Williams and Lewis 1993).

No one was spared the brutality by which wealth was garnered in the exploitation of Cubagua. The enslaved Native Americans were forced to dive for pearls until they met their untimely death in the waters filled with hammerhead sharks. Caribs were brought to Puerto Rico via the southeastern coast to be sold as slaves while conditions in Cubagua and Margarita continued to deteriorate. Antonio

Flores, who was sent to establish order, captured two *caciques*. The elder of the two was hanged, and the other was tied to the muzzle of a cannon. The dismembered body was fed to Flores's dogs (Muilenburg 1991:37).

By the mid-sixteenth century the native population in most of the Spanish-speaking Caribbean was decimated and prohibitions against the importation of indigenous slaves from other areas were being "enforced." An entire people was destroyed as the Spanish colonists acquired the necessary wealth that helped to finance the entry of ships illegally carrying slaves from Africa.

Upon the arrival of the Spanish conquerors, people of African descent contributed to the development of Puerto Rican society and culture. However, the importation of Africans throughout the initial stages of the Conquest was considered negligible and therefore not worthy of study. Luis M. Díaz Soler's seminal work, *Historia de la Esclavitud Negra in Puerto Rico* (1965), provides the basis for contemporary scholarship. Díaz Soler recognized that his work was a pioneering study in constant need of revision. Twenty years passed before Sued Badillo (1986), in a ground-breaking study co-authored with Angel López Cantos, *Puerto Rico Negro (Black Puerto Rico)*, challenged sixteenth-century Puerto Rican historiography. People of African descent have yet to be fully written into the historical texts of the seventeenth and eighteenth centuries.

Freed and free black men accompanied the Spanish explorers in their expeditions to various regions of the Americas. They did so as fellow explorers, soldiers, manual laborers, and servants. The free black population consisted of *ladinos*. These were free Iberian black men who served the interests of the Spanish conquerors and were rewarded with gold and indigenous slaves.

The Spanish elite in Puerto Rico and Hispaniola gathered financial resources and arms to engage in the capture of the indigenous population. *Baquianos*, hunters and guides with an intimate knowledge of indigenous settlements, were dedicated to hunting and capturing Carib slaves (Sued Badillo and López Cantos 1986:65; see also Murga Sanz 1960, Otte 1977:129). Expeditions to Lucayas (the Bahamas), Cumaná, the Lesser Antilles, and the South American coast resulted in the enslavement and death of huge segments of the indigenous population. Records provide us with accounts of free black men who established themselves within the military and obtained fortunes as they joined the European colonizers in the exploitation of the Americas.

Antón Mexía, a freed black man, provided services to Nicolás de Ovando, governor of Hispaniola, as an assistant to a crossbowman. He was later listed as an *encomendero* engaged in the extraction of precious metals with three indigenous slaves. His son, Francisco Mexía, gained prominence as a *soldado y cazador de fortuna*, engaging in battles against the indigenous population. He also was a noted slave catcher. Mexía hunted down and captured "Carib" slaves for a price. Testimony regarding the services of Mexía revealed that for one year he was contracted for forty-four *pesos de oro* to capture *caciques* and *indios*. He was contracted beginning on November 8, 1512. In an attempt to obtain indigenous laborers from the *cacica* Luisa, he was reportedly killed by "Caribs" in 1513. His father, Antón Mexía, appealed to the authorities for payment due for his son's services (Murga Sanz 1959:132; see also Sued Badillo and López Cantos 1986:19–21).

It is interesting to note that Puerto Rican historians have romanticized Mexía's "untimely" death among the Taíno, the indigenous Arawakan-speaking people of Puerto Rico, by arguing that in an act of courage, Mexía attempted to protect the *cacica* Luisa from the warring Caribs. Another noted soldier and slave catcher was the *ladino* Juan Garrido, who joined Ponce de León in the conquest of Puerto Rico, Mexico, and Florida (Murga Sanz 1959:35, Sued Badillo and López Cantos 1986:22).

In addition to the importation of these free men, black *ladinos* were imported as domestic servants, producers of subsistence crops, laborers in the sugar *ingenios*, and extractors of gold. *Ladinos* were often preferred over indigenous slaves as skilled manual laborers, given their previous experience in the Iberian peninsula (Sued Badillo and López Cantos 1986:67). Díaz Soler (1965:20) states that the Spanish Crown did not initially intend to transport African slaves to the New World. However, by 1501 the Crown had authorized the importation of black slaves. The instructions sent to Nicolás de Ovando stated that Moors, Jews, or persons recently Christianized could not travel to the Americas, with the exception of Spanish-born and Christianized slaves, *ladinos*. The enslaved *ladino* was forced to work side by side with indigenous slaves in the extraction of mineral resources. Sued Badillo (1986:69) argues that the "rigor and vicissitudes of mining life influenced the two *ladino* uprisings in Puerto Rico."

In 1503 Nicolás de Ovando requested that the *ladino* population be barred from entering the Americas because, upon their arrival, they joined the Indians and became fugitives from the law. However, by 1505 Ovando had requested that the importation of *ladinos* be reestablished in Hispaniola.

Ladinos joined forces with the Arawak population in an effort to overthrow Spanish rule. In 1514, a hurricane devastated the island. Food supplies were scarce. The availability of indigenous labor declined and the *ladinos* were forced to work in the mines. They retaliated and joined the Taíno in the interior of the island, waging war against the Spanish by raiding their settlements, destroying their crops, and further limiting their food supply.

Within this context, the Maroon emerged. According to Richard Price (1993:283), the word *cimarrón* has Arawak roots. The Spaniards adopted the word to refer to feral domestic cattle that had taken to the hills in Hispaniola, and soon after the term was applied to escaped Indian slaves. By the end of the 1530s it was beginning to refer primarily to African Americans and had strong connotations of "fierceness," of being "feral," "wild," or "untamed."

Although the indigenous population declined precipitously, indigenous people continued to wage war against the Spanish colonists. The forces of nature provided them with the opportunity to weaken the Spanish stronghold, albeit temporarily. In 1530 a hurricane again devastated the island of Puerto Rico, destroying haciendas, and the natives (in cooperation with runaway African slaves) seized the opportunity to further attack and destroy the settlements. This time, not even the dogs were spared (Sued Badillo 1983:28). In 1531, a second major uprising occurred involving the enslaved "black" population. This represented a greater threat to the colonizers because the number of people of color had increased, while the "white" population had decreased.

In addition to major uprisings, slaves in Puerto Rico as elsewhere engaged in day-to-day resistance against the social order. Black slaves were considered inferior beings. They were not simply captives of just wars; they were slaves paying a price for their conversion to Christianity (Rout 1976:20). Because slaves were considered intellectually and spiritually inferior beings, their ability to become fully Christianized was open to question. Moreover, their Afrocentric religious beliefs and practices were interpreted as dark sources of active *maleficia*. In 1549, several enslaved black women accused of sorcery and witchcraft were hanged in the main plaza in Caparra. Despite efforts to ban their religious expression, the enslaved people continued to resist.

It should be clear by now that the early history of conquest focused on white (Spanish) conquerors and the indigenous Arawak (often classed as "Carib") and black African and black Spanish. As the subsequent history of this island unfolded, so too did ethnic sets of classification emerge; these sets oscillate on the poles of racial mixture and blackness.

While, on the one hand, the Spanish-speaking Caribbean draws upon an ideology of *mestizaje* that is rooted in Iberian, indigenous, and African culture, in various social contexts many stress the distinctiveness of these "races" and of their influence on Caribbean history, society, and culture. Torres notes in her analysis of Puerto Rican racial ideologies: "Upon first glance, it appears that the national emphasis on *mestizaje* in Puerto Rico promotes processes of social integration. However, there is still a hyper-privileging of individuals of European descent with phenotypic features associated with whiteness." She demonstrates ethnohistorically and ethnographically how historical data are interpreted and misinterpreted to conform to racist ideological perspectives regarding the contributions of black people to the colonized nation. Further, by focusing on the ways by which the geographic terrain is culturally mapped and racialized, she demonstrates how categories and epitomizing symbols established in the Spanish colonial era such as *el negro esclavo*, the black slave, *el jíbaro*, a mythico-historical mountain peasant, and *la gran familia puertorriqueña*, the great Puerto Rican family, come together in contemporary Puerto Rican society to undermine attempts by Puerto Ricans not only to speak out against racism but also to assert their blackness *and* their Puerto Ricanness. In short, Torres argues that to be engaged with blackness is to be truly Puerto Rican; hence the title of her essay, "The Great Puerto Rican Family Is Really Really Black."

From Puerto Rico we move to an island society of the Lesser Antilles, St. Lucia, a nation-state comprising Grenada and the southern Grenadines, including Carriacou. The first of our two chapters on Grenada is by M. G. Smith. Smith's model of "the plural society" has attracted the attention of those interested in the phenomenon of "blackness" as a social construct affecting class, status, and political-bloc relationships. He offers here a sophisticated methodological and significant theoretical study of the community of elites in Grenada set within the polarity of what he calls the Grenadian "elite" and the "folk." This polarity becomes one of "white or near white" for the elite and mostly black for the folk, and includes most if not all of the oppositions that we discussed in the general introduction: light/dark, God/Devil, religious/superstitions, good/evil.

Douglas Midgett, a specialist in Grenada social structure and history as well as on the history and race relations of Grenadians in London, discusses relationships among literatures produced by West Indian people as a means by which to understand West Indian social relationships. An important dimension here is the use, in writing, of images of Africa and Europe. These relationships were formed through slavery and the struggle for freedom. Critical to Midgett's discussion is the creative use of language. His chapter problematizes the relationships among literature, history, and identity of West Indians. The very act of writing, he notes, is critically important in a social milieu characterized by "cultural ambiguity and social schisms" and influenced and shaped by institution of slavery and colonialism for centuries. He further states:

> This literature expresses a great awareness of the subtleties and complexities of social patterns of the islands. As such, it has underscored the absurdities of color and class distinctions, along with their destructive ramifications, with as much alacrity as it has condemned the role of the European colonizer as an historical and social malignancy.

Analyses of literary works from the Spanish and francophone Caribbean reveal similar themes (Benítez-Rojo 1995, Carpentier 1974, Glissant 1995).

Moving south to Trinidad, off Venezuela's northeastern coast, John Stewart, a creative writer of serious fiction and an anthropological ethnographer, illustrates some of the features brought forth by Midgett. Stewart's story, "Stick Song," set in a small community in his native Trinidad, reminds us once again of the latent power of dance awakened as Daaga, the protagonist, hears the distant rumble of drums in a Trinidadian village. With a stick in hand, Daaga dances, the drums summon him, compel him.

> The drums tell you what to do.
> "Aie but look, the American dancing!"
> "He ent no American: he's a born Trinidadian."
> "Aie, but he dancing sweet, man."
> "Bound to. No Yankee could dance this dance. Besides, he Daaga."
> "Who that?"
> "The fella what did kill all the Spanish and them before your grandfather time."

"He come back? He spirit come back?"
"Spirit like that don't bury, you know . . . "

In our introduction to volume I we wrote about the visit to the University of Illinois at Urbana-Champaign of two black leaders now becoming internationally known: Zulia Mena, the congresswoman from Colombia, and Fortunata Medina Pinedo de Pérez, the black Bolivian leader who led the recitation of the *saya* choral and dance form of that nation. The week following the visits in September 1996, Gloria Rolando, an Afro-Cuban filmmaker, visited the Urbana-Champaign campus. Rolando spoke of the vibrancy of Afro-Cuban traditions and of the common threads among black people throughout the African diaspora. She presented two documentary films: "Oguń: Eternally Present" and "My Footsteps in Baragua." In these films Rolando demonstrated how Cuban society was transformed by people who came to the island as enslaved Africans in centuries past and by poor laborers who migrated predominantly from Trinidad, Barbados, and Jamaica in the early twentieth century.

Cubans of West Indian descent who had migrated to Panama to construct the transoceanic canal were encouraged to settle there. When Cubans of West Indian descent speak of their homeland, they yearn to return to Trinidad, Barbados, or Jamaica to establish ties with their ancestors who fought against the Spanish, like Daaga in Stewart's story, before their grandfather's time and against the British in their own time.

Throughout this introduction, mobility and migration have been seen as dynamic phenomena that shape the structures and processes discussed. We offer one example out of hundreds in the chapter by Bonham C. Richardson, who focuses on migration cultures of the island communities of St. Kitts and Nevis (which became a unified nation-state in 1993). To underscore the importance of migration and remittances on these Caribbean islands, Richardson states, "Young people who go away are expected to provide financial support for family and friends left behind, *and almost everyone left on the two islands depends, at least in part, upon the success of those, old and young, who have emigrated*" (emphasis added). Once again we find the organizational feature of male migration complemented by female household nuclearity now clearly demarcated in all sections of these volumes (but not in all of the communities and regions discussed; see Richardson 1992, Fog Olwig 1993).

The next two chapters, by Kevin A. Yelvington and Faye V. Harrison respectively, deal with gender, ethnicity, and poverty in two nation-states—Trinidad-Tobago and Jamaica. In the first we come to see communal work in a factory in terms of broad structural and deep historical processes and learn that "gender and ethnicity are constructed in relation to each other." In the second, we are taken to the informal economy of a Jamaican slum and see what Harrison refers to as its "feminization." Her conclusion is that "sexual or gender inequality represents an essential and integral feature of social relations and cultural construction in Jamaica, where for the past four hundred years colonial and imperialist exploitation have governed the development of economic, political, and sociocultural patterns and structures." This certainly resonates with other observations in the literature we have been examining (McClaurin 1996, Bolles 1996).

Diane J. Austin, also writing about Jamaica, addresses issues of theoretical importance raised earlier and offers fresh viewpoints on relationships that obtain among class, traditions, history, and ideology.

"Celebration" is central to tradition and culture. In the plural societies composed of complex intersystems of the Caribbean, we find ritual, play, festival, and fantasy to derive from the European/African opposition that came to permeate the Caribbean scene with the demise of Native Americans almost everywhere on the islands (except Dominica). The late Frank Manning focuses on cricket in Bermuda (and by implication elsewhere in the Caribbean) to dramatize a situation detailed by the three previous chapters (and by others): "The total genre [cricket] dramatizes a fundamental, racially oriented conflict between cultural identity and economic interest—a conflict that is generalizable to the Caribbean (and perhaps other decolonizing areas) and that underlies the region's political situation." Throughout his chapter Manning demonstrates how Bermudans use figures of speech (metonymy, metaphor) attached to play to signify their awareness of structures of domination and patterns of resistance. Such play, in other words, is counterhegemonic within a structure of domination. These tropes form a metacommentary, he submits, that may be Caribbean-wide. He argues that "the [cricket] games reflect . . . a white power structure that has lost its traditional character but preserved its oppressive force" (see also Malec 1995, Mandle and Mandle 1988).

The subject of the next chapter, African-Latin dance traditions, has a long history. In 1962, Geoffrey Gorer reflected on his book *Africa Dances*, first published in 1935. True to the post–World War II Western hypostasis of African "tribalization" interfering with "modernization," Gorer looked back on his research as documenting the relics of folklore: "Serious dancing in West Africa is an important component of the tribal view of the world . . . [it] goes counter to the modernization, to the leap into the twentieth century, which is the goal of the present governments of the succession [from colonialist] states" (Gorer 1962: vi). He argued that if emergent West African governments attempted to "preserve" African dances as aesthetic phenomena, they would "dwindle into pettiness and quaintness." And, in frustration over the aesthetic attachment to varied dance forms by those espousing the new doctrine of West African *négritude*, with all its links to the Caribbean and to France, he simply wrote of the latter that it was something too elusive for him to grasp.

Some thirty years later Paul Gilroy (1993), focusing on black music, rethinks the issues, and writes:

The syncretic complexity of black expressive cultures alone supplies powerful reasons for resisting the idea that an untouched, pristine Africanity resides inside
these [musical] forms. . . . Today, this involves the difficult task of striving to comprehend the reproduction of cultural traditions not in the unproblematic trans-
mission of a fixed essence through time but in the breaks and interruptions which
suggest that the invocation of tradition may itself be a distinct, though covert, response to the destabilizing flux of post-contemporary world. (Gilroy 1993:101)

Gilroy's position has been stated by many writers, including Zora Neale Hurston
in the United States and J. Clyde Mitchell in Africa, using different genres of
expression, and they predate the radical tribalization formulations of Gorer. Since
the early 1960s writers such as Charles Keil in the United States and Nigeria and
later Christopher Waterman in Nigeria, have continued to understand black music in its multiple, transformable dimensions of creative communication. This
literature, through the mid-1970s, is reviewed by Anya Peterson Royce in *The
Anthropology of Dance* (1977).

For this volume we have chosen Yvonne Daniel's chapter, "Rumba: Social and
Aesthetic Change in Cuba." Here our attention is turned to one of the most
popular and enduring dances of Latin America, the Rumba (or Rhumba). Rumba
is a dance that foreign tourists like to see performed; it is a dance sponsored by
the socialist government of Fidel Castro. These forces of aesthetic performances
come from "above." Rumba is also a dance tradition "invented" and transformed
by black people of Cuba, most of them poor; it is a dance performed at local
levels; in this way the tradition bubbles up through nation-state ethnic and class
strata from "below." From above, Daniel tells us, "rumba's African and Spanish
movement sequences connect powerful physicality and aesthetic stimulation to
feelings regarding the Cuban nation and its people." And from below, she writes,
"the dark-skinned or black *rumbero* still sings of liberation and is concerned with
social dignity and personal artistic self-worth. . . ."

This second volume ends with a description and analysis of salient dimensions
of politics and voodoo during the era of François Duvalier (Papa Doc, 1957–
1971) and his son, Jean-Claude Duvalier (1971–1986). The Haitian-American
anthropologist and dependency theorist Michel S. Laguerre begins his chapter
with "Pilgrimage, Voodoo, and Politics" to demonstrate enduring relationships
among village structure, black pilgrimage to the "periphery" of Haitian society,
Vodún worship, and sociopolitical revelation. He then takes us to the "politicization of Voodoo" as discussed in 1928 by Jean Price-Mars with regard to its role in
the Haitian revolution of 1804. Following a review of this important subject he
proposes to look at it "as two poles of the same continuum . . . [reflecting] my way
of dissecting Haitian national culture as comprising, on the one hand, the dominant Western-oriented culture and, on the other, the mass-based popular culture,
both of them meshed together as each integrates selected elements from the
other."

One message that comes through this presentation is that Haiti may be viewed as a nation-state community of believers who have forged their beliefs repeatedly on the anvil of persecution. To understand Haitian beliefs and ritual activities one must set aside cherished Western dichotomies such as urban/rural, elite/folk, Christianity/Vodún, religion/politics, and class and ethnic hierarchy/egalitarian networks and think instead of intersecting continua. But the other side of understanding Haiti must also be clearly kept in mind. At this pole of tension the powerful dichotomies of the West—enforced in Haiti (as in other parts of the Caribbean and Central America) so often by North American military power—may also be seen as tearing the fabric of Haitian society apart. Both of these "poles" seem to be embedded today within a cosmographic-political structure of urban-rural Haiti, as manifest in the structures of temple relationships and in the relationships among secret police and Vodún priests—and, until recently, with the "President for Life."

Those who continue to think of Vodún as something akin to the mystical mumbo-jumbo of a "magic island" portrayed in much of Western literature should think seriously of Laguerre's sober presentation, based on meticulous scholarship. Vodún has its symbolic roots in West Africa (Dahomey) and early Catholic Christianity. Its ethnogenesis is found in the combination of plantation slavery and urban and rural *marronage*. Its American origins owe much to a fusion of African-European and native Arawakan systems of worship and belief, and it has been central to Haitian life since this part of Hispaniola was ceded to France by the Spanish in 1697. Its spiritual role in the second independence movement in the Americas (after that of the thirteen colonies to the north in 1776), resulting in the end of colonialism there in 1804, is best described as central. With regard to contemporary Haiti, Laguerre writes:

> One of the major consequences of the Duvalierisation of Voodoo is that it is a force to be reckoned with in the post-Duvalier era. The Voodoo church will continue to be a power base in the local community, and the Voodoo priest will maintain his role of broker or middleman to enhance his prestige, power and popularity. Thus, every constitutional president of Haiti will need a functional knowledge of Voodoo if he wishes to become a popular and successful leader. . . . Here is an instance where religious ideology was recuperated by the mainstream political system and used strategically to maintain a system of domination and inequality.

Vodún, in Laguerre's analysis, emerges as the soul of Haiti, an epitomizing symbol of the ideology of nationalist *négritude*: "Voodoo provides us in a very compact way with the political history of Haiti—which can be decoded through an analysis of titles used in the church. We find layers of historical sequences compacted in the titles and paraphernalia used by Voodooists within the realm of their church."

As noted in our general introduction, the sense of "community" was a key term in the choice of chapters presented in these two volumes. We ranged widely to draw together what we recognize as important, illustrative literature leading to genuine "comparative perspectives" with regard to communities throughout the Americas wherein "blackness," however defined, is significant to economic, social, political, ideological, aesthetic, ritual, or cosmological aspects of ongoing human life.

For the future, we see three major research priorities.

1. Researchers must develop techniques to understand cultural traditions, practices, and orientations where blackness is important to social life in the broadest and deepest possible dimensions of time and space. These techniques must include, we think, systematic attention to local-level details involving quotidian life, stylized activity, and epitomizing symbols and their embellishments. Above all else, talk—at all levels, about matters of concern to people living in communities, regions, and nation-states where blackness is important to human discourse—must be recorded, understood, and analyzed. Silences—at all levels—must be understood and analyzed as well.

2. Techniques must also be developed that draw from history, literature, the social sciences, experimental ethnography, and critical theory to affect the fluid movement from local-level microcosms to salient macrocosms and from the latter to the former.

3. And opportunities must be developed for people from communities, regions, and nation-states to study whatever they feel is necessary to enhance their technical abilities of self-identification of local and wide-flung problems attendant on issues of circum-Atlantic intersystems, including the Western sectors of the Americas.

In summary, we submit that the study of the conceptualizations of human blackness in the African diaspora and elsewhere must develop significantly into a sustained international, interethnic, intercultural effort. It must involve sharpening our critical perspectives on cherished paradigms forged over the past five centuries on the anvil of European and American racialism and racism and in the fires of black liberation.

En fin, el machete de Ogún que
anda por ahí cortándole la cabeza a viejos mitos
tiene de aliado a estos tiempos que vivimos,
a esta convulsa y nueva era donde todo es replanteado,
donde para reconstruir las nuevas y mejores sociedades a que aspiramos,
se vuelve la mirada al pasado,
criticamente, vívidamente—
macheteando la maleza del camino, cuando sea preciso—

para forjar, sólido y contundente,
el futuro.

—From Puerto Rican historicity and lore, *El Machete de Ogún*

At last, Ogún's machete
severs the heads of old myths
has as his ally these times we are living,
this convulsive new era when everything can be questioned,
when to build the better societies to which we aspire,
we turn our sight to the past,
Critically, vividly—
cutting the brush from our path when necessary—
to forge, firmly and forcefully,
the future.

—Rendition by Marilú de Laosa (1990:11)

REFERENCES FOR INTRODUCTORY CHAPTERS

Aguirre Beltrán, Gonzalo
  1946   La población negra de México (1519–1810). Mexico City:
                Ediciones Fuente Cultural.
  1958   Cuijla: Esbozo etnográfico de un pueblo negro. Mexico City:
                Fundo de Cultura Económica.

Albó, Xavier
  1994   And from Kataristas to MNRistas? The Surprising and Bold Alli-
                ance between Aymaras and Neoliberals in Bolivia. In Donna Lee
                Van Cott (editor). Indigenous Peoples and Democracy in Latin
                America. New York: St. Martin's Press and Washington, D.C.: Inter-
                American Dialogue, pp. 44–81.

Alegría, Ricardo E.
  1985   Notas sobre la procedencia cultural de los esclavos negros de
                Puerto Rico durante la segunda mitad del siglo XVI. La Revista
                del Centro de Estudios Avanzados de Puerto Rico y el Caribe
                1:58–79.

Arens, William, and Ivan Karp (editors)
  1989   Introduction. Creativity of Power: Cosmology and Action in Afri-
                can Societies. Washington, D.C.: Smithsonian Institution Press,
                pp. xi–xxix.

Arocha Rodriguez, Jaime
  1992   Afro-Colombia Denied. In North American Congress on Latin
                America (1992), pp. 28–31, 46–47.

Arrázola, Roberto
  1970   Palenque: Primer pueblo libre de América. Cartagena, Colombia:
                Ediciones Hernández.

Babcock, Barbara (editor)
  1978   The Reversible World: Symbolic Inversion in Art and Society.
                Ithaca: Cornell University Press.

Baralt, Guillermo, Carlos Collazo, Lydia Milagros González, and Ana Lydia Vega
  (compilers and editors)
  1990   El machete de Ogún: Las luchas de los esclavos en Puerto Rico
                (siglo xix). Río Piedras: Centro de Estudios de la Realidad Puertorri-
                queña, Proyecto de Divulgación Popular.

Barnet, Miguel
  1966   Biografía de un cimarrón. Havana: Academia de Ciencias de Cuba,
                Instituto de Etnología y Folklore.

Bascom, William R.
1951   The Yoruba in Cuba. Nigeria 37:14–20.
1952   The Focus of Cuban Santería. Southwestern Journal of Anthropology 6:64–68.

Bastide, Roger
1967   Les amériques noires: Les civilisations africaines dans le nouveau monde. Paris: Payot.
1969a   (editor) Les amériques noires. Special issue of the Journal de la Société des Américanistes 58.
1969b   État actuel et perspectives d'avenir des recherches afro-ambricaines. In Bastide (1969a), pp.7–29.

Beckwith, Martha
1929   Black Roadways: A Study of Jamaican Folklife. Chapel Hill: University of North Carolina Press.

Benítez Rojo, Antonio
1989   La isla que se repite: El Caribe y la perspectiva posmoderna. Hanover, N.H.: Ediciones del Norte.
1995   The Polyrhythmic Paradigm: The Caribbean and the Postmodern Era. In Vera L. Hyatt and Rex Nettleford (editors). Race, Discourse and the Origin of the Americas. Washington, D.C.: Smithsonian Institution Press.

Bennett, Lerone, Jr.
1987 [1962]   Before the Mayflower: A History of Black America. Chicago: Johnson.

Blanco, Tomás
1985 [1942]   El prejucio racial en Puerto Rico. Río Piedras: Ediciones Huracán.

Bliss, Peggy A.
1995   Black, White, Puerto Rican All Over. San Juan Star, Wednesday, March 22, pp. 30–31.

Bolles, A. Lynne
1996   Sister Jamaica: A Study of Women, Work, and Households in Kingston. Washington, D.C.: University Press of America.

Boon, James A.
1982   Other Tribes, Other Scribes: Symbolic Anthropology in the Comparative Study of Cultures, Histories, Religions, and Texts. Cambridge: Cambridge University Press.

Boorstin, Daniel J.
1983   The Discoverers: A History of Man's Search to Know His World and Himself. New York: Vintage.

Bourricaud, François
1962   Changements à Puno. Paris: Institut de Hautes Études de l'Amérique Latine.

Brandon, George
1993   Santeria from Africa to the New World. Bloomington: Indiana University Press.

Bugner, Ladislas (general editor)
1979   The Image of the Black in Western Art. 2 volumes. Cambridge: Harvard University Press.

Cabeza de Vaca, Alvar Núñez
1542a   Relation of Alvar Núñez Cabeza de Vaca. Translated from the original Spanish manuscript (1542b) by Thomas Buckingham Smith. New York: J. Munsell, 1851.
1542b   La relación que dio Alvar Núñez Cabeça de Vaca de lo acaecido en las Indias en la armada donde yua por gouernador Pamphilo de narbaez desde el año de veynte y siete hasta el año de treynta y seis que boluio a Seuilla con tres de su compania. Manuscript, Zamora, Spain.
1993 [1555]   Castaways: The Narrative of Alavar Núñez Cabeza de Vaca. Edited and with introduction by Enrique Pupo-Walker. Translated by Frances M. Lopez-Morillas. Berkeley: University of California Press.

Cabrera, Lydia
1969a   (compiler) Refranes de negros viejos. Miami: Editorial C.R. (Colección del Chicherekú).
1969b   La sociedad secreta Abakuá: Narrada por viejos adeptos. Miami: Editorial C. R. (Colección del Chicherekú).
1970a   Otán Iyebiyé: Las piedras preciosas. Miami: Mnemosyne, Ediciones Miami (Colección del Chicherekú en el Exilio).
1970b   Anagó: Vocabulario Lucumí (el Yoruba que se habla en Cuba). Miami: Cabrera y Rojas (Colección del Chicherekú).

Campbell, Mary B.
1988   The Witness and the Other Worlds. Ithaca: Cornell University Press.

Carmichael, Stokeley
1967   Quoted in Muhammed Speaks, December 15, p. 2.

Carmichael, Stokeley, and Charles Hamilton
1966   Black Power. New York: Vintage.

Carneiro, Edison
1946   Guerras de los Palmares. Translated by Tomás Muñoz Molina. Mexico City: Fondo de Cultura Economica.

Caro Baroja, Julio
1967   Vidas mágicas e inquisición. 2 volumes. Madrid: Taurus.

Carpentier, Alejo
1974   Concierto barroco. Mexico City: Siglo Veintiuno Editores.

Carrión, Juan M.
1993 Etnia, raza y la nacionalidad puertorriqueña. In Carrión, Teresa C. Garcia Ruíz, and Carlos Rodríguez Fraticelli (editors). La nación puertorriqueña: Ensayos en torno a Pedro Albizu Campos. San Juan: Editorial de la Universidad de Puerto Rico.

Carvalho Neto, Paulo de
1965 El negro uruguayo (hasta la abolición). Quito: Editorial Universitaria.

Castillo Mathieu, Nicolás del
1982 Esclavos negros en Cartagena y sus aportes léxicos. Bogotá: Instituto Caro y Cuervo LXII.

Césaire, Aimé
1947 Cahier d'un retour au pays natal. Paris: Editions Bordas.
1948 Discours sur le colonialisme. Paris: Présence Africaine.
1956 Culture et colonisation. Présence Africaine N.S. (8–10):190–205.

Chamberlain de Bianchi, Cynthia
1984 La enfermedad de gubida y el sincretismo religioso entre los Garífunas: Un analysis etnosiquíatrico. América Indígena 44 (3):519–542.

Chioma Steady, Filomina
1981 The Black Woman Cross-Culturally. Cambridge: Schenkman.

Collier, Simon, Harold Blakemore, and Thomas E. Skidmore (general editors)
1985 Cambridge Encyclopedia of Latin America and the Caribbean. New York: Cambridge University Press.

Columbus, Christopher
1960 The Journal of Christopher Columbus. Translated by Cecil James. New York: Clark N. Potter.

Córdoba L., Juan Tulio
1983 Etnicidad y estructura social en el chocó. Medellín: Editorial Lealon.

Corominas
1961 Breve diccionario etimológico de la lengua castellana. Madrid: Gredos.

Corsetti, Giancarlo, Nancy Motta González, and Carlo Tassara
1990 Cambios tecnológicos, organización social y actividades productivas en la costa Pacífica Colombiana. Bogotá: Comitato Internazionale per lo Sviluppo dei Popoli.

Cosby, Alfred W., Jr.
1972 The Colombian Exchange: Biological and Cultural Consequences of 1492. Westport, Conn.: Greenwood Press.

1986   Ecological Imperialism: The Biological Expansion of Europe, 900–
                1900. New York: Cambridge University Press.

Coulthard, G. R.
1962   Race and Colour in Caribbean Literature. London: Oxford Univer-
                sity Press.
1968   Parallelisms and Divergencies between "Negritude" and "Indige-
                nismo." Caribbean Studies 8:31–35.

Courtés, Jean Marie
1979   Preliminary Essay. In Devisse (1979).

Crahan, Margaret E., and Franklin W. Knight (editors)
1979   Africa and the Caribbean: Legacies of a Link. Baltimore: Johns
                Hopkins University Press.

Cuche, Denys
1981   Pérou Nègre: Les descendants d'esclaves africains de Pérou des
                grands domaines esclavagistes aux plantations modernes. Paris: Edi-
                tions L'Harmattan.

Cudjoe, Selwyn Reginald
1978   Resistance and the Caribbean Novel. Athens: Ohio University Press.

Curtin, Phillip D.
1969   The Atlantic Slave Trade: A Census. Madison: University of Wiscon-
                sin Press.

Dallas, Robert Charles
1803   The History of the Maroons from their Origins to the Establish-
                ment of their Chief Tribe at Sierra Leone. 2 volumes. London:
                Straham.

Davis, Martha Ellen
1981   Voces del purgatorio: Estudio de la salve dominicana. Santo Dom-
                ingo: Ediciones Museo del Hombre Dominicano, Serie Investiga-
                ciones Antropológicas No. 15.

Deive, Carlos Esteban
1980   La esclavitud del negro en Santo Domingo 1492–1844. 2 volumes.
                Santo Domingo: Museo del Hombre.

Dent, Gina
1992   Black Popular Culture. Seattle: Bay Press.

Desan, Suzanne
1989   Crows, Community, and Ritual in the Work of E. P. Thompson
                and Natalie Davis. In Hunt (1989), pp. 47–71.

Despres, Leo
1984   Ethnicity: What Data and Theory Portend for Plural Societies. In

David Maybury-Lewis (editor). The Prospects for Plural Societies. Washington, D.C.: American Ethnological Society.

Devisse, Jean
1979   1. From the Demonic Threat to the Incarnation of Sainthood. In Bugner (1979), volume 2.

Devisse, Jean, and Michel Mollat
1979   2. Africans in the Christian Ordinance of the World (Fourteenth to the Sixteenth Century). In Bugner (1979), volume 2.

Díaz Soler, Luis M.
1965   Historia de la esclavitud negra en Puerto Rico. Río Piedras: Ediciones Universidad de Puerto Rico.

Dolgin, Janet L., David S. Kemnitzer, and David M. Schneider
1977   "As People Express Their Lives, So They Are . . . " In Dolgin, Kemnitzer, and Schneider (editors). Symbolic Anthropology: A Reader in the Study of Symbols and Meanings. New York: Columbia University Press.

Drake, St. Clair
1987   Black Folk Here and There: An Essay in History and Anthropology. Volume 1. Los Angeles: UCLA Center for Afro-American Studies Publications.
1990   Black Folk Here and There: An Essay in History and Anthropology. Volume 2. Los Angeles: UCLA Center for Afro-American Studies Publications.

Drolet, Patricia L.
1980   The Congo Ritual of Northeastern Panama: An Afro-American Expressive Stucture of Cultural Adaptation. Ph.D. dissertation, University of Illinois at Urbana-Champaign.

Fernandes, Florestan
1972   O negro no mundo dos brancos. Sao Paulo: Difusão Européia do Livro.

Fick, Carolyn E.
1990   The Making of Haiti. Knoxville: University of Tennessee Press.

Filho, Mello Moraes
1888   Festas e tradiçes populares do Brasil. Rio de Janeiro: H. Granier.

Fog Olwig, Karen
1993   Global Culture, Island Identity: Continuity and Change in the Afro-Caribbean Community of Nevis. Philadelphia: Hardwood.

Forbes, Jack D.
1993   Africans and Native Americans: The Language of Race and the Evolution of Red-Black Peoples. Urbana: University of Illinois Press.

Franco Pichardo, Franklyn J.
1970   Los negros, los mulatos y la nacion dominicana. Santo Domingo:
                Editora Nacional.

Friedemann, Nina S. de
1984   Estudios de negros en la antropología colombiana: Presencia e in-
                visibilidad. In Jaime Arocha Rodriguez and Nina S. de Friedemann
                (editors). Un siglo de investigación social: Antropología en Colom-
                bia. Bogotá: Etno.

Friedemann, Nina S. de, and Jaime Arocha Rodriguez
1986   De sol a sol: Genesis, transformación y presencia de los negros en
                Colombia. Bogotá: Planeta Colombiana.
1995   Colombia. In Minority Rights Group (editor). No Longer Invisible:
                Afro-Latin Americans Today. London: Minority Rights Group Press,
                pp. 47–76.

Friedemann, Nina S. de, and Richard Cross
1979   Ma Ngombe: Guerreros y banderos en Palenque. Bogotá: Editora
                Carlos Valencia.

Fundación Colombiana de Investigaciones Folclóricas
1977   Primer Congreso de la Cultura Negra de las Américas. Bogotá: Fun-
                dación Colombiana de Investigaciones Folclóricas.

Geertz, Clifford
1973   The Interpretation of Cultures. New York: Basic Books.

Ghidinelli y Pierleone Massajoli, Azzo
1984   Resumen etnográfico de los caribes negros (Garifunas) de Hondu-
                ras. América Indígena 44 (3):485–518.

Gilroy, Paul
1993   The Black Atlantic: Modernity and Double Consciousness. Cam-
                bridge: Harvard University Press.

Glissant, Edouard
1995   Creolization in the Making of the Americas. In Vera L. Hyatt and
                Rex Nettleford (editors). Race, Discourse and the Origin of the
                Americas. Washington, D.C.: Smithsonian Institution Press.

González, Nancie L.
1988   Sojourners of the Caribbean: Ethnogenesis and Ethnohistory of the
                Garifuna. Urbana: University of Illinois Press.

Gorer, Geoffrey
1962 [1935]   Africa Dances: A Book about West African Negroes (with a new in-
                troduction by the author). New York: Norton.

Grafton, Anthony (with April Shelford and Nancy Siraisi)
1992   New Worlds, Ancient Texts: The Power of Tradition and the Shock
                of Discovery. Cambridge: Harvard University Press.

Greenblatt, Stephen (editor)
1993   New World Encounters. Berkeley: University of California Press.

Guillot, Carlos Federico
1961   Negros rebeldes y negros cimarrones (perfil afro-americano en la
               historia del Nuevo Mundo durante el siglo XVI). Montevideo:
               Fariña Editores.

Guss, David, and Lise Waxer
1994   Afro-Venezuelans. In Johannes Wilbert (general editor). Encyclope-
               dia of World Cultures. New Haven: Human Relations Area Files
               Press.

Harrison, Faye V.
1988   Introduction: An African Diaspora Perspective for Urban Anthropol-
               ogy. Urban Anthropology 17(2–3):111–142.

Helms, Mary W.
1988   Ulysses' Sail: An Ethnographic Odyssey of Power, Knowledge and
               Geographical Distance. Princeton: Princeton University Press.

Herskovits, Melville
1941 [1958]   The Myth of the Negro Past. Boston: Beacon Press.
1945   Problem, Method, and Theory in Afro-American Studies.
               Afroamerica 1: 5–24.
1948   Man and His Works. New York: Knopf.
1956   The New World Negro: Selected Papers in Afroamerican Studies.
               Frances S. Herskovits (editor). Bloomington: Indiana University
               Press.

Hill, Donald R.
1977   The Impact of Migration on the Metropolitan and Folk Society of
               Carriacou, Grenada. Anthropological Papers of the American Mu-
               seum of Natural History 52 (2).

Hill, Jonathan D. (editor)
1988   Rethinking History and Myth: Indigenous South American Perspec-
               tives on the Past. Urbana: University of Illinois Press.
1996   History, Power, and Identity: Ethnogenesis in the Americas, 1492–
               1992. Iowa City: University of Iowa Press.

Hobsbawn, Eric, and Terence Ranger (editors)
1983   The Invention of Tradition. Cambridge: Cambridge University
               Press.

Hoetink, Harry
1967   Caribbean Race Relations: A Study of Two Variants. Oxford Univer-
               sity Press.

Honigmann, John J.
1959   The World of Man. New York: Harper & Row.

Hulme, Peter, and Neil L. Whitehead (editors)
    1992   Wild Majesty: Encounters with Caribs from Columbus to the Pres-
                        ent Day. New York: Oxford University Press.

Hunt, Lynn (editor)
    1989   The New Cultural History. Berkeley: University of California Press.

Hurault, Jean
    1965   La vie matérielle de noirs réfugiés Boni et des indiens Wayana du
                        Haut-Maroni (Guyane Française). Paris: Office de la Recherche
                        Scientifique et Technique Outre-Mer.

Hurtado, Osvaldo
    1980 [1977]   Political Power in Ecuador. Translated by Nick W. Mills, Jr. Albu-
                        querque: University of New Mexico Press.

Ibarra, Jorge
    1972   Ideología Mambisa. Havana: Instituto Cubano del Libro.

Jeffreys, M. D. W.
    1971   Maize and the Mande Myth. Current Anthropology 12 (3):291–320.

Johnston, Sir Harry H.
    1910   The Negro in the New World. London: Methuen.

Kent, R. K.
    1979   Palmares: An African State in Brazil. In R. Price (1979), pp. 170–190.

Kerns, Virginia
    1983   Women and the Ancestors: Black Carib Kinship and Ritual.
                        Urbana: University of Illinois Press.

Knight, Franklin W.
    1974   The African Dimension of Latin American Societies. New York:
                        Macmillan.

Knight, Franklin W., and Colin A. Palmer (editors)
    1989   The Modern Caribbean. Chapel Hill: University of North Carolina
                        Press.

Kuper, Adam
    1988   The Invention of Primitive Society: Transformations of an Illusion.
                        London: Routledge.

Laguerre, Michel S.
    1976   Belair, Port-au-Prince: From Slave and Maroon Settlement to Con-
                        temporary Black Ghetto. In Norman E. Whitten, Jr. (editor). Afro-
                        American Ethnohistory in Latin America and the Caribbean. Wash-
                        ington, D.C.: American Anthropological Association, Latin
                        American Anthropology Group, pp. 26–38.
    1982a   Urban Life in the Caribbean. Cambridge: Schenkman.

1982b The Complete Haitiana: A Bibliographic Guide to the Scholarly Literature, 1900–1980. 2 volumes. Millwood, N.Y.: Kraus.
1987 Afro-Caribbean Folk Medicine: The Reproduction of Healing. South Hadley, Mass.: Bergin and Garvey.
1989 Voodoo and Politics in Haiti. New York: St. Martin's Press.
1990 Urban Poverty in the Caribbean: French Martinique as Social Laboratory. New York: St. Martin's Press.

Laosa, Marilu de
1990 Abolición de la esclavitud (review essay of El machete de Ogún). El Mundo: Puerto Rico Illustrado, March 18, pp. 9–11.

Larrazabal Blanco, Carlos
1975 Los negros y la esclavitud en Santo Domingo. Santo Domingo: Julio D. Postigo e Hijos.

Lea, Henry Charles
1908 The Inquisition in the Spanish Dependencies. New York: Macmillan.

Leach, Edmund
1982 Social Anthropology. New York: Oxford University Press.

Levine, Lawrence W.
1977 Black Culture and Black Consciousness: Afro-American Folk Thought from Slavery to Freedom. New York: Oxford University Press.

Lewis, Gordon K.
1983 Main Currents in Caribbean Thought: The Historical Evolution of Caribbean Society in Its Ideological Aspects, 1492–1900. Baltimore: Johns Hopkins University Press.

Lewis, Marvin A.
1983 Afro-Hispanic Poetry 1940–1980: From Slavery to "Negritud" in South American Verse. Columbia: University of Missouri Press.

Leyburn, James G.
1941 [1966] The Haitian People. 2d edition. New Haven: Yale University Press.

Lockhart, James
1968 Spanish Peru 1532–1560: A Colonial Society. Madison: University of Wisconsin Press.

Luciano Franco, José
1975 La diaspora africana en el Nuevo Mundo. Havana: Editorial de Ciencias Sociales.

McClaurin, Irma
1996 Women of Belize: Gender and Change in Central America. New Brunswick: Rutgers University Press.

MacLean y Esteños, Roberto
    1948   Negros en el Nuevo Mundo. Lima: Colección Mundo Nuevo.

Malec, Michael A. (editor)
    1995   The Social Role of Sport in Caribbean Societies. Amsterdam:
                    Gordon and Breach.

Mandle, Jay R., and Joan Mandle
    1988   Caribbean Hoops: The Development of West Indian Basketball.
                    Amsterdam: Gordon and Breach.

Marques, Gabriel
    1996   Brasil: Pasado, presente e as possibilidades futuras. Paper presented
                    at the Afro-Latin American Research Association Conference,
                    Bahia, Brazil.

Meennesson-Rigaud, Odette
    1958   Le rôle du Vaudou dans l'indépendance d'Haiti. Présence Africaine
                    17–18: 43–67.

Mintz, Sidney W.
    1966   Introduction to Leyburn (1941 [1956]), pp. v–xlii.
    1974   Caribbean Transformations. Chicago: Aldine.

Mintz, Sidney W., and Richard Price
    1976   An Anthropological Approach to the Afro-American Past: A Carib-
                    bean Perspective. Philadelphia: ISHI.

Mitchell, Michael
    1996   Human Rights and the Afro-Brazilian Predicament. Paper pre-
                    sented at the Afro-Latin American Research Association Confer-
                    ence. Bahia, Brazil.

Moore, Carlos
    1988   Castro, the Blacks, and Africa. Los Angeles: UCLA Center for Afro-
                    American Studies, Afro-American Culture and Society Monograph
                    Series No. 8.

Mörner, Magnus
    1967   Race Mixture in the History of Latin America. Boston: Little,
                    Brown.

Moya Pons, Frank
    1986a   Después de Colón: Trabajo, sociedad y política en la economía del
                    oro. Madrid: Alianza Editorial.
    1986b   El pasado dominicano. Santo Domingo: Fundación J. A. Caro Alvarez.

Muilenburg, Peter
    1991   Fate and Fortune on the Pearl Coast. Americas (English ed.) 43 (3):
                    32–38.

Murga Sanz, Vicente
    1959   Juan Ponce de León. San Juan: Ediciones de la Universidad de
                    Puerto Rico.
    1960   Puerto Rico en los manuscritos de Don Juan Bautista Muñoz. Vol-
                    ume 1. Río Piedras: Ediciones de la Universidad de Puerto Rico.

North American Congress on Latin America (NACLA)
    1992   The Black Americas: 1492–1992. NACLA Report on the Americas
                    25(4).

Nunley, John
    1988   Caribbean Festival Arts. Seattle and St. Louis: University of Wash-
                    ington Press and the St. Louis Art Museum.

Ortiz, Fernando
    1975a   El engaño de las razas. Havana: Editorial de Ciencias Sociales.
    1975b   Los negros esclavos. Havana: Editorial de Ciencias Sociales.
    1975c   Historia de una pelea cubana contra los demonios. Havana: Edito-
                    rial de Ciencias Sociales.
    1986   Los Negros Curros. Havana: Editorial de Ciencias Sociales.

Otte, Enrique
    1963   Cedulas reales relativas a Venezuela (1500–1550). Caracas: Edi-
                    ción de la Fundación John Boulton y la Fundación Eugenio Men-
                    doza.
    1977   Las perlas del Caribe: Nueva Cadiz de Cubagua. Caracas: Funda-
                    ción John Boulton.

Palencia-Roth, Michael
    1993   The Cannibal Law of 1503. In Williams and Lewis (1993), pp.
                    21–63.

Palmer, Colin A.
    1976   Slaves of the White God: Blacks in Mexico, 1570–1650.

Pané, Ramón
    1984   The Relación of Fray Ramón Pané. In Parry and Keith (1984). Vol-
                    ume 1, pp. 18–27.

Panger, Daniel
    1982   Black Ulysses. Athens: Ohio University Press.

Parry, John H., and Robert G. Keith (editors), with the assistance of Michael Jimenez
    1984   New Iberian World: A Documentary History of the Discovery and
                    Settlement of Latin America to the Early 17th Century. 5 volumes.
                    New York: Times Books and Hector & Rose.

Parry, J. H., and P. M. Sherlock
    1956   A Short History of the West Indies. London: Macmillan.

Pérez de la Riva, Francisco
1946   El negro y la tierra, el conuco y el palenque. Revista Bimestre Cubana 58 (2,3):97–139.
1952   La habitación rural en cuba. Havana: Contribución del Grupo Guamá, Antropolgía 26.
1979   Cuban Palenques. In R. Price (1979).

Pérez Sarduy, Pedro
1990   Open Letter to Carlos Moore. Afro Hispanic Review 9 (1–3):25–29.

Pérez-Stable, Marifeli
1990   In Pursuit of Cuba Libre. Report of the Americas 24 (2):32–48.

Pescatello, Ann M. (editor)
        New Roots in Old Lands: Historical and Anthropological Perspectives. In Black Experiences in the Americas. Westport: Greenwood Press.

Pitt-Rivers, Julian
1967   Race, Color, and Class in Central America and the Andes. Daedalus 96 (2):542–559.
1973   Race in Latin America: The Concept of "Raza." Archives Européennes de Sociologie 14 (1):3–31.

Pollak-Eltz, Angelina
1971   Vestigios africanos en la cultura del pueblo venezolano. Cuernavaca, Mexico: Centro Intercultural de Documentación (CIDOC).
1972   Cultos afroamericanos. Caracas: Universidad Catolica Andrés Bello.

Preciado Bedoya, Antonio
1961   Jolgorio: Poemas. Quito: Casa de la Cultura Ecuatoriana.

Price, Richard
1975   Saramaka Social Structure: Analysis of a Maroon Society in Surinam. Río Piedras: Institute of Caribbean Studies of the University of Puerto Rico.
1979   (editor) Maroon Societies: Rebel Slave Communities in the Americas. Baltimore: Johns Hopkins University Press.
1983   First-Time: The Historical Vision of an Afro-American People. Baltimore: Johns Hopkins University Press.
1990   Alabi's World. Baltimore: Johns Hopkins University Press.
1995   Executing Ethnicity: The Killings in Suriname. Cultural Anthropology 10(4):437–471.

Price, Richard, and Sally Price
1993   Collective Fictions: Performance in Saramaka Folktales. In Dorothea S. Whitten and Norman E. Whitten, Jr. (editors). Im-

agery and Creativity: Ethnoaesthetics and Art Worlds in the Americas. Tucson: University of Arizona Press, pp. 235–288.

Price, Sally
1983   Co-Wives and Calabashes. Ann Arbor: University of Michigan Press.

Price, Sally, and Richard Price
1980   Afro-American Arts of the Suriname Rain Forest. Berkeley: University of California Press.

Price-Mars, Jean
1928   Ainsi parla l'oncle. Paris: Imprimerie de Compiègne.

Quintero-Rivera, Angel G.
1987   The Rural-Urban Dichotomy in the Formation of Puerto Rico's Cultural Identity. New West Indian Guide 61 (3–4) 127–144.

Rohtner, Larry
1996   Close to Panama, Dreams of Rival "Canals." New York Times, November 10, pp. 1A, 6A.

Rout, Leslie B., Jr.
1972   Reflections on the Evolution of Post-War Jazz. In Addison Gayle, Jr. (editor). The Black Aesthetic. Garden City, N.Y.: Anchor, pp. 143–153.
1976   The African Experience in Spanish America: 1502 to the Present Day. Cambridge: Cambridge University Press.

Routte-Gomez, Eneid
1996   So, Are We Racists???? A Conspiracy of Silence: Racism in Puerto Rico. San Juan Star Magazine, December-January, pp. 54–58.

Royce, Anya Peterson
1977   The Anthropology of Dance. Bloomington: Indiana University Press.

Russell-Wood, A. J.
1995   Before Columbus: Portugal's African Prelude. In Vera Hyatt and Rex Nettleford (editors). Race, Discourse and the Origin of the Americas. Washington: Smithsonian Institution Press.

Sahlins, Marshall
1981   Historical Metaphors and Mythical Realities: Structure in the Early History of the Sandwich Islands Kingdom. Chicago: University of Chicago Press.

Scarano, Francisco A.
1993   Puerto Rico: Cinco siglos de historia. Santa Fe de Bogotá, Colombia: McGraw Hill Interamericana.

Schomburg, Arthur A.
    1928   Negroes in Seville. Opportunity 6:93.
    1970   The Negro Digs Up His Past. In Alain Locke (editor). The New
                    Negro. New York: Atheneum, pp. 232–240.

Shils, Edward
    1981   Tradition. Chicago: University of Chicago Press.

Shyllon, Folarin
    1982   Blacks in Britain: A Historical and Analytical Overview. In Joseph
                    Harris (editor). Global Dimensions of the African Diaspora. Wash-
                    ington, D.C.: Howard University Press.

Simms Hamilton, Ruth (editor)
    1990a   Creating a Paradigm and Research Agenda for Comparative Studies
                    of the Worldwide Dispersion of African Peoples. East Lansing,
                    Mich.: African Diaspora Research Project, Monograph No. 1.
    1990b   Toward a Paradigm for African Diaspora Studies. In Hamilton (1990a).

Sinnette, Elinor De Verney
    1977   Arthur Alfonso Schomburg, Black Bibliophile and Curator: His
                    Contribution to the Collection and Dissemination of Materials
                    about Africans and Peoples of African Descent. Ph.D. dissertation,
                    Columbia University.

Smith, Michael G.
    1965   The Plural Society in the British West Indies. Berkeley: University
                    of California Press.

Smith, Raymond T.
    1956   The Negro Family in British Guiana. London: Routledge & Kegan
                    Paul.

Stevens-Arroyo, Antonio M.
    1988   Cave of the Jagua: The Mythical World of the Taínos. Albuquer-
                    que: University of New Mexico Press.

Stutzman, Ronald
    1981   El Mestizaje: An All-Inclusive Ideology of Exclusion. In Whitten
                    (1981), pp. 445–494.

Sued Badillo, Jalil
    1983   Guayama: Notas para su historia. San Juan: Oficina de Asuntos Cul-
                    turales de la Fortaleza.

Sued Badillo, Jalil, and Angel López Cantos
    1986   Puerto Rico Negro. San Juan: Ediciones Huracán.

Taussig, Michael T. (writing under the pseudonym "Mateo Mina")
    1975   Esclavitud y libertad en el valle del Río Cauca. Bogotá: Fundación
                    Rosca de Investigación y Acción Social.

1978   Destrucción y resistencia campesina: El caso del litoral pacífico.
                Bogotá: Punto de Lanza.
1980   The Devil and Commodity Fetishism in South America. Chapel
                Hill: University of North Carolina Press.
1987   Shamanism, Colonialism and the Wildman: A Study in Healing
                and Terror. Chicago: University of Chicago Press.

Taylor, Douglas
1977   Languages of the West Indies. Baltimore: Johns Hopkins University
                Press.

Templeman, Robert
1994   Afro-Bolivians. In Johannes Wilbert (general editor). Encyclope-
                dia of World Cultures. New Haven: Human Relations Area Files
                Press.

Terborg-Penn, Rosalyn
1986   Women and Slavery in the African Diaspora: A Cross-Cultural Ap-
                proach to Historical Analysis. Sage 3 (2):11–15.

Thoden van Velzen, H. U. E., and W. van Wetering
1988   The Great Father and the Danger: Religious Cults, Material
                Forces, and Collective Fantasies in the World of the Surinamese
                Maroons. Dordrecht: Foris.

Thompson Drewal, Margaret
1989   Dancing for Ogun in Yorubaland and in Brazil. In Sandra T.
                Barnes (editor). Africa's Ogun: Old World and New. Bloomington:
                Indiana University Press, pp. 199–234.

Thornton, John
1995   Perspectives on African Christianity. In Vera Lawrence Hyatt and
                Rex Nettleford (editors). Race, Discourse, and the Origin of the
                Americas: A New World View. Washington, D.C.: Smithsonian In-
                stitution Press, pp. 169–212.

Tomoeda, Hiroyasu, and Luis Millones (editors)
1992   500 años de mestizaje en los Andes. Lima: Biblioteca Peruana de
                Psicoanálisis.

Trouillot, Michel-Rolph
1990   Haiti, State against Nation: The Origins and Legacy of Duvalier-
                ism. New York: Monthly Review Press.

Van Cott, Donna Lee (editor)
1994   Indigenous Peoples and Democracy in Latin America. New York:
                St. Martin's Press and Washington, D.C.: Inter-American Dialogue.

Varner, John Grier, and Jeannette Johnson Varner
1983   Dogs of the Conquest. Norman: University of Oklahoma Press.

Vasconcelos, José
    1925   La raza cósmica—misión de la raza iberoamericana—, notas de
                    viaje a América del sur. Barcelona: Agencia Mundial de Librería.

Verger, Pierre (editor)
    1953   Les Afro-Américains. Dakar: Institut Français d'Afrique Noire,
                    Mémoire 27.

Wade, Peter
    1993   Blackness and Race Mixture: The Dynamics of Racial Identity in
                    Colombia. Baltimore: Johns Hopkins University Press.
    (in press)   Music, Blackness and National Identity: Three Moments in Colum-
                    bian History. Popular Music.

Weber, Max
    1958   From Max Weber: Essays in Sociology. Translated and edited by
                    H. H. Girth and C. Wright Mills. New York: Oxford University Press.
    1964 [1947]   The Theory of Social and Economic Organization. Translated and
                    edited by A. M. Henderson and Talcott Parsons. Glencoe, Ill.: Free
                    Press.

Whitehead, Neil L.
    1988   Lords of the Tiger Spirit: A History of the Caribs in Colonial Vene-
                    zuela and Guyana 1498–1820. Dordrecht: Foris.
    1993   Native American Cultures along the Atlantic Littoral of South
                    America, 1499–1650. Proceedings of the British Academy 81:197–
                    231.

Whitten, Norman E., Jr.
    1965   Class, Kinship, and Power in an Ecuadorian Town: The Negroes of
                    San Lorenzo. Stanford: Stanford University Press.
    1981   (editor) Cultural Transformations and Ethnicity in Modern Ecua-
                    dor. Urbana: University of Illinois Press.
    1985   Sicuanga Runa: The Other Side of Development in Amazonian
                    Ecuador. Urbana: University of Illinois Press.
    1986a [1974]   Black Frontiersmen: Afro-Hispanic Culture of Colombia and Ecua-
                    dor. Prospect Heights, Ill.: Waveland Press.
    1986b   Review of books by Richard Price (First-Time: The Historical Vi-
                    sion of an Afro-American People and To Slay the Hydra: Dutch Co-
                    lonial Perspectives on the Saramaka Wars). Ethnohistory 33:91–94.
    1996   Ethnogenesis. In The Encyclopedia of Cultural Anthropology. New
                    York: Henry Holt and the Human Relations Area Files, vol. 2, pp.
                    407–411.

Whitten, Norman E., Jr., and John F. Szwed (editors)
    1970   Afro-American Anthropology: Contemporary Perspectives. New
                    York: Free Press.

Whitten, Norman E., Jr., and Arlene Torres
1992   Blackness in the Americas. In North American Congress on Latin America (1992), pp. 16–22, 45–46.

Whitten, Norman E., Jr., and Diego Quiroga
1990   Prefacio. In Giancarlo Corsetti, Nancy Motta González, and Carlo Tassara. Cambios tecnológicos, organización social y actividades productivas en la Costa Pacífica Colombiana. Bogotá: Comitato Internazionale per lo Sviluppo dei Popoli, pp. 9–16.
1994   The Black Pacific Lowlanders of Ecuador and Colombia. In Johannes Wilbert (general editor). Encyclopedia of World Cultures. New Haven: Human Relations Area Files Press.

Williams, Brackette
1989   A Class Act: Anthropology and the Race to Nation across Ethnic Terrain. Annual Review of Anthropology. Palo Alto: Annual Review, pp. 401–444.
1991   Stains on My Name, War in My Veins: Guyana and the Politics of Cultural Struggle. Durham: Duke University Press.

Williams, Jerry M., and Robert E. Lewis (editors)
1993   Early Images of the Americas: Transfer and Invention. Tucson: University of Arizona Press.

Wilson, Samuel M.
1990   Hispaniola: Caribbean Chiefdoms in the Age of Columbus. Tuscaloosa: University of Alabama Press.

Wolf, Eric
1982   Europe and the People without History. Berkeley: University of California Press.

Worsley, Peter
1984   The Three Worlds: Culture and World Development. Chicago: University of Chicago Press.

Wright, Winthrop R.
1990   Café con Leche: Race, Class, and National Image in Venezuela. Austin: University of Texas Press.

Zelinsky, Wilbur
1949   The Historical Geography of the Negro Population of Latin America. Journal of Negro History 34:153–221.

Zenón Cruz, Isabelo
1974   Narciso descubre su trasero (El negro en la cultura puertorriqueña). Volume 1. Humacao, Puerto Rico: Editorial Furidi.
1975   Narciso descubre su trasero (El negro en la cultura puertorriqueña). Volume 2. Humacao, Puerto Rico: Editorial Furidi.

PART TWO
EASTERN SOUTH AMERICA

1. BLACKS AND THE *ABERTURA DEMOCRÁTICA*

Michael Mitchell

A Brazilian returning from fourteen years in exile made this remark about his country's contemporary politics: "[F]oreign political scientists don't understand us because we don't appear to play politics by any established rules. . . . For example, in the strictest terms we shouldn't be gathered at this meeting of the opposition but that's exactly where we are . . . this is a strange land where our liberty hangs by a precarious thread . . . and where authoritarianism and democracy seem to exist side by side."[1,2]

This statement aptly expresses the feeling that most outside observers must have regarding the political trend referred to as Brazil's *abertura democrática*, or the transition to democracy. It seems to capture the sense of confusion and contradiction inherent in this recent development in Brazilian politics.

Since January 1979, a number of measures have been enacted to give Brazilians more freedom than they have enjoyed in sixteen years. Press censorship has been lifted. The great majority of political prisoners have been released and granted amnesty. Exiled political leaders, once considered enemies of the present regime, have been allowed to return without restrictions on their activities. The two-party system, created by the Castelo Branco regime to assure itself a more-or-less perpetual parliamentary majority, has been replaced by another which allows any group to form a political party (provided it meets rather stiff requirements of electoral strength) without government interference. Finally, Institutional Act Number Five, which gave juridical sanction to the institutions of repression and "internal security," has been abolished.[3]

Nevertheless, the shadow of authoritarianism continues to dwell over the Brazilian political process in the form of a constitutional amendment permitting the president (with the nominal consent of Congress) to invoke emergency powers which are perhaps harsher than those contained in the Fifth Institutional Act. Moreover, elections are still manipulated through "bionic" legislators and indirect elections for state governors. Severe chills have been created by a general who ventured out of institutional obscurity to warn the public against the imperfections of democracy. Winds of change are blowing through Brazil, but no one can be completely sure of whether they bring in their wake a new and vigorous

Originally published in Pierre-Michel Fontaine (ed.), *Race, Class, and Power in Brazil* (Los Angeles: Center for Afro-American Studies, University of California, 1985), pp. 75–119. Reprinted by permission of Michael Mitchell.

democracy, or an ever more sophisticated style of authoritarianism retrenching itself in the guise of democratic reform.[4]

Formal concessions to democratic liberties, however, are just one aspect of the abertura democrática. The process also encompasses the reemergence of mass-based organizations which, once timid, are now openly airing grievances and challenging the legitimacy of the authoritarian regime. Workers, students, prelates, women, and Blacks have, in the past several years, staged public demonstrations expressing opposition to authoritarian rule.

Perhaps one of the more surprising protests in recent times was the demonstration organized in July 1978 by Brazilian Blacks. Some 2,000 persons rallied in front of the Teatro Municipal of São Paulo to dramatize the depth of racial discrimination in Brazilian society. Speakers came from throughout Brazil to denounce specific instances of racial discrimination and to demand greater racial equality. This protest was somewhat unusual in that it provoked many into rethinking the long-held notion that Brazil was relatively free of the kind of racial tension that would generate such a protest. Contemporary Brazilian politics is indeed difficult to understand: elites of an authoritarian system benevolently offer to surrender a large share of their powers and prerogatives; workers engage in illegal strikes which are settled through negotiations with the government that banned them; and Blacks living in a "racial democracy" protest against racial discrimination.

This chapter will concentrate on one particular facet of the strange and complex process known as abertura democrática. It will explore the ways in which Blacks fit into the abertura and what they might expect from this period of political change. Specifically, I will attempt to give evidence in support of the following hypotheses: (a) that the styles of Black political activity will be determined by the prevailing political environment; and (b) that Blacks can make an impact on the abertura democrática despite their limited organizational and financial resources.

My choice of this topic might seem rather arbitrary, perhaps even artificial. Some might argue that it is inappropriate to speak solely of racial politics in a social system where Blacks, along with other groups, make up a large proportion of the lower classes and that "Black politics" should be strictly subsumed under the heading of class analysis. Others might suggest that the abertura democrática is itself the artificial creation of an authoritarian regime and hence an inaccurate focus for any discussion of real political change. These observations are no doubt valid, but their total acceptance obscures the existence of yet another curious reality: the apparent coincidence of broad changes in Brazilian politics and the emergence of a "new consciousness" among Afro-Brazilians. Are these "macro" and "micro" changes in any way linked? Are there elements in the process of abertura democrática that bear new and as yet unexploited political opportunities for groups whose power and influence have been virtually nonexistent in Brazilian politics? It seems advantageous to examine the manner in which broad political changes, the crystallization of group consciousness, and the activation of that consciousness into political form, mutually influence each other; to see whether new forms of political organization and expression can result from such a dialectic.

To facilitate the analysis, this chapter will be divided into two parts. The first section will attempt to trace the origins and development of the abertura democrática in broad strokes. In the second, I focus on the links between the abertura democrática and Black politics. Many of the remarks made here will be, of necessity, highly speculative since the abertura is still a new, confusing, and contradictory process. This analysis may prove to be useful despite the limitations imposed by the uncertainties of Brazil's present political atmosphere.

The Abertura Democrática

In order to trace the origins of a democratic tradition in Brazil one might profitably begin with the struggle for independence, when the ideals of the French Revolution were extolled by publications such as the *Revérbero Constitucional*, the *Malagueta*, and the *Sentinela da Liberdade*. Other bearers of democratic tradition, among them the Pasquins of the Regency period and Ruy Barbosa, should also be mentioned. The list is not impressively long, partially due to the hostility toward democratic ideals expressed by a rural, oligarchical society. Nevertheless, there is evidence of an indigenous democratic tradition in Brazilian history.[5] Although the present abertura democrática should be considered in this historical context, there is more value—but not great satisfaction—in beginning this discussion with the 1964 *golpe de estado*.

By that year, Brazil had reached a period when several economic, social, and political factors were simultaneously producing overwhelming strains on the political system. Economic stagnation in the industrial sector was becoming endemic. The persistence of archaic social structures (particularly in the countryside), the mobilization of workers, peasants, and students demanding social reforms, together with continual electoral impasses within a factionalized party system, all served to intensify social and political cleavages in Brazilian society.[6]

Prior to the 1964 coup, two presidents had tried to implement needed reforms but failed to establish a general consensus for doing so. The first, Jânio Quadros, resigned in frustration after only eight months in office. The second, João Goulart, was deposed in March 1964.

The forces that overthrew Goulart represented a curious collection of distinct, even conflicting, groups: military officers who resented Goulart's rejection of the necessity for honor and discipline in the ranks; both officers and civilians who perceived Goulart as a threat to the fundamental social order; and still others with personal ambitions they hoped to satisfy by participating in Goulart's overthrow.[7]

Rising above these factions was Marechal Humberto Castelo Branco who, because of his capacity for leadership, was chosen as the regime's first president.

Authoritarian by nature, Castelo Branco showed a commitment to correcting what were perceived as the worst abuses of the democratic era, and he promised to lay the foundation for an eventual return to a democratic political structure free of such abuses.

In Castelo Branco, Brazil once again produced a leader as complex as the political processes we are trying to unravel. How could an authoritarian military leader take a credible stance in favor of democratic ideals? The answer seems to lie in his military career. During World War II, Castelo Branco was a member of the Brazilian Expeditionary Force, which fought Italian fascism alongside the U.S. and other Western democracies. Moreover, he had been the head of the Escola Superior de Guerra, where prevailing military strategy allied Brazil with democracy and Western civilization, pitted against "anti-Christian" communism in an antagonistic international system.[8]

There were pragmatic reasons as well. In order to consolidate his political support, Castelo Branco had to contend with the great popularity still enjoyed by civilian political leaders. By leaning heavily on the concept of abertura, he was able to marshal support against both his military and civilian opposition.[9]

In the final analysis, however, the military man superseded the convinced democrat. Castelo Branco's commitment to democracy eventually gave way to pressures from a still untamed opposition. By the end of his term, he had begun to institutionalize authoritarian rule by establishing not only the indirect election of state governors, the reorganization of political parties, and the subjugation of Congress to the initiatives of the president, but also the conditions under which a state of emergency and suspension of civil liberties could be enforced. These measures were clearly designed to reduce popular participation in politics to a discreet minimum and silence any opposition to the new regime.[10]

Under the leadership of Castelo Branco's predecessors, Costa e Silva and Garastazu Médici, rapid economic development and "internal security" assumed a much higher priority than abertura. During this period (1967–1974), challenges to these regimes were handled with unprecedented severity. Workers' strikes, student demonstrations, and the Moreira Alves affair (an unusual display of legislative independence), served to intensify the authoritarian reaction. By December 1968, in response to a series of political crises, Costa e Silva outlined the extent of his dictatorial powers in the chilling Fifth Institutional Act.[11]

The Costa e Silva and Médici years were bitter ones. Individual rights were systematically violated and political participation repressed to an extraordinary degree. Torture became a routine means of intimidating and silencing the opposition. It was during this period that the regime attempted to halt the political process through appeals to national pride in economic and sports achievements. By 1974, when Médici's tenure in office ended, the authoritarian regime had become an institution.[12]

The democratic opening now under way can be viewed to some degree as a legacy of Castelo Branco. Many of his former advisers, such as General Golbery do Couto e Silva, former president Ernesto Geisel, and President João Baptista Figueiredo, became its architects.[13] When Geisel was inaugurated as the fourth military president since 1964, several factors emerged to put the issue of abertura democrática back on the political agenda. Not the least important of these was the need to resolve the problem of internal factionalism which had existed within the military since the days of Castelo Branco. The Castelo loyalists, among them Geisel himself, had considered the Costa e Silva and Médici presidencies humiliating defeats for the more politically sophisticated Castelistas. It was a simple matter for the latter to lay blame for unconscionable excesses on previous administrations, simultaneously raising the issue of democracy in order to discredit the opposition. The accession of Geisel was thus thought to be an opportunity to repudiate the "hard-liners" once and for all.[14]

Another factor which sparked interest in planning for a return to democracy was the sticky problem of legal status for civilian leaders cassados in 1964. If the ten-year suspensions of their rights were to be renewed, it would have to be done early in Geisel's administration. In the case of former president Juscelino Kubitschek, a popular figure whose original suspension of rights was considered unjust by many, a compelling reason would have to be given for extending it. To welcome such figures back into the political community might advance the cause of the regime and further isolate the hard-liners. The risk seemed minimal, as by 1974 virtually all armed resistance to the regime had been eliminated and with it one of the rationales for the "rule of exception."

Broader international events would also prompt a more "tolerant" attitude toward the political process. First, OPEC price increases were to have a severe impact on economic expansion. The consequent slowing of economic growth forced Geisel's government to function in a climate considerably less favorable than that enjoyed by previous administrations. Thus, by the time of Geisel's inauguration, several factors had emerged to make an abertura possible, and even advantageous. Still another external factor would emerge to influence abertura: the United States' foreign policy initiatives regarding human rights violations, which brought the issue of democratic freedom more sharply into focus for Brazilians.[15]

Geisel's initial moves in this direction seemed promising, if cautious. He named Armando Falcão as his minister of justice, signaling a potential reconciliation with those who still identified with former president Kubitschek and his Partido Social Democrático. But more encouraging still was Geisel's determination not to interfere in the congressional elections of 1974.

In short order these congressional elections became the first test of Geisel's intentions to carry out a plan of redemocratization. The election results went heavily against the government party and, for the first time, the prospect of an independent Congress had to be confronted. The results reflected a severe erosion of support for the government in the modern industrial areas, where the regime had claimed its most impressive economic successes. Furthermore, the vote tended to show that the government had virtually no support among the young, workers, and women, groups which had been historically excluded from political participation.[16]

Geisel and his advisers were quick to grasp the significance of the vote. Shortly thereafter, he announced that the process of abertura would come to an end. Nevertheless, Geisel was put on notice that he would have to confront the regime's eroding support.

During the remainder of his term, Geisel would feel still further pressures to expand political activity. These pressures, which had been building for some time and crystallized in the 1974 congressional elections, were to come mainly from businessmen, the Catholic church, students, and organized workers, who complained of the maldistribution of power and wealth and questioned the legitimacy of the authoritarian regime.

The first of these challenges developed out of the Herzog Affair, in which journalist Vladimir Herzog, after voluntarily surrendering to the authorities, was tortured and murdered in the presence of army security forces in São Paulo. Incensed by both the circumstances of his death and its attempted cover-up, public opinion exploded in outrage against the regime. When a similar incident occurred in the same army compound a few months later, Geisel was compelled to act. He responded by firing the army commander in whose jurisdiction the offenses had been committed. But the greater significance of the entire affair was that public opinion had established the limits of its tolerance. If the regime wished to maintain some semblance of legitimacy and support, it would have to end the violent intimidation of Brazilian citizens which had characterized the governments of Costa e Silva and Médici.[17]

At about the same time, the regime began to experience loss of support from its most loyal traditional ally. Brazilian businessmen began to complain that their participation in the economy was being threatened by large state enterprises (such as Petrobrás, Companhia Siderúgica Nacional, and Companhia do Vale do Rio Doce) and by multinational corporations.

At first, the debate between the business community and Geisel's regime was narrow in focus, with criticism also directed toward Geisel's efforts at redemocratization. As it grew, however, it seemed to take on a life of its own and paradoxically became linked to the cause of abertura democrática. As a result of the *estatização* controversy, Severo Gomes, considered a "liberal" in Geisel's cabinet, resigned as minister of industry and commerce.[18]

Ironically, this controversy was the legacy of Getúlio Vargas, who had recognized the political potential of state intervention in the economy decades earlier (1930–1945). Through the creation of various *institutos* to oversee the stabilization of prices and export of agricultural commodities, he was able to pacify rural oligarchical interests while he slowly drained their power. In the 1950s, Vargas used the artifice of state enterprises (specifically Petrobrás) to rally popular nationalist sentiment for his administration. He would no doubt have enjoyed the

irony of a regime whose objective was to eradicate all vestiges of his populist politics from national life fervently defending the economic structures he had set in
place.[19]

The Geisel regime was also beset by opposition from still another powerful
sector, the Catholic church. Relations with the Church, which had not been
cordial since 1964, grew increasingly tense under Geisel's government. They
reached their nadir in 1976, when the bishop of Nova Iguaçu, Dom Adriano
Hipólito, was kidnapped by government security forces. While in captivity, he
was humiliated by being stripped naked and painted red to symbolize his supposed political inclinations. A subsequent controversy arose concerning the death
of Jesuit Father João Bosco Brunier, who had been a supporter of the peasants'
fight for land in the Amazon. He was found to have been murdered by local
police.

Several issues divided church and state, but the most troublesome of these had
to do with the Church's renewed commitment to social justice and human rights.
As mentioned earlier, ordinary clergy were particularly forceful in speaking out
in defense of the dispossessed, and risked their lives as a result. More prestigious
religious figures, such as Helder Câmara and Paulo Evaristo Arns, also spoke out
against human rights abuses both individually and in forums such as the National
Conference of Brazilian Bishops (CNBB). Through organizations like the Commission of Justice and Peace, Church leaders also encouraged the laity to expose
the work of the semi-official death squads, and to bring suits against the torturers
of political prisoners. The work of Hélio Bicudo, Dalmo Dallari, and José Carlos
Dias was especially noteworthy in this regard.

For the Church to carry its criticism of government policy to the point of questioning the legitimacy of the regime due to its human rights abuses was a strong
indication that solid political support for the regime was sorely lacking in this
important sector of Brazilian society.[20]

By 1977 the process of abertura had come to a critical turning point where
Geisel felt compelled to reassert his "revolutionary powers" as a reminder to the
opposition. At issue was a matter of secondary importance, a proposed constitutional amendment reforming the judicial system of the states. For the Brazilian
Democratic Movement, the opposition party, the issue provided the first major
test of congressional independence since 1968. The confrontation came when
the MDB decided not to support the proposal and Geisel responded in the fashion of a stern authoritarian. He closed Congress for a period of two weeks and
announced a set of decrees which came to be known as the Pacote de Abril.
Among the measures were:

1. Indirect elections of one-third of the Senate by state legislatures: a process
   which, in effect, placed senatorial appointments in the hands of the president (those appointed have been referred to as "bionic" senators).
2. Indirect election of state governors.

3. Extension of the Lei Falcão limiting to two hours the amount of radio and television time available to *all* candidates in the 1978 elections, thus effectively eliminating the broadcast media as forums for political debate.
4. Extension of the presidential term of office from five to six years.
5. Reduction of the number of votes in Congress required for passage of constitutional amendments from two-thirds to a simple majority.
6. Legalization of divorce.
7. Enactment of the original judicial reforms which were the cause of the confrontation.

Disagreement inevitably arose regarding the motives behind the Pacote de Abril. Hugo Abreu, chief of the military household in Geisel's cabinet, attributed them to a "cynical" palace oligarchy headed by Golbery. Abreu claimed the latter was fearful of a poor showing in the forthcoming 1978 congressional elections. Walder Goes, columnist for the *Jornal do Brasil*, argued, on the other hand, that the Pacote was a skillful attempt by Geisel to steer a middle course between radical-right elements within the military, who pushed for a reimposition of the reign of terror, and the opposition whose challenges to the regime were gaining increasing respectability.[21] But whatever the motives, the net effect of the Pacote was to alter the course of redemocratization.

In order to impose his Pacote de Abril, Geisel had to expend a considerable amount of political capital, a commodity which he would be hard put to recover in the long term, despite the short-term gains envisioned. For one thing, Geisel's high-handed methods did not sit well with key supporters of the regime. Hugo Abreu eventually resigned, citing the "April Reforms" as one reason for leaving. Later, a once loyal ally, Senator José Magalhães Pinto, presented a still more serious problem by establishing a civilian presidential candidacy to oppose whomever the regime chose in the presidential succession process. Ultimately, a new democratic front was put together that placed even greater citizen pressure on the regime for redemocratization.[22]

The Pacote de Abril greatly stimulated a new round of reaction against authoritarian rule. In May 1977, confrontations reminiscent of 1968 occurred between the government and students. Initially student protests were confined to the issue of dwindling government allocations to higher education. But soon these protests blossomed into sweeping demands for (*a*) an end to military dictatorship and (*b*) unrestricted amnesty for political prisoners. And when police invaded the campuses of the Catholic University in São Paulo and the Federal University in Brasília, they discovered that the rules of political confrontation had changed substantially. Instead of quelling the protests, they were actually generating considerable support for the students' cause.[23]

Still another group was to make its entry into the political arena. Brazilian workers had been victimized consistently by government economic policies which artificially kept wages near subsistence levels. By May 1978, discontent reached dangerous proportions and for weeks striking automobile and metallur-gical workers held the government at bay. Rather than crush the strike openly, Geisel decided to "negotiate" a settlement. Although in real terms the workers won few substantial economic concessions, they gained a new sense of indepen-dence and a strong, politically astute leadership in men like Luiz Ignácio da Silva ("Lula"). From then on workers were to become vigorous combatants in the arena of Brazilian politics.[24]

Perhaps the severest crisis of Geisel's government erupted over the issue of presidential succession. This dispute exposed the most serious weakness of the bureaucratic-authoritarian regime, namely the tenuousness of the agreement among the military factions that held the regime together. No other crisis brought into sharper relief the unsubstantiality of this coalition, upon which political in-itiatives were predicated.

The crisis involved the firing of Army Minister Sylvio Frota, who, against Geisel's wishes, was believed to be positioning himself for a presidential candi-dacy.[25] The circumstances surrounding the affair are complex and because of their importance probably deserve a separate, more detailed, treatment else-where. What follows is a summary of these events.

Even before the political elites began gearing up to vie for the presidency in 1977, Geisel had anointed his chosen successor, the chief of the SNI, João Bap-tista Figueiredo. His attractiveness as a candidate stemmed from the belief that, as president, he would be willing to maintain in power the Castelista faction of the military and its principal spokesman, General Golbery. But Figueiredo had several serious drawbacks as a candidate. First, he was not well-known among civilians and could claim no popular base of support. Second, he was outranked by other generals, some of whom harbored presidential ambitions of their own — like Sylvio Frota.

Geisel faced several problems regarding the succession, which dictated his eventual course of action. Public opinion was beginning to coalesce around the prospect of an independent civilian candidacy and Geisel was determined to neu-tralize this effort. He was equally determined to outmaneuver a possible hard-line resurgence that might jeopardize the power of the Castelistas and bury what was left of his redemocratization policy. These problems could scarcely be resolved by supporting the candidacy of a hard-liner like Frota.

There was evidence of a personality clash as well. Ever since he became army minister, Frota had been a thorn in Geisel's side. The two disagreed on army administrative policy as well as more substantive issues such as redemocratization and the recognition of both the People's Republic of China and the MPLA gov-ernment of Angola. Furthermore, the strong-willed Frota seemed intent upon reversing Geisel's domestic political program. In an incident involving a journal-ist who was indiscreet enough to criticize the Duque de Caxias, patron of the Brazilian army, Frota actively sought the arrest and prosecution of the offender without first consulting the equally strong-willed president.

Whether Frota's dismissal was specifically due to this incident or not is unclear. What is certain is that long-standing discord existed between the two men, and the slight possibility of a Frota candidacy was probably sufficient cause for Geisel to act.

Because of the well-founded fear that Frota was capable of organizing a successful coup against him, Geisel orchestrated his dismissal with the utmost care. All members of the high command were provided with an explanation of the decision and a new army minister, General Fernando Belfort Bethlem (who shared Frota's critical opinions of redemocratization but was careful to operate within the army chain of command), was chosen before Frota learned that he was to be dismissed. When he left the government, Frota also left a demoralized hard-line military faction.

Despite Geisel's efforts to the contrary, Frota's dismissal was inevitably linked with the politics of presidential succession both in the public mind and among the political and military elites. Although it is doubtful that Frota could have acquired support outside of limited military circles, it appeared that Geisel had deliberately eliminated one presidential contender in order to advance the chances of his own protégé. Figueiredo would subsequently be obliged to prove the legitimacy of his rule as a result. His primary task in office was to establish a base of political support, particularly among civilians, and continuing his predecessor's efforts to reinstitute democracy had obvious political merits.

By the time Figueiredo assumed office in March 1979, several steps had already been taken by Geisel to ensure the continuation of the abertura process. Institutional Act Number Five, the primary instrument of repression, had been revoked (although so-called "constitutional safeguards" allowed Figueiredo to reimpose a "state of exception" virtually at his discretion), and press censorship was lifted. Clearly recognizing the damage done to him by the Frota affair, Figueiredo set out to create the public image of a man of the people by agreeing to a conditional amnesty and a reorganization of political parties.[26] Despite a momentary lapse during the campaign in which Figueiredo threatened to jail anyone who opposed redemocratization, expectations were heightened that the abertura would be extended further.

The question to be asked at this point is whether these expectations will be realized: how much further can and will the abertura be allowed to go? Because the political process depends on a precarious balance between authoritarianism and democracy, it is hard to arrive at a satisfactory conclusion. Dissidents can still be arrested and intimidated without due process,[27] and the constitutional safeguards give Figueiredo broad powers, a reminder to everyone that a state of exception can be reinstituted at any time.

Several factors help perpetuate the authoritarian-democratic predicament, one being Brazil's economic situation. A high inflation rate, estimated at 75 percent for 1979,[28] and chronic petroleum shortages will produce a continued economic slow-down and fierce competition for scarce goods. How the regime negotiates with groups that experienced relative prosperity during the boom years of the early 1970s will be crucial. Moreover, because of an extraordinarily large foreign debt (estimated at $60 billion) and the imposing presence of multinational corporations, the regime must respond to external actors whose major concern is not redemocratization—an unwieldy process at best—but a stable and predictable political environment in which business can go on as usual. Under such pressure the regime may see repressive controls as its only recourse.

A second factor has to do with the present realignment of political parties. As a consequence of the Party Reform Law, the opposition, once united in its efforts to abolish the most repressive features of the regime, has become factionalized. Natural constituencies such as labor are being courted by at least two *trabalhista* parties (those of Leonel Brizola and "Lula"), and issues once the domain of the democratic left are being usurped by parties of the center-right.[29] Perhaps the new parties will reflect the social divisions in Brazilian society more realistically than their artificially created predecessors. But if rivalries remain at present levels of intensity, the opposition faces diminishing prospects of coming to power or of altering the fundamentally authoritarian nature of the regime.

A third factor is the absence of any consensus about the definition of abertura democrática as a political concept. In the narrowest terms, abertura means a return to the "rule of law" and a minimal respect for civil liberties. In the broadest sense, however, it means creating a political order through a constituent assembly that would permit legitimacy to be conferred on any government which meets accepted standards of representation, even one which questions the premises of capitalist development. Brazilian elites have considered "the Spanish Solution" as well as "Mexicanization" as alternatives, and herein lies another grave affliction of Brazilian politics: confusion and uncertainty as to the new political model on which to build.

How long can this game of *abre-fecha* continue before tensions reach intolerable levels? Juan Linz has pointed out that since a redemocratization process means excluding old elites as well as incorporating new elements, current power holders can be expected to manipulate the redemocratization process indefinitely in order to maintain their positions of control. Furthermore, the Spanish experience suggests that an authoritarian system can withstand diverse opposition for a considerable length of time.[30] Thus, barring the unlikely occurrence of a miscalculated and protracted foreign military venture or a domestic military scandal of major proportions, the prospects of a radical solution to the abertura predicament appear to be slim.

In the final analysis, the abertura represents a distinct stage in Brazilian politics. Clearly, the naked repression of the past has come to an end, along with unified resistance to it. Nevertheless, with so many new and disparate elements added to the power equation of national politics, the abertura democrática constitutes a sort of *espaço de ninguem*, a political no-man's-land with new territories that will be vigorously contested in the months and years ahead.

Blacks and the Abertura Democrática

"The competitive social order," writes Florestan Fernandes, "emerged from a slave society and became an authentic and closed world of whites. . . . And, the structures of class society failed to eliminate, in any meaningful way, the racial structures of the previous social order. . . . This sociological dilemma is essentially a political one."[31]

Probably no other social thinker has penetrated the core of the Brazilian racial dilemma more deeply than Florestan Fernandes. In his several works he has shown that the predicament faced by Brazilian Blacks (that is, their lack of social opportunities and their victimization through racial discrimination) is fundamentally a question of the capacity of Brazil's social and political elites to preserve their power and privilege by suppressing a variety of social conflicts, while fully aware of the contradictions that give rise to these conflicts.[32] Fernandes points out that the mechanisms used to control social conflicts are formidable. Elites monopolize the instruments of coercion and ideological debate and traditionally have not hesitated to use these to suppress racial conflicts.[33]

On the other hand, Fernandes has also argued that if the racial injustices in Brazilian society are to be resolved, Blacks must force racial conflicts into the open. To expand on his argument, I would like to propose that (*a*) Blacks do exploit opportunities to generate racial conflicts, and (*b*) the current abertura democrática offers new possibilities for doing so. What follows is a discussion of the ability of Blacks to enlarge racial conflict through the mobilization of racial consciousness and racial protest. Some of the strengths and limitations of this approach to collective political action will also be reviewed.

RACIAL CONSCIOUSNESS AND RACIAL PROTEST

The abertura democrática has created a healthy climate for racial consciousness. With a number of other groups demonstrating their ability to confront an authoritarian and repressive regime, Blacks have also rediscovered the strength of collective assertiveness. In fact, one is tempted to label this recent blossoming of racial consciousness a Black renaissance comparable to that of the 1920s and '30s when the Black Brazilian press and the Frente Negra Brasileira flourished.

Some of the transformations brought on by this new consciousness are no less than astonishing. By the late 1970s, symbols of militancy which had belonged only to distant American cousins a decade ago were pervasive and commonly accepted by Afro-Brazilians. Afros and cornrow hairstyles were being worn by models appearing in the most established and fashionable Brazilian magazines; the intricate rituals of Black power greetings had been adopted by younger Afro-

Brazilians; and Black university students were quoting knowledgeably from Malcolm X and Frantz Fanon. Moreover, Afro-Brazilian poetry and fiction had begun to reflect significant aspects of the racial consciousness movement.[34]

Two occurrences mark the high points in the evolution of this Black consciousness. One is the development of the cultural phenomenon known as Black-Soul and the other is the creation of the Movimento Negro Unificado Contra Discriminação Racial (MNUCDR, or MNU). As these two phenomena have been described elsewhere in this volume, I will not attempt to discuss them exhaustively.[35] Nevertheless, I will sketch a few details of these movements in order to provide some background for the discussion which follows.

The Black-Soul movement is not, properly speaking, a political expression of racial consciousness, although it does have political overtones. It embodies the changes in fashion, popular music, and dance which closely resemble changes in Black American styles during the late 1960s and early '70s. The focal point of the movement is the disco soul club frequented primarily by working-class Black youths. Like their American counterparts, the soul clubs of Rio and São Paulo offer the music of Stevie Wonder, Aretha Franklin, and others, played with a heavy beat, an extravagant presentation of colors, and the opportunity to strike postures of personal ostentation. As a frequenter of one of these clubs put it, "The dances are like a parade of vanities."[36]

The soul movement is, above all, a commercial endeavor. Its music is intended to be sold in an entertainment market for profit. In fact, some have argued that it is a Trojan horse through which multinationals (particularly Warner-Electra-Atlantic Records) can gain a stronghold into a lucrative market. The promoters of soul were ambitious enough at one point to believe that the music would have the impact on Brazilian popular culture that jazz had on American tastes a half-century ago. Although these expectations have not been fulfilled, the movement still enjoys considerable, but less ostentatious, popularity, especially among the young.

The sociological significance of the movement lies in the fact that it reflects spontaneous feelings of racial assertiveness, and even, to a large extent, overt racial hostility. On one recent occasion in São Paulo, for example, a near riot broke out over the perceived arrogance of some whites who allegedly refused to follow the informal codes of conduct in a club. Thus, the soul clubs are rarely places where the myth of Brazilian racial harmony is realized. As one initiate explained the racial antagonism, "When poor Blacks have the audacity to leave their favelas to do something besides samba, the accusation is made that they are losing their negritude, and that they ought to keep on doing the samba. This is the same as saying, 'Stay in your favela, live there, suffer there, and die there.' "[37]

One criticism that has emerged because of obvious similarities is that the soul movement is an artificial transplant of 1960s Black America. To question the authenticity of this phenomenon seems to miss the mark, however. Afro-American and Afro-Brazilian cultures were shaped by institutions in slave societies that functioned in similar ways. It should come as no surprise that, given the reality of the global dispersion of mass consumer technology, a certain degree of cross-pollination occurs.

More important still is the fact that this movement represents a genuine search for new ways to express Black distinctiveness in Brazilian society. More traditional manifestations, such as samba clubs, are being abandoned because Afro-Brazilians see them as having been corrupted by the commercial and cultural dominance of whites. Black-Soul represents one new alternative that is revitalizing Afro-Brazilian culture. Such is the case with the Escola de Samba Quilombo, which uses a traditional vehicle of Black culture—namely, carnaval—to foster reappraisals of the Black Brazilian experience. One suspects, therefore, that criticism of the Black-Soul movement stems from the bitter feelings whites experience over attempts by Blacks to free their own cultural expressions from white domination.

Whatever proves to be the final judgment on the "authenticity" of the Black-Soul movement, one thing is clear. It is a sign of racial conflicts coming to the surface. Moreover, its visibility has helped to shape the evolving political consciousness of others.

The major shortcoming of the Black-Soul movement is that it expresses feelings of racial assertiveness in diffuse ways. Florestan Fernandes, in fact, referred to this stage in the development of racial consciousness as an "innocuous inconformity."[38] The movement lacks a structure through which to channel these feelings into constructive political action.

The crystallization of this consciousness occurred in São Paulo on July 7, 1978, when the MNU launched a public demonstration against racism that attracted some 2,000 persons. Black speakers came from various parts of Brazil to condemn several of the more recent and flagrant instances of discrimination and the pervasiveness of Brazilian racism in general. The manifesto read at the demonstration clearly stated the purpose of the event:

> Today we are in these streets in a campaign of denunciation!
> We are promoting a campaign against racial discrimination, against police oppression, against unemployment and marginalization. We are in the streets to denounce the terrible living conditions of the Black community.
> Today is an historic day. A new day begins for Black people!
> We are leaving the meeting rooms, the conference rooms, and we are going to the streets. A new step has been taken in the struggle against racism.
> Let the racists take cover, for we will demand justice. Let the assassins of Black people take cover, for we shall again demand justice. . . .
> We invite the democratic sectors of society to support us in creating the necessary conditions for a true racial democracy.
> —AGAINST RACIAL DISCRIMINATION
> —AGAINST POLICE OPPRESSION

—FOR THE GROWTH OF THE MOVEMENT
—FOR AN AUTHENTIC RACIAL DEMOCRACY[39]

The MNU has furthered its goals in several ways. Its *centros de luta*, now re-named action groups, work to raise Black consciousness on a grassroots level, while its leadership has attempted to establish a Black presence within the democratic Left. Moreover, the MNU has taken up the cause of the community of Cafundó, a village located near the city of Sorocaba, São Paulo, which has been involved in a bitter land dispute with a local *fazendeiro*.

Both the general ferment of the abertura and factors more directly related to the evolution of the race consciousness movement contributed to the creation of the MNU.[40] One of the events that precipitated its founding closely and sadly paralleled the Herzog affair. The incident in question involved the murder of a Black worker, Robson Silveira da Luz, while in police custody. Outrage against this injustice unmistakably called to mind the public reaction to the Herzog murder.

Another government action had its effect as well. Diplomatic recognition of the MPLA in Angola stimulated Black activism, just as the African independence movements had done for the American civil rights movement in the 1950s and '60s. The victory of a Luso-African colony after protracted fighting made the efficacy of militant political action more credible for Afro-Brazilians.

Moreover, Black university students were being exposed to the increasing militancy of the student movement in general, and the activities commemorating the ninetieth anniversary of the abolition of slavery, held on the campus of the University of São Paulo, did much to foster this kind of student interaction.

The Black-Soul movement also had its impact on the MNU. The limitations of such a movement had been apparent to many of the founders of the MNU for some time, however. They had participated in various forms of racial expression including theater, community organization, and cooperativism, and were cognizant of the limits of these approaches. In any event, the MNU was the outgrowth of several factors which saw protest activity as a logical step in the struggle to correct racial injustices.

Having thus described two important examples of the recent Black consciousness movement, I would like to raise the following questions: how do these recent manifestations fit the contours of the abertura democrática; and what possibilities does the abertura offer Blacks for effective political mobilization in the future?

I have argued that the abertura democrática is a process in which authoritarian elites are losing control over the management of social and political conflicts. The result of this is a general questioning of the nature of the present regime and a search for viable alternatives.

Can Blacks gain anything from this period of ambiguity and searching? Available evidence suggests that during periods of regime transition in Brazilian his-

tory, Afro-Brazilian race-consciousness movements do at least experience a broad-
ening of their ideological horizons. Thomas Flory, for example, has recently
called attention to the emergence of the "colored press" during the Regency period (1831–1841).[41] He points out that, besides raising the issue of racial discrimination, this press also actively took part in the intense debate regarding the legitimacy of monarchical institutions. And even though the "colored press" may have
been manipulated by stronger political forces as Flory asserts, it certainly stimulated questions about the type of political order, monarchical or democratic, that
would have best served free Blacks in the nineteenth century.

Similarly, the Vargas Revolution of 1930 kindled in Blacks a sense of liberation
from social control by the once-dominant rural oligarchs. This spirit allowed
them to contemplate what was then a novel way of participating in the political
process. The Frente Negra Brasileira translated this into an independent Black
political party whose purpose was to run racially conscious candidates for elective
office at all levels. While the Frente Negra could not completely free itself from
fascist corporatism, which the Vargas Revolution brought in its wake, some elements of the movement did break away to issue the *Manifesto in Defense of Democracy* at a time when the repressive Estado Novo was facing insurmountable
attacks.[42]

This recent abertura may have the same effect as those of previous eras. With
vigorous discussions now taking place about political relationships and controls
under authoritarian (1964–present [1985, ED.]) as well as democratic governments (1945–1964), Blacks are coming to understand the social and political
mechanisms that have frustrated their movements in the past. One small illustration of this is Eduardo Fereira de Oliveira's reply to the National Conference of
Brazilian Bishops regarding their intention to create a Negro Pastoral. Oliveira,
an ex-Christian Democrat and local São Paulo politician once closely associated
with the populism of Jânio Quadros, expressed the fear that the Church would
commit the error of extending the kind of paternalistic support to Blacks that it
had in the past. On other occasions Oliveira has also suggested that Blacks guard
against the reestablishment of the populism of a former era with which he was
associated.[43]

In this regard, the efforts of Abdias do Nascimento to elaborate what he calls
the ideology of Quilombismo can be enlightening. Quilombismo resembles the
work of Cheik Anta Diop and Chancellor Williams. This approach attempts to
construct a systematic explanation for the present condition of Black Brazilians
and to offer a plan of political action to alter that condition. Nascimento's purpose, like that of Diop and Williams, is to recapture from white control the collective memory of an African community by emphasizing the achievements of
Blacks in science, technology, and culture. In addition, Nascimento offers an explanation for the impoverishment of Blacks by attributing it to the impulses of
western man and his colonization of the non-European world. In this respect
Quilombismo represents an intellectual tool with which to shape the still-inar-

ticulate but genuine feelings of many Afro-Brazilians regarding the arrogated superiority of Western civilization and the presumed inevitability of its progress.

As mentioned previously, Quilombismo also lays out the blueprint of a new social and political order, some of whose main tenets are the following:

1. The realization of an anti-racist, anti-capitalist, and anti-imperialist revolution.
2. The transformation of the relations of production by democratic and peaceful means.
3. The promotion of human happiness through economic organizations based on communication and cooperative principles.
4. The collective use of the means of production (land as well as industry) and the just distribution of their products.
5. The establishment of a system of government based on egalitarian democracy.
6. Automatic apportionment of half of all important government posts to women.
7. Establishment of employment, education, and freedom of religion as basic human rights.[44]

While the eclecticism and utopianism in this program are clearly evident, it would be an obvious injustice to criticize the program strictly on these grounds, particularly because the ideology of Quilombismo is still at an inchoate stage of development. Moreover, the apparent similarities between Quilombismo and other, more established, ideologies should not detract from its unique origins as an Afro-Brazilian ideology and hence its applicability to the particular circumstances of Afro-Brazil. In any event, the test of its durability rests with the masses of Afro-Brazilians and the degree to which they will find it convincing enough to sustain them in drawn-out and often frustrating political confrontations. If Quilombismo inspires large numbers to political action, it can also affect the future course of the abertura democrática by making racial justice one of the goals to be achieved in a new political order.

There is still another way in which the abertura provides new directions for racial protest and racial mobilization. Abertura has been described as a political no-man's-land where no combination of political forces has yet established its legitimacy or ideological hegemony. Blacks can certainly enter this vacuum with their own redefinition of racial issues for political debate. Such a move raises the stakes in the struggle by escalating the demands Blacks can make in return for their allegiance and their fundamental political identity in the Brazilian nation. Rather than demand a "second Abolition," an issue that was basic to the movements of the 1920s and '30s, Blacks can make sweeping revisions in the substance of issues around which racial conflicts are fought in the political arena.

This process has in fact already begun with the articulation of "radical" issues

in the area of Brazilian race relations. An example is Abdias do Nascimento's
assertion that the Black-Brazilian experience is primarily one of genocide. One
solution is government repayment for the loss of life, limb, and liberty suffered
during slavery. If articulated forcefully and dramatically, the issue could compel
Brazilians to abandon their complacent notions about "racial democracy"; moreover, it could stimulate Blacks to rethink the extent to which their allegiance to
Brazil has been taken for granted in light of the validity of their claim to compensation due for past injustices practiced by the state.[45]

Another question which Blacks have begun to articulate in this regard is
whether to consider Brazil's entire inmate population as political prisoners. This
issue is of immediate concern to Blacks, who comprise an inordinate proportion
of the common prisoners in Brazilian jails. Again, if articulated forcefully, one
scenario might have this issue provoking a radical debate over the manner in
which social institutions marginalize Blacks by insidious means.[46]

The success of Afro-Brazilian protest, however, depends on more than analyzing the theoretical potential of enlarging conflicts or developing ideologies. Leadership, organization, and material resources are the more crucial components of
success, the lack of which places the severest constraints on current racial-con-
sciousness movements. Tensions have already emerged within these movements
over their future direction in light of these scarcities. Some have argued that a
practical course should be taken, such as the continuation of consciousness-raising efforts through cultural forms. Others insist on pursuing militant political action to guard against a recurrence of "innocuous inconformity."

Where resources are concerned, it might do well to recall the old saying that
"nothing succeeds like success." That is, any victory in a new area of conflict
might attract the leadership and organizational and material resources needed to
sustain a political movement. It must also be kept in mind, however, that the first
principle of successful protest depends on the shrewd calculation of risks to be
assumed in a protest situation. The continuing drama of Brazilian race relations
hinges on calculating and assuming the risks needed to "overcome" in new racial
conflicts.

Because of space limitations, this discussion has only skimmed the surface of
the issue at hand. Questions regarding the possibility of government initiatives
in race relations, or the potential role of electoral and coalition politics have yet
to be analyzed. I hope this chapter has succeeded in showing that the abertura
democrática does offer political outlets for an invigorated Afro-Brazilian consciousness.

In the final analysis, Afro-Brazilians will decide the course of their political
action. This writing is intended to reinforce the call to action made by the vet-
eran Afro-Brazilian activist Abdias do Nascimento: "It may be possible to create
a [Black] organization that isn't confined to research and analysis but that provides some direction to the Black Brazilian reality. We should participate on all
those fronts that are fighting for redemocratization on an equal footing, and not

remain outside of the process. That is what I see for the future. The destiny of the Black Brazilian is the same as that of the country."[47] For Afro-Brazilians, destiny remains open.

Postscript: This chapter was completed shortly after the Figueiredo government had initiated its program of political liberalization. At that early date the fate of this initiative appeared uncertain. Particularly during its early years, the direction of liberalization might have been driven off course by disgruntled elements of the authoritarian regime, which could at any moment have precipitated an unforeseen political crisis, as was the case of the Rio Center bombing incident in 1981. In this atmosphere of uncertainty, Brazilian politics continued to be calculated on the premise of overshadowing cycles of loosening and constraining of authoritarian control (abre-fecha).

After the gubernatorial elections of 1982, however, the pace of liberalization accelerated far beyond the designs of its architects. Throughout 1983 and 1984, mass mobilizations in favor of direct presidential elections and the convening of a constituent assembly thrust the process of democratization toward its conclusion. By 1985, with the inauguration of the first civilian president in more than twenty years, the possibility of a sudden closing of the political process or a return to authoritarian rule had become remote. Nevertheless, the sense of political uncertainty that had surrounded the previous regime promised to continue under the current regime. The new government would have to rise to the test of reestablishing relationships between the state and civil society along authentically democratic lines. One of these tests will occur when the new regime decides how it will handle the Black consciousness movement that emerged from the tensions of authoritarianism, the genesis of which has been described in this chapter.

Notes

1. The research on which this essay is based was supported by the William Hallum Tuck Fund and the Latin American Studies Program of Princeton University.

2. Dr. Plinio de Arruda Sampaio, in *Anais do encontro nacional pela democracia: Paneis da crise brasileira*, vol. 3, edited by the Centro Brasil Democrático (Rio de Janeiro: Editoras Avenir, Civilização Brasileira, Paz e Terra, 1979), 77.

3. *The New York Times* has been carrying accounts of these developments sporadically. See, for example, 17 September 1979, p. 2; 13 October 1979, p. 8; 13 January 1980, Section IV, p. 3; 10 February 1980, p. 3. See also *Veja* 539 (3 January 1979) for a report on Geisel's formal revocation of Institutional Act Number Five.

4. Abertura democrática is still an issue intensely debated by Brazilians. For a sample of opinions, see Centro Brasil Democrático, *Paneis da crise brasileira*; Tão Gomes Pinto, "O jogo do abre-fecha," *Isto é* 157 (26 December 1979); Nelson Werneck Sodre, "A ditadura acabou?" *Movimento* 159 (17 July 1978); and "Receta Brasil," *Veja* 523 (13 September 1978). "Receta Brasil" contains commentaries by Raymundo Foaro, Florestan

Fernandes, Francisco Weffort, Fernando Henrique Cardoso and others; Fernando Henrique Cardoso, et al., "Para onde vai o Brasil?" *Movimento* 217: 12–15 (27 August 1979). Whether democratic freedom is a truly "popular" issue has severely divided the Brazilian Communist Party recently; see *Isto é* 157: 12–14 (26 December 1979). Further commentaries can be found in "Oh Brazil," *The Economist*, 4 August 1979, 3–22 (a survey), and Robert M. Levine, "Democracy without Adjectives," *Current History* 78 (454): 49–52+ (February 1980). For more formal theoretical discussions of redemocratization, see: Guillermo O'Donnell, "Tensions in the Bureaucratic-Authoritarian State and the Question of Democracy," in *The New Authoritarianism in Latin America*, edited by David Collier (Princeton: Princeton University Press, 1979), 285–318; Fernando Henrique Cardoso, *Autoritarismo e democratização* (Rio de Janeiro: Paz e Terra, 1975); Philippe Schmitter, "Liberation by Golpe: Retrospective Thoughts on the Demise of Authoritarian Rule in Portugal," *Armed Forces and Society* 2(1): 5–33 (Fall 1975); Nicos Poulantzas, *The Crisis of Dictatorships*, translated by David Fernbach (London: NLB, 1976); Juan Linz, *The Breakdown of Democratic Regimes: Crisis, Breakdown and Reequilibration* (Baltimore: Johns Hopkins University Press, 1978); José Eduardo Faria, *Poder e legitimidade* (São Paulo: Editora Perspectiva, 1978).

5. Nelson Werneck Sodre, *Historia do imprensa no Brasil* (Rio de Janeiro: Editora Civilização Brasileira, 1966), 53–100; Thomas Skidmore, *Politics in Brazil, 1930–1964: An Experiment in Democracy* (London: Oxford University Press, 1967), 9, 79.

6. Alfred Stepan, "Political Leadership and Regime Breakdown: Brazil," in *The Breakdown of Democratic Regimes: Latin America*, edited by Juan Linz and Alfred Stepan (Baltimore: Johns Hopkins University Press, 1978), 110–137; Alfred Stepan, *The Military in Politics: Changing Patterns in Brazil* (Princeton: Princeton University Press, 1971), chapter 7; Thomas Skidmore, *Politics in Brazil*; Ronald Schneider, *The Political System of Brazil* (New York: Columbia University Press, 1971), 21–36; Helio Jaguaribe, *Economic and Political Development: A Theoretical Approach and a Brazilian Case Study* (Cambridge: Harvard University Press, 1968), 163–174; Octavio Ianni, *O colapso do populismo no Brasil* (Rio de Janeiro: Civilização Brasileira, 1971). Jan Knippers Black, *United States Penetration of Brazil* (Philadelphia: University of Pennsylvania Press, 1977) discusses U.S. involvement in the coup of 1964.

7. See Schneider, *The Political System of Brazil*, and Stepan, *The Military in Politics*.

8. Stepan, *The Military in Politics*, 234, 243–247; Schneider, *The Political System of Brazil*, 89–90, 120–121, 131–132. See also the brief analysis of Castelo Branco's political orientation contained in *Veja* 187: 36–47 (5 April 1972).

9. George-Andre Fiecheter, *Brazil Since 1964: Modernization under a Military Regime* (New York: John Wiley and Sons, 1975), 87–88.

10. Fiecheter, 89; Schneider, chapter 5.

11. Fiecheter, 155–162; Carlos Castello Branco, *Os militares no poder: O ato 5* (Rio de Janeiro: Nova Fronteira, 1977).

12. Fernando Pedreira, *Brasil política, 1964–1975* (São Paulo: Difel, 1975), 273–290; Alfred Stepan, *The State and Society* (Princeton: Princeton University Press, 1978), 104; Fernando Henrique Cardoso, *O modelo político brasileiro* (São Paulo: Difusão Europeia do Livro, 1973); Alfred Stepan, ed., *Authoritarian Brazil* (New Haven: Yale University Press, 1973).

13. General Golbery, reputedly the principal architect of abertura, left the Figueiredo

government, where he was chief of the President's civilian staff, expressing dire warnings against the authoritarianism and excessive powers of his own brainchild, the National Information Service (SNI), and its head, General Octavio de Medeiros (August 1981).

14. Hugo Abreu, *O outro lado de poder*, 3a edição (Rio de Janeiro: Nova Fronteira, 1979), 78. Abreu refers to the battles over presidential succession as world wars. The Castelistas lost the "First World War" with the election of Costa e Silva but won the "Second World War" with Geisel's election. Fernando Pedreira and Luis Perreira also suggest that Geisel's government represented return to one of the authentic goals of the 1964 movement, that is, the "perfection of democracy" which the "hardliners" under Costa e Silva and Médici had distorted through the repression of dissidents. See Fernando Pedreira, *Brasil política*, 274–278; and Luiz C. Bresser Perreira, *O colapso de uma aliança de classes* (São Paulo: Editora Brasiliense, 1978), 157. On the conflict between "hardliners" and the Castelistas see also Schneider, *The Political System of Brazil*, 254–255, 257.

15. Perreira, *O colapso de uma aliança de classes*, 38–41; Celso Lafer, *O sistema político brasileiro* (São Paulo: Editora Perspectiva, 1975), 115–123; Walder Goes discusses the Brazilian response to U.S. human rights policies in *O Brasil do General Geisel* (Rio de Janeiro: Nova Fronteira, 1978), 163–185.

16. "O modelo nasce das urnas," *Veja* 325: 20–45 (27 November 1974); "Eleições: A redescoberta da política," *Visão* (18 November 1974), 20+; Bolivar Lamounier and Fernando Henrique Cardoso, eds., *Os partidos e as eleições no Brasil* (Rio de Janeiro: Paz e Terra, 1975); Alfred Stepan, *The State and Society*, 104–106.

17. Hugo Abreu, *O outro lado de poder*, 107–114; António Carlos Fon, *Tortura: Historia da repressão política no Brasil* (São Paulo: Global Editora, 1979), 68–69.

18. "Os limites da estatização," *Veja* 359 (23 July 1975); "Estatização: O debate político," *Veja* 402 (19 May 1976); "O modelo em discussão," *Veja* 425 (27 October 1976); "A saida de Severo Gomes," *Veja* 441 (16 February 1977); Peter Evans, *Dependent Development: The Alliance of Multinational, State and Local Capital in Brazil* (Princeton: Princeton University Press, 1979), 265–273; Luiz C. B. Perreira, *O colapso de uma aliança de classes*, 127–128.

19. Peter Evans, *Dependent Development*, 85–92; Thomas Skidmore, *Politics in Brazil*, 41–47.

20. "A Igreja no Brasil," *Veja*, 434 (29 December 1976); "Dom Paulo Evaristo Arns: 'A Política e uma Necessidade," *Veja* 474 (5 October 1977); Georges-Andre Fiecheter, *Brazil Since 1964*, 149–155. On the Dom Hipólito Affair, see *Movimento* 231: 12–13 (3–9 December 1979).

21. Hugo Abreu, *O outro lado do poder*, 68–71. Goes argues further that Geisel's middle course should not be interpreted as a liberal or progressive one; rather it reflected a changing locus of power within the regime from military to civilian government bureaucracies. See Walder Goes, *O Brasil de General Geisel*, 105–112; Perreira, *O colapso de uma aliança de classes*, 129.

22. "Sucessão: O candidato civil," *Veja* 466 (10 August 1977). Subsequently, former general Eular Bentes Monteiro became the civilian presidential candidate of the MDB and the strongest challenger to date to the presidential successor handpicked by the regime.

23. "A presença do estudantes," *Veja* 453 (11 May 1977); Hugo Abreu, *O outro lado do poder*, 63–68. Abreu also served as chairman of the National Security Council and was

therefore the cabinet official in charge of coordinating government responses to the student protests. His self-portrait as a good soldier performing a reluctant duty is delineated in the following statement:

> Information supplied by the National Information Service suggested that the student movement could "push the government against the wall." . . . Thus, our purpose was to contain the strike movement in Brasília and to avoid larger demonstrations in other parts of the country . . . the thought of 1968 was uppermost in our minds. . . .
> One could ask: why didn't we have a dialogue with the students? Unfortunately, that was not part of my mission (Abreu, p. 65).

24. Labor militancy gained momentum in July 1979 when the construction workers of Belo Horizonte went on strike. This action was particularly significant because it diffused criticism that only the blue-collar aristocracy of automobile and metallurgical workers were involved in the new wave of strike activity. One of the construction workers actually lost his life in a confrontation with police during the 1979 strike. It should also be kept in mind that construction workers are among the lowest paid urban workers in Brazil. For details on the 1978 strikes see *Veja* 508: 68–72 (31 May 1978); and *Veja* 509: 87–90 (7 June 1978). On the Belo Horizonte strike, see "A revolte dos peões," *Veja* 570: 20–25 (8 August 1979); and "Porque Minas pega fogo," *Isto é* 137: 4–11 (8 August 1979). It should also be mentioned that as early as 1977 the Brazilian labor movement, under new leadership, was beginning to make serious challenges to government economic policy. See, for example, "Redemocratização: E os operarios?" *Veja* 471 (14 September 1977). For analyses of recent labor activity see José Alvaro Moises, "Current Issues in the Labor Movement in Brazil," *Latin American Perspectives* 6(4): 51–70 (Fall 1979); and John Humphrey, "Auto Workers and the Working Class in Brazil," *Latin American Perspectives* 6(4): 71–89 (Fall 1979). Interviews with Luis Inácio da Silva (Lula) can be found in *Latin American Perspectives* 6 and Centro Brasil Democrático, *Paneis da crise brasileira* 3: 159–170. For discussion of the politics of the labor movement in general in Brazil, see Kenneth Paul Erickson, *The Brazilian Corporative State and Working Class Politics* (Berkeley: University of California Press, 1977).

25. The following account of the Frota affair is based on Hugo Abreu, *O outro lado do poder*, 87–118, and Walder Goes, *O Brasil de General Geisel*, 63–102.

26. Before he was elected, Figueiredo made the unseemly remark that he preferred the smell of horses to the smell of people. (Figueiredo is a former cavalry officer.) To correct this mistake, after his inauguration he launched a public relations campaign to create the image of a simple man who felt at ease with the "common people." He changed his dark-hued glasses, which gave him a malevolent look, for clear ones and made several well-publicized visits to the *feiras*, commenting on the high price of beans and rice as he went. However, when Figueiredo tried this ploy in the city of Florianópolis in December 1979, he was confronted by elements of the Convergência Socialista who shouted epithets about the nature of his government and, reportedly, about his parentage. Incensed, Figueiredo tried to confront his critics. Eventually, he had to be restrained by his security guards from engaging in an exchange of fisticuffs with certain members of the "*povo*." After this incident, Figueiredo's Secretary of Social Communication declared that the "man of the

people" campaign had come to an end. See also *Isto é* 154: 3–5 (5 December 1979); and *Isto é* 155:8 (12 December 1979).

27. *Isto é* 155:10 (12 December 1979).

28. By 1981, it had reached 110 percent.

29. The Partido Popular, for example, advocated such "progressive" measures as the abolition of latifúndios, redistribution of wealth, and freedom of association for workers and students. But its constituency is the generally conservative business community and the middle classes of the major cities. See *Isto é* 162: 12–13 (30 January 1980), and *Isto é* 157: 7–8 (26 December 1979). Subsequently, the situation was aggravated by Brizola's loss of the Brazilian Labor Party (PTB) to Ivete Vargas by court order and his resultant founding of a third *trabalhista* party, the Democratic Labor Party (PDT).

30. Juan Linz, "Opposition Under an Authoritarian Regime: The Case of Spain," in *Regimes and Opposition*, edited by Robert Dahl (New Haven: Yale University Press, 1973), 171–259.

31. Florestan Fernandes, "Aspectos políticos do dilema racial brasileiro," in *O negro no mundo dos brancos* (São Paulo: Difusão Europeia do Livro, 1973), 259–260.

32. Florestan Fernandes, *A integração do negro na sociedade de classes* (São Paulo: Dominus Editora, 1965); *Circuito fechado* (São Paulo: Hucitec, 1976); with Roger Bastide, *Brancos e negros em São Paulo*, 3d edition (São Paulo: Companhia Editora Nacional, 1971).

33. Suppressing racial conflict through exhortations of the ideology of racial democracy does not occur very subtly or even justly at times. A case in point is the tragic circumstance of Maria Aparecida Rosa, who was barred from a night club in the town of Juiz de Fora in 1975 and complained loudly enough of the incident to have gotten the attention of then-President Ernesto Geisel. After Geisel learned of the fact he decreed that the offending club be closed immediately and that the perpetrators of the crime be prosecuted. Two points were instructive in this case: first was the swiftness of Geisel's action which was intended to forestall any questioning of the irony of such an incident occurring in a supposed racial democracy; and second was the cruel treatment handed out to Maria Aparecida Rosa for having caused a nation such public embarrassment. Maria Aparecida herself was ultimately accused of being a racist because she too aggressively pursued the case in her quest for justice, and she was fired from her job and forced to leave her home in Juiz de Fora for being a threat to social peace. See the *Jornal da tarde*, 13 May 1976, p. 16. On racial ideology and social control in Brazil, see Bolivar Lamounier, "Raça e classe na política brasileira," *Cadernos brasileiros* 47: 39–50 (May–June, 1968); and Thomas Skidmore, *Black into White: Race and Nationality in Brazilian Thought* (New York: Oxford University Press, 1974).

34. An example of this literature is Oswaldo de Camargo, *A descoberta do frio* (São Paulo: Edições Populares, 1979).

35. Reports of these movements have appeared in the American press. See Carol Cooper, "Black Rio: Race Consciousness Grows in Rio," *The New York Amsterdam News*, 2 December 1978; Larry Rother, "Brazil's Race Relations: In Theory and Practice," *The Washington Post*, 12 October 1978; and *Encore*, 5 March 1979.

36. *Veja* 429: 156 (24 November 1976).

37. *Ibid.* (my translation)

38. Florestan Fernandes, *Circuito Fechado*, 75–84.

39. Quoted in Abdias do Nascimento, *Mixture or Massacre?: Essays in the Genocide of a Black People* (Buffalo: Afro Diaspora Press, 1979), 213–214.

40. The following is based on Movimento Negro Unificado Contra Discriminação Racial, *Boletim informativo* 1(1) (São Paulo, n.d. xerox); Departamento de Jornalismo, Escola de Comunicação e Artes, U.S.P., Agência Universitaria de Noticias, *Boletim* 4: 41–44 (2d semester, 1979); Clovis Moura, A dificil trajetoria das organizações negras em São Paulo (São Paulo, 1979, Typescript, Commissioned by Centro Brasileiro de Analise e Planejamento [CEBRAP]), 29–33.

41. Thomas Flory, "Race and Social Control in Independent Brazil," *Journal of Latin American Studies* 9(2): 199–224 (November 1977). See also Nelson Werneck Sodre, *Historia do imprensa no Brasil* (Rio de Janeiro: Civilização Brasileira, 1966), 181.

42. See Michael Mitchell, "Racial Consciousness and the Political Attitudes and Behavior of Blacks in São Paulo, Brazil" (Ph.D. diss., Indiana University, 1977), 142–143.

43. Eduardo de Oliveira, "Pastoral do Negro Brasileiro," *Jornal da tarde*, 31 July 1979, p. 4.

44. Abdias do Nascimento, "Quilombismo: Um conceito científico emergente do processo histórico-cultural das massas afro-brasileiras," Documento No. 7 (São Paulo, 1979, Typescript); and Nascimento, "Princípios e propósitos do Quilombismo," *Folha de São Paulo*, Folhetim, 9 September 1979, p. 7.

45. The issue of genocide and reparations is discussed in Abdias do Nascimento, *O genocidio do Negro brasileiro* (Rio de Janeiro: Paz e Terra, 1978); see especially Florestan Fernandes' preface.

46. See, for example, Hamilton Bernardes Cardoso, "A vez dos presos comuns," *Isto é* 155: 42–46 (12 December 1979).

47. Abdias do Nascimento, "Nossos Negros solitários," *Veja* 512: 6 (28 June 1978).

2. THE NEGRO PROBLEM IN A CLASS SOCIETY, 1951–1960

Florestan Fernandes

Introduction

There is an integrationist pressure in Brazil to compel the Negro and mulatto to absorb the norms, patterns of behavior, and social values of the competitive social order. But this pressure does not draw on all the socializing forces of the larger society. Basically, it is clearly associated with the need to lessen the historiocultural distance between the sociocultural legacy of the black population and industrial civilization. In sociological terms, this pressure is measured by the need to absorb the Negro into the competitive social order, and as a result to develop his loyalty to the economic, juridico-political, and social foundations of this order. It does not cover other areas of socialization and participation in economic interests, social safeguards, or cultural riches. As a result, this integrationist pressure does not, strictly speaking, affect the prevailing patterns of the racial distribution of income, social prestige, and power. In the sphere of race relations, the class society is becoming an open social system, but the patterns of racial domination inherited from the past are not being updated. Within this broad picture, what might be regarded as the democratization of race relations is seen as a sociohistorical process that is heterogeneous, slow, and discontinuous.

These inferences are corroborated, empirically and theoretically, by the conclusions which may be drawn from the data in the Negro's collective protests and on the mechanisms of vertical social mobility inherent in the tendency toward classification of the black individual at the heart of the competitive social order. Collective protests unleashed sociopsychological tendencies among the Negro groups which corresponded in content and meaning to the integrationist pressures of the larger society. Nevertheless, they threatened the established patterns of racial distribution of income, social prestige, and power, for they aimed at the sudden universalization of those economic interests, social safeguards, and cultural values upon which rest the legitimacy and balance of the competitive social order. Thus, the Negro problem was equated with the ideal requisites for the integration and functioning of the class system, and racial unrest was granted the character of an organized and conscious struggle for racial equality. In other words, while it was reacting to the integrationist pressures of the larger society, the Negro's collective protest through the rights movements went too far. This explains why the protest found no echoes among whites and spread only through limited segments of the black population.

The mechanisms of vertical social mobility of the Negro and mulatto, in turn, could be and were measured by the duality and intensity of the integrationist pressure of the larger society. Society opened, suddenly and on a social scale, to the Negro and mulatto in the area of free labor and in the heteronomous positions of the occupational pyramid associated with the capitalist system. The integrationist pressure had direct structural and dynamic results on one level alone— that of the differentiation of the occupational and professional roles of the black individual. Yet the historical hiatus engendered by the conditions under which the bourgeois revolution and the consolidation of the competitive social order occurred in the city was closed. The Negro finally found normal and permanent ways of becoming part of the class society. Nevertheless, other positions in the system, with their corresponding social roles, were affected only indirectly, and in proportion to the socioeconomic vitality acquired by the developing strata of the black population. Not even the electoral roles associated with the national political power system were affected in any direct or immediate way. When the Negro is concerned with the obligations inherent in being a citizen of a republican national community, he does so haphazardly and strictly in terms of his material or moral interests. If the integrationist pressure of society were to be applied in this direction, we would have an objective and relevant index of the rise of sociohistorical forces which would tend to bring about with the greatest possible rapidity a socioeconomic and sociopolitical equalizing of the racial groups.

Given these external conditions, which would develop by stages the manner in which the competitive social order would be opened to the black population, the egalitarian impulses at work within this population would become subjected to a previous sociohistorical conditioning of a highly restrictive character and to a restricted, rigid, and unavoidable selection. It is not surprising, therefore, that the vertically mobile Negro should have cast his choice for a way of life as realistic as it is opportunistic, turning his back both on the rights movements and on the common interests of Negroes collectively. As some of them put it, "to think of collective movements brings bad luck," or "racial agitation takes a lot of work and is no use at all. It's like banging your head against the wall." They subscribed unconsciously to the rationale that "smart people don't ask for trouble," and they had grave reasons for doing so. To do otherwise would be to risk the security and the advantages of being part of the social order for the sake of mirages. Society has already shown the path to be followed, and with it the eventual solution to the Negro problem.

These results demand that we examine our subject matter from a broader perspective. First, it is necessary to discern whether racial tensions have repercussions of any sort on the pattern of integration of the competitive social order. We shall not deal with the broader picture of the manifestations of color prejudice, but merely determine how racial tensions are perceived and controlled socially. Second, we shall trace the actual configurations of what appears to be, in view of the contact situation, the *Brazilian racial dilemma*. In doing so, we shall come face to face with the central issue of our research and develop a stimulating perspective for the broadest conclusions we have reached.

Societal Reaction to Racial Tensions

The analysis carried out in the preceding chapter indicates that classification in the competitive social order is a structural and dynamic requisite for any change in the prevailing patterns of race relations. The reason for this is obvious. The relationship between color and dependent social position can only be broken if the Negro and mulatto attain a position of economic, social, and political equality with the white. Actually our analysis also suggests that such a position is not, in itself, sufficient to change the racial *status quo*. Whites ignore, consciously or unconsciously, the social effects of the Negro's classification on the social levels to which they themselves belong. Nevertheless, they cannot prevent socially rising Negroes from changing their conception of status, their mode of interaction with society, or their attitudes vis-à-vis the forms of racial adjustment inherited from the past. Gradually, imperceptibly, alongside the classification of Negroes and mulattoes in the competitive social order, patterns of race relations undergo sociologically significant changes. Over a long period of time, these changes (if the trends described are maintained) foster the slow but gradual adaptation of the system of race relations to the economic, juridico-political, and social requisites of that social order. We cannot say what would happen if the process were to gain intensive and constant momentum and were thus to become adapted to the pattern of integration of the class society and to the rhythm of its historical development in São Paulo. Under the circumstances of full employment and constantly rising actual average income at the moment, it would be probable that existing contradictions between norms, stereotypes, and actual behavior should cease. Because of the growing numbers of black individuals able to compete for and fulfill the social roles inherent in the positions they have achieved, the effective behavior of the whites ideally should be modified and channeled toward an accelerated democratization of the patterns of race relations.

So far, however, the sociological situation has been quite different. The absorption of Negroes and mulattoes into the structure of the class system has been so limited and hesitant that the old vicious circle remains relatively unbroken. Color continues to operate as a racial mark and as a symbol of social position, indicating simultaneously a dependent racial group and inferior social position. In addition, the majority of black individuals lack the means to break out of this confused state of affairs, which is both vexing and damaging. Even the vertically mobile

Negro—a privileged person among the Negro groups—must struggle heroically, uninterruptedly, and ingloriously in order to enjoy minute quantities of the pre-rogatives associated with his social position. This egalitarian trend, itself timid and hesitant, is canceled by the social context. As we have seen, in 1940 the cate-gory of employer comprised only 133 Negroes and mulattoes to 15,261 whites— 0.78 per cent to 97.04 per cent. Now, if we take as a point of reference the demo-graphic color pattern, this ratio ought theoretically to be quite different under a system of socioeconomic equalization of whites and Negroes. The number of Negro employers ought to be approximately 13.5 times greater (or about 1,609 individuals), and the number of white employers ought to be approximately one-tenth smaller (or 13,804 individuals)—not to speak of individuals of Asian ances-try, who overshoot our hypothetical ratio by more than one-sixth.*

Thus, we must work in terms of a reality that does not fit the conventional rationalizations defended by those whites who identify with the Brazilian racial ideology. They misrepresent the racial reality as they view the Negro's position through the ideal norms of behavior and the egalitarian potential of the competi-tive social order. On the other hand they are deceived in their own social outlook as they cling to the notion that there are no racial distinctions among the lower classes. This does happen, but only in those contact situations peculiar to social milieus molded by folk culture. There, the Negro is equal to the white for nearly all social purposes, through a leveling downward. This is a sociodynamic conse-quence of absorption into the network of human relations created by a subsis-tence economy. In a metropolitan society, however, downward leveling implies at least membership in the working classes, and this would require the systematic proletarianization of those segments of the black population which are involved in the free labor system outside of the occupations pertaining to the middle and upper classes. This is the case only in part and in a fragmentary and hesitant way. This results, in actuality, in serious limitation of the Negro's integration into the class system. Only a few segments of the black population have managed to achieve *typical class positions* in organized fashion. Other segments of the same population—presumably more than half even now—remain on the periphery of the free labor system and the class system, victims of anomic conditions of social existence or of sporadic association in the metropolitan subproletariat. In short, in the contact situation described, downward leveling is not the same thing as equalizing with the white. To the contrary, it implies an indefinite perpetuation of the two polarities which have traditionally upheld the parallel between color and minimal social position in Brazilian society: social anomie and socioeco-nomic dependence.

Editor's note: The author is referring to the Japanese immigrants to Brazil. In the first part of 1967, 73 per cent of the Japanese colony in Brazil were proprietors (Intercambio Cultural Entre Brasil e Japão, Japanese Consulate, São Paulo, mimeo., n.d.).

Although this does not explain everything (since we must also take into account residual forms of intolerance in the cultural traditions of the various ethnic and national groups of *Paulistana* society), it provides us with a general background for determining sociologically *how* and *why* this parallel possesses both historical viability at the present time and the external requisites for sociocultural survival. From this standpoint it seems that Negroes as a group will be able to change their patterns of societal reaction to the expectations and behavior of whites only when they manage to become fully integrated into the class society, and when this integration occurs on an equal basis vis-à-vis other racial groups. Even though these two conditions are not sufficient to alter the general situation—since the racial behavior of whites is motivated and controlled by cultural factors alien to the structuring of the class system—they are decisive on two counts. First, they serve as material and moral foundation for a change in the status representations of the Negro and mulatto, as well as in the mechanisms of societal reaction of the black population to characteristic manifestations of racial prejudice and discrimination. Second, they provide a sociodynamic requisite for the organization of the conscious behavior of Negroes and mulattoes as a group, rendering it appropriate to the typical requirements of the class situation in the present sociohistorical setting. In the view of these two points, it seems obvious that the Negro requires material and moral foundations in order to use in a different way and for his own benefit the safeguards bestowed by social position. As long as color prejudice[1] operates predominantly under cover of clearly defined class situations, its victims ordinarily have to contend with insuperable difficulties, and it is often impossible for them to defend their social interests through the social techniques, forms of behavior, and controls consecrated and guaranteed by the competitive social order.

This posing of the problem immediately suggests that racial tensions arise above and beyond the social interests and values inherent in the class positions which are found in São Paulo. The motivation for the nonconformist behavior of the socially rising Negro (for, as we have seen, the desire to rise is in itself a choice containing an element of protest) is the yearning to be someone, to rise, to become part of the system and of the established social order. As a rule, the achievement of a position (that is to say, of a class position) is involved. Nevertheless, where the Negro and mulatto are concerned, this yearning can only rarely be fulfilled from within a class situation. As far as the white is concerned, in turn, actual competition with the Negro is almost nil. It occurs only sporadically, in isolated cases which have no repercussions on the prevailing patterns of race relations. None of the class positions which developed historically up to the present time is endangered by the presence of competition of the Negro and mulatto. As a result it is not class interests that interfere with the expression of color prejudice. Proof of this is easy to obtain: the development of the competitive social order did not contribute in any way either to the intensification of expressions of color prejudice, or to a change in its sociocultural patterns. Actually the Negro does not enter, as a Negro, in the sphere of systematic social awareness and understanding of the white. It would seem that this is so, to a large measure, because the Negro is not regarded socially as a real or potential competitor for the enjoyment of the limited and highly desired safeguards of the class system. For this reason, the importance of color is secondary. Systematically meaningful are the external symbols of wealth, social prestige, and power which characterize the socioeconomic levels of the social pyramid or the personal characteristics and aptitudes of individuals independent of their social position. Nevertheless this general condition of awareness and understanding of one man by another does not make for neutrality in the adjustments of whites with Negroes, nor is it to be regarded as proof of the absence of color prejudice. The latter is unleashed, in unilateral and limited fashion, wherever and whenever the Negro comes forth and his presence becomes obvious and inescapable. Then, independent of any social motivations or controls related to the organization of the class society, there automatically come into play specific mechanisms which place the Negro's person or interests and forms of behavior in the direct line of awareness, understanding, and reaction on the part of the white individuals.

However, the Negro has not (at least not so far) become an inexorable reality which the white could not evade and had to face whether he liked it or not. To the contrary, the white can put the Negro in the background, ignore him, and plan the future as if society were racially homogeneous or if the powers of decision of the white racial group alone mattered within it. Now, it should be stressed in sociological terms that this factor, instead of arising as a positive requisite of racial integration along democratic lines, arose as a factor of inertia with profoundly negative results. Socially, it amounts to the general lack of interest of the white toward the Negro, which contributes to the indefinite perpetuation of certain archaic models of racial adjustment. The Negro is expected to adjust to the patterns of the prevailing civilization. But no heed is paid to what this means, materially and morally, to society, or how it might or should affect the equality of Negroes and whites in terms of the enjoyment of the social safeguards ensured by the class system. Further, and this is clearly sociopathic, wherever the Negro breaks through on his own to relatively high social levels, such occurrences are regarded and explained as if the traditional criteria of racial domination, which excluded the exception to the general rule and manipulated it to strengthen the rule, were still in full force and as if the parallel between color and minimum social position were a normal ingredient of relations between Negroes and whites.

We shall deal in this part of the present chapter with the following themes: the forms of expression of color prejudice in *Paulistana* society, and the mechanisms of societal reaction to dissimulated and open manifestations of color prejudice. The discussion of these themes, with selected empirical data, will permit us to complete our analyses and will help us determine the degree of dissonance that persists between the patterns of race relations and the forms of the organization of social life prevailing in São Paulo in the industrial era.

Sociohistorical analysis sees color prejudice[2] as a sociopsychological and sociocultural form typical of Portuguese-Brazilian civilization. It combines prejudiced judgments and attitudes of an ethnocentric and utilitarian nature with discriminatory social motivations and controls, and offers the eidetic and ethologic bases necessary to such judgments and attitudes.[3] It also links them to standardized forms of behavior which grant it minimal effectiveness, cohesion, and continuity. In this regard both prejudiced judgments and discriminatory practices are universals, being endowed with a certain homogeneity and generality. It seems obvious (although this is not acknowledged openly) that the irreconciliable contradictions and inconsistencies engendered by the conflict between these judgments and attitudes and the ideal patterns of Portuguese-Brazilian civilization have not really been eliminated. To the contrary, a unique compound has been formed which conceals this conflict and reconciles individuals to its repercussions on the affective and cognitive levels of social behavior. To limit ourselves to fundamentals, there are two chief dynamic results of this conciliating compound of incompatible and ideally exclusive sociopsychological and sociocultural elements. First, color prejudice does not appear on the social scene in a systematic way, but as a surreptitious, ambiguous, and vague social reality. Second, color operates as a dual frame of reference: it inseparably links race and social position, socially stigmatizing an entire racial category. This factor may appear to be secondary; nevertheless, it is crucial. It compels members of the stigmatized racial group to accept the forms of racial adjustment which are enjoined upon them. They develop attitudes, judgments, and forms of behavior which are ambivalent, vague, and contradictory because of the duality of the frame of reference; they become unable to differentiate racial stigmatization from socioeconomic dependence and sociocultural isolation; and thus they are unable to oppose such attitudes, judgments, and forms of behavior. As a result they are compelled to face prejudice in a state of great psychological confusion and without the means to group themselves into integrated racial minorities. Regarding themselves *de jure* and *de facto* as active members of the established social order, they learn to deal with the noxious effects of the racial contact situation only on the purely personal plane. Collective and organized recourse to radical techniques of exposure and protest are also closed to them, because racial tensions have been confined to the hidden level of race relations and are regarded socially as an incontrovertible threat to social peace. On the whole, everything contributes to regulate, dissimulate, and contain expressions of prejudice, subjecting them to the structural and dynamic requirements of a civilization that has made social accommodation the ideal goal of the societal integration of interacting racial groups. Expressions of prejudice cannot be carried far enough to endanger the interests, ideals of life, and social values associated with the historicocultural pattern of racial adjustment. On the other hand, however, they cannot be abolished without turning this complex automatically into a mere social equalizing of the racial groups involved.

This takes us to the heart of the structure and dynamics of the situation of racial contact prevailing in São Paulo. Expressions of prejudice prevent the differentiation, and consequently the aggravation of dissimulated color prejudice into systematic forms of racial prejudice and discrimination. At the same time, nevertheless, they tone down or cancel the repercussions in the sphere of race relations of the tendency to a democratization of wealth, social prestige, and power. Thus we uncover a very instructive aspect of our racial reality. It suggests that those who point to Brazil as an extreme case of racial tolerance have some justification. Yet, it also shows the other side of the coin, which unfortunately has been neglected: racial tolerance is not at the service of racial equality, and thus remains neutral to the human problems of the Negro related to the racial distribution of income, social prestige, and power. Indeed, this aspect is clearly linked to the protection and indefinite perpetuation of the racial status quo, through effects which foster the indirect preservation of the social disparities that condition the permanent subordination of the Negro and mulatto. The victims of prejudice and discrimination are regarded and treated with relative decorum and civility as human beings, but as if they were only half human. Their material and moral interests are not taken into account. What matters is social peace, with all it implies as an element of stability for the prevailing patterns of racial domination.

Those who consider racial relations superficially, without heeding the historicocultural pattern of social accommodation they involve or the implication of this pattern in terms of the racial distribution of income, social prestige, and power and the corresponding model of racial domination, do not really understand the existence, the deep complexities, and the persistent influence of the phenomenon. In the course of interviews and the experimental situations to which they lead, in the interaction of researcher and informant, obstinate and shocked denial was almost systematic. No one will accept the onus of being prejudiced. Only those who fall into the category of intolerant personalities and those who are typically neutral to color prejudice frankly admit its existence and its legitimacy or illegitimacy. Reality is uncovered gradually, through the accumulation of contradictions which do not affect the balance or behavioral tendencies of individuals. Questions such as "Would you bring a Negro to your home? Would you accept a Negro boss? Would you let your daughter (or sister) marry a Negro?" lead to a justification of inconsistencies, as a rule quickly perceived by the informant and accepted good-humoredly. "Yes, you're right. We *are* prejudiced. But what can we do?"

Not only has the opinion become widespread that color prejudice does not exist in Brazil, but this opinion has been enjoined on dissenters, white and Negro alike. Christian mores, in turn, have contributed to this tendency. The area of Portuguese-Brazilian civilization that suffers most from the sociocultural inconsistencies pointed out above is the religious one. Even though Catholicism prevented neither slavery nor color prejudice, it has spread a certain reluctance to face openly these dark aspects of human nature and of the organization of society.

The other two influences are secondary, but not unimportant. Through the influence of Catholicism, and to a large measure through the longing to identify with (European) civilization, prejudice and discrimination are viewed as degrading, as though they were one with incivility and barbarism.

We shall now endeavor to determine the existing relationship between racial judgments, attitudes, and forms of behavior which are prejudiced and discriminating to varying degrees, and the types of contact involved in possible situations of racial coexistence. Knowledge of this relationship is of great importance. It provides immediate evidence of the boundaries within which judgments, attitudes, and forms of behavior of this type are socially approved or tolerated. It also gives indirect evidence of the degree to which such judgments, attitudes, and forms of behavior are governed, standardized, and regulated socially—in other words, through a common historicocultural pattern.

The data gathered show that four typical kinds of contact underlie the immense variety of possible relationships between Negroes and whites.[4] First, there is a sort of contact by proximity. The mere coexistence of different racial groups leads to a web of interdependence which makes the members of these groups members of "our group." Although the overall point of reference becomes the national community, everyone being regarded as a Brazilian, the basis of interaction is provided by what might be called mass sociability. As a result Negroes and whites are seen as pure entities, as though contact were strictly formal and defined in terms of the identification of individuals with the racial categories pertaining to "our group." On this level color prejudice is expressed in an impersonal and mild form, which is at the same time insidious and corrosive. Color is firmly asserted as a social mark that links the Negro and mulatto inescapably to an inferior racial group and a degrading social position. The best example of this can be found in certain sayings already quoted above: "Negroes are not human"; "There is no such thing as a good Negro"; and so on. To these we might add the alternative sayings used by the Negroes themselves: "Whites are no good"; "White trash"; "Deceitful white"; "If I liked whites I would carry a sack of lime on my back"; "White soul"; "Stingy white"; "I'm a Negro but I'm my own master." There are even more expressive sayings which seem to stress positive attitudes and judgments: "Poor thing, it's not his fault if he's a Negro"; "You wouldn't know he was a Negro"; "He's a Negro only on the outside"; "When a Negro is good, he's good all the way"; "Negro with a white soul"; etc.; and "Good white"; "Wow! A straight white!"; "You wouldn't know he was white"; "A white as good as white bread." Most of the negative stereotypes which stigmatize the Negro and mulatto racially and socially are expressed in verbalizations of this type which permeate our behavioral expectations. For this reason, not only are such verbalizations transmitted unconsciously, but they condition the formation of persistent images (of the Negro by the white and vice versa) and eventually cause ethnocentric judgments to take the place of reality judgments.

Second, there is contact governed by convention, in accordance with the

premises of the traditional pattern of asymmetric race relations. The mask of civility places a wedge between personal feelings and deep-seated beliefs and the
conveniences and decorum of life in society. In accordance with the ethical duality that prevails in a caste society, the white has enjoined upon himself—and
thus upon the Negro as well—the general principle that each person must know
his place and behave in accordance with the corresponding external requirements. The affective, logical, and moral context of this type of interaction leads
men to regard the parallelism between racial and social stratification as natural,
necessary, and unavoidable. Thus, even while he uses every available means to
strengthen and retain the pattern of racial domination that engenders and maintains this parallelism, the white cultivates explicitly the prejudice that he is not
prejudiced. Since the sole basic aim is to preserve a certain pattern of racial domination, it becomes easy to conceal this objective behind defense of the social
order (or simply social peace). Color is brought into play as a racial mark only
insofar as it operates as a symbol of social status. We have two ways of uncovering
this dissimulated form of racial prejudice and discrimination. There is that which
arises when the conventions that govern racial adjustments are broken unilaterally by the "inferior" party; in other words, when the Negro or mulatto refuses "to
be treated like a Negro" (even as a "Negro with a white soul"). In this case, the
white endeavors mildly "to put the Negro in his place." (To recall an example
already cited, he may have the visitor's meal served in the kitchen, even though
the visitor is a mulatto, has a higher degree, and a white-collar profession.)

There is also that form which is disclosed when whites are compelled to reveal
"what is going on inside." A small traffic incident, an innocent prodding of the
informant's sensibilities, or a fight can contribute powerfully to a loosening of the
tongue. We can list some representative examples: We came across a taxi driver
drinking *pinga* with a Negro in a bar in Vila Nova Conceição. The scene appeared to be a friendly one. As soon as he was in his car, the driver said, "These
Negroes, you give them a finger and they want your arm."

"Why?"

"That Negro wanted me to lend him a hundred milreis till tomorrow. He said
it was to get him through the night."

"You didn't give it to him?"

"Of course not! He has some nerve."

"But isn't he your friend?"

"My foot! I don't even know him. I was having a drink and he asked me to treat
him to one. I said OK. And next thing you know he was ordering a three-milreis
pinga."

He confided further that he did not like Negroes because he found them im-
pertinent and dishonest. We asked whether he considered them inferior to
whites.

"That I can't say. I don't know enough about it. I only know that I've never
seen Negroes in important positions. They're only in low positions." Then he

recalled that he knew a "colored lawyer," but he added, "It's one in a thousand. All the others are illiterates. They don't know anything. You can't do anything with these people."

We pointed out the contradictions in his behavior. He had been drinking with a Negro, treating him in a friendly way, and yet these were the views he was expressing. He replied, "I don't like them. You have to accept them, or else they say you're stuck up. But I don't like them. What can you do? You have to live according to local custom. Here, this is our custom. I can't act differently from other people. People feel that you must accept Negroes—I don't accept them. I know they're not worth a damn."

In a group discussion among middle-class individuals of old Portuguese-Brazilian stock, we put up for discussion the opinion of one of the participants that "Negroes are inferior to whites." The person involved, who hires colored labor for his small industry, invites them for meals in his home, plays soccer with them, and associates on a friendly basis with those who appear to deserve his trust, did not hesitate to state without further ado: "Negroes are indeed inferior to whites. People who say they are not prejudiced are hypocrites. From the day I was in high school, I haven't come across a white person who wasn't prejudiced. But they hide it." He added upon further query, "As for the friendliness shown to Negroes by some people, especially in the upper classes, I think their behavior is comparable to their treatment of house pets. They treat Negroes as though they were pet puppies or kittens. They even give them their family names. Obviously they don't treat Negroes as equals. Then too, we can't confuse Negroes and whites. . . . Negroes know they are inferior and acknowledge that whites are more intelligent and must have authority over them. So they are meek and respectful and accept their place. They will never be able to attain the same position as whites, no matter what they may do." As he clarified his ideas, he emphasized spontaneously, "Prejudice is not due to color, but to the fact that Negroes are inferior to whites and have always served whites as slaves, servants, or laborers. Color serves to pinpoint people, and as a sort of frame of reference. It simplifies things by crystalizing the ideas that whites have about Negroes."

A barber of Italian-Brazilian descent told us about a brawl in which he had been involved and in which he had been hurt. (Circumstances led him to venture an "explanation" of his own accord.) "I was on my way home and Dito (a Negro who was a janitor at the school where they both worked) asked me to have a drink with him. We went into the Tabuleiro da Baiana and asked for two *pingas*. At this point a friend of Dito's came in. He was also a Negro, but a tall guy, a real giant of a man. He had hands *that* big, I'm not kidding. [He measured out a tremendous length.] He greeted Dito and said to him, 'What's up? You don't ask your friends for a drink?' Then we offered him a *pinga*. He accepted and talked for a while with Benedito. Then he turned to me and said, 'Look, give me five milreis. I want five milreis from you.' I answered, 'I haven't got five milreis. If you want, you can drink with us. But I can't give you money. All I have is the right change.' He answered, 'I already said I want five milreis from you!' He argued with me. He wanted me to give him the money. Dito stepped in. He tried to calm him down. But the friend didn't pay any attention and said, 'What's the matter? Are you turning against your own race?' Then I said, 'I don't give money to anybody. If you want to drink, drink. If not, get out! If you want five milreis, go and get some work!' The man didn't say a word. He gave me a hard blow on the nape of the neck which sent me face down on the bar and down to the floor. If there had been a glass there, I would have been killed. Instead of holding back his friend, Dito stepped away. At first I was dizzy. Then I came to, and I went half out of my mind. I was blind. I threw myself head first into his belly. He dived clear across the bar and hit his head on a marble corner. I was scared of him and kicked him in the shin. I wanted to kill the son of a whore. Then I kicked him twice in the face and I bent down and gave him a few more punches. If they hadn't torn me from him, I don't know where I would have stopped. He was bleeding from the mouth, the ears, and the nose."[5] "We ended up in the police station. But the officer knew me and let me go. I wasn't going to be arrested on account of a drunken nigger. I had hurt him, but I hadn't provoked him. . . . Later Benedito criticized me because I had hit his friend, who was drunk. I answered, 'You should talk. Your duty was to hold your friend back. Now you criticize me because I didn't get beaten up. That bugs you. You wanted him to beat me up because he belongs to your race. Well, let me tell you that as far as I'm concerned you no longer exist. I don't want to have anything more to do with you. This is it!' " The barber went on to make various comments about Negroes. "I have no sympathy for Negroes. I don't like those people. I say this to their faces. But they think it's a joke. . . . I don't take Negroes into my home. Do you think I'm going to take monkeys into my house?" He did not want them as friends because he regarded them as dishonest and immoral. "I have been going to Vila Matilde because my wife is ill and is staying with her mother. I've watched Negroes there. They're degenerates. They're not like other people. Whether they're married or single, they have no moral sense. If they have children they don't look after them. If they're married, it is as if they didn't have a wife. They live as if they were single. They have no notion of responsibility or decency like white people. Negro and mulatto women go with anyone who shows them cash. They'll go with anybody for any amount. It makes no difference whether he's married or single. I don't know if this is because they are very hot. It's a very different race, and it seems their women are hotter than others. Even married Negro women will have affairs with anyone who wants them. The washerwoman who works for us looks like she wants to eat me up with her eyes. It doesn't even matter if there are other people around."

Even in situations that demand caution, a breach of etiquette can cause a white person to lose his control. One of the women researchers described such an incident. A well-known physician was department head of a certain institute. On one occasion an informal party was organized in his honor. The social worker had the idea of entrusting a bookkeeper, described as a light mulatto and the employee with the longest tenure, with the words of greeting. "Dr. M.'s displeasure clearly showed on his face, and half-way through the speech he interrupted the speaker's praises and said drily, 'Dona V. [the social worker] has some funny ideas.' The bookkeeper was terribly upset. At the end of the party Dr. M. said to Dona V., 'So, that clerk was all you could find to make the speech? A mulatto!' "

To sum up, the two ways of uncovering prejudice permit us to lift a curtain which is neither very thick nor very heavy. There is a correct way of doing things in relations between Negroes and whites. This way is strictly conventional. It does not affect the deeper levels of sociability or the personality of the individuals involved. It seems easy to understand why whites should cling to such conventions. Even after the traditional patterns of racial domination had begun to break down, the rule of the white race was still at stake for them. Yet large numbers of Negroes and mulattoes—many of them partially or totally free from the traditional conception of the world—also prefer this model of racial adaptation. We shall cite as an example the ideas of a mulatto girl who made subtle distinctions between color prejudice and other mechanisms of appraisal, selection, and rejection.[6] Before coming to São Paulo, she had lived in Angra dos Reis and Rio de Janeiro. Here, she settled in Santo André, an industrial suburb of São Paulo. She was shocked by the attitudes of her neighbors, most of them first-generation European immigrants. She noticed that "they withdrew, in a way that might even be considered offensive, in order to avoid relations with Negroes. They will not under any circumstances make contact with colored people." Her "disappointment was such" that she "got to hate the city" and felt that "São Paulo is the worst place for Negroes. In Rio there is more tolerance than there is here. I noticed that some people disliked Negroes and avoided relations with them. But I saw more contact and more marriages between Negroes and whites."

Third, there is the contact that is flagrantly divergent from the traditional patterns of race relations, either on the white's or the Negro's part, or both. Even where the traditional conception of the world is in full force, racially intolerant whites stubbornly refuse to obey the rules governing race relations. We have already indicated in various ways how such persons "act in ornery fashion," expressing their deep-seated feelings and refusing to treat Negroes "as if they were human." Their golden rule is the well-known "like with like." Our research showed that the number of whites of Brazilian descent who still hold such attitudes is much larger than might be supposed.

Three facts may be inferred from the available evidence: (1) Aside from occasional instances of racially intolerant individuals, certain circumstances kept the "outbursts of frankness" on the part of "pure-bred *Paulistas*" from breaking the taboos governing race relations. (2) Such tendencies were clearly aberrant—i.e., they marked the racial attitudes, opinions, and behavior patterns of a minority. (3) Although it is impossible even to guess the size of this minority, our own experiences and the results of our investigations show that it included a considerable number of individuals. The sociological significance of such influences is clear. They show that the traditional racial code also prevailed fully in São Paulo (as we have already proved on other grounds in the first three chapters of this work). More important, they also prove that certain aberrant ways of expressing racial intolerance existed prior to and independent from the flow of immigration.

Nevertheless, immigration exercised a specific pull in the same direction. Immigrants were the bearers of cultural traditions of their own which did not offer Brazilian solutions to the problems posed by the mingling of races, but as they were absorbed into the national mainstream and in turn took over the local customs they reinterpreted the Brazilian cultural tradition. This is the truly crucial feature as far as the Negro is concerned. They never understood the two-faced game of an acceptance that was at the same time a rejection, or of a friendliness that was more apparent than real. They mistook form for content, thoroughly upsetting the foundations of racial interaction. They would accept the friendship of black neighbors or colleagues only to find themselves later astonished by the liberties and impudence arising from a fellowship that was ill conceived and ill planned in terms of the Brazilian tradition. Thus, in order to "put the Negro in his place" they found themselves compelled to break relations with him or to avoid him in an offensive manner.

The vertically mobile Negro, in turn, becomes a source of problems. He wants to be accepted by whites of the same social level and demands the same treatment accorded by the latter to other colleagues and friends. Here is an example, taken from an interview with a young woman journalist and civil servant.[7] "At the office we had a Negro co-worker, educated, cultivated, well-mannered, who held an official position. He would go out with us, go to dances at the professional club, and ask the white girls to dance. We had to grin and bear it! Often, he and I would leave together and he would walk me part of the way home. I would go on talking, and put up with it. But inside I would be thinking: If anybody sees us they won't think that we are co-workers. Once a group from the office went to Pôrto Alegre,* where we went to several nightclubs. He felt he had the right to ask us to dance, and we couldn't refuse and then go and dance with someone else. You can just imagine the situation!" White people, especially in the upper segments of the lower classes and in the middle and upper classes, are puzzled by such situations. The ambiguities of color and inferior social position disappear. Either they accept and treat the Negro as an equal, or they cannot have any relations with him. Here again, deliberate and systematic avoidance is the easiest solution.

The following opinions of a white accountant are characteristic of those that prevail among the middle classes: Color prejudice was being discussed among a group of friends. This man disagreed with those who insisted that " 'the Negro is

---

Translator's note: The capital of the southernmost state of Rio Grande do Sul.

to blame for his own situation and for color prejudice.' . . . Color prejudice was created by the whites. It wasn't the Negro who created this prejudice. A man isn't to blame for having been a slave. It was the whites who tore them from Africa and brought them to Brazil. But a man doesn't cease to be human because he's a slave. I don't think it's fair to blame the Negro. . . . The Negro's problem is one of education. If Negroes were educated, they could show their worth. Sociologically speaking [sic] there is no difference between races. They are all equal. Whatever whites can do, Negroes can do too!" When pressed with direct questions he frankly admitted, "Personally, I don't want any contact with Negroes. I don't like to have anything to do with them. . . . In my family no one likes Negroes. But this has nothing to do with my opinions." An obvious inference can be drawn from these examples. In some segments of the white population, the breakdown of the traditional patterns of race relations does not put an end to color prejudice. On the contrary, it permits it to be expressed in stronger, more obvious, and more offensive terms.

Fourth, we must discover the extent to which the development and differentiation of the competitive social order are reflected in the structuring of race relations. On those levels where this structuring followed normal integration patterns, Negroes and whites meet as potential equals. We have already noted the factors which undermine, limit, or neutralize this sociohistorical process. Nevertheless, when Negroes actually break through as competitors of the whites, they acquire certain minimal requisites for differential participation in the distribution of income, social prestige, and power. As we have noted, this phenomenon is not sufficiently extensive to make Negroes a collective threat to the security of whites. Depending on the shortcomings of the latter, the Negroes' reactions may be either indirect and impersonal or individualized and direct. The first category comprises those reactions induced by the recent success of Negroes in certain occupational areas, such as skilled labor. The thoughts of an elderly housepainter are characteristic. "You can't trust Negroes. They're too dishonest and wicked. They think only of money. They want to get it on Friday and to get a lot of it. They don't give a thought to the work. . . . They're bad employees. They're often absent, they're not careful in their work, and they're not conscious of professional duties. They know perfectly well that they can earn money painting, but they don't make the necessary effort. . . . They don't fulfill other obligations properly either. If you trust them, you're sunk! You have to put up quite a fight to make them do what they ought to do." His resentment was focused on what he called "the invasion of the trade by black people." Those concerned greet this news as disturbing, as though Negroes dishonored the trade. In the second category are the inevitable clashes engendered by interracial competition. As a rule the white treats his black colleague as though he were a subordinate and a hanger-on. He takes on the duty of protecting and guiding him. When he finds out that the Negro can paint, and furthermore might outstrip him in free competition, he resorts to various stratagems to secure permanent advantages. If these fail, there is no remedy but to accept things as they are. Of course, as he plots his little schemes, the white cannot always avoid an overt (and sometimes virulent) display of color prejudice. Most significant, however, is the fact that up to now such clashes and frictions have remained limited and have not caused color prejudice to develop into a conscious, sanctioned, and systematic social reality. We should also consider that the competitive social order is not yet sufficiently developed to do away with or to counterbalance the irrational eruption of racial factors in various spheres of human relations. If we consider both sides of the matter, it appears evident that the competitive social order tends to absorb the overt expressions as well as the concealed aspects of color prejudice, in the best sense of the Brazilian cultural tradition, thus dissociating them from typical sociohistorical patterns of racial conflict.

The following trends were easily identified: (1) a widespread distaste for discussion of matters relating to color and to the Negro situation, which made color prejudice a sort of forbidden subject; (2) the tendency to identify with manifestations atypical in Brazil (particularly with the experiences of other groups, as in the United States, where racial prejudice and discrimination ordinarily take on an open and systematic character), which made it possible to deny its existence in Brazil; (3) the tendency to reduce the basic elements in the expression of color prejudice to purely personal matters and to cover up thoroughly those elements which might be said to be stubborn residues of prejudiced or discriminatory opinions and behavior. This of course permitted an expansion in the levels of treatment and appraisal of the Negro: external decorum coupled with partial or total exclusion of the Negro from any long-range contact with whites.

We shall proceed to an analysis of the foundations of color prejudice as it is found in São Paulo, limiting ourselves to basic facts and dealing only with three factors: (1) the social consciousness of the forms of color prejudice acquired by both Negroes and whites; (2) the interpretations each group has for such forms; (3) the ethical elements in the standardized behavior of whites and Negroes in social situations where color prejudice is expressed.

As for the first topic, Negroes and whites differ strikingly in their capacity for awareness of color prejudice. This difference can be crudely measured by the unequal numbers of answers obtained for each group in written statements. Whites do not perceive clearly the different expressions of color prejudice and do not properly recognize their sociopsychological and socioeconomic effects. Among both Negroes and whites there exist tentative interpretations for these differences in the awareness and understanding of the prevailing racial reality. It is all said to result from a sort of "prejudice on the part of the Negro," who is victimized more by his persecution complexes and his compensatory or self-punishing fantasies than by "actual prejudice on the part of whites." Explanations of this sort have a flagrantly ethnocentric flavor. Although the white can remain unaware of or indifferent to the negative consequences, direct or indirect, of color prejudice, the Negro cannot. These consequences compel him to break through his cultural horizon and to ask questions that clash with our current ideas of the race situation. It should be made clear that, first, such questions arise from ever-recurring experiences and, second, the understanding to which they lead can be tested and sifted through the selfsame experiences and incorporated into the sociocultural heritage of the black population. In other words, there are culturally determined alternatives in the awareness and understanding of the racial reality. In addition, these alternatives are shared unilaterally by Negroes and mulattoes, who thus launch some means to lessen or do away with those influences that block the cultural tradition. The differences evident in the black population do not invalidate this general hypothesis.

The varieties of awareness and understanding of color prejudice developed by whites have certain common features. Among them, the most important and decisive deal with the irremediable confusions resulting from the traditionalist culture. Such confusions are expressed in various ways. First, in a generalized unawareness of the existence of a Negro problem. In a characteristic statement written by a white woman informant from a traditional family, we find the following assertion, "I assume that the Negro has no problem. He does not feel ill at ease among whites, while the latter do among Negroes. Whites have a color problem although it involves the color of Negroes."

Then there is the debate over whether color prejudice does or does not exist. One of the women researchers held a discussion among ladies belonging to traditional São Paulo families and got a good example of this. One of the ladies defended with great feeling the notion that there is no color prejudice in São Paulo, giving as an example a black physician in Santos* who is married to a white woman from an excellent family and who has principally white patients. Another of the ladies disagreed, saying that "prejudice does exist and is expressed more or less strongly, depending on the situation, the people involved, and so on." She gave two examples in turn: that of an engineer described as "a very dark Negro" who replied in writing to an ad placed by a company in the capital, enclosing excellent references from his alma mater. The response was favorable. "When he came to take up his duties, they told him cruelly that they couldn't take him because he was black, that they wouldn't have considered hiring him if they had known about his color."[8] The other example referred to the experiences of a delegation of physicians from São Paulo who attended a medical congress in Bahia. The receiving party included a black woman physician. This impressed the São Paulo delegation most unfavorably, for they felt they were being "treated with little courtesy." Eventually, however, the caliber of that doctor caused them to change their minds.

Finally, such confusions are associated with characteristic inconsistencies. A person will attest that he is "unprejudiced" and is in favor of racial democracy,

---

*Translator's note: A port city near the city of São Paulo.

and at the same time express attitudes and opinions that run counter to such statements. Here is how a university student descended from a traditional and militantly socialistic family discusses the matter. "I believe that after all, in a democracy, everyone is equal, and we must treat the Negro decently. Of course, everyone has his place, and you can't be involved with them at all times—you can't trust them too far, for the Negro always lets you down in the long run. It's the old saying, 'The Negro who doesn't mess as he comes in, messes on the way out.' But they have their right to get ahead in life if they make an effort, and you can't act as people do in the United States, where they even lynch Negroes and where everything is segregated. After all, this is inhumanity—no matter how you look at it, it's not their fault if they are black. I believe that we shouldn't act as though there was any difference between us and them. . . . As for color prejudice among us, I don't believe there is any. There are none of those weighty restrictions which exist, for example, in the United States. No one forbids the Negro from moving, studying, or making his way in life wherever he wishes. There may be a few individuals who are prejudiced and who feel the Negro should be treated as he was in the days of slavery. But on the whole, among my closer relatives, everyone acknowledges that after all differences of color are no reason for us to place restrictions on Negroes, since no one chooses the circumstances of his birth and it's not their fault if they are born black."

Another widespread feature is the tendency to reduce color prejudice to an individual and thus to negligible pecularity. Hamilton de Oliveira asserted in a public statement, "I am white and I believe that color prejudice does exist in Brazil, as it exists everywhere. I have both colored and white friends, and I know that prejudice is a personal matter. There are people who are repelled by colored individuals and vice versa. And there are people who do scientific research in order to find out whether Negroes and whites can reach some understanding." This tendency is apparent even in self-analyses. One of the women interviewers noted that a lady from a traditional family ". . . told me that she has no color prejudice. To her, Negroes and whites are exactly the same. She doesn't believe that color is associated with moral or intellectual attributes. Nevertheless, she has a physical revulsion for black skin. She cannot say why, since as a child she had a Negro nurse of whom she was very fond. The feeling is quite strong and she is ashamed of it, so if she steps into a streetcar and sees an empty seat next to a Negro man or woman, she deliberately sits there to see if she can overcome her feelings. But the revulsion persists to this day."

A third feature that deserves special attention because of its widespread nature is the tendency to equate color prejudice with class prejudice. Even the Afonso Arinos Law, which includes among "legal offenses all practices resulting from race or color prejudice" stresses that it is aimed at "a change in the racist attitude that prevails among us, especially in the country's upper social and governmental spheres."[9] Now, manifestations of color prejudice are a threat "to future social peace," as stated in the legislative bill because they are not restricted to "upper social spheres." This was stressed even in the clear judgment delivered by Counselor Plinio Barreto, as though the only fact involved were the socioeconomic inequality of the two racial groups. "While all have access to public affairs, not all have access to certain social circles. To many, the Negro remains an inferior being, unworthy of associating with whites and of competing in society for the respect accorded to whites. . . . As long as whites retain the economic supremacy they inherited from the slaveowners of old, Negroes, for lack of adequate means, will continue to make up the poorer classes and prejudice will be maintained. No laws can do away with it. No law ever eradicated deep-seated feelings or changed the psychological attitudes of a people."[10] In spite of the truth contained in this truly complete description of the situation, decreasing the social and economic distance between Negroes and whites is not enough to recast the pattern of race relations. The insistence on confusing the external features of color prejudice with what is sometimes underestimated as a mere class prejudice thus leads to a real deadlock.

There is yet a fourth general factor which is found in extreme and dramatic cases, where reality loudly contradicts the dogmas of the prevailing racial ideology. We might take as an example the incidents associated with the turning away of Katherine Dunham and her group from the Esplanada Hotel.[11] In dealing with the matter, the *Correio Paulistano* pointed out that ". . . there is no color prejudice in our country. This truth is known and understood by all Brazilians and also by all those who visit our country. Hardly ever do we come across a situation where the behavior of a Brazilian leads to circumstances of this sort."[12] Another newspaper was more explicit, as shown in the following excerpt: "It would seem that the hateful problem is finally appearing among us. It will be a crime if it does, and for this very reason we must raise a loud clamor against it. The hand that dared to close that door surely was a foreign one."[13] Such an approach makes the foreigner a scapegoat and proclaims the Brazilian race tradition to be genuinely democratic. The Negroes themselves have partly yielded to this distortion, which has disseminated a superficial and one-sided view of reality, as though ethnocentric attitudes and prejudiced racial behavior were rooted exclusively in the influence of immigrants and the descendants of immigrants.

Wherever the specific demands of the patterns of equilibrium of the class society clash with established custom, the latter is radically altered. The management of the Worker Placement Department of the Regional Labor Office, for example, made public facts which in the past were aired only by leaders of the Negro movements: "Our Department has not managed, to this day, to place a single one of the black workers who have applied for office jobs. As a result individuals with excellent qualifications sometimes remain unemployed. This applies to persons who came to us recently and who had graduated from the technical course in high school as well as to an accountant."[14] Interviews with the heads of the personnel departments of some large private organizations similarly revealed that some companies have been compelled to choose between the suppression of systematic racial restrictions and a permanent shortage of manpower. Although these pressures do not affect all organizations and all levels of employment to the same extent, they point to the great difficulty involved in perpetuating certain customs and to the curtains that concealed them.

We shall endeavor to show with the aid of a few examples how color prejudice is understood and expressed in different social classes. In the lower class we find some fluctuation in the content and forms of awareness, which is probably due to differences in socialization. The closer the individual is to the rural Brazilian world, the harder he finds it to make basic differentiations; the greater the ego-involvement of the urban individual, the clearer his understanding of the Negro situation. Thus, according to a bricklayer who had recently arrived from the interior and whose grandfather was black (described as a "light mestizo"), "In Brazil there is no color prejudice. Troubles are family matters. It's quarrels that make people fight. They bring division." Nevertheless, he noted that in the city, as in the interior, "There are lots of people who'd never let their daughter or their sister marry a Negro. They think it's offensive if a white woman walks down the street with a sack of coal. This can only be explained through color. It's not that they think black people are inferior to whites, or that they hate them. It's just the difference in color." As he saw it, "Austrians, Germans, Polacks, Czechs, etc., don't want to have anything to do with Negroes. They only hire dark labor if they can't get anything else.... They don't want to have anything at all to do with Negroes. Italians too, but not so much anymore. This craze is just about over with them."

A tradesman of Italian-Brazilian descent, also from the interior but who had lived long in São Paulo, showed greater insight. According to what he had observed at the company where he worked, "They would never hire a Negro for any job. The boss not only doesn't like Negroes, he's also afraid of them." In the town where he had lived there was a strict separation of Negroes and whites in the park. For this reason, he was interested in the situation in São Paulo. He found that "Negroes are not well regarded in society.... People think that Negroes are no good, that they are disorganized and dishonest.... It's easy to find good jobs in São Paulo, as long as you're not colored.... The foreigners especially, who have everything in their hands, won't make any room for the blacks. They think that Negroes are thieves, that they can't be trusted." He confessed that before he married he had black friends, although none of them was an "intimate friend." After he married he neither visited nor was visited by any of those friends. "This often happens. As long as we're single we often get together for all kinds of purposes. Marriage and family life put an end to bachelor life. If a Negro visited me at home, I would receive him well. But I don't take the initiative to resume contact with my former Negro friends." As for intermarriage, he said, "No one likes to marry off daughters, sisters, or other relatives to Negroes. I don't think it's a good idea myself. As a rule, in São Paulo, people I know do all they can to prevent this. It's only in the interior that you have marriages like this, out of fear of those voodoo men. People think they're hexed, that it's dangerous not to let a girl marry the voodoo fellow." The situation in the United States aroused his interest. He believed it proved that Negroes and whites are equal and that separation has acted as a stimulus on the former.

In turn, a carpenter of French-Brazilian descent, born and bred in a section of São Paulo, showed considerable understanding of the dilemmas that confront the Negro. "Negroes have good reason to be aware of prejudice and to react to it. What goes on is no joke." He gave an example relating to the chemical laboratory where he worked: ". . . they had this obsession about not hiring Negroes. It's only a while ago that they began to take them for physical labor. There were no other openings." He also told of several cases of candidates being rejected from modest jobs because of their color. "Prejudice against the Negro is very strong, although people claim that Brazilians are not prejudiced. There is [prejudice] even among poor people, but far less than among the rich. The poor have less prejudice because they have to live close to Negroes at work and at home." He thought that there was more contact at work because many white people avoid "inviting Negro fellow workers to their homes. . . . Whites treat Negro colleagues as if they were not prejudiced." Yet he felt that prejudice is expressed indirectly in three ways: "(1) In bad jokes against Negro colleagues, whom they treat in a disparaging and malicious way—as though they were joking, but meaning to snub them. (2) In their attempts to avoid close contact with Negro colleagues. Those are the ones who are most prejudiced. They avoid all intimate contact and limit their relationships to the demands of the job. (3) In the comments they make. Even those who seem not to have any prejudice and lead you to think that color is irrelevant to them, make it plain that they're prejudiced against Negroes, the way they talk behind their backs. This is the rule. They discuss everything their Negro colleagues do with malicious intent. They scorn the Negro's personality and behavior. These comments are always disparaging and nasty."

On the whole, concrete experience not only directs but limits the awareness of the racial reality. Two points nevertheless deserve emphasis in this connection. First, informants make a distinction between color prejudice and other influences at work. The results of an interview with an upholsterer are significant in this connection. He acknowledged that "most people avoid any contact or relations with them" and he knew that in the company where he worked, "the bosses don't like Negroes." Nevertheless, he emphasized that Negroes missed good jobs by not applying for openings in that company. Second, we must note that whites from different national and ethnic groups engage in reciprocal retaliation. They try to "pass the buck" when it comes to the more unpleasant or vexing aspects of the situation. The following excerpt from an interview with an office boy shows this quite clearly. "My family is prejudiced, and very much so. My parents are Portuguese and my brothers Brazilian, but they're all prejudiced.[15] We live in Brás, in the midst of the commercial district. I don't know if it was because they always lived there, among Italians, that they got this prejudice. This may be part of it, because Italians are the most prejudiced people I know. They're not just prejudiced, they don't try to hide it. For example, in Rio the people are good. They treat everybody well. I don't know if they're prejudiced, but at least they don't show it. They treat white people well, and they treat black people well. In São Paulo people are quite different, and I think it's because of the Italians. Italians think that everybody else is inferior to them. If they praise someone from another country or of another color, or treat him well, it's sheer hypocrisy and usually for calculated reasons. They feel contempt not only for the Negro but for every other race and nation. In conversation they show a complete lack of consideration. They sing their own praises and when they discuss anything, they do it in such a way that they end up giving you an inferiority complex."

We cannot go here into all the various personal statements gathered among middle-class individuals. As a rule such people only give up the stereotyped traditional view of the racial situation when they are brought face to face with characteristic incidents. There was the housewife who tried to help a black servant with a toothache. They went to several dental offices, some of them with empty waiting rooms, and did not manage to get any help. The lady insisted and was told that nothing can be done since no appointment was made. "I said that in this case we would make an appointment. They said we couldn't, that they were all booked up." Finally, the wife of a dentist who was not in his office administered first aid and then saw to it that her husband looked after the patient. "She got treatment because we were lucky to come across the dentist's wife. Women have more heart." There is the clerk who notices the behavior of his department head, manager, or boss, and sees how he keeps from hiring or promoting colored employees. There is the personal director or manager who gets strict orders "not to hire Negroes," sometimes "without exceptions," sometimes "with such-and-such exceptions." As a result, their understanding of the racial reality is very limited. But it does give them staunch convictions and a special viewpoint. A bank manager wondered how anyone could doubt the existence of color prejudice in São Paulo. It seemed strong and obvious to him. The personnel director of a large industry with its headquarters in São Paulo said that color prejudice varied from north to south of the country (from minimal to maximal intensity). According to his own observations, it is more moderate in São Paulo than in the extreme south of the country.

Those who lack an external system of reference sometimes have more acute intellectual perceptions. Starting from self-analysis, they reach equally interesting conclusions. A woman lawyer and civil servant of Portuguese-Brazilian descent, for example, notes her "physical revulsion for her Negro servant" and says that her husband feels the same way. "I can't stand walking through Rua Direita on Saturday or Sunday night because of the numbers of black people. They're all Negroes! Whites and blacks are not equal. Because I studied sociology and psychology, I know that differences of behavior derive from social circumstances rather than color. But they are different. I could never have a Negro boyfriend, much less a Negro husband." Another example comes from a lady who was a

college graduate and a language teacher. "Look, now that we're discussing prejudice in this intimate sense, I remember. About that couple who lived in Vila
Nova Conceição (a Negro physician married to a German woman). . . . Once, as
I was talking to a friend, she said to me, 'How could that woman take a Negro
husband? Even if he is educated, refined, everything a man should be . . . I don't
know! I don't think I'd have what it takes to be a woman . . . to sleep with a Negro!' I remember. At that moment I also thought of the intimacies of marriage
and I felt a shudder going through me. It's funny! . . . We think we don't have any
prejudice, and somewhere along the line we always do!" Even a small incident
can lead to some understanding of reality, as suggested in a statement written by a
teacher: "There should not be any prejudice against Negroes. I don't have any
prejudice except against intermarriage. But it is very difficult to be completely
'exempt.' The other day (I know it wasn't right) I got mad at the landlady and
said, 'She's acting like a nigger!' I was surprised at this myself, but I wanted to be
offensive."

The data gathered show the frequency of three types of viewpoints. First, it
reveals the combination of frank assessment of and indifferent complacency toward the racial problem. Thus, an educator stated that racial prejudice is very
strong not only in São Paulo but in the rest of the country as well. But it is fated
to disappear because of the gradual physical assimilation of Negroes into the
white population. "This is the trend. Obviously it will take centuries. But in the
future there will be no more prejudice among us."

In those segments of the middle classes that are most affected by the modernization of society, color prejudice tends to be expressed with nonconformist severity. A middle-aged woman teacher gave a characteristic answer: "I think that
prejudice is a mark of ignorance. Color is not responsible for social position or
the behavior of the individual. It's social conditions that act upon him and make
for a certain position or form of behavior." Among the younger generation caught
in this web of cause and effect, condemnation is often outspoken. A young
woman university student wrote, "Personally I regard prejudice as a foul stain
among us. I believe that prejudice is a stupid thing devoid of any logic. It is unseemly, especially among the civilized people that we claim to be. We know that
scientifically nothing has been proved about the superiority of the white over the
Negro—we know all this but we continue to regard the Negro as we would a
leper. When shall a true 13th of May* dawn in our country?" Such attitudes have
limited influence on the contact situation, because few segments of the middle
classes are deeply affected by the intellectual revolution wrought by modernization.

Members of the upper classes find it harder to attain an understanding of the
racial situation. Their area of informal and friendly contact with Negroes is so

---

*Translator's note: The date (May 13, 1888) when slavery was abolished in Brazil.

limited and so hedged in with restrictions that dramatic or shocking cases rarely become known. Even so, they offer glimpses of certain aspects of the situation independent of racial stereotypes or ethnocentric attitudes. The most hotly argued cases often refer to intermarriage. Painful experiences are remembered and used to prove that prejudice exists or that it is very strong. Unlike members of the lower classes, who describe everyday experiences, and members of the middle classes, who deal with key experiences, members of the upper classes have to rely on borderline experiences which place in jeopardy the very moral bases of the traditional conception of the world. A noted university professor from a wealthy and highly regarded family spontaneously told the interviewer, "There is no question that there is color prejudice in São Paulo. It may be that there is more harmony in other states. In São Paulo, however, prejudice exists and is very strong. But it is expressed without violence. There is no need for research in order to understand this. We all know it. There are even frequent instances of unpleasant contact between whites and Negroes. Even though prejudice is not violent, as it is in the United States, and takes a special form which permits contact with Negroes in certain areas, it becomes obvious as soon as you touch on certain intimate questions. Even in Bahia a white man would rebel against the idea of giving his daughter in marriage to a Negro."

The social outlook of a large portion of the upper classes is clearly governed by a view of the traditional pattern of racial interaction as being socially normal and necessary. This leads, in some circles, not only to the typical reaction already mentioned above—"there is prejudice and it's right"—but to an irrepressible tendency to distort the given data of concrete experience.

As we have already stressed, the Negro is no less a product of the sociocultural situation than the white. Nevertheless, he has additional resources that permit him to break through and even rebel against the limitations inherent in the prevalent understanding of the racial reality. Concrete experiences are not always interpreted in a strictly constructive way. But there is a powerful force working for him: social interests and ambitions conditioned or fed by his racial position broaden and deepen his ability to perceive and understand this reality. Suffering, shame, and rebellion, separately or together, lead him to the bottom of the abyss.

Nevertheless, the Negro's awareness and understanding of the manifestations and effects of color prejudice have certain characteristic shortcomings. First, as happens among whites, there are several chronic sources of partial or total blocking of the Negro's cultural horizon. Like the white, he is often inconsistent, confused, and bewildered. There is the Negro who shares the general, officially consecrated attitude, and who writes in his answer to the mass questionnaire, "Yes, happily, in Brazil there is indeed no color prejudice."[16] There is also the undecided Negro. Interviews with an accountant provide a typical example. "I'm not sure whether what exists in São Paulo is prejudice or something with some other name. Whites don't trust Negroes—that's for sure. Negroes don't know how to do things. They haven't had time to get going like the whites. That's how the whites' attitudes against Negroes arose. But if Negroes got on the ball and reached the same level as whites, they would be accepted by them and treated differently. I don't know if there really is prejudice or if it's something else that comes from the white's distrust and the Negro's incapacity to behave as the white expects him to."

Finally, there is the Negro who adopts contradictory attitudes. In our analysis we reduced the contradictions to three basic formulas:

(1) Informants deny with wavering vehemence the existence of color prejudice. But they acknowledge openly that "it's no use fighting prejudice." In an interview with a dark mulatto woman dancer, for instance, the following typical attitudes were expressed immediately following a meeting devoted to a discussion of the matter: "They told a pack of lies. I don't know how anyone can lie so blatantly. There is no prejudice in São Paulo. Negroes are received everywhere and are treated well by whites. I've been everywhere. As a dancer, I've performed my folk numbers in places where many classy whites don't go, among elite families and among French families." Later, however, she stated unself-consciously, "It's no use trying to fight color prejudice and to improve the Negro's position. There is no unity among Negroes."[17]

(2) The informants deny, also with wavering intensity, the existence of color prejudice, but at the same time they preach the advantages of open and systematic segregation. On interviewing a young Negro stoker, for example, the woman interviewer got the following typical ideas, "I don't think any differences are made, as long as the person is skilled. I don't think that Negroes are harmed by individual whites, but rather by the economic circumstances in which most of them live. I know something of the situation in the United States, of the struggles and prejudices. But I think that situation is better than the one here, because it leads Negroes to unite and to fight for better things."

(3) Informants do not deny the existence of color prejudice, but are afraid of raising the issue and compelling whites to become aware of the racial reality. In an interview with a mulatto accountant employed by a utilities company, for example, we find the following typical ideas: "The (Afonso Arinos) Law has its good points, because it gives Negroes and mulattoes a weapon with which to fight prejudice. But it's chief flaw is the fact that it emphasizes prejudice. It used to be like a needle in a haystack. No one had any clear awareness of its existence, especially whites. Now the law has accentuated it. And many whites won't like being compelled to accept the Negro."

Inconsistencies and nonconformities of this sort are, however, easily understood and explained. The Negro absorbs in various ways the prevailing racial ideology and sees himself, the whites, and the world in which he lives through the prism of this ideology. He achieves a victory when he manages to separate concrete experiences from this ideological context and to analyze them, with varying degrees of perceptiveness, without the direct or indirect pressures they exert upon him. In any case, the burden of socialization and cultural conditioning is quite clear. The blocking of any awareness or understanding of the situation follows a

descending scale. It is intensive where the Negro is fully involved in the traditional cultural horizon. We shall recall at this point that two human types must
be kept in mind simultaneously: the rural Negro who recoils with mistrust and
caution from contact with the white, and the refined Negro who identifies fully
with the interests, values, and world of the white. Both tend to deny the existence
of color prejudice—the former out of inexperience, the latter because it would
make his own acceptance an exception. However, while the former conforms
inadvertently to the asymmetric pattern of racial relations because he was molded
by the customs of rural culture, the latter plays a deliberate game aimed at social
enlightening.

Beyond this, we must consider the cases of black persons who overcome the
obstacles of color prejudice through the devious paths of marginal society. This
applied on a large scale to Negro delinquents in the past, and is still often the
case for the same. The delinquent is far from indifferent to external pressures,
since the adaptive and integrative mechanisms he uses individually or common-
ally are reactions to these pressures. It would be correct to state, however, that he
does not face the psychological dilemmas which consciously or unconsciously
torture those Negroes who accept the rules of the game of society and become
victims of the "complex."

Finally, we cannot omit mention of the illusions of the middle-class Negro who
is stubbornly oriented to the effects of social mobility and who asserts himself by
means of compensatory or real mechanisms, through the external appearances of
his social position. As we pointed out in the preceding chapter, he knows—from
hard personal experience—what is and what is not color prejudice, and he is also
familiar with all its ramifications. But he has no intention to redress them or to
become involved in a crusade. The immediacy of his objectives alienates him
consciously or unconsciously from racial problems. The fact is that out of sheer
social calculation he attains a new form of passive capitulation. Flagrant contradictions expressed through polite rationalizations and which do not preclude the
simultaneous disclosure of painful incidents or experiences serve as escape devices: "It exists, but I never experienced it"; "I watch my step—I never go where
Negroes are not wanted"; "You must differentiate between prejudice and selectivity"; "Our people are very sensitive, they see persecution everywhere." At this
pole, we are very far from the mental blocks engendered by the traditional conception of the world. The individual "sees the situation with his own eyes." Nevertheless, his awareness and understanding of reality are filtered through social
illusions and hopes which, if they do not blind him, may silence and disarm him.

There is a basic ambiguity in the characterization of the white as the source
of color prejudice. Of course, in the various equations of color prejudice devised
by the Negro, the white is always the active agent of ethnocentric appraisals and
discriminating behavior (whatever the direct or indirect responsibility of the
Negro for its origin). Certain gradations suggest the generalized character of

color prejudice (it exists among the poor as well as among the rich) and show its varying intensity (it is stronger among the latter than among the former).

It seems clear that the old pattern of racial domination is on the wane. It is also clear, however, that this pattern (at least under the sociohistorical circumstances under consideration) is becoming adapted to an open-ended social order where income, social prestige, and power remain concentrated, from a racial stand-point, at strategic points and levels. The chief results of these changes were reflected at once in a negative way among Negro groups. On the one hand the social classification and vertical mobility of the Negro and mulatto were dissoci-ated from the gradual formation of a racially identifiable, integrated, and autono-mous Negro minority. On the other hand the elites were separated from the masses, fostering an insensitivity on the part of the Negro himself to the Negro problem which is without parallel in the cultural history of the city. To summa-rize, the attainment of typical class positions did not grant the black population any possibility of creating a social race situation compatible with the economic, social, and power structure of the class society. The Negro remains inarticulate and powerless before the white, without specific means of directly influencing the current reshaping of the patterns of racial domination. To confine ourselves to essentials, this leads to the following: (1) The nonexistence of a racial situation fashioned historically by the competitive social order deprives Negroes collec-tively of all sociopsychological sources of differentiation, reorganization, and uni-fication of the perceptive and cognitive foundations of conscious social behavior. (2) The Negro attempts to fill the resulting vacuum by means of the perceptive and cognitive resources he has accumulated in the course of his struggle against slavery and against the patterns of racial domination inherent in the traditional social order, as though we were still in the first quarter of the nineteenth century. (3) These perceptive and cognitive resources have proved adequate for a much deeper, more realistic, and freer understanding of the racial reality than has been developed by whites, but it has not permitted understanding of this reality as a changing whole. Thus, basically, the yearning to belong to the system has re-stricted the cultural horizon of the Negro and mulatto and confined their social ambitions and aspirations—and with them their capacity for awareness of the sur-rounding racial reality—to the destruction of traditional patterns of racial domi-nation. According to our hypothesis, this explains both the ambiguity of their con-scious characterization of the white's active role in color prejudice, and their alienation from the meaning of this prejudice in terms of the collective destiny of the Negro group within society. Paradoxical as this may seem, the Negro un-masks the white, checking the rationalizations which conceal the sources and the visible results of color prejudice. Nevertheless, he submits spontaneously to the white man's game, confining his own awareness of racial reality to a historical context. Obviously the prospects would be different if the social perspectives of Negroes and mulattoes were any other than they are. If the starting point of their conscious social behavior granted basic significance to the sociopathic con-sequences of the racial distribution of income, social prestige, and power in the structuring of social relations, the yearning to belong to the system would be ex-pressed socially in connection with the ideal goal of changing the system.[18]

This simple reversal of the social perspective makes it possible for the Negro to overcome the basic alienation that interferes with his awareness of color preju-dice. Meanwhile, this awareness serves to compensate for the inconsistencies in the current racial thinking of the whites, as well as to give the Negro a realistic and pragmatic conception of the world which fulfills his need for social self-affirmation. If such a reversal of perspectives were to occur, however, the Negro would achieve the subjective requisites needed to regard his present and his fu-ture as those of an identifiable, integrated, and autonomous racial minority—i.e., he would gain the intellectual capacity to broaden his view of the world to the point required for a socially constructive role in the hesitant development of ra-cial democracy in Brazil.

The Negro fought the manifestations and results of color prejudice on the level of his struggle for survival in the big city of the capitalistic era. Thanks to the breakdown of the seignorial and slaveholding order, to the establishment, expan-sion, and consolidation of the competitive social order, he was gradually able to alter his social goals. Nevertheless, color prejudice blocked his move from a pe-ripheral, marginal position to the heart of the class structure. The social context thus compelled him to find out *why* he was rejected before he could succeed in his endeavors to belong to the system. Here we can see the positive influence of the social context which compelled the Negro to rise out of his lethargy, break into the white's world, and destroy his idols.

Our analysis of various types of written documentation showed that the Negro's awareness and understanding of color prejudice as a sociopsychological and historicocultural reality is surprisingly deep. Even though the intensity of con-crete experiences, the maturity of the social outlook, and the firmness of the in-dividual's basic convictions range from unabashed neutrality (among a small but significant minority) to racial fanaticism (in rare and isolated cases), if the evi-dence gathered covers practically every important aspect (such as motive, condi-tion, and consequences) of the expression of color prejudice. It seems that on the level where the Negro responds dynamically to the demands of the situation, which is the level of the struggle for survival in the midst of the community and thus for the acquisition of those institutionalized social positions to which he has ready access, he has a clear-cut, distinct, and consistent idea of the racial reality. We must stress in particular what this means in sociological terms. The common-sense understanding amassed by the Negro in recent times, over less than two generations, involves a quite sensible conception of the prevailing patterns of color prejudice and makes it possible for him to do something about its effects, whether in the sphere of the organization of race relations or in that of voluntary controls which might direct those effects into socially desirable channels.

As for the first point, such common-sense understanding involves (*a*) criteria by which to recognize color prejudice, (*b*) awareness of the structural and dynamic links which connect color prejudice and patterns of racial adjustment, and (*c*) certain factors external to color prejudice which nevertheless exacerbate it. In recognizing prejudices the Negro has developed a deceptively simple technique: he draws the dividing line along the obvious (and thus irrefutable) differences between the treatment accorded to the Negro and that accorded to the white under similar circumstances. From this standpoint the basic factor is the social position and the prerogatives (rights and duties) this social position implies. Therefore, at the deepest level of his social awareness, the Negro sees color prejudice as a system of discriminatory practices used by whites in their social intercourse with black individuals. The subtlety of this awareness of reality does not reside here, however, but in the manner in which he solves concretely the problem of knowing what is and what is not color prejudice. The chief point of reference ceases to be the white. The victim is taken into account—rather than the executioner—and examined to see whether he might indeed qualify for the equality which he pleads for from the whites. There exists already a veritable folklore in connection with false prejudice, which recommends extreme prudence and moderation: "Not everything the Negro regards as prejudice really is"; "Our people are very sensitive"; "You would have to make sure whether it was prejudice or lack of ability"; "We have to differentiate between prejudice and selectivity," and so on. The Negro does not shun the use of color prejudice as a mechanism of self-defense, as a compensatory mechanism, or even as an outright scapegoat.

This complex of attitudes, expectations of behavior, and social techniques does not prevent him from attributing color prejudice to certain unchanging factors. Even if here too there is a certain amount of confusion, the chief trend is to regard color in a broader sense, as though it were a symbol both of the racial origins and of the social position of Negroes and mulattoes; and to feel that the white has categorically defined color as an index of overall inferiority (be it racial, economic, social, cultural, moral, or political). This demonstrates how much farther the Negro has traveled than the white in his understanding of racial reality. The white gets angry at the Negro and does not even want to hear of color prejudice because he is afraid that he is being accused of practicing some degrading form of racism. Not only is the Negro free of such designs, but he forges ahead, fusing the various factors which have always linked relations between whites and Negroes with the equation of racial and social stratification. With sharp and penetrating discernment, he places color in a sociohistorical category, thus linking what whites separate in theory but associate in actual behavior. For this reason the white claims that the Negro, when he attains a class position, finds that the social prestige he has gained does away with all limitations and restrictions associated with color. The Negro preaches the exact opposite: it is after gaining an education, skills, and a certain position that he meets the white face to face and finds all doors closed. It is easy to test this—all you need do is to subject the white person to certain contacts which might be called experimental. Nevertheless, the moral frame of reference is a complex one. Let us take one example. A young Negro told his mulatto friend that "the girls at the University probably are not prejudiced." He planned to invite them to a cheap dive to see what happened. The friend retorted, "They won't go, and it won't have anything to do with color prejudice. They wouldn't go to a cheap white dive either. This is not their environment." When such a test is carried out, the Negro sees to it that the frame of reference is adequate to the purpose at hand.

In understanding the structural and dynamic foundations of color prejudice which permit the Negro to project his relations with whites onto the societal organization, nine items are of special importance.[19]

(1) The Negro is fully aware of the importance of concealment in the white's behavior. His description of this propensity involves two harsh words—the two-faced or false quality of the white. This is expressed with more neutrality and courtesy among the educated Negro groups, where it is said that the white's friendliness is superficial—"a matter of polish." As already indicated, however, no clear-cut rejection is associated with this state of affairs. To the contrary, as stated by a mulatto girl as she described her relations with her teachers, "I don't know whether the courtesy and kindness of my teachers are real or put on. It may be that they're not sincere but this doesn't bother me. The important thing is that they treat me well and that I get consideration from them."

(2) Negative stereotypes in all their forms—whether ideas of a folkloric and popular nature (as in the words set to popular music), or white conceptions of the Negro's character which restrict his acceptance—are understood in a formal and concrete as well as a functional sense. Although awareness of concealment leads to hesitancy—but does not as a rule interfere with the external course of social relations—an understanding of stereotypes is the very foundation of the Negro's self-defensive mechanisms and of what might be called his "reactive prejudice."[20] In some cases, this understanding even leads to stubborn mistrust which poison all relations with whites.

(3) There is a clear awareness of the dual nature of the white's ethical code, linked with an irrepressible reactive tendency to regard the prevailing racial ideology as a false and misleading view of reality. Even though the data given from Chapter 4 [of Fernandes's original study] onward do not require empirical support, the importance of this factor to the attitudes and patterns of behavior of the Negro and mulatto leads us to transcribe part of one of the typical statements we gathered. In a public discussion organized by a Negro lawyer who had been a leader of the rights movements, we heard the following thoughts: "The white could not, and still cannot, get used to the idea of regarding his lost property as a citizen on an equal footing. He had tried, through every possible means, to retain his lordly attitudes and to keep the Negro in his place, in the kitchen of the house, bettered by illiteracy, and feelings of inferiority, without providing him with a single opportunity. . . . There is a perfect technique, perhaps the fruit

of tacit agreement, to conceal and subdue the collective guilt of the ruling group
. . . a truly negative technique which even now, in the present day, is used successfully in Brazil's official international relations. This is the use of a tired cliché
which has been discredited within our national boundaries. Actually, this method
of publicity, of making unilateral history, is meant to create a sort of pressure, a
certain psychological conditioning of our less wary and more susceptible foreign
visitors, and deliberately leads them to view the problem of race relations through
a distorting prism. Through this prism, everything is a bed of roses. The white is
white, the black is white, the yellow is white. Everything conspires to an atmosphere of immaculate whiteness in which the various contacts of the various ethnic groups in the country—already assimilated or in the process of assimilation—
have been and are being carried out beautifully, without clashes, mildly and
placidly. . . . The matter was and is still disguised in such a way that the pressure
is exercised even on certain learned sectors of the society, thus palming us off to
the world as the most perfect example of racial democracy. This . . . is the version
for foreign consumption. The prevailing atmosphere, our history books, our public media, our formal statements, all assert that we have no color problems or
color prejudice. This assertion, shared naïvely even by outstanding citizens and
personalities, is the handsome cloak for foreign eyes, the sweet-sounding voice of
popular sayings. In fact, however, the Negro is a marginal person and as such a
discontented one."

(4) As a result of these forms of understanding, the Negro tends to see the emergence and perpetuation of discriminatory practices. He is prone to regard them
as an inherent part of the situation. One Negro accountant pointed out expressions of color prejudice in the business world, saving, "The owners of stores and
bars (there are no black waiters) are not to blame for these barriers. It is the cus-
tomers who compel them to act as they do when they turn down a Negro. Obviously the Negro is prejudicial to business: a customer comes in and there are two
salesmen, one white and one Negro—if the white one is busy, the customer waits
until he is free. This, besides making service difficult, also brings financial losses
to the owner."

(5) The Negro also becomes objectively aware of the sources of the white's
differential racial attitudes, judgments, and behavior. He not only knows to what
extent differences in social level and cultural tradition (associated with the racial,
ethnic, or national origins of the various population groups) are reflected in the
intensity of color prejudice, as noted above, but he also takes into account two
other variables: the relationship between tolerance or intolerance and the personality type of the white; and the variations due to the skin shade, sex, age, etc., of
the Negro or mulatto.

(6) Such understanding of the overall situation fosters in the Negro a strong
tendency to differentiate between individuals, values, and opportunities on the
one hand, and his own general opinions and judgments of the white, of the latter's prejudice, and of its consequences (the concealed isolation of black persons)

on the other hand. This encourages the amassing of valuable understandings in a society where selective acceptance of the Negro hinges on the whims, sympathy, or tolerance of the whites, and where the Negro can become with relative ease the exception that confirms the rule. It also leads to a certain maturity of judgment thanks to which men and women, adults and young people try to separate the chaff from the wheat—i.e., to pick out among their white acquaintances those who could be true friends or on whom you can count. Incidentally, we heard in various interviews the same statement that, in spite of color prejudice, there can be "a deep, disinterested and true friendship" between whites and Negroes. This belief, which is at the same time a hope, does not baffle the Negro. On this point, he shows an acute awareness of the potentialities for racial coexistence in a society where color prejudice is diffuse and unsystematic.

(7) The Negro is unable fully to catch all the variations in the attitudes, hesitancies, and concealed forms of behavior of the whites. Coexistence with whites has not yet gone far enough to permit this. Nevertheless, he differentiates with great insight between the two most frequent varieties of the expression of color prejudice—the concealed and the obvious—and he discloses that he knows something more—namely, that the latter variety is alien and contrary to Brazilian tradition. So, whenever he can, he would rather use the evidence provided by this variety in order to criticize and fight color prejudice generally.

(8) Inevitably, the Negro is highly sensitive to the nuances of the ingroup situation as they are reflected in the forms of adjustment and awareness of the black individual himself. The important thing here is his objective understanding, influenced by suffering and widespread disappointment because of external conditions, his lack of participation in the larger culture, or the white man's success. The degree of the Negro's awareness, his moral autonomy, and loyalty to his own group are regulated by these disappointments. As a result, substantial disagreements—even as to the existence or nonexistence of color prejudice and the manner in which to fight it—acquire a suprapersonal frame of reference and can be placed on levels which lessen the potential danger of misunderstanding and conflict. The data gathered show that this frame of reference has been ineffective in the overcoming of differences. But it creates a modicum of respect and understanding for the other—if not for his motivations—in the never-ending frictions. In short, the Negro directs upon himself the formula he has used to understand the white and the overall situation, thus uncovering and adjusting intellectually to the various forms of differential sociocultural behavior, of personality, and of the orientation of his racial counterideology.

(9) There is one item which is not universal, but which is frequently linked to the most radical and intolerant interpretations of the Negro situation. This is the explicit role played by exploitation in the formation and retention of color prejudice. Understanding operates on three distinct levels: (1) the abolitionistic process as a historic despoliation and as the irremediable expulsion of the Negro to the periphery of organized society; (2) the material and psychological bases of the

perpetuation of racial inequality, and thus of the connection between color prejudice and the defense of the privileges of the dominant race; (3) the different levels of the Negro's participation, rewards, and promotion in the free labor system, thus defining exploitation in terms of the retention of a reserve of manpower for undesirable jobs and of the lowering of Negro workers' levels of remuneration. This item, although it appears unsystematically and only in specifically nonconformist contexts, is of almost unique significance because it is the only factor in the revelation of racial attitudes which is not concerned with moral arguments and which points openly to an apparent link between color prejudice and the material interests of the dominant race.

As regards the factors external to color prejudice which contribute to its exacerbation, three points deserve special emphasis. It would seem that the Negro tends to stress his own ability to deal with the white. Those who lack experience in coexistence with the whites, and especially those who cling stubbornly to certain deleterious beliefs induced by the "complex," are said to aggravate the expressions of color prejudice and to convince whites that the best policy (not to say the only adequate policy) would be exclusion or ultra-exclusive acceptance.

Another point which is approached with relative insight relates to internal migrations.* Many of those interviewed broached the subject spontaneously, trying to hint at the difficulties inherent in the continuous turnover of the black population. Gradually the Negro learns to live in the city, to make use of its resources, and to shield himself from the concealed or obvious expressions of color prejudice. Nevertheless, the Negroes who come from rural areas without technical skills, financial resources, or experience cannot adjust to the city as a group. In short, the same problems are posed anew with each generation, as though the experience amassed collectively were useless. Finally, the Negro also becomes aware of the fact that the urban community has unforeseen drawbacks. Racial, ethnic, and national groups, as well as social classes, acquire new forms of autonomy and self-affirmation. As a result, they acquire the freedom to disobey socially consecrated rules and to enjoin their specific conceptions of the world. Thus, the Negro has become aware that concealed prejudice, bad as it may be, is preferable to obvious prejudice, and he has tried to understand the latter as part of the developing new situation.

As for the second point, the effects of color prejudice are seen, as we have pointed out, on two separate levels. Let us consider first those that rose to the social consciousness in the light of the organization of racial relations in *Paulistana* society. There, color prejudice is regarded as "the great problem of the Negro." Although it is clearly understood that prejudice does not operate in isolation and that the chief barrier to integration is economic inequality, the rights movements

---

Editor's note: The author is referring to the constant migration of poverty-stricken people, mostly Negro and mulatto, from northeast Brazil to São Paulo in search of employment.

have spread the firm belief that eradicating color prejudice precludes rectification of the economic problems which lower the income and standard of living of the black population. On the other hand, it is emphasized that the distortion of racial consciousness fostered by the dominant race catches the Negroes themselves in its web, disarming them and impelling them to passivity. Here is a representative example of this attitude: "There is color prejudice . . . and it is quite severe, because aside from being prejudice it is hypocrisy. In the United States, where such prejudice is open, it has benefited the Negro, led him to have a look at himself and solve his own problems. In Brazil the very opposite occurred. The denial of color prejudice caused the Negro to fall ever lower. This is clear for all to see. The Negro has no opportunities. He has no opportunity to rise. This is a situation which, if it continues, the Negro race will be doomed to an inglorious disappearance from the racial scene." Such a logical, emotional, and moral context was naturally bound to give rise to a grim view of the effects of color prejudice. Whatever the limitations of its sociocultural legacy and its intellectual roots, in this area the exposure of old racial myths achieved its true aim. If things did not change, it was not the Negro who was to blame but the absence of effective communication and organized solidarity between the racial groups in social coexistence.

On this level, at least five basic opinions prevalent among Negroes require mention. First, there is one which is cultural and which boldly outlines the Negro's view of the open function of color prejudice. Through it, the white attempts to keep the Negro in his place, that is to say, to retain the social distance that prevails among the racial groups and to maintain racial inequality both in the relations between individuals and in succeeding generations. Second, there is the understanding that even selective acceptance involves a certain degree of isolation, that it does not arise from the black individual's restraint but from the attitude of his white friends. The third and fourth opinions are oriented toward those effects of color prejudice which make for psychological and moral drama. The third regards the inferiority complex as a reactive sociopsychological phenomenon. In this viewpoint, three factors are emphasized: its dynamic formation under pressure of ethnocentric judgments and discriminatory practices on the part of whites; the formative experiences of children and youths in their relations with whites of the same or of older generations; and the evidence that the complex is not an "atavism or something that might be transmitted from father to son . . . but something that arises from the various forms of behavior of the white toward the Negro."[21] This answers the argument, which enjoys some currency among whites, that the Negro "carries a servile attitude in his blood." The fourth opinion regards apathy and what might be called the passive capitulation of the Negro to the white. Both are ascribed without rancor to the root of subservient relations—the link between master and slave—and to those later circumstances which prevented the resocialization of the Negro into the order of liberty and equality. As a result a historical explanation is sought that would not be operative in those social configurations where the Negro can affirm himself. Apathy and passive capitulation are thus defined as anomalies that reflect not the Negro's will but an ineluctable destiny against which he intends (and hopes) to fight according to a nonconformist philosophy: "It is the Negro himself who must solve the Negro problem."[22] Fifth, the Negro makes a connection, although he does so in a somewhat confused way, between the expressions of color prejudice and the monopoly of power by the whites. Not only does he shrewdly point out that moral pressures indirectly engendered by such expressions of prejudice bring discord among black individuals and strengthen their tendency to flatter whites, but he understands that the rule of "divide and conquer" is part of an unstated code that makes color prejudice a portentous weapon of racial domination.

On another level, the Negro moved on to value judgments which had practical applications. The situation was not a simple one. As a group that was heir to a highly heteronomous racial condition and that did not have access to the mechanisms of solidarity of other ethnic or racial segments, even the path to self-enlightenment appeared difficult. Thus, it is not surprising that the great practical descriptions for the Second Abolition arose within the climate of racial turmoil engendered by the rights movements. Actually, no one went much beyond that in subsequent times. There was merely a change of attitude which is worthy of mention. As part of an authoritarian outlook, it was believed in some circles of the black population that the best course would be to "make the white swallow his color prejudice." This was the first expression of a simplistic answer to the white's own racial philosophy: What matters is not what you as a white person think or do, but what is possible for the Negro to achieve independently of the innermost preferences of the dominant racial group. Later this entire philosophy was toned down, but at the same time it acquired greater vitality and practical effectiveness. The Negro prefers to undermine the white's capacity for resistance by destroying those arguments that lend meaning to discriminatory practices. Thus he continues to deal with the same set of practical predescriptions: stabilization of the Negro family; elevation of women; education; acceptance of social controls that would compel obedience to the minimal standards of responsibility and solidarity that prevail among whites; fostering of a higher income and living standards; indirect reeducation of the white through the dissemination of the ideal personality types of the larger society among Negro groups; encouragement of collective action on the Negro's part toward the solution of his problems and toward the union of the Negro race. Nevertheless, the degree of maturity shown in the use of these social techniques, especially those that can be used on the personal level, has increased considerably. Even though he is not involved, or involved only slightly in collective disturbances or great collective debates, the Negro is beginning to face more effectively certain crucial and inevitable challenges. He perceives more objectively the connection between the quality of behavior and the type of adjustment to be developed. He faces with integrity (and sometimes also with shrewdness) the problem of adjusting his personality to the material and psychological demands of a class society. He tries to learn how to compete without too much personal stress and without provoking the white to open resistance, thus skillfully averting the danger of racial conflict.

We now shall turn to the other two aspects under consideration. It will suffice to present here the explanations offered for color prejudice by whites and Negroes, and for the ethical factors which govern the behavior patterns of whites and Negroes in those social situations where color prejudice is expressed.

We were able to single out sixteen explanations of color prejudice considered logical by whites, of which fifteen are typical and one is atypical. Among the typical explanations, seven give special consideration to the social images imputed directly to the Negro:[23] (1) "It's the fault of Negroes, because they act in a cringing way, as though they were still slaves"; (2) "They're not accepted because of their color"; (3) "They're a degenerate race"; (4) "Prejudice arises from the Negroes' lack of education"; (5) "Negroes are not inferior, but they feel that their color makes them inferior"; (6) "They are treated like this because of the conditions in which they live"; (7) "What they call prejudice is their own bias against the whites." The other eight typical explanations are based on qualities imputed directly to the white himself: (1) "Whites despise Negroes";[24] (2) "Negroes are held in low regard by whites and are therefore avoided"; (3) "Whites don't give opportunities to Negroes"; (4) "It's the white's rudeness"; (5) "It's a rich man's thing, copied by poor whites"; (6) "What matters is money"; (7) "This came from abroad. It's an immigrant's thing"; (8) "It's an imitation of the United States." None of the explanations cites qualities imputed to both Negroes and whites in terms of interdependence or reciprocal action. The one atypical explanation, in turn, was given by an intellectual. It regards color prejudice as the result of deep-rooted feelings independent of social or cultural conditioning: "Color prejudice stems from positive and negative tendencies which lead individuals of the same race to come together and individuals of different races to reject one another."

We were able to single out fifteen explanations of color prejudice considered logical by Negroes, of which fourteen are typical and one is atypical. Among the typical explanations, six are based on qualities directly imputed to whites:[25] (1) "Color prejudice is a defensive weapon of the white"; (2) "Prejudice is explained by the pride of the former slave masters and by the hatred they had for Negroes"; (3) "It's an artificial prejudice born of the biases brought by immigrants"; (4) "An imitation of the United States, fostered by the hatred of Negroes that prevails among whites"; (5) "It arises from the white's hypocrisy"; (6) "It is the result of the white's backwardness and bad manners." Three other typical explanations are based on qualities directly imputed to the Negro:[26] (1) "It is the fault of the Negro, who doesn't know how to do things and how to behave properly"; (2) "The Negro is responsible because he doesn't rebel against white tactics"; (3) "Color prejudice is explained by the Negro's resentments (or 'complex')." Six typical explanations are based on qualities imputed both to whites and to Negroes, or to forms of social interaction between both groups.[27] (1) "It is a class prejudice, since color points to the economic and social inferiority of the Negro to the white"; (2) "The Negro was the white man's slave and never had resources comparable to those of immigrants. Abolition gave him liberty, but not economic or social freedom. He remained, as before, a helpless victim of the stereotypes that degraded him as an individual, as a person, and as a race"; (3) "The white race created for itself the concept of superiority, and for the Negro race the concept of inferiority. In accepting both concepts, the Negro sanctioned the use of color as a sign of the superiority of the white race and the inferiority of the Negro race"; (4) "Prejudice exists because the white never allowed the Negro to achieve true equality"; (5) "It's a mixed prejudice, of race and of class. It's not of race alone, because there are whites who accept Negroes. Nor is it of class alone, because certain limitations are applied to all Negroes, even wealthy ones. As a mixed prejudice, it's a prejudice of color"; (6) "The whites removed the Negroes from their lives and got used to living apart from them. Now Negroes think that they're forbidden from going to certain places." The one atypical explanation is a development of an ultrapessimistic theme that characterizes "color prejudice as one of the miseries of human nature." It emphasizes that even after they become rich and integrated into respectable strata of society, Negroes may struggle under the restraints of prevailing avoidances and limitations.

What should be stressed in these data is the basic contrast in the use of awareness and understanding of color prejudice on the part of Negroes and of whites. Both work with the same conceptual tools. The Negro's understanding of the situation, however, is clearly governed by the direct or indirect assumption that color prejudice involves a sort of social exploitation practiced by one race against another. Thus, his conceptual tools are part of a social perspective that regards as equally important the endeavor to define prejudice and the attempt to correct it. As we see it, it is thanks to this social perspective that the Negro manages to lend a specific meaning, a generic meaning, and some historical insight to his conceptual tools, forging them so they will be at the same time a source of enlightenment and an instrument of individual or collective action.

The analysis of the ethical elements involved directly or indirectly in the expression of color prejudice yields results that are basic to a characterization of the dynamics of white and Negro racial behavior. The white's racial behavior is still largely (though unconsciously) governed by *ambiguous ethics*. This is made clear primarily by the very nature of the socially persistent expressions of the duality of the white's ethical code. Let us list eight typical aspects of these expressions, which reveal the sociopsychological context of the racial attitudes of whites: (1) The contrast between the overt and covert attitudes, judgments, and forms of behavior of the white toward the Negro continues to be characteristic and open, so that apparent outer friendliness exists alongside deep currents of aversion and avoidance. (2) The chief result of the dual ethical code is the partial or sometimes total clouding of the white's moral outlook, leaving the field wide open to ethnocentric judgments and discriminatory behavior. (3) To this result must be added the tacit distortion (prevailing among all prejudiced people) of the criteria of personal judgment of the Negro, thus fostering an influx of negative stereotypes about the Negro and the Negro race in general. (4) Similarly, the customary patterns of composure, thoughtfulness, and justice lose their meaning (usually in a partial and variable way) where the Negro is concerned. (5) Among whites there is a near-automatic combination of three related tendencies: applying exclusive or unilaterally demanding criteria of control to the Negro's accomplishments; recalling evidence concerning negative cases (or the negative aspects of specific cases), and generalizing from them to all black individuals, as though the resulting conclusions were proven, true, and indisputable. (6) In comparing whites and Negroes, criteria are taken from the patterns of the whites, without the consideration that Negroes do not enjoy the same material, intellectual, or moral advantages—in other words, proper perspective is often completely overlooked. (7) Even in positive cases of acceptance, in instances of contact with Negroes that fall within the category of the exception that confirms the rule, there remains the tendency to use controlling limits which are not universally applied to whites under similar circumstances. (8) There is a strong tendency to admit that irrational impulses ("a deep dislike," "an uncontrollable negative feeling," "an unrestrained revulsion") operate freely or under limited self-control in relations with "Negroes who don't know their place."

Ambiguity is also seen in the very nature of those moral influences that determine the social perspective of whites in race relations. Actually, whites use ambiguous ethics because they are still governed by the traditional pattern of asymmetric race relations. There is no other explanation for their attitudes and behavior. They are extremely insensitive, in the face of human dramas engendered by discriminatory practices, to the indisputable contradictions between negative stereotypes and the culture's conflicting ideal patterns, and to the obvious inconsistencies between the racial attitudes, judgments, and forms of behavior inherited from the past and the axiological, consciously shared bases of the competitive social order. They are extremely stubborn in the defense and perpetuation, on the ethological level, of the traditional patterns of race relations, through which they foster the Negro's psychological alienation (what lies behind statements such as "Negroes aren't human"; "The Negro must be put in his place"; "Negroes are not capable of self-discipline"; and so on, if not the white's moral autonomy and the Negro's total moral heteronomy?). They are extremely self-righteous, which is made clear in their endeavor to save face, that is to say, to channel criticism or anger not against prejudice or discrimination in itself, but against its open expression. This leads to a sort of acute hypocrisy openly tolerant of color prejudice.

Such ethics explain the limited extent of the moral revolution. This revolution is now expanding, but it encounters a barrier in the lack of enthusiasm with which the standards of the competitive social order are applied to race relations. There are those who show violent disapproval, who define color prejudice as "a foul stain," "a stupid thing," "behavior unworthy of civilized people," etc. Yet in concrete situations such statements do not prevent those who utter them from making moral decisions that are ambiguous and sometimes shockingly contradictory. On the other hand, those who feel some responsibility for other people are not always sure of their own ground. One of the women researchers was confronted with a dilemma—to side with the Negro mother who would not let her daughter go to school, or to side with the daughter? And later, what could she offer her? Thus, many hesitations arise from the nature of the situation. Even when he wishes to be rid of the traditional patterns of morality, the white carries them with him and is compelled to take them into account. Society has not yet overcome them, for in this area it retains many archaic structures. The harmonious elements of the dynamics of the white's racial behavior are not altogether a product of the present time. There is a compromise with the recent past and even with the remote past, so that the moral universe of the white is strongly determined (and in view of the demands of the situation, clearly distorted) by the traditional patterns of asymmetric race relations.

Although the Negro does not altogether escape this unavoidable situation, we find quite a different picture when we turn to an analysis of his moral code as it relates to expressions of color prejudice. It would be impossible to deny that the Negro's racial behavior is governed by an ethic mirroring that of the white. He has assimilated the patterns of the white man's morality, and views himself, thinks, and acts in terms of a morality of the dominant race. Nevertheless, especially since the second decade of this century, he has not used this morality to hide behind. To the contrary, his interests and social goals led him to a complete change of perspective. Now that the socioeconomic structure that plunged him into a state of total and irremediable psychological alienation has broken down, he intends to follow those patterns of morality fully and without any reservations. He thus confronts the white with an impasse. He claims for Negroes, collectively and individually, the right to enjoy the white man's morality without any restrictions. As a result, besides being a reflection his ethics are egalitarian, holding as their supreme goal the endeavor to equal the white socially.

Like the white, the Negro is bound to the traditional conception of the world and its race relations. Nevertheless, the dynamics of his racial behavior are not determined by impulses in favor of the *status quo* and thus of stability in the prevailing system of race relations. It is caught up with and filtered through the complexities of the present to the point where moral responsibility turns to the present reality, and in a certain sense to the future as well.

The Negro builds up an entire ethical code that anticipates, qualifies, or forbids capitulation to the white. Passive surrender, with all the factors that governed and regulated it in accordance with the norms of the traditional pattern of asymmetric race relations, is decried as "despicable," "degrading," "revolting." This does not merely condemn the master-slave morality, but also dictates that the link for whites between the individual and his prerogatives as a human being be fully valid for Negroes as well. The white's standard and style of living, with its social interests and values gains importance, and not the white man himself. As a result, as the Negro identifies with the social order that prevails in the larger society, he severs himself from a racial stratification that originated neither through nor for this social order. He can thus loudly proclaim himself to be the herald and champion of racial equality. As he differentiates between white behavior and the white individual, the Negro elects to fight not the human practitioner of color prejudice, but the traditional asymmetric pattern of race relations, and the kind of domination of one man by another that derives from it. All this presupposes a characteristic zeal in most egalitarian ethics, at least during the period of their implantation and consolidation. The Negro endeavors to attain a strategic combination of objectivity and responsibility, both to disarm his opponent on the moral plane and to infuse social criticism with the relentless weight of moral indignation.[28]

From what may be inferred, the revolution in the Negro's ethical outlook has gone much farther than the evidence might suggest. There is actually a positive moral environment with potentials both for the unmasking of the opponent (or of the mere defender of the social order, in the case of those who still identify with the traditional pattern of asymmetric race relations) and for the exposure of ethnocentric judgments and discriminating practices to public censure (as sources of substantial and irreparable damage to the dignity of the individual and to the preservation of his psychological autonomy). No matter how much it may be stressed that such tendencies will remain ineffective as long as the moral patterns of the white's and the Negro's interracial behavior do not synchronize, one thing remains clear and indisputable. The moral pressures coming from the victims of color prejudice arise as dynamic forces that work toward the undermining of the functions of racial distinctions in the organization of the entire society.

The Brazilian Racial Dilemma

The preceding analysis completes our investigation of racial contact. It shows that the position of the black population still does not structurally or functionally match the class positions possible within the competitive social order of São Paulo. An explanation for this cultural lag was furnished in the process of a careful description and interpretation which combined a synchronic and a diachronic analysis of the present racial conditions. On the one hand, the breakdown of the caste and estate system associated with slavery had no direct repercussions on the forms of racial adjustments developed in the past. Not only did the traditional mechanisms of racial domination remain intact, but the reorganization of the society failed to affect in any significant way the preestablished patterns of racial distribution of income, social prestige, and power. As a result the freedom achieved by the Negro bore no economic, social, or cultural dividends. On the contrary, in view of certain specifically historical aspects of the city's economic development, this freedom met with the direct and indirect pressures of the population succession. The limited forms of sociability and integrated social life inherited by the black population from the slaveholding, seignorial days, met with destructive forces, and this population was faced with a long and intensive phase of social disorganization. These facts contributed decisively to the aggravation of unfavorable dynamic effects on the racial distribution of income, social prestige, and power. Anomalous as this may seem, a racial situation typical of the vanished social order remained unaltered, and the black population in its near totality became a substitute for the former rural and urban masses. On the other hand, the establishment and development of the class system did not follow a path beneficial to the gradual reabsorption of the former slave. The competitive social order arose and developed as an authentic and closed white world.

During the first period of the bourgeois revolution—which went on approximately from the breakdown of the slaveholding order to the beginning of World War II—it met the economic, social, and political demands of the large planters and the immigrants. During the second phase of this revolution, begun under the auspices of a new style of industrialization and the adoption of financial, technological, and organizational patterns characteristic of an integrated capitalist system, it was subordinated to the economic, social, and political interests of the bourgeoisie which arose during the previous phase—that is to say, in large measure, to the interests of the white upper and middle classes. The situation of the black population would have remained unchanged had it not been for the changes incurred by population succession. The gradual but drastic decline of immigration and the intensification of internal migrations engendered certain changes on the labor market and in the techniques of occupational selection. This phenomenon is recent, however, and as yet has had no significant repercussions on the patterns of racial distribution of income, social prestige, and power. Yet it is of enormous heuristic importance, because it shows that over the last twenty-five years the racial situation of the black population has undergone a clear change owing to the attainment of typical class positions by some segments of the population. This occurred, for the majority, through proletariatization; for a thin and heterogeneous minority, through incorporation into the middle classes; and in a few individual and sporadic cases, through incorporation into the upper classes.

The dynamic importance of this process derives from the sociopsychological relationship of the collective behavior of Negroes and mulattoes. As long as the competitive social order seemed totally closed to his longings for social classification and social ascent, the Negro either withdrew and isolated himself, thus aggravating the anomic effects of social disorganization prevailing among the Negro groups, or he joined racial associations and movements which provided an outlet for his unrest and collectively organized the Negro protest. As the pressures of the labor market gradually opened the competitive social order to Negroes and mulattoes, and as certain opportunities for social classification and vertical mobility arose, the Negro and the mulatto focused on the struggle to become part of the social order. They left the racial movements and threw themselves wholeheartedly into egoistic and individualistic competition. Both processes so far have had but meager repercussions on the situation of racial inequality. Nevertheless, they point to certain racial changes in the organization of the Negro's cultural outlook, behavior, and personality. The change in his cultural outlook caused him to become familiar with and react to the world in which he lived. It provided him with a racial counterideology which equipped him to expose the existence and the effects of color prejudice and which helped him to lessen effectively the cultural distance which separated his social longings from the demands of the situation. The change in his behavior gave continuity and effectiveness to the process of reeducation unleashed by the rights movements, and it reoriented his collective grievances, focusing them on viable and far-reaching goals. It offered the Negro the probability of entering the historical stage as a human being, with new societal supports, in order to compete on an individual basis with the white man and perhaps to fight collectively for the Second Abolition.

While all this is of considerable importance, the black population as a whole is merely on the threshold of a new era. In the past, out of sheer inertia, the distribution of income, social prestige, and power was sufficient to safeguard an absolute pattern of racial inequality. Now that this distribution begins to show signs of variety, other mechanisms come into play to safeguard and strengthen the economic, social, and cultural distance which always separated whites and Negroes in São Paulo. The worst is that the Negro has neither the economic, social, and cultural autonomy nor the political vitality to confront safely the disastrous repercussions of these mechanisms on his endeavors to become part of the social order. Powerless and bewildered, he witnesses the penetration of color prejudice into the byways of class relations, undermining his most constructive yearnings for social integration and adulterating the moral context of racial adjustments. In short he finds out that to become part of the social order, to become human, and to become equal to the white are different things with multiple gradations. Like a hydra, racial inequality is reborn after every blow. While common interests and bonds between social classes might unite individuals or groups above and beyond racial differences, the racial question divides and opposes them, condemning the Negro to a subtle isolation and undermining the foundations of the development of the competitive social order as a racial democracy.

The Brazilian racial dilemma is thus clearly outlined. Seen in terms of one of the industrial communities where the social class system developed most intensively and most homogeneously in all of Brazil, it is characterized by the fragmentary, unilateral, and incomplete manner in which it has managed to embrace, coordinate, and govern race relations. These relations have not been totally absorbed and neutralized, and have not vanished behind class relations. Instead, they have been superimposed upon the latter, even where they contradict them, as though the system of social adjustments and controls of the class society had no means at its command to regulate them socially.

Viewed from this standpoint, the Brazilian racial dilemma appears as a structural phenomenon of a dynamic character. It is expressed on the various levels of race relations. For this reason it would be easy to identify it in the behavioral lapses of individuals who believe they are not prejudiced; in the inconsistencies in the norms and patterns of interracial behavior; in the contrasts between negative stereotypes, ideal norms of behavior, and actual behavior in racial adjustments; in the conflicts between ideal culture patterns which are part of the axiological system of Brazilian civilization; in the contradictions between personality ideals and the basic personality types molded by this civilization. Yet it arose from a generalized and common cause: the structural and functional requisites of the class society apply only in a fragmentary, unilateral, and incomplete way to those situations of social contact where the social participants appear, regard themselves, and treat one another as whites and Negroes. In other words, the structures of the class society have not thus far succeeded in eliminating in a normal way preexisting structures in the area of race relations. The competitive social order has not been fully effective in motivating, coordinating, and controlling such reactions.

The descriptions given above permit us to understand and to explain genetically this cultural lag. It keeps recurring because the Negro undergoes persistent and far-reaching assimilationist pressures, and although he reacts to them with ever more reaching and persistent integrationist aspirations, he does not find adequate means of access to the social positions and roles of the social system. For the opposite to occur, it would be necessary for both pressures to be allied at least with a gradual social equalization of Negroes and whites. This teaches us something of great importance. The Brazilian racial dilemma is a phenomenon of a sociopathic character, and it will only be possible to rectify it through processes that will remove the obstacle introduced into the competitive social order by racial inequality.

This explanation permits us to place the Negro problem in a truly sociological perspective. It is a social problem not only because it shows irremediable contradictions in the racial behavior of the whites; because it manifests the indefinite persistence of unjust patterns of racial distribution of income, social prestige, and power; or because it proves that a considerable segment of the black population undergoes material and moral damage incompatible with the laws of the established social order. These are symptoms of chronic illness, which is more serious and more malignant: the minimal conditions of normal differentiation and integration in the social system. The plasticity of the human social response and of the functioning of social institutions permits a society to operate satisfactorily even under conditions of chronic social imbalance. However, as long as such conditions remain irremediable, such a society is condemned to abnormal or subnormal forms of internal development. It can never expand to the limits of normal differentiation and integration it might ideally achieve. In Durkheimian terms, we would say that it does not fulfill the developmental potentialities guaranteed by the corresponding type of civilization. Now, the Brazilian racial dilemma faces us with a situation of this sort. The development of the competitive social order met with an obstacle, is being impeded, and is undergoing structural distortions in the area of race relations. From this standpoint, the rectification of such an anomaly is not primarily and exclusively relevant to the actors in the tragedy, including those who are affected most directly and irremediably. It is basically relevant to the very balance of the social order, that is to say, to its normal functioning and development.

As we know, where human collectivities face social problems of this magnitude, they also show special difficulty in finding and using appropriate techniques of social control. São Paulo, of course, is no exception to this rule. The very situation that prevails arises in large measure from the fact that racial inequality is socially understood, explained, and accepted as something natural, just, and inevitable, as though the competitive social order had not altered the old patterns of relationship between Negroes and whites. The sole unrestrained dynamic source of rectification is thus the development of the competitive social order. But this makes the homogenization of the social order dependent on spontaneous impulses which are of their very nature too slow and too instable, not to speak of the obvious and thus foreseeable risk. The tendencies uncovered do not exclude the possibility of a conciliation between the forms of inequality inherent in the class society and the inherited patterns of racial inequality.

From this we may infer the importance of the practical aspect of the problem. The mechanisms of societal reaction are innocuous or ineffective to varying degrees. Either they do not capture racial reality in the sense of a transformation of the competitive social order, or else they do—as with some of the social techniques used by Negroes—but they have no repercussions on the historical scene. Even so, two things become evident. First, the only truly creative and nonconformist influence which operates in accordance with the requisites for integration and development of the competitive social order arises from the collective endeavors of Negroes. In this sense, the reorganization of the rights movements and their updating is basic. Today, Negro groups are more highly differentiated. These movements should take into account the varieties of social, economic, and cultural interests which have grown among the Negro groups. Nevertheless, if greater heed were given to the need to involve whites in these movements, this variety of focuses of interest would be a positive fact, for it would accelerate understanding of democratic pluralism in a multiracial class society. Second, a large measure of the bewilderment of whites and Negroes alike arises from the lack of a democratic philosophy of race relations that would be socially acceptable and applicable by both groups. Within the moral context that prevails at the moment in racial adjustments, it is doubtful that anything of the sort might be attained.

The white clings, consciously or unconsciously, to a distorted view of the racial contact situation. The Negro, in turn, when he breaks through this barrier, is not only heard but gives rise to irrational misunderstandings. Furthermore, through the very element of protest in his egalitarian longings, he struggles to rectify the inconsistencies and contradictions of race relations within a context of immediacy which is drawn by his impaired or unsatisfied economic, social, and cultural interests. For this reason, any broader constructive innovation would have to arise from rational techniques of control. Many countries have already faced similar problems, and show the way. It would be necessary to establish special services, on a national, regional, and local basis, to deal with the practical problems of absorbing varied population groups into a democratic society. Unfortunately the problem has been underestimated in Brazil, and there has prevailed the irrational approach of leaving such groups to a thankless fate which has almost always been unproductive to society as a whole. It seems obvious that we must think in terms of a radical change of approach that would also take into account population groups located in the big cities. In setting down a policy of racial integration along these lines, the various segments of the black population deserve special attention and strict priority. On the one hand it would be difficult otherwise to reclaim totally this important segment of the national population for the free labor market. On the other hand we cannot continue without serious injustice to keep the Negro at the margin of the development of a civilization he helped to create. As long as we do not achieve racial equality, we will not have a racial democracy, nor will we have a democracy. Through a historical paradox, the Negro today has become the test for our capacity to erect in the tropics the foundation for a modern civilization.

Notes

1. We repeat here that we are using the concept as a sociohistorical category, that is to say, as it is found in the Negro's social consciousness and in the mind of more or less tolerant whites.

2. We have already indicated repeatedly that we use the term "color prejudice" as a sociohistorical category forged by the Negroes and shared to a large measure by the whites. As we have mentioned, this category is characterized by its comprehensive character. It merges the two technical concepts of racial prejudice and racial discrimination.

In view of the purposes of this chapter, we must stress how the two concepts are differentiated and how we have used them in our research. Racial prejudice may be defined as "a social attitude propagated by an exploiting class with the aim of stigmatizing a certain group as inferior, so that the exploitation of this group or its resources may be justified." (Cox, 1948, p. 393). In turn, "racial discrimination only appears when we deny individuals or groups the equality of treatment they may wish for" (Allport, 1954, p. 51). (Aside from the bibliography provided by these two works, important books will be found in the bibliography at the end of this work.)

The controversies surrounding the conceptualization of and approach to both phenomena cannot be discussed here. Nevertheless, we must stress that we do not regard racial prejudice as falling within the specific domain of personality, and racial discrimination as being exclusively pertinent to social structure, as do many American sociologists and social psychologists. Both may be viewed on the various levels of sociological analysis (of social action and relations; of collective behavior; of the socialization and organization of personality; of social norms, representations, and values; and of the differentiation and integration of social systems). In the course of our research we focused our analysis on the structural and dynamic aspects of the connections among racial prejudice, racial discrimination, and the patterns of integration of the social order. Thus, racial prejudice was viewed explicitly in terms of its functions, as a source of legitimation for social opinions, judgments, and representations which motivate, define, and govern social attitudes and forms of behavior. Racial discrimination, in turn, was explicitly regarded as part of the complex of processes which define, develop, and regulate the disparities resulting from the overlapping of social stratification and racial stratification within the larger social system.

3. On the concepts of *eidos* and *ethos* in sociopsychological and socioethnological analysis, see Bateson, 1958, pp. 29–30.

4. The documentation was obtained in various ways. Most of the data was gathered through interviews, mass observation (in the form of statements written by informants or given verbally in group situations), and meetings or seminars with various types of individuals drawn from the Negro groups for the purpose of debating the topic of color prejudice as a social problem. These data were supplemented by questionnaires; life histories; case studies of dramatic, obvious, or irrefutable instances of discrimination; and some written statements excerpted chiefly from the daily press.

5. This account was confirmed by the other protagonist, Sr. Benedito.

6. At the time of the interviews the girl had finished high school and a typing course and was about to graduate as an accountant. She had worked to support herself through her studies.

7. This interview was given in mid-February, 1956.

8. The lady added that he committed suicide as a result.

9. *Diario do Congresso*, Rio, July 18, 1950.

10. *O Estado de São Paulo*, August 8, 1950.

11. The incident occurred in July, 1950, and gave rise to a big scandal. [*Editor's note:* Katherine Dunham, the American Negro dancer, was refused rooms in a luxury hotel in São Paulo presumably because of her skin color.] Renato Jardim Moreira made a case study of it from clippings taken out of 55 different newspapers in São Paulo and other parts of the country. We shall use only a few data from this manuscript study.

12. *Correio Paulistano*, July 13, 1950.

13. In view of the use to which we have put this excerpt, we shall not identify the newspaper.

14. Interview in A *Folha da Manhã*, São Paulo, May 22, 1959.

15. He would not bring home black friends or girlfriends (even light mulatto girls) for fear that his parents and brothers might mistreat or snub them.

16. In the personal statements, an average of three black persons out of ten expressed similar opinions or remained undecided.

17. We have similar statements made by men and women of various ages that we deemed unnecessary to give here.

18. It should be noted that to change the system, on the level of race relations and in

the terms considered here, is tantamount to extending the principles that govern the integration of the competitive social order to the sphere of racial coexistence. We are thus dealing literally with "revolution within the order." If the expansion of the class system were more rapid and more homogeneous, and the absorption of the black population occurred at a constant rate, this process would be spontaneous—though of course governed by the interests and aspirations of the members of that population.

19. We could not find any order of importance for these items in the Negro's understanding of racial reality. The order used is thus arbitrary.

20. Here is a typical example taken from interviews with a mulatto woman teacher: "One day, after work, I went out with a white woman colleague. The following day she told me, 'My fiance liked you.' I answered, 'Don't worry, I might feel the same way about him, but I'm not interested.' 'But he didn't say that to offend you!' 'Whenever he came around I would say, 'Look, here is your fiance,' and she would always say, 'He said he liked you.' " We can easily see the myriad hidden assumptions that motivated the mulatto teacher's reactions, and how they affected her normal relations with her colleague and the latter's fiance.

21. Excerpt from a statement by a Negro intellectual and civil servant.

22. This saying was disseminated by the first newspapers of the Negro press and by the rights movements. It appears in numerous personal statements.

23. The explanations will be given in order of frequency.

24. This explanation is given three times as frequently as those that follow.

25. Explanations (1) and (4) were given with the same frequency.

26. These explanations occur more frequently than the preceding ones (from one-and-a-half to three times as often). They are given in decreasing order of frequency.

27. These explanations are given in decreasing order of frequency. The first three occur two or three times as often as the others.

28. This will be fully appreciated if we bear in mind the force of such criticism when it is appropriately addressed to those inconsistencies in interracial behavior which bring into play the ideal culture patterns and the dynamic equilibrium of the prevailing social order.

3. RACE, CLASS, AND POLITICS IN GUYANA

The Role of the Power Elites

Ralph C. Gomes

Introduction

The tripartite concern with race, class, and politics in Guyana in the study of power elites rests upon our concern with the ways in which such factors "determine" the life chances and life styles of Guyana's elites, the extent to which race and class cleavages persist through the development of race and class consciousness and organizations, and the relative permeability of such structured cleavages. Specifically, this paper will discuss the Guyanese setting, the development of the new coalition of Guyanese elites, their objective interest and nationalist politics, and the social profile of the new elite in Guyana.

Because of the similarities in the struggles experienced by developing nations, this paper may have applicability to other Third World countries.

The Guyanese Setting

The spread of commercial capital—the growth of a work market—colonial expansionism—all resulted in the colonization of Guyana (formerly called British Guiana). The colonization process also resulted in the suppression of the indigenous American Indian communities which at that time practiced simple forms of natural economy and communalism. From its first conquest in 1595 until 1803, the territory belonged to several conquerors, reflecting the colonial rivalries of the time. In 1803, Guyana capitulated to the British colonialists under whom it remained until its independence in 1966.

The period of early colonialism began with simple exchanges and coastal settlements. This era witnessed the establishment of slavery, based on the movement of African peoples as the principal mode of labor in the country. This mode of production, in embryo, was organized into an institution which took the form of sugar plantations. These plantations were characterized by a rigid social and eco-

Originally published in *The Western Journal of Black Studies* 3 (Spring 1979), pp. 57–65. Copyright © 1979 by Washington State University Press. Reprinted with permission.

nomic hierarchy, the brutalization and near destruction of its workforce, and arbitrary and authoritarian forms of social relationships.

The persistent slave revolts which erupted in 1763, 1808, and 1826, in addition to the rise of industrial capitalism in Britain, *legally* forced the colonialists to abolish slavery in 1883. The termination of slavery resulted in financial compensation to the planters rather than the slaves. The white planter class used their control of the state and the authority of the colonial office, in combination with their unquestionable economic power, to delay the elimination of slavery. This delay was accomplished by the introduction of indentured contract immigrants from other parts of the world (e.g., Portugal, China, Madeira, and, principally, India) as a modified form of slave relations. From 1838 to 1917, these indentured relations dominated British Guiana's form of work force. However, the struggles by the natives to become independent, to diversify away from the plantation, and to create a free labor market continued. Moreover, these struggles were fused with internal strengths in the metropolitan power structure, in particular. The factors which led to the destruction of the use of indentured immigrants were diverse and manifold. For instance, the rise to prominence of industrial capitalists, their ideology of free trade and laissez-faire, in combination with the growth of competition from other capitalist countries (e.g., U.S., Japan, and Western Europe), eventually forced an end to these pre-capitalist forms of surplus extraction.

The new dimension of economic structure which was formed in Guyana freed the labor market. In addition, more contemporary means of agricultural production became somewhat diversified from the refining of sugar, and, later, other activities (e.g., trading, commerce, construction, and, later, the mining of bauxite), grew in importance.

It is important to note that each new variation of the dominant modes of production—plantation slavery, indentured workers, modified slavery, and peripheral capitalism—was dialectically related to modifications in the political superstructure. Despite the more or less continued dominance by the white planter class until the end of the Second World War, the natives' struggles for state control and political hegemony were consistently waged. The participants in these struggles were the plantation workers, and, later, the miners and other workers. As a national offensive, the two groupings of the petty bourgeoisie and the masses often merged. Thus, in 1923, despite a limited property-based suffrage, the urban petty bourgeoisie gained great influence because of the popular support of the masses over the local state. This development forced the metropolitan power structure to remove the existing constitution and to introduce the form of direct colonial rule. This move resulted in little local interference, i.e., Crown Colony government as it had evolved during slavery.

In the period preceding the world wars, even until fairly recently, Guyana was a colony under the domination of an alien power, namely Britain, which claimed various rights and privileges. Both Smith (1962) and Newman (1964) raised the question of how a small minority of Europeans could successfully control a much larger non-European majority. They concluded that this control was not accomplished exclusively by strict discipline and employment of a trained militia, but by the setting up of a rigid hierarchial social structure (class stratification) bounded by two extremes. At the apex of the structure were the colonialists who reigned supreme with an air of superiority. The status and power of the elite were inversely proportional to its numbers. At the base of the social scale were the masses who were looked down upon and whose condition was, in general, pitiable.

However, the colonial system had its critics, and the most ego-involved of all the critics was the working class. As Walter Rodney (1966) correctly pointed out, there were several expressions of the awareness of the fundamental class contradictions in the colonial society. These expressions were manifested in such movements as the 1920s Critchlow (British Guyana Labour Union) movement, which later mushroomed into a colony-wide workers' organization, and the Co-Operative Credit Bank movement.

Later, the need to escape the clutches of colonialism and the need to achieve self-determination through independence became crystalized into concrete issues. Predominant in the cry were the demands for workers' rights to organize trade unions; universal education and other welfare benefits; universal suffrage; and for natives to be appointed into decision-making positions in the civil service. All of these demands were made in the context of a call for independence. From a crystallization of the issues, came a range of actions such as civil disobedience, selective violence against property, organized strikes, and demonstrations.

Over the years, the cumulative result of alienation, and socio-cultural disorganization, together with their social and psychological consequences, provided the background from which emerged social cohesion, and a significant comprehensive mass-based nationalist movement for independence. This movement evolved into political activities which manifested themselves in the formation of the People's Progressive Party (P.P.P.) in the early nineteen fifties. The leaders of this party were Cheddi Jagan, Forbes Burnham, Martin Carter, Eusi Kwayana (then Sydney King), and others who were young, lower-middle-class, Black, or Indian intellectuals, most of whom had just returned home from studying in various metropolises (Western-educated elites).

Rather than staunchly defending the status quo, these Western-educated elites openly challenged the established power structure and provided the leadership in the incipient nationalist movement, thereby establishing a new role for themselves. Fanon, in commenting on the new role of the Western-educated elites, in his book, *Black Skin, White Masks*, noted that "the Black man who has lived in France for a length of time returns radically changed, that is, if he goes to Europe, he will have to reappraise his lot, and that he will learn there that he is a Negro. For the Negro there is a myth to be faced. . . . The Negro is unaware of it as long as his existence is limited to his own environment; but the first encounter with a white man oppresses him with the whole weight of his Blackness." Blocked and rebuffed in their quest to identify with the dominant culture (as their major reference group), they come to identify with their despised group, a switch similar in function to what Brinton in the *Anatomy of Revolution* calls the "transfer of allegiance of intellectuals," a process which constitutes a necessary prerequisite of revolutions.

The Western-educated elites also provided the leadership due to the facts that:

1. During their studies and travels abroad, they came into contact with a dominant culture that awakened a desire for equality and freedom from the superimposition of "Englishness" on their way of life;
2. Coming into contact with nationalists from other countries who were in the same predicament, these elites came to the realization that the time for change in the mode of government had come; and
3. On their return home, they were most directly affected by the motivational base—those who were the most marginal and alienated from the established order.

The rank and file members of the P.P.P. was made up of the urban masses, mostly Black, and the rural peasantry, mostly East Indian. The party was a mass-based progressive party that consisted of the hitherto powerless classes in Guyanese society. These members were opposed by the old oligarchy of white and near-white planters, businessmen, and upper-middle-class professionals and civil servants who made up the core of the old Client-Elite.

If the party had persisted in its efforts as a national liberation movement in which strong cadres were organized throughout the country, and as a consequence, new values and parallel institutions were developed in the course of the struggle, then one may surmise that the course of Guyanese history could have been radically different. But, as it unfolded, the People's Progressive Party succumbed to a combination of opportunistic politics, personal ambitions, class interest, and British and American manipulations. Within six months of an impressive electorate victory in 1953, the P.P.P. was railroaded out of office by the British Government. They (the British) suspended the constitution. By 1955, the P.P.P. was hopelessly split, revealing a complete separation of the radical "sheep" (Jaganites) from the conservative and reactionary "goats" (Burnhamites). The final blow came when the colonialists jailed Jagan, an Indian, and left Burnham, a Black, free, causing an exacerbation of racial tensions. These tensions had already been manipulated in the party power struggle between the Burnhamites and the Jaganites.

From 1955 to independence in 1966, "coalition politics" or the "politics of compromise" became the order of the day, and strange bedfellows became "normal" in Guyana's politics. Why did some progressive leaders consistently align themselves with confirmed reactionaries to achieve unity? The answer lies partly in the idealism of these progressive leaders, and this idealism itself stemmed from the fact that they were not guided by the scientific principles of socialism.

After the P.P.P. split, Jagan remained with the original nucleus and rallied most of the Indian support to form a reconstituted P.P.P. Concurrently, Burnham attracted most of the Black urban masses and formed a new party: the People's National Congress (P.N.C.). Both of these parties were coalitions with more limited agendas than the original mass-based P.P.P. Both political parties compromised the ideological basis of the original P.P.P. and recruited some of the most reactionary elements of the middle class and the old oligarchy in competing nationalist coalitions.[1]

In the initial phases of the competition between these two nationalist coalitions, the P.P.P. won the battle against the P.N.C. but lost the war to the British with whom it (the P.N.C.) was aligned. As Cheddi Jagan (1971) puts it:

> If the years of the suspended constitution, 1953 to 1957, were a period of *colonial dictatorship*, the years 1957 to 1964 were the period of the P.P.P. in office but not in power. (p. 188)

First, the P.P.P. captured the elections of the 1957 balloting in what was up to then the most racist and bigoted election that Guyana had yet to witness. Race became a more important focal point than class, thereby helping to cement coalitions of hitherto antagonistic class interest.

It is quite clear at this point that the racial issue had clearly obscured some of the very significant differences of class orientation and class interest in the policies of the two parties. Mulattoes and other "coloreds" who had hitherto aligned themselves with the "Black" voters joined the P.N.C. party, taking not only themselves, but in some cases whole right-wing parties (i.e., the National Democratic Party, United Force, etc.). The P.N.C. became the "responsible" nationalist party of the Christian middle class, made up of such disparate elements as petty bourgeois intellectuals, junior civil servants, the urban masses, and elements of the old oligarchy that had seen the writing on the wall. All of these factions were united by their fear of "Indian dominance" and "communist control."

Although the P.P.P. frequently had difficulty in obtaining and retaining the support of Indian businessmen and professionals, the P.N.C. found it increasingly difficult to hold on to the loyalty of the urban masses, as the politics of the party operated against their interest. Thus, a mere *racial analysis* of the dynamics of Guyana's politics definitely obscures the historical class contradictions inside and outside the two major parties.

Jagan and the P.P.P. won the 1961 elections, subsequently bringing internal self-rule. However, shortly after, the United States and the British initiated a master plan to topple the "Communist P.P.P." This plan included destabilization techniques, propaganda, racial incitement, and a most extreme form of proportional representation for the 1964 elections, among other machinations.

In the 1964 elections, it was anticipated that none of the major political parties, namely the P.P.P., P.N.C., and the United Force (U.F.), would gain the minimum 50 percent of the votes, so that a coalition government would have to be formed. Although both Jagan (leader of the P.P.P.) and Burnham (leader of the P.N.C.) espoused a similar ideology, the Marxist-Socialist exposition of Jagan was less acceptable to the Americans and the British than the moderate socialism proposed by Burnham and his P.N.C. party. Also, it was clear that the system of proportional representation was designed by the American and British to keep Jagan and the P.P.P. out of office.

In 1965, Professor Schlesinger, a former member of the White House Advisory Staff to President John F. Kennedy, pointed out that:

> Burnham's visit left the feelings, as I reported to the President, that "an independent British Guiana under Burnham (if Burnham will commit himself to a multiracial policy) would cause us many fewer problems than an independent British Guiana under Jagan." And the way was open to bring this about, because Jagan's parliamentary strength was larger than his popular strength: he won 42.7 percent of the vote. An obvious solution would be to establish a system of proportional representation. . . .
>
> Thus, after prolonged discussion, the British government finally did it in October 1963; and elections held finally at the end of 1964 produced a coalition government under Burnham. With much unhappiness and turbulence, British Guiana seemed to have passed safely out of the communist orbit. (pp. 778–79)

Professor Schlesinger also pointed out that there was a 50 percent chance of Jagan going "communist." Does this mean anything more than that there was an equal chance of Jagan "going American"? And was it not the American government that made the decision about which way things in Guyana went, anyway? In the 1964 election, the P.N.C. coalition carried the day even though Jagan's party won the single largest block of votes under the Proportional Representation electoral system, and, thus, Jagan was forced out of office.

In 1965, the stage was set for the P.N.C. coalition, made even broader by the inclusion of a right-wing party (U.F.) of the old oligarchic reactionary businessmen. Since the 1964 elections, there have been allegations of systematic erosion (voting rigging) of the freedom at the ballot. In 1966, Guyana became independent from Britain, under a coalition government of the P.N.C. and the U.F. led by Burnham. The coalition, however, was short-lived since differences between Burnham and D'Aguiar (leader of the U.F. party) emerged, leading to the eventual demise of the coalition government.

Four years later, on February 23, 1970, Guyana became a Cooperative Republic, marking the 207th anniversary of a slave revolt in Guyana. In the election of 1973, the P.N.C. increased its parliamentary majority to two-thirds with 37 of a total of 53 in the Assembly.

The New Coalition: Objective Interest and Nationalist Politics

The ideas of Guyanese nationalism emerged out of the ravages of imperialism, slavery, colonialism, and racism. At the forefront of the thrust of Guyanese Nationalism was the seemingly objective interest of the masses. Amongst the Guyanese masses were the petty bourgeois who, having access to ideas, rode on the backs of the masses and other progressive leaders, expounding nationalism while selfishly and deceptively maintaining their class interest.

"In spite of nationalization and the establishment of co-operatives, in spite of free education and aid to African liberation movements" (Rodney, 1977, p. 9), the petty bourgeoisie never advanced beyond the periphery of nationalism. Hence, when the struggle for political independence was crystalized and the masses yearned for revolutionary leadership to liberate them from imperialism, they were fed with rhetoric, reformism, and, later, in some cases, were subjected to outright repression, denial of democratic rights, and discrimination in employment practices along party and racial lines. As a class without an economic base, the strength of the petty bourgeoisie came from its control of the reins of state machinery and other national organizations, such as trade unions.

The new coalition that Burnham and the P.N.C. had forged was not unique to Guyana. Throughout the former British and French territories such coalitions could be found in the wake of broad-based nationalist struggles. With independence, the various elements of the coalition now had to be paid off in "coin" that corresponded to their objective interests. The various factions of the victorious P.N.C. coalition in Guyana and their objective interests are outlined as follows:

1. *The Old Bourgeoisie*, i.e., the old Client-Elite that had done the bidding of the British, and had been rewarded with titles, and other trinkets of the empire. This group of upper-middle-class people included: (a) Mulatto and white businessmen; (b) Mulatto, Black, and Indian professionals; and (c) Senior Mulatto and white civil servants and managers.

2. *The Middle-Class Intellectuals*: (a) Black professionals in the classic professions, such as law, medicine, dentistry, etc.; (b) teachers and middle- and junior-level civil servants; (c) self-taught or formally educated labor leaders; (d) technical personnel (i.e., both in terms of physical as well as mental skills).[2]

3. *The Masses*, which were made up of the urban Black working class and a small element of the rural peasants (Indians) and laborers who were also Black.

Very clearly, the objective interests of these various classes and the strata within these classes were different, but "independence" was seen as a goal which would advance the interests of all members of the various factions.

THE OLIGARCHIC INTERESTS

In the case of the more "progressive" elements of the old oligarchy (Client-Elite), a sizable number recognized that the old order was changing and opportunistically moved to align themselves with the forces that they knew would ultimately prevail. They understood that they could offer money and "legitimacy" to the coalition, and realized that with "independence" they stood to reap huge benefits due to the decreased competition from expatriates in business, and, in other money-making pursuits, such as the top echelons of the civil service and the more lucrative professions. (In Guyana, as in most capitalist societies, the classic professions are "Business.") However, other elements of this old oligarchy felt that they need not make such a concession, since they anticipated out-organizing and out-maneuvering the relatively new Black intellectual politicians at the opportune time. After all, this precedent had been set with British tutelage. Moreover, they were historically positioned in upper echelons of the decision-making machinery.

With independence, this grouping came into its own, not only in Guyana but throughout the Caribbean. The titles at their disposal multiplied so as to provide financial and status rewards necessary to keep them happy. This grouping was the backbone of the "neo-colonial" strategy of the British and other colonialists, and of the coalition strategy of Burnham, Williams, Manley, and other West Indian political leaders. Constitutional coalition politics and the "independence" which it brought, when viewed from an objective standpoint, benefited the middle class more than any other grouping in Guyana and other Caribbean states.

THE MASSES

The masses had everything to gain and nothing to lose with the advent of "independence." "Independence" meant Black instead of white and/or colored rulers. Whether these Black rulers were middle-class intellectuals or not, there was a rising sense of Black identity, which was pregnant with meaning for Guyanese and West Indian society[3] and which predisposed the masses to identify with Black leadership. Certainly, in their minds, being governed by their own was one step forward psychologically, and would also probably usher in economic, social, and political benefits for them. In essence, the mobilization of Black identification on the part of the masses was exactly what the Black intellectuals were espousing. In fact, the whole philosophy of the P.N.C. coalition was built on "making the small man a real man," as well as the promulgation of other pro–working class utterances.

Conceivably, the masses looked forward to "independence" as a panacea, and were encouraged in this vision by their leaders. Politics in Guyana had by this time become the preserve of the middle-class intellectuals, and they continued

in their efforts to ensure the loyalty and support of the all-important masses. However, unlike the middle class, the masses of Guyana did not benefit substantially
from "independence." Rather, their benefit was circumscribed to that of the psychological. As a consequence of this development, Blacks now strut where whites
once did, and the insidious racism of the British was henceforth no longer tolerated. The notion that Black is indeed beautiful in Guyana gained acceptance.

Nonetheless, that is exactly the problem, because class interests become unclear. Moreover, this newly achieved racial ideology allows the Black middle-
class intellectual to say to the Black masses, in all honesty, that we are all "one"
people, united by the bond of color and common oppression. In spite of the fact
that a qualitatively better health care and educational system and meager efforts
at land reform have occurred, the masses of Guyana are still poor, unemployed,
and powerless. It is clear that the masses of Guyana, relatively speaking, have
been the big losers in the Competitive Constitutional Coalition politics of "post-
war" Guyana.

The New Elite in Guyana

A PROFILE

This paper has noted the emergence of the middle class as the core of the
ruling coalition in Guyana and has summarized some of its gains with the advent
of "independence." It suggests that the leaders of this coalition emerged from this
middle class, and that this class was qualitatively different from the old Client-
Elite of the pre-independence days of Guyana. It has also been pointed out that
the emergence of this essentially Black middle class was an improvement towards
a social balance in Guyana. However, the analysis cannot stop here if there is to
be an adequate understanding of the nature of political power in Guyana. The
various strata of the "middle-class core" of the ruling coalition of Guyana must
be further examined. The strata of immediate importance is the *leadership strata*,
that is, the organizing and decision-making intellectuals who staff the highest
decision and policy-making levels of the state bureaucracy, the para-state organizations, the trade unions, and military and para-military forces. The combinations of these groups are those that form the *New Elite* in Guyana.

THE NATURE OF THE NEW ELITE

What, therefore, are the psychological characteristics and the cognitive orientations which this New Elite in Guyana seem to share in common? By means of
inductive generalizations based on observations, it is possible to derive a set of
psychological and sociological predispositions, which can be taken to be the necessary characteristics of the New Elite in a dynamic context. These predispositions are, of course, not unique to any one ethnic group.

1. The New Elite are superbly confident and notoriously ambitious. They display some organizational ability, and are "intellectually" knowledgeable about the world. They are authoritative, purposeful, and zealous in the pursuit of their goals. They display unrelenting drive, energy, and persistence, the quality of "never giving up," of having "staying power," which is perceived by some as stubbornness and "pushiness," but by others as dedication. They are bold, loyal to their cause, assertive, defiant, and sufficiently aggressive and adventurous to take risks on behalf of their principles and the "cause."

2. The New Elite in Guyana is basically middle class or petty bourgeoisie, and, as such, does not own the means of production as do the ruling elites in advanced capitalist states. Their power and wealth has its source in their control of the state bureaucracy and the higher level positions of the state corporations in Guyana. Any serious analysis must point out that the question of the ownership of capital becomes almost irrelevant if an entrenched bureaucratic-elite controls the decisions of who gets what, when, and can give themselves all the wealth and privileges that capital ownership entails in an industrial capitalist society.

3. The New Elite is a first generation "money" elite. Due to this absence of an established economic base, the New Elite tends to indulge itself in conspicuous consumption and financial accumulation of a type that can at times be somewhat embarrassing. An extension of this analysis also embraces the area of status symbols and other "status pay." The tendency for top officials in Guyana to display their status, in sometimes petty ways, his become a fact of life. The same can be observed in other Caribbean and Third World countries.

4. The New Elite is a westernized elite. The education of this group is as homogenous as could be expected. Almost to a person, they have gone through the British high school system, particularly Queens College or Bishops High School. (The "British Public School" system modeled the "learning centers" that can be found throughout the environs of the British Commonwealth.) Many of them have also gone through the Western university system, where the overriding paradigm is an acceptance of Western technological rationality, i.e., the notion of the universal application and superiority of Western technology. In the acceptance of this Western technological paradigm, this group can be considered an "International Elite." In all fairness to the ruling elite in Guyana, however, they have probably gone further than the elites of any other former British Caribbean territory to break out of this Western technological paradigm by more recently encouraging Chinese and Soviet technology transfers to Guyana.

5. The New Elite is a modernizing elite. By its very nature, as an embodiment of the middle class, the New Elite must continue to create new bureaucratic and other state machine functions if it is going to continue to pay off the middle-class core with jobs and status. While a certain proliferation of bureaucratic functions, independent of economic development is possible, this situation has inherent limitations. Economic development becomes, at some critical point, a precondition of further bureaucratic and state machine expansion. This situation is

true regardless of whether one is referring to a capitalist society on the Jamaican model or to a capitalist society such as Guyana. Economic development then becomes a logical "must" for this Ruling Elite in order to pay off the middle class and to provide better social and economic services to the masses. Unlike the old oligarchy, the New Elite is progressive and liberal, and is not anti–working class *per se*. The problem is one of pragmatic priorities in the competing objective interests of the different classes represented in the coalition. The middle class is the core. Their interests are attended to first by the Ruling Elite. If the Ruling Elite of Guyana show an inability to provide the "status jobs" for this middle class, then the core of their coalition may crumble. The masses come second in the coalition, and therefore the "trickle down" benefits of "Economic Development" are left for them.

One final point should be made about the progressive-liberal nature of the New Elite. The need for the proliferation of bureaucratic and state functions under their control is a partial explanation of the nationalization of foreign enterprises like ALCAN and Reynolds Metal Company—generally accepted as progressive measures.

6. The New Elite is a culturally ambiguous elite. Whereas the old Client-Elite merely mimicked the Europeans, this is far from the case with the New Elite. This New Elite is culturally progressive in that its members have rejected most of the symbols of Western European culture, and have reasserted the positive and rich traditions in African, Asian, and South American cultures. Dress, language, heroes, curricula, and many other transmitters and elements of culture have been radically changed on the part of the New Elite. Such is an expression of the "manhood" of a formerly despised and oppressed people, and it is probably the most genuine expression of nationalism of the New Elite. Let the record show that the P.N.C. coalition did not compromise on the issue of the cultural identity of the Guyanese people and the decolonization of cultural symbols. When the balance sheet is totaled, it will be found that in this sphere, a lasting contribution was made. Guyanese are today much more comfortable with their Blackness or Indianness, respectively, as compared with the old oligarchy in particular, and whites in general. This redefinition of culture is a two-edged sword that obfuscates class lines and interests, and subtly subordinates them to the issues of race and ethnicity.[4]

In further reference to the cultural ambiguity of the new elite, the fact that while they have progressively redefined culture in Guyana, they have maintained certain core elements of their Western orientation in terms of their penchant for titles; their need for heirarchy, and the status derived from being near the top or on the top of the hierarchy as well as their need for Western status symbols, all of which have further underscored this cultural ambivalence. This total and sincere commitment to progressive cultural redefinition while maintaining insidious Western value elements may be termed Cultural Schizophrenia.[5]

7. Finally, and by no means exhaustively, the New Elite is an amorphous and

flexible elite in which upward mobility is an important part of the game. Unlike the old Client-Elite, which jealously guarded the entrance to its ranks, the very strength and maintenance of power of the Ruling Elite depends on being able to co-opt anyone who carves out a niche in the national life, which is outside of the sphere of legitimacy of the New Elite. So, for example, when a labor leader emerges as a strong independent force on the horizon, he or she is incorporated—in many cases as a minister or other high-level functionary.

The result, of course, is to defuse any threat from the particular co-optee, who is, in many cases, from some segment of the working class, and whose interests are then bartered as the price of entry into the Ruling Elite. A vicious cycle then ensues in which middle-class intellectuals attempt to enter the higher echelons of the Ruling Elite, carve out a niche which then leads to a co-opting response and the bartering deal. But this is a full cycle—the end being the constant manipulation and "selling out" of the interests of the masses of Guyana by the people who continually claim to be representing those interests.

With Guyana's evolution from colonialism to a fully recognized political state, the nature of the elites has been transformed. Whereas, in the past, a handful of white planters composed the power elite, contemporary Guyana is increasingly led by an expanding group of indigenous Western-educated elite (petty bourgeoisie), who ride the backs of the masses, espousing nationalism while selfishly and deceptively maintaining their class interest.

The Cult in Guyanese Society

A social system affects the structure of the personality, no matter what the system is. In the United States, for example, the "open system," characterized by individualism and egoism, affects personality needs of some people through the deterioration of the system, which alienates individuals from the political community. The social character of life in America, with its class contradictions and racial discrimination, can force the development of certain psychological adjustments. These adjustments may be the rejection of American values and norms, consequently encouraging individuals to join any social group or religious organization that provides immediate psychological or sociological gratification. An example is seen in the case of the People's Temple of California and the subsequent Jonestown, Guyana, tragedy of 1978. This situation may be thought of as "escapism" from an unsympathetic and impersonal society.

An opportunistic leadership, such as the New Elite in Guyana, would accept the notion that their country could provide the setting for a utopia. Opportunism may be the only plausible explanation for the Guyanese government cooperating and offering incentives for the People's Temple religious group to locate in Guyana. Jim Jones, the cult leader, had gained significant acceptance in America, having been recommended by persons such as Rosalyn Carter, the U.S. president's wife, and by several members of the political establishment of San Fran-

cisco. Mutual benefits were obtained by all the participants in the religious colony at Jonestown. Choosing an isolated location gave the cult leaders greater control over the members. The cult members found the geographic and physical
isolation ideal for avoiding the "contamination" and "distraction" of the wider
society.

The ruling party of the New Elite could not have been ignorant of the economic and political ramifications of the Jonestown encampment by this Ameri-
can-dominated religious group. There were rumors that ships were carrying
goods in and out of Jonestown without reference to Guyana's customs regulations, and that Jonestown residents were entering the country without submitting
to the normal immigration procedures. In combination, these actions were violations against the laws of Guyana and can only be interpreted as the ruling party's
greed and political opportunism which created blinders for the Guyanese officials toward the activities of Jonestown.

The Guyanese government, which claims to be socialistic, may have seen the
evangelistic, agriculturally based mission as leading the way to socialism. However, for theorists and proponents of true socialism, it would be ludicrous to suggest that Jonestown was a socialist "state." Although some of the principles of
communal living were being employed, the experience at Jonestown must be
viewed as merely an anti-capitalist exercise.

The events which surrounded the People's Temple cult reflect a growing trend
of disenchantment with Western society. However, social engineering, such as
the kind presently taking place in Guyana, does not alleviate the basic societal
problems if the underlying causes are not determined and dealt with rationally.
Artificial control mechanisms often backfire, regardless of the number of psychological factors that are programmed. In any event, opportunism in politics by
Guyana's New Elite should be recognized and eliminated.

Conclusion

From the foregoing, it can be seen that while the ruling class of the New Elite
of Guyana changed in its social composition, the status of the masses still remains largely impotent, reflecting yet another manifestation of the "iron law of
oligarchy." Furthermore, this petty bourgeoisie leadership does not serve the interest of the masses of people irrespective of whether they are Black, Indian,
Amerindian, or Chinese.

Consequently, it is evident that racial politics has effectively masked a class
struggle which is currently seething in what Shivji (1970) calls "the silent class
struggle." This struggle will continue until the masses realize that only they can
legitimate the power of the New Elite, whose current position of compromise
with known "imperialists," such as America and the Jonestown experience, is
against the fundamental interest of the working class.

Progressive leadership must come from the masses to alleviate the class struggle in Guyana, to mobilize the workers, and to train and develop a cadre that will work to bring the masses their rights. Guyanese of the calibre of Walter Rodney, Clive Thomas, Cheddi Jagan, Moses Bhagwan, Eusi Kwayana, to mention a few, have already developed sound analyses to aid the cadre in their development of liberation ideas. Providing these ideas, founded upon the interest of the whole, take precedent over the insular middle-class or racial interest, then the people of Guyana will triumph.

Notes

1. See J. E. Greene, *Race vs. Politics*, Institute of Social and Economic Research, University of the West Indies, 1974, Chapters 2 and 3, for further discussion.
2. Note the broad definition of intellectuals.
3. See Anselm Remy, *The Duvalier Phenomenon* (Fisk University, Mimeo, 1974). This paper is an excellent analysis of how Duvalier was able to use racial politics, not of his own making, to come to power.
4. Note that while Guyanese are culturally decolonized and comfortable and confident, *vis-à-vis* whites and coloreds this is not so in Afro-Indian relations.
5. See Anselm Remy, *The Duvalier Phenomenon, op. cit.*

References

Brinton, C. 1965. The Anatomy of Revolution. Englewood Cliffs, N.J.: Prentice-Hall.
Fanon, F. 1967. Black Skin, White Masks. New York: Grove Press.
Greene, J. E. 1974. Race vs. Politics in Guyana. Kingston, Jamaica: Institute of Social and Economic Research, University of the West Indies.
Jagan, C. 1971. The West on Trial. Berlin: Seven Seas Publishers.
Newman, P. 1964. British Guyana: Problems of Cohesion in an Immigrant Society. London: Oxford University Press.
Remy, A. 1974. "The Duvalier Phenomenon." Fisk University, Mimeographed.
Rodney, W. 1966. "Masses in Action." New World. Georgetown, Guyana: New World Group Publishers.
———. 1977. "Open Letter to C.C.C." In Caribbean Contact, Newspaper, vol. 5, no. 7, p. 9.
Schlesinger, A. 1965. A Thousand Days: John F. Kennedy in the White House. Boston: Houghton Mifflin Co.
Shivji, G. 1970. "Tanzania: The Silent Class Struggle." Cheche. Mimeographed. Dares Salaam, September.
Smith, R. T. 1962. British Guiana. London: Oxford University Press.

4. ETHNICITY AND RESOURCE COMPETITION IN GUYANESE SOCIETY

Leo A. Despres

Ethnicity and ethnic group relations, often assuming dimensions of racism, are subjects that have received considerable research attention from all denominations of social scientists.[1] Nevertheless, a great many substantive problems remain unresolved even to the point of theoretical clarification. Not the least of these problems is the widespread persistence of ethnicity as an element of structural significance in the organization of societies of varying types. Ethnicity persists most obviously in those societies that have been labeled, inter alia, complex, multiple, multi-ethnic, segmented, heterogeneous, urban, industrial, pre-industrial, or plural.[2] However, quite apart from the problem of their classification, these societies engage processes of social differentiation and incorporation which are evident in societies usually considered more homogeneous from a cultural point of view. And if, following Barth (1969: 13), one defines ethnicity as a categorical ascription presumptively determined by origin and background, elements of ethnicity may be in evidence at the organizational interface of group relations in some of the most simple societies of record.[3]

It very well may be that ethnicity and ethnic group relations implicate problems that override the specificity of particular cultures, historical circumstances, polities, and ecologies. Indeed, this is suggested in much of the current literature.[4] Assuming this to be the case, it follows that the persistence of ethnicity and the various forms of interethnic accommodation that accompany it cannot be explained completely by reference to conditions or circumstances peculiar to one society or another at a particular historical moment. And, considering the variability of cultures, institutional systems, polities, ecologies, and demographic circumstances, typological efforts to disclose the processes involved seem rather misspent (e.g. van den Berghe 1970: 21–41; Schermerhorn 1970). What is needed is some set of propositions, even if tentatively derived, giving issue to generalizations of invariant order in respect to the conditions that favor the selection of ethnic ascriptions and identities for the purpose of organizing human activities.

Accordingly, the focus of this paper is simultaneously theoretical and substantive. Substantively, it presents a case study of ethnicity and ethnic group relations

Originally published in Leo A. Despres (ed.), *Ethnicity and Resource Competition in Plural Societies* (The Hague: Mouton, 1975), pp. 87–117. Copyright © 1975 by Mouton de Gruyter. Reprinted by permission of Leo A. Despres and Mouton de Gruyter.

in Guyanese society. In developing this case, it will be suggested that the persistence, organization, and differential incorporation of ethnic groups in Guyanese society is very much determined by the competition for material resources that exists among the various populations that were settled in this area as a consequence of European exploration and exploitation. To further enhance the comparative assessment of this general thesis, by way of concluding, more specific hypotheses will be presented in respect to the conditions affecting resource competition on the one hand and incorporation processes on the other. Thus, theoretical considerations of a more general nature will follow upon the presentation of data.

Regarding the analysis of data, it will be convenient to focus attention mainly on three dimensions of ethnicity and ethnic group relations: first, that pertaining to the overall social system and the persistence of culturally differentiated populations; second, the nature and character of organized ethnic group relations; and third, the role of ethnicity as it affects individual encounters within varying situational contexts. Although related, each of these dimensions may be dealt with separately.

1. At the level of the overall social system, one must begin by taking note of census data and the much-discussed problem of census classification. Guyana is said to be a land of six peoples. As of 1964, the population was comprised of: East Indians (50.2 percent), Africans (31.3 percent), Amerindians (4.6 percent), Portuguese (1.0 percent), Chinese (0.6 percent), and white (0.3 percent). For some curious reason, in 1960 the category "European" was dropped in favor of the category "white." A residual population, the mixed (12.0 percent), is also given categorical recognition.

Students of Guyanese society have proclaimed the ambiguity and empirical invalidity of these census categories. Guyanese who count other Guyanese sometimes give note to subjectively asserted ethnic identities for purposes of classification. In other instances attention is drawn to ambiguously defined cultural diacritica that are assumed to be generally standardized: e.g. dress, religion, house form, or style of life. In still other instances, persons are counted in reference to equally ambiguous phenotypical variations, particularly skin color, facial features, or hair texture. All of this underscores the fact that in the final analysis these census categories are stereotypic. Thus, it has been argued, they are inconsistent with the variation in observed institutional and cultural practices and with the actual distribution of phenotypical diacritica.[5]

Notwithstanding the stereotypic nature of census categories, Guyanese often do accord identities to other Guyanese that generally correspond to the ethnic categories in question. Moreover, individual Guyanese do this even when they are inclined to reject for themselves the ethnic identities which others accord them. This is to suggest that the categories in question are not entirely devoid of objective significance. Following Barth (1969: 9–38), it would seem that the critical question is whether or not these ethnic categories enjoin imperative statuses and, if so, how these statuses are structured within the overall social system.

There is substantial evidence to suggest that ethnic categories do enjoin imperative statuses in Guyana. As indicated elsewhere (Despres i.p.), unofficially and sometimes officially, these ethnic categories are the foci of differential consideration within the public domain. One recent example of this is provided by the 1965 inquiry into the problem of "racial" imbalance in the public services. The rather exhaustive study made of this problem was commissioned by the government of British Guiana and carried out by the International Commission of Jurists. Quite apart from its procedures and findings, three points need to be emphasized regarding this inquiry. First, the Burnham government of 1965 commissioned this inquiry in order to alleviate political pressure arising from the widespread belief in the East Indian community that an imbalance among Africans and East Indians existed in the public service. Second, the measure of that imbalance was made in reference to population ratios that were derived from the application of the stereotypic ethnic categories under discussion. Finally, the investigation itself, and the circumstances surrounding it, gave implicit expression to a set of norms according to which a great many Guyanese, including some who are important leaders, are inclined to support the view that within the all-inclusive public domain, the structure of Guyanese society should disclose what M. G. Smith (1969: 434–435) has called a "consociational" form of incorporation.

That is to say, many Guyanese are inclined to view their society as one comprised of diverse ethnic and/or racial collectivities of unequal status and power. Paraphrasing a title borrowed from the Prime Minister's recent book (Burnham 1970), to mold from these one people with one destiny, many Guyanese would maintain that these collectivities need to hold equivalent corporate status in the common public domain. Therefore, regarding recruitment into the public service, consideration needs to be given to ascribed ethnic criteria in addition to criteria of individual achievement. At the very least, achievement criteria should not be developed and administered in a manner that would contribute further to the corporate inequalities that are perceived to exist among ethnic populations as a consequence of their former colonial domination. It follows from these views that Africans and East Indians should be given entitlements not only in reference to their numbers, but also in relationship to the inequalities that are thought to exist in respect to their collective status in the overall social system.

Being somewhat relative to the ethnic population with which one is most generally identified, the definition of corporate inequalities among ethnic populations in Guyana contains a subjective component. But these perceptions also are not entirely without an objective base. If one takes as an objective measure of status inequality the relationship of individuals and groups to the material resources they own, control, or otherwise manage, a definite order of inequality exists among ethnic populations. Moreover, this order of inequality is of such historical depth that the statuses it enjoins are institutionalized and imperative and they correspond to the competition for resources that has obtained among the populations in question. The historical data supporting this view have been detailed elsewhere (Despres 1967: 30–67; 1969: 14–44). A brief summary will satisfy the purposes of this analysis.

It is evident that the populations that came to Guyana from Africa, Asia, and Europe differed not only phenotypically but also in their cultural traditions and practices. It is equally evident that other differences developed according to whether such populations were imported as slaves or indentured workers, or whether they arrived as immigrant planters, merchants, public servants, or commercial agents. It is certain also that these differences of origin were modified by early adaptive experiences. Miscegenation occurred, particularly between Europeans and Africans. Languages were lost. And many traditional practices gave way to the agro-industrial demands of an expanding colonial economy.

However, regarding ethnic populations, the process of readaptation in the coastlands of Guyana was itself differentiating. That is to say, while all Guyanese shared the experiences of colonialism and the plantation economy, ethnic populations disclose different historical careers in respect to these influences. More specifically, ordered by the competition for resources that existed within and across varying micro-environments (i.e. plantations, villages, and towns), Europeans have remained dominant in their control of the most productive environmental resources available, particularly land, minerals, employment opportunities, and markets. At the same time, since they were first imported as indentured workers, East Indians have slowly but steadily alienated from Africans the control of those environmental resources that have remained accessible primarily to non-Europeans.

For example, between 1840 and 1900, East Indian indentured workers all but displaced Africans from the labor market which the sugar plantations provided. It is true that following emancipation a great many Africans gravitated away from the sugar plantations. But not all of them did so simply because they wanted to flee the source of their former bondage. On the contrary, the first migratory wave from the estates was created by a general strike in 1842, when the planters attempted to reduce the wages of African workers to the pre-emancipation level in order to help defray the cost of importing more than 50,000 indentured workers. Strikers, it seems, were summarily ejected from estate lands. A more severe strike developed in 1847, when the planters again attempted to reduce wages (Young 1958: 15–21). Except in special job categories such as pan boiling and seasonal cane cutting, Africans could not or would not compete for the wages paid indentures. Thus, by 1911, the African proportion of the estate population had dwindled to 10 percent while the number of East Indians increased to 86 percent. Since 1911, the African proportion has stabilized between 10 and 15 percent.

Similarly, East Indians have displaced Africans from most of the coastal agri-

cultural lands not taken up by the sugar estates. In the years immediately following emancipation, Africans came to occupy virtually all of these lands. Living in
villages under various forms of local government organization, they put these
lands under ground crops, coconut, and fruit trees. In 1881, only 13 percent of
the village population was made up of East Indians and a few Chinese. The African proportion comprised 65 percent and most of the rest was counted as
mixed. By the time A. H. Marshall (1955) reported his study of local government
in British Guiana, East Indians contributed 54 percent to the village population
and the African proportion had declined to 37 percent. In 1960, the East Indian
proportion of the rural population (including the population of sugar estates) was
60 percent compared to 25 percent for Africans.

While 93,000 Africans, compared to 379,000 East Indians, continue to live in
rural areas, more than half of them are located in the East and West Demerara
districts, where the best agricultural lands are occupied by sugar estates and much
of the rest by East Indians. Being relatively close to Georgetown and its environs,
most of the Africans living in these districts are directly or indirectly dependent
upon sources of urban employment for their livelihood rather than agriculture.
The agricultural lands they do work provide more by way of subsistence value to
children, to the elderly, and to the unemployed than they provide by way of employment in the production of cash crops (Despres 1969: 33–37). Almost all of
the coastal agricultural lands in Berbice and Essequibo have been taken up by
East Indians.

In the face of these pressures, over the years Africans have turned increasingly
to urban employment opportunities in order to secure some sort of resource base.
As is shown in Table 1, in 1891 only 21 percent of the African population resided in urban areas, compared to 5 percent of the East Indian population. At the
same time, Africans contributed 36 percent to the urban population, compared
to the 8 percent contributed by East Indians. By 1960, almost half of all Africans
resided in urban areas, and they comprised 50 percent of the urban population.
If the mixed population, which sees itself as predominantly African, were to be included in these figures, the proportion of Africans in the urban population would
increase to 71 percent.

It should be noted also that in recent years the East Indian population has
experienced considerable change in both size and distribution. Apparently as a
result of the eradication of malaria in 1945, a disease that was endemic on the
sugar estates, the East Indian population has virtually exploded. Between 1946
and 1960, the proportion of East Indians in the total population increased from
44 to 48 percent (it passed 50 percent in 1964), whereas it had increased less than
one percent during the previous fifteen-year census period (1931–1946). At the
same time, the African proportion of the total population decreased from 38 to
33 percent. Moreover, not all of this decline can be explained by a shift in African
ethnic identity, because the proportion of mixed population increased from 10 to

Table 1. Africans and East Indians in urban population, 1891–1960

Period	Percentage of Africans in urban areas	Percentage of Indians in urban areas	African proportion of urban population	Indian proportion of urban population
1891	21	5	36	8
1911	28	6	42	11
1921	29	6	51	11
1931	34	7	54	12
1946	39	10	54	16
1960[a]	49	14	49	21

[a] In addition to Georgetown and New Amsterdam, figures for 1960 include the Mackenzie-Christanburg-Wismar (Upper Demerara River district) as an urban area. Were this area excluded, the rural-urban composition of Africans and their contribution to the urban population would remain approximately the same (49 percent), but the East Indian proportion of the urban population would increase to 23 percent. In other words, the inclusion of this district significantly expands the urban population base but because East Indians are more concentrated in Georgetown and New Amsterdam, it diminishes their contribution to the total urban population.

only 12 percent between 1946 and 1960. Attending this growth in the East Indian population has been a change in its distribution, probably related to the widespread unemployment that followed upon technological changes in the sugar industry after World War II. Thus, as shown in Table 1, while the number of Africans living in urban areas increased from 39 to 49 percent between 1946 and 1960, the African proportion of the urban population actually declined from 54 to 49 percent. On the other hand, the proportion of East Indians in the urban population increased from 16 to 21 percent.

All of this is to suggest that the resource competition that had obtained for more than a century between Africans and East Indians in rural areas has now become a feature of urban life as well. Perhaps the magnitude of this competition can be revealed in reference to the public service.

Although the available historical data are inadequate for the precise kind of comparisons that would be most useful, it is quite evident that the public service in Guyana has been a most important source of employment, particularly for urban Africans, during all of this century and much of the last. In 1891, for example, Africans and a few Europeans made up almost the entire teaching profession. As early as 1900, Africans comprised an overwhelming majority of the unpensionable staff in practically every department of the public service. In 1940, they represented 67 percent of all pensionable public servants. And by 1960, they ranked second only to Europeans among departmental heads in the public service. By way of contrast, in 1931, only 12 percent of all Guyanese professionals and public servants (6,202) were East Indians. Also in 1931, East Indians contributed only 7 percent to the 1,397 Guyanese employed in the teaching profession.

Table 2. Total racial percentages in the security forces, the civil service, government agencies and undertakings, and areas of governmental responsibility.[a]

Body	European	Portuguese	Indian	African	Amerindian	Mixed	Chinese	Others
The security forces	0.35	0.8	19.9	73.5	1.1	4.19	0.16	—
The civil service	0.29	0.76	33.16	53.05	2.08	9.52	1.15	—
Government agencies and undertakings	0.39	1.05	27.17	62.49	0.14	8.02	0.91	—
Local government	0.06	0.57	49.68	38.89	0.11	10.46	0.23	—
Teachers in primary education	—	1.72	41.27	53.87	1.06	1.46	0.58	0.04
Land development	—	0.4	85.49	13.06	0.17	0.66	0.11	0.11
Percentage of total	0.22	0.88	39.97	50.64	1.16	6.35	0.75	0.03

[a] The data reported in Table 2 have been adapted from figures given in the report of the British Guiana Commission of Inquiry, *Racial problems in the public service* (1965: 33).

As late as 1960, East Indians comprised but 16 percent of all pensionable civil servants and only six Indians, compared to twenty-six Africans, could be counted among the fifty-seven departmental heads.

Returning to the previously mentioned study of racial imbalances in the public service, Table 2 presents data indicating the extent to which this resource domain has been invaded recently by East Indians. Considering total employment by the government in 1964, Africans remained in the majority—50.6 percent compared to almost 40 percent for East Indians. This figure, however, reflects the population of land development schemes in the rural sector, and East Indians comprise more than 85 percent of the population to whom these lands have been allocated.[6] Nevertheless, East Indians have increased their proportion of the public service from 12 percent in 1931 to 33 percent in 1964. They now represent almost 50 percent of the persons employed in local government and they make up more than 41 percent of the teachers employed in primary education. It should be added that the number of teachers employed in government and government-aided primary and all-age schools is now 5,301, considerably more than the 1,397 employed in 1931. This mobility is even more remarkable when it is considered that most of it has occurred since 1950.

The pattern of mobility, however, has not been confined only to resource domains under the control of government. Still another important resource base for Africans has been the internal marketing system which, in Georgetown, is centered in three large marketplaces: Stabroek, Bourda, and La Penitence. In 1971, a survey of the records kept for persons required to pay rent on market stalls, trays, and the like was made in order to determine the ethnic composition of hucksters, peddlers, and stall proprietors as well as the size and types of enterprises in which they engaged. Comparative data were collected for 1960 and 1970 and, in order to provide some check on the records, an actual census of market operations was made for 1971.

Only some of the data in respect to Stabroek, the largest of the three markets, have been analyzed, but preliminary findings are in keeping with those reported above. In 1960, weekly or monthly rent was being paid on 623 enterprises in Stabroek. Of these, 48 percent were operated by Africans and 52 percent by East Indians. These figures are exclusive of the relatively small number of enterprises operated by Portuguese, Chinese, and others. By 1970, the number of enterprises for which rent was being paid had increased to 755. However, the enterprises operated by Africans had declined from 48 to 33 percent while those operated by East Indians increased from 52 to 67 percent. Perhaps of equal import is the observational impression, yet to be supported by a complete analysis of data, that Africans tend to operate the least substantial of these enterprises. They are more commonly observed operating sidewalk enterprises and selling from trays and boxes than occupying market shops and stalls.

It is clear from these data that, in respect to environmental resources in Guyana, categorically identified populations have been competitively aligned since early in the seventeenth century, when the Dutch West India Company first imported slaves from Africa for the purpose of developing its possessions. The plural character of this system deepened in the nineteenth century when, following emancipation, Portuguese, Chinese, additional Africans, and large numbers of East Indian indentured workers were imported by the British in order to maintain at a low level of cost the manpower resource requirements of an expanding mercantile economy based on plantation agriculture. All of these populations differed in their racial and cultural origins and they continued to differ as a consequence of their particular historical careers. Thus, while the ethnic identities ascribed to these populations are in part stereotypic, they are by no means entirely putative. Accordingly, such identities have persisted quite apart from the subjective inclination of particular individuals to assume a wide range of other social identities. Moreover, in respect to environmental resources, ethnic identities enjoin imperative statuses and these, in turn, disclose an order of inequality among the populations so identified. This order of inequality is no less evident today than at any time in Guyana's history. In support of this view, it is instructive to conclude this portion of the analysis with data revealing the position occupied by ethnic populations in the current Guyanese economy.

Table 3 reports the percentage contribution of various industries to the Gross Domestic Product (GDP) and to the employed labor force for the period 1964–1965. It may be noted from these data that six industries generate approximately 78 percent of the GDP and also contribute 78 percent to the employed labor force. These industries are: sugar and sugar processing, mining, distribution and trade, rice agriculture and mixed farming, services (particularly banking and insurance), and government. How Guyanese stand in relationship to these industries reveals not only that there is an order of inequality among individuals and groups but, more important for our purposes, that the individuals and groups so ordered cluster significantly within the categorical ethnic boundaries under discussion.

Table 3. Percentage contribution to the gross domestic product and employed labor force by industry[a]

Industry	Percent contribution to GDP (1964)	Percent contribution to employed labor force (1965)
Agriculture and food processing:		
Sugar	17.0	18
Rice	5.7	14
Other	5.2	7
Total Agriculture	(27.9)	(39)
Forestry	2.4	2
Fishing	1.9	2
Livestock	2.6	1
Mining	17.1	3
Manufacturing: other than food processing	3.3	5
Distribution	12.8	14
Transportation and communications	6.4	7
Construction	5.1	5
Services: rental, financial and other	10.2	3
Government	10.3	19
Total	100.0	100.0

[a] The data presented here in reference to the Gross Domestic Product have been abstracted from David (1969: 1–42). Data in regard to the employed labor force have been abstracted from various tables presented in the Ministry of Labour and Social Security's publication, *Survey of manpower requirements and the labour force* (1965).

It is difficult to define precisely the collective status which Europeans and other non-Guyanese enjoy by virtue of their relationship to the resources that these industries employ or generate. However, some indication of the situation is provided in an unpublished project proposal circulated by the Agency for International Development at the University of Guyana in 1970. Inter alia, the proposal stated that the importance of foreign control in these areas is indicated by the fact that for 1968 exports of sugar, molasses, rum, bauxite, and alumina totalled $89.1 million, or about 75 percent of total exports. In the same year the "investment income" line item in Guyana's balance of payments showed a net outflow of $17.7 million, largely reflecting the transfer of profits to overseas owners. The report continued: "In the raising and slaughtering of beef cattle, British interests account for about 20 percent of the national herd. . . . About 45 percent of the insurance business is in foreign hands. The local match company is British owned, and the local flour mill is American owned. Retailing and the import-export trade are both largely in foreign hands." In regard to banking, the report noted: "Except for the new National Cooperative Bank, commercial banking is entirely under foreign control, servicing sugar and distributive trades in an amount equal to about 66 percent of total credit extended to business firms. If credit extended to mining were identifiable, this percentage would, of course, be larger." And finally, the report emphasized: "A 1966 UN survey of manpower requirements indicated that there were about 500 expatriates employed in Guyana in the private sector, concentrated largely in professional and managerial positions." These expatriates and their families comprise a substantial proportion of Guyana's "white" population.

In response to political changes over the past ten years, the employment of Guyanese in the higher echelons of these industries has reduced the number of expatriates in the overall population. Nevertheless, these enterprises remain firmly in the hands of "whites."[7] By virtue of this control, "whites" disclose the characteristics of a corporate economic elite rather than those of a population element in a generalized social class structure. Regarding recruitment into this elite, national, ethnic, and/or racial criteria continue to be important quite apart from criteria of achievement. A variety of epithets—some racial, some ethnic, and some denoting social and political class—are applied by Guyanese to other Guyanese who work and live on the fringes of this elite.

An undetermined but certainly marginal proportion of the resources exploited and produced by these core industries are available to Guyanese, mostly by way of taxes, duties, and wages.[8] Such taxes, duties, and wages serve to differentiate ethnic populations. For example, while the bauxite industry contributes 17 percent to the GDP and only 3 percent to the employed labor force, 95 percent of all bauxite workers are African. Sugar, on the other hand, contributes as much to the GDP, but it contributes significantly more to the employed labor force (18 percent), and 85 percent of all sugar workers are East Indians. While rice agriculture and mixed farming, including food processing, contribute less than 11 percent to the GDP, they contribute even more than does sugar to the employed labor force (21 percent). As previously indicated, these also are primarily domains of East Indian employment. Still another important source of employment is the distribution industry. It contributes 14 percent to the employed labor force. Much of this employment is taken up by the export-import trade, particulary in bauxite, sugar, and rice, and it provides work for dockworkers, most of whom are African. However, wholesale-retail trade is primarily in the hands of expatriate firms and East Indian merchants and shopkeepers. The latter particularly are inclined to give employment to East Indians.

Considering the imbalance of Indians and Africans employed in these core industries, it is not surprising that Africans comprise a majority of the unemployed in Guyana. It also is not surprising that they define their interests corporately and with particular reference to government. As an industry, the government generates 10 percent of the GDP and contributes 19 percent to the employed labor force. Thus, apart from agriculture, the government is the largest consumer of labor in the country. While all elements of the population look to the government for favors and support, the overwhelming majority of Africans view their control of the government as an absolute prerequisite of their economic survival. As a consequence, competition for the government and for the resources which the government commands is fierce among Africans and East Indians.

To summarize the situation in respect to the overall social system: Guyana has an economy encapsulated within the sphere of European, Canadian, and American domination. Its core industries are foreign-owned and controlled and they leave only a marginal share of the country's material resources unexpropriated and available to Guyanese. The whites who manage these industries are a group apart from the rest of the Guyanese. Over the years, the competitive allocation of Guyana's unexpropriated resources has served to order categorically identified elements of the Guyanese population in an arrangement of unequal status and power. Amerindians are marginal to the whole economy and they exist at the bottom of this stratification structure. Africans, on the other hand, are a sizeable population holding practically no investment in land or commercial enterprises. Outside the bauxite industry, Africans have had little security of employment except in the government service. Thus they have looked, and continue to look, to government for status. Because the East Indian population is made up of businessmen, merchants, shopkeepers, rice farmers, sugar workers, and, more recently, public servants, and in view of its size, Africans are very much inclined to consider the East Indian population as a threat to their material well-being. East Indians, of course, express reciprocal views. So many racial diacritica attend ethnic identities that most of the mixed population has little choice but to identify with African interests. And finally, because of their number, their racial identity with Europeans, and their threatened position in the economy, the Portugese are of their own accord leaving the country.

2. Inevitably, the structure of inequality among ethnic populations in Guyana has promoted the organization of a variety of special interest groups and associations which, in turn, impart to ethnic group relations much of their political interface. Important among such groups have been the East Indian Association, the Sanatana Dharma Maha Sabha, the Arya Samaj, the Hindu Society, the United Sad'r Anjuman-E-Islam, the Islamic Association, the Muslim Youth Organization, the Sword of the Spirit (Portuguese), the Chinese Association, the Afro-American Association, the League of Coloured Peoples, the Mahatma Gandhi

Organization, the Young Socialist Movement (African), and the Progressive Youth Organization (East Indian), to name but a few. Also important in this regard have been various business and professional associations, labor unions, and a variety of special interest organizations, such as the Sugar Producers Association and the Rice Producers Association. And perhaps more important than all of these are Guyana's ethnically based political parties, particularly the Indian-dominated Peoples Progressive Party and the African-dominated Peoples National Congress.

Given the limitations of space and the fact that the political activities of some of these associations are frequently concealed by intriguing alliances and all manner of rhetorical pronouncements, it is not possible to describe fully here the many ways in which such organizations have functioned to promote the exclusive interests of ethnic constituencies.[9] However, perhaps some feeling for the situation can be conveyed in reference to a few examples. Consider, first, the Rice Producers Association.

The Rice Producers Association (RPA) was established by authority of the legislature in 1946 (Ordinance Number 7) to represent the economic interests of rice farmers. In this capacity, the RPA not only negotiated prices for rice with the Guyana Marketing Board, a government-appointed statutory commission, but it secured various subsidies with which rice farmers were provided low-cost seed, fertilizer, insecticide, and even gasoline. Although the officers of the RPA were elected by the farmers, invariably they were active members of the Peoples Progressive Party (PPP). By virtue of the close relationship between the RPA and PPP, the latter was able to secure public resources with which it promoted its political programs in the Indian community. Subsequently, when the Burnham government assumed power in 1965, efforts were made to break this link between the RPA and the PPP.

According to African informants, the Burnham government "bribed" a few Indian rice farmers and with their assistance organized the Guyana Rice Corporation. Ostensibly, as a public company, the Guyana Rice Corporation was designed to supersede the Guyana Development Company, a similar company that had been organized by the colonial government in the 1950's. However, by withdrawing subsidies from the Rice Producers Association and investing them in the new Guyana Rice Corporation, an organization ostensibly run by Indians but controlled by Africans, the resource link between the Peoples Progressive Party and East Indian rice farmers was effectively broken. In the meantime, the Rice Producers Association still negotiates prices on behalf of rice farmers with the government-appointed Rice Marketing Board. However, the RPA has failed to negotiate an increase in the price of rice for more than seven years under the Burnham government. This has driven many Indian rice farmers to give up some of the lands they have occupied, particularly the more marginal lands on which they paid rents. In 1970–1971, the rice industry was in a state of economic de-pression. Nevertheless, as one informant put it, ". . . if rice farmers want favors from the government they must learn to share with the Africans. After all, we once had most of the land they now occupy."

Africans in Guyana are inclined to view almost any form of corporate organization in the Indian community as somewhat of a threat to their political interests. This is particularly the case in respect to any association that might disclose ties with the Peoples Progressive Party. Thus, as a general strategy, the Burnham government and the Peoples National Congress have bent every effort to dissolve or otherwise disrupt whatever organizational links might exist between the PPP and various elements of the Indian community. The situation regarding the Rice Producers Association is one example of this strategy. Another may be provided in reference to the Maha Sabha.

The Maha Sabha is a religious association, ostensibly apolitical. However, since the 1950's, its officers have been politically active in the Peoples Progressive Party. In 1970, a power struggle developed within the Maha Sabha between its president and certain PPP activitists who felt the president was too closely associating himself with the Burnham government. Subsequently, the president arranged an election of officers in which only his delegates were allowed to participate. With the help of the police, who kept opposition delegates from invading the meeting, the president succeeded in having himself re-elected. The Burnham government moved immediately to have the president of the Maha Sabha appointed Speaker of the House in the Legislative Assembly. Moreover, contrary to traditional procedure, which is to appoint as Speaker a person acceptable to both the government and the opposition, this appointment was made without the consent of the opposition. As a consequence of these developments, while the PPP continues to maintain its support among the Maha Sabha's membership, it no longer controls the Maha Sabha's corporate offices. However, by virtue of its relationship to the Maha Sabha's president, the Peoples National Congress and the Burnham government have effectively disrupted an organization that once served to join important elements of the Indian community to the Peoples Progressive Party.

One of the most significant ethnic organizations to appear in recent years is the African Society for Cultural Relations with Independent Africa (ASCRIA). The forerunner of ASCRIA is the Society for Racial Equality, essentially a black separatist movement organized by Sidney King (now called Eusi Kwayana) in the early 1960's, when Guyana suffered wave upon wave of racial rioting and killing. As a separatist movement, the Society for Racial Equality sought to have Guyana partitioned into a consocation of three territorial units: one reserved for Africans, one for East Indians, and a third to contain a voluntarily mixed population of whites and non-whites, including Africans and Indians who might not want to live among their own. Failing to win support for this scheme, the Society for Racial Equality incorporated elements of the League of Coloured Peoples and reorganized itself as a black power movement.

To be sure, ASCRIA is militantly black. However, in defining black it combines elements of race, social class, and cultural elements that are visibly African. Membership rules are said to prescribe a six-month course in black studies as prerequisite for full membership status. As one member explained this requirement: "A black who does not think black is a 'redneck' and cannot belong to ASCRIA. A light colored person who thinks black can belong." East Indians, Portuguese, Chinese, Amerindians, or whites cannot belong at all. In keeping with these views, ASCRIA is dedicated to the revitalization of African culture. Thus, it maintains a rather extensive educational program, importing materials and sometimes teacher-volunteers from Africa and the United States. This educational program is based in Georgetown but it reaches into several rural areas of black population concentration. It offers lectures in history, journalism, economics, cooperative organization, and even agricultural practice. It encourages the adoption of African names, values, and dress. It also encourages the use of what are thought to be African rituals in regard to religious practice, weddings, funerals, and other celebrations. And it discourages close associational ties between blacks and other elements of the population, particularly whites.

If ASCRIA were simply a cultural revitalization movement it probably would not be of much concern to other Guyanese. However, this is not the case; ASCRIA is also a political and economic movement with considerable muscle. Its membership is required to be active on many fronts and in 1970 its active membership was estimated to be in excess of 2,000 Africans and still growing. By 1971, at Mackenzie, ASCRIA had assumed such complete control of African bauxite workers that the president of the Guyana Mine Workers Union could not attend a meeting of his own union without ASCRIA's consent. Many of ASCRIA's members are prominently placed in government and in such public corporations as the National Bank of Guyana and the National Co-operative Bank. In 1970–1971, ASCRIA's coordinating elder, Eusi Kwayana, chaired the National Land Settlement Committee and the Executive Board of the National Marketing Corporation. In addition to these and other positions, he also served as a close advisor to the Prime Minister.

Apart from rhetoric and loose ideological pronouncements, ASCRIA's political program is quite clear in its intent and purpose. As ASCRIA defines the situation, all Guyanese have been exploited by British colonialism and American imperialism. In addition, Afro-Guyanese have been further exploited and discriminated against by East Indians and the Portuguese. Because of this, Afro-Guyanese are forced to struggle with poverty and unemployment at the bottom of the power structure. Accordingly, from ASCRIA's point of view, this situation must be changed. Africans have to be re-established on the land, and it makes little difference whether it is land presently occupied, by the sugar industry or by East Indians, or new land in the interior. Africans have to be given an equal share in business, in government, and in other resource opportunities. Again, it makes little difference whether they assume control of enterprises presently owned by

Europeans, Indians, and Portuguese, or they are given control of new enterprises developed with government assistance.

In order to accomplish these things, according to ASCRIA, Africans must assert their own independent cultural identity. They must draw upon the historical traditions that are being drawn upon by such contemporary African leaders as Jules Nyerere. They must be educated in the techniques of communal or cooperative management. And above all, at least in the foreseeable future, Africans must retain control of the government.

The close relationship between ASCRIA, the People's National Congress (PNC), and the Burnham government is a source of considerable anxiety among ethnic populations in Guyana.[10] In 1970–1971, many Guyanese would have been inclined to agree with the view expressed by one informant: "Burnham is ASCRIA as much as Eusi Kwayana is ASCRIA. ASCRIA is the cultural and economic arm of the government: the PNC is its political arm." Charges of ethnic and racial discrimination were both prevalent and widespread, particularly in the East Indian community. Thus, in November of 1970, still another association came into being. It called itself the Anti-Discrimination Movement (ADM). Organized and financed primarily by East Indian businessmen and professionals, its leaders held public meetings at which they proclaimed themselves opposed to "gross acts of discrimination and corruption at all levels of the government." The ADM published a weekly, called *Liberator*, which it distributed freely in all parts of the country. By May of 1971, many African political leaders believed that the ADM either was an instrument of the Peoples Progressive Party or that it was in the process of giving birth to a new East Indian political party.

This type of organized interface among ethnic populations can be found in most parts of the society and among virtually all elements of the population. It can be found even among university students. For example, at the end of the 1970 academic year, three groups contested the elections for student government at the University of Guyana. One comprised an all-Indian slate of candidates, another an all-African slate, and the third group presented a carefully balanced slate of Africans and East Indians. As it happened, the all-Indian slate won the election. Subsequently, Africans from the balanced slate accused the Indian candidates with whom they ran of having secretly campaigned in favor of the all-Indian slate. Eventually, a petition was circulated among African students requesting that the vice-chancellor of the university declare the election null and void for a variety of manufactured reasons. The following academic year, 1970–1971, this issue was kept alive and it served to divide the student body for the entire year in respect to every program which the student government sponsored. Student strikes were threatened unless the vice-chancellor moved to resolve the problem. However, his hands were tied by the fact that the election had been properly conducted under the supervision of faculty from the Department of Political Science. In the end, the situation resolved itself when a factional dispute developed within the student government over the misappropriation of funds. This provided the vice chancellor with an opportunity to remove the student president from office and put the student government in the hands of the university administration until books could be audited and new elections scheduled on the basis of PROPORTIONATE REPRESENTATION.

To summarize, the competition for resources in Guyana has served to order categorically identified populations in a system of unequal status and power. As a consequence, the identities of the populations so ordered have become politically charged. Thus, they have provided a basis for the corporate organization of a variety of ethnically exclusive groups and associations. As these groups and associations seek to secure resources for the constituencies they purport to represent, they must also seek to disrupt the order of inequality that obtains among ethnic populations. In the process, however, such groups not only reinforce the ethnic identities according to which their membership is recruited, but they also serve to align competitively those corporately organized segments of the populations from which their membership is drawn. It remains to be shown how these developments relate to individual inter-ethnic encounters.

3. It has been noted elsewhere (Despres i.p.) that, viewed from the vantage point of individual encounters, ethnic relations in Guyana assume dimensions that do not make readily apparent the structure of inequality that has been previously described. Social interaction is commonplace among all elements of the general population. In the markets and shops, in government offices, at various places of work, in the schools, at public celebrations, at cricket and football matches or the like, and sometimes in private homes one can observe Guyanese of virtually all ethnic categories interacting, and it does not appear immediately that their behavior is in any way modified by ethnic identities or the imperative statuses that might attach to such identities.

Gradually, however, this general impression begins to change. It may begin with observations at the seawall where people gather to enjoy the evening breezes, or in the Botanical Gardens where couples and families take Sunday afternoon walks. On these occasions, it will be observed that Africans and Indians sit or walk separately and they do not frequently greet one another or join in conversation. Where people dine in public places, particularly where they also dance, but even in the university cafeteria, groups are inclined to be ethnically exclusive. Friends who meet one another at the cinema, the band concert, or on the street are usually of the same ethnic category. So also are the peer groups that walk the streets after school. Then, at the barber shop or some other casual setting where one may be engaged in semi-private conversation, it may be detected how easily the subject swings, without prompting, to matters having to do with ethnic populations and their differences. On such occasions, one may also note how the substance of conversation changes according to who the speaker is and what other persons happen to be in hearing distance. Then, even in private conversation with a doctor, a dentist, a barrister, or a school teacher, the ease with which disparaging remarks are drawn in respect to one ethnic group or another cannot pass undetected.

The observer need not search out these episodes. They will engage his attention at the filling station, the dry-cleaning establishment, the market stall, or the faculty lounge. He will observe them also at the Police Officers Club, the Georgetown Club, the Army Staff Club, the Civil Service Association Club, or at a luncheon meeting of the Rotarians. A casual mention of virtually any subject, whether it be automobiles, cricket, the Mashramani celebration, housing, the cost of living, seawall construction, or even the bloom in the Botanical Gardens, may elicit an unexpected ethnic remark or a drawn out commentary on ethnic politics or the comparative achievement of ethnic populations. For example, a comment on the bloom in the Botanical Gardens caused a filling station attendant to give a five-minute lecture on how the Gardens had deteriorated because the Burnham government had attached a section of the Gardens to the Prime Minister's private residence "for the purpose of entertaining the African masses." Of course, Africans are not the only people the Prime Minister entertains but it is true that his residence incorporates a section of the Gardens which is no longer accessible to the general public.

Clearly, the occasions of inter-ethnic encounters are not only episodic but they are also extremely variable in respect to situation, circumstance, and personnel. This makes their structuring difficult to discern. Nevertheless, as observations are drawn together, it is evident that such encounters disclose a generalized pattern. A few selected examples may serve to illuminate the characteristics of this pattern.

First, in most situations involving non-Guyanese and Guyanese of different ethnic origins, Guyanese of virtually every category tend to obfuscate or submerge their respective ethnic identities in favor of asserting a common national identity. The imperative status that becomes operative under such circumstances incorporates all Guyanese in a manner as to suggest that as a people Guyanese conduct themselves in terms of values that clearly set them apart from non-nationals, particularly Europeans, Americans, and Canadians. Even other West Indians are given to understand that the Guyanese are nationals to be differentiated from Jamaicans, Trinidadians, or Barbadians. Of course, this national identity, and the imperative status that attaches to it, is reinforced by constitutionally defined legal codes.

In other situations, for example a public meeting sponsored by a new and somewhat radical political group called Movement Against Oppression (MAO), it may be observed that Guyanese of different ethnic origins will merge their respective ethnic identities in opposition to other Guyanese, also of different ethnic origins, who are epithetically labeled as "white niggers," "house slaves," or "red people." This latter group may include East Indians, Afro-Guyanese, Guyanese of mixed ancestry, Portuguese, and Chinese. Collectively, they form a special status category because of their relationship to Europeans or because of their style of life. This group is thought to discriminate against other Guyanese by virtue of their exploitive economic practices and also in terms of their associational proclivities.

What emerges in this instance is an imperative social class status which combines in its definition phenotypical images and cultural diacritica. This is reminiscent of the color-class continuum that has been reported to be widespread in the West Indies (Lewis 1968; R. T. Smith 1970: 43–76; Lowenthal 1972). When it is observed that the distribution of resources is more perfectly correlated with generalized ethnic identities than with specifically defined phenotypical and cultural diacritica, it seems rather difficult to attribute pervasive structural significance to a color-class continuum. For example, at the meeting reported above, there were forty-four people in attendance, including two whites (one Portuguese and one European married to an Afro-Guyanese), seven East Indians, and at least five persons that might easily have been considered mixed. None of these people identified themselves as "white niggers" or "red people," nor were they considered as such by the rest of the group.

These and other observations suggest that elements of a color-class differentiation are perhaps functional, particularly in situational contexts where the submergence of ethnic identities facilitates interaction among persons who have in common something more important than their ethnic differences. More specifically, in the situation cited, ethnic identities were submerged by the assertion of a more generalized "white/non-white" dichotomy which is thought by many Guyanese, including certain ideologically inclined intellectuals, to correspond to a historically derived pattern of economic exploitation in terms of which particular phenotypical images and life styles tend to be associated with certain status groups, particularly Europeans. Thus, the use of such images facilitates interaction among ethnically diverse Guyanese who commonly see themselves apart from such status groups. In other situations, these very same Guyanese may be observed asserting their respective African, East Indian, or Portuguese ethnic identities rather than a generalized identity expressive of their common economic status.

In still other situations, specifically those involving encounters among persons of only two ethnic groups, ethnic identities are asserted to lay claim to special status consideration. The effect of this is to declare the opposition of the group with which one identifies to a third group, no member of which is participating in the encounter. Accordingly, it frequently may be observed that when one or two Africans, or alternatively one or two East Indians, are interacting with non-Guyanese, they will seize the opportunity to assert their African or, as the case may be, their Indian identity by drawing negative stereotypes in reference to a population not represented in the encounter. Similarly, when East Indians have encounters with Portuguese, negative reference may be made to Africans. The variations on this type of episode seem endless but, always, they seem to involve a special status claim for the collectivity with which one identifies.

Invariably, status claims arising from one ethnic identity serve to diminish the claims arising from another. Thus, less commonly observed are situations in which individuals of different ethnic origins counterpose their respective ethnic identities. When such situations are observed, they generally occasion a verbal or a physical quarrel. The exception is when one party to the encounter ignores or dismisses the claim asserted by the other, often in a joking manner. An increasingly common variant on this pattern is when members of militant ethnic associations, ASCRIA for example, seize opportunities to express their militancy. This often occurs in contexts that are organized and, therefore, under control. Under such circumstances, the assertion of conflicting ethnic claims is usually ignored rather than rebutted by persons who might otherwise rise to the offense.

It is evident from these few illustrations that sensitivity to ethnic claims and identities tends to be rather pervasive in Guyana. As a consequence, a rather elaborate code of etiquette has developed in respect to inter-ethnic encounters. The details of this code are imperfectly known but it becomes readily apparent to even the most casual observer that on most occasions it is simply impolite to assert ethnic identities. Such assertions almost always involve claims which diminish the status of one group or another. Thus, unless the situation is appropriate, the assertion of an ethnic identity can be a source of embarrassment to the individual who asserts it. In view of these circumstances, unless observation is more than superficial, it would seem that ethnic identities are more apparent than real and that such identities do not enjoin imperative statuses affecting the interaction of individuals and groups. As suggested here, the opposite is the case.

The question remains: What kinds of situations tend to evoke the assertion of ethnic identities and claims? To answer this, it must be kept in mind that the assertion of such claims establishes a mode of competitive opposition between one ethnic group and another. And invariably, when such a mode of competitive opposition is effected, it reflects upon the fundamental status inequalities that have been previously described. Accordingly, situations which call into question the rights, privileges, and entitlements that are thought to attend the status inequalities existing among ethnic populations, or situations that give issue to the resource allocations from which these inequalities derive, tend to evoke ethnic identities and claims in respect to individual encounters.

The overall pattern that emerges from all of this is one of segmentary opposition. That is to say, some situations evoke national claims which override the claims of ethnic populations. In these situations, the status claims of all Guyanese are joined in opposition to Europeans, Americans, Canadians, and even other West Indians. Some situations bring into focus claims which serve to join Africans and East Indians in opposition to other ethnic and/or racial elements. Still other situations summon forth claims that divide individual Africans and East Indians in opposition to one another. In fact, when some Africans refer to other Africans as "red people," an epithet which combines racial and cultural criteria to define a generalized social class status, it needs to be recognized that some situations evoke identities that serve to divide Africans among themselves. For the most part, this pattern of segmentary opposition corresponds to and reflects both the continuities and discontinuities which the differential incorporation of ethnic populations enjoins in the overall structure of Guyanese society.

4. To summarize the situation regarding ethnicity and resource competition in Guyana, it may be stated that practically all Guyanese declare themselves in support of a political system which defines the rights and obligations of citizenship without reference to ethnic considerations. In fact, such considerations are absolutely proscribed by Guyana's present constitution. However, for reasons that have been stated, this pattern of universal incorporation does not obtain. Rather, since early in the seventeenth century, competition for resources in Guyana has served to order a system of inequality in terms of which categorically differentiated populations have been joined in competitive opposition. Accordingly, most Guyanese are inclined to view their society as one comprised of diverse ethnic and/or racial collectivities of unequal status and power.

The cultural and sometimes phenotypical diacritica which Guyanese use to identify these ethnic collectivities are stereotypic, but they are by no means completely devoid of historical foundation and empirical significance. The populations to which such diacritica are applied are populations of different origin. During the course of Guyana's colonial history, these populations have been differentially exploited and they have differentially adapted to the conditions of their exploitation. This process of differential adaptation, in turn, has been productive of cultural developments which also facilitate the categorical identity of these populations. Similarly, the inequalities of status which Guyanese ascribe to these ethnic populations are real inequalities when measured against the material resources they command. And it is a fact that both within and across various resource domains these ethnic populations continue to be competitively aligned.

Over the years, the competitive alignment of ethnic populations in Guyana has been productive of considerable tension and conflict. In response to this, and in an effort to achieve stability, particularly in recent times, both colonial and independent Guyanese governments have been inclined to concede to ethnic populations corporate, but equal, entitlements in the public domain.[11] In other words, in the absence of universal incorporation, ethnic populations have been accorded consociational status. However, the definition of what in fact constitutes equal entitlements is a matter on which there exists a great deal of ethnic dissension. This dissension has contributed significantly to the corporate or political organization of the ethnic populations in question.

Thus, existing between the overall structure of Guyanese society and the level of individual encounters is a variety of groups and associations that seek to promote the corporate interests of ethnic populations. These include political parties, ethnic organizations, business and professional associations, religious societies, and in some instances labor unions. The public interests of some of these groups are avowedly ethnic while the ethnic interests of others are disguised by constitutional charters and public rhetoric. Some of these groups and associations have been more successful than others in achieving their objectives and, therefore, they have been more continuous in their efforts. These groups also vary in the extent of their organization and the size of their active membership. However, quite apart from these variable features, the political and economic activities of such organizations as ASCRIA and the Anti-Discrimination Movement simultaneously bring into sharp focus the corporate interests of ethnic populations and the competition for resources that obtains among them.

It follows from these considerations that ethnicity in Guyana enjoins a system of ascribed statuses of considerable historical depth. This system has been particularly functional in respect to the competition for material resources. However, the persistence of this system has not precluded the development of still another status system according to which individual Guyanese are socially differentiated in reference to their particular achievements. These two status systems are entangled but they are not coterminous. Thus, quite apart from their respective ethnic identities, individual Guyanese may assert a relatively wide range of other social identities. Whether or not particular Guyanese will suppress some or all of these other status identities in favor of asserting claims which attach to their ethnic status is largely a function of the circumstances surrounding different interactional situations.

To state the matter differently, the domain of individual transactions is both situational and episodic but it is not without patterning. Ethnic identities and status claims enter selectively into this domain in that they tend to be asserted whenever circumstances bring into focus the status inequalities that exist among ethnic populations. The pattern is characteristically one of segmentary opposition. It corresponds to and reflects both the continuities and discontinuities between the two status systems under discussion. And it would appear that these two status systems will persist in Guyana as long as ethnicity confers upon individual Guyanese competitive advantage in respect to material resources.

5. It is not the better part of wisdom to generalize too extensively from a single case. However, among anthropologists, it is a *sine qua non* that case studies have heuristic value for comparative purposes. Thus, it is appropriate to conclude this analysis with considerations of a more general nature.

Perhaps the most difficult questions that may be posed regarding ethnicity and ethnic group relations are questions that have to do with the problem of ethnogenesis. Why do populations come to be culturally differentiated in the first place? Why do such differentiations persist? Under what circumstances might we expect ethnic collectivities to become corporately, or politically, organized? What forces tend to promote the differential incorporation of ethnic populations within the all-inclusive public domain? In other words, when and under what conditions will ethnic populations become the object, de jure or de facto, of political discrimination?

At the risk of oversimplification, research in regard to the problem of ethnogenesis is particularly informed by three theoretical orientations which are current in anthropology. Following Barth, one approach directs our attention to the interactional processes by which ethnic boundaries are defined and made operative. The focus of investigation is the ethnic boundary that defines the group and not, as Barth (1969: 15) notes, "the cultural stuff that it encloses." This is not to minimize the fact that ethnic groups only persist as significant units when they disclose marked cultural differences. Rather, it is to emphasize that such cultural differences presuppose a structuring of interaction: they presuppose a relatively stable set of prescriptions and proscriptions governing situations of contact. It is consistent with this approach that ethnic groups cannot be adequately delineated in reference to historically derived cultural systems. Except perhaps for brief historical moments, such systems tend to transcend group boundaries. Moreover, ethnic boundaries often express cultural differences that are more putative than real in an historical sense. Thus, it is also consistent with this approach that the essential feature of ethnicity is its ascriptive character. For example, Barth states: "To the extent that actors use ethnic identities to categorize themselves and others for purposes of interaction, they form ethnic groups in this organizational sense" (1969: 13–14).

A second approach to the study of ethnogenesis may be derived from the work of those anthropologists who have been concerned primarily with the plural features and overall structure of multi-ethnic societies. The conceptions of social and cultural pluralism which inform this orientation are attributed to Furnivall (1939, 1942, 1948), an economist who was struck by the ethnic divisions characteristic of Southeast Asian societies. However, the leading exponent of this approach among anthropologists has been M. G. Smith (1957: 439–447; 1960: 763–777; 1965). Without belaboring conceptual problems that have been thoroughly worked over in the literature, the critical focus of the plural society approach lies in the institutional orders which presumably attend the interactional process of which Barth writes.[12] These institutional orders are taken to be expressive of cultural systems. These systems, in turn, serve not only to differentiate populations which may be called ethnic, but they serve also to delineate the system of relationships that exists both within and across these populations.[13]

Still another approach to the study of ethnogenesis may be derived from the work of anthropological ecologists who have underscored the relationship of material resources to the evolution of cultural systems.[14] In the context of ecological research, cultural systems are viewed as transgenerational behavioral codes, the

organization and persistence of which disclose processes of adaptive selection.
Regarding the evolution of such codes, it is neither necessary nor logical to assume that those which persist are entirely adaptive or maladaptive, functionally
unified, or internally consistent in their institutional organization and expression.
Nor is it necessary to assume that these codes are impervious to the influence of
individuals. Probably to a significant degree, the adaptive selection of these behavioral codes is a function of factors influencing the extent to which they impede or facilitate the acquisition of environmental resources.

It is not appropriate in the present context to elaborate the merits and limitations of these theoretical orientations. However, assuming a culture to be a set of
ways of occupying and using an environment, it follows that a population will
become culturally differentiated to the extent that segments of that population
differentially exploit whatever resources are available in the same environment.
Building upon this assumption, and combining elements derived from each of
the three approaches under discussion, generalizations of invariant order may be
ventured in respect to the conditions that seem to favor the genesis and persistence of ethnic ascriptions and status identities for the purpose of organizing certain relationships among groups as well as among individuals. Phrased in the
form of hypotheses, such generalizations may be stated as follows:

a. A system of ascribed ethnic statuses will follow the differential adaptation
   of population segments and persist to the extent that the assertion of ethnic
   identities serves to confer competitive advantage in respect to environmental resources.
b. Ethnic identities will tend to confer competitive advantage in respect to
   resources when (1) the quantity of resources available is severely limited
   relative to demand and (2) the accessibility of such resources does not require individual command of complex technological skills and knowledge.
c. Whenever resource domains vary significantly in the complexity of their
   technological requirements, there will exist corresponding systems of status
   ascription and status achievement. The coexistence of such systems will engage a pattern of structural continuities and discontinuities according to
   which ethnic status claims will enter selectively into the domain of interpersonal transactions.
d. To the extent that phenotypical, rather than cultural, diacritica attend the
   expression of ethnic identities, boundaries will remain rigid and boundary
   crossing will be minimized.
e. The selective advantage of pluralism in a differentiated but relatively stable
   techno-environment is the reduction of competition among populations for
   which ethnicity confers competitive advantage.
f. The corporate or political organization of ethnic populations will follow
   upon any techno-environmental changes that are productive of increased
   competition both within and across varying resource domains.

g. Finally, the differential incorporation of ethnic populations will obtain to the extent that one population segment succeeds in monopolizing control of all resource domains within any circumscribed environment.

Obviously, the validity and comparative utility of these generalizations need to be established. By way of conclusion, and without recapitulating what has been previously summarized, it is suggested that the data in respect to Guyana are sufficiently supportive of these generalizations as to commend their further discussion among social scientists interested in the comparative study of ethnic phenomena.

Notes

Some of the data presented in this paper were collected with support provided by the Social Science Research Council in 1960–1961. Thanks to the support of a Fulbright Fellowship, additional research was conducted in Guyana over a twelve-month period in 1970–1971. A very preliminary draft of this paper was presented to the 1971 meetings of the International Studies Association in San Juan, Puerto Rico, where it benefited considerably from critical comments offered by Harmannus Hoetink, Wendell Bell, and Leo Kuper. I also wish to thank Burton Benedict, Pierre van den Berghe, and Melvyn Goldstein for the benefit of their wisdom in respect to subsequent drafts.

1. The literature in this field is much too extensive to summarize here. For a general review, see the following: Banton (1967); Schermerhorn (1970); Shibutani and Kwan (1965); van den Berghe (1967, 1970); and Zubaida (1970).

2. See particularly M. G. Smith (1969: 416–419). In this context M. G. Smith cites, among others: Radcliffe-Brown (1940); van Lier (1950); Sjoberg (1952); Nash (1957); Speckman (1963); and Hoetink (1967). Also see M. G. Smith (1960, 1965); Despres (1967, 1968); and the work edited by Kuper and Smith (1969).

3. M. G. Smith (1969: 106–111) discusses ethnicity in reference to "mobile" societies, a category that includes collectors, pastoralists, and some agriculturalists. He suggests that pluralism may not be significantly evident in societies that approximate a pure form of band organization. However, his definition of ethnicity, giving emphasis to exclusive units of social and biological reproduction, is much more restrictive than Barth's. If the more general definition is employed, then clearly relationships between territorial bands often assume elements of an ethnic character. See, for example, L. Marshall (1960, 1965) on the Bushmen. To my knowledge, ethnicity is not often discussed in reference to band populations. However, as Barth has noted, most of the research done by anthropologists rests upon the assumption that there are relatively discrete differences between cultures and that these differences correspond to the organization of groups and societies. Indeed, how these ethnic units might be classified to facilitate their comparative study is the whole point at issue in an article by Narroll (1964).

4. I interpret the development of a more general theory to be the thrust of Barth's recent discussion of ethnic groups and boundaries. A more general theory is also the objective of Kuper and Smith's (1969) comparative effort in respect to pluralism in Africa. And more recently, to develop a more general framework than is thought to be suggested

by such notions as the "plural society," Cohen and Middleton (1970) have suggested that these phenomena be subsumed under the study of "incorporation processes."

5. See, for example, Braithwaite (1960: 816–831); R. T. Smith, (1962: 98–143; 1970: 43–76); Lewis (1968: 35–46); and Cross (1968: 381–397). Although some of these works do not treat census categories as such, they do treat the difficulties associated with any effort to categorically differentiate populations in reference to institutional differences or the distribution of racial diacritica.

6. The allocation of newly developed agricultural lands, particularly to East Indian rice farmers and retrenched East Indian sugar workers, occurred primarily under the Jagan government between 1957 and 1963. In many instances these land development schemes incorporated Crown lands occupied by Africans whose leases had lapsed.

7. The Demerara Bauxite Company is Guyana's largest producer of bauxite and alumina. Owned by Aluminium Ltd. of Canada (ALCAN), this company was nationalized in 1971. The politics of this take-over are extremely complicated but, in the end, the government of Guyana was forced to borrow substantial funds from the United States to maintain the company's inventory and it had to employ a South African marketing firm to gain access to the international bauxite market.

8. It is difficult to determine precisely how much the Guyanese actually derive from foreign-owned industries. In the case of bauxite, according to one generous estimate, Guyana realized over a fifty-year period 39 percent of the sale value of bauxite from the Demerara Bauxite Company in the form of taxes, duties, and wages. However, according to Guyana's Prime Minister, the amount quoted represents less than 3 percent of the total profits realized from Guyanese bauxite by Demba's parent firm, Aluminium Ltd. of Canada. The first percent was reported by Demba in the August 27, 1970, edition of the *Guyana Graphic*. The second percent was quoted in a speech by the Prime Minister, as reported in the February 25, 1971, edition of the *Guyana Graphic*. Because bauxite prices are fixed by the parent company according to its own calculations, the true value of the bauxite extracted by this firm may never be known.

9. The organization and political activities of many of these associations have been described elsewhere (Despres 1967: 121–176, 221–267).

10. The anxiety which ASCRIA has generated among East Indians is such that even the notable East Indian historian Dwarka Nath (1970: 209–214) felt compelled to address the problem in a postscript to his revised history of the East Indian population in Guyana. Nath considers the relationship between Indians and Africans in Trinidad much less explosive and much less infused with racialism than is the case in Guyana.

11. One example of this is the constitutional provision for an electoral system based on proportionate representation. This provision was prescribed by the British in Guyana's independence constitution and it has been maintained by subsequent Guyanese governments. Although proportionality is calculated on the basis of votes achieved by political parties and not on the basis of ethnicity, it was the ethnic organization of political parties which prompted the adoption of this electoral system in the first place. Proportionate representation tends to secure a competitive position for the African population which comprises a large minority vis-à-vis the East Indian population.

12. For a discussion of these conceptual problems, see M. G. Smith's most recent statement (1969: 415–458).

13. It should be noted that M. G. Smith (1969: 427–430) does not equate social and cultural pluralism with ethnic or racial differences, nor does he consider such differences

as sufficient or requisite features of social orders based on sectional disjunctions and in-equalities.

14. The literature on human and cultural equality is too extensive to relate. However, the views expressed here have been particularly informed by the following: Harris (1964); Alland (1967); Vayda and Rappaport (1968); Geertz (1968); Bennett (1965, 1969); and Vayda (1969).

References

Alland, Alexander, Jr.
    1967   Evolution and human behavior. Garden City: The Natural History Press.

Banton, Michael
    1967   Race relations. New York: Basic Books.

Barth, Fredrik
    1969   Introduction, in Ethnic groups and boundaries. Edited by Fredrik Barth,
            9–38. Boston: Little, Brown.

Bennett, John W.
    1965   Ecology in anthropological and ethnological sciences: man-culture-habitat
            relationship, in Proceedings of the Eighth International Congress of An-
            thropological and Ethnological Sciences, 237–241.
    1969   Northern plainsmen, adaptive strategy and agrarian life. Chicago: Aldine.

Braithwaite, Lloyd
    1960   Social stratification and cultural pluralism, in Social and cultural plural-
            ism in the Caribbean. Edited by Vera Rubin, 816–831. Annals of the New
            York Academy of Sciences 83.

British Guiana Commission of Inquiry
    1965   Racial problems in the public service. Report of the British Guiana Com-
            mission of Inquiry. Geneva: International Commission of Jurists.

Burnham, Forbes
    1970   A destiny to mould. Trinidad and Jamaica: Longman Caribbean.

Cohen, Ronald, John Middleton
    1970   Introduction, in From tribe to nation in Africa: Studies in corporation
            processes. Edited by Ronald Cohen and John Middleton, 1–34. Scranton:
            Chandler.

Cross, Malcolm
    1968   Cultural pluralism and sociological theory: A critique and re-evaluation.
            Social and Economic Studies 18:381–397.

David, Wilfred
    1969   The economic development of Guyana 1953–1964. London: Clarendon
            Press.

Despres, Leo A.
    1967   Cultural pluralism and nationalist politics in British Guiana. Chicago:
            Rand-McNally.

1968   Anthropological theory, cultural pluralism, and the study of complex socie-
        ties. Current Anthropology, 9:3–26.
1969   Differential adaptations and micro-cultural evolution in Guyana. South-
        western Journal of Anthropology 25:14–44.
i.p.   Ethnicity and ethnic group relations in Guyana, in Proceedings of the
        American Ethnological Society, 1973.

Furnivall, J. S.
1939   Netherlands India: A study of plural economy. Cambridge: Cambridge
        University Press.
1942   The political economy of the tropical Far East. Journal of the Royal Cen-
        tral Asiatic Society 29:195–210.
1948   Colonial policy and practice: A comparative study of Burma and Nether-
        lands India. London: Cambridge University Press.

Geertz, Clifford
1968   Agricultural involution: The processes of ecological change in Indonesia.
        Berkeley and Los Angeles: University of California Press.

Guyana Graphic
1970   Article appearing in the Guyana Graphic, August 27.
1971   Article appearing in the Guyana Graphic, February 25.

Harris, Marvin
1964   Patterns of race in the Americas. New York: Walker.

Hoetink, H.
1967   The two variants in Caribbean race relations: A contribution to the sociol-
        ogy of segmented societies. London: Oxford University Press.

Kuper, Leo, M. G. Smith, editors
1969   Pluralism in Africa. Berkeley and Los Angeles: University of California
        Press.

Lewis, Gordon K.
1968   The growth of the modern West Indies. London: MacGibbon and Kee.

Lowenthal, David
1972   West Indian societies. New York: Oxford University Press.

Marshall, A. H.
1955   Report on local government in British Guiana. Georgetown: Argosy.

Marshall, Lorna
1960   !Kung Bushman bands. Africa 30:325–355.
1965   The !Kung Bushmen of the Kalahari Desert, in Peoples of Africa. Edited
        by James L. Gibbs, Jr., 241–278. New York: Holt, Rinehart and Winston.

Ministry of Labour and Social Security
1965   Human resources in Guiana, volume two: Manpower requirements and
        the labour force. Georgetown, Guiana: Ministry of Labour and Social Se-
        curity.

Narroll, R.
1964   On ethnic unit classification. Current Anthropology 5:283–312.

Nash, M.
   1957   The multiple society in economic development: Mexico and Guatemala.
          American Anthropologist 59:825–838.

Nath, Dwarka
   1970   A historic of Indians in Guyana. London: published by the author.

Radcliffe-Brown, A. R.
   1940   On social structure, reprinted in Structure and function in primitive soci-
          ety, by A. R. Radcliffe-Brown, 184–204. London: Cohen and West.

Schermerhorn, Richard A.
   1970   Comparative ethnic relations: A framework for theory and research. New
          York: Random House.

Shibutani, Tamotsu, Kian M. Kwan
   1965   Ethnic stratification. New York: Macmillan.

Sjoberg, Gideon
   1952   Folk and feudal societies. American Journal of Sociology 58:231–239.

Smith, M. G.
   1957   Ethnic and cultural pluralism in the British Caribbean, in Ethnic and cul-
          tural pluralism in intertropical countries, 439–447. Brussels: INCIDI.
   1960   Social and cultural pluralism, in Social and cultural pluralism in the
          Caribbean. Edited by Vera Rubin, 763–777. Annals of the New York Acad-
          emy of Sciences 83.
   1965   The plural society in the British West Indies. Berkeley and Los Angeles:
          University of California Press.
   1969   Some developments in the analytic framework of pluralism, in Pluralism
          in Africa. Edited by Leo Kuper and M. G. Smith, 415–458. Berkeley and
          Los Angeles: University of California Press.

Smith, Raymond T.
   1962   British Guiana. London: Oxford University Press.
   1970   Social stratification in the Caribbean, in Essays in comparative social
          stratification. Edited by Leonard Poltnicov and Arthur Tuden 43–76. Pitts-
          burgh: University of Pittsburgh Press.

Speckman, J. D.
   1963   The Indian group in the segmented society of Surinam. Caribbean Studies
          3: 3–17.

van den Berghe, Pierre L.
   1967   Race and racism: a comparative perspective. New York: John Wiley and Sons.
   1970   Race and ethnicity. New York: Basic Books.

van Lier, R. A. J.
   1950   The development and nature of society in the West Indies. Amsterdam:
          Royal Institute for the Indies.

Vayda, Andrew P. (editor)
   1969   Environment and cultural behavior, ecological studies in cultural anthro-
          pology. Garden City: The Natural History Press.

Vayda, Andrew P., Roy A. Rappaport
    1968   Ecology, cultural and non-cultural, in Introduction to cultural anthropol-
            ogy. Edited by James A. Clifton, 476–497. New York: Houghton Mifflin.

Young, Allan
    1958   The approaches to local self-government in British Guiana. London: Long-
            mans.

Zubaida, Sam (editor)
    1970   Race and racialism. London: Tavistock.

5. THE CULTURAL CONTINUUM

A Theory of Intersystems

Lee Drummond

Introduction

The principal task of this article is to demonstrate the relevance of work in creole linguistics for current anthropological problems concerning ethnicity and the culture of polyethnic societies. Linguistic and ethnographic material on Guyana suggests that such societies pose theoretical problems which can be resolved only by a thorough reworking of the concept of culture. The key idea here is the *intersystem*, or *continuum*, a theoretical formulation of creole linguistics[1] applied specifically to Guyanese Creole in Derek Bickerton's *Dynamics of a Creole system* (1975).

Bickerton argues that Chomskyan transformational linguistics views languages as discrete systems which embody discrete sets of rules, whereas the creole languages of Guyana and other postcolonial emigrant societies cannot be analyzed as such. Instead he proposes that their combined or intersystemic features be accorded first priority in constructing a theory of language, and not be dismissed as evidence of marginal, non-natural linguistic status. Creole linguistics thus provides a metaphor of culture that contrasts sharply with the metaphor of cultural structure often evoked by anthropologists striving to translate structural linguistics into anthropological discourse. Unlike the structural metaphor, the creole metaphor of culture places primary emphasis on internal variation and diachrony or change within the cultural system. The cultural intersystem contains no uniform rules or invariant properties, but derives its systemacity from a set of transformations which cover the variability of the data. Speakers of creole languages and learners of second languages routinely generate utterances according to the transformational rules of a linguistic continuum. I argue that members of a creole society similarly operate with understandings and expectations concerning fundamental *differences* that set apart persons in their society, and that those differences comprise a cultural continuum. In the emigrant society of Guyana differences are most clearly articulated in terms of racial or ethnic cate-

Originally published in *Man* 15:2 (1980), pp. 352–74. Copyright © by The Royal Anthropological Institute. Reprinted by permission of The Royal Anthropological Institute.

gories, so that the Guyanese cultural continuum is primarily organized around variable concepts of ethnic identity. Internal variation and change in the creole continuum are tied to the symbolic processes of ethnicity.

Intersystem and Ethnicity

Perhaps the most convincing argument for applying Bickerton's linguistic analysis to cultural theory is its fit with situations prevailing in many parts of the world today. His elevation of the little-esteemed process of second language learning to the status of an intersystemic phenomenon critical to linguistic theory forces the anthropologist to reflect on the prominence of intersystems in his own research. Four centuries of massive global migration, voluntary and involuntary, and the recent impetus to modernize and urbanize have transformed most societies. In the Americas especially, European, African, Amerindian, and Asian languages and cultures were initially brought together under an economic system — slavery or indentured labour—that scarcely favoured either the preservation of indigenous lifeways or the smooth merging of differences into a unified and harmonious whole. The resulting combination, as I have argued elsewhere (1978), is neither a "plural society" as that concept has been advanced to describe the Caribbean (M. G. Smith 1965; Despres 1967) nor an integrated totality in the Parsonian sense (Parsons 1951). It is instead an intersystem, or cultural continuum. Variation produced by incorporation of diverse groups in a strongly class-structured society is very much in evidence, taking the form of political divisiveness, economic privilege or privation, and contrasting ethnic stereotypes. Diversity and divisiveness are fundamental to the system. Differences can operate as representations because they take their significance from a pool of shared myth and experience. Individuals are cognizant of much or all the possible range of behavior and belief in the continuum, although need not behave or act as the other does, just as speakers of a creole language can generally understand utterances at either extreme of the continuum but rarely control both extremes in their own speech. The reality of the system is, therefore, the set of bridges or transformations required to get from one end to the other. Hence the emphasis on the notion of intersystem.

Since the continuum model focuses on intra-societal differences, it can handle the intriguing and difficult phenomenon of ethnicity. The creation of emigrant societies and their subsequent departure from the colonial world have paved the way for a contemporary situation in which notions of ethnic identity are widely and intensely held. Ethnicity is a major factor in modern world politics, and has recently attracted much attention from anthropologists and other social scientists on both sides of the Atlantic.[2] The internal heterogeneity characteristic of creole languages is tied to the diverse backgrounds of members of a creole society, and so it is not surprising that creole culture should encompass a comparable heterogeneity. The mode of expressing that heterogeneity assumes multiple forms, but

it is very often part of a generalized belief system based on the principle of ethnic difference: the notion that the social setting is populated by distinct kinds of
people, who are what they are as a consequence of inborn qualities or deeply held
beliefs manifest in their everyday behavior and difficult or impossible to re-
nounce. A particular attribute, such as physical appearance, dress, speech, mode
of livelihood, or religion, has ethnic significance, or marking, only by virtue of
the system of meanings in which it is embedded. While being Catholic in Mont-
real is not a critical attribute of identity, it is in Londonderry. On the other hand,
it does not matter much in Londonderry if one cannot speak French.

It is a curious fact that just as social scientists in the 1950s and early 1960s
were preparing for a post-colonial world dominated by the interlocking forces of
nationalism and modernization, the world began to fragment into ethnic sodali-
ties.

> But primordial groups have frequently conflicted with the emergent nationality
> of new states—or even the existing nationality of old states . . . —for the domina-
> tion of individuals' highest loyalty and provide alternative ways of organizing and
> identifying. Sometimes they are smaller in scale than the state itself and promote
> separatist tendencies, sometimes they are larger and promote a sense of political
> dismemberment and a desire for unification on a larger scale based on primordial
> ties such as the cases of pan-Arabism, greater Somalism, or pan-Africanism.
> Yet the relationships between nationality and ethnicity are complex. There is
> the rare instance where the boundaries of the state are nearly coterminous with
> the boundaries defined by ethnicity or race, although the absolutely perfect fit may
> exist nowhere even among the old states. More characteristically, ethnicity and
> race, even while competing with the emergent nation, have sometimes become
> redefined on a larger scale than before as a result of nation-building activities.
> (Bell & Freeman 1974: 288)

Social thought in the immediate post-colonial period set out to bring new nations into a framework of analysis already in place. And since that framework was
constructed around what Bickerton would call "static system" models[3]—unified,
bounded cultures of putatively monolectal nation-states—it was a natural assumption that newly independent members of the world community would pursue their own nationhood without delay. Then began an unending series of racial
incidents, civil war, and religious discord in the Third World. The rise of ethnic
consciousness signified to some that these new political entities, largely put together at conference tables and traded repeatedly during European wars, were
not true societies, but an unstable approximation, a congeries of peoples and customs lacking the coherence and integration displayed by the real thing.

I believe something like this reaction is at the root of plural society theories,
which rest on the premiss that certain post-colonial social systems are special
cases in that they lack a kind of social mortar which non-plural systems possess.
Yet, such theories cannot adequately deal with the plural origins of societies that

are supposed to exemplify cohesion and stability. Migration proceeded on a different scale from the seventeenth century onwards, but it did not begin then; contemporary Western societies—and languages—were fabricated by creole processes like those Bickerton describes for Guyana. Plural society theories mostly predated the beginnings of widespread urban racial strife in the United States and clearly did not anticipate the recent popular appeal of ethnic ties. Watts, "Chicano Power," *Roots* (Haley 1976) and numerous other events and cultural productions serve to underscore Bickerton's persuasively simple argument that the most well-defended typologies fail to conceal an underlying uniformity. For him uniformity is manifested by the human faculty of language (1975: 179–80); for me it is the universal cultural formulation of systems of essential similarity and difference that we call kinship and ethnicity (Drummond 1977b: 849–50).

The Guyanese Cultural Continuum

If we take creole linguistics as anthropological metaphor, how are its concepts, notably those of internal variation and change, to be applied in substantive analyses of cultural processes in a particular society? Bickerton's arguments are precise and rigorous because he confines his analysis to verb tense and aspect markers. The regularities he discovers in Guyanese speech are grammatical and often well beyond the ability of native speakers to articulate for themselves.[4] For the student of Guyanese culture, however, it is impossible to identify relationships among cultural categories that do not already contain local exegesis. The analysis of culture must proceed on the levels of semantics and discourse, and there the native speaker usually has definite ideas about the meaning and direction of his utterances. Thus while I shall claim that transformational relationships exist within the Guyanese cultural continuum, I will not pretend that these can be demonstrated with the rigor of grammatical regularities.

An initial clue to the Guyanese cultural continuum is provided by the series of surprises and unsettling incidents that the white English-speaking anthropologist experiences on beginning fieldwork in Guyana. The time-honored technique of presenting oneself as an outsider interested in learning the local language and acquiring information about the culture of one's hosts simply does not work. For, as a former British colony, the language of the nation is English, and the stereotype of "English" customs and behavior built up during a century and a half of colonial rule is still much in evidence. The ethnographer thus finds himself in the curious and often perplexing situation of being taken as an adept of the culture he has come to study. His English speech conforms to the emulated standard or acrolect, even if it is unintelligible (the child of one of my informants was once heard to remark, "Mr Drummond talk so good you kyan [can't] understand he"). And as a "whiteman" the ethnographer finds himself pegged into a complex set of ethnic categories whose terms sound familiar as individual items (although there are numerous exceptions: "buck," "bacra," "dugler," "boviander"), but which possess unexpected semantic contents. During the first months the embarrassing situation occurs again and again of trying to have a conversation with someone whose native language is English and failing miserably at it. And much worse than the ethnographer's frustration is the informant's sense of status degradation, for within the terms of the colonial value system an inability to communicate does not reflect the foreigner's ignorance of the local tongue but the native speaker's dependence on speech habits he has learned to regard as "broken" language.[5]

The ethnographer's first experiences lead him to postulate highly diverse speech communities, one consisting of government officials, educators and radio commentators, the other of ordinary "men in the street." This observation itself may alert him to internal variation in the system, but the subtlety of variation becomes apparent only later, when he realizes that those same officials, educators and commentators are fully capable of speaking with the fluent Creole of the "men in the street," who themselves can often dress up their speech if they wish.[6]

Linguistic variation within the Guyanese continuum is accompanied by cultural variation in the form of ethnic stereotypes that divide the already small population (about 800,000) into discrete but interlinked categories. "Coolie" (East Indian), "black" (Negro), "buck" (Amerindian)[7], "potugee" (Portuguese not equivalent to "white" in the Guyanese system), "chinee" (Chinese) and "white" or "English" are primary terms for identifying and relating to people in the course of daily life. The differences are real, but they are continuously subject to transformation. Ethnic categories can be understood by direct analogy to the situation of the creole language learner. Just as one can speak English to another who believes he is responding in English and yet find communication severely impeded, so one can be English (in the sense of origin, customs, tastes, etc.) and find oneself on unfamiliar ground with another who considers himself to be English or to be doing the things that English people do. To paraphrase Bickerton, the dilemma that the foreigner faces in learning creole culture is different only in degree from dilemmas handled daily by persons native to the culture.

Changes in Guyanese social structure have increased, not decreased, internal variation in the former colony. The ethnic categories, "English" (or "whiteman") and "African" (or "blackman") are particularly good examples. R. T. Smith (1962) has described how Guyanese society was integrated under the political authority and cultural hegemony of the English. Things "English" were intrinsically good and the goal of social aspirations for over a century. Then in the postwar years an independence movement led by an East Indian, Dr. Cheddi Jagan, drew attention to the many contradictions involved in trying to become what was in fact one's own colonial master. Before the independence movement could attain its goal, however, a complex chain of events resulted in Jagan's former lieutenant, Forbes Burnham, an Afro-Guyanese barrister, defeating Jagan in the 1964 elections (Despres 1967). Jagan and Burnham's parties were by then racially divided, so that the election issued in what was in effect a black minority government. During his sixteen years in office, Prime Minister Burnham has created a highly centralized State and proclaimed that Guyana has undergone a "socialist revolution." Yet there was no political revolution; only an election in which western powers were implicated and subsequent elections that have brought widespread accusations of unfairness. The most cathartic events of recent times have been the race riots of 1963–4 and Jonestown, scarcely inspirations to a new cultural identity. But the government, represented in the highest places by Afro-Guyanese, does control the economy and is present in every aspect of daily life. If one needs a job or a political favor, it is usually an Afro-Guyanese who has the power to grant it. The "revolution" is socially and culturally ambiguous. While the English have departed and "English" values are everywhere denounced, the nationalist government has not been seen to have had conspicuous success in finding convincing images with which to construct a Guyanese identity. The ethnic categories, "whiteman" and "blackman," are consequently infused with a great deal of ambivalence: each is at once powerful and good *and* powerless and evil. Given the high degree of polarization in the conceptual system of Guyanese ethnicity, it is to be expected that people will assign a wide range of meaning to a single ethnic category.

Because Amerindians, Europeans, Africans, East Indians, Chinese and others entered British Guianese society at different times and on different stratification levels, it is not surprising that they assimilated English culture at different rates and in different ways. Again, the language learning analogy works nicely: a small proportion of the population became well-versed in English customs and manners, another small proportion acquired the barest rudiments of them, and the majority were spread out between the two extremes. Despite great differences in the assimilation of English ways, most Guyanese were prepared to assert at some point that they were behaving just as the English did.[8] The semantic content of the ethnic category "English" or "white" is thus both rich and internally inconsistent. "English" ways are sometimes opposed to "creole" or "African" customs, sometimes to "coolie" customs, sometimes to "buck" customs, and so on. Classification of an actual slice of behavior depends greatly on who is doing the classifying and where the behavior is taking place. The very practice that is regarded as "coolie" or "creole" in Georgetown may be held up as a fine example of "English" behavior in the countryside or bush.

Weddings provide a good illustration of the internal variation and contradiction characteristic of Guyanese ethnic categories, for they are occasions when persons of some genealogical, and often ethnic, difference participate in a single rite. Historically the situation was brutally simple. Since marriage among slaves would interfere with the slaveowner's traffic in human property, anything approaching formal wedlock was forbidden to most of Guyana's pre-emancipation population. Later, when freed blacks or indentured East Indians married, the colonists described their ceremonies with pejorative terms such as "bush wedding" or "bamboo wedding." With the spread of Christianity among late pre- and post-emancipation blacks, however, essential features of the "English" wedding could not be denied non-English Guyanese.

The stereotype of a proper, English wedding took root early in Guyanese co-lonial history and continues to be an important aspect of the cultural scene. It is possible to identify several elements of the "English" wedding in Guyana. These include "standing up in church," the bride's white dress and veil, and a reception at which "sticking the cake" and "toasting" occur. The first two elements are con-siderably more than the second two, since a Christian service conforms approxi-mately to an international format and the bride's attire to available photographs of metropolitan fashion. "Sticking the cake" and "toasting" occur at a social gath-ering following the ceremony, and there is much latitude in the arrangements of these events. Where the gathering is held, what kind of cake is provided, what refreshments are used for the toasts, the presence or absence of music and danc-ing, and even who dances with whom (boys with girls or boys with boys) are all significant indicators to the Guyanese host or guest of the kind of occasion he is attending.

One of several paradoxes contained in the subject of Guyanese weddings is that performances specifically called "English" weddings are usually staged by Afro-Guyanese descendants of persons forbidden by law to participate in such ceremonies. Although "English" customs continue to figure in contemporary speech and behavior, the exodus of whites from the country during the past thir-teen years has diminished the resident population of that group to a minute frac-tion of the total, perhaps 2,000 at most. Long before the English departed physi-cally, however, "English" weddings stopped being ceremonies with participants from England and, with the additions I have mentioned, became equated with Christian services. And since Africans were first and most thoroughly Christian-ized, it was they who assumed the mantle of "English" culture at the altar. This situation altered the meaning of the wedding ceremony. As R. T. Smith's (1956) detailed study of Afro-Guyanese family structure demonstrates, marriage in the sense of church vows was regarded more as a celebrated culmination of a long period of conjugal residence than as a sanction to take up that status. A couple with several children and perhaps grandchildren would have a church wedding to enhance their position in the community, clarify inheritance rights of their offspring, entertain their friends, and, often, resolve an inner conflict with their growing sense of religious obligation. The "English" wedding was both socially prestigious and religiously correct, so that its format, modified to fit local exi-gency, was taken up by Christianized blacks and has since become an important index in the culture of ethnicity in Guyana.

Variation in this kind of intersystem is pronounced. The simple fact that one "stands up in church" to be married is itself a claim to prestige in a society that regards consensual cohabitation as a usual arrangement ("dey live home" being a common way of acknowledging such a relationship). And because some ele-ments of the ritual format—principally those associated with the reception—are less constrained, there is ample room for invidious comparison. Each wedding is like a weather balloon which a family launches into the turbulent Guyanese cultural atmosphere, and it is promptly buffeted by the strong cross-currents of prevailing ethnic stereotypes.

For if a wedding is not "English," then it is almost invariably "coolie," that is, a ceremony and associated social gathering that signal membership in the numerically dominant Hindu and Muslim communities. The "coolie" wedding takes place at the bride's home, not in a church, and involves either Hindu rites and dress or the Muslim custom of paying for the bride with a *nika*. Following the ceremony, a meal of curry, rice, dhal and roti is served to everyone present, and generally there is enough remaining to share to neighbors. If the "coolie" features of the event are sharply drawn, then the meal is eaten with the fingers from a banana leaf rather than a plate.

East Indian indentured laborers were brought to British Guiana after the Christianizing process had begun among Africans, so that they entered a society in which both the dominant minority and the subordinate majority shared a set of religious values that excluded the "pagan" beliefs of Hinduism and Islam. East Indians were physically and socially confined to plantations as a condition of their servitude and were culturally isolated from both English and African as a consequence of their language and religion. The churches held the colony in their grip throughout the colonial period, and it was only gradually that an independent Guyana was able to wrest control of the school system from ecclesiastical hands. To be East Indian or "coolie" was therefore a great liability.

Although the English as a group have disappeared from the country, Christianity has not; indeed, public expression of religious views is more common in Guyana and throughout the West Indies than in Europe or North America.[9] Persons of African descent have filled the void left by the departing colonists and become culturally "English," thereby retaining Christianity in an important social role and reinforcing the divisiveness between believer and non-believer. Because African and East Indian in Guyana have been traditional opponents from the beginning, the "English" *v.* "coolie" distinction figures in the complex of politics, economy and "race" that define the system.

If Guyanese society were divided into Christian blacks and Hindu or Muslim East Indians, a case could perhaps be made for some type of pluralist interpretation. The actual cultural processes are, however, not that straightforward, and to describe them as the effect of conflict between discrete groups with discrete traditions merely repeats the folk wisdom of ethnic stereotypes without analyzing the connecting themes, or transformations, that make Guyanese culture a "dynamic system," in Bickerton's phrase.[10]

There is first of all the peculiar inversion of identity whereby blacks become "English." This phenomenon, since it issues from a history of oppression and false consciousness, is shot through with contradiction and ambivalence: the contemporary nationalist Guyanese is faced with the dilemma of embracing a religion that was an integral part of his historical subordination or renouncing it in favor of fabricated and uncompelling appeals to national unity couched in a non-Guyanese idiom. There is a second cultural process which involves the East Indian community in a similar transformation of identity. Recognizing that plantation agriculture was a dead end, East Indian migrants endeavored to educate their children and secure them in professional occupations. Yet because the schools and professional community were dominated by colonial values, upwardly mobile families found themselves stigmatized as "coolie" in a Christian milieu. Inevitably many East Indians accepted Christianity, adopted English names, and set out in pursuit of a lifestyle based on a perceived modernity. The boundary separating "coolie" and "English" established at the beginning of the indenture system in 1838 has dissolved and stretched until it is currently not a line but a continuum. Thus while the "coolieman" and the "blackman" possess distinct cultural images, those images overlap in the important areas of religious and occupational status. Indeed, it might be said that "coolieman" is now the most "English" figure in the Guyanese continuum, for East Indians have been steadily buying up Georgetown businesses put on the market by Portuguese and English businessmen opting out of Prime Minister Burnham's Cooperative Republic.[11]

Yet the diversity of attributes assigned the "coolieman" ranges from contemptuous remarks about his country bumpkin ways to envious references to his wealth and social position. This internal variation is precisely what vitiates pluralist interpretations of Guyanese ethnic categories and requires some type of creole continuum hypothesis. The need for such an approach mounts when one considers that the category, "coolie," is further differentiated internally by the presence of Hindu and Muslim religious communities. Although both East Indians and Africans experienced similarly dehumanizing conditions on the plantations, the former have survived indenture with their basic religious institutions in place. Not that they are intact or unchanged by migration and plantation work, but internal rearrangements of the code are still read as cultural constructs of "Hindu" or "Muslim," however heterodox Guyanese practices might seem to, say, a Madras Brahim or a Karachi mujtahid. The approximately 410,000 Indo-Guyanese do not preserve all the beliefs and practices of their two world religious traditions, but instead emphasize different ones at different times to communicate their understanding of what is at issue in particular events. It is the very corruption or heterodoxy of the Hindu and Islamic traditions that unites Indo-Guyanese in a system of shared differences. Guyanese Hindus and Muslims recognize their doctrinal differences, but they also realize their tenuous relationship to world religious communities. The centripetal force of the Guyanese intersystem overcomes the centrifugal force represented by ties with world religious communities.

The intersystem created in cultural relations between Hindu and Muslim identities is distinct from that created when "coolie" and "black" identities are involved. The content of ethnic stereotypes varies from case to case, which results in the society or culture itself being continuously redefined. For this reason Guyanese society or culture cannot be considered as a fixed system. Instead, it is a set of transformations which encompasses significant variation and thus defines the continuum.

The Continuum in Practice

Weddings again illustrate the kind of categorial interaction through which persons define themselves and provide contexts for the definition of their offspring. Material from two occasions reveals some of the complex interplay of identities responsible for the dynamics of the system. The first occasion involves an East Indian Muslim woman and an East Indian man whose parents reared him as a Christian, although they themselves had a Hindu background. The second is a Christian wedding in which the bride was mixed Amerindian–East Indian and the groom an East Indian Hindu.

The first wedding was performed in a village about five miles from Georgetown on the East Coast of the Demerara River. I had been invited by a co-worker of the bride's father, a Christian living in Georgetown who was herself invited. As we drove out to the "wedding house" with other guests, there was some conversation about whether the ceremony was to be "coolie" or "English." This kind of ethnic-situating speech occurs routinely. My companion said that while Muslim practices would be observed she felt much of the afternoon would follow "English" custom. For one thing, she had been asked to bake the "English" wedding cake—a white, tiered affair topped by a figurine of a bridal couple. And at the office she had taken part in conversations about the bride's white wedding gown and the gowns of sisters who were to act as attendants.

The wedding house was already crowded when we arrived. A few girls in their recently acquired gowns were the only other sign that a ceremony was under way. We waited. The groom arrived about an hour late and had obviously been drinking, not the most auspicious way to begin a Muslim service. He was dressed in a Western style suit and tie and wore sunglasses. Even for a wedding a suit and tie are rather unusual in Guyana today, for the Government has successfully replaced that vestige of colonialism with the "shirt jac." The groom and numerous guests, including myself, were invited upstairs, where the ceremony was to be held. Everyone wearing shoes removed them at the foot of the stairs. The groom took off his shoes, but left on his socks. The upstairs room was cleared of all furniture except an ornamental corner cupboard holding dishes and an assortment of calendar pictures. The floor had been covered with white sheet cloth. Officiants were the bride's father, two witnesses, and an elderly *maji*, all dressed in black pants, a flowing white long-sleeved tunic that extended to the thigh, and a black skull cap.

As guests arranged themselves on the floor, the *maji* and the groom sat together on a sheet near the center of one wall. The *maji* asked several rhetorical questions about the boy's intentions, and interspersed his Creole English with a few phrases from an Arabic prayer book which he carried. It was resolved that the groom would pay a *nika* of $100 (£16). The bride's father and his two witnesses then went into an adjoining room where the bride was making her preparations and ascertained that the *nika* was sufficient. A guest seated beside me explained at this point that the purpose of the *nika* was to provide the bride with a source of independence after the marriage, thus rejecting the idea that the man was "buying" the woman. When the three men returned the bride's father informed the *maji* that the arrangement was satisfactory. The *maji* then proceeded to ask the groom more questions—whether he knew the meaning of marriage, that it was sanctioned by Allah, and so on—and to intone an Arabic chant. The groom responded in what can charitably be described as a lighthearted manner, interrupting more than once to ask that he be allowed to "pay de money and leh de wedding done." The chant and a prayer ended the ceremony.

The women present filtered downstairs as the bride's brothers started to pass around plates for a meal of beef curry, dhal, roti and Pepsi Cola. The men upstairs were served first and ate with the fingers sitting on the floor. Downstairs the women sat at table and used cutlery. During the meal the bride remained in the room where she had been from the start. As guests finished eating and went downstairs others took their place. After everyone had eaten, a period of relaxed conversation and simply killing time lasted about an hour.

During that period the bride evidently made her final preparations. Downstairs preparations were also under way, the first strictly ritual activity that had occurred there all afternoon. A wicker couch where guests had sat earlier was covered with bridal linen—a white quilt and two large pillows embroidered in pink, "Love" and "Best Wishes." This was to be the seat of honor during the "toasting." Finally the bride descended, outfitted in white floor-length gown and veil, followed by her attendants. She and the groom sat in the prepared spot and immediately became the focus of a Guyanese "toasting" session, although without toasts since it was, after all, a Muslim house. A plate was placed on a low table before the couple, and when individuals came forward to offer their best wishes they deposited a five- or ten-dollar bill. It was a subdued affair: no one held forth long or theatrically. The "toasting" lasted fifteen or twenty minutes and when it was finished the bride and groom were ready to go. They bundled the money together with the bride's trousseau waiting in a suitcase by the door and said their farewells as they strolled out to a waiting car

The performance was an intriguing piece of syncretism, but in its wider context reveals even more of the cultural intersystem. For the bridal couple were on their way to a reception at the groom's parents, Christian-convert East Indians absent from the Muslim rite. It seemed that this event was to be the destination of the wedding cake provided by my friend; "sticking the cake" would be done in Christian territory. Whether a small Christian service was also planned I do not know. I found it significant, though, that the bride was absent from her "wedding" (according to conventional Muslim practice) yet donned a wedding gown to leave home—a nice opposition between the "English" Guyanese wedding and the "English" English ceremony. It appeared that a wedding party also waited at the groom's home; drinking, dancing and music would take place after all.

In this kind of split ceremony, the groom's role is an interesting example of the Guyanese continuum. Conjugal relations across racial and religious lines are a fairly common occurrence, but the Muslim community attempts to hold fast to the principle of marriage within the faith. Consequently, before the bride's father would consent to a marriage, the prospective groom had to be converted to Islam. This involved a period of religious instruction, administered by persons who, like the *maji* in the ceremony just described, were themselves native speakers of Creole English and familiar only with a greatly reduced "church Arabic." At the end of that period the prospective groom took a Muslim name. The degree to which social identity is transformed by this name change obviously varies from individual to individual, but its consequences cannot be denied: the names of children and their relationship to grandparents, for example. The concessions demanded of the young man were, in effect, redeemed by his rather churlish behavior—being late, wearing a suit and sunglasses, cracking jokes. These affirmations of modernity, together with the fact that he had planned a more festive reception elsewhere, point to the tension and ambivalence underlying the afternoon's events. There was no clear division between Muslim and non-Muslim or English and non-English elements of the ritual, nor was it simply a matter of some of each being lumped together in a mechanical fashion.

It is rather that the sequence of events drifted back and forth between stereotyped poles of "Muslim" *v.* "English." And the definition of particular events in those streams depended largely on who was doing the defining. Certainly the *maji* would give a different interpretation of the wedding gown and the "toasting" than would the bride or one of the Georgetown Christian guests. Most importantly, the peculiar syncretism of the ritual cannot be seen as in any way anomalous: far from being an exception, it is distinctively Guyanese. While outside observers from Muslim or Christian countries would hesitate to identify the East Coast Demerara wedding as an example of their religious tradition, almost any Guyanese would be at home in the concatenation of images and ideas.

Other intersystemic features of Guyanese culture are illustrated by the second case, a wedding and attendant social drama in the interior. The Pomeroon River in northwestern Guyana is populated by representatives of all the coastal ethnic groups, as well as Arawak and Carib Amerindians. The presence of Amerindians, commonly if derogatorily known as "bucks," complicates an already complex coastal interethnic system. While economically and politically deprived in the Guyanese stratifaction system, their physical appearance and long association with white colonial officers, missionaries, and explorers endow Amerindians with several attributes of once-esteemed "English" culture. Individual Amerindians are often quick to emphasise this cultural affinity, identifying themselves with the "English" in opposition to "black people" and "coolie people" (see Drummond 1977a; 1977b). Paradoxically, the very aspects of behavior and ideology that Amerindians embrace as "English" are acquired from their intimate involvement with similarly isolated and impoverished non-whites of the interior—farmers, prospectors, rubber collectors. Thus in distinguishing themselves from blacks and East Indians living downriver, the Arawak in particular single out characteristics that most ally them with syncretic, non-white creole culture. Weddings are an especially apt example, since few indigenous Arawak practices attended the formation of a conjugal union. There was an open field here for the interacting cultural forces that have shaped the Guyanese system.

The Pomeroon area has a long tradition of "moving and mixing." Coastal people have immigrated to the river steadily since the early nineteenth century, settling among and marrying local Amerindians. These dual principles are nicely illustrated in the lives of the bride, her mother and grandmother. The bride's grandmother, an Arawak, was once involved with an East Indian man who lived a short distance downriver with his East Indian wife and children. She became pregnant by him and bore a daughter. This girl was thus what Guyanese would call an "outside child" of the East Indian man—the distinction between children born inside and outside marriage. Although she grew up in an Arawak household, she recognized her kinship ties to half-brothers and half-sisters who were members of an East Indian family. As a young woman, she also bore a daughter—the bride of the story—to an East Indian man. She later married a mixed man from outside Pomeroon, whom I will call "Williams" (a common name in the area), and her daughter spent the final years of her childhood in that context. The daughter, like her mother and grandmother, formed an attachment for a young East Indian that resulted in her bearing his child. The boy was from Pomeroon, a Hindu living not far downriver from the Williamses. Mrs. Williams insisted that the two "stand up in church" and be properly married, the church in question being a Catholic mission at the Arawak and East Indian settlement of Siriki. As Hindus the boy's parents were opposed to a Catholic service, but there was the fact of the child and the young people's continued interest in each other. They permitted their son to consent to a Christian wedding but refrained from attending themselves.

The service was accomplished with as much fanfare as possible. A large river launch brought the sizeable wedding party, while the bride, in full white dress and veil, and her attendants arrived at the mission in the sportiest speedboat on the upper river. The groom came dressed in a black suit, again unusual for Guyana. After the missionary priest had conducted the formal service, the wedding guests formed in a kind of processional at the riverside. The bride and groom walked through these parallel lines of well-wishers, boarded the speedboat, and were whisked downriver to a reception planned by Mrs. Williams.

Mrs. Williams was in a state of near-exhaustion when the first guests arrived.

Apparently there were few women living nearby on whom she could rely for assistance in the laborious task of feeding at least fifty persons. The meal was the first item on the afternoon's agenda. It was curry, rice and roti, served at table with cutlery in a series of sittings. Mrs. Williams was the chief server, and as she dashed about handing out plates of food she happened to deliver one with her left hand. For a few moments she was even more flustered than before, apologizing to the individual she had served with her left hand.

Following the meal the reception moved on to the "toasting" phase. The table was cleared for the final time and the bride and groom, still in wedding dress and suit, were seated at one end. A platter appeared at the other end, along with a decanter of white rum (not a bottle, which would have been usual in that area) and a number of shot glasses. In roughly the order that guests had taken their turn at the table, they came forward to extend their congratulations and often stayed on to give some advice, tell a humorous off-color story, or sing a song. The toaster then placed a money offering on the platter before him. Each person's toast was punctuated with a snap of rum around the table, so that the guest who stayed for a round of toasting left the table in a considerably altered state. Each departing toaster was replaced by another member of the party until everyone had spoken, drunk, and offered his gift.

Although I did not sense it at the time, the drink and merriment stirred some ill feelings among a section of the wedding party—Mrs. Williams's East Indian half-brothers. A minor social drama unfolded that expressed some of the complexities and difficulties of the situation. Mrs. Williams, linked with East Indian tradition by birth and experience, was intent on an "English" wedding for her daughter. Yet her daughter was marrying a Hindu and her own Hindu half-brothers were there at her invitation. The next phase was too much for one of the half-brothers: the wedding reception began to change into a "spree" common to Pomeroon social life. Social drinking, music, and mixed dancing were to follow. The half-brother began to quarrel. Even in the not-infrequent cases where Guyanese Hindu weddings are accompanied by male drinking, any public dancing is strictly male—usually a few drunken boys swaying to music on the open ground floor while the women and respectable men are upstairs. If women dance, it is with one another, secluded in a sleeping room of the house. But as the music started up at Mrs. Williams's that evening and couples began to pair off, an awful row broke out between her and the irate half-brother. He had said enough to touch a nerve and she shouted back both justification and insult, "Dis an English wedding! Dis na coolie ting!" At that the half-brother retreated into a sulk, and shortly afterwards he and his brothers found an excuse to leave the quickening festivities.

It did not become a real Amerindian spree at that point, however, for after a few dances the bridal couple were bundled into the waiting speedboat and set off for the groom's home. I was informed that things would be quieter there. At the Williamses' the reception, deprived of its last ceremonial emblems, became indistinguishable from any Pomeroon spree. Dancing went on until "the drinks finish," in this case late the next morning.

"Dis an English wedding! Dis na coolie ting!" captures the contradictory nature of ethnic stereotypes that fold back on themselves, collapsing and confusing the social patterns, religious beliefs, and ethnic identities of Guyana's heterogeneous population. "English" in the sense that the service was Christian (and performed by an English missionary), the entire event was strongly infused with "coolie" attributes—the life histories of the participants, the meal, the prohibition on serving with the left hand, and the ever-present counterbalance of the groom's Hinduism. But at the moment of crisis, when Mrs Williams stridently defended the "English" nature of her affair, the afternoon was at the point of reaching out for its greatest common denominator—the "spree" with all the "buck" associations that entails. Amerindian ways of party-giving have left their imprint on all the people who live on the upper river, and are in fact responsible for many of them being conceived and brought into this world. The curious thing is that ambivalence and a kind of false consciousness combine to deny any importance to Amerindian customs as such. They are honored, not in their absence, but after they have been redefined, reconstituted as "English." The point, of course, is that the dancing and drinking that followed the "toasting" at Mrs. Williams's was neither "buck" nor "English" (and it was surely not "coolie"); it was a creole synthesis which owes its vitality, paradoxically, to an insistence on defining behavior and belief according to persistent ethnic stereotypes. The mixed people of the Pomeroon insist on an ideology of pure types, which are constructed out of the only available material—processes of interethnic mixture.

Internal Variation and Change

The two weddings support my claim that Guyanese culture can best be understood as a creole continuum. In them, as in virtually every aspect of daily life, ethnic ascription is a spontaneous feature of interaction. People are on their way to a wedding: Is it going to be a "coolie" or "English" ceremony? You ask a friend about someone he has just mentioned: "Oh, he is that *fula* man (Muslim) who drives a hire car on the East Coast road." You are inquiring into the economic situation of Georgetown shopkeepers: "Well, you know dem Coolie people mus' gat money." Ethnic labelling carries both ostensive and evaluative meaning; it is employed simultaneously as a convenient means of sorting out social actors and assigning them qualities that help to explain what is happening, why someone is behaving in a certain way. An ethnographer of a Guyanese community is inevitably forced to pay close attention to the way his informants employ ethnic terms, regardless of the theoretical position he takes on the concept of ethnicity.

Guyanese ethnic categories form a system. While terms like "white man," "black man," and "chinee man" at first sight would appear intelligible to any English speaker, on closer inspection it proves impossible to separate them from the contextual meanings they have acquired in Guyanese society. The way the category "English" was handled at both weddings is a case in point. Why a "potugee" (Portuguese) is not "white," why someone the North American or European visitor assumes to be Afro-Guyanese turns out to be "buck" (Amerindian), and where intermediate categories such as "dugler" and "boviander" fit, are questions that cannot be answered without considering the mutual interaction of ethnic categories in Guyanese culture.

If one accepts the prevalence and systematic nature of ethnic categories, a possible next step would be to search for distinctive features of those categories. Such an analysis might proceed by discovering relationships that held across the category set (invariant properties), and would conclude by ordering those relationships in the most parsimonious fashion. There are serious problems with this procedure. Very few ethnographic studies have even attempted to construct a detailed picture of how persons in a polyethnic society communicate ideas about human distinctiveness, that is, how they actually assign ethnic identity and agree implicitly on its significance on particular occasions.[12] Although publications on ethnicity have mushroomed in recent years, most assume a narrow sociological perspective that views ethnic groups or interest groups as already established and designated by a set of labels. The research problem then becomes: How do members of group X act and feel with respect to members of group Y? I am suggesting that this approach disregards a prior question: How do persons define and identify X-ness and Y-ness? A methodology is therefore required to investigate ethnicity as a cultural system, in much the way that one treats the content and interrelationship of ideas in a religious belief system (Geertz 1966).

As the methodological problem yields to systematic research on the content and ascription of ethnic categories, a theoretical problem—to identify something like distinctive features within an ethnic category set—becomes even more acute. My investigations indicate that Guyanese indeed use a common set of ethnic terms, although they employ them in ways that are mutually inconsistent or contradictory. Ethnic categories quite simply possess a property that is characteristic of all symbols—they are ambiguous.[13] The crisis at Mrs. Williams's reception occurred because she and her half-brother viewed social dancing as a kind of conceptual boundary marker between notions of appropriateness tied to being "English" or being "coolie." Yet at the Muslim wedding people were quite prepared to see "English"/"coolie" contrasts in other events of the afternoon, and it was generally known that social dancing would be on the agenda at the groom's home.

With data like these in mind it is interesting to consider the plight of early attempts to write grammars for creole languages. The simplest approach was to separate speakers of the "standard" language from those of the "Creole" language and proceed to analyze the latter's speech. As Bickerton (1975) notes, however, when such a procedure is attempted the linguist soon finds himself with an assortment of perplexing material. Certain speakers identified as creole users will insert what appear to be standard language items, but which are used according to creole (or basilectal) rules. For example, *bin*, an anterior, punctual marker, as in *dem bin gat wan lil haus* ("they had a little house"), is replaced by *did* in the transition from basilect to mesolect. But while *did* looks standard, it is used by some speakers in decidedly non-standard environments, and occasionally occurs with *bin* in the same utterance: *wi bin tretn, yu no, wi did fraikn laik koward* ("we were threatened, you know, we were frightened like cowards") (Bickerton 1975: 70). Which grammar is this speaker following? While an orthodox treatment might be to discard such "contaminated" data in favor of "pure" creole, the fact is that most Guyanese display a similar range of grammatical competence in their everyday speech. And they employ ethnic categories in much the same fashion. They appear to be following multiple and incompatible rules. The question, "which culture is this person following?," therefore calls for an answer formulated within a theoretical framework that gives due recognition to internal variation in the system. There are no definitive criteria for any ethnic category, and hence no invariant relationships between categories. It is possible to begin to accommodate internal variation within a continuum model, but without that theoretical construct one is forced to disregard "idiosyncracies" in specifying a small number of structural "regularities."

Internal variation in the Guyanese cultural continuum is sustained by the dynamism of interethnic mixture. Even had ethnic categories once possessed univocal meanings and stood in one-to-one relationships with bounded social groups, four centuries of interethnic mixture would rule out any possibility of such a situation existing in contemporary Guyana. The second wedding illustrates this point. It would be a serious error to interpret the miniature social drama at Mrs. Williams's reception as a result of conflict between two ethnic groups. Amerindian and East Indian are not suddenly forced into confrontation by having to participate in the same ceremony; they have been interacting in the most intimate ways for generations, as the physical existence of Mrs. Williams and her daughter attest. Just as Mrs. Williams is mixed Amerindian–East Indian, so her reception is strung between conceptual polarities. Indeed, had she, the participants, and the ceremony itself been less "mixed," the conflict would probably not have occurred. Mrs. Williams's behavior and its cultural significance are analogous to Guyanese Creole speakers' productions and their grammatical significance: she controls a range or segment of the cultural continuum, but cannot operate within it without sometimes stumbling over conflicting rules, much as Bickerton's informant cited above combines *bin* and *did* constructions. The extent and duration of interethnic mixture in Guyana, together with the diversity of established ethnic stereotypes, gives Guyanese the routine choice of constantly bringing into operation a range of ethnic identities.

Ethnicity as Symbolic Process

In applying ideas from Creole linguistics to anthropological topics, I have produced a cultural analysis of Guyanese ethnic categories. The justification of this approach is primarily ethnographic; I continually found Guyanese employing ethnic stereotypes in the course of their daily affairs, yet could not disentangle conflicting usages of the same term nor relate it back to observed behavior in any systematic fashion. Rather than disregard a portion of the ethnographic material in favor of parts that seemed to manifest structural regularity, I have sought instead for systematic features that endow ethnic categories with meaning. The result is the notion of a Guyanese cultural continuum, which possesses three characteristics.

1. Ethnic ascription is a spontaneous and central feature of Guyanese social life;
2. Guyanese ethnic categories form a system of inter-connected meanings;
3. The systematic nature of ethnic categories derives from their heterogeneous or multivocal meanings. Internal variation and change are methodologically and theoretically crucial to understanding how Guyanese culture operates.

Informing the development of this continuum model is the idea that ethnicity may be treated as a cultural system, that is, as a set of compelling ideas about one's own and others' distinctiveness that provide a basis for acting and for interpreting others' actions. Treating ethnicity as a set of symbolic processes is clearly not in keeping with those approaches being followed in contemporary theoretical discussion such as transactional analysis, cultural ecology, and certain lines of Marxian critique. Particularly for the latter, ethnicity is regarded as a spurious topic, a part of the ideological smokescreen laid down by the ruling class to obscure the economic realities of the class struggle. While my argument concerns itself with the content and interplay of cultural categories, this does not mean that its conclusions are irrelevant to an understanding of Guyanese social structure and intergroup antagonism. With the Guyanese ethnography in mind, I would go further and say that ethnicity as somehow disconnected ideology versus ethnicity as somehow engaged class conflict is a distinction that cannot be sustained. Ethnic categories have had the most fateful consequences in Guyanese history; from the beginning of the colonial era through the disturbances of 1963–64 people have fought and died in the context of ideas about race.

The arguments I have presented in favor of a notion of cultural continuum may help to integrate idealist and materialist approaches to ethnicity. The phenomenon of internal variation is useful in explaining why ideology and action do not always make a good fit. Rather than disregard activities that do not coincide with the structural regularity of a symbolic system or, at the other extreme, disregard stated beliefs that seem to be vitiated by the harsh realities of economic activity, I believe it is more realistic to see meaning and action operating within a range of variation, so that the two sometimes mesh nicely and at other times appear irreconcilable. A recent paper by Salzman (1978) is extremely helpful in bringing the present discussion of internal variation into line with theoretical developments in political anthropology. In discussing conflicting theories of lineage organization, Salzman performs an admirable synthesis by arguing that empirical evidence about the relative importance of lineages in the daily life of particular societies must be interpreted from the perspective of what he terms "social structures in reserve" (1978: 621–5). At any one time lineage ideology may or may not dictate observed behavior, but the fact that it does not cannot be taken to mean that ideology is an empty sham obscuring an infrastructural reality of political and economic relations. For the situation of a group may change dramatically. If so, a seemingly irrelevant ideology can speak directly to daily needs and concerns. Lineage ideology is thus a "social structure in reserve," cumbersome and embarrassing at times but on hand should the need arise. Realizing ethnic identity in Guyana is a similar process of taking up or leaving aside parts of a rich repertoire of beliefs about what is involved in being "coolie," "black," "buck," and so on.

Nearer still to the notion of internal cultural variation discussed here is Galaty's analysis (1978) of an "ethnosociology" among the Maasai. Galaty argues that the identity, "Maasai," rests on an idealized pastoral praxis which subsumes and coordinates several distinct subsistence and occupational strategies—hunters, horticulturalists, blacksmiths, and diviners. Maasai are thus differentiated according to their mode of production (as Marxist theory would expect), but their mode of production is itself a function of conceptual interplay among categories of identity. The intertwined strands of production and symbolization can only be separated artificially; in reality both contribute to the articulation of what it means to be Maasai. Distinctions that matter to an insider (gradations of pastoral praxis) may well seem insignificant to an observer not immersed in the system, for whom "Maasai" are a group of East African pastoralists with shared economic interests and techniques. This is certainly the case in Guyana, where the distinctions that matter are internally generated categories of cultural difference: Indo- and Afro-Guyanese are first of all Guyanese and West Indian, rather than Indian and African. A Guyanese "ethnosociology" of the kind begun here would consequently explicate the salient categories of identity and their co-variation as Guyanese employ them in interpreting their experience.

Creole Language and Creole Culture: Implications for a Theory of Culture

In suggesting points of comparison between work in Creole linguistics and anthropological studies of polyethnic societies, this article argues that analytical concepts developed for the former are appropriate to problems currently faced by the latter. The linguistic analogy has been a prominent feature of anthropological argument, but to date anthropologists have largely drawn their inspiration from some branch of structural or transformational linguistics. Yet that theoretical framework is ill-suited to the features most characteristic of complex societies—cultural heterogeneity and change. Creole linguistics, because it makes internal variation and change its central methodological and theoretical concerns, is a better source of ideas for the ethnographer who must make sense of a body of highly diverse and seemingly conflicting data. But an anthropology which incorporates the concept of creole continuum does not merely increase its descriptive adequacy for a small set of societies; it poses questions about the very nature of culture. If variation and change are fundamental aspects of cultural systems, as they appear to be of linguistic systems, then we must consider the possibility that ethnographic studies of small, post-colonial, ethnically fragmented societies such as Guyana illustrate creole processes found in societies everywhere. What were presumed to be marginal, atypical societies requiring a separate, pluralist theory become central to discussions of general theory. The concept, "cultural system" or "culture," will have to be redefined so that a particular human population ("society") is no longer thought to possess an ideational component ("culture") characterised by uniform rules and invariant relationships. The "elementary structure" of such a cultural system is not an isolated proposition, but an intersystem—the pragmatic residue of persons seeking to define their identity *vis-à-vis* one another. The systematic nature of culture is thus to be found in relationships which, through a series of transformations, connect one intersystem to another. A cultural continuum, like a linguistic continuum, may be identified by inserting arbitrary boundaries within a transformational series. Structural linguistics inspired a structural metaphor of culture as in the work of Lévi-Strauss and others; creole linguistics could suggest a creole metaphor of culture that replaces invariance with transformation, boundedness with internal variation, and center with periphery. In the spirit of creole metaphor, Bickerton's critique of linguistic theory may be read as a critique of cultural theory.

> Hitherto, it has been generally supposed that language, in its most general sense, could be divided into a number of entities called languages, which could be further subdivided into entities called dialects. Doubts about the validity of the latter term were quoted [earlier]; these can now be extended to the former as well. For Guyanese Creole clearly does not constitute a language, insofar as one end of it is indistinguishable from English. Yet it cannot be a dialect, since dialects are supposedly more homogeneous than the language that contains them, while Guyanese Creole is less homogeneous than English. So what is it? . . . Is there any sense in which we can call Guyanese Creole a system? I believe so, even though it may involve interpreting the "system" in a way rather different to that of common linguistic usage. When a linguist speaks of languages as constituting systems, he is usually thinking of static systems, systems with a fixed number of parts which hold invariant relations with one another. But there is no *a priori* reason why a system should be static, and indeed we know perfectly well that languages are not static. Guyanese Creole can claim to be a system by virtue of the fact that relationships within it, though not invariant, are systematic. There is, as I have shown, no trace of anything that could be called random mixing of elements; on the con-

trary, the rule-changes that give rise to different outputs are tightly interrelated and capable of principled description. The only difference between it and what have traditionally been called systems is that it is dynamic, not static. (Bickerton 1975: 166)

Bickerton demonstrates that many Guyanese speakers in his sample have the routine facility to switch between lectal levels of creole with radically different grammatical rules, more different, in fact, than the separate grammars of familiar Indo-European languages (see for example 1975: 182–4). And since he is unwilling to attribute the flexibility of Guyanese creole speech to unique historical conditions—and provides convincing documentation to support his claim—it is necessary to question the basic principle of invariance, the oneness of deep structure, that informs the structural metaphor of culture. Anthropologists are engaged in the comparison of entities called cultures, and, in the role of ethnographer, establish an intimate association with a particular group of people. This procedure has made it tempting to endow the notion of *a* culture with concrete meaning. Once that has been done, there is the further temptation to get down to bedrock, to say what a particular culture is "really" about. The structural metaphor of culture thus "affords well" with our professional intuitions, and it is not surprising that it has been so well received.

The creole metaphor of culture I extrapolate from Bickerton's work[14] runs counter to both professional and commonsense intuitions. It forces us to question whether, or in what sense, cultures are wholes. Apart from the considerable intellectual capital invested in the idea of discrete societies and cultures, the counterintuitiveness of the creole linguistic metaphor is troublesome because it would seem to issue in an insupportable atomism. If cultures were as internally varied and changeful as Bickerton says creole languages are, then the ethnographer would exhaust himself describing and comparing every little pocket of informants in order not to miss any essential variation. The further theoretical task of putting such patchwork monographs into a coherent comparative framework would be hopeless. Where does that leave the creole metaphor? At this seeming impasse it is interesting to note that Bickerton himself offered an intriguing solution as far as linguistic systems are concerned:

> Thus, if the creole continuum constitutes a system (as we have given good reason to believe), the language-learning continuum between two distinct languages must equally constitute a system, and the "Anglo-Chinese" and "Anglo-Spanish" of native English-speaking learners of Chinese and Spanish must have as much right to the title "system" as English, Spanish and Chinese (themselves all clearly "multilectal" languages, it should be noted). But if the reader quite naturally revolts from innummerable new "systems" of this kind, there is a preferable solution. . . .
>
> This is to regard neither Anglo-Chinese or Anglo-Spanish, on the one hand, nor English, Chinese or Spanish, on the other, as constituting systems—not because

they are too pluralistic, as one would have to conclude from a static, monolectal definition of "system," but because they are only partial and arbitrary interpretations of the unique repository of System—the human *faculté du langage* itself. (1975:178)

Yet, while "languages" come to be perceived as increasingly overlapping and ill-defined, "language" emerges as an ever more readily definable object. It is probably already true that we can say with more confidence "*x* is or is not a feature of human language" than we can say "*x* is or is not a feature of language A." Fairly soon we may be able to specify with absolute precision what human language can and cannot contain. Indeed, it begins to seem as though there is a Second Saussurean Paradox. Saussure regarded *la langue* as principled and describable, *le langage* as unprincipled and *"inconnaissable"*; a reverse situation may well turn out to be closer to the truth (1975: 179).

As such theories [natural phonology and generative semantics] develop, both creole continuums and intersystems will increasingly be seen as objects of study potentially more revealing than supposedly discrete natural languages, insofar as they pose more stringent tests of what language (as distinct from languages) can contain. At the same time, acceptance of the fact that there are no systems but only System, and that any arbitrary interpretation of that system (i.e., any so-called "natural language") has the potential of merging into any other in a principled way, will enable us to reconcile the apparent paradoxes which arise from the four best-attested facts about human language: that all languages seem different, but that all are somehow alike; and that all languages are systematic, and yet that all are subject to continuous change (1975: 179–80).

To be consistent with the creole metaphor, one would have to assert that there are no cultures, only Culture. Any cultural system would contain analytical specifications—or invariant properties in the structural metaphor—already contained in some other, supposedly distinct, cultural system. It thus becomes impossible to specify rules of the system ("structures" in Lévi-Strauss's sense) that operate in all or even most domains of the system. Cultures come to be seen as overlapping sets of transformations or continua, that together hold the secrets to humanity's unique faculty of Culture. In devising a program to identify the constituent transformations of Culture, we shall have to pay particularly close attention to material too often dismissed as fragmentary or in some way "spoiled." Mosaic societies of the Caribbean, bursting cities of the Third World and rapidly changing contemporary Western civilization all provide valuable examples of creole processes that shape cultural intersystems.

Notes

Field research on which this article is based was conducted in December 1969–January 1971 under a National Institute of Health Field Training Grant, in September 1975–January 1976 under a Social Science Research Council fellowship, and in February–

August 1979 under a National Science Foundation award (BNS 78-07394). The author gratefully acknowledges this support. In Guyana opportunities to interact with local scholars have contributed significantly to the views expressed here. Professor John Rickford of the Linguistics Program at the University of Guyana and Mr. Wordsworth McAndrew and Mr. Michael Gomes, poet and educator respectively, have been particularly stimulating analysts of their own society.

1. Treatments generally known to anthropologists include Hymes (1971), Bickerton (1976), Bailey (1976), and DeCamp & Hancock (1974).

2. A lengthy paper would be required simply to chart the main currents in writings about ethnicity over the past decade. Barth's now classic treatment (1969) began a dialogue that in the past few years has produced several major works used in preparing this article (Bennett 1975; Brewer & Campbell 1976; Cohen 1974; de Vos & Romanucci-Ross 1975; Glazer & Moynihan 1975; Mason 1970).

3. Radcliffe-Brown's analogy (1952) of social to physiological morphology is a pertinent example. The tradition continues in the Parsonian corpus.

4. He distinguishes three levels in Guyanese creole: basilect, mesolect and acrolect. These cover the range from least to most standard English. An important example of internal structural difference is the presence of a stative/non-stative distinction in basilectal creole and its absence from the acrolect.

5. For an eloquent account of this distressing aspect of life in independent Guyana, see "A question of self contempt" by the Guyanese poet Martin Carter (1966).

6. It is curious that Bickerton, for all his insistence on the importance of intersystems and the analogy of creoles to second language learning, has nothing to say about the predicament of a standard English-speaking outsider trying to learn Guyanese creole. Although he suggests (p. 178) that Guyanese are better at speaking and understanding "down" (in the direction of the basilect) than "up," it has always seemed to me that the foreigner learning creole finds his opportunities to converse in it further restricted to a group of close acquaintances who have some idea of what he is trying to do. Trying one's ill-formed creole expressions on a stranger may well seem absurd and insulting, something in the way of a middle-aged, middle-class white trying to use "street talk" with a black teenager. In both situations English has become a foreign language for the English-speaker. DeCamp provides an excellent description of the complex process of "speaking up" and "speaking down" in Jamaican creole:

> But no one can deny the extreme degree of variability of Jamaican English. There are many middle-class St. Andrew housewives who claim that they can speak the broad creole because they can converse with their maids, yet they can understand very little of the conversation if they overhear the maid talking with the gardener. Further, in Jamaica there is not a sharp cleavage between creole and standard. Rather there is a linguistic continuum, a continuous spectrum of speech varieties ranging from "bush talk" or "broken language" of Quashie to the educated standard of Philip Sherlock and Norman Manley. Many Jamaicans persist in the myth that there are only two varieties: the patois and the standard. But one speaker's attempt at the broad patois may be closer to the standard end of the spectrum than another speaker's attempt at the standard. The "standard" is not standard British, as many Jamaicans claim; rather it is an evolving standard Jamaican (or perhaps standard West Indian) English which is mutually intelligible with, but undeniably

different from, standard British. Each Jamaican speaker commands a span of this continuum, the breadth of the span depending on the breadth of his social contacts; a labor leader, for example, commands a greater span of varieties than does a suburban middle-class housewife (1971: 350).

7. See Benjamin (1978: 53–63) for suggested etymologies of this ethnic term.

8. This process is quite complex, for as I argue elsewhere (1978: 37) much of the "pluralism" in Caribbean culture can be attributed, not to discrepant traditions of emigrant groups, but to internal contradictions in English social structure that were magnified by the colonial process.

9. In its official guise the Jonestown settlement in 1977–78 appeared to some Guyanese government figures as a commendable synthesis of strong religious conviction and socialist ideology. In attempting to view the events of November 1978 from a Guyanese perspective, it is important to consider that religious sects proliferate there and that all benefit from a Guyanese disposition to avoid public criticism of religious activities.

10. Despres's academically respectable treatment of "cultural pluralism" (1967) was preceded by Michael Swan's Colonial Office–commissioned British Guiana: land of six peoples (1957), which abounds in uncritical passages on the traits or personalities of the major ethnic groups — most of them drawn from Guyanese who were conscious that they were speaking to an Englishman there on an official mission and no doubt careful to phrase their remarks within a colonial idiom.

11. Emigration is probably the most significant social phenomemon in Guyana in recent years. Although official figures are unreliable, it is indisputable that import bans, currency restrictions, high unemployment, street crime, and a general decline in social services of all types have caused large numbers of skilled and semi-skilled workers to leave Guyana.

12. Alexander's (1977) paper on the "culture of race" in Jamaica and Whitten's two monographs (1974; 1976) on ethnicity among Ecuadorian Amerindians and Blacks are notable exceptions. I have linked the analysis of ethnicity with that of myth in a previous paper (1977b). The "sociological perspective" criticized here is typified by Brewer and Campbell's (1976) study of East African intergroup attitudes. While the subject afforded an excellent opportunity to discover the constantly shifting boundaries of ethnic categories in an extremely heterogeneous social milieu, the researchers approached it with the assumption that ethnic groups were already well-defined. The point here is that it is the cultural nature of the definitions which is the intriguing problematic, and not sets of correlations of attitudes towards pre-defined groups.

13. The ambiguity, however, is not randomly distributed, as Harris (1970) maintains in arguing that the concept of ethnicity yields its interpretive or explanatory force to something else — such as economic competition or physical adaptation. The ambiguity of ethnic categories derives from their being employed to give form to situations that change rapidly over time, evoke powerful needs and emotions (sexual, aesthetic, and religious as well as economic) and involve persons with ascriptive or performative rights to dual or treble classification. Ethnic categories cannot be dismissed or relegated to a class of sociocultural epiphenomena, but need to be scrutinized for the meanings which people invest in them in the course of fixing their bearings in the storm-lashed seas of the Third World.

14. And he bears no responsibility for my interpretation of his analysis.

References

Alexander, Jack 1977. The culture of race in middle-class Kingston, Jamaica. Am. Ethnol. 4, 413–35.

Bailey, Charles-James N. 1976. The state of non-state linguistics. Ann. Rev. Anthrop. 5, 93–106.

Barth, Fredrik (ed.) 1969. Ethnic groups and boundaries. Boston: Little, Brown.

Bell, Wendell & Walter E. Freeman (eds) 1974. Ethnicity and nation-building. Beverly Hills, California: Sage.

Benjamin, Joel 1978. Loss of person: Some etymological notes on "buck." Release 1, 53–63.

Bennett, John (ed.) 1975. The new ethnicity (1973 Proc. of Am. Ethnol. Soc.). St Paul, Minnesota: West Publishing House.

Bickerton, Derek 1975. Dynamics of a Creole system. Cambridge: Univ. Press.

—— 1976. Pidgin and Creole studies. Ann. Rev. Anthrop. 5, 169–93.

Brewer, Marilynn B. & Donald T. Campbell 1976. Ethnocentrism and intergroup attitudes: east African evidence. New York: Halsted.

Carter, Martin 1966. A question of self-contempt. In New world: Guyana independence issue. Georgetown, Guyana.

Cohen, Abner 1974. Two dimensional man. Berkeley: Univ. of California Press.

DeCamp, David 1971. Towards a generative analysis of a post-Creole speech community. In Pidginization and creolization of languages (ed.) Dell Hymes. Cambridge: Univ. Press.

—— & Ian F. Hancock (eds) 1974. Pidgins and Creoles. Washington, D.C.: Georgetown Univ. Press.

Despres, Leo 1967. Cultural pluralism and nationalist politics in British Guiana. Chicago: Rand McNally.

de Vos, George & Lola Romanucci-Ross 1975. Ethnic identity: Cultural continuities and change. Palo Alto: Mayfield.

Drummond, Lee 1977a. On being Carib. In Carib-speaking Indians: Culture, society and language (ed.) Ellen B. Basso. Tucson: Univ. of Arizona Press.

—— 1977b. Structure and process in the interpretation of South American myth: The Arawak dog-spirit people. Am. Anthrop. 79, 842–68.

—— 1978. The Trans-Atlantic nanny: Notes on a comparative semiotics of the family in English-speaking societies. Am. Ethnol. 5, 30–42.

Galaty, John 1978. Being "Maasai", being "under cows": Ethnic shifters in East Africa. Ms. Department of Anthropology, McGill University.

Geertz, Clifford 1966. Religion as a cultural system. In Anthropological approaches to the study of religion (ed.) Michael Banton. London: Tavistock.

Glazer, Nathan & Daniel P. Moynihan 1975. Ethnicity: theory and experience. Cambridge, Mass.: Harvard Univ. Press.

Haley, Alex 1976. Roots. Garden City, New York: Doubleday.

Harris, Marvin 1970. Referential ambiguity in the calculus of racial identity. SWest. J. Anthrop. 27, 1–14.

Hymes, Dell (ed.) 1971. Pidginization and creolization of languages. Cambridge: Univ. Press.

Mason, Philip 1970. Patterns of dominance. London: Oxford Univ. Press.

Parsons, Talcott 1951. The social system. New York: Free Press.

Radcliffe-Brown, A. R. 1952. On social structure. In Structure and function in primitive society. London: Cohen & West.

Salzman, Philip 1978. Ideology and change in tribal society. Man (N.S.) **13**, 618–37.

Smith, M. G. 1965. Plural society in the British West Indies. Berkeley: Univ. of California Press.

Smith, R. T. 1956. The Negro family in British Guiana. London: Routledge & Kegan Paul.

——— 1962. British Guiana. London: Oxford Univ. Press.

Swan, Michael 1957. British Guiana: The land of six peoples. London: H.M.S.O.

Whitten, Norman E. Jr (1974). Black frontiersmen. New York: Halsted.

——— 1976. Sacha Runa: Ethnicity and adaptation of Ecuadorian jungle Quichua. Urbana, Illinois: Univ. of Illinois Press.

6. THE HISTORICAL CONTEXT OF NENGRE KINSHIP AND RESIDENCE

Ethnohistory of the Family Organization of Lower Status Creoles in Paramaribo

B. Edward Pierce

The family system of lower status Creoles, or the Nengre of Paramaribo, Surinam,[1] is similar to that of other Afro-American proletariats. The common characteristics of these systems include: (1) variable mating forms, including legal marriage, nonlegal coresidential unions, and nonlegal extraresidential unions; (2) a high degree of conjugal instability; (3) a high incidence of households headed by single females; (4) the pivotal position of females in kinship, domestic, and residential groups; and (5) the frequent inclusion of distant consanguineals in the household. In addition, the factors that have provided the bases for causal explanations of these characteristics in other Afro-American family systems (i.e., the West African heritage of polygyny, the slave and plantation systems, economic marginality, systems of land tenure, and a high incidence of migratory wage labor) are all pertinent in the Surinamese case.[2] Since all of these factors are apparently relevant to an explanation of Nengre family organization, none of them, taken singly, is an adequate causal explanation of this particular family system, or for that matter, of Afro-American family organization in general.

My initial research on Nengre family organization resulted in a contemporary, synchronic analysis of kinship and residence with the aim of demonstrating that distinctive patterns of kinship provide the Nengre with important referents for manipulating their domestic and residential relationships (Pierce, 1971). As work on this synchronic study progressed, I developed an interest in gaining a diachronic or historical perspective on Nengre family organization. This essay represents my initial attempts to come to grips with some of the problems involved in reconstructing the (ethno) history of Nengre family organization.

As is the case in other areas of Afro-America, there is little direct historical evidence on the family system of the Surinamese slaves or their emancipated descendants, the Nengre. Consequently, a diachronic perspective on Nengre family

Originally published in Ann Pescatello (ed.), *Old Roots in New Lands* (Westport, Conn.: Greenwood Press, 1977), pp. 107–31. Copyright © 1977 by Ann Pescatello. Reprinted with permission.

organization can only be acquired through heavy reliance on inference from indirect evidence. This inferential reconstruction will be successful only if the conceptual framework within which it occurs is rigorously defined. Published studies
of Afro-American family organization are of limited aid in this regard since they
generally rest on inadequate concepts of "the family" and simplistic ideas about
causal factors that account for continuity and change in family organization.

Family organization is defined here as the sociocultural system which results
when a society's members participate in the groups and networks formed by the
articulation of the kinship, domestic, and residential domains. Kinship is the collective cultural or cognitive map of the biological network. Domesticity refers to
the domain of activities that must be performed in order to sustain the lives of
the members of a household. Residential relationships are concerned with the
problem of who lives with whom.

Buckley (1968:490) describes sociocultural systems as being complex and
adaptive, and he defines complex adaptive systems as being negentropic and internally and externally open. Thus, it may be suggested that the important characteristics of a family system are that it maintains its structural integrity through
time, it consists of components or domains that are reciprocally related and mutually interdependent, and the system as a whole persists or changes in response to
external influences or causal factors. Externally derived change-producing factors
can impinge on the domain(s) of kinship, domesticity and/or residence, and changes
in any of these domains will produce corresponding changes in the others.

The external influences or causal factors include ecological and demographic
variables which have a significant effect on residence and domestic patterns, and
externally derived cultural inputs which have a significant effect on the ways that
a society's members think about the family. These constitute the environing field
of the system of family organization. Considerable insight into the historical development of the Nengre system of family organization can be acquired by determining significant changes that have occurred in its environing field.

The point of departure for our consideration of the historical development of
Nengre family organization will be a discussion of significant aspects of the contemporary system. The data on which this summary discussion is based were
gathered by means of the traditional anthropological techniques of participant
observation, intensive interviews of key informants, and a household census. This
discussion of the contemporary system will be followed by a consideration of the
historical development of Nengre family organization in the context of its environing field. It must be emphasized that this reconstruction is tentative and preliminary. There are enormous collections of relevant archival materials in Surinam and Holland that I have not had the opportunity to examine.[3]

The Contemporary Nengre Family

Nengre families manifest variable conjugal, domestic, and residence patterns.
This variability is closely associated with ranked status. As is the case in other

Caribbean societies, the Nengre manifest and evaluate status in terms of what Wilson refers to as the respectability prestige system (1969:71). Respectability encapsulates societywide status-determining criteria which are based on metropolitan (i.e., Dutch) behavioral norms. In a familial context, respectability entails the maintenance of a neolocal, primary household based on a legally sanctioned monogamous marriage in which the husband-father provides support and the wife-mother engages in domestic and child-rearing activities.[4]

Statements by informants indicate that the Nengre consider the respectable form of household as ideal and that most attempt to organize their own domestic and residential relationships accordingly. However, because of such factors as poverty, the necessity of supporting and caring for dependent consanguineals, conjugal dissolution, and early pregnancy, many Nengre households manifest one or more of the following Afro-American patterns: single female headship, nonlegal coresidential conjugal union, matrifocality in kinship, domestic, and residential relationships, and consanguineal extension. Several scholars have interpreted these patterns as a reflection of social disorganization or pathological deviation from Euro-American norms (Frazier, 1939; Glazer and Moynihan, 1963). However, evidence on Nengre social organization indicates that this population has a viable kinship system which is distinctive, and provides a charter for both respectable Euro-American and typical Afro-American households.

The Nengre currently consider three types of conjugal union to be socially significant: legal marriage, living-together unions, and outside unions. Legal marriage is formalized by religious and civil ceremonies and an elaborate wedding reception, and is considered to be maximally respectable. Living together, a nonlegal coresidential conjugal union, is not considered particularly prestigious, but it is regarded as completely legitimate. An outside relationship is a nonlegal union between a male who is a partner in a legal marriage or living-together union and an extraresidential female; such unions are not approved of despite their frequent occurrence.

Living together and outside unions do not entail binding legal rights or obligations, and they can be dissolved at will by either spouse. On the other hand, legal marriage involves rights and obligations that can only be terminated through divorce, which is prohibitively expensive. Because of the expense and permanence of legal marriage, Nengre couples generally establish living-together unions initially. They delay legal marriage until they are financially secure and have assured themselves that their relationship will endure.

Many adult Nengre of both sexes are conjugally unstable. Some of these are without mates, while others are in the process of establishing or dissolving living-together unions, in which case the partners are not coresident but refer to each other with reference terms for spouses.

Surinamese law requires a mother to register the names of her children with the civil government at birth. A father who is not legally married may grant legal recognition to his children by a living-together or casual mate if she grants him permission to do so. A child who receives paternal recognition inherits a patrinymic and is considered to be legitimate. If a man is legally married, paternal recognition of all children born to his wife during the marriage is automatic.[5] A man who is a partner in legal marriage or a living-together union never recognizes his children by outside mates. Paternal recognition is currently becoming more important than it was in the past, but even today the stigma that attaches to children who bear their mothers' surnames is minimal.

The potential for conflict between affinals is high. While the Nengre have reference terms for close affinals, they are not considered to be "family people" or true kinsmen. Relevant genealogical space is bilaterally structured and includes all third ascending and descending generation and closer lineals and all parents' parents' siblings' children's children (second cousins), and closer collaterals. The incest taboo is bilaterally extended to include second cousins and closer consanguineals. A Creolized reference terminology of English, Dutch, and Portuguese provenience embraces all known kinsmen within this domain.

The Nengre consider two types of consanguineal kinship groups to be significant. All living kinsmen within two ascending and descending generations and five degrees of genealogical distance are members of the "closeby family." The closeby family is an exogamous, kindred-type network, the members of which are tied to ego by reciprocal rights and obligations. Few, if any, Nengre know all of their relatives within the theoretical limits of the closeby family, and ties between fourth- and fifth-degree consanguineals are very weak, even when knowledge of the relationship exists. The "root" is a cognatic descent group of four generations which consists of all the descendants of a great grandparent. Roots are identified with the plantations or rural areas in which they originated, and are of religious significance in that they are the groups within which possessing spirits and ancestral ghosts are inherited and worshipped. Roots are frequently spoken of as if they were corporate, but at present, they do not have corporate functions.

The bilateral structure of Nengre kinship occurs because descent is simultaneously traced through agnatic and uterine linkages in the patrilateral and matrilateral segments of genealogical space. However, the relationship between a father and child is considered to be fundamentally different from that between a mother and child. This difference is reflected in the fact that different terms are used for the two types of relationships. The Nengre consider themselves to be related to their fathers through "blood" and to their mothers through the "belly" or the womb.

According to the Nengre folk theory of reproduction, a male deposits blood in the belly or womb of a female at conception. The blood is the essence from which the fetus is formed and the medium through which immutable physical and behavioral characteristics are transmitted. Food taboos are also inherited patrilineally because foods that are incompatible with a father's blood are thought to be incompatible with the blood of their children. After depositing his blood in the belly of the mother, the father's active involvement in prenatal development ceases.

The mother's womb is the receptacle within which the fetus develops. When impregnated, she assumes the task of providing a suitable environment within which the fetus develops. In addition to maintaining her own health through proper diet, cleanliness, and the like, she must avoid eating foods that are prohibited to the father of her child since they will produce skin irritations and ultimately leprosy if ingested in great quantity.

Paternal and maternal obligations to dependent children are analogous to male and female reproductive roles. Ideally, fathers provide support for their dependent children while mothers care for, nurture, and nourish them. Care, nurture, and nourishment provide the basis for more cohesive and intimate relationships than support. As a result, virtually all Nengre feel a closer relationship to their mothers than to their fathers, and ties between kinsmen related through belly or uterine linkages are stronger and more cohesive than those joining kinsmen through blood or agnatic linkages. Genealogical knowledge of matrilineal relatives is usually much more extensive than that of other segments of genealogical space. Kinship and domestic activities tend to occur within uterine networks, and if consanguineal household extension occurs, uterine relatives are much more likely to be incorporated than those joined to the household head by agnatic or mixed networks.

In the spring of 1969, a household composition survey was carried out on fifty-eight randomly selected Nengre households that were located in the residential district in which my dissertation field research was based. The results are summarized in Tables 1 and 2.

The composition of sample households varies considerably. Typical Afro-American patterns of household organization occur frequently.[6] Peripheral household members are joined to female core members most frequently, to both members of conjugal cores less frequently, and to male core members least frequently. Household extension involves consanguineals much more frequently

Table 1
Core Structure and Basic Household Type among the Nengre

	Type of Household			
Core Structure	Nonextended	Primary	Extended	Total
Single Male	3	0	3	6
Single Female	3	8	8	19
Living Together	3	9	5	17
Legal Marriage	2	5	9	16
				58

Core = single household head or household head and coresident spouse.
Nonextended household = household containing only core members.
Primary household = household containing a core and children.
Extended household = household containing a core and relatives other than or in addition to children.

Table 2
Patterns of Household Extension

Total number of household members	317
Total number of core members	91
Total number of peripherals	226
Affinal peripherals	4
Bilateral children of conjugal core	93
Primary or uterine consanguineals of female core member	110
Nonuterine consanguineals of female core member	9
Primary or uterine consanguineals of male core members	10
Nonuterine consanguineals of male core members	0

than affinals. Consanguineal extension occurs through uterine networks much more frequently than through nonuterine networks. These data indicate that there is a close correlation between Nengre kinship and residence.

Historical Perspective

The first successful attempt to settle Surinam was made by Lord Willoughby of Parnham, who claimed it for England in 1650 and established a sugar colony there. The colony was taken over by a Dutch fleet in 1666 during the second Anglo-Dutch war. From 1667 until 1975,[7] Surinam was a part of the Kingdom of the Netherlands, with the exception of two brief periods during the Napoleonic wars, 1795–1802 and 1804–1814, when England again established control. During the early stages of Surinamese colonization, a plantocracy of diverse provenience developed consisting of British, Dutch, French, Germans, Northwest European Jews, and Sephardic Jews from Brazil. Van Lier (1949:33–48) indicates that planters of differing national origins tended to form separate subsocieties.

The Dutch conquest of Surinam was initiated by the Dutch West India Company after it had lost control over the Pernambuco Region of Brazil in 1650. From 1667 until 1794, the Dutch West India Company maintained a monopoly on the importation of slaves to the colony, after which the slave trade was opened to traders from all Western European countries. In 1808, when she had reconquered Surinam for a brief period, England outlawed the importation of slaves from Africa to her colonies in the New World. Holland reaffirmed the British position when she again gained control of the colony in 1814, but the clandestine importation of slaves continued for more than a decade thereafter.

Several authors of early descriptions and travel accounts of Surinam have discussed sources of provenience of the slave population. Van Lier (1949:122–124) and Wooding (1972:17–50) have synthesized this information. The provenience terms indicate that slaves were imported to Surinam from the West African coast between Senegambia and Angola. However, on the basis of clusterings of tribal provenience designations, it appears that a majority of the West Africans who were shipped to Surinam came from the region of the Ivory, Gold, and Slave Coasts.[8] This hypothesis is supported both by the fact that, after 1650, Dutch military and commercial activities were centered in El Mina on the Gold Coast, and by a consideration of the provenience of Africanisms in Nengre supernaturalism.

The urban Nengre believe the soul consists of dual aspects: the *kra* and the *djodjo*. *Kra* is an Akan and Ewe term for soul, and *djo* is the Fon term for god. Two larger categories of *winti* or possessing spirits are *Kromanti* and *Papa*. *Kromanti* is an altered form of Coromantyn, the slave port on the Gold Coast, and *Papa* or *Pawpaw* was an important slave port on the Dahomean coast. The names of many particular *winti* come from the same general area: Vodu (Fon), Loko (Fon), Opete (Akan), and Leba (Fon) are some of these. The urban Nengre have a system of day names which is almost identical to the Ashanti system.[9] Anansi, the Akan spider trickster, is the major character in a genre of folk tales told by the Nengre at wakes. While numerous explicit African elements have been retained in the Nengre magico-religious complex, it is important to note that these are combined into a total configuration that is Surinamese rather than African.

In spite of the retention of explicit Africanisms in Nengre supernaturalism, West African cultural patterns are not manifest in Nengre kinship and residential patterns. No Nengre kinship terms appear to be of African provenience. Genealogical space is bilaterally structured and the incest taboo is bilaterally extended. The frequent occurence of conjugal instability and a variety of mating forms can be more plausibly explained in terms of the Surinamese external environing field than as a survival of West African polygyny. It is tempting to interpret the differentiation of agnatic and uterine linkages in Nengre descent and the relative cohesiveness of relationships in uterine and sororal networks, as opposed to agnatic and fraternal networks, as being derived from the Ashanti descent system. As will be seen presently, however, this descent system can be explained as a consequence of customs and laws connected with the Surinamese system of slavery.

Most scholars who have interpreted the Afro-American family in terms of systems of slavery have minimized or completely discounted the importance of African cultural influence to its development. The fact that research has failed to yield explicit African cultural survivals in Nengre kinship and residence does not indicate that African cultural influence on this family system was negligible. Rather, it indicates that explicit manifestations of kinship and residence at a surface level are responsive to change in the Surinamese external environing field. Comparative analysis of Surinamese and various West African kinship systems at a deeper structural level would probably reveal a close relationship between them.[10]

Until the end of the eighteenth century, Surinamese society consisted primarily of masters and slaves. According to Stedman (1796:280), an estimated slave labor force of 50,000 at the height of the plantation period in Surinam declined at the rate of 5 percent per year so that it was necessary to import 2,500 Africans annually. The abolition of the slave trade in the early nineteenth century forced Surinamese planters to rely on reproduction within the Surinamese slave population to renew the labor force. The significant consequences of these changes were a noticeable improvement in the treatment of slaves during the nineteenth century and the simultaneous increase in the ratio of births to deaths within the slave population. Despite this improvement in the condition of slaves, this population was never able to maintain itself.

A major distinction within the slave population was drawn between "Saltwater Negroes" who were imported from Africa and Creole Negroes who were born in Surinam. During the seventeenth and eighteenth centuries, when a large proportion of the slave population consisted of Saltwater Negroes, tribal loyalties appear to have provided an important basis for the organization of interpersonal relationships among slaves. As the number of Saltwater Negroes decreased, tribal loyalties were supplanted by plantation affiliation as a determinant of social organization (Van Lier, 1949:162). The attachment of Creole Negro slaves to their plantations is reflected in the following statement by Teenstra (1848:42): "Negroes are extraordinarily attached to the place of their birth, the graves of their elders and their close relations. The yard on which they have played as children is holy to them so that they dislike leaving the plantation on which they were born."[11]

It should be noted that contemporary urban Nengre consider themselves to be mystically attached to the places where they were conceived and to the plantations where their cognatic descent groups or roots developed.

A second basic distinction within the slave population was between slaves owned by individuals, a majority of whom lived in Paramaribo, and slaves who were owned by the plantations to which they were attached. The proportional representation of the urban slaves to the total population of Paramaribo, and to the total slave population of Surinam, varied. In 1791, 8,000 of a total Paramaribo population of 11,500 were slaves, and the total Surinamese slave population was 53,000. In 1830, there were 8,500 slaves in the total urban population of 15,265, and the total slave population of the colony was 48,784 (Van Lier, 1949:31, 151). While the proportional representation of slaves in the population of Paramaribo declined during this period, the percentage of urban slaves in the total slave population increased largely as a result of a decline in the colonial slave population. Freed slaves continued to move toward Paramaribo in increasing numbers following emancipation in 1863.

According to Van Hoevel (1854:138), individually owned urban slaves were much more fortunate than those who were bound to plantations, although their circumstances were also wretched. Some of these slaves worked as domestics in the households of their masters, but a large number were made to go out and seek jobs, or were rented out to others by their masters. Salaried and artisan slaves were required to bring their masters a specified amount of money each day. Some masters permitted these slaves to keep the remainder of their pay, but others took all that their slaves earned and gave them provisions, or more frequently, a set amount to be used for the purchase of provisions for themselves and their children. Van Hoevel (1854:76) estimates that the funds that slaves received for their provisioning generally varied between fifty and seventy cents per week. He states that this amount was completely inadequate, especially for women who had to support and care for themselves and their children. Many slave women were forced to work for their masters on Sunday, the only free day that was allowed them, or to turn to prostitution in order to acquire the funds necessary for minimal survival.

Working conditions for slaves varied on different types of plantations. Conditions on sugar plantations were generally the worst, especially during the relatively short seasons during which cane was harvested and sugar was refined. On coffee and cotton plantations, workloads were lighter. On wood plantations, which were situated further from the coast, conditions for slaves were most favorable because of light workloads and isolation and independence from masters who resided closer to the coast (Van Hoevel, 1854:144).

Most plantations had a few domestic and artisan slaves, but the great majority of plantation slaves worked in the fields for at least nine hours per day, six days a week. Instead of the money which many individually owned slaves received for their provisioning, plantation slaves were given minimal provisions which were supposed to be supplemented by their own spare time efforts at raising food on small plots provided by the plantations. Generally, slaves on plantations with resident owners received better treatment than slaves on plantations run by administrators because the administrators were more interested in the quick maximization of profits than in the maintenance of the capital that the plantation's slave force represented.

The Surinamese slave system was based in part on Roman law, in part on custom, and in part on colonial proclamations and statutes. Adequate provisions for enforcing the proclamations and statutes pertaining to slavery were never made, however. It was only in 1851, when it was certain that Holland would emancipate the slaves in the near future, that anything resembling a comprehensive slave code was developed.

During the seventeenth and eighteenth centuries, most of the measures that were passed appear to have been designed to maximize the difference in status between free and slave, and to keep the slaves under control. Sexual relationships between white females and slave males were forbidden and were punishable by the death of the latter. Slaves who met whites on the street were required to stand aside and make way for them. Whites and slaves were prohibited from keeping company or gambling with one another. Slaves were forbidden to carry weapons. Slaves darker than mulattoes were not allowed to wear shoes, stockings, or jewelry. Each slave was to be branded with the mark of his master. Slaves could not go onto the street at night without a letter of permission from their masters, and they were required to carry lighted lanterns to announce their presence.

Throughout the period of slavery, religious dances of all types were forbidden, as was the gathering of large crowds of slaves at funerals (Van Lier, 1949:141–142).

The growth of abolitionist sentiment in the Netherlands and the emancipation of slaves in the British colonies in 1834 and the French colonies in 1848 caused a reevaluation of the Surinamese slave system. At the insistence of the Dutch metropolitan government, the colonial government of Surinam passed a comprehensive slave code in 1851. The code defined rights and obligations between masters and slaves, minimal requirements for the care and provisioning of slaves, maximal workloads for slaves, maximal punishments that could be exercised against slaves, and penalties for the infringement of these rules. The Surinamese planters accepted this code with a surprising degree of willingness because it was seen as a means of postponing the inevitable emancipation of slaves and because it was not at all stringent.

The slave code of 1851 made inadequate provisions for the welfare of slaves. Van Hoevel maintains that the stipulated workloads for field slaves were almost twice as onerous as maximal workloads for manual laborers in the Netherlands (1854:213), and that the minimal food allowance for adult slaves according to the law contained a tenth of the protein consumed by an ordinary Dutch soldier (1854:183). The maximal punishments that could be given slaves were extremely severe, and the penalties for slaveowners who exceeded these limits were very light. The major inadequacy of the slave code was that the governor, who was given the responsibility for enforcing its provisions, was not given the means for doing so.

Throughout the period of slavery, Surinamese slaves could secure their freedom through manumission. Manumission occurred in one of three possible contexts. It occurred most often when European males purchased the freedom of their common-law slave wives and children. In other cases, manumission was granted by masters as a reward for faithful service by domestic slaves. During most of the period of slavery, it was possible for slaves to purchase their own freedom, but relatively few of them were able to do so (Van Lier, 1949:100).

In spite of various governmental attempts to control manumission through the imposition of manumission taxes, requirements that manumission requests receive governmental approval, and the outlawing of self-purchase between 1832 and 1851, the free Creole population grew steadily. In 1738, there were an estimated 598 free Creoles in Surinam. By 1812, this population had grown to 3,075 and was larger than the European population. By 1830, there were 5,041 free Creoles in Surinam as compared with a European population of 2,500 (Van Lier, 1949:97–98; Teenstra, 1842:5–9). Almost all of the free Creoles resided in Paramaribo.

The free Creole population was differentiated on the basis of phenotype and legal position into four status categories: freeborn colored, manumitted colored, freeborn Negro, and manumitted Negro. As was the case in other colonial slave

societies in the New World with significant populations of free Creoles, Caucasoid phenotype and free birth were accorded more prestige than Negroid phenotype and freedom through manumission. The colonial government issued proclamations which placed restrictions on free Negroes but not on freeborn or
manumitted coloreds, and free Creoles who had been manumitted were subject
to restrictions that did not apply to those who were freeborn. It is not possible
to determine whether phenotype or legal status was the more important status-
determining criterion, but it can be assumed that phenotype was of more immediate relevance in ascribing status because of its visibility as compared with the
relative difficulty of determining legal status.

As of 1830, the free Creole population consisted of 3,974 individuals categorized as colored and 1,094 classified as Negroes (Van Lier, 1949:98). No data are
available on the relative sizes of the manumitted and freeborn segments of the
free Creole population. However, it is probable that the rate of manumission was
always much lower than the birth rate within the free Creole population. As a
result, Creoles born into freedom almost certainly outnumbered those who were
manumitted throughout the period of slavery.

Within the free Creole population, there was a colored elite that mixed relatively easily with Europeans, and a "middle class" consisting of Jewish, colored
and a small number of Negro clerks, bureaucrats, and shopkeepers. Lower status
free Creoles, most of whom were manumitted Negroes, formed a proletariat consisting of manual laborers and gardeners who sold produce raised on provision
grounds close to the city (Van Lier, 1949:114–116).

New World slave systems have been compared in terms of economic factors
(Williams, 1944) and the distinction between Iberian and Northwest European
cultural heritage (Tannenbaum, 1947). Hoetink (1967, 1969) has effectively
demonstrated that these approaches should be combined. In a comparison of the
slavery and race systems of Curaçao and Surinam, he suggests that, although both
of these areas were subject to cultural influence from the same colonizing
power—i.e., Holland—ecological, demographic, and geographic differences in
the two areas caused significant differences in severity of treatment of slaves, frequency of manumission, relative size of free and slave populations, and the like.
While the comparison suggests that Surinam's slave system conformed more
closely to the Northwest European model than Curaçao's, it is necessary to recognize that the slave society of Surinam was similar in certain respects to those
based on Iberian cultural influence.

A substantial racially mixed free Creole population developed early in Surinam and was maintained until emancipation through extensive sexual relationships between European males and slave females and frequent manumission.
High-status free Creoles interacted freely with Europeans and occupied important political positions because of the transitory nature of European society
(Hoetink, 1969:183). It is important to remember that the size, importance, and

relatively great social mobility of the free Creole population were attributable to ecological and demographic factors rather than to Latin influence via Iberian colonizing powers.

The civil and legal aspects of the Surinamese slave system were clearly of Northwest European provenience. During most of the period of slavery, the colony lacked a comprehensive slave code. Governmental control of the treatment of slaves by masters was minimal, and governmental decrees and proclamations pertaining to slavery were aimed at maintaining repressive control over the slave force. Slaves were legally defined as property rather than as persons. Unlike the Spanish and Portuguese colonies where the Roman Catholic church and the crown were protectors of slaves, Christian denominations had little, if any, influence on the Netherlands' colonial policy. Moreover, Dutch royalty did not become concerned with the welfare of slaves until abolitionist sentiment became very strong in the nineteenth century. While the baptism of slaves was mandatory in the Iberian colonies, the government did not encourage missionary work among the Surinamese slaves by Moravians and Roman Catholics until emancipation was recognized as inevitable.

Little information is available on the mating patterns of Surinamese slaves. Because they were not legally recognized as human beings, slaves could not enter into legally recognized marriages, and consorts could be sold separately if their master desired (Van Hoevel, 1854:52). Blom reports that conjugal unions between plantation slaves were not ceremonially sanctioned, and he implies that both male and female slaves frequently had continuing sexual relationships with several mates at the same time (1787:393). It can be assumed that mating patterns among urban slaves were similar to those of plantation slaves in most respects. However, the proportion of Europeans and free Creoles to slaves was greater in Paramaribo than in rural areas, with the result that slave females mated and formed conjugal unions with free males much more frequently in the city than on the plantations.

Most Europeans who went to Surinam were single, or they left their wives at home. Usually, they bought or rented female slaves or established nonlegal conjugal unions with free Creole women whom they took as housekeepers and sexual consorts. While these unions were not legally recognized, many of them were extremely durable and stable.

Teenstra (1842:48) describes mating among free Creoles as follows: "Most Creoles live unmarried, having in addition to a housekeeper, two or three concubines outside of the house, for the colored women are nowhere less proper in their behavior to men than in Surinam although they are very faithful in the absence of legal marriage.[12] He also states that because some free Creoles considered marriage as too final and permanent, they prevented their daughters from marrying legally until they had lived together with their prospective husbands and were sure that their unions would endure.

While this information is not extensive, it suggests that important features of the system of mating among contemporary urban Nengre were already present during the period of slavery. Among the slaves and free Creoles, conjugal relationships appear to have been unstable. The data presented indicate that members of both of these populations formed conjugal unions that were comparable to the living-together and outside relationships that are entered by the Nengre today. Religiously but not legally sanctioned unions became possible for slaves in the nineteenth century. Legal marriage, while comparatively rare among free Creoles, was theoretically possible and was engaged in by members of the elite segment of this population.

Surinamese slaves were not regarded as having any relatives other than a mother, and the status of the mother determined the status of her children. In speaking of the children of European fathers and slave mothers, Stedman (1796:88) makes the following comment: "In Surinam, all such children go with their mothers: that is, if she is in slavery, her offspring are her master's property should their father be a prince, unless he obtains them by purchase."

In the same vein, Teenstra (1842:23) says that white directors were generally discouraged from creating stable unions with female slaves belonging to the plantations on which they were employed since this caused a loss of authority and could tempt them to purchase their consorts and children from the establishment.

It was customary in Surinam not to sell slave children and their mothers separately, although it sometimes occurred if a plantation was to be liquidated or if the owner was returning to Europe (Teenstra, 1848:102; Van Lier, 1949:157). Proclamations forbidding the separate selling of mothers and children were issued in 1782, 1821, and 1850. The last of these proclamations stated:

> Slaves, during the life of their mother and as long as they belong to the slave class, may never be separated from her through purchase, barter, giving or in any other manner be placed in the ownership of a third party in such a way that they will not be reunited with their mother. — Children can never be separated from their mother, or the mother from her children. (Van Hoevel, 1854:52)[13]

This proclamation did not apply if a mother or her children were manumitted, since, legally, a slave and a free person could not be related. In addition, if a mother were convicted of a crime, her children could be sold away from her as punishment. In spite of these exceptions which could provide legal justification for the separate selling of slave mothers and children, it is probable that the customs and proclamations forbidding it were generally adhered to.

The inviolability of the bond between a slave mother and her children was the only feature of the family organization of slaves that was legally validated by the Surinamese slave system. As a result of this feature, households and kinship groups had a matrifocal or matricentric character that was externally imposed. Given the high degree of conjugal instability that characterized the slave population, it is logical to assume that male consorts would be peripheral or absent in many Surinamese slave families.

The Proclamation of 1850 specified that the slave mother and her children should remain together for as long as she lived. Following her death, it is probable that her children would continue to reside on her plantation in some cases. Intergenerational extension of matrifocal ties would produce descent groups consisting of a core of uterine relatives with children of male members who selected mates from their own plantations. While they are not localized or corporate, urban Nengre roots are structurally equivalent to these descent groups which can be hypothesized to have existed among slaves on plantations.

In retrospect, many important features of urban Nengre family organization appear to have been present, or at least were foreshadowed, during the period of slavery in Surinam. These include: a high degree of conjugal instability and the possibility of legal marriage for free Creoles; emphasis on the closeness of uterine and sororal as opposed to agnatic and fraternal linkages; and the probable existence of matrifocal households and cognatic descent groups with a supernatural attachment to their place of origin.

Three population segments of the Surinamese slave society are relevant to this analysis: lower status free Creoles, individually owned slaves from the urban area, and plantation slaves. Demographic, ecological, and status differences between these segments undoubtedly caused differences in modes of family organization, but the historical data are not sufficiently detailed to enable systematic comparison. Distinctive characteristics of kinship and residence of all three of these population segments were probably combined as emancipated plantation slaves migrated to Paramaribo and mingled with emancipated urban slaves and lower status free Creoles to form an urban proletariat.

During the period of slavery, Dutch colonial policy was directed toward the maximization of profits from plantation agriculture and the maintenance of as great a difference as possible between the slave and free statuses. As plantation agriculture became less profitable and abolitionist sentiment in Europe increased, Holland's colonial policy in Surinam underwent significant change. Following emancipation in 1863, a colonial program of "Assimilation Politics" was adopted. The aim of the new program was to make Surinam an overseas replica of Holland and to impart Dutch culture to the Surinamese Creole population. Behavior patterns such as conjugal instability and nonlegal conjugal unions, speaking Surinamese Creole, and going without shoes and stockings were now discouraged. The Dutch language, Christianity, formal education, and European manners and morals became highly valued and, at least theoretically, were accessible for the first time to a large majority of the Surinamese population.

The program of Assimilation Politics was naïve in its basic assumptions and impossible to execute without the expenditure of tremendous resources. It was abandoned before it had a chance to work because it was realized that Hindustani and Javanese indentured laborers, who were imported to Surinam following emancipation, were unwilling to abandon their own cultures. The result of Assimilation Politics was to establish the Dutch behavior patterns that it sought to inculcate as highly valued respectable forms of behavior for Creoles, and later, for upwardly mobile members of other ethnic groups.

Prior to emancipation, Surinamese planters feared that, when given their freedom, slaves would abandon the plantations to which they had been attached because of laziness and an aversion to their former owners. During the late nineteenth and early twentieth centuries, a majority of the previous plantation slave population did, in fact, migrate to Paramaribo. However, the evidence suggests that the urban migration of Creoles was not a result of the causes advanced by the planters. Rather, it was a result of the continuing decline in Surinamese plantation agriculture that had begun at the turn of the previous century, and of the replacing of the slave labor force by the importation of approximately 72,000 indentured laborers between 1853 and 1939.[14] While it is probably true that many slaves disliked plantation agriculture and were attracted to the city, the economic situation in Surinam following emancipation was such that most ex-plantation slaves were forced to become urbanized regardless of their wishes.

After emancipation, previous city slaves were joined by those who were moving in from the plantations to form a rapidly growing urban proletariat which was the nucleus of the contemporary Nengre population. The number of uneducated and unskilled Creoles seeking work was much greater than the number of non-agricultural jobs available. The urban unemployment problem became more acute when, following the expiration of their contracts of indenture, Chinese, Hindustani, and Javanese indentured laborers began moving to the city and into nonagricultural pursuits.

The slave forebears of the contemporary Nengre population were economically powerless in that they had no control of the profits produced by their labor. While emancipation gave them this control, it did not assure them a secure economic position. For most of the period that has elapsed since emancipation, the Nengre have been economically marginal because of low wages and limited occupational opportunities. Emancipation did produce a very significant change in the legal status of ex-slaves and provided them with a limited number of opportunities for upward mobility. Yet, it did not appreciably alter the external environing field so as to produce sudden dramatic alterations in Nengre kinship and residential patterns.

Since emancipation, Surinam has been faced with a problem of chronic unemployment. From time to time, increased economic activity and foreign aid have provided temporary relief. Between the 1870s and 1930s, gold mining and the harvesting of wild rubber were important nonagricultural industries. During the 1920s, bauxite mining became a major industry, and its importance has increased continually since then. Several long-term construction projects such as the Zanderij Air Field, which was built by the U.S. Army during World War II, and the Afobakka hydroelectric dam, which was built after the war, have provided large numbers of jobs for skilled and unskilled laborers. In addition to these indigenous sources of employment, the petroleum refining industry of Curaçao, and the postwar reconstruction and industrial boom that followed it in Holland, opened up many jobs for the Surinamese.

Most of the occupational opportunities mentioned above are for males and involve spending considerable periods of time in the interior of Surinam or in other countries. The urban Nengre have taken these jobs more frequently than members of other ethnic groups. As is the case in other Afro-American populations, male absenteeism has been an important factor in perpetuating matrifocal patterns of kinship and residence within the Nengre population.

While matrifocality and other traditional Afro-American patterns of mating, domesticity, and residence are manifestations of continuity in the historical development of the Nengre family system, the system has undergone significant change since the period of slavery, and particularly since the 1930s. As will be recalled, the Nengre have adopted selected Dutch social patterns as canons of respectability during the postemancipation period. In a familial context, respectability requires the maintenance of a neolocal primary household based on legal marriage in which the husband-father provides support and the wife-mother engages in domestic and child-rearing activities. With the rapid development of educational and occupational opportunities in Surinam since the 1930s, increasing numbers of Nengre have been able to conform to standards of respectability in family organization. The contemporary Nengre kinship system, described in the first part of this essay, is sufficiently flexible to provide institutional validation for a wide variety of domestic and residential arrangements ranging between traditional Afro-American and respectable Euro-American polar extremes.

Conclusions

The historical development of the Nengre family system has been conceived of in terms of adaptation to a complex, changing environing field. The foregoing analysis suggests that factors affecting the organization of Nengre families can be subsumed within three general categories: (1) African cultural survivals of a general nature which have subsequently operated to selectively filter adaptive responses at a deep structural level; (2) Euro-American acculturation in general and Dutch cultural influence in particular which have become increasingly significant in the postemancipation period; and (3) historical events, phenomena, and ecological and demographic factors that are unique to Surinam. Cultural influences from China, India, Indonesia, and the parent nations of smaller Surinamese ethnic segments appear to have had negligible effects on Nengre family organization. In this regard it can be noted that African slaves and European masters co-existed in Surinam for two hundred years before the importation of indentured laborers, and that the boundaries between ethnic segments are very impermeable.

Because past conditions and responses to them have limited the possible variety of responses to subsequent changes in the external environing field, a consideration of historical factors is essential to an adequate analysis of Afro-American family organization. However, as this study has demonstrated, simplistic historical explanations are inadequate. All factors cited as causes in the literature on the Afro-American family are relevant in the Nengre case. No single historical source or condition or contemporary ecological or demographic factor can be expected to provide an adequate explanation of the urban Nengre or any other Afro-American system of family organization.

Notes

The information on which this essay is based was gathered during two field trips to Paramaribo, Surinam. The first of these (October 1967–May 1969) was devoted to the gathering of data on contemporary urban Nengre family organization, and provided the basis for my dissertation on the articulation of kinship and residence among the urban Nengre. The second (Summer 1971) was devoted to the gathering of primary data on urban Nengre supernaturalism and library research on the history of Surinam. The first field trip was financed by NIMH Fellowship 1F1-MH-35, 792-01 and Grant Attachment MH 13,771-01. The second was financed by grants from the National Geographic Society and the Committee on Faculty Research Support of the Florida State University, Tallahassee, Florida. I am grateful to these agencies for making the research possible.

1. In Surinam, the term *Creole* is utilized to designate an ethnic segment that is defined in terms of European and/or African descent, and participation in the national social and cultural system of the coastal area. Approximately 70 percent of the Creole population resides in and around Paramaribo, the capital and only true urban center of the country, and a substantial majority of this population is lower status, economically marginal, and Afro-Caribbean in cultural orientation. Lower status Creoles are referred to as Nengre both by themselves and by others.

2. During the 1930s and early 1940s, explanations of the Afro-American family stressed historical factors such as the survival of West African cultural patterns (Herskovits, 1941) and disorganizing effects of slavery systems (Frazier, 1939). Later, contemporary ecological and demographic patterns provided bases for explaining salient features of Afro-American family organization. These explanations are based on factors such as: systems of land tenure (Cohen, 1954; Clarke, 1953), a division of labor that causes prolonged separation of the sexes or migratory wage labor (Gonzalez, 1969; Kunstadter, 1963; Otterbein, 1965), and economic marginality (Clarke, 1957; Smith, R. T., 1965). M. G. Smith (1966) compares the family systems of five Caribbean communities in terms of differences in the structuring of relationships of conjugality and parenthood. Valentine (1968) critically

evaluates analytical schemas which emphasize the disorganization of Afro-American families and those which focus on poverty as a cultural determinant of family organization.

3. Since this essay was submitted for publication, two important analyses of Surinamese Creole family organization have appeared. William F. L. Buschkens (1974) has amassed an extensive body of ethnohistoric data on the family organization of Paramaribo Creoles in a much more ambitious analysis than is represented here. My criticisms of Buschkens's work stem from his definition of family organization which is based primarily on residence, secondarily on domesticity, and peripherally, if at all, on kinship. This definition results in what I consider to be a superficial analysis of contemporary Creole family organization, and in an overemphasis on patterns of continuity in Creole family organization as manifest in such patterns as instability of conjugality, consanguineal household extension, and matrifocality. I am unwilling to conclude, as Buschkens seems to, that the family system of Paramaribo Creoles has not changed significantly since the early stages of the period of slavery.

I would agree with Buschkens that there have been numerous important continuities in the historical development of the Creole or Nengre family system. I think, however, that it is also necessary to recognize that historical events and phenomena such as the decline of the plantation system, emancipation, the migration of many lower status Creoles to Paramaribo, Dutch colonial policies such as Assimilation Politics, and the decreasing isolation of Surinam from U.S. and Western European acculturative influences have had significant effects on Creole residential, domestic, and kinship patterns.

Brana-Shute (1974) has studied the organization of familial and extrafamilial relationships of lower status Creole males in Paramaribo. His concept of family organization is similar to that of Buschkens, but Creole family organization is not the primary focus of his analysis. Brana-Shute's research deals with the important problem of the articulation of males within an Afro-American society. With regard to this focus, his analysis is detailed, thorough, and sophisticated.

4. When missionary work was begun among Surinamese slaves by Moravians and Roman Catholics in the latter part of the eighteenth century, missionaries encouraged converts to become partners in religiously sanctioned marriages. These marriages were not recognized by the colonial government since slaves were not permitted to enter into legal contracts. Older informants stated that religious marriages persisted until as late as the 1950s.

5. The legally married husband of a female is the father of her children by different males. In the field, I encountered a case in which a legal wife deserted her husband for another man who was older and richer. During the ten years that she lived with the latter, she bore him four children. Since divorce had not occurred, the children had the surname of their mother's husband, rather than their own father, and the husband was theoretically the children's legal guardian.

6. For concise summaries of the literature on recurrent patterns of Afro-American household organization, see Kunstadter (1963) and Otterbein (1965).

7. From 1667 until 1954, with the exception of two brief periods of British control, Surinam was a colony in the Kingdom of the Netherlands. From 1954 until 1975, it was an internally autonomous commonwealth partner in the Kingdom of the Netherlands. On November 25, 1975, Surinam became a completely independent country.

8. Wooding deals extensively with the tribal provenience of Surinamese slaves. His data are summarized in the following table (adapted from Wooding, 1972:36).

Tribes from Which People Were Imported to Surinam

| Sengambia | Ivory Coast | Togo | | Cameroon |
| Sierra Leone | Ghana | Dahomey | | Congo |
Liberia	(Gold Coast)	(Slave Coast)	Nigeria	Angola
Foela	(Tebou)	Abo	Nago	Abo
Foeloeppoe	(La Hoe)	Ayois	Ibo	Congo
Conia	Aqueras	(Ardra)		Loango
Sokko	Alquirasche	Fida		Goango
Riemba	Akim	Foin		Pombo
Temne's	Annamaboe	Jaquin		Demakoekoe
Mendees	Asiantijn	Mallais		(Angola)
Pre-Negers	(Accra)	Papa		Guiamba
Gola	Coromantijn	Dahomansche		
(Sierra Leone)*	Delmina			
(Goree)	Fantijn			
(Cabo Monte)	Gango			
Konare	Tjamba			
	N. Zokko			
	Sokko's			
Sokko's	Wanway			

* Names in parentheses are place-names, not tribal names.

9. Following is a comparison of day names in Surinam and Ashanti:

	Surinam		Ashanti (Source: Smith, R. T., 1956:131)	
	Male	Female	Male	Female
Sun.	Kwasi	Kwasiba	Kwasi	Akwasibu
Mon.	Kodjo	Adjuba	Kwaduo	A'duowa
Tues.	Kwamina	Abeni	Kwabena	Abenaa
Wed.	Kwaku	Akuba	Kwaku	Akuwa
Thurs.	Yaw	Yaba	Yaw	Yaa/Yawa
Fri.	Kofi	Afi, Afiba	Kofi	Afuwa
Sat.	Kwami	Amba	Kwame	Amma

10. The concepts of surface and deep structure have been developed by the Transformational Grammar School of Linguistics. In the present context, it is sufficient to define surface structure as being manifest at the level of empirical reality, and deep structure as underlying and accounting for the appearance of the empirical manifestation. This distinction is relevant in social anthropology because it clarifies the differences between structural-functionalists such as Malinowsky and Radcliffe-Brown and structuralists such as Lévi-Strauss with regard to the definition of structure. Structural-functionalists have been concerned with surface structure of sociocultural phenomena, while structuralists

are primarily concerned with deep structure. For an excellent demonstration of such deep structure similarities, see Wilbert (1975).

11. Author's translation.

12. Author's translation.

13. Author's translation.

14. Between 1853 and 1872, 5,400 indentured laborers were brought to Surinam through individual initiative. These included 500 Maderian Portuguese, 2,500 Chinese, and 2,400 British West Indians. In 1872, the Dutch government took control of the importation of indentured laborers to Surinam. Between 1873 and 1916, approximately 34,000 Hindustani indentured laborers were brought in from India, and between 1891 and 1939, approximately 33,000 Javanese indentured laborers were imported from Indonesia (Malefijt, 1963:21–22).

References

Bascom, W. R. 1941. Acculturation Among the Gullah Negroes. American Anthropologist 43:43–50.

Blom, A. 1787. Verhandeling van den Landbouw in de Kolonie Suriname. Amsterdam: J. W. Smit.

Brana-Shute, Gary. 1974. Streetcorner Winkels and Dispersed Households: Male Adaptation to Marginality in a Lower Status Creole Neighborhood in Paramaribo. Ph.D. dissertation, Gainesville: University of Florida.

Buckley, W. 1968. Society as a Complex Adaptive System, in W. Buckley, ed., Modern Systems Research for the Behavioral Scientist. Chicago: Aldine, pp. 490–513.

Buschkens, Willem F. L. 1974. The Family System of the Paramaribo Creoles. The Hague: Martinus Nijhoff.

Clarke, E. 1957. My Mother Who Fathered Me: A Study of the Family in Three Selected Communities in Jamaica. London: George Allen Unwin.

Cohen, Y. A. 1954. The Social Organization of a Selected Community in Jamaica. Social and Economics Studies 2:104–134.

Frazier, E. F. 1939. The Negro Family in the United States. Chicago: University of Chicago Press.

Glazer, N., and Moynihan, D. P. 1966. Beyond the Melting Pot: The Negroes, Puerto Ricans, Jews, Italians and Irish of New York City. Cambridge: M.I.T. Press and Harvard University Press.

Gonzalez, N. L. 1969. Migration and Modernization: Adaptative Reorganization in the Black Carib Household. Seattle: University of Washington Press.

Herskovits, M. J. 1941. Myth of the Negro Past. New York: Harper.

Hoetink, H. 1967. Caribbean Race Relations: A Study of Two Variants. London: Oxford University Press.

Hoetink, H. 1969. Race Relations in Curaçao and Surinam, in L. Foner and D. Genovese, eds., Slavery in the New World: A Reader in Comparative History. Englewood Cliffs, N.J.: Prentice-Hall, pp. 178–188.

Kunstadter, P. 1963. A Survey of the Consanguine or Matrifocal Family. American Anthropologist 65:56–66.

Malefijt, A. de Waal. 1963. The Javanese of Surinam: Segment of a Plural Society. Assen: Van Gorcum and Company.

Otterbein, K. F. 1965. Caribbean Family Organization: A Comparative Analysis. American Anthropologist 67:66–79.

Pierce, B. E. 1971. Kinship and Residence Among the Urban Nengre of Surinam: A Re-evaluation of Concepts and Theories of the Afro-American Family. Ph.D. dissertation, New Orleans: Tulane University.

Smith, M. G. 1966. West Indian Family Structure. Seattle: University of Washington Press.

Smith, R. T. 1956. The Negro Family in British Guiana: Family Structure and Social Status in the Villages. London: Routledge & Kegan Paul.

Stedman, J. G. 1796. Narrative of a Five Year Expedition Against the Revolted Negroes of Surinam. London: J. J. Johnson and J. Edwards.

Teenstra, M. D. 1842. De Negerslaven in de Kolonie Suriname en de uitbreiding van het Christendom onder de heidensche bevolking. Dordrecht: H. Lagerweij.

Valentine, C. A. 1968. Culture and Poverty: Critique and Counter-proposals. Chicago: University of Chicago Press.

Van Hoevel, W. R. 1854. Slaven en vrijen onder de Nederlandsche wet. Zaltbommel: John Norman and Son.

Van Lier, R. A. J. 1949. Samenleving in een grensgebeid. The Hague: Martinus Nijhoff.

Wilbert, Johannes. 1975. Kinsmen of Flesh and Blood: Is the Goajiro Kinship System Indigenous or African? Paper presented in a symposium on Ethnohistory of Afro-Americans in Latin America, 74th Annual Meeting of the American Anthropological Association in San Francisco, December 5, 1975.

Wooding, C. J. 1972. Winti: een Afroamerikaanse Godsdienst in Suriname: een cultureel-historische analyse van de religieuze verschijnselen in de Para. Meppel, Holland: Krips Repro b.v.

7. SEXISM AND THE CONSTRUCTION OF REALITY

An Afro-American Example

Sally Price

Throughout their history, the Suriname Maroons (often called "Bush Negroes") have excited the romantic imaginations of outsiders—from the 18th-century soldiers who fought against them in their original wars of liberation to the 20th-century anthropologists who live among them, and from the coastal Surinamers who see them walking barefoot in the streets of the capital city to the foreign tourists who sign up for one-day jungle excursions to the interior. All of these observers have been captivated by the story of the Maroons' heroic struggle for freedom from slavery, by their striking independence in the South American rain forest, and by the visible debt their way of life owes to the many African societies from which their early ancestors came.

Two aspects of Maroon society—the place of women and the role of art in social life—have attracted considerable attention and have contributed importantly to the image of Maroon life as it is constructed by non-Maroons. This paper, based on long-term fieldwork with the Saramaka Maroons, suggests that the social and artistic life of women has generally been misunderstood by outsiders at least in part because of ideas about gender that are held by both outsiders and by Maroons themselves.

The fascination of Westerners with the place of women in Maroon societies can be traced to two central features of Maroon life: a strongly matrilineal kinship system and the evident independence of women in many contexts. Because residence, political succession, ritual involvements, marriage prohibitions, land tenure, and countless other aspects of their life are regulated by a kinship system centered on relations traced through women, outsiders are often inspired to speculate as to the political/ritual/social influence that they imagine Maroon women must exercise within their communities. Because they often see Maroon women conducting themselves quite independently—maintaining a household separate from their husband's, growing their own food in an individually owned garden, rearing children largely as single parents, and, in the most literal sense,

Originally published in *American Ethnologist* 10:3 (August 1983), pp. 460–76. Reproduced by permission of the American Anthropological Association. Not for further reproduction.

paddling their own canoes—many outsiders assume that Maroon women's freedom from the domination of men extends over the whole of their domestic life.
In other words, the pivotal position of women in defining the basic structure of
social relations has often been misread as a central role for women in directing
social life itself; matriliny has been read as matriarchy.

The evident independence of Maroon women in housing, subsistence activities, child rearing, and intervillage transportation is occasionally misinterpreted
as a kind of 1970s-style liberation; women's independence is viewed as their own
conscious choice. As a result of this kind of speculation, the literature on Maroons is sprinkled with characterizations of the following sort:

> The women essentially rule the entire people because they are the main ones who
> deal with the gods. (Kersten 1770:137)

> It is chiefly the women who see that the ancestral and village customs are en-
> forced. They are the guardians of the ancient traditions and customs of the race.
> (Kahn 1931:98)

> . . . the [Maroon] woman, . . . jealous of her independence from the man, places
> her pride in being able to get along on her own. (Hurault 1961:158)

> The women . . . participate fully in the . . . major decisions about village life.
> Women sit on the high councils, equal to the men. (Counter and Evans 1981:92)

This image, frequently reinforced by an ideologically motivated glorification
of Maroon society, sometimes leads to ironic distortions. For example, the explicit
purpose of the custom of menstrual seclusion is to protect men's ritual powers
from pollution. This period of seclusion is viewed by Maroon women as one of
the more distasteful, inconvenient, and burdensome necessities of their life. However, two recent male visitors whose only verbal contact with the Maroons was
through an interpreter misrepresent the periodic banishment of women from social life by presenting the menstrual hut as the location of a kind of feminist escape from the burdens of daily life, asserting that

> rules governing the practice [of menstrual seclusion] are made by the women
> themselves . . . the women seem to enjoy this opportunity to get away from the
> village chores and family and join their friends in the woman's *oso* [house] for
> several days of gossip and laughter. (Counter and Evans 1981:133)

Outsiders give even more attention to Maroon art than to Maroon women,
resulting in a large body of literature, both popular and scholarly, published in
English, Dutch, French, German, Spanish, and other languages. Books and articles on "Bush Negro art" have always been devoted to decorative woodcarving—the stunning and elaborately developed medium that every Maroon man is

expected to master (see, e.g., Dark 1954; Herskovits 1969 [1930]; Kahn 1931; Hurault 1970; Muntslag 1966). The received wisdom about Maroon art (i.e., woodcarving) is that it functions importantly in the context of male-female relations, especially in courtship and marriage. Such gift giving is traditionally viewed as a one-way street, with men actively producing and proffering artistic objects and women passively receiving and admiring them. Herskovits (1969:159), whose first foreign fieldwork was among the Saramaka in the late 1920s, offered a quotation in pseudo-Saramaccan to support this picture of Maroon art: " *'Tembe no muje sundi,'* . . . 'Woodcarving is not a woman's affair.' " Another writer, working with secondary sources, generalized confidently that "the role of the men is primarily concerned with creation, that of the women with appreciation" (Dark 1951:57).

My own experience with Maroons does not contradict the image of Maroon women as enthusiastic and admiring connoisseurs of men's woodcarving, nor does it lead to doubts as to how meaningful these decorated objects are to them as symbols of sexual love. At the same time, however, my experience makes it very clear that artistic creativity and productivity are not confined to men; Maroon women have developed forms of artistic expression that are every bit as richly elaborated. If we look at what is actually happening in Maroon villages, we see women as active artists, producing beautifully carved calabashes and a wide range of textile arts that rival their more well known counterparts in other areas of the world. We also see that the use of art in courtship and marriage is very much a two-way street, with Maroon women expressing their love through artistic gifts just as men do.[1]

Over the past 16 years, in the course of general ethnographic research with Saramaka Maroons, I have attempted to understand women's social and artistic life from their own perspective.[2] Particularly in informal settings—while cutting rice in their gardens, sewing clothes and carving calabashes on their doorsteps, preparing meals in their cooking sheds, doing laundry at rocks in the river, and gossiping together in the menstrual hut—Saramaka women have provided interesting clues as to how their place in the society is reflected in their arts, as well as how their arts are used in social life. They have spoken eloquently and perceptively about their place in the society, about their view of men's arts and women's arts, and about the potential of decorative and verbal arts for expressing their joys and sorrows.

The image that Maroon women present of themselves is quite different from that of defiantly independent matriarchs who run council meetings, preside over social and religious life, and delight in the conviviality of the menstrual hut. Rather, when women speak of their participation in public life it is with recognition of the dominant role of men as social and religious leaders. When women speak of menstrual seclusion it is with resignation rather than joy. The bulk of their conversations center on their involvements in a polygynous marriage system

that strongly favors men. Moreover, their daily life during the years I spent in the
field offered strong support for these views, in the form of countless specific incidents.

Art in Social Life

Several features of Saramaka social life are particularly relevant to a full understanding of their arts. First, husbands are scarcer than wives. Second, women
are more dependent on their husbands, in terms of material well-being, than men
are on their wives. Third, women attach more affective value than men do to
both the giving and the receiving of conjugal gifts.

THE RELATIVE SCARCITY OF
HUSBANDS COMPARED TO WIVES

Even though many Saramaka men have two, three, or even four wives, there
are at any one time many more women without husbands than men without
wives. Furthermore, while being unmarried is for men virtually always a temporary state to be altered more or less when they choose, women's opportunities for
remarriage decline sharply with age, so that women who are widowed or divorced
in their 40s face a very real prospect of remaining permanently without a husband, and women past menopause virtually never remarry. Several different features of Saramaka life are responsible for this surplus of older, marriageable
women, but the two most important contributing factors are (1) that women enter into their first marriage in their mid-teens, while men do so in their mid-20s
and (2) that Saramaka men spend long periods of their life earning money on the
coast, effectively removing themselves from the marriage pool. With teenage girls
and non-Saramaka women acquiring a significant portion of the potential husbands, the scarcity of marriageable men for older Saramaka women is not only a
perceived problem but a statistical reality.[3]

THE GREATER MATERIAL DEPENDENCE OF A WOMAN
ON HER HUSBAND THAN OF A MAN ON HIS WIFE

A Saramaka woman is dependent for a wide range of goods and services on *one*
man, her husband, who should provide her house, her canoe, her household furnishings, the bulk of the fish and game in her diet, and the male labor needed
for clearing gardens in the forest. When she has no husband, or when her husband is absent for long periods of time, her standard of living is significantly lowered. During these times she is put in the position of "begging" a kinsman—a
brother or an uncle, for example—to help out. When a woman's house is built
by a kinsman, however, it is not expected to be as beautifully decorated as the

one her husband would have provided; fish and game are supplied by her kinsmen only when there is some left over from what they give their own wives; and
unmarried women must often make do with reworking old gardens rather than
planting newly cleared ones, because their male kinsmen are too busy to spend
time felling trees and cutting underbrush for them.

By contrast, there is very little variation among Saramaka men in how adequately they are supplied with the goods and services for which women are responsible. The most important material contributions that women make to men
are meals and clothing, and it is rarely difficult for a man to obtain either of these.
Not only are men generally married for most of their lives but because of widespread polygyny a man is frequently in the position of being provided for by two
or three women at a time, all of whom are consciously competing for his favor.
As a result, men often have valises and trunks filled with beautifully decorated
clothing, much of which they have never worn. In terms of food, the practice of
communal meals for the men of a neighborhood, as well as for any men visiting
in the neighborhood, means that meals are always available to men whether or
not their wives are around to cook for them.

Sexual opportunities are similarly tilted in favor of men. Ideals for women's
behavior require sexual fidelity to one husband at a time, sexual abstinence during that husband's years away from Saramaka, and resignation to a sharply reduced sex life during old age. By contrast, men are expected to have several wives
at a time, to engage in frequent extramarital affairs, to take lovers and wives during their years away from Saramaka, and to continue to be sexually active well
into old age.

In short, women sometimes have access to the goods and services that are supplied by men and sometimes not. But men are almost never deprived to any significant extent of the goods and services that are provided by women.

WOMEN VALUE CONJUGAL EXCHANGES MORE THAN MEN DO

There is no doubt that Saramaka women are more insecure than Saramaka
men when it comes to pleasing their spouses in terms of both the proper fulfillment of their own obligations and the adequate reciprocation of their spouses'
offerings. It is perhaps significant that a special phrase, *nyá papái*, which refers
to the shame of not being able to reciprocate a gift properly, is used frequently by
and about women but is not generally applied to men. Even the etiquette of conjugal exchange is different for men and women. Saramaka women, upon receiving a gift from a husband, are expected to offer more effusive expressions of gratitude, to display it to a wide range of other people, and to indulge in dramatic,
excited behavior similar to that of American women on television game shows
who win fur coats or washing machines or trips to Hawaii. Saramaka men who
receive a conjugal gift are also expected to express thanks, but in a much more
subdued style. The main contribution women make to men's life—prepared

food—is treated not as a gift that must be acknowledged but rather as the simple fulfillment of a woman's duties.

Male and Female Artists

Just as husbands are scarcer than wives in Saramaka, so too are male-made woodcarvings scarcer than female-made decorative textiles. This alone confers on woodcarvings a special value. Inventories of a number of women's possessions indicate that although women may have two or three carved combs and up to five or six carved stools, they tend to own only one or two examples of most kinds of decoratively carved objects—paddles, food stirrers, peanut-grinding boards, and so forth. These objects are displayed in the woman's house, and women are always able to supply a detailed account of which man made each one and when it was presented. Woodcarvings, then, represent to women tangible and very visible symbols of specific personal relationships.

Textiles are a very different matter. Because most men have two or three wives at a time, as well as a large number of lovers who also offer decorated textiles as gifts of affection, their storage trunks tend to be filled with literally hundreds of capes, breechcloths, dance aprons, calfbands, and neckerchiefs. When I discussed these collections with their owners, it became clear that only a very few of the individual textiles retained specific romantic meanings. Men often did not know which wife or lover had sewn a particular textile, and they tended to see their clothing as a largely undifferentiated accumulation of gifts from the women in their life.[4]

Women's carved calabashes are also intended for use in the context of marriage, but unlike woodcarvings and textiles, they are never conjugal gifts. Decorated calabashes are understood primarily to reflect the care and aesthetic taste of the woman who sets them out when serving her husband's meals; as such, they form an important part of the Saramaka conception of a woman's role in marriage. The display of calabashes is also an important aspect of the ceremonial presentation that occurs when a woman pays her first formal visit to a new husband's village. Women often decorate the interior of their house with extensive arrays of carefully selected calabashes that they have carved (see S. Price and R. Price 1980:Figures 23–24).[5]

Woodcarving, decorative sewing, and calabash carving—the three main artistic media in Saramaka villages—thus play complementary roles in social life. Woodcarvings are highly valued by women, and each carved object is understood as a specific symbol of the relationship between the man who created it and the woman to whom he gave it. Textiles offer an idiom for women to express their love for a man, but they do not generally retain individualized romantic associations by the men who own them. And carved calabashes communicate the care with which a woman fulfills her conjugal duties, without ever serving as a conjugal gift.

Saramakas not only have firm opinions about the relative value of artistic media, such as woodcarvings and textiles, they also have definite ideas on a more general level about the "natural" artistic aptitudes of men versus women. Even when considering the arts that women have developed and personalized, such as embroidery or interior-carved calabashes, there is still a general belief among both men and women that men could do them better. Women like to ask men for help in laying out an embroidery design, sometimes even seeking instructions as to which lines to execute in which colors.[6] Men often say they are too busy to help, but when a man does sit down to draw out the lines of a design with pencil, the woman embroiders it extremely conscientiously, treating it as a valuable asset. As one woman commented, "Embroidered neckerchiefs that men design are more handsome than women's because they design them like a woodcarving." What she was referring to was the achievement of geometric precision and exact symmetry in men's designs, for these are the features of men's carving that women consider themselves incapable of producing. Men have always used imported tools, such as compasses, in their art, and they produce designs with rigorous geometric regularity, a quality that is strongly valued by all Saramakas, both men and women.

Women's more flowing free-form designs are also admired, but to Saramakas they reflect a lesser artistic accomplishment. Women see themselves as striving in their arts toward the kind of symmetry and geometric precision that characterize men's woodcarving, but generally failing to achieve it. Their narrow-strip textile compositions are consciously planned in terms of symmetry around a vertical center strip, but they exhibit a tendency—viewed by Saramakas as typically feminine "mistakes"—to stray from the perfect regularity of a pattern (e.g., by the insertion of an extra bit of embroidery or the reversal of one of two "matching" strips of cloth). Capes embroidered by women are similarly designed around a center, but the sides rarely come out perfectly even. Figuring out how to balance the elements of a calabash design in order to produce a proper mirror image between the two sides is seen by women as one of the most difficult parts of getting the design the way they want it. Those few women who teach themselves how to mark out geometric embroidery designs, rather than asking a man to help or embroidering a more typical woman's design, show pride in their accomplishment, but their behavior is considered by most people to be rather unfeminine. Young girls who show an artistic inclination in this direction (like girls in a traditional community in the United States who aspire to an expertise in physics or construction work rather than in literature or nursing) are made to understand that the precision involved in such designs represents a somewhat "unnatural" skill for their sex.[7]

Men's Art, Women's Doodling

In the hands of Western observers (brought up with their own definite notions about men and women), the Maroons' cultural bias toward male artistic styles has been accepted not as an aesthetic preference but rather as a statement of ethnographic reality. The consequences of this interpretive error have ranged from the academic to the economic: men's woodcarving is the only Maroon art treated seriously in the literature and it is the only Maroon art that has any commercial value in the tourist shops of coastal Suriname.

Even when outsiders *do* acknowledge the existence of women's arts, their perceptions still tend to reflect Western preconceptions about men and women. For example, in one of the very rare attempts to deal seriously with Maroon women as artists, Philip Dark (1951) projected some traditional Euro-American notions about women onto Maroon calabash arts and reached some rather questionable conclusions about what he called the "personality configurations" of Maroon men and women.[8] In an analysis of the differences between men's calabash carving (executed on the exterior surfaces of two-piece containers, with compasses, chisels, and knives) and women's calabash carving (executed on the interior surfaces of bowls and ladles, with pieces of broken glass), Dark evaluated their distinctive features in the following terms. The men's designs were described as "always clearly marked," "always well considered and apt," and "always conceived as having to fill a definite surface," and they were said to exhibit "apt consideration of the relationship of design to design space" (Dark 1951:58–59). By contrast, the women's carvings were described as "alien" (to the men's), and it was said that they "may or may not" overflow the design space, "may or may not" be conceived as having to fill a definite surface, and "may or may not" be "apt" in terms of the relationship of design to design space (Dark 1951:59).

To understand the differences that he perceived between men's and women's styles of carving, Dark looked to published ethnographic reports on Maroon life. There he found comments that allowed him to characterize Maroon marriage as a "tenuous" relationship in which "women appear to have the whip hand" (1951:59) and "divorce is quite an informal matter, a woman being able to break a union on some slight pretext" (1951:57). Combining his own museum analysis of calabash carvings with these impressionistic ideas of Maroon social life (provided by Morton Kahn, a physician who visited Suriname in the 1920s), Dark (1951:59) arrived at the remarkable speculation that both indicate

> a distinct difference in temperament between the men and women of this culture. The men would appear to be definite in their actions and probably more conservative than the women. The women may perhaps be thought more fickle and more easily susceptible to novelty. Perhaps the decoration of calabashes by the women is their form of doodling.[9]

Although based purely on secondary sources, Dark's reading of the contrast between the "personality configurations" of Maroon men and women as artists presented ironic similarities to the ideas of Maroons themselves. His comparative assessment of male and female styles of carving led to the notion that one is art, the other doodling. Maroon "sexism," while not reaching such an extreme position, also encourages the view that women's art is inferior to men's art. We are told by Dark that women's designs are less consistently "well considered and apt" than those of the men; we are told by Maroons that women's designs exhibit less technical skill than those of the men. We thus have two independent assessments of these decorative styles that strongly reinforce one another—one from a museum researcher and another from the artists themselves. In both cases, however, it might be useful to attempt to disaggregate the visual properties of women's art (such as features of design and technical control) from the cultural and social settings in which it is being evaluated, after which we should be able to reintegrate them in a more perceptive understanding of the ways in which they interrelate. For the fact that Dark's evaluation of male versus female arts in a sense corresponds to that of Maroons does not make either one of them any less a culturally conditioned aesthetic response.

Having observed the production, evaluation, and uses of Saramaka arts over an extended period of field experiences, I have come to the firm conclusion that the differential status of men's and women's arts stems more from social dynamics and gender constructs in that society than from the Saramakas' abstract aesthetic preferences.[10] If we do not simply assume that Maroon women are fickle doodlers, it becomes possible to appreciate the arts they produce and the ways in which they use art in their daily lives. Women's calabash carvings and textile designs, viewed from a more purely aesthetic perspective, represent richly elaborated artistic traditions.[11] Regardless of the status of women's arts relative to men's, the appreciation of women's artistic expression among both men and women is still a strong, positive aspect of Saramaka life. The importance of these arts in social life is equally undeniable. We can no longer accept the idea that Maroon men are active artists and Maroon women are passive connoisseurs, that Maroon men give art and Maroon women receive it. On the contrary, women spend a great deal of time engaged in artistic activities and most of what they produce is used to express and reaffirm the love that they feel for a man. By embroidering a handsome cape for her husband, a woman communicates her affection; by carving beautiful calabashes to set out at his meals, she reasserts her commitment to their marriage. Their arts, like men's woodcarving, are used to express love and solidarity.

Popular Songs

When love turns sour, when jealousy over a rival builds, when anger dominates, and when divorce threatens, however, the decorative arts are not viewed by Saramakas as a proper expressive outlet, and people turn instead to the performing arts. In the remainder of this paper I present Saramaka women's songs as a reflection of their self-image and an example of the gap between the way these women view their social position and the way it is traditionally portrayed in the literature. I suggest that their social position, as they themselves view it, has exerted a fundamental influence on the Saramaka construction of the relative merits of men's and women's arts.

Popular songs *(sêkêti kandá)* are the preferred artistic medium for the expression of love and hate, joy and despair, desire and rejection. Two representative examples give an idea of the range of emotions that these songs cover. In one a man expands the standard Saramaka "good morning" (*I wéki nô?*, "Did you awake?" or *Fá i wéki?*, "How did you awake?") into a song of admiration for his tall wife:

Gadja mazó, a póbiki búka,	Statuesque nun, with the mouth of a doll,
Un fá i wéki-o, mama?	How did you awake, momma?
Mi wéki-o, mi wéki-é.	I awoke, I awoke [the reciprocal greeting].
Mama, i wéki hánse sèmbè.	Momma, you awoke [as] a beautiful person.

In another, a woman calls out for help after a dramatic verbal and physical fight with her husband, mother-in-law, and co-wife; this song employs the standard term for a co-wife adversary and addresses a plea for help to Gaan Gadu, the "supreme deity" of Saramaka whose "voice" is heard in the form of thunder.

Kabitén, baáa-o. Kéé!	Headman, oh brother. *Kéé!* [expression of alarm]
Di soni miti mi,	The thing that's happened to me,
Un tá yéi-ó?	Do you hear?
Di gaamá-dê,	The tribal chief there,
Di soni miti mi,	The thing that's happened to me,
Un tá véi, nó?	Do you hear?
Téé u mi véi di Gaán Gádu bai	When I hear the thunder roll
Mi kái Gaán Gádu-éé,	I call out to Gaan Gadu,
Mi bái goón liba-o.	I shout out to the world.
U di vavó u mi édi	It's because of that slut-of-mine [co-wife]
Mi kái ên-éé.	That I'm calling him.

Sêkêti songs are created spontaneously by both men and women, usually about specific incidents in their own lives. In some songs people deal with problems that they share with others. For example, there were many songs in the 1960s about the hydroelectric dam that flooded about half of Saramaka territory and forced some 6000 people to evacuate to government-built towns near the coast. There were also many songs composed after a man tried to assassinate the Saramaka tribal chief that commented on the event and offered condolences to the chief. Most songs, however, are more personal and refer to the ups and downs of individual relationships. A Saramaka woman once suggested to me that all *sêkêti* songs are either songs of love, songs of cursing, or songs of hardship; that is, they either express the passions of a particular relationship, attack a specific enemy, or voice despair over personal hardships such as loneliness or poverty.

People most often compose new *sêkêti* songs in solitary and relaxed settings— for example, while paddling a canoe, cutting rice in a garden, or daydreaming at home. A person sitting idly on a doorstep may break into a spontaneous song as a way of commenting on the passing scene. An appropriate way to react to a gift is through a sung expression of delight. Even very young children are actively encouraged to invent *sêkêti* songs. One girl set the name of a kinsman to a little melody when she was three or four years old, singing "*Peléki-éé, Peléki-oo*," and was warmly embraced by everyone around, who interpreted this simple song as the beginning of a promising *sêkêti* career. Children just a few years older enjoy performing their own songs in groups, with a soloist, a choral response, and an accompaniment of rhythmic handclapping.

If a person's new *sêkêti* song catches the fancy of others, it is sung and talked about and eventually performed for the community at large, usually at one of several types of all-night funeral ceremonies. In the presence of perhaps a hundred or more people, a carefully groomed and attired performer sings the solo while executing a special dance. A line of women and girls, bent forward at the hips, provide a steady beat of handclapping and punctuate the soloist's phrases with a simple choral response. At the end, the performer is embraced and congratulated by others and another *sêkêti* song begins, either by the same person or by someone else.

Because of the frequency and spontaneity of *sêkêti* song composition, many are almost immediately forgotten and even those that become popular have a relatively brief active life. There were several hundred *sêkêti* songs being sung in Saramaka during 1967–68, but a year or two later these had all gone out of style and had been replaced by new ones that reflected incidents of more current interest—from love affairs and divorces to gift presentations and petty crime. When asked to do so, Saramakas can still sing the songs of the past decade, and the older women I worked with derived great pleasure from providing me with nostalgic renditions of songs that were popular in the early 20th century. But in the absence of an anthropologist's urging, the performance of outdated songs is limited to an occasional brief session at the very end of a wake, when most of the participants have already gone home to sleep.

Unlike some genres of Saramaka singing, *sêkêti* songs are composed in the everyday language of Saramaccan, but their verbal style is subtly different. Occasionally a person introduces a new word or phrase that becomes part of *sêkêti* vocabulary, more for the way it sounds than for what it means. *Sêkêti* lyrics also include more metaphorical words and expressions than does ordinary speech. For example, various kinds of Western-style communication that Saramakas view partly as foreign novelties are used to symbolize irresponsible gossiping: when a nonliterate woman sings that her name is "written down in a book," or when a man who has never used a telephone sings to someone, "Your mother just phoned," they are very explicitly accusing another person of spreading malicious rumors. Similarly, a faithful wife is often referred to metaphorically as a nun (mazó); a beautiful woman may be called Queen Wilhelmina (Kónu Wemina) because of the romantic attitude that Saramakas have toward Dutch royalty.

Women's Songs

The spontaneity of sêkêti composition allows these songs to express emotions directly and forcefully through phrases that are also used in gossip sessions and other conversational settings. The commentary in songs closely parallels the attitudes that people voice in other contexts. The emotions that women's songs express are extremely varied, from tender love to bitter jealousy, but there is a statistical tendency for them to be more negative than those composed by men.[12] The image of life that women project in their songs, like that expressed in other settings, contradicts quite strongly the notion that they hold the "whip hand" in marriage. Rather, they tend to present themselves as individuals deeply involved in love relationships that constantly run into snags and inspire intense rivalries. They also make clear that they are rarely in a position to control their personal lives as much as they would like to. Women's love songs are generally simple lyrical expressions of affection; they require no social science analysis. However, some commentary about women's other songs, which make up the statistical majority, may offer partial support for my argument that the position of Maroon women in their own society is not as privileged as some outsiders have imagined.

Women most frequently focus their songs on relationships with their husbands, their husbands' kin, and their husbands' other wives (their arch enemies in this polygynous society). While relations with their own kinswomen (especially mother, sisters, and mother's sisters) tend to be friendly, solidary, and relaxed, those relationships acquired through marriage are more often distinctly strained, and women view themselves as relatively impotent in dealing with the conflicts thereby produced. A woman's husband may fail to provide well for her, or he may show preference for another of his wives, but she is acutely aware that if she leaves him she not only will suffer in terms of material goods but she may well never have a chance to remarry. A woman's in-laws may spread malicious gossip about her, but if she leaves their village to establish full-time residence in her own village, she loses status in her husband's eyes and weakens her marriage. A woman's co-wives may make life extremely trying for her, but there is nothing she can do about the fact that her husband enjoys spending time with them. Many women's sêkêti songs address these dilemmas, not as general social problems but in terms of particular situations and individual relationships.

Several songs that one Saramaka woman made up in despair and anger over a particular rival are illustrative. In the first one, composed while she was cutting rice in her in-laws' horticultural camp, the woman attempted (at least rhetorically) to elicit sympathy from her husband through exaggerated self-deprecation:

Kiólo-éé,	Young dandy,
Wómi án dê a kamia kê mi môó-nô.	There's no other man around who wants me anymore.
I wánwan si mi kê.	Only you have ever wanted me.
Wé di fési Gaan Gádu dá mi,	Well, the face that God gave me,
Di u hónyó-hónyó.	That of a wasp,
I wánwán si mi kê.	Only you have ever wanted me.
Wé, di fési Gaán Gádu dá mi,	Well, the face that God gave me,
Di u mbéti u mátu,	That of a forest beast,
I wánwán si mi kê.	Only you have ever wanted me.
Wé, di fési Gaán Gádu dá mi,	Well, the face that God gave me,
Di u zandibô, wé,	That of a cartoon character, well,
I wánwán si mi kê.	Only you have ever wanted me.
Wé, di fési Gaán Gádu dá mi,	Well, the face that God gave me,
Di u basikáanu,	That of a funeral mask,
I wánwán si mi kê.	Only you have ever wanted me.

A second song was inspired when people told her husband that she had taken a lover; she called out to the gods in despair at being the victim of ugly rumors:

Di gádu a di lio,	Oh god that presides over this river,
Mi bái helú dá i,	I call out in despair to you
Di sondi miti mi a múndu	[About] the thing that's happened to me in the world
Sôndò mi sábi.	Without my even knowing.

In a third song she accused her husband's kin of making life in their village unbearable for her.

M'án ó téi ên,	I won't take it,
Bigá ná mi á di lio.	Because this isn't my river [home village].
Sèmbé sitááfu u tjái . . .	Accepting punishment from others . . .
M'án ó tjái di f'ên môò.	I'm not going to take *his* anymore.

And finally, when her efforts to save her marriage failed, she sang a bitter concession of defeat to her co-wife:

Kambósa-éé,	Co-wife,
Ná wái dá mi môô.	Don't celebrate to me anymore.
Muyêè,	Woman,

I ku i mánu toóu.	You and your husband have a church marriage.

(Or, more freely, "Co-wife, you don't need to strut around so smugly for my benefit anymore. Woman, it's clear that you and your husband have as monogamous a pact as city people who get married in a church.")

Many women's songs about marital problems have a distinctly bitter, sarcastic tone. In one a woman effectively characterized her co-wife as the kind of person who could have committed the worst atrocities of World War II, referring to her as a "German" *(Alumá).* In another song a woman inquired solicitously whether her husband was in menstrual seclusion, since that would explain why he never came to her house to sleep anymore. One woman sarcastically addressed her husband's sister by the term for a co-wife, feigning understanding for the sister's hostility toward her by pretending that they were both married to the same man. Another woman ridiculed her husband's obsession for assuring her sexual fidelity by singing a song of mock gratitude for his assistance in keeping her virtuous:

A púu mi a yayó-yéé.	He saved me from promiscuity.
Disi-puu mi a môntjo-éé,	This one saved me from becoming a whore.
A á mánu f'i téi,	When you marry certain kinds of men,
Nòò, i án tá yayó môô.	You don't fool around anymore.

Women frequently compose sarcastic songs extolling the passionate love of their husband and their co-wife:

Fá a namá ku i dê,	The way she's pressed up against you,
Fá a namá ku i dê,	The way she's pressed up against you,
Sébitaa ku vái, Sébitaa ku vái,	From May to January, from May to January,
Un án ó lúsu môò.	You two will never break apart.
A dóu a búnu;	He's arrived at [something] good;
Di wómi téi sindó muyêè.	The man's taken a "sit-still" [faithful] wife.
Di wómi táa mi yayó,	The man said I was fooling around,
Téé án tá véi m'wootu seéi.	So he wasn't even hearing my words [of protest].
A dóu a búnu.	[But now] he's arrived at [something] good.
Di wómi téi sindó muyêè.	The man's taken a "sit-still" wife.

Saramaka women commemorate both their victories and their defeats in song. One woman, for example, sensing that her co-wife's marriage was on rocky ground, suggested to her that she should admit defeat quickly and gracefully:

Adjóisi u gó dá di wómi	Saying goodbye to the man
An taánga môô-éé.	Isn't so hard.
Adjóisi u gó dá di wómi	Saying goodbye to the man
An taánga môô-éé.	Isn't so hard.
Di a dá i pási f'i sa gó,	Since he's given you an opportunity to leave,
Nôô, i gó dé ên,	Just go and say it,
Nôô, i tooná-éé.	And then be on your way.

Another woman, recognizing that her own marriage was falling apart, composed a song of concession:

Mi pii lái-éé.	I've packed my things.
Mi pii lái-éé.	I've packed my things.
A di wán wósu nôò	It's just at that one house [the co-wife's]
I tá kê duumi.	That you keep wanting to sleep.

Art, Gender, and Social Consciousness

One of the most important contrasts between Saramaka men and women is their differential involvement in the world beyond their tribal territory. This involvement has left its mark on their respective material lives, sexual histories, linguistic patterns, personal styles, and philosophical orientations. It has also been a crucial influence on their respective artistic styles and on the ways that art fits into their social lives.

Saramaka masculinity, in addition to specific expectations regarding sexual virility, hunting skills, verbal eloquence, and ritual competence, has long required an ability to function in "foreign" settings, as well as an active enthusiasm for dabbling in non-Saramaka culture. Whether in the streets of Paramaribo, the construction sites at Afobaka, the Djuka villages in eastern Suriname, the towns of French Guiana, or the diamond-mining camps of Brazil, Saramaka men must know how to converse in foreign languages, deal with people from other ethnic backgrounds, hold down a job, and make wise purchases for the return home. Men enjoy displaying symbols of this aspect of their lives, mixing into their speech words they have picked up from different languages, decorating their houses with nonfunctional items of Western culture (e.g., light bulbs in villages with no electricity), working the antics of coastal personalities into their songs, and reminiscing about the novelties of life outside Saramaka, from elevators and supermarkets to prostitutes and motorbikes. Men sometimes ostentatiously consume foods they have imported from the coast; one man, for example, occasionally opened a can of evaporated milk and poured it into a cup of coffee, enjoying it especially because of the reaction of his great-grandmother, who considered imbibing the bodily fluids of a cow to be the ultimate sign of the decadence of city life.

By contrast, women's lives have always been envisioned by Saramakas more purely in the context of their home environment. While men often talk about their own alternation between Saramaka and coastal societies, women tend to see their life experiences as an alternation between villages and horticultural camps. Women's subsistence activities require a higher proportion of native materials and locally made tools than do men's, and their houses have fewer manufactured furnishings. Their speech is less sprinkled with foreign terms, and their dress includes fewer store-bought items. Their view of city streets, buses, stores, and other features of life outside Saramaka exhibits a stronger ratio of apprehension to fascination. While men take pride in mastering appropriate etiquettes and styles of interaction for their dealings with outsiders, women tend, in the presence of non-Saramakas, either to become very withdrawn or to adopt a crude brashness, both of which reflect their lack of confidence and their discomfort in such situations.

The different orientations of Saramaka men's and women's lives vis-à-vis the outside world are reflected quite directly in their arts. In terms of tools, men's use of store-bought compasses, chisels, and knives for both calabash decoration and woodcarving contrasts with women's use of broken glass for calabashes and threads pulled from scraps of cloth for embroidery. In terms of design styles, men's compositions tend to be rigorously geometric, with straight lines, perfect arcs and circles, and exacting symmetry—the very features that they are familiar with from printed signs, machinery, and Western architecture; by contrast, women's design styles more often center on free-form "organic" shapes, with stubby appendages and irregular symmetries. In terms of the place of the various arts in social life, the long-term absences of men from tribal territory, which are a fundamental influence on the nature of male-female relationships in this society, are also crucial in delineating the social meaning of the artistic gifts that flow within these relationships.

In Saramaka, the value of men's artistry is closely linked with the value of men. The explicit association that women make between particular woodcarvings and particular relationships contrasts with the less attentive attitude of men toward the social origins of their decorative textiles, in a way that corresponds directly to the respective concerns of women and men about marriage itself. The insecurities that women express in their songs are the same insecurities that inspire their unbounded joy at receiving a carved comb or food stirrer. The security that men enjoy in terms of ongoing marriage prospects is similarly related to their more subdued reaction to the artistic gifts they receive from women.

From an anthropological perspective, it should not be surprising that women in Saramaka villages express fundamental dissatisfactions in their personal lives without generally going on to assess critically the cultural attitudes and institutions that lie behind their difficulties. In most cases, a Saramaka woman suffering material deprivations because she has no husband does not wish that her culture provided equal money-earning opportunities for men and women; she wishes only that she could find a husband. Because of their relative isolation from other ways of life, the cultural setting in which these women grow up has provided the framework for their social consciousness; alternatives have traditionally carried connotations of deviance and impropriety for women as much as they have carried a sense of excitement and adventure for men. During my residence in Saramaka, women reacted with strong moral indignation to stories of women from villages closer to the city who "hid their periods" in order to avoid the inconveniences of menstrual seclusion; they expressed resentment about their husbands' sexual freedom in the same culturally prescribed rhetoric that their grandmothers had used; they never failed to distinguish their husbands' meals from their own through rigorous attention to special details of service, such as smooth mounds of rice and specially chosen calabash bowls; and they were rearing their daughters to expect the same satisfactions and frustrations in life that they were experiencing.

As Michelle Rosaldo (1980:417) has argued, the relevance of sexual asymmetries for social scientists is not that they exist but that they are closely linked, like other phenomena such as racism and social class, to the particulars of women's (and men's) lives, activities, and goals. The strong sexual asymmetries of Maroon life—material, social, and conceptual—are as deeply embedded in the arts as they are in subsistence practices, in marriage patterns, or in religious beliefs. Each Maroon woman's life experience represents, in part, a response to the attitudes and institutions that define her as a woman. The creative arts, whether calabash carving, decorative sewing, song composition, body cicatrization, or any other medium, form a dynamic and richly expressive part of that response.

Notes

This paper has benefited from constructive criticisms by Richard Price, Roberta Johnson (commentator on an earlier version presented at the 1982 Caribbean Studies Association Conference in Kingston, Jamaica), and participants in the Johns Hopkins Seminar in Atlantic History, Culture, and Society.

1. Perhaps because of the strong association of each medium with maleness or femaleness, the decorative arts are not considered appropriate as gifts within same-sex dyads. That is, a man would not make a woodcarving for another man, and a woman would not embroider a textile for another woman.

2. My fieldwork, conducted jointly with Richard Price, has been largely in Saramaka villages on the Pikilio, an upriver tributary of the Suriname River (see S. Price and R. Price 1980:Figures 3–4); the demographic and ethnographic details in this paper refer primarily to that region. My comments on gender and the arts reflect observations on the life of Suriname Maroons more generally. In this paper, Saramaccan words are written with a modified version of the orthography developed by Jan Voorhoeve: vowels have "Italian" values except that e represents the vowel in English "met" and ó represents the vowel in

English "all"; vowel extension is indicated by double vowels; and high tones are indicated by acute accents, while low tones are left unmarked.

3. For a more detailed discussion of the effects of labor emigration on Saramaka marriage, see R. Price (1970, 1975).

4. The only portion of a man's personal textile collection that is certain to evoke memories of specific women is a small, distinctly private and rarely contemplated set of memorabilia. Somewhere in each man's trunks is a tied kerchief containing all the adolescent girls' aprons that he has been given during his life, either on wedding nights with never-married girls or as gifts from adolescent lovers. For example, one 92-year-old man, who kindly spent three days opening his trunks of clothing for my inspection, came upon such a kerchief in the course of the project. Excusing himself with obvious delight and commenting that he had not seen this bundle in over 25 years, he turned his back to me (and to one of his wives, who was also present) and unfolded each cloth in turn, reminiscing silently and announcing proudly at the end, in the language that he associated with his youth as a wage laborer in French Guiana, "*Quinze!*"

5. For a comparative discussion of Maroon and West African calabashes, see S. Price (1982).

6. The reliance of women on men for help in planning designs dates to the very beginning of Maroon decorative sewing (see van Panhuys 1899:81). Until several decades ago, men also lent their artistic skills to the designing stage of women's body cicatrizations, but this practice was discontinued as men allegedly proved increasingly unable to resist the sexual temptations it presented.

7. The style of Saramaka women's arts has changed visibly over the past century, with symmetry becoming more precisely executed by each succeeding generation of artists. At every point, however, women's designs have been less geometric and less perfectly symmetrical than those of men. See S. Price (1983) for a detailed discussion of these developments and the aesthetic attitudes and perceptions that have changed along with them.

8. My commentary on this analysis of Maroon "personality configurations" is in no way intended as an attack on Dark. Rather, it is a caution about the power of any observer's social and cultural environment to color his or her perceptions of other societies, especially in the absence of first-hand fieldwork. It seems unlikely that Dark's paper, published in 1951, would have reflected the same perspective if he had written it in 1981. Similarly, the idyllic feminism that Counter and Evans (1981:92, 96, 133) imagine to exist among the Maroons—with men and women sharing political responsibilities and domestic chores and women fashioning the rules of menstrual seclusion as a way of liberating themselves periodically to relax in the company of other women—is clearly a product of its time.

9. Dark's (1951) characterization of Maroon marriage inspired a cryptic but vehement rebuttal by Melville Herskovits (1951), whose book on Maroon life (Herskovits and Herskovits 1934) would have provided a somewhat more sophisticated firsthand description of Maroon marriages than Kahn's (1931). See also Dark's (1952) reply.

10. This is clearly a judgmental assertion, proof for which would require discussion of many facets of Saramaka social and artistic life and their development through time, a task undertaken at some length in S. Price (1983).

11. For several hundred examples, see the illustrations in S. Price and R. Price (1980).

12. A sample of songs from the Pikilio region reveals that about half of those composed

by men expressed positive emotions such as admiration or love and only about one-fourth expressed negative feelings such as anger. By contrast, those composed by women were about one-fifth "positive" and about three-fourths "negative." In general, about two-thirds of *sêkêti* songs are composed by women. The corpus on which this discussion is based includes 178 songs, a minority of which cannot be classified as either "negative" or "positive." A more detailed discussion of *sêkêti* songs, including several dozen transcriptions/translations, is contained in S. Price (1983). See also S. Price and R. Price (1980:174–178) and, for ten recorded examples, R. Price and S. Price (1977).

References

Counter, S. Allen, and David L. Evans
1981 I Sought My Brother: An Afro-American Reunion. Cambridge: MIT Press.

Dark, Philip J. C.
1951 Some Notes on the Carvings of Calabashes by the Bush Negroes of Surinam. Man 51:57–60.
1952 Bush Negro Calabash-Carving. Man 52:126.
1954 Bush Negro Art: An African Art in the Americas. London: Tiranti.

Herskovits, Melville J.
1951 Bush Negro Calabash Carving. Man 51:163–164.
1969 [1930] Bush Negro Art. In The New World Negro: Selected Papers in Afroamerican Studies. Frances S. Herskovits, ed. pp. 157–167. New York: Minerva Press.

Herskovits, Melville J., and Frances S. Herskovits
1934 Rebel Destiny: Among the Bush Negroes of Dutch Guiana. New York: McGraw-Hill.

Hurault, Jean
1961 Les Noirs Réfugiés Boni de la Guyane Française. Mémoires de l'Institut Français d'Afrique Noire (Dakar) 63.
1970 Africains de Guyane: La Vie Matérielle et l'Art des Noirs Réfugiés de Guyane. The Hague: Mouton.

Kahn, Morton C.
1931 Djuka: The Bush Negroes of Dutch Guiana. New York: Viking Press.

Kersten, Christoph
1770 Letter of 12 February. In Die Mission der Brüdergemeine in Suriname and Berbice im achtzehnten Jahrhundert (1913–19). F. Staehelin, ed. 3(1):137–139. Herrnhut: Vereins für Brüdergeschichte in Kommission de Unitätsbuchhandlung in Gnadau.

Muntslag, F. H. J.
1966 Tembe: Surinaamse Houtsnijkunst. Amsterdam: Prins Bernhard Fonds.

Panhuys, L. C. van
1899 Toelichting Betreffende de Voorwerpen Verzameld bij de Aucaner

Boschnegers. In Catalogus der Nederlandsche West-Indische Ten-
toonstelling te Haarlem, pp. 74–82. Haarlem.

Price, Richard
1970   Saramaka Emigration and Marriage: A Case Study of Social
            Change. Southwestern Journal of Anthropology 26:157–189.
1975   Saramaka Social Structure. Analysis of a Maroon Society in Suri-
            nam. Caribbean Monograph Series 12. Rio Piedras: Institute of Car-
            ibbean Studies of the University of Puerto Rico.

Price, Richard, and Sally Price
1977   Music from Saramaka: A Dynamic Afro-American Tradition. Phono-
            graph record with ethnographic notes. New York: Folkways Records
            FE 4225.

Price, Sally
1982   When Is a Calabash Not a Calabash? Nieuwe West-Indische Gids
            56:69–82.
1983   Co-wives and Calabashes. Ann Arbor: University of Michigan Press.

Price, Sally, and Richard Price
1980   Afro-American Arts of the Suriname Rain Forest. Berkeley: Univer-
            sity of California Press.

Rosaldo, M. Z.
1980   The Use and Abuse of Anthropology: Reflections on Feminism and
            Cross-cultural Understanding. Signs 5:389–417.

8. DANCING FOR ÒGÚŃ IN
YORUBALAND AND IN BRAZIL

Margaret Thompson Drewal

Dance is an integral part of African ritual.[1] Addressing metaphysical beings or powers, it is a poetic, non-verbal expression continually created and re-created by countless performer/interpreters over generations. In its formulations of time, space, and dynamics, dance transmits a people's philosophy and values; it is thought embodied in human action. A primary vehicle for communicating with the spirit realm, it is at the same time perceived to be an instrument of the gods through which they communicate with the phenomenal world. As such, ritual dance is an unspoken essay on the nature and quality of metaphysical power. Indeed, for the Yoruba, dance — in certain contexts — is metaphysical force actualized in the phenomenal world.[2]

In western Yorubaland this is dramatically illustrated in ritual dances associated with Ògúń, the deity whose quick, aggressive actions may bring violent death and destruction or, by contrast, may bring the birth of children. It is also evident in dances of Candomblé in Bahia, Brazil, where during the early nineteenth century Yoruba captives were sold into slavery (Pierson 1942:35) and where, as a result, the influence of Yoruba culture, and of Ògúń, is strong (Bastide 1978:66, 205–206, and 253–55). To place these ideas about dance into a broader Yoruba philosophical context, the following discussion considers the Yoruba concept of metaphysical power and its more well known relation to utterances.

The power of utterances has been widely documented in Africa (cf. Ray 1973; Peek 1981) and in Yorubaland (Prince 1960; Beier 1970:49; H. Drewal 1974; Verger 1976–77; and Ayoade 1979:51). Prince observes, for example, that among the Yoruba "to utter the name of something may draw that something into actual existence . . . not only within the mind and body of he who utters and he who hears the word, but also in the physical world as well" (1960:66). And Ayoade points out, "to the initiated the sound of the words is the audible manifestation of its innate force" (1979:51). In certain contexts, voicing action verbs literally activates dynamic forces. Thus Verger reveals that, in Yoruba incantations (*ọfọ̀*) chanted during the preparation or application of medicines (*òògùn*) to invoke the dynamic essences of all their ingredients, a monosyllabic action verb drawn from

Originally published in Sandra T. Barnes (ed.), *Africa's Ogun: Old World and New* (Bloomington: Indiana University Press, 1989), pp. 199–234. Reprinted by permission of Indiana University Press.

each ingredient's name is pronounced following that name to set the ingredient into action. For example:

1 ewé ọ̀ọ́yọ́ àjẹ́ bá wa yọ àrùn kúrò n'ìhà
2 ewé awùsá sà àrùn ìhà
3 ìyẹ́ agbe gbé àrùn ìhà kúrò
4 ìyẹ́ àlukò kó arun ìhà kúrò

1 ọ̀ọ́yọ́ àjé leaf chase away (yọ) the disease of the flank for us
2 awùsá leaf heal (sà) the flank disease so it may go away
3 agbe feather carry (gbé) the flank disease outside
4 àlukò feather pick (kó) the disease out of the flank (Verger 1976–77:254)

Verger suggests further that appellations are attributed to ingredients based upon particular actions described by verbs used in formulating them. It is thus the action or, more accurately, the *acting* verbs inherent in names and incantations which, when voiced, enable them to mobilize the inner essence of a spirit or force. Beyond this, however, it is the sound qualities of the acting verbs which make them dynamic.

The sound qualities of verbs, nouns, adjectives, and adverbs in Yoruba incantations often correspond to the dynamic qualities of actions in the natural environment. In the following invocation, utterances simulate actions in evoking the way an Egúngún spirit called Àgàn becomes manifest.[3] Serving as a formula for bringing the Egúngún festival into the world (ayé) (H. Drewal and M. Drewal 1983:2–4), this invocation uses an analogy to rainfall, playing upon its dynamic qualities—not just one quality, but a whole repertoire of qualities—to convey the spirit's elusiveness. Like rain, the spirit Àgàn comes to the world qualitatively in a myriad of ways:

1 Mo dé wẹ́rẹ́wẹ́rẹ́ bi eji orì alẹ́
2 Màrìwòoo! Àgànóoo!
3 Mo dé kùtùkùtù bí ejí òwúrọ̀
4 Màrìwòoo! Àgànóoo!
5 Mo dé pápàpá bi ejí ìyálẹ̀ta
6 Màrìwòoo! Àgànóoo!
7 Ojú alágbẹ̀dẹ kò tó'lẹ́ arọ́
8 Màrìwòoo! Àgànóoo!
9 Ojú amọ̀kòkò kò tó'lẹ̀ amọ̀
10 Màrìwòoo! Àgànóoo!
11 Mẹ̀mẹ̀mẹ̀ nigbe ewúrẹ́
12 Màrìwòoo! Àgànóoo!
13 Bọ̀bọ̀ nigbe àgùtàn
14 Màrìwòoo! Àgànóoo!

15   Mojí lóòrò kùtùkùtù[4]
16   Mogbé inini òrun w'aiyé
17   Mo wò rùrùrùrùrù
18   Màrìwòoo! Àgànóoo!
19   Mo dé t'ogbó t'ògo t'àkò t'idà
20   Màrìwòoo! Àgànóoo!
21   Gbámù! Òfo!
22   Gbámù! Òfo!
23   Gbámù! Òfo!
24   Amamamamamamama!
25   Ẹ má a wá!
26   Ẹ má a wá!
27   Ẹ má a wá! (Recorded in Ilaro, 1977)

1   I come wẹ́rẹ́wẹrẹ́ [small, quick, and light, i.e., drizzling] like the early night
      rain
2   Màrìwòoo! Àgànóoo!
3   I come kùtùkùtù [forceful and quick, i.e., pouring] like the early morning
      rain[4]
4   Màrìwòoo! Àgànóoo!
5   I come pápàpá [large, heavy, slow sporadic drops] like the rain at sunrise
6   Màrìwòoo! Àgànóoo!
7   The eyes of the blacksmith cannot see underneath the ground of his shed
8   Màrìwòoo! Àgànóoo!
9   The eyes of the potter cannot see the inside of clay
10   Màrìwòoo! Àgànóoo!
11   Mẹ̀mẹ̀mẹ̀ cries the female goat
12   Màrìwòoo! Àgànóoo!
13   Bòbò cries the female sheep
14   Màrìwòoo! Àgànóoo!
15   I get up early in the morning
16   I bring dew from the otherworld to earth
17   I become rùrùrùrùrù [all pervasive, literally the sound of walking over dewy
      grasses]
18   Màrìwòoo! Àgànóoo!
19   I come with cudgels, a sheath, a sword
20   Màrìwòoo! Àgànóoo!
21   Grasp it! Nothing's there!
22   Grasp it! Nothing!
23   Grasp it! Nothing!
24   Amamamamamamama!
25   Be looking! We are looking!

26   Be looking! We are looking!
27   Be looking! We are looking!

That Yoruba acknowledge a relationship between the dynamics of speech and the dynamics of action is evident in their verbal characterizations of dance, particularly in the use of evocative words, or what Babalola (1966:67–68) calls word-pictures, words which by their very sound and intensity evoke mental pictures or images. Hence, a dance for the ancient female deity Oòduà, perceived to be cool, patient, and calm, is described by Ọ̀họ̀rì Yoruba as gentle (ijó jẹ́jẹ́). In addition to its definition—gentle—the sound jẹ́jẹ́ is evocative. Its oral dynamics in this context evoke light, moderately and evenly paced, effortless motion. In contrast, a dance associated with the god of thunder and lightning is described by an Ẹ̀gbádò priestess as being very powerful (ijó kíkan kíkan tó l'abgára), literally "a dance performed kíkan kíkan with forcefulness." Kíkan connotes a forceful release of energy as if under pressure (personal communication, Rowland Abíọ́dún, 1981). Like jẹ́jẹ́, the phrase kíkan simulates verbally the effort quality of the dance, that is, one in which a dominant motif is raising (kí) and percussively dropping (kàn) the shoulders repetitively, i.e., kíkan kíkan. Kí is quick, sharp, and high (or up) in tone; kan is forceful, full, and heavy, dropping in tone. The dance further evokes, in its speed and thrust, the dynamics of lightning and thunder—in that order—associated with Ṣàngó. In fact, from this perspective, the image of lightning and thunder can be seen, like the analogy to rainfall illustrated above, to derive meaning from its actual dynamic qualities, qualities which in turn reflect the nature of Ṣàngó's own power.

In Yoruba thought, there is a direct correlation between the dynamic qualities of both dance and oral performance and power known as àṣẹ. According to Beier (1970:49), "Yoruba believe strongly in the power of the word, or rather in a mysterious force called ashe . . . that quality in a man's personality which makes his words—once uttered—come true." One Yoruba singer alluded to this concept of voiced àṣẹ in referring to certain songs he performs which have efficacy because, when voiced, they operate as "wind (ẹ̀fúùfù) combatting wind"; that is, the force exerted in voicing a song acts upon other forces permeating the world that are believed to be creating a particular situation (cf. H. Drewal 1974). Going a step further, Verger (1964:16) states that àṣẹ is "the principle of all that lives or acts or moves . . . everything which exhibits power, whether in action or in the winds and drifting clouds, or in passive resistance like that of the boulders lying by the wayside."[5]

In its broadest sense, àṣẹ is metaphysical power. It has been translated as "authority" or "command" (Abraham 1958:71), "a coming to pass . . . effect; imprecation" (Crowther 1852:47).[6] However, when Yoruba speak of an individual with àṣẹ, aláṣẹ, a person with authority, they usually mean one with innate metaphysical power who by virtue of this power maintains complete and awesome control over spiritual realms and, by extension, over social ones. In and of itself, *àṣẹ* has no moral connotations; it is neither good nor bad, positive nor negative (Verger 1964:16). It is the principle of realization (dos Santos 1976:71). It is absolute power and potential, present not only in utterances, but in all things—rocks, hills, streams, mountains, leaves, animals, sculpture, ancestors, gods, and actions. It is through voiced power, or *àṣẹ*, that devotees of Ògún call him and seek his advice. It is also with voiced *àṣẹ* that they bring him into the phenomenal world.

For the Yoruba, evidence of the presence of *àṣẹ* in the various things of the natural and supernatural realms is displayed in their qualitative aspects. Thus Yoruba define and classify plants used in medicines by taking into account their odors, their colors, their textures, their responses when touched, and their effects upon those who touch them (Verger 1976–77:249). According to Warren et al. (1973:ii), "If one asks herbalists why they select certain ingredients [for their medicines] one learns that it is because they are bitter or sweet, red or black, hard or slimy, or that they possess some other quality." The qualities of inanimate objects, such as leaves, rocks, ores, or other natural elements, as Warren and Verger indicate, are inherent in their tastes, textures, shapes, and colors. Animated beings such as humans and animals express innate power in their behavior, that is, in their everyday actions and utterances.[7] In performative phenomena, such as in ritual utterances and dance, these qualities are expressed dynamically through patterned time. To a great extent, utterances and actions carry this power precisely because they are intrinsically dynamic.

If oral recitations possessing *àṣẹ* invoke supernatural forces, bring them into existence, and set them into action, then dance represents more literally the materialization of those forces in the world. It is through dance, through what Langer (1953:187) refers to as "a play of powers made visible," that metaphysical forces become manifest. Nowhere is this relationship between words and actions more explicit than in the verbal and kinetic exertions associated with the deity Ògún, the hot, vengeful warrior who kills with quickness and directness.

The Dynamics of Ògún

The *àṣẹ* personified by Ògún is driving force—that which thrusts into new realms, breaks new ground, and achieves the ordinarily unachievable. Ògún represents accomplishment, exploration, and innovation (Barnes 1980:7, 28–29). He penetrates the frontiers of the unknown—the forest, the battleground, and the fringes of society. He both benefits mankind and on occasion destroys parts of it, and in his quests he is insatiable, tenacious, and unyielding. His path is often fraught with unexpected hazards. It is Ògún's nature to be quick, direct, and strong. Whether creative or destructive, his dynamic can be characterized as explosive.

Many of Ògún's symbols, such as the *àgbaadú* snake, represent his *àṣẹ*. Small and black, with a red stripe on its neck, the *àgbaadú* or *òṣúùró* snake reportedly is very quick, vicious, and deadly and, because of its small size, is able to attack people completely by surprise.[8] Iron also embodies Ògun's *àṣẹ* (cf. H. Drewal, chapter 10). Consistent with the nature of his power, iron implements when used by people to perform work demand actions of quickness, forcefulness, directness, and an explosive release. Like Ògun's acts, these acts can be creative, but they can also be destructive, whether by intent or by accident. Working with iron, man thus partakes of Ògun's dynamic force. Hence, human action can be seen to derive ultimately from metaphysical force, or *àṣẹ*. Indeed, this relationship between human action and metaphysical force to a large extent accounts for the need of people who use iron implements to sacrifice to Ògun. Individuals revitalize Ògun through sacrifice so that they may partake of that vitality and manage it safely.

Ògun's *àṣẹ* can, therefore, be heard and observed. It is expressed physically and audibly in the dynamics of dance and oral performance. Both dance and utterances are physical exertions which express attitudes toward time, space, weight, and flow (Bartenieff 1980:51).[9] Some combination of quickness, forcefulness, and directness expressed in an explosive release of energy recurs frequently in Ògun's performative imagery; these same qualities are also alluded to in the physical and behavioral properties of the many objects and beings, like iron and the *àgbaadú* snake, which make up his symbolic complex. The following analysis of the dynamic qualities of oral texts and dances specific to Ògun demonstrates how they display the *àṣẹ* of Ògun.

One of Ògun's dominant images is that of destruction. Barnes, in fact, views Ògun as "a metaphor for the dangerous and destructive powers of mankind" (1980:28). An oral praise poem reinforces the destructive image:

1   O p(a) ọkọ s(i) oju ina
2   O p(a) aya s(i) madiro
3   O p(a) wọn wẹrẹwẹrẹ sa l(i) (o)de
4   Ogun ni ẹjẹrengun ile alaigbọran
5   O gbe ori olori sawisa
6   O wo (o)ko oloko rojo rojo
7   O pọn (o)mi si (i)le fi ẹjẹ wẹ
8   Ogun l(i) ọn jẹ agbe (i)rin omo pa omo
9   Sare m(u) omi wa o pa meje
10   Ọkunrin giri bi ẹni ṣi lẹkun
11   O pa s(i) otun o ba otun jẹ
12   O pa s(i) osi o ba osi jẹ

1   He kills the husband before the fire,
2   He kills the wife in the foyer,
3   He kills little ones as they flee outside.

4   Ogun is the *ẹ̀jẹ̀rengun* leaf in the house of the proud, fierce man.
5   He seizes the head of another freely,
6   He stares at the penis of men.
7   With water in the house he washes with blood.
8   Ogun who makes the child kill himself with the iron he plays with;
9   While carrying water he kills seven (people).
10   Man trembles like someone who opens the door.
11   He (Ogun) kills on the right and destroys on the right,
12   He kills on the left and destroys on the left. (Verger 1957:176, my translation)

The action verb *pa*, to kill, is common in praise poetry and invocations for Ògún, and its dynamic in oral performance is analogous to the visible dynamics of movement. Hence the oral expression can be subjected to the same analytic treatment that is given to physical effort.[10] The verb *pa* pronounced in oral texts conveys a blow which is spatially direct, sudden, and powerful, executed with an explosive release. Armstrong uses the spelling *kpa* to underscore the vocal force of the Yoruba "p" sound.[11] Its repetition, "*Ó pa ọkọ. . . . Ó pa aya. . . . Ó pa wọn wẹrẹwẹrẹ*" (lines 1–3) and so on, conjures up an image of Ògún with cutlass in hand slashing out at those around him. Indeed, one of his most widely known praises is, "He killed them with one blow (instantly)" (*Ó p'awọn bere kojo*). This verbal image is enacted physically in Ilaro, where, on certain occasions, a hunter possessed by Ògún rushes through the town, cutlass in hand, and decapitates any dog in his path with one stroke of his iron blade. Another invocation for Ògún declares:

1   Ó pa oko síbi iná
2   Ó pa aya si bálùwẹ̀
3   Ó pa omo pa ìya
4   Adamolore kège kège
5   Kùtùkùtù l'ògún ba
6   Àiyí gọlọtọ s'oko oloko
7   Ekun oko eke wo

1   He kills the husband near the fire,
2   He kills the wife in the bath house,
3   He kills the child, kills the mother.
4   Sword-cuts-off-heads *kège kège*.
5   Early in the morning, Ògún met them;
6   They were found stone-dead in the farm of another farmer.
7   Ogun will punish those who don't fear him. (Olúpọ̀à 1975)

The phrases above play upon harsh *p* and *k* sounds pronounced with explosive energy. They possess a dynamic that is unleashed in the act of pronouncing them, and convey force through the effective patterns of stress placed on consonants, words, or phrases, that is, the combination of tone, speed of syllables, vocal force, and flow—all of which combine to simulate physical effort. Again, the word *pa* (kill) is direct, quick, and explosive. In another phrase containing a word-picture, "Sword-cuts-off-heads *kège kège*," the image of heads rolling is conveyed. The sound *kège* has a heavy, sluggish quality and, when repeated, suggests continuous motion. The syllable *kè* interrupted by the sound of *ge* followed by a short pause and repetition sets up a rhythm which evokes an image at once horrific and humorous, that of a heavy, irregularly shaped sphere—the head—rolling after the quick, powerful thrust of Ògún's cutlass. It is evident from these examples that Yoruba have a great sensitivity to dynamic qualities and that they use them quite deliberately in verbal performance—and, as we shall see, in dance—to evoke, and thus ultimately to invoke, the vital force of Ògún.

Throughout Yorubaland there are many different Ògún dance styles. For the purposes of this paper, however, one distinct style and its context will be discussed: Ògún possession trance dance associated with a ritual festival for the gods in western Yorubaland. A comparison then will be made with Ògún possession trance dance in the Yoruba-derived Candomblé houses of Bahia, Brazil.[12] These examples provide us with insight into the role of dance and the significance of its dynamic qualities in ritual. Using the body as an expressive instrument, the Ògún dancer evokes, and thus invokes, the actual dynamic qualities which constitute the essence of the god and accomplishes this by manipulating and controlling time, space, energy, and flow in accordance with traditional precedent.

Possession Trance in Western Yorubaland

Invocations, praise poetry, music, and dance are essential to nearly all Yoruba ritual in which spiritual forces are actualized. Invocations and drumming performed before the onset of possession trance both in Yorubaland and in Brazil serve to bring Ògún into contact with devotees. Through dance, spiritual forces materialize in the phenomenal world. The god is said to mount (*gùn*) the devotee (*eléégún*, literally, "one who is mounted") and, for a time, that devotee becomes the god. Temporarily, then, the animating spirit of the deity (*èmí òrìṣà*) displaces that of the individual being mounted (Ọsitola 1982). Whatever the priest does from the moment he enters the trance state is thought to represent the god's own actions. Among the Yoruba, possession trance states are expressed through the medium of dance. To my knowledge, there is no instance of possession trance among the Yoruba which does not occur as dance or in association with dance.

Spirit mediumship is the most significant role of a priest. The uniting of devotee and deity into one image often causes some confusion for researchers who, for example, try to establish the identity of figures represented in Yoruba sculpture. Sculpture represents the union of the priest and deity in the depiction of the former with the costumes, hairstyles, and paraphernalia identified with the

latter (M. Drewal 1986). Likewise, these identical fashions are observable in ritual dance. It is through dance, however, that the priest brings the active deity (not
a symbolic representation) into the phenomenal world for the community. To
become possessed by the gods is, therefore, the primary role of the medium.

As in all initiations into priesthoods throughout Ègbádò and Òhọrí areas,
Ògún devotees go through extensive training, which in large part is devoted to
preparing them for spirit mediumship. They metaphorically die and are reborn.
According to Verger:

> An initiation always begins with a symbolic death and resurrection which marks
> the novice's break with his past and shows his birth into a new life consecrated to
> the deity. . . . During the period which separates the day of resurrection from that
> on which the novice receives a new name, . . . [the novice] seems to lose all rea-
> son, he is plunged into a dazed state of mental paralysis; he has forgotten every-
> thing, no longer knows how to speak and talks only in unintelligible sounds. The
> novice in this state is called *Omotun,* new child. (1954:337)

Mediums become differentiated in the particular dances, music, and songs attributed to their personal deities and in their performance styles. Throughout Ègbádò and Òhọrí areas, however, there is consistency in the practice, initiation,
and training of mediums, as well as in the broad style of entering trance. The
novices' clothes are taken away, their heads are shaved, and they are secluded in
a dark shrine, where they must remain quiet and still for some weeks. During this
period, the head is bathed regularly in the *àṣẹ* of the deity, made up of an amal-
gam of leaves, blood of animals, and pulverized minerals (Verger 1954:324 and
1969:n.2, p. 65). Furthermore, the *àṣẹ* of Ògún is rubbed into incisions made in
the shaven head. This is thought to fix the power of the deity in the head of the
devotee and to stimulate possession trance. The initiate is now known as *adóṣù,*
one who has received the medicine, or *òṣù,* of the god. Later, special hairdos are
worn by the newly initiated to identify them with their particular god and to show
that this is a head endowed with power. Finally, the devotee receives a special new name which suggests Ògún's hold or claim on the initiate, such as
Opelajumiedebo, "The-one-who-kept-late-and-came-speaking-a-new-language,"
or Omulel'okiti, "The-one-whose-deity-carried-her-to-Omolu's-mound (shrine)."
Both names refer to possession trance; the first refers to a ritual language spoken
during trance which reflects the dialect of the Òhọrí Yoruba subgroup from
which this particular Ògún practice spread, and the second refers to the notion
that Ògún took charge of or claimed a devotee by carrying her to Omolu's shrine.
The verb here implies that she was "carried" via a trance state.

In possession trance performance, the left side is stressed to symbolize the spirit
realm. Ògún mediums in Yorubaland carry iron implements in their hands, often
in their left hands.[13] Likewise, the priest of Ẹlẹgba, the divine messenger, carries a
cudgel in the left, and the priest of Ṣàngó also carries in the left a staff represent-

ing a neolithic axe of paired thundercelts (M. Drewal 1986). The left in Yoruba society is used in many other ritual contexts: inside the Ògbóni lodge on special meeting days, Ògbóni members greet each other and guests with the left hand;[14] when òjẹ̀ don the Egúngún masquerade they step into the cloth with the left foot;[15] and deities greet the community with the left hand, that is, the possessed priest, whose head has been mounted by the deity, greets the community with the left.

These contexts of lefthandedness have a common purpose. In every case they involve spiritual communication. As one devotee put it, "The right is used by men; the left is used by the gods." Hence, when one enters the Egúngún cloth to make the Egúngún spirit manifest, one must step in with the left foot, and when offering a gift or sacrifice to deities one presents it with the left hand.

The prevalent interpretation in the literature on the Yoruba of the unclean, antisocial left hand is misleading in that it does not allow us to perceive the importance of the left for spiritual communication in a ritual context. The left is reserved for ritual and must not, therefore, be used in ordinary social discourse. In this way the sacred is kept separate from the profane to protect the integrity of both worlds at once (Hertz 1973:7); as Yoruba would put it, the world (ayé)— a domain where people reside only temporarily—is ritually separated from the otherworld (ọ̀run), a metaphysical realm of permanent existence. Seen from this perspective, it is then possible to understand why the social use of the left is unacceptable and even considered to be deviant behavior.

Handheld objects particular to Ògún and carried in the left hand inevitably signal a possession trance context, when the deity mounts the head of his priests. The priest literally becomes Ògún, and whatever the possessed priest says and does is taken to be Ògún's own words and actions. In the left hand, possessed priests carry objects symbolic of the god's powers, the iron blades of Ògún, the cudgel of Ẹlẹ́gba, the bow and arrow of Ọ̀ṣọ́ọ̀sì, or the thundercelts of Ṣàngó. These power symbols in the left hand signal a visitation from the spirit realm, but at the same time they assert the authority and the responsibility of the medium to be the god's conduit in this world.

In any ritual where iron or iron implements are required, particularly in blood sacrifices performed with iron blades, Ògún must be dealt with first, for iron itself is Ògún. It represents Ògún's vital power, his capacity for quick, forceful, overt action concretized in iron tools and implements of all varieties (cf. H. Drewal, Art or Accident: Yorùbá Body Artists and Their Deity Ògún, in Africa's Ogun: Old World and New, Sandra T. Barnes (ed.), Bloomington, Ind., IUP, 1989, pp. 235–60). Iron implements are a symbol of Ògún's worldly accomplishments, whether those accomplishments are destructive or productive, whether they involve the iron cutlasses, arrows, and guns of warfare, automobiles and motorcycles, the blades of circumcision, the hoes of farming, or the adzes and knives of carving. Iron implements and Ògún get things done quickly and forcefully. That is the nature of their power. Thus, while iron implements carried by the mediums symbolize Ògún's nature and his dynamic potential, the left hand which wields them speaks of his ability to penetrate the phenomenal world allowing devotees to tap his force.

In western Yorubaland, a religious group whose principal deity is Omolu, an earth deity in charge of contagious diseases, especially smallpox, believes that all deities, including Omolu, have their own Ògún and their own Ẹlẹ́gba (also known as Èṣù, the trickster). Ẹlẹ́gba is the divine mediator who must receive the first invocations and sacrifices; he is the "god of the crossroads" who makes initial contact with other gods on man's behalf. He personifies the intersection of the world and the otherworld. Ògún, on the other hand, represents the path itself. He facilitates Ẹlẹ́gba by "clearing the way." Therefore, ceremonies which involve Ògún often place him first in the ritual order together with Ẹlẹ́gba, the divine mediator.[16] Ẹlẹ́gba and Ògún work hand in hand. Informants explain that, as the god of iron, Ògún is first to enter and clear the bush where the shrines of all the other deities are installed (Ògún ló ṣàlè f'òrìṣà dó)—a way of saying that without Ògún no other deities can be worshipped on earth. He is in front, unyielding and "courageous like the road" (Anaya pátá bí ọnà). As an ambitious, courageous warrior he is determined to go first. This is communicated explicitly when, during a procession to the bush, the site of Omolu's shrine on the outskirts of town, the female medium possessed by Ògún Igbó, "Ògún of the Bush," charges to the front of the line intent upon commandeering the group. Consistent with his perceived personality, Ògún acts quickly, directly, and forcefully. His inclination to rush forth quickens the pace of the entire group. Because Ògún's courage and tenacity can place the female medium, who is mortal, in great physical danger, attendants continually restrain her from fully asserting Ògún's prerogatives.

Dancing for Ògún in Western Yorubaland

In Igbogila, an Ẹgbádò community northeast of Ilaro toward Nigeria's western border, a religious group that combines many olórìṣà, literally "owners of deities," performs rituals for those deities every five days (every four days by a Western count).[17] These are essentially danced rituals, the primary object of which is possession trance. Deities represented among the olórìṣà cluster around and symbolize the realm of the bush. In order of their ritual performance, they are Ògún, Eyinlẹ, Ìrokò, Ondo, Omolu, and Ẹlẹ́gba.[18] Eyinlẹ (Erinlẹ) is a deity associated with streams and hunting; Ìrokò is a bush deity associated with the African teak tree of the same name. Omolu appears to be the dominant deity in this group; he is the god of contagious diseases, particularly smallpox. Not specifically identified with the bush, however, is Ondo, the deified founding forefather of the town of Pobẹ in Benin (R.P.B.).[19]

In the shade of a large tree, the group sets up chairs for its own members and for spectators. The mediums, with shoulders bare and chests bound with cloth, stand side by side to open the ceremony and invoke Ẹlẹ́gba, by placing their left feet forward. Attention is focused on the spiritual (left) side, since what is to follow is direct communication with the spirit realm. The mediums slowly and repetitively place their left feet forward, returning each time to their starting position with both feet side by side. Turning to face the opposite direction, they repeat the exercise. With this formulaic opening, they then form a circle, dance counterclockwise, invoke each deity in the aforementioned order, and sing his praises. The songs, the dances, and the drum rhythms are particular to each god or set of gods. The song determines what the drums play and how the devotees dance.

After a process of honoring and invoking each deity in song and dance, beginning with Ògún, the mediums break out of the circle, and the drums again invoke Ògún. Ògún's mediums gaze downward; their dance movements diminish. A change in attitude occurs, from outgoing and playful to concentrated, serious, and inwardly focused. As if bound to the spot, the mediums stop moving their feet; upper torsos veer to the side; heads drop; and left knees quiver, causing their bodies to tremble. The priests in this state are called "horses of the gods" (ẹṣin òrìṣà). Attendants rush to straighten their cloths and bind their waists and breasts tightly, in much the same way a rider saddles a horse, pulling the straps tightly to secure the saddle in place, for Ògún must "mount" (gùn) and ride his medium. At this point, the mediums are fully transformed into the deity. They repeatedly lick their lips in an agitated fashion. Their upper torsos drop, the heads roll back, and eyes roll upward. Attendants quickly close the mediums' eyelids and bring their heads forward. The final sign that Ògún is present is signaled when the medium emits a deep guttural yell. It is said that when the god mounts the medium's head he roots the medium's feet to the earth; thus, attendants release the possessed mediums by slapping or stepping on the tops of their feet. The possessed mediums then take giant steps, leading with the whole left side of their bodies, and make their way to the gathered crowd. Hands are placed on the hips, and knees and feet are lifted and extended forward. After greeting the entire assemblage with "Ẹ kú o!" the mediums sing, dance, and pray. Ògún in this way directs the drummers.

During the performance, spectators give money to Ògún and the drummers. The amount ranges from several cents to one dollar with an average of about twenty cents. By "spending money" (nínáʼwó) for Ògún, spectators receive special recognition and blessing from him. In a sense they invest in his dynamic power, and in return they receive the benefit of that power.

More than one Ògún priest may be possessed simultaneously, but only one comes forth at any given time to sing. An Ògún may step forward to sing, for example:

1	I am afraid of everybody.
2	But if anybody claims to be higher than Ògún,
3	I shall lower him down. (Verger 1969:60)

A ceremony's progression is spontaneous in that the mediums decide on the spur of the moment which song to sing, and this in turn determines what the drums play and what dance is performed. Likewise, the mediums determine at what point they will stop a dance and begin a new one.

The Ògún mediums perform several dances, which are rhythmically and visually distinct, and these can be in any order as long as they are appropriate to Ògún. In none of the dances are the mediums' orientations in the dance space predetermined; rather, they tend to scatter themselves and face any direction. Further, they do not relate to each other physically. They dance simultaneously, yet independently.

As noted above, Ògún mediums carry various instruments in their hands to identify the power of their deity. Iron blades of various descriptions evoke Ògún's role as hunter and warrior; miniature flintlock guns suggest similar ideas; miniature iron pincers evoke the work of the blacksmith. For example, Ògún mediums (Olóògún) may carry an iron spade in the left hand. In this context, the mediums usually carry a combination of implements in both hands, which are held rather statically, moving only in response to active shoulders. Whatever the particular combination of instruments, one is usually iron. Ògún's presence then is implicit even before the onset of possession trance. The implements speak of Ògún's acts; the dance on the other hand evokes the dynamics required for those acts.

Ògún's dances express the nature of his vital force. In all of them, the head is calm; in contrast, the shoulders are active, especially the shoulder blades or scapulae, which are repetitively raised and lowered, a special characteristic of Ọ̀họrí style dancing.[20] Known as èjìká, a term which refers both to the shoulders and the movement associated with the shoulder blades, these gestures have an amazing range of dynamic possibilities, from gentle and subtle to forceful and exaggerated, and from fluid and smooth to sharp and angular. As performed by Ògún, however, they are distinctly forceful, quick, sharp, and exaggerated, in keeping with his explosive manner. The èjìká of the thundergod Ṣàngó is performed similarly to convey similar attributes of power (M. Drewal 1986). Knees are flexed, and torsos are pitched forward from the hips at approximately a 45-degree angle. From this position, and with active shoulders, a number of different stepping patterns and rhythms are performed. These patterns are fairly short, often in counts of four, and repetitive.

Ògún's dances range from extremely rapid to moderately paced. The most moderate of them conveys a stalking dynamic. Its overall quality can be characterized as cautious, that is, a combination of hesitancy and determination. The movement bursts forth with a quick, strong step, and is then held back, restrained for an instant before it bursts forth again; a third step exhibits an even more sustained movement with a final large burst of energy that ends in a crouching position, again held. The medium steps on one foot and places the other slightly to the back side in a wide stance, pausing for an instant in a very deliberate fashion. Stepping then on the other side, she repeats the pattern. On the third step, instead of placing the foot, she slides it past the other; it skims the ground, then goes out and around so that the medium changes direction toward the sliding foot. The slide is suspended and, at the last possible moment, in time to the music, the medium lunges forward in a slight crouch onto the other foot. This position is held again in a long pause to give it emphasis. Thus the medium steps: &1 hold, &2 hold, &3_slide 4 hold, and so on. The implements carried by the mediums are held motionless in front of the torso. While there is a clear emphasis on pauses and sustained movements, these are interspersed with strong bursts of energy which are sudden and emphatic that ultimately evoke an overall dynamic of stalking.

Another of Ògún's dances uses similar elements to produce slightly different qualities and rhythm. It, too, has a stalking dynamic. But this time the medium takes three long, low strides at a pressing pace and then with a catch step either continues in the same path or changes direction; thus, stepping 1 2 3&4; 1 2 3&4. With each step, the scapulae jump forcefully outward and upward and then plunge emphatically in again, thus double-timing the feet. The forcefulness and directness of this dance give it a feeling of determination. No matter which way Ògún travels, he does so with a sense of pressing urgency and self-confidence.

In both dances, Ògún is forceful. In the first, restraint combined with bursts of energy evokes both force and quietude and conveys a sense of caution. In the second, he is the epitome of Ògún as a driving force. Pursuing a direct path quickly with long, low strides, he is "courageous like the road," as his praise name recalls.

A third and final dance, the àgèrè, can be performed both for Ògún and for Eyinlè, who is also found widely throughout Yorubaland.[21] The name refers at once to the dance and to a traditional hunter's drum (Abraham 1958:30), even though any one of a number of different drums can play the àgèrè rhythm and accompany the dance. Àgèrè can be performed anytime either Ògún or Eyinlè is honored. For example, it can be performed by the hunter/warrior association during rituals at the shrine of Ògún Ilu, also known as Ògún Àjobo, that is, the Ògún for the Town, or the Ògún Everybody Worships Together;[22] by priests of other deities, like Ṣàngó, during rituals in which Eyinlè is invoked; and by certain masquerades known as Eléyinlè (Owners of Eyinlè), who dance during Egúngún "performances of miracles" (ap'idán) (cf. Drewal and Drewal 1978:34–35, pl. 15). While the first two dances are fairly localized within western Yoruba groups influenced by the Ọhọri, the àgèrè Ògún appears to be more widespread, often associated with Ọyọ-derived institutions, although this may be the result of a historical melding of traditions from different regions.

The àgèrè has a quality distinct from the others. Its rhythm is rolling: one foot essentially remains in place while alternately the other foot shifts backward and forward and backward and forward—each time assuming full body weight. After the second forward step, the moving leg then becomes the stationary one so that the sequence is repeated on the other side. If the dance progresses at all, it does not travel far. This dance in different contexts is performed with varying degrees of energy. Female caretakers of Eyinlẹ shrines, who are not necessarily mediums, dance it very gently with small, easy steps, whereas Ògún mediums in possession trance perform it powerfully with large leg gestures so that, instead of a rolling feeling, it jumps. Quickness and forcefulness in combination once again speak of Ògún's innate power.

As mediums begin to tire from being "ridden" by Ògún, an attendant stretches out their arms over their heads. When Ògún finally leaves the female medium's head, he withdraws suddenly. Her body tenses all over and, if near a spectator, she grabs hold tightly. Attendants must be ready to catch the medium and help her to the sidelines to be seated, or the medium will have a difficult time coming out of the trance state. With the attendants' aid, the medium leaves the performance space, and a number of measures are taken to clear her head and return her to normalcy. Attendants pour gin over the medium's head and rub it in to revive and alert the inner head; they blow into the ears and onto the top of the head, press the base of the neck, press their foreheads against the medium's forehead, stretch the medium's arms upward and then place them on the knees, and pull the legs forward by the big toes, all the while calling the medium's special name bestowed at initiation. The medium revives as if from a deep sleep and sits quietly gazing into space.

Dancing for Ògún in Bahia

In Bahia,[23] initiates of Candomblé go through a ritual death and rebirth (Herskovits and Herskovits 1942a:10 and 1942b:273). They are secluded for three to twelve months; their clothes are taken away, never to be worn again, and their heads are shaved (Pierson 1942:286–87); they are innoculated on their heads with sacred cuts to infuse them with the vital force of their deity (Herskovits 1943:501); the head is further washed regularly in a solution of leaves and other natural ingredients to attract and stimulate the vital force of the deity (Verger 1955); and the initiates are given new names (Herskovits 1943:501; Verger 1954:337). During this time, the devotees learn, among other things, the songs and dances of their particular deity. This spiritual retreat serves to dedicate the devotees to their deities and to prepare them for receiving the vital force of their god through possession trance (Omari 1984:23).

Among the Ketu and Nago Candomblé houses, danced ceremonies known as *obrigação* begin publicly as the "daughters of the gods" enter the *barração*, the ceremonial house, accompanied musically by the drummers.[24] Holding their two fists together in a manner in which one holds a horse's reins while riding, the daughters enter single file to a rapid cadence with small cantorlike steps, the *mae de santo* (literally, "mother of the saint," the female head of Candomblé) in the lead.[25] The entrance is said to represent a horse and to serve the purpose of dispatching Exu, god of the crossroads, for Exu is "a messenger boy" (*menino de recado*) between men and the gods. The horse is a symbol of mediation, a symbol which recurs in possession trance when the mediums are said to be literally the "horses" of the gods.

With tiny, quick steps, the devotees circle counterclockwise and, as the *mae de santo* reaches the spot closest to the front door, she raises her arms toward it and, crossing her two index fingers at a right angle, makes the sign of the cross-roads, the metaphorical intersection between the world and the spirit realm. Twice more, she steps back, whirls around quickly, and gestures toward the door, crossing her index fingers to open the ritual, that is, to mark the time and place to begin spiritual communication.

When the devotees have formed their circle, they invoke the gods with three chants each, beginning with Ogun. This segment of the ritual is known as a *xire*, the same as the Yoruba word *şiré*, indicating "a play" or "an entertainment" for the gods, for it is the purpose of this portion of the ceremony to coax the gods from their otherworldly domain into the phenomenal world. The *mae de santo* sings in Yoruba, *A xire Ogun o! A xire Ogun!* "We play for Ogun oh! We play for Ogun!" The devotees join in the chant and dance. Led by the *mae de santo* and accompanied by the drums, the devotees honor and invoke the gods one by one.[26] After Ogun comes Oxossi, god of the hunt; Osanyin, god of herbalism; Omolu, god of disease; Nana, goddess of deep water; Oxumare, goddess of the rainbow; Yewa, goddess of water; Yemanja, goddess of the salt water; Oxun, goddess of fresh surface water; Yansan, goddess of wind and war; Xango, god of thunder and light-ning; and Oxala, god of creativity.

When the devotees have finished invoking the gods, the *mae de santo* starts again and this time the devotees begin to fall into a trance. They kick off their shoes, and they begin to quiver. Their upper torsos and heads drop forward, and their chests rock back and forth rapidly in short, sharp motions. Sometimes a devotee may become instantly possessed, as if suddenly struck with the full force of the deity. This is visibly communicated by an unexpected burst of energy from the devotee which seems to thrust her out into space, body rigid, and which sends attendants scrambling to keep her from falling or landing on other participants. Attendants adjust the possessed's cloth by tying it tightly around her breasts, in the case of female deities like Yansan, Oxun, and Yemanja, or, in the case of males, either over the left shoulder or over both shoulders, crisscrossing on the chest (Omari 1984:22); they also assist the "horses" until they have regained con-trol and are transformed into the deity. Fully possessed, the mediums prostrate themselves before the drummers and the *mae de santo* and, as the manifestation of the deity, greet the spectators. In trance the possessed mediums stand with hands either on their hips or folded behind their backs. After dancing to a song associated with the deity, the possessed mediums are led out of the dance enclo-sure. The particular god honored at any given ceremony determines which other gods will "visit"; thus, if Xango is honored, his wives—Oxun and Yansan—are likely to visit and, if Omolu is honored, chances are his mother, Nana, will make an appearance.[27]

A break in the ceremony occurs while attendants prepare the mediums in the clothes of the deities. When ready, the deities form a single line led by the *mae de santo*. In the ceremonies in which Ogun visits, he always comes first. A slow processional song is played by the drummers as the *mae de santo* sings.

Ago, ago l'ona.

Make way, clear the way.

The line of deities enters slowly. As the Herskovits's (1942b:277) recall, "First comes the god of war, in green, wearing as a male deity, lace-edged pantalettes, a short wide skirt over them, dagger in hand, a sash about the waist tied in a wide bow, a brilliant cap as of a prince in an Arabian Nights tale."

The dances which characterize Ogun, in contrast to those performed in western Yorubaland, are mimetic. They act out in a stylized way Ogun fighting with his cutlass. Crucial to this mime, however, are the dynamics of Ogun's actions, and indeed this is what seems to capture the imagination of observers. Thus:

> The outward manifestations of the ecstasy of the children of Ogun, god of war, are much more forceful than those of the children of Oxun, goddess of fresh water. The former have something of the brutality of armies in battle, some of the hardness of steel, while the latter have a liquid, amorous quality—the fascinating sensuality of lazy rivers or still lakes sprinkled with sunlight. (Bastide 1978:377)

Whether or not Ogun carries a scythe or a sword:

> He brandishes it with eyes closed, slashing about wildly on all sides in his dancing. Sometimes, in a thrilling mock duel, he will fence with an agile devotee who has nothing but her bare arms to use as weapons. Such a brave daughter will be rescued from him, just in time to prevent injury, by being drawn away from the fray by several alert *ekedes* [assistants]. (Leahy 1955:9)

This dance, reflecting the nature of Ogun's vital power, is quick and direct with an explosive thrust.[28] As Ogun, the medium slashes, but does not do so "wildly on all sides." Inclining his body toward a diagonal, he takes two large steps, closes his feet to change to the opposite diagonal, and repeats the pattern in the opposite direction. While his stepping carries him back and forth diagonally forward, his bent arms, which carry metal blades (*espada*), slash powerfully in opposition up and down in the direction of the diagonally inclined torso and in time to the quick paces of his feet. As one *mae de santo* (Olga do Alaketu, 1974) explained: "He eats raw [food] and doesn't throw anything away; he kills, eats, and doesn't throw anything away, doesn't repent for what he has done" (*Ele come cru e não lança; ele mata, come e não lança, não se arrepende do que faz*).[29] Ogun moves between the seated audience and the drums, and, when reaching one or the other, spins around forcefully and returns in the opposite direction. Olga do Alaketu called this dance *pada* Ogun (1974), perhaps "Ògún's return" (Abraham 1958:539).

There is a popular story in Yorubaland about how Ogun sank into the ground alive leaving a long chain emanating from the spot and instructing his people that, if they ever needed him to defend them, they should pull on the chain that he left anchored in the earth. To test Ogun's allegiance, one day a citizen tugged on the chain, and Ogun came out slashing with his cutlass, in the process decapitating his own townspeople. Realizing what he had done, he vowed never to return. The *pada* Ogun of Brazil may relate to this well-known Yoruba motif of Ogun's absolute aggression, for it is said to represent gestures of war (*gestos dos guerreiras*).

Another of Ogun's mimes is similar to dances for other "hot" or dueling deities, such as Xango and Oxossi, called *ecu* (Pierson 1942:304). Two people face each other: two Oguns, or Ogun and another "hot" deity or other participant. Slightly shifting the right foot backward in four counts while pivoting on the left, and then repeating on the other side, each dancer prepares for a mock duel. Then, the dancers shift their bodies slightly from side to side alternately kicking the feet backward. All the while facing each other, they thrust their cutlasses, carried in the right hand, back and forth laterally, cutting across the left wrist in a rapid cadence in time to the music.

Sometimes the preparatory steps described above can be used to lower the knees to the ground to a seated position. From that position, sitting on their knees, the dancers move their torsos in a circular direction so that, at its farthest extent backward, they are practically lying horizontally on the ground. After circling one way and then the other, the dancers slowly work their way back to a full standing position in the same fashion as they descended. Such dances express Ogun's identity as a warrior.

It is perhaps significant in the Brazilian context, where the Yoruba language is no longer well understood, that the dances are mimetic, representing Ogun in a literal way. With the possible exception of a few elders, devotees are unable to give translations of Yoruba-derived songs; rather, they prefer to explain the dances which accompany the songs (M. and F. Herskovits 1942a:12; Binon 1967:165). In the Bahian context, where the oral liturgy is only vaguely understood by its users, dance can define and characterize the deity in a more precise way than the oral texts. Thus in addition to stressing *how* Ogun operates, that is, his dynamic qualities, the dances in Bahia become more literal by miming precisely *what* Ogun does.

Bastide felt that "Ogun's persona as a brutal and aggressive warrior and beheader . . . won out" over that of hunter, blacksmith, or farmer in Brazil, where he has become more widely known as the patron deity of slave revolt (1978:254). Indeed, warrior plays and dances are traditionally popular in Brazil, where they have become odd mixtures of elements from the *cucumbys*, the *congos*, and the *quilombo*—mystery plays patterned after the Portuguese *autos* (Portuguese mystery plays)—which usually depicted battles between two opposing groups (Ramos 1939:111). An 1888 illustration in a book by Mello Moraes Filho shows a group of Os Congos performing a war dance which appears to be quite similar to the mock battle in which Ogun mediums engage. Moraes Filho states,

> In transit, following a religious litter, a struggle ensues between the two lines of blacks, that were in dispute, defending themselves, ...
> And, fighting each other with iron swords, making complete turns and cadencing the flanks, the *Congos* advancing in procession, singing, in heat of battle, in bitterly contested combat:
>
> *Fire on the earth,*
> *Fire in the sea,*
> *That our queen*
> *Us has to help!* . . .
> (Moraes Filho 1888:95)

As in performances of the *congos* and *quilombos*, Ogun engages in mock combat in which two people face each other wielding swords. Ogun dances, as well as *quilombos* performances, symbolize slave revolt (Ramos 1939:110; Bastide 1978:254). Since these mystery plays tended to be mimetic and preceded the Candomblé by nearly a century, it is quite possible that Os Congos, *cucumbys*, and/or *quilombo* war dances were appropriately grafted onto the Yoruba war deity Ogun.[30] Further evidence for this suggestion lies in the Portuguese-inspired costumes worn by the possessed mediums. Like the older Os Congos' costumes, the vestments of Ogun, as well as other male deities, consist of a long tunic, belted by a wide sash, over full-legged pantalettes.

By the same token, the *àgèrè* dance, which is associated with hunters and is performed to honor Ògún and Eyinlè in Yorubaland, appears to have been incorporated into the repertoire of dances for hunting deities Oxossi and Yansan in Bahia. In Bahia, Inle (Eyinlè) represents an aspect or quality of Oxossi (*qualidade*).[31] Thus, as Bastide (1978:254) suggests, Ogun's persona as hunter seems to have dropped out in favor of his persona as warrior, or rather seems to have been usurped by Oxossi, who in Yorubaland is also traditionally a hunting deity.

Ògún in Western Yorubaland and Brazil: A Comparison

There are marked similarities between ritual performances for Ògún in Igbogila, Nigeria, and in Bahia, Brazil. Like those in Igbogila, cult groups or Candomblés in Bahia honor diverse Yoruba deities collectively during a single ceremony. The rites of initiation are similar too, including symbolic death and rebirth, seclusion, and practices of taking away the clothes, bestowing new names, shaving and bathing the head, and embedding medicines to stimulate possession trance. After honoring Ẹlégba, both groups dance in a counterclockwise circle to invoke each of the deities in sequence with a minimum of three songs each. In addition to Ẹlégba, other deities represented in the cult group of Igbogila which are also found in Bahia are Iroko, Omolu, and of course Òguń. Inle, the Bahian version of the Yoruba deity Eyinlè, is considered a manifestation of Oxossi—both are associated with hunting. In Yorubaland and in the more traditional cult houses of Bahia, Òguń is always invoked first after Ẹlégba, and explanations for his coming first are much the same: he "opens the way."

Devotees of Òguń in both places carry instruments symbolically associated with the deity. The sword is more common in Brazil, but in Nigeria Òguń mediums also carry iron pincers, spades, flywhisks, or miniature guns. Although Òguń is acknowledged in Brazil to be the god of iron, the cutlasses carried by the possessed mediums are made of laminated chrome, as are many of the ritual instruments of Candomblé which require metal. Emphasis on the left in the context of possession trance is not as evident in Brazil as in Yorubaland. Yet, Pierson (1942:289) notes that, when a deity wishes to take leave of the ceremony, he clasps left hands with another participant tightly.

The style of the onset of possession trance is quite similar, including the practice of greeting members of the audience individually, keeping the hands on the hips, and exaggerated stepping. In Brazil as in western Yorubaland the possessed devotees are called the horses of the gods.

A further comparison may be made in the marked distinction between dance which serves to invoke spiritual forces and dance which follows the invocation and represents the materialized force itself. Both in Yoruba country and in Brazil the distinction is made in terms of dynamics. In Bahia, when devotees invoke the deities at the beginning of the performance, gestures are minimalized. Rather than portraying the deities fully, they merely give an indication of the movements which represent them. Thus Òguń's large, forceful movements are reduced to small, vague, effortless gestures. In a subtle way, index fingers that serve as cutlasses offer a gross understatement of underlying warlike intent. This minimalization of movement conserves energy for the long service which culminates in possession trance, when the deities are given full expression. For as the horses of the deities, the devotees are ridden hard. Nonetheless, the marked difference between dances performed as invocations and as actual possession serves to concentrate energy in the part of the dance which actualizes the deity.

The important point here is that the dances, however understated, were nevertheless performed. Like liturgical texts, the import of which is not always fully understood by listeners, their significance lies in their actual performance. Whether or not the dances are literally understood, the performance is thought to carry power. What is vital, then, is the actual effort—the verbal and kinetic exertions which, when minimally stated, invoke metaphysical forces but, when fully asserted, activate and even embody those forces. Both in Brazil and in western

Yorubaland, the dances which manifest Ògún indeed reinforce the verbal images of him in myths and praise poetry. They show him to exert explosive force—powerful, quick, and direct.

Conclusions

Because dance and oral performance express, and are even thought to conduct, spiritual force, an analysis of the use of dynamics in ritual is essential to our understanding of the total religious framework of the Yoruba; it allows us to perceive the gods as power personified, each embodying a particular locus of dynamic qualities which remain coherent and consistent no matter the context. By focussing on *how* deities act (the qualities of their actions) as distinguished from *what* they do (the acts themselves) it is possible to resolve apparent contradictions in their personalities. We can go beyond the creative/destructive dichotomy and examine the wellspring of power that underlies both creation and destruction: Ògún's àṣẹ. The dynamic configurations expressed in Ògún's dances and verbal arts serve as models of and for humans so that, as Bartenieff (1980) puts it, they may cope with the environment. Through ritual performance, people tap and use power that is appropriate for meeting life's demands.

Notes

1. The data for this paper were gathered during fieldwork in Nigeria in 1975, 1977–78, and 1982 and in Bahia, Brazil, during the summer of 1974. The 1982 research trip was sponsored by the National Endowment for the Humanities (RO-20072-81-2184). I wish to thank in particular the *Olóriṣà* of Igbogila, Nigeria, for welcoming me at their rituals. I am also indebted to Joçelina Françisca Barbosa of Ile Olga do Alaketu, Matatu, Salvador, for teaching me the Candomblé dances for the deities, and Olga do Alaketu and Antonio Agnelo Pereira, Elemaso, Ile Caṣa Branca, Salvador, for discussing Candomblé ritual and dance with me. Special thanks also go to Juana and Didi dos Santos and to Pierre Verger for many courtesies during my stay in Bahia. I also wish to thank Rowland Abiodun for reading and commenting on this paper and Henry John Drewal, who assisted in all phases of this project.

2. In Yoruba thought, the phenomenal world is *ayé*, usually translated simply as world. *Ayé* is a domain where people reside temporarily. In addition it includes a number of spirits who can become manifest in human or animal form. The realm of the gods and ancestors is known as *òrun*, a permanent otherworldly reality. The relationship of *ayé* to *òrun* is expressed in the proverb "The world is a market, the otherworld is home" (*Ayé l'ọjà, òrun n'ilé*).

3. Egúngún refers to masquerades which honor the ancestors in Yorubaland and also to the society which produces them. Cloaked in cloth and embellished with other items such as carved masks, bones of animals, or feathers, they are thought to be spirits manifest in the world (*ayé*).

4. *Kùtùkùtù* means "early in the morning" and, in this context, also evokes the quality of the rain. It conveys the dynamic of just beginning something; it implies an initiating

action which has not yet reached its full potential (personal communication, Rowland Abiodun, 1982).

5. Rudolph Laban's theories of effort are based on similar kinds of observations. Thus, "the weighty power of a rock with its visible potential for impact speaks of the tremendous impetus with which it might plunge into the valley as an avalanche. The grace of a plant speaks of the readiness to move which drives a flower out of its stem from which fruit and new seed will sprout. . . . Animal movement speaks of the fine adaptations with which a particular species has immersed itself into its surroundings to fit increasingly finer, more differentially into the workings of nature" (Laban cited in Bartinieff 1980:1).

6. For the most elaborate discussions of àṣẹ, see Verger (1964), dos Santos (1976), and M. and H. Drewal (1987).

7. For a discussion of behavior as it relates to concepts of inner power, see H. Drewal (1977).

8. Informants say this snake is the Black Mamba; however, Abraham (1958:153) points out that "the Spitting Cobra (Blacknecked Cobra) is often wrongly called the Black Mamba." Indeed, salmon-pink and black cross-bars, according to Abraham, usually alternate on the underpart of the Spitting Cobra's neck and front part of its body.

9. Utterances express attitudes toward time, space, weight, and flow audibly through the combination of: 1) speed of sounds or syllables, 2) their degree of directness—whether they are voiced in a straightforward manner or are gliding, 3) their vocal force or thrust, and 4) their flow—whether the stream of energy is free-flowing or bound, held back, or restrained.

10. In analyzing movement and its corollary oral expression, I follow Laban and Lawrence, who identified four factors which, in varying degrees, combine to produce effort or dynamic qualities: exertion (from light to strong), control (from fluent to bound), time (from slow to quick), and space (indirect or direct). In the authors' view: "A person's efforts are visibly expressed in the rhythms of his bodily motion. It thus becomes necessary to study these rhythms, and to extract from them those elements which will help us to compile a systematic survey of the forms effort can take in human action" (1947:xi).

11. However, I have followed the practice of the Department of African Languages and Literatures at Ọbafemi Awolowo University (see, for example, Oyelaran 1976–77).

12. Candomblés are Afro-Brazilian cult groups organized for the worship of African deities, primarily those of the Yoruba (see Omari 1984).

13. The right hand sometimes carries percussion instruments shaken initially to invoke the god and ultimately to pronounce àṣẹ, àṣẹ, àṣẹ, "so be it," in response to prayers. As one participant in traditional Yoruba religion noted, "When townspeople hear the bells and gongs of the priest performing ceremonies inside his shrine, they will be saying in their homes as they are working, 'àṣẹ, àṣẹ, àṣẹ' to accompany the ringing in support of whatever the priest is saying." Lending efficacy to prayers and invocations, the sound of the bells helps to induce possession trance and later in the ceremony to enforce the words of the gods, spoken through the mediumship of the priest.

14. Ògbóni is a society of elders which functions as a governing body together with the king. For more information on Ògbóni, see Morton-Williams (1960) and H. Drewal (in press).

15. Òjè is the name given to members of the Egúngún society.

16. This holds true in the United States among practitioners of Yoruba religion who were originally trained by Cubans (Edwards and Mason 1985:iii). Thus, at sacred ritual

parties (*bembe*) for Yoruba deities in the New York metropolitan area, drummers begin by saluting Ẹlẹ́gba first and then Ògún. For an American practitioner's perspective on Ògún, see Edwards and Mason's booklet (1985:16–20), written primarily for English-speaking initiates of Yoruba religion.

17. The cult is found in an Ẹ̀gbádò town, but it originated among the Ọ̀họrí Yoruba. Thus devotees sing and pray in the Ọ̀họrí dialect. The Ọ̀họrí Yoruba live on the border between Nigeria and Benin (R.P.B.) in the area of the Kumi swamp. Because of their relative inaccessibility during the rainy season, they are considered by their neighbors to be among the most conservative Yoruba. Their dialect is quite distinct. The members of this cult group indicate that their practices had earlier roots among the Gùn (Ègùn), an Àjà-speaking people of southern Benin (R.P.B.). The deity Omolu is said to have come from Gun country and, indeed, one of Omolu's dances is called *ègùn Omolú*, meaning the Omolu of the Ègùn people, who, according to cult members, are from Àjàṣẹ (Porto Novo).

18. Although Ògún is the dominant deity in this cult group, any medium can join, and thus conceivably any deity can be included. Other deities represented within the group are Ṣàngó and Ọya, whose priests are no longer possessed, because they have grown too old and feeble to perform.

19. For another ceremony which features the deity Ondo, see M. Drewal (1975).

20. Western physicians refer to this movement as "winging of the scapulae," which implies a neurological disorder and a lack of control. However, these movements performed in western Yorubaland, quite to the contrary, are superbly controlled. Not only can they be performed with a wide range of dynamics, but they also can be intentionally varied rhythmically.

21. For more details on the deity Eyinlẹ̀ (Erinlẹ̀), see Thompson (1969) and Babalọla (A Portrait of Ògún as Reflected in Ìjálá Chants, in *Africa's Ogun: Old World and New*, Sandra T. Barnes [ed.], Bloomington, Ind., IUP, 1989, pp. 147–72).

22. One of the association's titleholders, Aṣípa, holds a position on the king's council of chiefs. The society was probably at its peak during the nineteenth century, when during the Yoruba civil wars hunters became warriors to defend the town.

23. The analysis of Candomblé dance comes from observations of 14 ceremonies in 6 different houses during 1974. For consistency, the English spelling of Ògún is used throughout, without tone marks.

24. *Obrigação* are analogous to *bembe* in the Cuban Lucumi, or Santería, tradition, which are now held in the United States by Hispanic peoples as well as both black and white Americans.

25. Saint here is a euphemism for an African deity. In Brazil, Catholic saints have been syncretized with African deities. To a large extent, this occurred to mask Candomblé during a time of religious repression (Omari 1984:14).

26. For a discussion of the role of the drums and drummers in Candomblé, see Herskovits (1944).

27. This is also the case in Afro-American *bembe*, sacred parties held for the Yoruba deities.

28. Tempo is one of the factors that make up dynamic qualities thereby helping to characterize the vital force of deities. Béhague notes in his examinations of Candomblé songs that "the idiosyncrasies attributed to a given orixa (whether young or old, temperamental or peaceful, and so on) influence the tempo of such songs" (1975:75). As in the Old World, the song determines the drum music, which in turn sets the pace of the dances.

29. Lépine (1981:23) presents some personality traits that are common to Ogun mediums, suggesting at the same time that after initiation they become more like the deity. It seems clear that one's personal deity licenses the expression of certain distinctive personality traits associated with that deity. And dance is one of the mechanisms through which Ogun power is expressed and felt.

30. According to Pereira da Costa (cited in Ramos 1939:106), the earliest documented date of a Congos or Cucumbys is June 24, 1706. This is found in a document belonging to a religious association in the town of Iguarassu in Pernambuco; whereas, Carneiro (1954:48) calculates a date of circa 1830 as the foundation of Candomblé. Furthermore, Ramos says of the *quilombos* of Palmares, formerly a community of runaway slaves who banded together in collective resistance, that their plays recall "the opposing camps, the dances, chants, struggles ending in capture, intrigues and trickery and finally the siege of the Negro position and with its fall, the reenslavement. . . . When the queen is introduced into the plot, there seems to be a close relationship between these plays which I have called *quilombos* and the Congo plays" (1939:110). Moreover, in a revised reprint of Moraes Filho's 1888 work, Câmara Cascudo observes (1979:72, n.28) that the performance of Os Congos is very similar in detail to that of "os 'Mouriscos' " (Moors) associated with processions on São João's Day in Portugal. Such warrior dances involving battles with swords as part of Catholic processions, he suggests, can be traced to fifteenth-century Europe.

31. These shifts in emphasis and fusions in Brazil reflect the need to systematize deities from diverse locations in Yorubaland who have similar attributes in order to show how they actually are integral parts of one unified system.

References

Abraham, R. C. 1958. Dictionary of Modern Yoruba, London: University of London Press.

Ayoade, J. A. A. 1979. The Concept of Inner Essence in Yoruba Traditional Medicine, in African Therapeutic Systems. Z. A. Ademuwagun, J. A. A. Ayoade, I. E. Harrison, and D. M. Warren (eds.), Waltham, Mass.: Crossroads Press, pp. 49–55.

Babalọla, S. A. 1966. The Content and Form of Yoruba Ìjálá, London: Oxford University Press.

Barnes, Sandra T. 1980. Ogun: An Old God for a New Age, Philadelphia: ISHI.

Bartenieff, Irmgard, with D. Lewis. 1980. Body Movement: Coping With the Environment, N.Y.: Gordon and Breach, Science Publishers, Inc.

Bastide, Roger. 1978. The African Religions of Brazil: Toward a Sociology of the Interpenetration of Civilizations (Helen Sebba, trans.), Baltimore: The Johns Hopkins University Press.

Béhague, Gerhard H. 1975. Notes on Regional and National Trends in Afro-Brazilian Cult Music, in Tradition and Renewal: Essays on 20th-Century Latin American Literature and Culture. M. H. Forster (ed.), Urbana: University of Illinois Press, pp. 68–80.

Beier, Ulli. 1970. Yoruba Poetry, Cambridge: Cambridge University Press.

Binon, Giselle. 1967. La Musique dans le Candomblé, in La Musique dan la Vie, Tome 1. T. Nikiprowetzky (ed.), Paris: pp. 159–207.

Carneiro, Edison. 1954. Candomblés da Bahia, Rio de Janeiro: Editorial Andes (2nd ed. revd.).

Crowther, Samuel. 1852. A Vocabulary of the Yoruba Language, London: Seeleys.
do Alaketu, Olga, Mae de Santo. 1974. Interview, Matatu, Salvador, Bahia, August 17.
dos Santos, Juana E. 1976. Os Nago e a Morte: Pade, Asese e o Culto Egun na Bahia, Petropolis: Editora Vozes.
Drewal, Henry J. 1974. Efe: Voiced Power and Pageantry, African Arts 7(2):26–29, 58–66.
———. 1977. Art and the Perception of Women in Yoruba Culture, Cahiers d'Etudes Africaines 68(37–4):545–67.
———. In press. Meaning in Oshugbo Art among Ijebu Yoruba, in Festschrift, Ethnologisches Seminar, B. Engelbrecht and R. Gardi (eds.), Basel: Universität Basel.
Drewal, Henry J., and Margaret T. 1983. Gẹlẹdẹ: Art and Female Power among the Yoruba, Bloomington: Indiana University Press.
Drewal, Margaret T. 1975. Symbols of Possession: A Study of Movement and Regalia in an Anago-Yoruba Ceremony, Dance Research Journal 7(2):15–24.
———. 1986. Art and Trance among Yoruba Shango Devotees, African Arts 20(1):60–67, 98–99.
Drewal, Margaret T., and Henry J. 1978. More Powerful Than Each Other: An Egbado Classification of Egungun, African Arts 11(3):28–39, 98–99.
———. 1987. Composing Time and Space in Yoruba Art, Word and Image 3, 4.
Edwards, Gary, and John Mason. 1985. Black Gods—Orişa Studies in the New World, Brooklyn: Yoruba Theological Archministry.
Herskovits, Melville J. 1943. The Southernmost Outpost of New World Africanisms, American Anthropologist 45(4):495–510.
———. 1944. Drums and Drummers in Afro-Brazilian Cult Life, The Musical Quarterly 30(4):477–92.
Herskovits, Melville, and Francis Herskovits. 1942a. Afro-Bahian Religious Songs, (Album XIII Notes), Folk Music of Brazil issued from the Collections of the Archive of American Folk Song, Library of Congress Music Division.
———. 1942b. The Negros of Brazil, The Yale Review 32(2):263–79.
Hertz, R. 1973. The Pre-eminence of the Right Hand: A Study in Religious Polarity, in Right and Left: Essays on Dual Symbolic Classification, R. Needham (ed.), Chicago: University of Chicago Press, pp. 3–31.
Laban, Rudolph, and F. C. Lawrence. 1947. Effort, London: Macdonald & Evans.
Langer, Suzanne K. 1953. Feeling and Form: A Theory of Art, New York: Charles Scribner's and Sons.
Leahy, J. G. 1955. The Presence of the Gods among the Mortals: The Candomblé Dances, Brazil 29(4):4–11.
Lépine, Claude. 1981. Os Estereótipos da Personalidade no Candomblé Nàgó, in Olóòrìṣà: Escritos sobre a religião dos orixás, C. E. M. de Moura (coordinator and trans.), São Paulo: Editora ÁGORA, pp. 11–31.
Moraes Filho, Mello. 1888. Festas e Tradições Populares do Brasil. Rio de Janeiro: H. Garnier. [Reprinted in 1979 with preface by Silvio Romero and revisions and notes by Luís da Câmara Cascudo. São Paulo: Editora da Universidade de São Paulo and Livraria Itatiaia Editora.]
Morton-Williams, Peter. 1960. The Yoruba Ogboni Cult in Oyo, Africa 30:362–74.
Olúpọnà, A., Aṣòguń. 1975. Interview, Ibaiyun, November 13.
Omari, Mikelle Smith. 1984. From the Inside to the Outside: The Art and Ritual of Ba-

hian Candomblé, Monograph Series, no. 24, Los Angeles: Museum of Cultural History, UCLA.

Oṣitola, Kolawole, Babaláwo. 1982. Interview, Ìjẹbu-Òde, July.

Oyelaran, Ọlasope O. 1976–77. Seminar Series, no. 1 (2 vols.), Ifẹ: Department of African Languages and Literatures, University of Ifẹ.

Peek, Philip M. 1981. The Power of Words in African Verbal Arts, Journal of American Folklore 94(371):19–43.

Pierson, Donald. 1942. Negroes in Brazil: A Study of Race Contact at Bahia, Chicago: University of Chicago Press.

Prince, Raymond. 1960. Curse, Invocation and Mental Health among the Yoruba, Canadian Psychiatric Association Journal 5:65–79.

Ramos, Artur. 1939. The Negro in Brazil, Washington, D.C.: Associated Publishers.

Ray, Benjamin. 1973. "Performative Utterances" in African Rituals, History of Religions 13(1):16–35.

Thompson, Robert F. 1969. Abatan: A Master Potter of the Ẹgbado Yoruba, in Tradition and Creativity in Tribal Art, D. P. Biebuyck (ed.), Berkeley: University of California Press, pp. 120–82.

Verger, Pierre. 1954. Rôle Joué par l'État d'Hébétude au cours de l'Initiation des Novices aux Cultes des Orisha et Vodun, Bulletin Institut Fondamental d'Afrique Noire 16(3–4):322–40.

———. 1955. Bori, Première Cérémonie d'Initiation au Culte des Òrishàs Nàgó à Bahia au Brésil, Revista do Museu Paulista (São Paulo), n.s., 9:269–91.

———. 1957. Notes sur le Culte des Orisa et Vodun à Bahia, La Baie de tous les Saints au Brésil et à l'Ancienne Côte des Esclaves en Afrique, Mémoires de l'Institut Fondamental d'Afrique Noire, no. 51.

———. 1964. The Yoruba High God—A Review of the Sources, Paper prepared for the Conference on The High God in Africa, Ibadan, December 14–18.

———. 1969. Trance and Convention in Nago-Yoruba Spirit Mediumship, in Spirit Mediumship and Society in Africa. J. Beattie and J. Middleton (eds.), N.Y.: Africana, pp. 50–66.

———. 1976–77. The Use of Plants in Yoruba Traditional Medicine and its Linguistic Approach, in Seminar Series, No. 1, Part I, Ọ. O. Oyelaran (ed.), Ifẹ: Department of African Languages and Literature, University of Ifẹ, pp. 242–95.

Warren, Dennis M., A.D. Buckley, and J. A. Ayandokun. 1973. Yoruba Medicines, Legon: The Institute of African Studies, University of Ghana.

PART THREE
THE CARIBBEAN

9. LA GRAN FAMILIA PUERTORRIQUEÑA "EJ PRIETA DE BELDÁ" (THE GREAT PUERTO RICAN FAMILY IS REALLY REALLY BLACK)

Arlene Torres

This chapter explores how the seminal work *El país de cuatro pisos* (1980) by José Luis González (1926–1996) challenged historiographers and ethnographers to critically examine the relationship between "race," racializing practices, ethnicity, and national identity in Puerto Rico. González argued that the formation of a Puerto Rican national identity could be divided into several tiers. The first of these was the Afro-Antillean tier. It constitued the basis of Puerto Rican society and culture and was rooted in the experiences of enslaved and free people of African descent who inhabited the island shortly after the arrival of the Spanish.

The second tier consisted of an influx of *extranjeros*, "white" Europeans, encouraged to migrate to Puerto Rico in the early to middle nineteenth century via the 1815 Cédula de Gracias in order to allay fears about a black takeover following the Haitian Revolution. Another objective was to *blanquear*, to whiten, the island with foreigners. Despite these attempts, as sugar plantations developed in the nineteenth century with black enslaved laborers from Africa and the Antilles and free black and *mulato* laborers who settled on the island, the Afro-Antillean component of Puerto Rican society and culture became further solidified.

The third tier emerged with the 1898 invasion of Puerto Rico by the United States. And the fourth, González argued, was grounded in the populist movements of the 1940s, a critical period in the construction of a Puerto Rican nationalist identity (see Quintero Rivera 1981[1979], J. González 1989[1980], 1986, Alvarez Curbelo and Rodríguez Castro 1993).

Juan Manuel Carrión (1993) argues that the tiered structural model of González is static and essentializing. He accuses González of adopting a hispanophobic stance in his effort to demonstrate that Puerto Rican culture is rooted in the experiences of enslaved and free blacks. He states (Carrión 1993:7) that just because blacks and *mulatos* for the most part occupied the island in the latter part of the eighteenth century, it does not mean that Puerto Rico is culturally African. He also states that González is exploiting in his work inherent contradictions found when the construction of an ethnic imagery has a racial component. Finally, by doing so, Carrión argues, González erroneously conflates race with culture. The four-tiered structural model simply does not work.

Carrión suggests, by contrast, that the *ajiaco* (*sancocho*, callaloo) metaphor invoked by Fernando Ortiz (1939) to describe the Cuban nationalist identity might be more appropriate. He states (Carrión 1993:9): "Cuban nationalist identity is a process always in formation where a number of cultural factors conjoin to create new forms." Unlike González, Carrión argues that Ortiz does not dispense with the view that "la cultura proviniente de España constituye la 'troncalidad' de la cultura cubana (Spanish culture constitutes the root of Cuban culture)." Carrión does not dispense with this view, either.

Carrión's criticisms of the static and essentializing view of culture presented by González are well taken; however, Carrión falls into the same trap. While González privileges the roots of African heritage in the formation of a Puerto Rican national identity, Carrión continues to give special consideration to Spanish culture. Contradictions loom large. Carrión's posture cannot be maintained if, as he suggests, we are to adopt the *ajiaco* (*sancocho* in Puerto Rico) metaphor precisely because *el sancocho* is a stew made up of spices, meats, and tubers from the Old World and the New. Moreover, the stew can no longer be separated into disparate elements. It is a creation of people of the Americas.

Puerto Rican nationalist practices draw upon an ideology of *mestizaje* (the *sancocho*) that is rooted in the blend of Spanish, indigenous, and African cultures. Upon first glance, it appears that a national emphasis on *mestizaje* in Puerto Rico promotes processes of social integration; however, there is still a hyper-privileging of individuals of European descent with phenotypic features associated with "whiteness." As Miriam Jiménez Román notes in a critical analysis of race relations in Puerto Rico (1996:10),

> There is the institutionally sanctioned and popularly reinforced belief in distinct races with identifiable, essential traits, with a corresponding notion of a "multiracial" society whose citizens enjoy harmonious relations, not least because of their evolutionary trek toward "whiteness."

This contradiction was poignantly expressed in 1988 when Rafael Hernández Colón, governor of Puerto Rico at the time, placed himself in a compromising position when he addressed the Institute of Iberian-American Cooperation in Madrid. In what is now an infamous speech, he stated (*El Nuevo Día*, June 21, 1988, p. 45): "The contribution of the black race to Puerto Rican culture is irrelevant, it is mere rhetoric" (see Flores 1993, Torres 1995, Rodríguez Castro 1995).

Upon his return from Spain, Hernández Colón had to answer to charges of racism. In an article entitled "España, San Antón y el ser nacional (Spain, San Antón, and our national identity)," he stated (*El Nuevo Día*, June 6, 1988):

> While in Central and South America indigenous cultures continue to enrich and form part of the national cultures of the respective countries (Mexico, Guatemala, Peru, Bolivia), in the Greater Antilles only archaeological artifacts remain.

Centuries ago indigenous peoples were assimilated by the Hispanic culture, and together with a rich African contribution, integrated our Puerto Ricanness.

While in some islands of the Caribbean or, for example, in a country such as Guyana, the black culture and its population was preponderant, in Puerto Rico given historical circumstances that scholars have already addressed, this rich heritage was assimilated, as in the case of the indigenous heritage, by the Hispanic culture, producing our national culture which cannot be classified as Taino, African, or Spanish, but as the harmonious synthesis of the three that constitutes the Puerto Rican identity. . . . [1]

This ideological perspective became the cornerstone of the quincentenary commemoration on the island in 1992 with one caveat: there were two worlds instead of three. The commemorative event was called "Encuentro de dos mundos (An Encounter between Two Worlds)." By recognizing the Americas, this so-called encounter departed from the 1908 celebration, "El Cuarto Centenario de la Civilización Cristiana (Four Hundred Years of Christian Civilization)," a celebration held shortly after the North American invasion of Puerto Rico. These commemorative events, among others, were riddled with contradictions as tensions surfaced and other cultural practices and interpretations oscillated between a collective identity and an identity primarily rooted in the Spanish or Spanish and Amerindian past (see Rodríguez Castro 1995:22). There was, however, a common thread. The Spanish encounter with Africa and the forced and violent encounter of enslaved Africans with the Americas in each of these historic events was deliberately concealed.

As Torres and Whitten indicate in the general introduction to this volume, processes of pernicious pluralism activate and perpetuate the clash of three symbols of nationalism as *mestizaje, indigenismo,* and *blanqueamiento* in Latin America and the Spanish-speaking Caribbean. Powerful symbols of nationhood coupled with ideologies of *mestizaje* and *blanqueamiento* exemplify the Puerto Rican paradox. The "mixture" is embraced, provided that the essence of Puerto Rican society and culture is still rooted in Spain and later in the Americas. The Caribbean dilemma is also writ large. As John Nunley (1993:290) notes in his analysis of Trinidadian culture and callaloo,

> Just as the soup improves in taste, becoming sweeter as diverse ingredients blend, so has Trinidadian culture become better as it has increased in diversity. . . . Cultural diversity, though it sometimes causes severe social tensions in the community, remains positively valued.

While Puerto Ricans on the island have tended to focus on the blend in particular historical moments, in other contexts they have sought to establish and maintain boundaries between groups that are racially defined.

Carrión (1993:9) is quite right when he says, "Puerto Rico, no cabe negarlo, es una nación mulata (We cannot deny that Puerto Rico is a mulatto nation)."

However, the crux of the matter is that Puerto Rico is *mulato* as a nation *cuando nos conviene* (when it is convenient to be so). The ethnographer's challenge, then, is to demonstrate historically and ethnographically how racialized social and cultural categories are invoked without conflating race and culture despite the fact that *en la vida cotidiana* (in everyday life) they are constantly conflated.

In an insightful overview, "The Persistent Power of 'Race' in the Cultural and Political Economy of Racism," Faye V. Harrison (1995:47) notes that as critiques of race as a biological concept were launched, anthropologists adopted a "no-race" posture and therefore did not address why racism continues to exist. Anthropologists, she argued, focused on ethnicity and "for the most part, euphemized or denied race by not specifying the conditions under which those social categories and groups historically subordinated as 'racially' distinct emerge and persist." She further stated (Harrison 1995:48): "Other analysts showed how ethnicity and race can be interrelated but distinct dimensions in the formation of individual and group identity, and how depending on the context, one dimension may modify or take precedence over the other."

In the past, scholars who compared the racial–color continuum in Latin America and the Spanish-speaking Caribbean to the racial bifurcation in the United States and elsewhere demonstrated how race and class are interrelated (Hoetink 1967, Mintz 1971, Duany 1985). However, for the most part, these scholars argued that class relations in Latin America and the Spanish-speaking Caribbean took precedence over race relations, and thereby they failed to analyze how discourses about class relations euphemize race and provide a means to deny the existence and persistence of racist practices.

The purpose of this chapter is to work against the silencing of a critical discourse on race relations and color prejudice in Puerto Rico. I discuss precisely how ideas and perceptions of self and other are reproduced and/or changed over time in a racist and class-based society. I go on to suggest the ways by which we may begin to critically analyze how the historical terrain and the contemporary Puerto Rican cultural landscape are racially mapped in daily discourse, a discourse that continually seeks to silence and marginalize *el puertorriqueño, que ej prieto de beldá*, the Puerto Rican who is really black.

I further propose to show how members of communities defined by others as black challenge the criteria by which they are so defined by drawing upon a wide range of their experiences. As they celebrate their black identity, they draw upon contradictory and complementary paradigms that emphasize their cultural autonomy. In other social contexts they emphasize their identity as *negros* and *mulatos* who constitute an integral part of the nation, *la gran familia puertorriqueña*, the great Puerto Rican family (Quintero-Rivera 1981, Rodríguez Juliá 1983, 1988).

I argue that the great Puerto Rican family *ej prieta de beldá* as opposed to this same family as *es prieta de verdad*. The negative ascriptions associated with blackness are brought to the fore in this contrast between vernacular Spanish and standard Spanish.

The use of the black vernacular as opposed to *la lengua castellana*, the Spanish language, by the black Puerto Rican poet Fortunato Vizcarrondo in the poem titled *¿y tu agüela, ónde ejtá?* and in the title of this essay ironically contests racist ideologies that seek to silence *el negro y el mulato*. An engagement with cultural practices that are stereotypically viewed as unrefined, culturally lacking, or confined to the realm of popular culture reveal that Puerto Rican nationalist ideologies simultaneously "whiten" and "darken" the Puerto Rican cultural landscape.

Despite this critical commentary on Puerto Rican society, *¿y tu agüela, ónde ejtá?* has received national and international acclaim. Poems such as these are recited and performed in contexts where a Puerto Rican nationalist heritage is celebrated provided that the celebration of blackness is limited to the expressive realm.[2] Such a strategy obfuscates the intent of the author, and of the performers of the piece. Blackness is not only manipulated, it is rendered powerless.

Racialized Terrains

The cultural mapping of the landscape in Puerto Rico is critical because it is racialized and class based (Jackson and Penrose 1993). In Puerto Rico the opposition between the coast and the interior and between coastal/urban and rural laborer positions are subsumed by the tripartite classification of *el negro, el blanco*, and *el jíbaro* in society. In Puerto Rico, a mythico-historical figure, called a *jíbaro* and represented by a light-skinned peasant living in the mountainous interior, seized the Puerto Rican imagination. He has become the bearer of a nascent Puerto Rican identity and symbolically represents blacks who are marginalized.

I conducted anthropological fieldwork intermittently from 1984 through 1988 on the southeastern coast of Puerto Rico. The boundaries where the communities of Maunabo, Patillas, Arroyo, and Guayama begin and end were not readily apparent given the similarities in the geographical and cultural landscape, but subtle differences are mapped out in the architectural landscape, place names, and roadways.

The southeastern coast can be divided into the wet littoral valley encompassing the towns of Yabucoa and Maunabo and the alluvial plains extending from Patillas to Ponce. Maunabo is closely aligned with municipalities to the east. Given its terrain, however, it is also an integral part of the cultural geography and landscape of Patillas Arroyo and Guayama, its neighbors to the west. The central mountain ridge blocks access to these communities; they are relatively isolated. When sugar reigned, these communities were accessible via the sea. With the demise of the sugar industry, they remained spatially, socially, and economically marginal. However, throughout the history of these communities an intricate web of social relations can be teased out of the landscape. This web extends into the present.

The Afro-Antillean peoples of the southeastern coastal towns of Maunabo, Patillas, Arroyo, and Guayama were to be the population for study in this region. They are people who yearn for recognition on their own terms. Such a yearning is manifest in an imagery that challenges the Puerto Rican imagination. This imagination constitutes a collective cultural identity that primarily emphasizes a Spanish heritage and secondarily that of indigenous Caribbean, always privileged over African descent. The whole southern coast is populated by dark-skinned black people of Afro-Antillean descent, and their recognition requires Puerto Rico to come to grips with the phenomenon of blackness.

Before we can critically engage in an analysis of the intersection of race, class, and social status in Puerto Rico, we need to critically examine the historical terrain for the reference points established vis-à-vis *negro*, *blanco*, and *jíbaro* during the Spanish colonial era. It is with these colonial categories that euphemisms for race emerged and became located within Puerto Rican economy, society and culture.

Historical Background

Throughout the eighteenth and nineteenth centuries, black people, slaves and their kindreds, constituted the coastal labor force on the sugar plantations as well as the urban labor force that met the needs of the "white" plantation owners and the creole elite. Black people, who were descendants of freed slaves or maroons living on the coast in subsistence-oriented fishing communities or in the interior of these coastal municipalities as rural laborers, were recognized only when they represented a threat to the established social order.

The 1815 Real Cédula de Gracias contributed to the economic growth of Puerto Rico and promoted the development of the valley of Guayama.[3] There was a major influx of *extranjeros*, foreigners, in the area. Many settled in the barrio of Arroyo with their capital, black slaves, and technology. Among the foreigners were French planters who had fled Haiti after the revolution of 1804. They sought to recover their losses by engaging in the production of sugar on the southeastern coast of Puerto Rico (Sued Badillo 1983:72, J. González 1981 [1979]:47). Other foreigners also settled in the valley of Guayama.[4] However, they did not settle in the area on a permanent basis. Their objective was to acquire the wealth to be had from the production of sugar with the use of a slave labor force. As Charles Walker, a North American *hacendado* and owner of the Hacienda Concordia in Arroyo stated, "Los dueños de plantaciones son principalmente extranjeros e independientes de la gente del país, ya que todos usan trabajo esclavo (The owners of the plantations are primarily foreigners. They work independently of the people of the Island, since they all use slave labor)" (Sued Badillo 1983:89). The growth of plantations in Arroyo initially helped to sustain the subsistence

agriculture in the interior and the fishing communities on the coast and contributed to the development of an urban sector that served the needs of the planters.
As foreigners appropriated larger parcels of fertile land in the coastal areas for the
production of sugar, *estancias*, small farms dedicated to the production of goods
for subsistence, were displaced. Maunabeños and Arroyanos who engaged in subsistence agriculture were forced to move farther into the interior of the municipality. Some of these laborers continued to engage in subsistence activities, while
others became part of an urban labor force. These laborers engaged in carpentry,
masonry, coopering, and iron work (Sued Badillo 1983:73).

In the mid-nineteenth century, Catalans, Corsicans, and Mallorcans settled in
Puerto Rico. This second wave of foreigners, José Luis González (1981[1979]:
50) argued, had a profound influence on race relations and the development of
a Puerto Rican national identity. Catalans in particular became involved in commercial activities in the valley of Guayama. These merchants, government officials, and military officers constituted a conservative group that sought to maintain Spanish rule. As the most economically and politically influential people in
the area, they maintained their social distance from other foreigners and from the
free and enslaved laborers; these free and enslaved laborers were black people
who contributed to the economic wealth of the area. This second wave of Europeans bought and settled on land in the interior of the island. They were primarily engaged in the production of coffee and other goods for export. Like their
coastal counterparts, these entrepreneurs relied on a slave labor force. As black
slaves became more difficult to acquire, however, European immigrants relied
on the labor of the displaced peasants in the coastal areas and in the interior of
the island (Scarano 1981, 1984).

The Growth of a "Nation"

Puerto Rico, formerly a colony of Spain, is a territory ("commonwealth") of
the United States. It is neither state nor nation. Nonetheless, Puerto Ricans
think of themsleves as constituting *una nación*, a nation. Hereafter the word *nation* in English or *nación* in Spanish is used without quotation marks in the self-
idenitfying Puerto Rican sense of the nationhood of its people. With this in mind
we can understand the ambiguities and contradictions inherent in the cultural
construction of "nation" within this island territory.

In the early to mid-nineteenth century the displaced black and *mulato* artisans,
laborers, and subsistence farmers and the *jíbaros* in the interior of the island did
not constitute part of *una nación*. They were viewed by *peninsulares*, foreigners,
and the growing *criollo*, creole elite, with contempt because they did not constitute a labor force that would readily meet the needs of the expanding plantations
and *haciendas*. As a result, plantation owners, *hacendados*, and the professional
elite in the urban areas supported local and regional policies and practices that
controlled both the enslaved and the free labor force. González (1981[1979]:51)

poignantly summarized the effects of European colonization in the nineteenth century as follows:

> The conquered on this occasion were not the indigenous Taínos, extinguished three centuries ago by the genocidal policies of the first conquest. They were the white inhabitants of the mountainous interior of the Island, a group that was out of touch with the civilized urban and semi-urban milieu of the coast. These mountainous peasants—the original *jíbaros*—became a massive labor force of agregados, sharecroppers, tied to the land via the institutionalization of the *libreta*, pass-book, a legal instrument created to satisfy the needs of a developing economy. The subsistence economy that prevailed in the region was soon displaced by an hacienda economy that focused on the production of coffee. The developing economy was in need of a labor force that was prohibited from migrating to other areas of the Island. The hacienda economy provided the material base for the emergence of an elite Creole class.[5]

As the *señorial* class, the *hacendados,* began to lay claim to Puerto Rico in opposition to the interests of the Spanish colonial government as well as against conservative merchants in the southern littoral, a nascent Puerto Rican identity began to take shape that reflected the values and beliefs of the *hacendados.* The Puerto Rican nation was constituted as a paternalistic class of *hacendados* who provided the *jíbaro* with the means to engage in productive labor for the good of the nation. Blacks and *mulatos* were still not considered part of the emerging nation. Santiago-Valles (1994:44) stated there were two major factors that influenced how these laboring classes were defined. First, even until the 1830s, many of the enslaved laborers had been born in Africa. Second, the development of sugar plantation in the eastern and southern coasts relied on slave labor from the English and French Caribbean. He further stated:

> The racialization of these topographic and class boundaries was not as coherent or as tidy as the post-1940s historiography has legendarily assumed. The latter tended to imagine a "white" peasant majority nostalgically representative of Puerto Rican national culture vs. a handful of "dark" coastal laborers who were in but not of the Island. On the contrary, important segments of this mountainous peasantry were of mixed African and Iberian heritage, harking back to the period between the sixteenth and late eighteenth centuries when runaway slaves (of both sexes) settled and intermingled with fugitive galley prisoners and former soldiers of various backgrounds and with remnants of the indigenous population. (Santiago-Valles 1994:44)

Historical data demonstrate that free black and *mulato* laborers constituted a majority in the municipalities located in the southeastern littoral. They not only engaged in subsistence activities on the coast; they also constituted a black yeomanry that lived in the mountainous interior of Guayama, Arroyo, Patillas, and Maunabo (see Woofter 1930).

By positioning *jíbaros* on the *haciendas* in mountainous interior of the island and *negros* and *mulatos* on the plantations on the coast, the historical contributions of free black people prior to the abolition of slavery and thereafter is left unwritten.

Puerto Rican Historiography

Puerto Rican historiography and ethnography have focused primarily on the effects of changing political and economic forces in the development of Puerto Rican society and culture. Until recently, few scholars have attempted to grapple with the political-economic structures and the intricate webs of symbolic representations that constitute and are constituted by culture (L. González and Quintero Rivera 1984, L. González 1992, Santiago-Valles 1994). The oppositions between the plantation and the *estancia*, the coast and the mountainous interior, urban and rural, slave and free yeoman, black and *jíbaro*, economy and livelihood, permeate the historical and ethnographic literature on Puerto Rico and form part of everyday discourse among Puerto Ricans (Lewis 1983, Mintz 1974a, 1974b, J. González 1981[1979], Quintero Rivera 1987, 1988).

These symbolically charged categories perpetuate the construction of a black identity that is tied to a coastal plantation economy that relied on a black and enslaved labor force and a romanticized *jíbaro* identity of "white" peasants in the mountainous interior of the island who engaged in subsistence activities and were later incorporated as *agregados*, sharecroppers, on the expanding coffee haciendas. Because people conceive of history selectively and are constrained by relations of power, alternatives to these oppositional categories are scarcely found in the historical and ethnographic literature.

For example, historiography and its fixed categories did not allow for the growth of a free black yeomanry engaged in subsistence activities in the mountainous interior of the municipalities on the southeastern coast of Puerto Rico and elsewhere. But the historical data clearly show that there was a larger percentage of free blacks and *mulatos* as compared to black slaves in the southeastern coast of Puerto Rico. The existence of free black and mulatto communities that were adjacent to the sugar plantation economy or whose residents participated in it as temporary laborers needs to be explored further.

Recently, scholars have begun to examine the role of black slaves and free black and mulatto laborers and artisans in the coastal and urban milieus of eighteenth- and nineteenth-century Puerto Rico (Duany 1985, J. González 1981[1979], Moreno Fraginals et al. 1985, Quintero Rivera 1987, 1988, Scarano 1981, 1984, 1993, Negrón Portillo and Mayo Santana 1992). These analyses challenge previous historical interpretations because blacks and *mulatos* are located in varied social, economic, and political arenas.

Jíbaros negros were located on the coast as well as in the interior of coastal municipalities of the island. The fusion of *jíbaro* and *negro* in Puerto Rico radically alters the ways by which these categories have been essentialized in the Puerto Rican cultural imagination precisely because this union represents a movement toward blackness. Processes of *blanqueamiento* are negated. The *jíbaro* is no longer just a white-skinned peasant; he is a *jíbaro negro*. The mythico-historical figure is also a female. She is a black *jíbara*.[6] Some were tied to the plantation and *hacienda* economies, others were engaged in subsistence strategies and practices to ensure their livelihood, and still others were part of each of these economies (see Ortiz 1940, Steward et al. 1956, Price 1966, Whitten and Friedemann 1974, Whitten 1974). Rather than arguing that free blacks, *mulatos*, and *jíbaros* became landless laborers and sharecroppers following abolition, it can be argued that enclaves of free blacks and *mulatos* also existed and developed prior to and following the emancipation of slaves in Puerto Rico.

Once we gain such a perspective, blacks and *mulatos* are perceived not as marginal to but rather vital to the development of the nation. This seriously revised perspective differs from previous interpretations of historical data because it does not simply define black people as former slaves and laborers who became assimilated as members of the nation. It challenges scholars to critically assess how blacks and *mulatos* throughout the history of Puerto Rico engaged in strategies to gain acceptance by nonblacks, on the one hand, while maintaining their black autonomy, on the other hand, in particular and specifiable social and economic arenas.

Reinterpreting History, the Family, and the Nation

The association between the great family and the nation harks back to the development of a Puerto Rican nationalist ideology in the late nineteenth and early twentieth centuries. This ideology was symbolically represented as *la gran familia jíbara*, the great *jíbaro* family, with the *hacendado* as the paternalistic and benevolent head who provided his children with means by which to engage in productive labor for the good of the nation. As the *criollo* elite sought to establish a nation in opposition to the Spanish colonial government, the subordinate but transformed *jíbaro* represented the nation. Manuel A. Alonso's novel, *El gíbaro*, captured the imagination of the *criollo* elite, a mythico-historical imagination that failed to reflect the racial and socioeconomic composition of nineteenth-century Puerto Rico. As J. González (1981[1979]:57) stated,

> *El gíbaro*, as we all know, is a collection of picturesque customs. This description fails to shed light upon the existence of numerous black and *mulato* inhabitants in the Island. However, the account does reveal a fundamental reality; the *criollo* class Alonso represented was not able to project its vision of the Puerto Rican

identity to include the various segments that constituted the basis of Puerto Rican society.[7]

The image of *la gran familia jíbara* became further solidified in the early twentieth century as members of the creole elite sought to establish their Puerto Rican identity in opposition to the new colonial power, the United States. Within this context, the Puerto Rican family consisted of the creole elite, the *jíbaro*, and the marginalized black laborer on the coast. The creole elite and the nonblack laborers defined blacks and *mulatos* as displaced laborers who were now part of the nation. Given the demise of the sugar industry and the encroachment of U.S. economic and political interests in the area, the argument was made that all members of the Puerto Rican family suffered under U.S. tyranny.

Blacks and *mulatos* themselves, however, were actively involved in political struggles to assess and define the extent to which they were truly part of the Puerto Rican nation. Black and *mulato* people in many ways understood that they were within the geopolitical boundaries of the nation but were not really considered part of that cultural construction. They were the family members who, Fortunato Vizcarrondo argued, were hidden from view; hidden because they revealed that the *jíbaro, "ej prieto de beldá,"* the great family, hence the nation, is truly black. The *criollo* elite understood that a lack of cohesion among the laboring classes undermined their attempts to promote and maintain national solidarity. Within this context *la gran familia puertorriqueña*, the ideology of *mestizaje* and processes of *blanqueamiento* came together to undermine attempts toward the development of a black consciousness (Whitten and Torres 1992, Torres 1995; also see the general introduction to this volume).

The Racialization of the Social and Economic Terrain

In contemporary discourse and practice an opposition between San Juan (Puerto Rico's capital on the north coast) and *la isla*, the island, forms part of everyday discourse (Quintero-Rivera 1987). When the question ¿*De dónde eres?* (Where are you from?) is posed, the reply is either *De San Juan* or *De la isla*. Communities *dentro de la isla*, within the island, are considered less cultured than communities located in the San Juan metropolitan area. And communities located on the coast are considered even less cultured. *Jíbaros*, country peasants, reside in the rural areas, and darker-skinned people live on the coast. The oppositions are even further delineated in localized settings. This dichotomy notwithstanding, people throughout the southeastern coast of Puerto Rico recognize the existence of black communities in the coastal areas as well as in the interior of Maunabo and Arroyo, where I conducted ethnographic fieldwork.

As the southeastern coast is racially mapped by Puerto Ricans, *barrios*, municipalities, and regions are also socially and culturally defined as *negro*, black. At the local level there is an opposition between *arrabales* and *caseríos*, on the one hand, and *urbanizaciones* on the other. Most Puerto Ricans, particularly those who do not reside in the area, believe that poor, dispossessed, and dark-skinned Puerto Ricans reside in *arrabales*, sectors of towns or villages with substandard housing, and in *caseríos*, public housing complexes. While there is a whole range of phenotypical variation in these housing facilities, a disproportionate number of black people reside there and they are blamed for many of the social ills present in the community.[8]

The working poor, the working class, and the middle class live in *urbanizaciones* in the urban area. Puerto Ricans quickly associate the name of an *urbanización* with the class status of the people who reside there. Even though there is a whole range of phenotypical variation in these housing developments, the people there are not categorized as *genta negra*, black people. The residents of *urbanizaciones* are perceived to be socioeconomically better off, better educated, and *mas culto* (more refined) than residents of *caseríos*. In fact, the working poor in the *urbanizaciones* are not always economically better off than those living in *caseríos*. However, their social status is higher precisely because they are located in a particular sociogeographical space, that of the *urbanización* as opposed specifically to the *arrabal* or *caserío*.

Maunabeños and Arroyanos define themselves primarily as Puerto Ricans from particular regions or communities within a municipality. This sense of belonging to a particular place is closely tied to their national identity, on the one hand, and to their social identity, on the other. People often remark, *Soy d'aquí* (I am a native). Others say, *Soy de Guayama, pero llevo quince años en Maunabo* (I am from Guayama, but I have spent the last fifteen years in Maunabo). These individuals refer to their place of birth as a primary identity referent, despite the fact that they reside elsewhere.

As Puerto Ricans engage in discursive practices they situate themselves and others within a racialized terrain and a particular social framework that once again oscillates between a collective identity and one rooted in a particular cultural heritage. People are categorized based primarily on physical attributes, family ancestry, geographic location, class, and status. Individuals who are phenotypically black may be accepted by the larger society, but their acceptance is conditional on cultural "lightening." This is so because it is assumed that the person has engaged in culturally adaptive strategies that promote *mestizaje* and *blanqueamiento*. *Mestizaje*, the ideology of racial mixture, is an integral part of national discourse and practice throughout Latin America and the Spanish-speaking Caribbean. In Puerto Rico, the ideology of *mestizaje* acknowledges the contributions of people of African, indigenous, and Spanish descent in the formation of the nation, but it also maintains and promotes racialist ideas and practices.

The process of *blanqueamiento* specifically encourages Puerto Ricans to identify with the *mestizo*, the *jíbaro* as oriented toward lighter skin, and culture. By employing these ideologies of *mestizaje* and *blanqueamiento* to gain conditional acceptance by nonblacks, racism is perpetuated. These ideologies and processes of "whitening" refer to whiteness and blackness in cultural terms. Whiteness is associated with *la cultura*, culture. The view here is that upward mobility cannot be achieved if a black identity is maintained because there are negative cultural ascriptions associated with blackness. *Gente negra*, black people, are perceived to be culturally unrefined and lack ambition. As Torres and Whitten state in the general introduction,

> *Culture* is an ambiguous but important term. In Spanish, the feminine article *la*, as in *la cultura*, elevates a concept to something refined, European, civilized. When one goes to an expensive opera in Bogotá, Colombia, for example, wearing "fine" clothes and speaking in a "refined manner," one is participating in *la cultura* and one is *muy culto*, very civilized. Today, in most Latin American societies, to affix *cultura* to blackness without the article *la* is to demean traditions and lifeways to something "vernacular," worthy of study by folklorists but insignificant in processes leading to higher and higher levels of Latin American civilization.

Such a perspective does not negate the existence of black culture but confines it to the realm of the "popular." In the Puerto Rican context, by defining black cultural contributions within the context of slavery and the expressive realm, naturalized stigmata that set black people apart from the rest of Puerto Rican society are continually reproduced.

Class stratification in Puerto Rico is delineated because people incorporate markers of social status that include geographic locality, family lineage, social and moral conduct, and current socioeconomic status (Lauria 1964). Individuals with similar family backgrounds, economic status, political affiliation, and phenotypical variation in the family are considered equals. Income, occupation, education, social relationships, and material wealth are all taken into account in identifying the economic and social standing of individuals and their families. This view of a local-level stratified system blurs distinctions and perpetuates the view that socioeconomic status overrides concerns regarding an individual's racial and family heritage. But indicators of social status are racialized. The people of the southeastern coast of Puerto Rico, where I conducted ethnographic fieldwork, are well aware of family histories and economic successes or failures. They ideally state: *Todos somos iguales, algunos más blanquitos otros más trigueñitos* (We are all equals, some of us are whiter and some of us are darker).

For example, Maunabeños and Arroyanos, who are not classed as *gente de bién* or *gente de dinero*, elites, often look with contempt upon the old elite, *blanquitos*, because such members of the upper stratum firmly hold onto their hereditary status. In particular, those people who are classed as elite because they have acquired wealth and claim to be white are often ridiculed. Fortunato Vizcarrondo's penetrating question is invoked: *¿y tu abuela dónde está?* (and your grandmother, where is she?). Individuals *de una buena familia*, from a good family, with refined tastes who do not flaunt their hereditary or monetary status are considered ideal.

By collapsing racial and class distinctions under the broad concept *una buena familia* or *una buena persona*, Puerto Ricans can neatly avoid the extent to which issues of race, gender, and class permeate everyday life. However, in casual conversations issues of race and class and a sense of place come to the fore. When a farmer and landowner from the interior boasted about the acquisition of a fine horse, he was asked, "¿Quien te lo vendío? (Who sold it to you?)" The man replied, "De un hombre de la costa, negro pero bueno. (From a man on the coast, a black one, but a good one.)" In other words, by definition coastal people, *negros*, are bad unless they engage in behaviors or activities associated with *gente buena*.

A Black Identity: The Family and the Nation

In Puerto Rico, respectable families known as *gente buena* constitute the nation. In the southern littoral many blacks and *mulatos* are asserting their identity as part of the nation but are aware of the fact that socioeconomic survival means developing strategies and exercising options that may contradict national, collective, and self-interests (Silvestrini 1989). In addition, Maunabeños and Arroyanos migrate and develop subsistence strategies to benefit their families and by extension their communities and the nation. By engaging in behaviors that strengthen family ties, they challenge the status quo.

Karen Fog Olwig (1993), in her study of continuity and change in an Afro-Caribbean community of Nevis, argues that many of the social and economic problems that plague a community on Nevis are resolved to a great extent within the Nevisian transnational community. Irresolvable conflicts in the local society are resolved in the transnational context because individuals seek to improve their socioeconomic conditions elsewhere. Since Afro-Caribbean culture remains critical to the transnational community, maintaining social relations and engaging in exchanges from distant locations affect the local community. Fog Olwig (1993:156) states: "the mutual rights and obligations that tie Nevisians situated in distant locations together in global networks are thus informed by Afro-Caribbean culture, in particular its family system. The cultural identity which sustains the Nevisian global community draws, to a considerable extent, on the Afro-Caribbean rural life which has formed the context within which Afro-Caribbean life has emerged."

In the case of Puerto Rico, particularly in the communities within which I focused, social and economic problems are only partly resolved by outward migration. There is simply no guarantee of socioeconomic success abroad, and individuals may or may not be able to elevate the social and economic status of their families on the island. Individuals who are successful, though, assert their Puerto Rican identity by traveling to and from the island on a regular basis, by maintaining local family and community ties, and by demonstrating to others that they have resisted assimilation by adhering to local family values.

Decades of short-term and long-term migrations to the U.S. mainland and return migrations to the island have had many effects on localized communities. Family members who send remittances and consumer goods to relatives living in Puerto Rico try to elevate the social status of their family members in three principal ways. First, they demonstrate that they are hard-working individuals who have acquired success abroad. Second, as sociable and respectable members of a family, they fulfill their responsibilities toward them by providing them with consumer goods and economic resources. Third, the consumer goods in and of themselves become markers; they stand as emblematic symbols of a higher class and social status. However, elite or middle-class nonblacks consider these goods not as gifts but as purchases that place the families in severe debt and further support the stereotypic view that poor black people cannot manage resources properly and are therefore always in debt. All Puerto Ricans, however, participate in a consumer culture that affects their values and ideas, social relations, and exchange patterns (see West 1992).

As previously discussed, Puerto Ricans draw upon a host of criteria to categorize an individual or a group of people. Consequently, social relations and exchanges can be interpreted in complementary and contradictory ways. The expanded family network and the strategies black people engage in to improve their socioeconomic conditions contradict the prevailing stereotype view that black people are poor, lazy, and dependent. It can also perpetuate the view that black people engage in behaviors that are associated with Puerto Rican culture in general and not with stereotyped black culture. By so doing, familial practices among blacks can still be viewed stereotypically as disorganized, even though there is strong evidence to the contrary.

The multifaceted discourse on the family, the nation, blackness, and *mestizaje* is complicated even further. The U.S. presence on the island, migration to the mainland, and return migration to the island provide the impetus to challenge racist and class-based ideologies. As Maunabeños and Arroyanos have been exposed to discourses on race in the mainland and have been categorized as "minorities" and "people of color," they have become even more conscious of alternative ways by which to represent themselves.

As these challenges take place, problems in the local communities and throughout Puerto Rico are viewed by most Puerto Ricans as a result of negative external influences of *los norteamericanos*, and by return migrants who introduce such ways to the island. There is no acknowledgment that ideas that challenge and contradict the national ideology are rooted in the continual struggle of many black people on the island to assert their identity as members of the nation (Chatterjee 1993, Handler 1988, Dominguez 1989, Fox 1990).

At present, a Puerto Rican nationalist identity that continually places emphasis on the "harmonious synthesis" of whites and indigenous and black people throughout history fails to convince people who define themselves as black that they are equal partners in the making of the nation. They are conscious of the fact that *mestizaje* can never be fully achieved because nonblacks do not accept the fact that *negros, mulatos, trigueños, jabaos* are all truly members of the nation.

The people of the southern littoral who embrace an ideology of blackness argue that most Puerto Ricans are not willing to accept the quality of blackness, and hence most dark-complexioned people as part of the Puerto Rican cultural construct of nation. Such people, they argue, place a premium on strategies and practices that promote *blanqueamiento*. More important, these people of color argue that black people who struggle to affirm their contributions to *la gran familia puertorriqueña* want to do so on their own terms and not under the conditions set by nonblacks. As Whitten (1995) states in his discussion of ethnogenesis, cultural hegemony is not absolute. There are "people who do not entirely share nation-state ideologies of culture, personality, and society and consciously begin to enact counter hegemonic strategies, increasing their own sense of distinct history and altered destiny."

On March 22, 1995, the people of Puerto Rico commemorated the 122nd anniversary of the abolition of slavery. Peggy Ann Bliss (1995) reported:

> Puerto Ricans will "bleach away" many of the physical traces to its African past by the year 2200, with the other Spanish-speaking Caribbean following a few centuries later. "Puerto Ricans are whitening (*blanqueando*) faster than any other *mestizo* (hybrid) country," said Luis Díaz Soler, a specialist on island slavery. "In two centuries, there will hardly be any blacks in Puerto Rico."

Anthropologist Ricardo Alegría echoed this sentiment by stating that in the Spanish-speaking Caribbean, Puerto Rico will "become white" faster than the Dominican Republic. Cuba, he argued, will slowly whiten, since Cuba liberated 300,000 slaves as compared to the liberation of 27,000 slaves in Puerto Rico. Remarks by learned scholars, particularly by scholars whose work has focused on slavery, the black experience, and Puerto Rican society and culture on the 122nd anniversary of the abolition of slavery, reveal the ways by which ideologies of blackness, *mestizaje*, whiteness, and processes of *blanqueamiento* permeate the academy, the media, and the Puerto Rican cultural landscape.

Contrary to these prevailing views, Puerto Ricans who define themselves as *negros* and *mulatos* argue that those who promote ideologies of *mestizaje* and *blanqueamiento* fail to consider that Puerto Rican culture is being darkened. As a result, many Puerto Ricans, they argue, fail to understand how black people have engaged in cultural practices that have truly transformed Puerto Rican culture, the nation, and its people.

In the blackened cauldron, *el sancocho*, the stew, is boiling over; black Puerto Ricans are continually creating themselves anew, as they continually engage in debates about the rootedness of Puerto Rican culture, the Puerto Rican family, and the Puerto Rican nation.

Notes

1. Here is the original Spanish version:

> Mientras en Centro y Suramérica las culturas indígenas siguen enriqueciendo y formando parte importante de las culturas nacionales de los respectivos países (México, Guatemala, Perú, Bolivia), en las Antillas Mayores sólo quedaron sus restos arqueológicos, biológicos y culturales que desde hace siglos fueron asimilados por la cultura hispánica, para junto a la rica contribución africana, integrar nuestra puertorriqueñidad.
> Mientras en algunas islas del Caribe o países como Guyana, por ejemplo, la cultura negra y su población fue preponderante, en Puerto Rico, por las circustancias históricas que ya han señalado los estudiosos, esa rica herencia fue asimilada, al igual que la indígena, por la cultura hispánica, produciendos así nuestra cultura nacional que no puede ser clasificada como taína, africana o española, sino como la armoniosa síntesis de las tres, que es la puertorriqueñidad. . . .

2. Musical celebrations in particular continually pay homage to the contributions of black people to Puerto Rican culture. This is expressed in the video *Al compás de un sentimiento* (1996). It is the most recent musical tribute produced under the auspices of El Banco Popular celebrating the life and work of Pedro Flores, an Afro–Puerto Rican who migrated to the U.S. mainland in the 1930s. The nationalist sentiments expressed in his lyrics emphasize a collective Puerto Rican identity. In this musical context Flores, like his Afro–Puerto Rican counterparts, is a Puerto Rican son precisely because he celebrates his Puerto Ricanness even though he is steeped in a black musical tradition and heritage and is living in the mainland.

3. This chapter focuses on ethnographic data gathered in municipalities located in the southeastern coast of Puerto Rico, where I conducted fieldwork in 1984 and 1985. The communities of study include the municipalities of Maunabo, Patillas, and Arroyo. See Torres (1995).

4. The 1842 Census revealed that Guayama's population consisted of naturales, 5,019; europeos, 170; de America, 329; canarios, 8; franceses, 413; ingleses, 27; daneses, 458; alemanes, 22; holandeses, 77; italianos, 71; and otras naciones, 3,797; for a total of 10,391. (Cited in Sued Badillo 1983:87)

5. Los conquistados en esta ocasión no fueron obviamente, los aborígenes taínos, extinguidos hacía tres siglos por la política genocida de la primera conquista, sino el campesinado blanco que habitaba la región montañosa de la Isla, virtualmente incomunicada de la civilización urbana y semiurbana de la costa. Ese campesinado montaraz—los "jíbaros" originales—se convirtió entonces en masa de agregados atados a la tierra por la institución de la "libreta," ejemplo elocuente de un instrumento legal creado para satisfacer las exigencias de un determinado desarollo económico. Y es que la economía de substancia que había prevalecido en esa region fue remplazada por una economía de ha-

ciendas basadas en el cultivo de café, necesitada de mano de obra estable e impedida de migrar a otras regiones. Esa economía de haciendas fue el sustento material de un nuevo sector de la clase dirigente criolla.

6. The role and the contributions of black women to Puerto Rican society have yet to be fully addressed in the scholarly literature. Groundbreaking analyses include Elisabeth Crespo (1996) and Félix V. Matos Rodríguez (1995).

7. *El gíbaro*, que es como todos sabemos una colección de cuadros y costumbres, arroje tan escasa luz sobre la existencia de la numerosa población negra y mulata del país, nos revela una realidad fundamental, a saber, que la clase representada por Alonso no era todavía capaz de proyectar su propia concepción de la identidad puertorriqueña a los amplios sectores que constituían la base social del país.

7. See Santiago-Valles (1994) for an analysis of how crime is gendered, racialized, and class based in Puerto Rican discourse.

References

Alegría, Ricardo E.
1954   La Fiesta de Santiago Apóstol en Loíza Aldea. Madrid, Spain: ARO-Artes Gráficas, Colección de Estudios Puertorriqueños.

Alvarez Curbelo, Sylvia, and María E. Rodríguez Castro
1993   Del nacionalismo al populismo; cultura y política en Puerto Rico. Río Piedras, Puerto Rico: Ediciones Huracán.

Bliss, Peggy Ann
1995   San Juan Star. March 22, 1995, pp. 30–31.

Carrión, Juan Manuel
1993   Etnia, raza y la nacionalidad puertorriqueña. In Teresa C. Garcia Ruíz and Carlos Rodríguez Fraticelli (editors). La nación puertorriqueña: ensayos en torno a Pedro Albizu Campos. San Juan: Editorial de la Universidad de Puerto Rico.

Chatterjee, Partha
1993   The Nation and Its Fragments: Colonial and Postcolonial Histories. Princeton: Princeton University Press.

Crespo, Elizabeth
1996   Domestic Work and Racial Divisions in Women's Employment in Puerto Rico, 1899–1930. Journal of the Centro de Estudios Puertorriqueños 8 (1–2):30–41.

Domínguez, Virginia R.
1989   People as Subject, People as Object: Selfhood and Peoplehood in Contemporary Israel. Madison: University of Wisconsin Press.

Duany, Jorge
1985   Ethnicity in the Spanish Caribbean: Notes on the Consolidation of Creole Identity in Cuba and Puerto Rico, 1762–1868. Ethnic Groups 6:99–123.

Flores, Juan
1993   Cortíjo's Revenge: New Mappings of Puerto Rican Culture. In Juan Flores, Divided Borders: Essays on Puerto Rican Identity. Houston: Arte Público Press, pp. 92–110.

Fog Olwig, Karen
1993   Global Culture, Island Identity: Continuity and Change in the Afro-Caribbean Community of Nevis. Philadelphia: Hardwood.

Fox, Richard G. (editor)
1990   Nationalist Ideologies and the Production of National Cultures. Washington, D.C.: American Anthropological Association, American Ethnological Society Monograph Series no. 2.

González, José Luis
1981 [1979]   Literatura e identidad nacional en Puerto Rico. In Angel G. Quintero Rivera et al. Puerto Rico: Identidad Nacional y Clases Sociales. Río Piedras, Puerto Rico: Ediciones Huracán.
1989 [1980]   El país de cuatro pisos y otros ensayos. Río Piedras, Puerto Rico: Ediciones Huracán.
1986   Nueva visita al cuarto piso. Madrid: Libros del Flamboyan.

González, Lydia Milagros
1992   La tercera raiz: Presencia africana en Puerto Rico. San Juan, Puerto Rico: Centro de Estudios de la Realidad Puertorriqueña, CEREP Institute de Cultura Puertorriqueña ICP.

González, Lydia Milagros, and A. G. Quintero Rivera
1984   La otra cara de la historia: La historia de Puerto Rico desde su cara obrera. Volume 1. 1800–1925. Río Piedras, Puerto Rico: CEREP.

Handler, Richard
1988   Nationalism and the Politics of Culture in Quebec. Madison: University of Wisconsin Press.

Harrison, Faye V.
1995   The Persistent Power of "Race" in the Cultural and Political Economy of Racism. Annual Review of Anthropology 24:47–74.

Hernández Colón, Rafael
1988   España, San Antón y el ser nacional. El Nuevo Día, June 6, 1988, p. 53.

Hoetink, Harmannus
1967   Caribbean Race Relations: A Study of Two Variants. New York: Walker.

Jackson, Peter, and Jan Penrose (editors)
1993   Constructions of Race, Place and Nation. Minneapolis: University of Minnesota Press.

Jiménez Román, Miriam
1996   Un hombre (negro) del pueblo: José Celso Barbosa and the Puerto Rican "Race" toward Whiteness. Journal de Centro de Estudios Puertorriqueños 8 (1–2):8–29.

Lauria, Antonio
    1964   "Respeto," "Relajo" and Interpersonal Relations in Puerto Rico. An-
                    thropological Quarterly 37:53–67.

Lewis, Gordon K.
    1983   Main Currents in Caribbean Thought: The Historical Evolution of
                    Caribbean Society in Its Ideological Aspects, 1492–1900. Baltimore:
                    Johns Hopkins University Press.

Matos Rodríguez, Félix V.
    1995   Street Vendors, Pedlars, Shop-Owners and Domestics: Some Aspects
                    of Women's Economic Roles in Nineteenth Century San Juan,
                    Puerto Rico (1822–1870). In Verene Shepherd, Bridget Brereton,
                    and Barbara Bailey (editors). Engendering History: Caribbean
                    Women in Historical Perspective. New York: St. Martin's Press,
                    pp. 176–93.

Mintz, Sidney, W.
    1971   Groups, Group Boundaries and the Perception of Race. Compara-
                    tive Studies in Society and History 13:437–43.
    1974a   Caribbean Transformations. Baltimore: Johns Hopkins University
                    Press.
    1974b [1960]   Worker in the Cane: A Puerto Rican Life History. New York: Norton.

Moreno Fraginals, Manuel, Frank Moya Pons, and Stanley L. Engerman (editors)
    1985   Between Slavery and Free Labor: The Spanish-Speaking Caribbean
                    in the Nineteenth Century. Baltimore: Johns Hopkins University
                    Press.

Negrón Portillo, Mariano, and Raúl Mayo Santana
    1992   La esclavitud urbana en San Juan. Río Piedras, Puerto Rico: Edicio-
                    nes Huracán.

Nunley, John
    1993   Peter Minshall: The Good, the Bad, and the Old in Trinidad Carni-
                    val. In Dorothea S. Whitten and Norman E. Whitten, Jr. (editors).
                    Imagery and Creativity: Ethnoaesthetics and Art Worlds in the Ameri-
                    cas. Tuscon: University of Arizona Press, pp. 289–308.

Ortiz, Fernando
    1939   La Cubanidad y los Negros. Estudios Afrocubanos 3(1–4):3–15.
    1940   Contrapunteo cubano del tabaco y del azúcar. Havana: Consejo Na-
                    cional de Cultura.

Price, Richard
    1966   Caribbean Fishing and Fishermen: A Historical Sketch. American
                    Anthropologist 68:1363–1383.
    1983   First-Time: The Historical Vision of an Afro-American People. Balti-
                    more: Johns Hopkins University Press.

Quintero-Rivera, Angel G.
    1981 [1979]   Clases sociales e identidad nacional; notas sobre el desarrollo na-
                    cional puertorriqueño. In Quintero Rivera et al. Puerto Rico: Identi-

dad nacional y clases sociales. Río Piedras, Puerto Rico: Ediciones Huracán.

1987   The Rural-Urban Dichotomy in the Formation of Puerto Rico's Cultural Identity. New West Indian Guide 61(3–4):127–44.

1988   Patricios y plebeyos: Burgeses, hacendados, artesanos y obreros las relaciones de clase en el Puerto Rico de cambio de siglo. Río Piedras, Puerto Rico: Ediciones Huracán

Rodríguez Castro, María Elena

1995   Divergencias: De ciudadanos a espectadores culturales. Postdata 10–11:18–28.

Rodríguez Juliá, Edgardo

1983   El entierro de Cortíjo. Rio Píedras, Puerto Rico: Ediciones Huracán.

1988   Puertorriqueños (Álbum de la Sagrada Familia puertorriqueña a partir de 1898). Editorial Playor, S.A.: Biblioteca de Autores de Puerto Rico

Routté-Gómez, Eneid

1996   So, Are We Racists????? A Conspiracy of Silence: Racism in Puerto Rico. San Juan Star Magazine, December–January, pp. 54–58.

Santiago-Valles, Kelvin A.

1994   Subject People and Colonial Discourses: Economic Transformation and Social Disorder in Puerto Rico, 1898–1947. Albany: State University of New York Press.

Scarano, Francisco A.

1981   Inmigración y clases sociales en el Puerto Rico del siglo xix. Río Piedras, Puerto Rico: Ediciones Huracán.

1984   Sugar and Slavery in Puerto Rico: The Plantation Economy of Ponce, 1880–1850. Madison: University of Wisconsin Press.

1993   Puerto Rico: Cinco siglos de historia. Mexico City: McGraw-Hill.

Silvestrini, Blanca G.

1989   Contemporary Puerto Rico. In Franklin W. Knight and Colin A. Palmer (editors). The Modern Caribbean. Chapel Hill: University of North Carolina Press.

Steward, Julián H., et al.

1956   The People of Puerto Rico. Urbana: University of Illinois Press.

Sued Badillo, Jalil

1983   Guayama: Notas para su historia. San Juan, Puerto Rico: Oficina de Asuntos Culturales de la Fortaleza.

Torres, Arlene

1995   Blackness, Ethnicity and Cultural Transformations in Southern Puerto Rico. Ph.D. dissertation, University of Illinois at Urbana-Champaign.

Vizcarrondo, Fortunato

1976 [1942]   Dinga y Mandinga poemas. San Juan, Puerto Rico: Instituto de Cultura Puertorriqueña.

West, Cornel
    1992   Nihilism in Black America. In Michele Wallace and Gina Dent
                (project editors). Black Popular Culture. Seattle: Bay Press.

Whitten, Norman E., Jr.
    1995   Ethnogenesis. In David Levinson and Melvin Ember (editors). Ency-
                clopedia of Cultural Anthropology. New York: American Publishing
                Company for the Human Relations Area Files.
    1974   Black Frontiersmen: A South American Case. New York: Wiley.

Whitten, Norman E., Jr., and Nina S. Friedemann
    1974   La cultura negra del Litoral Ecuatoriano y Colombiano: Un modelo
                de adaptación étnica. In Revista del Instituto Colombiano de Antro-
                pología 17:75–115.

Whitten, Norman E., Jr., and Arlene Torres
    1992   Blackness in the Americas. NACLA 15(4).

Woofter, T. J., Jr.
    1930   Black Yeomanry: Life on St. Helena Island. New York: Holt.

10. STRATIFICATION IN GRENADA

M. G. Smith

We set out to pursue three objectives: to describe the conditions of status distribution among Grenadian elite; to illustrate a method for the field study and analysis of social stratification that seems especially appropriate to small societies, or to small segments of large societies; and finally, to test the theories of action and pluralism by analyzing stratification among the Grenadian elite. To test these theories we have to explore the general problem of the nature and place of common values in social stratification. The latter problem will occupy us throughout this chapter. . . . Method and data are equally relevant to the theoretical discussion; I shall therefore review my method briefly before assessing the significance of the data.

Method

This study rests squarely on four sets of data, each distinct in source and reference. These may be listed summarily. (1) Classifications of the 1946 Directory personnel provide the basic sample frame of ranked individuals. (2) A catalogue of personal associations and club memberships serves to define the association or isolation of classified personnel. (3) Inventories reveal the distributions of such conditions as income, occupation, employment, organizational status, ratable house values, commercial directorships, and phenotypes among the classified personnel. (4) Finally a genealogical study of eighty-three descent lines represented in this sample provides data on kinship, descent, inter-marriage, legitimacy, mating patterns, occupational inheritance, educational background, religion, immigrant status or origin, social mobility, affinal connections, and genotypes. None of these four bodies of information could have provided a satisfactory account of elite stratification separately, nor indeed would any three of them, but together they describe this structure comprehensively and accurately. Moreover, all four sets of information are equally free from bias and theoretical presumptions. Inventories, genealogies, classifications, and clique lists were collected without any selective emphases or special instructions to informants. All data remained unanalyzed until the field work was over; the procedure was as objective as I could make it.

From the Directory classifications we obtained a ranked distribution of listed

Originally published as ch. 9 of M. G. Smith, *Stratification in Grenada* (Berkeley: University of California Press, 1965), pp. 228–66. Reprinted by permission of Mary Smith.

personnel whose attributes and relations we could study independently. Instead of arbitrarily dividing the listed population into "classes" by criteria of our own selection, with this status distribution at hand, we sought to examine the distribution of various conditions among the sample of ranked individuals. We found that such conditions as occupation, income, ratable house value or land fluctuated irregularly in their distribution. We also found that the status divisions derived from the sample dispersion correspond roughly to certain ranked social strata, each quite distinct in its "racial" status, phenotype, associations, intermarriage, and kinship ties. Although they overlap, these social strata are not completely congruent in their boundaries or membership with the status levels derived from the classification. One of these distributions is an analytic construct devised for research; the other is an actual unit and feature of the social structure.

Several questions arising at this point merit discussion. One may ask whether individuals or roles are the appropriate units of ranking. The thesis that roles are the units of stratification is discussed briefly below; but insofar as social stratification refers to the ranking of individuals in society, the answer seems clear; even though individuals are the units ranked, the framework for this ranking is some set of categories by which the rankers seek to represent the existing distribution of these individuals in socially significant units whose composition and alignments are the main features of the stratification.

A second question asks whether stratification consists in a ranking of individuals in one or more scales. To this there are various answers. At the operational level, all nineteen classifiers employed only one scale each, so that in all cases a single scale seemed appropriate to them. I have merely collated these separate classifications into a single scale, the accuracy of which is tested against the patterns of association, kinship and marriage, by which individuals form themselves into groups. At the theoretical level, as Talcott Parsons says, "unless there is to be a functionally impossible state of lack of integration of the social system, the evaluations by A and B of their associate C must come somewhere near agreeing; and their relative ranking of C and D must broadly agree where the necessity for comparison arises."[1] Moreover, in small populations where people either know or know about one another, these evaluations often tend to reflect the associational behavior of the individuals ranked.

An analyst may stratify a population in as many scales as he cares, distinguishing its occupational, economic, and political stratification, among others. These separate scales are analytic constructs, of problematic meaning and uncertain relevance to the population concerned. Members of a society may construct these ideal-type scales themselves, but they are also quick to distinguish them from the system of social stratification as it actually operates. The main reference of these analytic one-factor scales is to Marx's "economic" theory of social stratification and change. Following Weber, modern sociologists have replaced Marx's gross economic classification by a number of scales based on criteria more or less independently defined, such as occupation, education, wealth, and style of life.

In large industrial towns, these single-factor scales may be useful for a preliminary classification of the population, but such analytic "stratifications" should be
sharply distinguished by the researcher from the rank order the people actually
use to regulate their interaction and relate to one another. Unless this popular
order obtains, we cannot usefully study it.

Among Grenadian elite, as the classifications show, people perceive such an
order, rank one another differentially within it, and regulate their associations,
marriages, and activities accordingly. We have reviewed many facts confirming
this. We must therefore conclude that, however heterogeneous it may be, Grenadian elite evaluate one another and are themselves evaluated in terms of a
single scale, the existence of which they assume, while their assumption gives
it existence. Thus even if our panel disagrees on the forms of their classifications and on individual placements as an effect of the difficulties involved in simultaneous reduction of different dimensions to a common single scale, this
disagreement merely underlines their insistence that such a basic scale prevails;
and of course, their differing schemes and placements may have quite other
bases. . . .

The third problem that concerns us now is the relationship between our statistical classes and the actually existing social divisions. We have seen that intimate association in cliques, kinship connections, and intermarriage are especially
useful in distinguishing the boundaries and memberships of real social units. Distributions based on these relations correspond very closely with one another as
well as with differences of modal genotype and phenotype. At both ends of the
elite status scale, these solidary social strata present extreme differences in the incidence of other significant conditions, such as occupational inheritance, immigrant status or origin, and local or foreign schooling. The distribution of status between these solidary differential biosocial groupings does not correlate as closely
with the distributions of income, acreage, ratable house value, occupational, and
employment status among this population; but these latter conditions are variable
attributes of individuals rather than attributes of a social unit as such. As individual characteristics, they are also primarily economic rather than social. But our
present interest lies in the relations between our analytic categories, the status
divisions of the sample dispersion, and such ranked social groupings as actually
exist in Grenada. To identify the latter, intermarriage, kinship, and personal association are clearly the best indices.

A very common index of solidary social units is intermarriage. Rigidly prescribed, this produces endogamy, as is typical of caste, but when preferred rather
than obligatory, intermarriage is often identified with class. "Members of a class
tend to marry within their own order, but the values of the society permit marriage up and down."[2] For Schumpeter,

a suitable definition of the class—one that makes it outwardly recognisable and
involves no class theory—[lies] in the fact that intermarriage prevails among its

members socially rather than legally. This criterion is especially useful . . . [when] we limit our study to the class phenomenon in a racially homogeneous environment, thus eliminating the most important traditional impediment to intermarriage.[3]

For Parsons, too, kinship, which is a function of marriage, is also important. "The class status of an individual is that rank in the system of stratification which can be ascribed to him by virtue of those of his kinship ties which bind him to a unit in the class structure. Kinship affiliation is thus always a basic aspect of the class status of an individual."[4]

Schumpeter's qualification identifies a basic problem. In a racially homogeneous environment, classes are intramarrying units, but in a racially mixed society, such intramarrying units may differ from classes in character, function, and form. The Grenadian elite are racially heterogeneous. They are divided . . . into a number of relatively closed endogamous units, aligned vis-à-vis one another at an angle to the horizontal divisions of the status scale. Besides marrying within their own ranks, their male members also mate hypergamously with folk women. By criteria of kinship, marriage, association, genotype, and phenotype, each elite stratum is homogeneous and solidaric, externally distinct. But the nature of these elite strata and of the status structure itself remains obscure. It would be premature to assume that such strata represent either castes or classes as these terms are commonly used. And to illustrate the difficulties which arise when general theories rely solely on concepts of caste and class in analyzing all varieties of stratification, we may cite Parsons once more. He defines caste as "a type of class structure . . . where the only relevant criterion of class status is birth. . . . All hierarchical status is ascribed. From this type there is a gradual transition to an opposite pole—that in which birth is completely irrelevant to class status."[5] This statement is neither consistent with the general sociological view of caste, nor with Parsons's earlier definition of class status by reference to kinship and birth. The source of Parsons's difficulty here is his attempt to generalize from racially homogeneous to racially heterogeneous environments without adequate allowance. In the process the class categories that may be appropriate in a racially homogeneous environment are extended so widely as to lose meaning. Thus at one moment, "birth is completely irrelevant to class status"; at another, "kinship is always a basic aspect of the class status of an individual";[6] at a third, "caste . . . is the case where the only relevant criterion of class status is birth."[7] This example may serve as a warning. In racially mixed societies, caste may not be the only type of ranked endogamous unit, nor should we expect to find only classes in the sense of Schumpeter's definition. We have already described Grenadian mating patterns as typical neither of class nor caste, though recalling both. Hutton's observation that while pluralism "has much in common with the caste system, . . . it is clearly not caste in the Indian sense"[8] applies to the class alternative also.

In basing our analysis of elite stratification on individuals rather than on positions, we diverge most clearly from the conceptual framework of those sociologists who interpret stratification as a ranking of roles or positions rather than of individuals. But since those writers claim that stratification expresses the common values on which societies depend for integration and order—the basic assumption we are concerned to test—this divergence may be inevitable. This difference is purely formal nonetheless. For even if roles are the critical units to which stratification relates, they can only enter into such a ranking if they are currently filled by individuals. Stratification neither subsumes the ranking of corporate organizations—though these have evident roles—nor can it include roles which are neither allocated nor institutionalized within the society. Thus at most stratification can only refer to those roles which are currently distributed among the members of a given social unit; but since each individual simultaneously holds many roles, and since many roles are simultaneously indefinite, unfamiliar, and distributed among many individuals, in ranking the elements of their social systems, individuals with their different combinations of role and other differentiating attributes are normally selected by members as the appropriate units to be ranked. Our sample classification merely illustrates this.

In any event, the presumed consensus and "integration of ultimate values"[9] from which these writers derive distributions of rank and reward was not very evident in Grenada from 1951 to 1953. Instead, during 1951 there were riots, bloodshed, looting, and arson; and with the introduction of universal suffrage, the formerly disfranchised "peasants" voted solidly against every representative of the elite who stood for election; with two exceptions, all these lost the cash deposits required of candidates. Throughout 1952 and 1953 strikes, arson, and threats continued. These disturbances led many Grenadians to wonder openly whether their society had any ultimate values or goals in common; but to examine this question empirically, we need precise measurements of the differing values of given variables and criteria at different levels of the social hierarchy. To derive these measures of value, we have had to employ procedures of the kind used above. Otherwise, we should simply predicate common or differing values to suit our own interpretations.

In describing Grenadian stratification, I have drawn on facts of local history, economy, culture, and political organization which, together, provide the developmental context of the system under study; I have avoided individual references and illustrative anecdotes because these are patently unsatisfactory for the present analysis, and because I wish to describe this structure in distributional terms as objectively as I can. I have omitted from this study the data yielded by classified counts because they are redundant; I have also omitted the civil service, as well as official and quasi-official role distributions current during field work, because the political structure was then changing rapidly and the significance of these roles was ambiguous. Under the Crown Colony regime, power was vested in the governor and his senior officials, who administered the island by a policy of *laissez faire*. With the introduction of universal suffrage in 1951, following a major strike, the trade union leader, Mr. E. M. Gairy, dominated the Legislature, and Grenada began to move toward internal autonomy in spite of dissensus, as a possible member of the problematic West Indies Federation, which emerged in 1956 and dissolved in 1962. For part of this period Gairy dominated the Legislature, and for the rest, he was excluded from it on various charges of misconduct. Being reëlected in 1961, he again took charge of the administration. Shortly after, at the request of the Island Administrator, a Commission of Inquiry was appointed to investigate charges of misuse of public funds leveled against Gairy and some of his ministers.[10] In consequence of the Commission's report, the British government briefly revoked the Grenada constitution, dismissed the Legislature, and returned power to the Administrator. The Federation had by then collapsed. Gairy went to Trinidad, and a new government with different orientations was elected. The stability of the traditional stratification after eleven years of uncertainty and turmoil is thus as obscure as ever; but in 1952–1953 it seemed quite clear that effective political power rested with Gairy and the British government, rather than with the Grenadian elite.

Perhaps the most important data on which our analysis rests are provided by the genealogies. It seems strange, given the recognition by sociologists that "class" is based on kinship and intermarriage, that so many laborious studies of stratification have been made without systematic use of genealogical inquiry. Here again, Marx's influence is evident. In challenging his "economic" interpretation of society, many students have tended to develop and multiply alternative scales, some of which combine several indices while others rest on one criterion, such as occupation. While some scales are psychological, most are economic in their emphases, and both divert attention from social relations. But clearly, if solidary social strata are based on kinship and intermarriage, then any adequate study of social stratification must make use of genealogical inquiry as well as other resources.

The Plural Society

One aim of this study is to test the thesis that Grenada is a plural society by examining its integration in the sphere of values. A plural society is one in which sharp differences of culture, status, social organization, and often race also, characterize the different population categories which compose it. An important feature of this societal type is the subordination of the majority to a dominant minority which is also culturally distinct. The conditions of dominance and subordination are expressed institutionally as well as in personal relations. They hold primarily between social categories, rather than individuals. The dominant minority generally exercises control through the government. It furnishes the models on which justice, administration, welfare, and development are institutionalized, and it typically controls these. It regulates the form, content, and organization of education. Its institutions provide the dominant economic and religious framework for the society, and are buttressed further by protective laws. The dominant minority either holds most of the local property, or receives the largest portion of the social income. Under its laws, this minority imposes its own distinctive modes of property, marketing, and work organization, as well as its occupational specialties. By law, religion, and economy, it institutionalizes those modes of mating and kinship representative of its culture, while denying equal status to others. With varying content and success it seeks to impose the basic attitudes and values that are conditions of the status quo, including the maintenance of its own specially privileged position. By various social, economic, and political arrangements which together constitute the basic system of social control, the dominant minority maintains its special position and privileges, and seeks to isolate those who challenge it. Insofar as its wealth, influence, personal qualities, and cultural skills attract support from subordinate sections, the institutional system and status of the dominant minority evoke a consensus; and those subordinates who support the system will then seek to attach themselves to the dominant group by corresponding disassociation from other sections. However, the distinctive feature of the plural society is the identification of its major structural units by cultural differences expressed in their institutional systems, values, and networks of social relationships. These differences embrace kinship, mating, family, work organization, property forms, education, voluntary associations, religion, ritual, belief, and values. Differences of wealth usually accompany such differences in institutional culture. Where institutional, political, and economic differences coincide, the separation of culturally distinct sections is greatest; and, given their hierarchic ranking, the distributions of sectional status exhibit sharp discontinuities. Such sectional ranking is perhaps the most obvious and important single feature of the plural society. It is at once the basic condition of continuity in its current form and a prime source of instability. Since the dominant minority represents a small fraction of the total population, the gradients of status and numbers are also imbalanced. In these conditions we can expect plural societies to exhibit dissensus rather than consensus about values, means, and ends. For continuity they usually depend on distributions of power sufficient to regulate popular protests, rather than on integration through voluntary adherence to common values and ends.

Ethnographic Implications

The Grenadian population falls into two quite distinct divisions, which I have called the *elite* and the *folk*. Of 80,000 in 1953, at least 75,000 persons belonged to the folk section in their own view, in the view of the elite, and according to any principles of sociological classification. The members of this folk section are typically black, illiterate or barely literate, poor in property, resources and skills, "superstitious," illegitimate, and of very low status. Of this folk population, about 3,000 were of East Indian descent, distinguished from the rest by race and cultural origin, but not by social status.

In Grenada, elite and folk are sharply distinguished by their behavior, ideas, speech, associations, appearance, color, housing, occupation, status, access to resources, and in other ways. Folk differ from elite in their use of the French Creole patois, in modes of mating, domestic organization, child-rearing, socialization, and kinship; in their social institutions, such as *maroon, jamboni, susu,* "bouquet," or company dance,[11] and in their local organization as dispersed communities. They differ also in their folklore, in their wakes, the third-night, nine-night, forty-night, and other funeral ceremonies, in their cults of Shango, Congo, Shakerism, and the Big Drum—all cults which were prohibited by laws passed in 1926 with elite support—in their faithful maintenance of Yoruba as a sacred or classical tongue, in their general fear and manipulation of obeah, or sorcery, their beliefs in witches, "dealers," spirits of the dead and of the wild, in divination, and in *saraca* or sacrifice as the means of dealing with the supernatural. They differ also in their work and working conditions, which typically involve dependence on the customary perquisites with which Grenadian estates supplement their low cash payments to workers. They trace their descent wholly and directly from the slaves emancipated in 1838, or from the indentured Indian laborers imported shortly thereafter. The folk lacked industrial and political representation or organization until 1951, when these forms were institutionalized in the midst of considerable upheaval, despite strong elite hostility and opposition. They hold property in familial groups and through procedures at variance with Grenadian law, and they regulate inheritance and settle disputes without resort to the official courts, by use of community "peacemakers," divination, obeah, and other mechanisms of their folk culture. They differ from the elite in maintaining a domestic economy based heavily on subsistence production of household food supplies and on migration to Trinidad, Venezuela, and elsewhere. They differ in technology, occupational skills and expectations, in standards of living, education, school attendance, income, type of house, dress, and so on. Their modes of celebrating childbirth, baptism, and marriage are also distinctive. They place special weight on ritual, and have aspirations, beliefs, and values that contrast sharply with those of the elite.

With these basic cultural differences, we find parallel differences of status, organization, modes of social relation, phenotype, wealth, knowledge, interest, and orientation that sharply distinguish folk and elite. Each group observes different patterns of interaction with its own members; between the two sections, modes of interaction are distinctive and heavily formalized. The subordination of the folk and the cultural and social dominance of the elite are expressed and stressed in all their associations. In consequence, the sections form two sharply different populations whose association traditionally presumed subordination of the majority to the regulating institutions and power of the few. Insofar as the coexistence

of social sections with these demographic and cultural attributes approximates
the model of the plural society just outlined, Grenada in 1953 was an excellent
instance of Creole plural society in which political and economic control was
traditionally vested in a numerically small, culturally dominant, and socially exclusive section. This order having been challenged, the society was then in turmoil.

Among themselves, Grenadian folk make several status distinctions, among
which sex and age are primary, though differences of education, property, and
behavior are also important. Although these folk distinctions do not enter into
the present study directly, they differ clearly from those which regulate status
placement among the elite. The coexistence of these two diverse stratification
systems involves dissensus concerning the values on which individual rankings
should be based, and this serves to deepen the status discontinuity between the
folk and the elite.

Our data show the status cleavage between elite and folk quite distinctly. On
our status scale this break appears at the vacant interval, .835. Few intimate associations between members of the same sex cross this line; but one large estate-
owner who ranks below it is classified as a "peasant," or member of the folk. Of
403 classified individuals, only twenty-five were folk, and these all owed their inclusion in the Directory to some moderate economic prominence as shopkeepers, produce dealers, farmers, or craftsmen. Some classifiers, as we saw, refused
to rank folk representatives on a scale designed for elite, holding that this was
impossible. Others simply described these folk members as "representatives of
the *saraca* class"—that is, members of a category defined by the use of sacrifice
for worship and for the solution of personal problems. The population ranked
above .835 on our scale differs modally from that which ranks below in language,
appearance, housing, property form and value, occupation and organizational
status, employment conditions, kinship, birth status and descent, intermarriage, education, recreation, settlement patterns, religious belief and practice,
and modes of voluntary association. They differ also in political and occupational
organizations for the pursuit of special or sectional interests. It would be truly
remarkable if they do not also differ in values and behavioral norms.

The two extremes of this sociocultural scale may now be summarized. Holding
the highest positions are whites or near-whites of "good family," superior income
or property, occupational opportunity, education, and housing; such persons derive their position through birth in established families that trace legitimate descent over several generations. Their heirs have an identical position. They inter-
marry with families of similar condition and status or with whites from overseas.
Law sanctions and defines their modes of property, employment and labor recruitment, mating, and kinship. By birth they belong to one or another of the
leading Grenadian churches. Like their parents before them, they are customarily
educated abroad and have at best a limited understanding of the local French
patois spoken by the folk. They exercise important indirect political influence

through expatriate and native officials with whom they associate, as well as through friends and kin in Britain who, in turn, exercise influence through Members of Parliament. They have long withdrawn from direct involvement in local politics, business or executive roles other than those which devolve on them privately, as by inheritance. Socialized abroad, they regard Britain or Barbados as their cultural base and look upon Grenada as a distinct society with which they have to deal in order to protect or promote their own interests. They are thus conservative and defensive in their orientations, associationally exclusive, and careful in their contacts with members of other groups. In place of identification with the society in which they hold the highest status, they see themselves as white settlers in an essentially foreign and unpredictable tropical country, whose people differ from them in race, language, culture, ideas, and in other ways.

At the opposite pole are the "unpredictable" folk, who believe in ancestral spirits, nature spirits, witches, sorcerers, dealings with the Devil, divination, sacrifice, spirit possession, revelation, and other "African" ritual figures and forms. Most live on or near estates, where they work for low wages, but enjoy a wide range of ancillary benefits characteristic of slavery, maintained by custom, and known as "privileges." Their economy is almost uniform, with its basis in subsistence production of household food supplies, supplemented by the sale of labor or crops at low rates for cash. Their school education is marginal at best, while their informal socialization to folk culture is intensive.[12] Most are born out of wedlock and bear or beget children likewise. Mating is initially extraresidential, and marriage is usually deferred until the principals are already grandparents, or will shortly be so. Status placements within this group emphasize differences of sex and age. Property is held conditionally and without title by family groups whose compositions vary structurally as well as over time. Work organization has special forms, such as *maroon* and *jamboni,* in which cash has no place. Local disputes are either settled by local "peacemakers," by magic, or by kin and community elders. Law is avoided as unpredictable and punitive. The norms and procedures of elite law are neither understood nor approved by the folk. The majority of these people are black, nominally Roman Catholic, speak a French patois among themselves, emphasize *rites de passage,* and have no tradition of political or industrial organization.

To illustrate the depth of this contrast and the divergence of interests and values which it involves, we may again cite Simon Rottenberg's observations in 1952, when Gairy's union was less than two years old. Rottenberg remarks of the planters that " 'getting out production at low cost' which is the first principle of entrepreneurial conduct in the developed countries, here becomes submerged by the principle of preserving a customary social pattern."[13] Of the "workers" he notes many grievances that

> evoke more emotional response than insufficiency of the daily wage rate . . . are not capable of adjustment by the ordinary process of collective bargaining. . . .

The membership pattern of the Union [includes people] . . . who are exclusively engaged in "own-account work". . . . Disputes are enormously varied . . . the Union's grievance book is filled with them. There are complaints about cows doing damage to gardens; unjust accusations of thefts of coconuts; the cutting into land by road builders; the failure to compensate for damages suffered by collision with vehicles; attacks by dogs and the like. . . . There is a real question whether the Union can operate ... . in a community in which disputes which have no relevance to job relationship are so important, and in which the difference between the wage worker and the self-employed peasant is a purely formal one.[14]

Clearly, neither the planters nor the peasant-workers regarded the conflict of 1951–1953 as primarily economic; perhaps both were right.

The polar contrast just developed is not simply an ideal antithesis. These contrasting types are highly standardized realities. The sections they represent are separated by wide and coincident differences of status, interest, culture, resources, and race. Differences in each of these dimensions reinforce and are reinforced by differences in the others. However, the interval between these social extremes is not a vacuum. Like nature, society abhors this. Centuries of association under slavery and since have inevitably produced some biological and cultural mixture. In this Creole society racial and cultural hybrids occupy the interval between the extremes. Race mixture and its products are rather obvious and easy to identify. Persons of hybrid or dual culture are less easily identified and described and may also vary widely in status. It is thus useful to sketch the distinctive characteristics of this category.

Besides its main white and Negro racial stocks, Grenada also includes an assimilated handful of Portuguese, and an East Indian minority. These are the only other ethnic groups. The Indians are distinguished as "East Indian" by other natives, who reserve the term "Creole" for themselves. In fact, very few Indians of unmixed descent had managed to enter the elite by 1953, and none ranked above .440. Indian members of the elite share the institutional forms of Creole cultural hybrids, while differing in limited areas that reflect their Indian heritage. They are few in number and so dependent on the Creole elite for acceptance and status placement that they do not form a distinct ethnic enclave, but associate individually with Creoles of equivalent status and observe these Creole norms. Thus the cultural hybrids are almost entirely colored Creoles. They vary as widely in their social and cultural characteristics as in genealogical derivation and phenotype. In many cases these variations correlate with one another, but not in all.

The Creole intermediate range thus includes some persons whose cultural and social characteristics approximate those of the white social pole, others whose characteristics approximate those of the black social pole, and others whose cultural and social characteristics place them squarely in between. It is best to describe this central intermediate type first. People with this mixture of cultural skills manipulate Standard and dialect English and the French patois with equal ease. They accept and manipulate formal Christianity and folk beliefs equally. Tension between these belief systems is partly reduced by Christian emphases on the immediate concern of God, His Saints and Angels, in individual struggles against the forces of evil which obeah, *lougarou*, "dealers," and the Devil represent. While typical Creoles do not themselves take part in the prohibited folk cults of Shango and Shakerism, their attitudes and beliefs combine folk elements with Christian practice, and private magic with priestly exorcism.

Bicultural Creoles also manipulate property forms typical of both cultural extremes, and usually combine individual possession held under legally valid conditions with property rights of folk derivation which the law does not recognize. In the same way they use both types of saving institution—the bank and the *susu*; both types of work organization—wagework by task, or day, and *maroon* or free groupwork; all forms of mating—marriage, concubinage, and extraresidential liaisons; and both folk and elite kinship forms, freely admitting paternity of their illegitimates, though leaving these with their mothers and often ignoring their interests, while imposing sexual restrictions on their womenfolk. They distinguish legitimate from illegitimate issue sharply, though stressing their own illegitimate links to higher-ranking paternal kin, while minimizing ties of kinship with the folk. They operate all forms of voluntary association, from cliques and athletic or social clubs to lodges and friendly societies, recruiting members from among themselves. Educationally, they combine some informal socialization in the folk culture with formal education in local primary and secondary schools. Occupationally, and in terms of employment status, they are widely scattered through the range of available positions; some have executive status on their own account or supervisory roles in other enterprises; many hold routine subordinate positions as typists, shop assistants, overseers, teachers, nurses, dressmakers, foremen, clerks, and the like. The distinctive features of this categorical type express their relatively equal and superficial acculturation to both extremes. For this reason they may seem to embody and express the forms of either cultural alternative in almost equal measure; but since these sectional values differ in base and focus, their conduct and valuations vary situationally, and the most constant principle regulating their behavior in different situations is preoccupation with their own social status. While specialists in neither alternative culture and, accordingly, by their performance often giving dissatisfaction both to the culturally white and the culturally black, they claim to bridge the gap as cultural "middlemen."

As these characteristics define the bicultural Creole, divergences from this type will tend to fall into two clusters, one approaching the "white" cultural pole, the other, the "black." From the preceding summaries of these alternative modes, the form these divergences will take and the content each will have becomes evident. What requires explicit recognition is the incidence of some "white" elements or conditions among people whose institutional position and practices are mainly "black," and the distribution of some "black" elements and conditions among people whose traditions and practice are mainly "white." Granted variability in the specific individual combinations of elements drawn from these alternative cultural traditions, it follows that there will be corresponding variability in the rankings made by and of such people. Naturally, these variations are not entirely random. Some social and cultural conditions tend to be linked with others. For example, legitimate descent over several generations in this milieu implies lineage membership, stable family organization based on marriage, and adequate economic opportunities or resources. As we have seen, these conditions tend to be associated with relatively high income, good housing, some tradition of land ownership, secondary education, sometimes overseas, high organizational status in local commerce or government, moderate or light skin color, intensive clique and club activities, high rates of kinship marriage and "class" endogamy, highly routinized and predictable behavior, and a corresponding divorce from "black" cultural patterns, which such persons disvalue and oppose.

From biculturalism the modal deviation toward the folk pole includes illegitimate birth status and ambiguous ancestry, cohabitation without marriage, lower income, rather poorer housing, little formal education in elite schools and more intensive informal education in folk culture, less property and more reliance on folk patterns of tenure, lower organizational status, and explicit rejection of ascriptive criteria such as lineage, maternal ancestry, light skin color, schooling abroad, and immigrant derivation. Participation in elite cliques or clubs tends to be marginal, while attendance in the proprietary clubs of lower-status townsfolk may be frequent. We have already noticed how one exceptionally wealthy ex-policeman of folk background established a proprietary club for his gambling activities. Folk values and beliefs regarding sex, fertility, spirits, magic, kinship, ritual, health, and prosperity are dominant within this group. In short, apart from the ideally bicultural mean, we can discern modal deviations among this hybrid Creole elite toward either cultural extreme. Given the initial ranking of European and African traditions and races based on history, status differences should correspond with these cultural alternatives.

Model and Reality

To test the proposition that Grenada is a plural society, we have to examine the hypothesis just advanced. In terms of the definition of plural societies given above, Grenada seems clearly to be one. The deep social cultural, and demographic disbalances and antitheses that characterize plural societies have been shown to prevail in Grenada. We now have to determine the validity and significance of this description by examining the Grenadian elite to see whether its character is unitary or pluralistic. By employing ideal-type models we have shown that, if Grenada is a Creole plural society, between its "white" and "black" cultural poles there should be a variable Creole population organized in three culturally and socially distinct strata, one of which approximates the "white" sociocultural pole and another the "black," while the third occupies the range between. On the other hand if Grenada is not a plural society, we should not find the elite divided into four ranked strata such as our model requires; and even if we do find four elite divisions, they should not exhibit the value difference and institutional patterns our model requires. It is necessary therefore to find out whether such modally differentiated social strata exist by reëxamining the characteristics of persons ranked at the various status levels in the sample population.

As the local "white" stratum, I identify that group the majority of which ranks above .265, and which also includes the majority of those ranked above .265. These people are recruited by immigration from Britain and Barbados and by several generations of legitimate descent in both lines. They are white or near-white. They are systematically disassociated from positions of public responsibility in Grenada. On a per capita basis they own most of the local land, have the highest average incomes, are usually educated in Britain, and educate their children there. As regards marriage and kinship, their disassociation from other strata is complete, but they also form a distinct associational unit, and few of them participate in cliques with members of other strata, whom they meet mainly in the club they control. Most of their families live on estates in the country, and their male members commonly have illegitimate issue by folk women. They associate easily with immigrant settlers and white visitors and more frequently with expatriate officials than do other local groups. They exercise influence on local affairs through native as well as expatriate officials, through contacts in London, and through executives who rank in the strata below. Though mainly Anglican, they include some French Catholic families, but among them religion is no barrier to intermarriage. Socialized in Britain or Barbados, but seldom in Grenada, they see and conduct themselves as a small group of settlers in a relatively alien society, where many are born and most will probably die. Within the stratum, prestige correlates closely with color and with the maintenance of paternal status and occupation. Functionally, this stratum specializes in maintaining the traditional bases of status ascription in Grenada, and in interpreting the local society to important white guests. Accordingly, within this group, color, descent, school background, British ancestry or immigrant status, behavior, and associations outweigh differences of income, occupation, acreage owned, ratable house value, religion, employment, and organizational status. Grenadians describe this group as "the planter class," but although white planters form the core, they account for less than half the membership of this group; and altogether it represents less than a third of the people Grenadians classify as "planters." The "economic" classification is thus really social and cultural at base.

Despite internal differences of income, ratable house value, acreage, and land-owning status, most of the people ranked between .265 and .435 form the core of the second stratum. Most members of this stratum rank at this level on our status scale, and most persons ranked at this level on the scale belong to this social stratum. It forms a single unit with a well-defined network of cliques, agnatic descent-groups, and affinal connections which link its members together.

It is characterized by unusual rates of first-cousin marriage and childless spinster-hood. Bastards begotten by male members with folk women have no place in this group. Some members are independent landed or business proprietors, others are professionals of reasonable income by Grenadian standards, others are executives in charge of government departments or local branches of overseas firms. Some members are recent immigrants or of recent immigrant descent. The prevailing skin color is medium to light brown, and the stratum is relatively homogeneous in genotype and phenotype. Most native executives are drawn from this group, which stresses the education of its young, some families sending their children to Barbados or Britain for schooling, though higher education is little valued. The stratum exhibits considerable internal diversity in occupation, organizational po-sition, employment status, income, area of residence, property ownership and style of house, educational background, immigrant or Creole ancestry, but some-what less diversity in color and style of life. Most families belonging to it are Prot-estant and trace legitimate descent further back in the paternal than in the ma-ternal line. The unit is highly endogamous, seldom marrying immigrants or members of inferior strata. It is distinguished by uniquely high rates of social in-teraction and participation in executive affairs, and may be described as the "col-ored executive class." Its members are distinguished by their intense emphasis on observance of "white" cultural forms, and by their contempt for those of the folk. In this stratum, the dominant conditions and correlates of social status are kin-ship, descent and marriage, color, association, behavior, organizational role, edu-cation and income, in that order.

The next social stratum is even more diverse. On our status scale, this division is represented by most of the people who rank between .435 and .605. Its mem-bership is rather heterogeneous. It includes some planter families tracing illegiti-mate descent to British immigrants who educated their children abroad, but the great majority have been educated in Grenadian secondary schools and most are themselves of shallow legitimate ancestry and birth status. It has a fairly high in-cidence of illegitimate descent and an even higher rate of social isolation. The prevailing pigment is medium brown or mulatto, club life is desultory, and cliques are by no means general. Many at this level engage as executives in com-merce, government, or agriculture; others are professionals or operate shops and farms on their own account. The rates of endogamy and kinship marriage are lower than in the stratum above; so is the average income of this group. Religious affiliation is rather diverse; Catholics and Protestants are unequally represented, and denominational affiliations carry great weight in social interaction.

The distributions of property, income, and ratable house value are more vari-able here than in the stratum above, and so are occupations and organizational status. Occupational inheritance is not highly valued, and has a low incidence. Some members of this stratum emphasize individualistic achievement orienta-tions, others resist them. Some individuals and families are downward mobile, while others are pursuing upward mobility, and many feel insecure about their personal rank. High status aspirations and their frustration make many ill at ease. In consequence, associational life in this stratum is rather weak, a reflex of its heterogeneity. Its members vary in employment status and place differing values on these alternatives. Unmarried females are expected to remain childless, though not all do. Married and single men beget children freely by folk women in liaisons of varying form. Many in this stratum retain folk beliefs in witchcraft, obeah, Divine interference, dealers, and the powers of folk cultists, but many are also Christian fundamentalists, while some are rationalists. *Susu* and banks are used equally for saving.

Such a heterogeneous collection of culturally differentiated individuals is clearly uniform neither in its valuations of status criteria, nor in their incidence. Accordingly, status criteria vary in their values most widely between individuals in this stratum, and social rankings here are notably relativistic. Intergenerational occupational change is valued as expressing individual achievement, to which status increments may attach. In practice, as we have seen, organizational position has greater status significance than occupational role. Accordingly, many occupational mobiles who emphasize criteria based on achievement suffer frustration in their search for higher status.

The fourth and lowest-ranking elite stratum has prevailingly dark pigmentation, prevailingly illegitimate ancestry; purely local education, mainly in secondary schools; a high proportion of Roman Catholics; very little intermarriage between kin, and rather irregular mating patterns, which include high rates of extramarital mating by both sexes, illegitimate issue, and some concubinage. Incomes are relatively low; property is small and mainly held under folk tenure; dependence on wagework, salaries or on small-scale business and farming is typical; representative clubs are proprietary with few members exercising executive roles; despite much variation the emphasis on housing is strong; and stress on the achievement of status by individual merit is general. Persons at this level display a greater incidence and variety of folk practice and ideas than do those of any other elite stratum. Many in this stratum, both individuals and families, have been recruited through illegitimate descent from higher-ranking elite males. In the townships, traditions of occupational inheritance are absent; in the rural areas, family farms and shops are modal. Hardly any undergo foreign schooling and socialization. Representative associational groupings at this level are lodges of Foresters and Odd Fellows, Friendly Societies and certain sporting clubs, while women stress church associations and societies. From this stratum the estates recruit overseers, and government and commerce draw subordinate clerics and shop assistants also.

Members of this group are usually critical of the ascriptive bases of elite stratification, and have high individual status aspirations; however, these criticisms and aspirations do not directly include the folk, except insofar as men of this level assume that they are the natural leaders of the underprivileged. Representatives of this stratum were important actors during the conflicts of 1951 to 1953. Thus at this level the symbols of status—money, housing, relief from manual work, leisure, dress, dancing, and carefree behavior—are highly valued, while the local determinants of such status are rejected. Kinship, descent, intermarriage, association, legitimacy, and light skin-color are positively disvalued as criteria for status placement in this stratum; and its members exhibit less internal diversity than those immediately above, perhaps because they share a common marginal position in elite society as a whole. As their status and cultural characteristics separate them associationally both from the folk below and the stratum above, they represent a separate social unit of their own.

Thus our analysis of the classified sample has identified a number of real social strata distinguished from one another in status, culture, values, and associational patterns precisely as the hypothesis of elite plurality requires. Moreover, each of these strata corresponds, as a unit, directly to an equivalent stratum in the model of elite pluralism we set out to test. Thus, the white planters postulated by the model are represented by the stratum centered above .265 on our scale, while the black "folk" are represented by that below .835. The intermediate bicultural Creoles of this model are to be found mainly in the stratum centered between .435 and .605 on our scale, while the groups that deviate from this mean in the direction of the "white" and "black" extremes have their centers between .265 and .435, and between .605 and .835, respectively, on our scale. It is highly unlikely that such an exact correspondence could derive accidentally, or that we have misunderstood its meaning. In this regard, the objectivity of our materials and methods are equally essential and valuable. Given the two major cultural traditions and racial groups on which Grenadian society is based and their historical relations, the categories we have derived by the plural hypothesis follow inevitably. To test these inferences empirically, one simply has to see whether the field data confirm the model, and for this it is only necessary to summarize data already reported about each of the social strata in elite society. By pulling together the various bodies of information analyzed above for each stratum in turn, we have been able to describe their characteristic features and differences. When this is done, we find a complete concordance between these data and the model of elite pluralism which is itself a special instance of the wider condition of Grenadian pluralism. This concordance applies to social forms as well as to their content, and to the ranking of the social strata these differentiate. Their correspondence sufficiently establishes the validity of the hypothesis we set out to investigate.

Measures of Values

We have yet to demonstrate the significance of this plurality by identifying characteristic value differences among these strata; and for this we must examine the measures of correlation and regression for various criteria of status placement, noting their variability at different status levels. The essential ratios are presented in tables 1 and 2. Together, these tables measure variations in the valuations of the criteria to which they relate at different levels of the elite scale. They define the problems of integration raised by the nature and number of these criteria and strata in concrete quantitative terms; and they also indicate in detail, as well as in outline, the modalities of integration that obtain.

Table 1 sets out the correlation and regression coefficients that hold between differences of social status and such factors as taxable income, acreage owned, ratable house values, phenotype, genotype, and weighted associational score, for various subsamples drawn from the classified population. Negative coefficients for the first four factors in table 1 indicate corresponding positive associations between increases of status expressed by declining scores and increases in the values of the variables concerned. Correlations between increases in status and increases of acreage owned, taxable income, or ratable values of urban and rural housing are all positive, moderate, and of similar strength. However, the regression coefficients for logarithmic income and acreage yield angles sufficiently close to 45° to indicate intense relations between changes of these factors and of status placements. Relations between differential status and ratable house values in town or country are more irregular.

The three remaining variables represented in table 1 are phenotype, genotype, and weighted associational score. All three have high positive correlations with social status, and for genotype and phenotype the regression angles that approach 45° indicate very intense relations. For the weighted associational score, which has the highest correlation coefficient in table 1, .865, the regression angle indicates a less intense relation.

Of the subsamples, those which describe distributions of income, urban house values and phenotype are more fully representative of the classified population as a whole than are those which refer to genotype, acreage, rural housing, and weighted associational scores—these latter being more representative of the upper and middle elite strata. In this agricultural setting, however, acreage and income are often linked economically, as phenotype and genotype are, biologically. Comparison shows that the more obvious ascriptive criteria, such as genotype and phenotype, correlate more closely with differential status than do less directly ascriptive criteria such as acreage, income, and housing, even though these may partly derive from inheritance. Most closely linked with status is associational pattern, and we have used this above, with good effect, to test the significance of status intervals and the validity of the individual rankings. In sum, these correlations reveal the predominance of ascriptive criteria. The regression angles derived from correlations of phenotype, genotype, acreage owned, and taxable income are virtually identical; in this way they indicate very similar relations among this elite between these factors and differential social status.

In table 2, I set out for each of these seven variables and social status the correlation and regression coefficients by status level, as well as by subsample. With-

Table 1

Summary of Product-Moment Correlations for Status Scores (x) and Selected Variables (y)

Sample measures	Log Status/acreage (x) (y)	Log Status/income (x) (y)	Rural house Status/rates (x) (y)	Urban house Status/rates (x) (y)	Phenotypical Status/color (x) (y)	Genotypical Status/color (x) (y)	Weighted associational Status/score (x) (y)
Number in Sample	76	264	64	64	376	171	146
Mean Status ($\bar{x}$)	0.43	0.51	0.40	0.53	0.54	0.44	0.42
Mean of y Variable ($\bar{y}$)	2.192	3.333	0.32	0.90	0.63	0.53	0.41
ρ	−0.34	−0.31	−0.37	−0.38	0.68	0.73	0.865
b_{yx}	−0.962	−0.925	−0.533	−1.717	0.926	1.142	0.756
θ	136.1°	137.2°	151.9°	120.2°	42.47°	48.47°	37.1°
c	2.610	3.807	0.532	1.813	0.13	−0.08	0.092

Table 2
Product-Moment Correlations and Regression Coefficients for Status and Selected Variables by Divisions

Status divisions	(1) Log Income			(2) Log Acreage			(3) Rural house rates			(4) Urban house rates		
	N	ρxy	$b^y x$	N	ρxy	$b^y x$	N	ρxy	$b^y x$	N	ρxy	$b^y x$
0–0.265	20	–.144	–2.3918	14	–0.65	1.764	13	–.059	–.3442	—	—	—
0.265–0.335	26	–.0434	–1.0233	12	–.3377	–8.494	10	.301	1.6807	5	.7374	7.6313
0.335–0.435	45	–.1154	–2.1358	14	.0992	1.2672	14	.453	4.9254	15	.0703	1.4331
0.435–0.605	82	–.7368	–1.5913	24	–.2589	–3.0225	21	–.0211	–.0938	24	–.0310	–.4453
0.605–0.835	82	–.2412	–1.1351	11	–.0630	–.4877	6	–.2491	–.5832	18	–.2067	–3.9153
0.835–1.00	5	–.769	–4.6707	1	—	—				2		
Total	264	–.31	–0.925	76	–.34	–0.962	64	–.37	–0.533	64	–.38	–1.717

Status divisions	(5) Phenotypical color			(6) Genotypical color			(7) Weighted associational score			
	N	ρxy	$b^y x$	N	ρxy	$b^y x$	N	ρxy	$b^y x$	θ
0–0.265	31	.267	1.5321	21	.41	1.3645	20	.5485	1.050	46°24′
0.265–0.335	33	.145	0.1148	28	–.033	–0.1903	24	–.1610	–.4430	–23°53′
0.335–0.435	56	–.054	–0.3195	41	–.031	–0.1682	37	.0829	.1435	8°11′
0.435–0.605	103	.098	0.3034	51	.26	1.159	51	.6594	1.0471	46°19′
0.605–0.835	135	.274	0.7722	27	.265	1.1487	14	.3033	.5038	26°43′
0.835–1.00	18	–.543	–1.8754	3	—	—				
Total	376	.682	0.926	171	.734	1.1416	146	.865	0.756	37°14′

out exception, this table reveals sharp changes in all these correlations at different levels of the scale. Thus, even though table 1 indicates a close integration between certain factors and status, when we examine their distributions at different status levels, we find marked variability in the extent to which each correlates with status placement. Thus logarithmic income, which shows the most even and continuous association with status, varies in its correlation coefficients from $-.0434$, or indifference, in the second status level, to $-.769$ in the last. Regression coefficients for this factor, which has the most stable distribution, vary from 1.0233 to 4.6707. For logarithmic acreage they vary from $+1.764$ to -8.494. For housing they are too variable to require comment. For phenotype they vary from $+1.53$ to -1.87; for genotype, from $+1.36$ to $-.19$; for weighted associational score they vary from $+1.05$ to $-.4430$. These divergent measures of correlation and regression are found as often between proximate strata as between those farther removed; yet, even though these strata are distinguished by sharp differences in their modal correlations with each of these seven criteria separately and all together, the several subsamples yield results that indicate general correspondences in the distribution of these various factors and status.

It is clear that differences in the correlation and regression coefficients between social status and given variables at different levels of the status scale express differences in the significance of those variables for status allocation within these differing strata. It is also clear that the differing significance of these variables at different strata expresses differing valuations of these criteria for status placement at these levels. Thus even though a given variable has a high correlation with status for the subsample as a whole, it usually has a very variable significance for status at different points of the scale, corresponding to the different valuations placed on it at each level by the people themselves. Table 2 accordingly provides a quantitative description of the differing valuations of status criteria which characterize the various levels of the Grenadian elite. Without doubt, this table demonstrates that value differences prevail over value agreements, as between different elite strata. It accordingly expresses the differences of value systems that characterize the real social strata.

Underlying the numerous differences of correlation and regression coefficients represented in table 2 are two antithetical and dissonant sets of value orientations. One set is ascriptive and stresses racial descent and family ties, inheritance of status, property, education abroad, quasi-hereditary organizational position, and associational exclusiveness; the other rejects this basis for ranking in favor of individualistic achievement of status, income, occupational, and organizational roles, standards of living, and so forth. This value set rejects claims to high status based on light skin color, inherited wealth, family tradition, and influence. These two sets of values are directly contrasting and opposed.

Members of the executive stratum ranked between .265 and .435 may claim that they owe their positions to their own individual achievement and training. Quite apart from the historic recruitment of Grenadian executives from these families over the generations, and granted that those ranked above are not interested in these positions, under local conditions members of this social stratum enjoy a virtual monopoly of requisite training and background for such roles. The historical record also shows that they have done very little to extend these educational opportunities to other strata. Thus the annual scholarship established for university training in 1916 with a value of £175 a year was first suspended in 1924 and then converted in 1926 to a biennial scholarship valued at £100 per year. In 1931 after much argument a board of education was instituted, and only in 1938 were new directions in education adopted.[15] Likewise, initiatives to liberalize the constitution and institute adult suffrage both came from Britain. In 1944, at the last election under the Crown Colony regime, 4,004 people were eligible to vote, the vast majority being members of the elite.

Our data demonstrate a basic disagreement about the values relevant for status placement among the elite. Some strata emphasize criteria that others reject; and even when different strata use the same criteria, they give them different values. The significance of a given status criterion changes absolutely and relatively for individual rankings within and beyond each analytic stratum, since each status level contains members of two or more mutually exclusive social strata.

The analytic strata defined by our sample dispersion do not correspond exactly with the social units into which the elite are grouped. Real social strata are identifiable by their tendencies to form separate units for association, clubbing, intermarriage, and kinship. In this they recall the social classes that Schumpeter described. But as each elite stratum tends to be ethnically homogeneous, it is also to some degree ethnically distinct from those above and below it; and as we have seen, these ethnic criteria, both biological and cultural, are given considerable emphasis to preserve group boundaries. The result is, as Rottenberg sensed, a series of abrupt social cleavages.

It is possible, as we have seen, to indicate the boundaries of these ranked groupings, and the ways in which they are aligned to one another and to the horizontal divisions of our status scale. Since such units are distinguished associationally, by intermarriage, by kinship, and by marriage between kin, and since these relations correlate highly with individual status, congruence in the limits of these relational networks provides the decisive index of unit boundaries.

The regression angles for status and associational scores at each status level may also indicate the alignment of the axis of the social unit centered there. For the stratum ranked above .265, this angle is 46° 26'. For that ranked between .435 and .605 it is 46° 19'. Both angles approach 45° and the maximum possible intensity between association and status placement. However, the factors that underlie this correspondence differ at each level. As already shown, the group centered above .265 maintains its position by disassociation from most of the elite. That centered between .435 and .605 consists of the modally bicultural Creoles who are most exposed to contradictory standards of status ascription and achievement and to competing demands from the different cultural traditions. They are at once the most culturally heterogeneous stratum and the least secure in their personal status. Accordingly, they display the highest rate of social isolation among these elite, as the chief alternative to exclusive association with social peers. Between .605 and .835 the regression angle for weighted associations and personal status is 26° 43', a gradient consistent with the marginal position of these people in the elite.

The strata ranked between .265 and .435 are of special interest. In the level ranked above .335 the regression angle for association is −23° 53', a complete reversal of patterns found elsewhere. In the level ranked between .335 and .435 this angle is +8° 11', which is virtual indifference. These very irregular alignments derive from the subdivision into two ranked halves of an associational field dominated by a single social stratum. Taken together, the groups ranked between .265 and .435 have a regression coefficient for association and status of +.4468 which gives an angle of 25° 5', similar to that found in the stratum below .605. Here, also, different conditions account for these similar alignments; people ranked between .605 and .835 may associate with one another, despite relatively wide difference in status, for lack of others to associate with. People ranked between .265 and .435 associate intensively, across and beyond this status range, in a network of kinship and affinal relations that binds them into a solidary endogamous group.

Concluding Remarks

Our analysis indicates a substantial divergence of values among the Grenadian elite. The strata that hold different values differ also in institutional practices and commitments. At one extreme, among the highest-ranking Westernized Creole "whites," we find an undiluted ascriptive orientation with solidary particularistic stress; at the other, in the dark, low-ranking elite levels above the folk, the prevailing set of values is individualistic and achievement-oriented. These two value sets challenge and clash with each other. Their coexistence at different levels of the elite hierarchy represents dissensus rather than the prevalence of a common system of values. In effect the Grenadian elite exhibits these pluralistic features as a direct function of its position in the plural society of Grenada. The exact correspondence of its composition with that derived from our model of Grenada as a plural society based on primary cleavages between elite and folk, simultaneously identifies the nature of this society and confirms the thesis that institutional uniformities and differences entail corresponding communities and differences of values.

We set out to study the assertion that a common value system is the indispensable basis of all society. Furnivall explicitly denied that such overarching systems of common values are to be found in plural societies. He based his distinction between plural and unitary societies on the lack of common values and a common will in the plural society, as against their central role in other types. For action theory, however,

It is a condition of the stability of social systems that there should be an integration of the value standards of the component units to constitute a "common value system." . . . The existence of such a pattern system as a point of reference for the analysis of social phenomena is a central assumption which follows directly from the frame of reference of actions as applied to the analysis of social system.[16]

We can now set out the essential data and their implications. (1) Social alignments identify four solidary ranked strata among the elite and show that the axes of these social strata diverge from the horizontal intervals between status levels. Thus individual status and social affiliations often diverge. (2) These solidary social units represent Grenadian elite organization more accurately than the analytic scheme of horizontal status levels. (3) They also correspond directly with the model of elite organization deduced from folk-elite differences and relations. (4) These deductions implied that the elite are stratified in groups that differed in racial character, in status, in institutional observance, and in values. (5) The four elite strata we have identified perfectly illustrate this model in three respects; namely, ranking, racial, and institutional differences. For these differences, various tables already discussed furnish direct data. (6) The differing value sets of these elite strata are also shown by their differing regression and correlation coefficients for a wide range of status conditions.

These facts demonstrate the plural character of Grenadian society quite clearly. If Grenada is a plural society based on folk and elite, and if these have the ethnographic features attributed to them, then our analysis of these social and cultural differences should reveal four elite divisions with the characteristics that the four elite strata actually show. The empirical confirmation of these deductions validates the assumptions on which the model was based—namely that Grenada is a plural society composed of two basic sections, the folk and the elite, distinguished by the relations and institutions reported above. But if Grenada is a plural society, on the basis of Furnivall's thesis and my institutional interpretation of this, its elite should also exhibit dissonance rather than community of values. The evidence for this is to be found in table 2. The decisive test consists in the sharply variant valuations of differing status factors at differing status levels, as shown by the variability in their correlation and regression coefficients. These show that the values of given conditions differ at different status levels, and are often reversed. In consequence, the scale of elite stratification represents an unstable hierarchy of value differences, rather than a stable system of common values. This conclusion is quite consistent with the thesis Furnivall advanced, and contradicts the basic assumption on which the theory of action rests.

On the evidence we have just reviewed, the Grenadian elite do not display the common value system that action theory predicates. Instead they exhibit a dissensus which reflects the deeper and wider value cleavages presented by the society's two main cultural traditions. However, despite this disunity of values, Grenada has a very fair record of historical stability. From 1796 until 1951 there were no local disturbances. Emancipation in 1838 passed very peacefully. "The conduct of the liberated people of Grenada on that day was most exemplary. . . . There was no drunkenness, or disorderly conduct."[17] Shortly afterwards, the exodus of ex-slaves to Trinidad began. Of the majority who remained, some became small holders and peasants, while others worked on the same estates they had once served as slaves, under new arrangements. During the years immediately following Emancipation, a new kind of labor relation gradually took shape, which, when fully developed, served to integrate the planters and "peasants," and through them the elite and folk, and thus the total society, from 1860 to 1950. But though this relation ensured the orderly coöperation of planters and "peasants," it neither rested on common values nor served to promote them. Asymmetrical in form, its function was symbiotic, and its prerequisite was a sufficiently basic difference in the values of the "peasants" and planters to permit their symbiosis. These Grenadian data suggest that, besides political domination or a common value system, symbiotic relations between people whose values differ may also provide a viable basis for social order.[18]

By 1890 the mutual accommodation of planters and peasants was sufficiently assured for the colonial government to permit removal of the British garrison which usually undertook to maintain local order. Thereafter, until 1939, the island was ungarrisoned, as it was again in 1950, on the eve of violence. Grenada's history shows that throughout this period the basis of social order and stability was the symbiosis of planter and peasant. As this symbiotic relation decayed progressively after 1930, discord increased to the point of violence. Differences of value and goals that had long been muted and diverted by this symbiotic accommodation then emerged in opposition.

This island's history shows that stability and social order may have various bases. Grenada has known an older type of social order based on force and slavery—before and after Fedon. We should not therefore assume too lightly that social order invariably rests on common values, or presupposes them.

The results of our inquiry may be challenged on various grounds, of which we may discuss two briefly, in closing. It may be said that our statistical evidence does not indicate any real differences in value between elite status levels, but that it represents an illusory artifactual product of our analytic method rather than data. This is ultimately a matter for mathematicians to settle. For my part, I can see no ground for holding that correlations for such variables as income or phenotype in a limited status range, say .265 to .435, will generate spurious or artifactual results, while the same correlations for a larger status range will not. In both cases the formula and principles of calculation are the same; so is the type of association which the correlation seeks to measure. The results are thus of identical logi-cal status, whether the computation refers to a larger or lesser sample; and for this reason we can usefully compare these results for various strata to ascertain their similarities and differences.

When one stratum yields a negative correlation for a given variable and status, the second indifference, and the third a high positive coefficient, it is also unde-niable that these differing measures express differing valuations of the variable as a condition or correlate of status within the various strata. I confess that I can see no other interpretation of correlation ratios, whether variable or not, and whether for a total sample or for its subdivisions. But in this case, our general conclusion seems unavoidable. A review of table 2 shows such sharply differing coefficients of correlation and regression for these variables and differential status among suc-cessive strata, that the onus of proof would seem to rest on those who maintain that these distributions express a common system of values among this elite. Moreover, when stratum coefficients for the several variables are considered to-gether, they seem to reveal an ascriptive, solidaristic, and particularistic set of values among the strata that rank above .435, as opposed to a relatively universal-istic, achievement-oriented, and individualistic set of values among strata ranked between .435 and .835. This contrast is fully confirmed by the distributions of other status factors such as education, legitimate descent, immigrant origin, oc-cupation, and so forth, for which correlations have not been calculated. A differ-ing value system seems to be dominant in either half of the elite hierarchy. Ac-cordingly we cannot claim that this stratification rests on a common system of values throughout. The evidence seems clearly against this.

A technical version of the argument that our results are spurious and artifactual may point to the small number of observations in most of the strata whose varying correlations we treat as indices of similar or variant valuations. To statisticians, reliable correlations require samples with three or four hundred observations. As units, our various subsamples approximate this condition in differing degrees, while the strata correlations clearly do not. The smaller the number of observa-tions for which correlations are computed, the less exactly does this measure de-fine the relative dispersion of the variables in the sample. Its value as a basis for prediction is correspondingly reduced.

Recognizing this, besides using various standard tests of significance, I have also relied on regression coefficients, which indicate the intensity and form of the association between the variables correlated by strata, rather than on the correla-tion alone. These regression coefficients vary as an effect of differences in the standard deviations of the distributions for the two variables in the samples drawn from each stratum. They restate the association between these variables for each stratum in ways that minimize the probable errors inherent in correlations based on small numbers of observations, and at the same time, they specify the exact intensity of the association between the variables at each status level.

A second, rather different, type of criticism might hold that even if our conclusions do reveal the value differences we claim, they cannot prove the absence of common values in other areas among elite or between elite and folk. From this viewpoint, any catalogue of value differences, however lengthy, must fail to substantiate this conclusion on the ground that it is incomplete. Thus on this argument it is impossible ever to "prove" the absence of common values; at best we can merely measure differences with regard to particular values in any given case: but to show a lack of common values in certain areas does not prove their absence in all.

The validity of this argument is open to doubt. First, it ignores the distinctions originally mentioned between common, shared, similar, and universal values and goals. It also ignores recent work in the theory of action and values. In the light of our opening discussion it seems possible that the unidentified "common values" on which such criticism rests are really similar, or universal values, rather than common values as such. Such similar values may either have the same status as Furnivall's "common wants"—"all wants that all men want in common . . . they share in common with the animal creation";[19] or, alternatively, they may correspond to Kluckhohn's universal values of reciprocity—truth, beauty, and the like—which all people are said to hold, though neither identically nor always in common.[20]

It seems highly probable that this simple error may underlie the infinity of common values to which this argument leads if logically extended, in view of the elaborate theoretical work by Professor Parsons and his colleagues on value systems, especially in relation to social stratification. These theoretical inquiries identify the limits within which various values may enter into a common value system. In the Parsonian scheme common values relevant to social action are definable by reference to five dichotomous pattern variables or dilemmas which confront all social action. With the aid of this scheme of pattern variables, the two divergent value sets revealed by our data are easily identified; and in terms of this scheme, which is central to the theory of action, these divergences are directly opposed. Moreover, for action theory the exclusive antithetical combinations of these pattern variables define the range of values which may or may not be held in common. Thus, at least in terms of that view of common values which is central to current action theory, our conclusion seems to hold.

The patterns of elite recruitment and socialization discussed above are directly relevant here. We have seen that at both extremes the Creole elite are insulated against internal mobility. Elite can hardly so lose "caste" that they are identified as folk in Grenada. Where an individual's behavior suggests this possibility, the deviant's kin are expected to export him promptly—and regularly do so. On the other hand, folk traditionally recruited into the elite are the bastard offspring of elite fathers. Thus, there is virtual closure of the lower elite threshold against unattached folk.

At the upper limit, an even more stringent closure obtains. The "white planter class" maintains its diminishing strength through recruitment from abroad. It prohibits intermarriage of its members with other elite. It educates all its children abroad. Its members by birth or association retain their status within it even when their status in the wider society has fallen through some irreparable deviance on their part. In these conditions status-ranking and social mobility differ clearly. Even eminent Creoles whose official rank sets them a notch or two above these planters in status never cross this social barrier. Thus at both ends this Creole elite is sealed against mobility. Such simultaneous social and status mobility as occurs can only proceed within it. Thus the Creole elite is distinguished from the superior white planters and from the inferior black folk as an exclusive range of social mobility closed to outsiders. This closure expresses its value distinctness and exclusiveness. Without common values, social mobility cannot occur, and where these obtain, mobility is inevitable. Only where we find that social mobility is possible can we expect to find common values. In Grenada this index distinguishes three ranked social sections, each with distinctive values.

It would clearly be premature to pretend that we have resolved a problem that in one guise or another has been central to sociological theory and research for more than a century. We have at best tried to translate it into operational terms and to study it in a context selected to test two critically conflicting formulations. This experiment indicates that, at least among Grenadian elite, the value dissensus by which Furnivall identified tropical colonies as plural societies prevails. Thus, in this case the theory of action which assumes that only common values can furnish the basis of social order and social stratification is evidently invalid; and this conclusion suggests that action theory urgently needs testing in field studies of other contemporary societies. Its claim to universal validity should no longer be taken for granted; in any society its appropriateness and validity requires proof.

The sort of modification by which action theory may be adapted to plural societies and mixed populations is perhaps latent in Talcott Parsons's remarks on American stratification. In discussing these phenomena, he notes that in America

> the ethnic problem seems to modify the system of stratification through two principal types of process. In the first place, the value-system of an ethnic group may vary from that paramount in the dominant society. Then, within certain limits of tolerance, it may tend to form a variant sub-society within the larger society, more closely approximating implementation of its own values. In these respects, the actions of an ethnic group should be interpreted in terms of its own distinctive culture, including its own internal stratification and the ways in which it can, according to its values, appropriately articulate with the main class system. The second mode of modification derives from the fact that the ethnic group, with regard both to its value patterns and to any other aspects of its status in the larger society, constitutes an entity somewhat apart, to which non-members react in patterned ways, which in turn help to determine the reactions of the group.[21]

Here Parsons virtually recognizes that differing and opposed value systems may coexist in an ethnically mixed society of the sort we have been discussing; but without explicit attention to these situations, the action framework and its theory of stratification can deal only with systems of a limited range, namely, those which meet certain rather special conditions and assumptions. Whether societies with such consensual normative bases are not a minority of the units with which sociology has to deal must thus remain an open question.

It is necessary therefore to recognize the significance of plural societies as a distinct societal type, with distinctive though variable properties of structure, function, order, and development. Especially in the study of plural societies which are defined primarily by their relative "lack of a common will," the assumption of common values may easily replace analysis by ideology, and thus obstruct understanding. On Furnivall's argument, many recently independent nations have this plural basis and character, as certain recent studies tacitly admit.[22] While action theory may be useful for understanding certain types of social system, given its distinctive assumption of normative consensus, it is not appropriate everywhere; and at least in plural societies, of which Grenada is a representative Creole case, its validity seems lower than the thesis Furnivall advanced.

Notes

1. Talcott Parsons, "An Analytical Approach to the Theory of Social Stratification," *American Journal of Sociology*, vol. 45 (1940; reprinted in Talcott Parsons, *Essays in Sociological Theory, Pure and Applied* [Glencoe, Ill.: Free Press, 1949], p. 167).

2. W. Lloyd Warner and Paul S. Lunt, *The Social Life of a Modern Community*, Yankee City Series, vol. 1 (New Haven, Conn.: Yale University Press, 1941), p. 82.

3. Joseph Schumpeter, *Imperialism and Social Classes* (New York: Meridian Books, 1955), p. 108.

4. Talcott Parsons, *Essays*, p. 173.

5. Ibid.

6. Ibid.

7. Ibid.

8. J. H. Hutton, *Caste in India* (London: Cambridge University Press, 1946), p. 117.

9. Kingsley Davis and Wilbert E. Moore, "Some Principles of Stratification," *American Sociological Review*, vol. 10 (1945), p. 244.

10. *Report of the Commission of Enquiry into the Control of Public Expenditure in Grenada During 1961 and Subsequently* (London: H.M.S.O., May, 1962), Command No. 1735.

11. For a description of the "bouquet," or company dance, see M. G. Smith, *Kinship and Community in Carriacou* (New Haven, Conn.: Yale University Press, 1963), pp. 10–11, 73.

12. M. G. Smith, *Dark Puritan* (Jamaica: Extra-mural Department, University of the West Indies, 1963).

13. Simon Rottenberg, "Labor Relations in an Underdeveloped Economy," *Caribbean Quarterly*, vol. 4, no. 1 (January, 1955), p. 56.

14. Ibid., p. 55.

15. *Report of the Education Officer and Senior Inspector of Schools for 1952*, Grenada Council Paper No. 1 (St. George's: Government Printer, 1954), pp. 2–3.

16. Talcott Parsons, "A Revised Analytical Approach to the Theory of Social Stratification," in Reinhard Bendix and Seymour Martin Lipset, eds., *Class, Status and Power: A Reader in Social Stratification* (Glencoe, Ill.: Free Press, 1953), p. 93.

17. *The Grenada Handbook and Directory, 1946* (St. George's, Grenada), p. 41.

18. S. F. Nadel, "Social Symbiosis and Tribal Organization," *Man*, vol. 38, art. 85 (1938), pp. 85–90.

19. J. S. Furnivall, *Colonial Policy and Practice* (London: Cambridge University Press, 1948), p. 310.

20. Clyde Kluckhohn, "Values and Value-Orientations," in Talcott Parsons and Edward A. Shils, eds., *Toward a General Theory of Action* (Cambridge, Mass.: Harvard University Press, 1951), pp. 418–419.

21. Talcott Parsons, "A Revised Analytical Approach," pp. 118–119.

22. Edward A. Shils, *Political Development in the New States* (The Hague: Mouton, 1960), pp. 14, 16, 35, 58, 64, 70 ff.

11. WEST INDIAN VERSION

Literature, History, and Identity[1]

Douglas Midgett

Poets and satirists are afflicted with the superior stupidity which believes that societies can be renewed, and one of the most nourishing sites for such a renewal, however visionary it may seem, is the American archipelago.

—Derek Walcott[2]

Perhaps one of the most perplexing issues concerning West Indian societies is that of identity. This issue has occupied the talents of many writers and political thinkers and has drawn the attention of scholars of the history and society of the area. Some commentators maintain that its resolution would lead variously to healthy psyches, political stability and independence, a sense of social community, and the integration of a potentially major region of the New World. The continued failure to arrive at a distinctive, positive identity is blamed for everything from alcohol abuse to the repeated failure to achieve political and economic integration.

A brief glance at the historical origins of these societies may shed some light on the bases of these problems.[3] The people of the West Indies are products of the most sustained and intense European colonial domination undergone by any present-day population. For some, at least, that process has not yet ended. Moreover, they are products of a process that has resulted in the formation of new societies, that is, the population segments that came to be constituent parts of these societies were none of them indigenous. They arrived from the Old World, and the society that developed very much reflected the relationships between populations resulting from the initial economic structures on which European interests in the area were predicated. West Indian society, viewed as a whole, was always fragmented in terms of political administration and economic ties to the metropole. As the British Colonial Office administered the units separately, so the plantocracies in the individual islands were engaged in economic competition with one another. Internally, too, these were fragmented societies, divided

Originally published in Ann Pescatello (ed.), *Old Roots in New Lands* (Westport, Conn.: Greenwood Press, 1977), pp. 209–42. Copyright © 1977 by Ann Pescatello. Reprinted with permission.

initially between slave and free, white, colored, and black, and evolving (some with subsequent additional population segments) into entities characterized by social, cultural, and structural pluralism. This situation produced an atomized regional structure of increasingly economically peripheral units tied to Great Britain like unconnected points to the hub of a wheel, each internally divided into sections that were often culturally antithetical. Hence, the possibility of integration of the region was severely limited. As Gordon Lewis has noted, in view of this historical development it is ridiculous to criticize West Indians "for their insularism, when in harsh fact the basic responsibility is that of the English themselves who kept the islands unnaturally apart from each other for three centuries or more and then expected them to come together in less than fifteen years."[4]

The kind of integration which many have envisioned and worked toward for decades depends on some basic factors. Some of these factors may well be beyond the realm of West Indian influence. If, for example, continued fragmentation serves the continued "development" of the region as a source of cheap labor for import substitution industries and as a market for consumer products from North America and Europe, then area politicians, however pure their motives, will find it very difficult to buck that tide. On the other hand, much has already been done in one field, although perhaps not specifically directed to the ends suggested here. This endeavor concerns the difficult issue of identity, the creation or manifestation of a vision and unity of purpose that transcends the pettiness of the micronationalism of the current post-Federation West Indies. In this chapter some of the directions that this endeavor has taken and might take are elaborated.

In another area, East Africa, Ali Mazrui has discussed the concept of cultural engineering—the process of constructing institutions and ideologies that will enable new nations in that part of the world to embark on nationhood with integrity and sense of purpose.[5] The parallels with the West Indies, while not overwhelming, are suggestive. Until recently, both areas were under colonial control; both are composed of heterogeneous populations, separated during the colonial period by the nature of the administrative apparatus; and, in both cases, the partial integration of individual members of the non-European population into the colonial political and economic structure was facilitated by an educational process of European design, a programmed alienation process. In his study, Mazrui suggests the utility of the concept for this study of identity in the West Indies:

> Cultural engineering becomes the deliberate manipulation of cultural factors for purposes of deflecting human habit in the direction of new and perhaps constructive endeavors. Sometimes the effort consists in changing cultural patterns enough to make it possible for certain institutions to survive. At other times the purpose of cultural reform is basically attitudinal change. Ultimately, there is the paramount issue of identity, of how people view themselves and how far self-conceptions can be modified in the direction of enlarged empathy.[6]

In applying some of Mazrui's approaches to the West Indian situation, the scope of this essay has been limited to include just two of the areas of his concern, the writing of history and creative literature. These two topics were chosen for a number of reasons, the most important of which is the abundance of literary and historical material available to the researcher. The creative literature of the West Indies is the product of an especially prolific group of writers, particularly during the last quarter century. Historical accounts of the region, abundant and mostly written from a Euro-centric point of view, have begun to attract the attention of many young historians of the area who are bringing decidedly different orientations to the interpretation of these data.

Literature

In his discussion of the relationship between creative literature and nationalism or nationalistic identity, Mazrui suggests three dimensions for consideration: the act of writing itself, the themes employed, and the linkages between, in his case, African literature and other literary traditions, particularly those European.[7] An examination of West Indian writing along these dimensions reveals a number of aspects that have implications for the formation of identity. The very act of writing in societies that are as profoundly colonial as those in the West Indies is initially an assertion of identity. If that writing moves in directions that diverge from those of the colonizer and are counter to that sector of the society which has controlled access to literacy, then the assertion has particular salience. In a society such as the West Indies which is characterized by cultural ambiguity and social schisms, a number of themes are of obvious importance: the issue of race, the connections with Africa and Europe, and the impact of centuries of slavery, to name just a few. Finally, the relationship to European literature may be viewed from different perspectives: the determination of criteria by which this newly emerging literary output is to be judged, or the development of an indigenous, unique style of expression within the confines of a European literary language. These perspectives, especially indigenous style, are closely tied to questions of particularistic versus universalistic interpretation, a question hardly confined to literature of West Indian expression, but nonetheless one that must be considered after the following discussion.

In the West Indian creative literature appearing during the past twenty-five years, many of the issues noted above have consistently arisen. In these societies where the European custodians of literacy produced almost nothing of artistic merit, much of this recent literary output is the product of blacks and East Indians. Consequently it deals in various ways with the social cleavages and psychological disorientation common in a colonial situation.

Although any consideration of literature from a thematic approach results in some distortion of the works considered, examining the literary output from the perspective a number of themes relating to identity will illuminate these issues significantly. Accordingly, five broad themes that have been given some attention by West Indian writers are discussed, with exemplary material given in each case. These five themes include (1) the relationship of the people to the West Indian physical environment; (2) the use of Africa and Europe as metaphor, the invocation of cultural continuity and racial memory; (3) the reference to historical events in the islands, including the examination of slavery and the struggle for freedom; (4) present-day issues, including class and color schisms in the societies; and (5) the use of language, particularly the role of Creole or dialect.

THE ISLAND ENVIRONMENT

The writer who has gone farthest in an attempt to define the relationship of the West Indian to environment is the St. Lucian poet and playwright Derek Walcott. For Walcott this relationship must be understood if West Indians are to make sense of their position and comprehend their existence. He directly addresses the question of whether the West Indian experience, rooted in a history characterized by human destruction and dehumanized relations, can ever result in anything more than a derivative identity, neither creative nor in harmony with the island landscape.

So it is that Walcott explores features of that landscape, physical and human, and expresses at times a deep love for his homeland. Separation, so much a part of the West Indian experience, evokes the following response:

> I watched the shallow green
> That broke in places where there would be reef,
> The silver glinting on the fuselage, each mile
> Dividing us and all fidelity strained
> Till space would snap it. Then after a while
> I thought of nothing, nothing, I prayed, would change;[8]

As Gerald Moore observes, Walcott is a writer of the small islands; his poetry frequently focuses on those dazzling beaches fronting the rusting, galvanized roofed fishing villages that rim his native St. Lucia.[9] Despite the penetration of his vision (or perhaps because of it), Walcott's portraits of Anse-la-Raye and Dennery reveal an ambiguity that aids in our understanding of the motives of migrants who, in flight from villages in austere London council houses, assert their longing for these small, somnambulant places.[10]

With the exception of *The Sea at Dauphin*, Walcott does not, however, confine himself in his plays to the sea and the villages. Other works explore the aspects of the countryside environment of the peasantry and evoke even more basic elements of the West Indian setting. A striking case is the continual presence of the heavy rain in *Malcochon*, a feature that becomes a device for measuring the pace of the play. Another example is the treatment of the mountainous interior of the island, the domain of the charcoal burner, Makak, in *Dream on Monkey Mountain*; this image was fully realized in the televised production of the play by Trinidad and Tobago Television.[11]

Other West Indian writers, mostly novelists, explore the island environments and experiences through vivid portrayals of rural and village life. These works, occasionally referred to as childhood novels, deal in varying detail with coming of age in these settings. In the process, they examine the relationship between the growth of their actors and their comparatively diminished settings. The most important of these works is George Lamming's first novel, *In the Castle of My Skin*.[12] A "childhood novel" only insofar as its protagonist and occasional narrator is a boy growing up in a Barbadian village, this work is a portrait of West Indian society in flux during that period of labor unrest and growing demand for popular political participation before World War II. Despite his preoccupation with these themes, Lamming frequently details the human communion with environment in this setting.

The novels of Michael Anthony, particularly *The Year in San Fernando* and *Green Days by the River*, lack the pointedness and concern with larger issues that characterize Lamming's work.[13] In their depiction of coming of age, or perhaps in just the vignettes of adolescent experience, however, they are particularly attuned to the features of the surroundings that circumscribe these identifiable activities. In the first-named novel the setting, richly mined for metaphorical checkpoints on the year's seasonal changes, is urban Trinidad, a world of streets and houses, buses and strangers. In contrast, *Green Days* explores the world of the peasant and village. It evokes a fecund, slower paced milieu which, until the rather terrifying final episodes, contrasts with the tempo of rapidly emerging adolescence.

The exploration of themes involving relationships with the West Indian natural environment has received considerable elaboration. Whether this relationship is peripheral to other concerns or is seen as a central problem for resolution by West Indian man, as in Walcott's work, these writers have repeatedly turned to the island settings as foci for playing out their literary directions. Perhaps the emphasis on this focus leads inevitably to Dennis Scott's conclusion:

> It is time to plant
> feet in our earth. The heart's metronome
> insists on this arc of islands
> as home.[14]

AFRICAN CONNECTION[15]

Undeniably African references are frequently encountered in West Indian writing. Some kind of cult activity is depicted in novels in both urban and rural settings. Although not a few of these lean heavily on the spectacular, orgiastic aspects of these events, recalling the more ludicrous effects of old jungle movies, some have dealt with the African element in an attempt to examine what possibilities exist in the definition of identity.

A particularly ambitious attempt to portray the cultural collision of Africa and Europe is Lamming's *Season of Adventure* in which the conflict centers in the person of Fola, the middle-class mulatto girl.[16] Kenneth Ramchand has called this book "the most significant of the West Indian novels invoking Africa."[17] There are compelling arguments for this judgment. Lamming is not content to use ritual as a device either to demonstrate a cursory familiarity with the occult or as a dazzler for the reader searching for bits of local color. Rather, the question is very directly posed as to what are the existential considerations for a people divided between a remembered and still vital, if altered and attenuated, African past and a present direction that involves the denial of that heritage. This question is an enormously difficult one and Lamming makes clear that it has no facile resolution.

Derek Walcott, too, has dealt with Africa, to the greatest extent in *Dream on Monkey Mountain*, where the invocation of this heritage finds its fullest expression in the tribal ceremony toward the end of the play.[18] The "primitive" quality of this scene is pronounced, a feature which as a dramatic device is more acceptable in a play than in a novel. Moreover, the play is a dream, a series of images, which means that the scene need not be evaluated in terms of its ethnographic accuracy.

Another of Walcott's plays, *Ione*, is the only piece of West Indian writing known to me which includes African social patterns.[19] The two families, headed by patriarchs and descended from a common male ancestor, are portrayed as lineages in opposition. Despite these forays into African survival and memory, the key issue for Walcott seems to be how to incorporate the African and European, as expressed in the following:

> how choose
> Between this Africa and the English tongue I love?
> Betray them both, or give back what they give?
> How can I face such slaughter and be cool?
> How can I turn from Africa and live?[20]

For one writer, the Barbadian poet and historian Edward Brathwaite, the question of identity, at least at one level, is not such a vexed issue. No single body of work in West Indian literature goes further toward exploring and resolving the African heritage and presence as does Brathwaite's trilogy, *Rights of Passage, Masks,* and *Islands*.[21] In the first of these volumes of poetry, which deals with slavery and its legacy, Brathwaite concludes with the rhetorical question:

> Should you
> shatter the door
> and walk
> in the morning
> fully aware
> of the future
> to come?[22]

Although his answer is direct—"There is no turning back"—it is not simply arrived at, for a conception of the future requires an understanding of the African experience, past and present. Thus, in *Masks* the author must remove himself in time and space to reacquaint himself with his cultural antecedents. It is only after this journey that he can return to confront the contradictions of a West Indian existence in *Islands*. For Brathwaite, then, the invocation of Africa is not just a stylistic trick, or even an anthropological search for retentions, but a means to deal with the existential problems posed in his society. The environments of Brathwaite's concern are not the landscapes and seascapes of the islands but the inner visions, products of culture and history.

LITERATURE AND HISTORY

Apart from some examination of recent historical events dealing with nationalism and regional political issues, West Indian writing has rarely taken the historical tradition of the islands seriously in its purview. Perhaps this may reflect a general acceptance (albeit loud public denial) of Naipaul's contention that the West Indies has no historical tradition worthy of serious consideration.[23] Nevertheless, there is a marked absence of interest in themes that center on slavery and the trade, resistance, rebellion, and the effects of European power struggles in the area on social life in the islands.

One historically important area that occasionally surfaces in literature is that of the stereotypic depictions of black people, slave and free, which have in the past so influenced the interpretations of history and images in literary sources. Brathwaite, for example, takes the figure of Tom, the slave Uncle Tom, and expands on a role that has been the source of much malign expression.[24] Brathwaite's Tom is not just a bowing, servile darky, but he has a range of personality characteristics; he is a psychologically assaulted, but whole individual, however mocked by his history.

Stereotypic figures are also presented in Walcott's *Ti Jean and His Brothers*, in which appear three black figures, frequently encountered in literary and other accounts.[25] Gros Jean is the buck nigger, strong-backed, but weak in the head, whose witlessness and reliance on brute strength are his final undoing. Mi Jean is the prototypical Afro-Saxon, the sycophant who is the exemplification of imitation being the sincerest form of flattery. His comeuppance occurs only after he realizes, too late, that the colonizer is not about to admit the imitator into the inner circle. That leaves Ti Jean, a figure who appears rather less frequently in those accounts describing the "character and social manners of the negro," and only then during periods of turmoil and rebellion when the planters' paranoia surfaces in print. Ti Jean is the realist, unresponsive to the destructive flattery of the master, the realist who understands that the only way to change the system is to destroy it. That he is the hero and ultimate victor in the play, defeating the plantation owner/devil, is a measure of Walcott's recreative hope, only rarely achieved in the West Indian reality.

In a quite different direction, a most significant novel dealing with the literary interpretation of actual historical events is V. S. Reid's *New Day*.[26] The action of the novel spans the period in Jamaican history from the Morant Bay Rebellion in 1865 to the "new day" of the constitutional revisions of 1944 which promised a new political order. As the story is told through the eyes of an old man who was a participant in the 1865 rebellion and a witness to the 1944 events, it provides a view of a people who are the inheritors of their own unique history. It is in this effort that the book's significance lies, for Reid lends a heroic quality to these people and events that is entirely absent from the history lessons most Jamaicans learned at school. Although in *New Day* Reid has opened up a new direction for others intent upon mining historical sources, none has followed his lead. It may be that the enterprise must await the day when these writers attain a more complete understanding of this history.

COLOR AND CLASS

The issues of color and class that presently divide West Indians and frustrate attempts to develop a sense of community did not receive extensive treatment in literature until recently. The disinclination in the past to confront these social issues directly is best exemplified in the contrast between the poetry written a generation ago and that contained in some recent collections.[27] With the exception of some iconoclastic writers like E. M. Roach and Martin Carter, the poetry of the 1950s and before did not touch on the themes of conflict and struggle.

These issues *were* the subject, however, of some novels, especially those of Roger Mais. His milieu is the city, Kingston, and the yard culture of the poor urban dweller. In two novels, *The Hills Were Joyful Together* and *Brother Man*, Mais portrays the reality of what it is like to be poor and black in the city, the one locale in the island where the material opulence of the wealthy is continually on display.[28] Mais depicts this existence not as a nether world, as some have suggested, but as a functioning community, constrained by and confronting a situation where wealth and skin color are the only marks of status.

Another writer who characterizes the poor is Orlando Patterson, whose first novel, *The Children of Sisyphus*, also focuses on the urban poverty scene of Kingston.[29] Patterson's writing has occasionally been criticized and unfavorably compared with that of Mais. If it is lacking, it is only a matter of style, not of sociological accuracy, a characteristic that Patterson strives for, sometimes at the expense of readability.

If the characters in Mais's and Patterson's urban shanties have in most cases come to some kind of terms with the harshness of their environments and the constraints that limit their chances, then the protagonists in novels of the colored middle class appear to be continually searching for *persona*. There is a strong hint that survival for these people, Naipaul's mimic men,[30] lies in the assumption of some guise that masks the conditions of inequality in the society and blinds them to the aimlessness of their own civil servant existence. In *Nor Any Country*, Paul Breville explains to his brother his escape to schizophrenia: "They think I'm mad, . . . All right. I encourage them to think so. I behave as if I am. Deliberately. . . . This is the only world I can inhabit now, where they can only laugh and tolerate. I can never fail or disappoint now. Nobody expects anything of me. Not even myself."[31]

These novels convey the notion that the colored middle class is in a cultural limbo—denied full membership as Englishmen, a status that would be commensurate with their education and training, and unable or unwilling to respond to the vitality of the urban and rural folk culture that surrounds them. Even when a return to these roots is attempted, as in the instance of Jerry Stover in Andrew Salkey's novel, *The Late Emancipation of Jerry Stover*, the experiment frequently culminates in disaster.[32]

In this discussion, one more work deserves mention because it deals directly with the issue of race and the pathological consequences it can engender in a setting where color and privilege have for so long been interrelated. John Stewart's *Last Cool Days*, set in his native Trinidad, confronts the subject of racial awareness with a starkness unusual in West Indian literature, a directness that belies the author's long residence in the United States.[33] Perhaps like Trumper in *In the Castle of My Skin*, the West Indian writer must leave the islands "to know what it mean to fin' race,"[34] to comprehend an identity that is every bit as profound a reality in his homeland.

THE USES OF LANGUAGE

As indicated earlier, the mere production of literature in the language of the colonizer is in itself a political act in societies so markedly colonial as the West Indian. In the West Indies, creative literature has been written in English; the problems of creating an indigenous written art form in the foreign language of the colonizer, which are problems common to African and Asian writers, are not paramount for the West Indian artist. But the specific use of language, the decision whether to use dialect and Creole in the effort to deal with themes and to create a distinctive, even nationalistic literature, is most certainly at issue here.[35]

Some works have employed Creole speech extensively. Walcott and Garth St. Omer, both St. Lucians, have produced works rich in the use of patois, the Creole of that island.[36] The difficulty of such an effort appealing to any but a very select readership is evident in the development of St. Omer's novella, *Syrop*, which was originally written with dialogue in patois but was later published with translation into roughly equivalent English dialect.[37] Another earlier use is in Reid's *New Day*, where the narration by the old man, John Campbell, is almost entirely in dialect, a device used with great effect, particularly in descriptions of the Jamaican landscape.[38]

Others have used dialect sparingly, most often in dialogue to catch the "flavor" of verbal exchange in the island setting. Often enough, however, some of this use of dialect is for humorous effect, to present a particular character as ludicrous. Employed in this fashion, the use of dialect differs little at times from the linguistic atrocities attributed to blacks in travelers' accounts written during and just following the slavery period.

Recently, the use of dialect has taken a decidedly different turn, particularly in works of poetry. This change was signaled in the 1971 special literature issue of *Savacou*,[39] the organ of the Caribbean Artists' Movement. The outcry which greeted the publication of dialect poetry in that issue is indicative of the embarrassment some felt in confronting the artistic use of "bad talk," "bad English," or "broken English." It is also indicative of a larger issue, the one of particularistic as opposed to universalistic criteria for the critical evaluation of literature.[40] Without going into this issue at great length, there appears to be no reason why at one point in time much West Indian writing, published and read primarily outside the islands, did not take a universalistic bent. Given the current political ferment in the area, however, the direction toward particularistic concerns and themes, especially in poetry, is both understandable and necessary.

History

Mazrui notes that a controversy concerning the writing of history in East Africa focuses on three levels: methodology, content, and application.[41] The West Indian historian has somewhat different problems, and this difference relates to some basic contrasts between the two regions. One of the principal questions in Africa, as Mazrui indicates, concerns the validity of oral tradition as source material, or, put another way, whether nonliterate traditions can be said to have histories at all. Such a problem is not so compelling for the West Indian historian. Although an examination of oral sources might aid the historian—and the issue of time dealt with in terms other than past, present, and future may prove just as troublesome in the West Indies as it has for African historians—the basic problems seem to be at Mazrui's level of application.

Mazrui raises the issue of the commitment of scholarship; specifically, he questions whether the study of history is to be directed toward an accretive or a corrective enterprise.[42] This distinction speaks directly to the most important problem for West Indian historians, namely, the correction of historical interpretations that have been heavily Eurocentric in their conceptions. The problem is not just one of counterbalancing some distorted data selection, but is also one of deriving new orientations with which to approach the data. This observation is not new, for West Indians from J. J. Thomas through C. L. R. James and Eric Williams pointed out these necessities before the advent of the current group of historians. Nonetheless, this task must be accomplished if West Indians are to make history serve a new and heightened self-image.

The following sections, one concerned with events in the Eastern Caribbean, specifically St. Lucia, and the other with a series of situations in Jamaica, demonstrate two points. The first section is an examination of how to proceed in the reinterpretation of historical events and figures. The second involves a people's sense of their own history through the presentation of themes in the popular realm, themes that have to do with popular notions of historical postures which nations or peoples assume or with relationships between nations or population segments within a nation. The second section examines a popular theme through which Jamaican society has been interpreted and contrasts it with the "official" portrait of that society.

VICTOR HUGHES AND THE BRIGANDS' WAR

In the last decade of the eighteenth century, the tremors that spread from the Haitian Revolution and the French Revolution touched nearly all of the islands of the Lesser Antilles in the form of violent confrontations. The last bitter struggle of the French and English for control of the area and the glimpse of release from servitude by an awakened black population combined to fashion the most turbulent period of the three centuries since European exploration had begun in the Caribbean.

During this time, a series of developments led to what has been termed the "Brigands' War," an especially bloody set of engagements between forces composed of British militia opposed by an army made up of a few French revolutionaries and large numbers of black and mulatto freedmen and ex-slaves. Adolph Roberts, in a relatively dispassionate discussion, notes that the confusion prevalent in the Antilles following the French Revolution so weakened the French position that by early 1794 the British, often in consort with French Royalists, were in control of most of the Eastern Caribbean.[43] By the latter part of that year, however, many of these same islands were controlled or under siege by a new force in the region. Under the direction of Victor Hughes, a mulatto born in France, the revolutionary forces first took Guadeloupe, and from that base Hughes sent missions to many of the other islands to enlist blacks and incite slave rebellions. The strategy worked in St. Lucia, St. Vincent, and Grenada, all of which fell into Hughes's hands. Matters remained thus for two years until the islands again returned to the immensely superior forces of the British; Hughes retained only Guadeloupe. The fighting did not end with these defeats, for the black armies continued to wage guerrilla campaigns against the British and in so doing controlled large portions of the interiors of some of the islands.

Let us now turn to a discussion of how these events are interpreted and how the character and singular accomplishments of Victor Hughes and his associates are assessed in the histories of this era.

For many writers of West Indian history, the events in the islands were mere adjuncts to the European history of that period.[44] Consequently, the events described above are most often dealt with in terms of French-British oppositions or, within the French sphere, in Royalist-Republican terms. The inaccuracies resulting from such an orientation are pointed up in Burns's description of the Brigands as comprising "whites of extreme revolutionary views, and escaped slaves."[45] In fact, these armies were mostly black and were composed of men legally free under the Republican regime. The incorrect identification of these forces is not as serious an error as the inability to recognize the importance of these struggles for people who realized that their newly found freedom would exist only as long as they could defend their territories against superior forces. Roberts reports, for example, the following situation in Guadeloupe upon the restitution of slavery and the trade: "A great many [Negroes] committed suicide rather than return to bondage. Four hundred former slaves locked themselves up in a fort, and when they became convinced that they would not be exempted from the abhorred decree they touched off the gunpowder magazine. All were killed."[46] Such accounts ought to provide some clue as to the degree of the blacks' commitment to maintaining a political situation that would insure their continued freedom.

In their treatment of Hughes, the historians certainly cannot be accused of ignoring the man. Indeed, they seem to take special relish in applying the most florid adjectives whenever his name appears. Brian Edwards found it difficult to deal with Hughes in any but the most scurrilous terms, stating that "his name has since become proverbial for every species of outrage and cruelty . . ." and that he was "savage, remorseless, and bloody" and an "inexorable tyrant."[47] Burns saw him as "an audacious and bloodthirsty revolutionary leader,"[48] and in local histories of the period in St. Lucia Hughes is described as "a ruffian" and is characterized by his "violence and greed."[49] Alec Waugh, the popularizer of West Indian history, provides us with the most colorful account of Hughes's character and bloody proclivities:

> Of less than medium height, with a corpulent torso that he encased in clothes that were too tight for it, with thick, stocky legs and a plebian, sensual mouth, pitted by smallpox, abrupt in manner, jerky, with a Southern accent, Victor Hughes rarely looked anyone in the face, but when he did, his small grey eyes inspired either terror or repulsion.[50]

Other revolutionary leaders, associates of Hughes, who occupy prominent positions in the struggles of the ex-slave populations, come off little better in the

hands of the historians. For example, Julian Fedon, Hughes's lieutenant in Grenada, is variously characterized as a "skillful but barbarous leader" and "as ruth-
less and brutal as Hughes himself."[51]

The problems created by this kind of writing and interpretation of West Indian
history are almost self-evident. These problems are not relegated to difficulties in
orientation (which are recognized by some of these writers, although limited to
such designations as "Anglophile" versus "Francophile"), or to the tendency to
ornament descriptions of certain personalities. Rather, they are of a more profound nature, for in explaining the conflicts of the time in terms of their significance for what was happening in Europe, these writers have failed to take account of the largest category of people directly involved and the ones for whom
these events were most significant. Moreover, the view of this history provided in
these accounts prevails in the islands today, and it is this interpretation of their
histories that islanders see symbolically represented throughout the West Indies.
For an example let us now turn, within the general context of the preceding historical discussion, to a local situation, a particular event, and the manner in
which it is represented symbolically.

In St. Lucia, the period preceding the revolutionary era is described as one of
"peaceful colonisation," and it is noted that "great advances were made."[52] These
"advances" were, of course, accomplished through the expansion of plantation
agriculture employing a slave labor force. This golden era of peace and prosperity
came to an end following the conclusion of the American Revolution and the
subsequent resumption of full-scale hostilities between the British and French in
the Eastern Caribbean. The instability produced by these conflicts enabled others to seek their own solutions to the question of who would control their desti-
nies. That all residents of the colony did not share in the prosperity of that time
is evidenced in the following account from Breen. In about 1784, "the island had
been infested by the Maroon Negroes, who taking advantage of the defenceless
situation of the planters, had committed the most wanton depredation on different estates, and even cruelly murdered some of the inhabitants."[53] These insurgents were brought under control during a brief period of French rule in the
island, but the impetus for internal revolt did not abate and was renewed less than
a decade later.

In 1793, after a visit from an emissary of the new French Republican regime,
the following situation ensued: "The work of the estates was discontinued, the
plantations were deserted, and nothing prevailed but anarchy and terror, in the
midst of which the Negroes under arms were discussing the 'rights of man'."[54]
The abolition of slavery was decreed on February 4, 1794, and the self-interest of
the vast majority of St. Lucians was served. The emancipation was shortlived,
however, as a British force recaptured the island two months later and set the
stage for the entry of Victor Hughes.

Although the British captured the fortress on Morne Fortune overlooking Castries Harbor, they failed to pacify much of St. Lucia. The ex-slaves-turned-libera-

tors moved their arena of operations to the interior of the island where they continued to harass the British troops for a year. By this time, in early 1795, Hughes, in Guadeloupe, had received sufficient goods and troops from France to make new incursions into the Southern Caribbean. In St. Lucia the garrison, weakened by disease and the effects of repeated battles with the black insurgents, capitulated without much struggle, and the island was once again in the hands of the blacks.

In the months that followed, this controlling army fiercely repulsed all British attempts to recapture the island. Moreover, military operations were pursued to the point that the whole island was pacified and subsequently served as a base for launching revolutionary forays into other islands of the Antilles. Expeditions embarked from St. Lucia for St. Vincent, Grenada, and Martinique to join with revolutionary forces in those islands in their common cause of liberation. The British could hardly tolerate these military losses for long, and in 1796 an invasion fleet with 12,000 men moved on St. Lucia, which had been out of British hands for more than a year. Again they moved toward the symbol of military control of the island, the fortress on Morne Fortune above Castries. Converging on the promentory, they were engaged by the revolutionary army which had liberated the island. In the ensuing struggle, both sides battled fiercely for the fortress; the blacks, outnumbered more than five to one, resisted the superior force for a month. When the British army finally captured the hill and forced the defenders to surrender, it did not mark the end of resistance, for some of the blacks again took to the interior where they fought a guerrilla campaign for over a year. The storming of the Morne did, however, signal the end of a period of freedom for St. Lucian blacks, a condition they would not achieve again for over forty years. Today many remnants and edifices mark the many struggles for control of the Morne Fortune and, ultimately, control of the island. Some bear plaques and some are noted in guidebooks, while others are merely piles of debris, the importance of which has gone unremarked. An exception is a column erected in 1932 to commemorate the event of the capture of the hill described above. An inscription on the stone reads:

> On the 24th May, 1796, the 27th. Regt. stormed and captured Morne Fortune. As a mark of the Regiment's gallent conduct Sir Ralph Abercrombie ordered the French garrison to lay down their arms to the 27th. Regt. and directed that the King's colour of the 27th. Regt. be hoisted at the fort for 1 hour prior to the hoisting of the Union Flag.

The continued recognition of this event in the form of an annual ceremony attended by members of the St. Lucia Police Force is symbolic of the kind of irony that has become a part of the blacks' popular expression of their histories. This kind of self-mockery ought not to escape a people engaged in the reinterpretation of their own history. Perhaps it is best summed up in the words of a St. Lucian who has written: "Today we have a monument to mark this reintroduction of slavery in St. Lucia. Black officials pay tribute to it. It may perhaps be a demonstration of the native irony of our people. On the other hand it can be looked upon as an insult to Black people."[55]

A particular image of Jamaican society and the relationships it has engendered among its sectors has prevailed for well over a century. This image grew directly out of the tandem institutions of plantation agriculture and African slavery. Since emancipation in 1838, it has been held up to mirror a society which, through official channels, has sought to foster a public model of progress in the achievement of egalitarian ideals and interracial harmony. The counterversion that has occupied a continual place in the minds of most Jamaicans, and that has repeatedly been invoked in the numerous popular movements of self-liberation and expression, is at considerable variance from that of the racial paradise.

Briefly stated, Jamaican society is portrayed as rigidly divided between exploiter and exploited, between oppressor and oppressed, opposed categories that correspond with the racial opposition between white and black in the society.[56] Thus, the position blacks in Jamaica have occupied through time is directly analogous to that defined during slavery. This image has often been characterized in biblical terms: the island is seen as a Babylon for the blacks. Most political movements have emphasized the image and have claimed to seek its resolution.[57] The proposed solutions have ranged from that of socialist revolution to an apocalyptic cleansing to "evolution not revolution." Nonetheless, the image has remained, capitalized upon by politicians seeking votes and employed by large numbers of Jamaicans in interpreting their society and its history. The brief portraits that follow examine examples of this persistence, how the image has been reinforced, and how people have acted upon it.

1831: The "Baptist War."[58] In 1831, the island, after more than two centuries of slavery and associated acts of resistance, erupted in what became the largest rebellion during the pre-emancipation era. Despite the fact that these events marked the culmination of the nineteenth-century trend toward the acceleration of resistance and rebellion, and that the intention of the 1831 action was to involve all of the slaves of the island, there was initially little violence except the burning of several estates in the western parishes. The response of the authorities operating through the militia was immediate and overwhelming. During the next fortnight, the retribution heaped upon slaves through outright killing and subsequent executions left over 500 dead.

In examining the underlying factors leading to this rebellion, writers have stressed the importance of the Baptist missionary movement and its activities among the slaves which involved discussions of human rights and the emancipation debates in England.[59] The division in the society is expressed in more than ecclesiastical terms, however, for as Patterson notes, the slaves in their response to the missionizing influence had Africanized the Baptist faith that was being offered them.[60] It was this syncretic process that gave rise to the religious movement known as "Native Baptists." This development represents more than just a curiosity for students of acculturative processes, for, as Patterson suggests, "Among those of the non-white population who developed a genuine interest in Christianity, religion became inseparably linked with social status *and political action*."[61] [My emphasis.] Thus, the "Baptist War" was actually a struggle that was underlined by the most fundamental structural, racial, and cultural divisions in the society.

1865: Morant Bay. The series of events leading to the Morant Bay Rebellion in 1865 have been the subject of much debate and printed controversy, much of which revolves around the governor of the period, John Eyre. This is unfortunate, for a discussion focusing on the character and deeds of an individual tends to obscure an understanding of how these events reflect the relationships and recurrent actions that have long characterized Jamaican society.

In the quarter century following emancipation and the end of the apprenticeship period in 1838, the society and economy of Jamaica underwent some profound, if impermanent, changes. The decline in sugar production and the abandonment of estates were complemented by a dramatic rise in the number of independent smallholders and the production of foodstuffs for subsistence and local markets. The abundant indications of the growth of a resourceful, independent peasantry constituted an ominous sign for the oligarchic element that had held the reins of economic and political power in the island during much of its colonial history.[62]

The prosperity depicted here, that of smallholders released from bondage and managing through initiative and hard work, is not the kind of prosperity that the historical accounts of the area have portrayed. Moreover, in view of the continual decline of sugar and the abandonment of estates, it was not the kind of prosperity the Jamaican government was to allow to continue. By the early 1860s, the rising prosperity of the peasantry had been reversed; the government had levied taxes with a view to driving labor back to the plantations and had succeeded in creating a desperate situation for many Jamaicans. The government's wretched treatment of the smallholders was noted by E. B. Underhill who sounded a warning after a visit to the island in 1860. He mentioned particularly the heavy taxation, absence of justice, and denial of political rights as conditions making life unbearable for the peasantry.[63]

With this situation as a backdrop, the rebellion at Morant Bay took place in October 1865. After a confrontation between police and residents of the parish concerning the release of prisoners, violence broke out and a number of people, including some policemen, magistrates, and the *Custos* or local administrator, were killed. Retribution by the government under orders of Governor John Eyre was devastating. The number of dead after a two-week siege is unknown, but over

400 were executed with or without trial and more than 1,000 houses and properties were destroyed in the parish of St. Thomas in the East.[64]

Two aspects of the event, the actions leading up to it and its aftermath, particularly concern us here. First, the conditions that confronted the peasantry were made known to those who had the power and the responsibility to act on their behalf. Their impossible situation was regarded as totally inconsiderable by that sector of the society charged with maintaining the public good.[65] Second, a small incident, confined to a single parish, was dealt with as if it were an all-out attack on the foundations of the society; the governor's action, with subsequent acquiescence by most of the Jamaican establishment, was intended to demonstrate where the locus of power lay.

Marcus Garvey in Jamaica.[66] Despite the persistence of an official version which has repeatedly suggested progress and growth in Jamaican society, the relationships between population segments during the immediate postslavery period underwent very little change until Marcus Garvey appeared in the public life of the island. The Jamaica of 1915 is described in dismal terms by Brown: "Although seventy-eight years have passed since the total abolition of slavery, however, the condition of laborers in Jamaica remains practically the same as it was then." He characterizes the laborer's position as "still an economic slave."[67]

This is the society into which Garvey was born and grew to young manhood, one in which the lot of most people of similar origins was fundamentally unchanged, despite the introduction of "stable government" following the Morant Bay massacres in 1865. Two brief periods of Garvey's career when he was resident on the island are examined here, and his reception and treatment by the custodians of power in the society in each instance are contrasted. The two periods are from 1914 to 1916, when Garvey was active in pan-African efforts in Jamaica before departing for the United States, and from 1927 to 1934, after his deportation from the United States.

The first period was a time of intense effort and creativity for Garvey, during which he founded and widely publicized the aims of the United Negro Improvement Association. This activity followed Garvey's odyssey which had brought him into contact first with black workers throughout the Caribbean and next with continental and African advocates of the pan-African ideal in London. His zeal and dedication to the task of forming an international association for the expression of African solidarity and the uplift of black peoples elicited curiously divided responses in his native island. He reported some cooperation from influential white officialdom and clergy and disdain from the Jamaican colored middle class for whom any hint of an African connection was anathema. His decision to quit Jamaica for the United States was not the result of abject failure of his efforts, but rather stemmed from his realization of the importance of directing such a movement from a central, powerful nation like the United States, which had the largest black population in the Western Hemisphere.[68]

The second period was marked by a somewhat different response to Garvey as an individual and to his pan-African efforts. In 1927, he had returned to Jamaica, no longer a bright, if untried, young man initiating an ideal, but the persecuted leader of the largest black mass movement in history, branded by the establishment press and government of the United States as a dangerous (if only because demented) figure. His reputation as a danger to the established order followed him to Jamaica and gave his opposition an excuse to frustrate his efforts over the next seven years.[69] This time, however, it was the Jamaican colonial establishment which continually attempted to hamstring Garvey's operations. The colored sector of the population may still have been queasy about an identification with blackness or Africa, but Garvey's essential problem was that he *was* a threat. By then, through word and accomplishment he represented a decided contradiction to the underlying assumptions on which Jamaican society was based.

Labor Unrest and the Modern Political Era. The labor riots that occurred in the West Indies in the late 1930s had more direct political effect in Jamaica than elsewhere.[70] The 1938 riots again provoked a massive display of force by the colonial government, even as they demonstrated once again the correctness of all those reports of successive Royal commissions which had cautiously suggested that all was not well on the Jamaican labor scene. At this juncture, however, the stage was set for the emergence of a new political force: the urbanite, middle-class labor leader and/or lawyer who, representative of a growing city-based collectivity and supported at the polls by an expanded electorate, came to power throughout the islands. As an immediate consequence of the 1938 disturbances, two men, through their personalities and political organizations, came to dominate Jamaica's electoral politics over the next quarter century.

The institution of a universal adult franchise in 1944 set the stage for the rise of Alexander Bustamante and Norman Manley to power in Jamaican electoral politics.[71] Bustamante, in particular, employed some of the same tactics of mass appeal that others had before him, some of whom had arrived too early to capitalize on the new expanded electorate and others who had chosen other avenues. But the two leaders and their political parties formed the movement of the time; they shared mass support of the electorate; and they were the vanguard of the organized labor movement. The promise for changing the society was there in their rhetoric and their presence. Yet, twenty-five years after the riots both men had grown old. Whatever dreams they had had they had compromised, and the promises for societal transformation had faded. The "new day" many had envisioned had not become a reality.

A preoccupation with personalities can frequently impede the writing of history and the analysis of political developments, particularly when these personalities are still living or their memories remain fresh. The examination of Jamaican progress in the years following the 1938 riots and the institution of universal suffrage provides a case in point of this kind of obscurant analysis. Lewis, in drawing comparisons between personalities, suggests that Garvey would have had the same fortune with an expanded electorate as Bustamante, but that "the development of modern Jamaica might have been fundamentally different," presumably in the direction of a fundamental transformation of the society.[72] Manley's biographer, on the other hand, indicates the singular achievements of his subject and lays the blame for Jamaica's and the West Indies' retarded political maturity on the pettiness of others.[73] Both of these approaches are misplaced.

Lately, the standard for studies of recent political and social change has risen with the publication of a series of monographs by social scientists resident in and committed to the area. In the case of Jamaica, this trend is exemplified by Trevor Munroe's analysis of the island's political life in the modern era.[74] Proceeding from a picture of the structural situation at the time of the riots and the elections of 1944, Munroe charts events since that time without extensive reference to the character and personal idiosyncrasies of Bustamante and Manley. Rather than demonstrate the importance of their personalities, Munroe concentrates on the nature and interests of those sectors of the society that they came to represent. In this regard, Munroe is able to account for the paucity of structural change generated by these two principal figures and the political battles they waged. His conclusion concerning the role the middle and working classes would have had to play in any societal transformation during this period again illustrates the facile nature of analyses focused on personalities.[75]

The Jamaican Present. The question remains whether Jamaican society has been transformed in the period since World War II. Certainly, much has happened internally and in the larger world that impinges on the life of the island with even greater insistence. But what evidence exists for the alteration of those basic divisions in Jamaican society, repeatedly indicated in the historical events depicted above? To what extent is the image of Jamaican society sketched at the outset still a valid one, and does it remain useful in informing the behavior of the majority of Jamaicans?

A striking example of how patterns of inequality have persisted to the present in Jamaica is evidenced in the following excerpt from a 1962 report on the Jamaican economy to the prime minister. After detailing some "remarkable" characteristics of the previous ten-year period of economic growth, the writer states:

> This proud trend is only marred by the undeniable increase in inequality in the island, despite the efforts of the government. The income in agriculture has hardly increased—the production of food seems to have actually declined. The problems of the small farmer are especially acute, though the extensive and costly Farm Development and Settlement Schemes were directed precisely at the relief of this sector. In the urban scene, too, the share of wages has diminished, while total company profits have increased. Within the wage sector, the discrepancy between the earnings of the skilled workers in the organized trades and the rest have also shown striking increase. While unemployment has been reduced, it remains a grave problem. This increase in inequality might explain, at least partially, the less than complete economic psychological impact of the magnificent economic record of the Government of Jamaica.[76]

The preceding account could not be a better example of tongue-in-cheek irony if it were so intended. Its obvious message is that the negative aspects of the economic picture most directly affect the well-being of the overwhelming majority of the population, rural smallholders, and the urban unskilled. Thus, despite the modern growth of the Jamaican economy, the same sectors of the labor force that have contributed work out of proportion to their rewards in the past remain outside the benefits accruing from this remarkable growth. What is more, it is precisely the area of the traditional basis of the economy, the sugar industry, where modernization is phasing out workers who for generations have maintained and have depended upon the plantation.[77] There is ample indication that the industry, itself symbolic of the divisions in the society, remains incapable of self-examination, still demanding special privilege in the economy, and still unresponsive to assertions of workers' rights.[78]

Today, then, much in the structure of Jamaican society represents a continuation of basic, long-standing schisms. The emergence of the Rastafarians as exemplifying a spiritual mirror to catch the reflection of this society and the widespread appeal of the cultural aspects of this movement are indicative of the continued currency of the image. The startling fact is that the seriousness of the situation has not mitigated the manipulation of images by contemporary politicians, a situation reminiscent of that which followed the 1938 unrest.[79] These politicians recognize that these trends in Jamaican self-recognition are serious, but whether they will formulate programs commensurate with the gravity of the situation remains an unanswered question.

Nonetheless, there are now a few realities that the Jamaican power elites can ill afford to ignore. The image of the society depicted in Rastafarian dogma and implicit in the actions of Jamaicans for over a century now seems to have much greater popular support than in the recent past.[80] Moreover, many young, educated Jamaicans espouse this characterization, and all the more firmly as a result of the repressive actions of recent governments. Finally, it is an image which informs political action; it has done so in the past and, unless important changes are effected, it will do so in the future.

Conclusion: Symbols and Identity

The discussion of literature in this essay surveys a few directions West Indian writers have already charted and suggests others that have only been minimally explored. While it is difficult to predict the future course of creative endeavor, two related trends may eventually alter the relationship between the artist and the West Indian public. First, younger intellectuals and artists are now remaining in the islands or are returning after brief periods abroad rather than maintaining an expatriate existence as so many did in the past. Whether this trend will continue obviously depends partly on the growth of a local readership.

Closely linked with this trend is the second, the enthusiasm of younger writers for poetry and their use of the language of the masses. This trend is an important one, for poetry lends itself, much more than prose, to performance; thus, the artist can be assured a wider audience and the influence that the written word has historically had in West Indian society.

In sum, West Indian writers have often sought to define an identity for their people, not so much in a patriotic or historical sense as in an attempt to explore (1) the relationship of the individual to the natural environment, (2) racial identity, and (3) an acceptance, if less than exhaltation, of indigenous cultural forms. Mazrui has noted the tendency of African writers to move beyond the patriotic themes evoked during nationalistic struggles to dealing with "postnational" issues.[81] Whereas writers of the earlier period emphasized the African/European contrasts in an effort to celebrate indigenous forms, the more recent trend is self-critical and focuses on topics such as postcolonial political corruption. In contrast, much of West Indian literature has never had to under go this transition, for it has contained an element of self-criticism from its inception. This literature expresses great awareness of the subtleties and complexities of the social patterns of the islands. As such, it has underscored the absurdities of color and class distinctions, along with their destructive ramifications, with as much alacrity as it has condemned the role of the European colonizer as an historical and social malignancy.

The discussion of the events of the late eighteenth century in the Eastern Caribbean suggests the possibilities that historical information can be reinterpreted to serve West Indian self-interest. Reinterpretation of the historical data is needed not only to better serve propagandistic interests of nationalistic movements, but also for its scholarly value. The earlier accounts, bound by Euro-centric interpretation, are inimical to regional self-pride, and in addition are frequently inaccurate or misinformed. Application of a West Indian perspective can help correct erroneous misconceptions and can contribute to a fuller historical understanding of the region.

The question with which the writer of Jamaican history—and perhaps of all West Indian history as well—must concern himself is whether the popular image of Jamaican social life is correct. This is not to say that it may be verifiable by historical evidence on every count but rather whether the popular image is a view which, taken into consideration, might more fully inform the historian. Can it be that black Jamaicans have had a better informed view of social and political realities than have some of the scholars who have sought to interpret the historical evidence?

This view is also related to nationalistic symbols. If Paul Bogle has been elevated to the status of national hero on the basis that he was simply an individual who opposed an inept and cruel governor, Edward John Eyre, then the symbol is ephemeral, amounting to little more than recognition of an interesting historical event over which much ado was made in England.

If, on the other hand, Bogle is seen as symbolic of the oppression of black people and the event of Morant Bay as epitomizing the profound historical divisions in Jamaican society, then the symbol of the national hero has a decidedly different character. If Jamaicans come to view their history in those terms, the results may be a strengthened national identity and an informed revolutionary nationalism as well.

Mazrui writes of five processes fundamental to nation-building: cultural fusion, economic interpenetration, social integration, conflict resolution, and shared national experience.[82] Since this essay on West Indian history and literature has not specifically addressed economic and political issues, the processes of economic interpenetration and conflict resolution are of little concern here. The other three processes are more pertinent to our discussion, however. The creation of literature and the interpretation of historical experience are both directly concerned with these issues; they may contribute to and inform action designed toward these processes as ends.

One of these processes may bear a somewhat different relationship to the work of writers and historians. The achievement of social integration, the "process by which gaps between the elite and the masses, the town and the countryside, the privileged and the underprivileged, are gradually narrowed,"[83] may not be positively related to the efforts described above. With regard to the discussion of historical events in Jamaica, the direction in which some historical interpretation may influence this process seems questionable. A tendency—whether in literature or the writing of history—to throw into sharper focus the divisions of the society may, at least in the short run, exacerbate the conflict and the gaps between collectivities who see their interests as opposed.

Writers of literature and history can help a people to achieve cultural fusion and positive self-definition. Specifically, in the West Indian situation, they can help the people to see themselves as more than mere adjuncts to the history of other nations and to realize that their cultural tradition is not stunted and derivative. In turn, these achievements can lead to the kind of collective introspection from which a heightened sense of peoplehood can emerge. While the question of whether history is shaped through the actions of the masses or through the thoughts of the intellectuals is moot, it seems that if the West Indian renewal Walcott envisions is possible, the contribution of writers and historians toward cultural fusion and positive self-definition must be sustained and continually experimental.

Notes

1. This essay is largely part of my continuing study of matters of identity among black people in the Caribbean and in Great Britain. Any insights that may be found here are attributable to conversations with many people, most importantly John Stewart in Illinois, George Odlum and Fergus Lawrence in St. Lucia, and John La Rose in London; persisting blind spots are my responsibility. The use of the terms *West Indies* and *West Indian* refers

to that part of the Caribbean archipelago that was under the recent colonial domination of Great Britain.

2. Derek Walcott, "The Caribbean: Culture or Mimicry?" *Journal of Interamerican Studies and World Affairs* 16 (1974):13.

3. A full background to the issues and problems of the contemporary West Indies may be found in the introductory chapters of two excellent general works on the region. See Gordon K. Lewis, *The Growth of the Modern West Indies* (London: MacGibbon and Kee, 1968), pp. 15–68; and David Lowenthal, *West Indian Societies* (London: Oxford University Press, 1972), pp. 1–75.

4. Lewis, *The Growth*, p. 18.

5. Ali A. Mazrui, *Cultural Engineering and Nation-Building in East Africa* (Evanston, Ill.: Northwestern University Press, 1972).

6. Mazrui, *Cultural Engineering*, p. xv.

7. Ibid., p. 23.

8. Derek Walcott, "Tales of the Islands, Chapter X," in *In a Green Night* (London: Jonathan Cape, 1962), p. 30.

9. Gerald Moore, *The Chosen Tongue* (London: Longmans, 1969), pp. 20–26.

10. See Walcott, "Return to D'Ennery, Rain," in *In a Green Night*, pp. 33–34; idem, "Homecoming: Anse La Raye," in *The Gulf* (London: Jonathan Cape, 1969), pp. 50–51; idem, *Another Life* (New York: Farrar, Straus, and Giroux, 1973), pp. 32–38.

11. The three plays mentioned are collected in a volume, *Dream on Monkey Mountain and Other Plays* (New York: Farrar, Straus, and Giroux, 1970).

12. George Lamming, *In the Castle of My Skin* (London: Michael Joseph, 1953).

13. Michael Anthony, *The Year in San Fernando* (London: Andre Deutsch, 1965) and idem, *Green Days by the River* (London: Andre Deutsch, 1967).

14. Dennis Scott, "Homecoming," in *Uncle Time* (Pittsburgh: University of Pittsburgh Press, 1973), p. 8.

15. In a recent publication, Edward Brathwaite pursues the topic of Africa in Caribbean writing in much greater depth. The interested reader is advised to consult his "The African Presence in Caribbean Literature," *Daedelus* 103, no. 2 (1974):73–109.

16. Lamming, *Season of Adventure* (London: Michael Joseph, 1960).

17. Kenneth Ramchand, *The West Indian Novel and Its Background* (London: Faber and Faber, 1970), p. 149. As noted above, a thematic approach necessarily results in some distortion of the purposes of a writer, a suggestion that seems most justified with respect to the work of Lamming. Because his writing is so many-faceted, and because he is working with ideas at different levels of reality and consciousness, his work is often misrepresented by critics. A contrast, however, is the fine insight into his art given in an interview with George Kent. See Kent, "A Conversation with George Lamming," *Black World* 22, no. 5 (1973):4–15, 88–97.

18. Walcott, *Monkey Mountain*, pp. 308–320.

19. Walcott, *Ione* (Mona, Jamaica: Extra-mural Department, University College of the West Indies, 1953).

20. Walcott, "A Far Cry from Africa," in *In a Green Night*, p. 18.

21. Brathwaite, *Rights of Passage* (London: Oxford University Press, 1967); idem, *Masks* (London: Oxford University Press, 1968); and idem, *Islands* (London: Oxford University Press, 1969).

22. Brathwaite, "Epilogue," in *Rights of Passage*, p. 86.

23. See V. S. Naipaul, *The Middle Passage* (London: Andre Deutsch, 1962) and idem, *The Overcrowded Barracoon* (London: Andre Deutsch, 1972).

24. Brathwaite, "All God's Chillun," in *Rights of Passage*, pp. 16–20.

25. Walcott, in *Monkey Mountain*, pp. 81–166.

26. V. S. Reid, *New Day* (New York: Knopf, 1949).

27. For examples of recent trends in poetry, see Andrew Salkey, ed., *Breaklight* (Garden City, N.Y.: Anchor/Doubleday, 1973) and *Savacou*, no. 3/4 (1970/1971).

28. Roger Mais, *The Hills Were Joyful Together* (London: Jonathan Cape, 1953), and idem, *Brother Man* (London: Jonathan Cape, 1954). These two are now collected along with a third novel in *Three Novels* (London: Jonathan Cape, 1966).

29. Orlando Patterson, *The Children of Sisyphus* (London: New Authors, 1964).

30. V. S. Naipaul, *The Mimic Men* (London: Andre Deutsch, 1967).

31. Garth St. Omer, *Nor Any Country* (London: Faber and Faber, 1969), pp. 104–105.

32. Andrew Salkey, *The Late Emancipation of Jerry Stover* (London: Hutchinson, 1968).

33. John Stewart, *Last Cool Days* (London: Andre Deutsch, 1970).

34. Lamming, *In the Castle*, p. 295.

35. For discussions of the use of language in West Indian writing, see Moore, *The Chosen Tongue*, pp. xviii–xx, and Ramchand, *West Indian Novel*, pp. 77–114.

36. There is a problem of readership here because lexically patois is of mostly French derivation. For treatments of the language, see Mervin Alleyne, "Language and Society in St. Lucia," *Caribbean Studies* 1 (1961):1–10, and Douglas Midgett, "Bilingualism and Linguistic Change in St. Lucia," *Anthropological Linguistics* 12 (1970):158–170.

37. St. Omer, *Syrop*, in *Introduction 2: Stories by New Writers* (London: Faber and Faber, 1964). For another example of the alterations the writer must make to accommodate his work to a larger audience, compare Walcott's *The Sea at Dauphin*, collected in *Monkey Mountain*, with an earlier version (Mona, Jamaica: Extra-mural Department, University College of the West Indies, 1958).

38. Reid, *New Day*.

39. *Savacou*, no. 3/4 (1970/1971).

40. The particularistic-universalistic controversy is characteristic of black American literature as well. This is not surprising considering that literature is used as a vehicle for self-assertion and for the definition of community. Interestingly, metropolitan critics in both the United States and Great Britain are perfectly happy with black writers who employ universalistic themes as long as they stick to parochial settings in black America and the islands. The paradox of the writer seems to be that, to achieve critical acclaim, the topics he chooses and his approach to them must not confuse the critic, and at the same time he must not become overly ambitious and overextend to areas with which he is not familiar. Understandably, many writers in both areas have chosen to ignore the critics altogether, and the result has been a growing indigenous literary criticism. Examples are Ramchand, *West Indian Novel*; Wilfred Carty, *Black Images* (New York: Teachers College Press, 1970); Louis James, ed., *The Islands in Between* (London: Oxford University Press, 1968); John La Rose, ed., *New Beacon Reviews Collection One* (London: New Beacon Books, 1968); Sylvia Wynter, "One Love—Rhetoric or Reality?—Aspects of Afro-Jamaicanism," *Caribbean Studies* 12 (1972):64–97; and a number of articles by Gordon Rohlehr.

41. Mazrui, *Cultural Engineering*, pp. 3–22.

42. Ibid., pp. 14–16.

43. W. Adolph Roberts, *The French in the West Indies* (New York: Bobbs Merrill, 1942), pp. 223–232.

44. See Eric Williams, *British Historians and the West Indies* (New York: Scribner's, 1966), especially Chapter 5.

45. Sir Alan Burns, *History of the British West Indies* (London: Allen & Unwin, 1954), p. 542. Under the subheading "The War in the Lesser Antilles," Burns repeatedly characterizes the opposing forces in terms of "British" and "French."

46. Roberts, *The French*, p. 229.

47. Brian Edwards, *The History, Civil and Commercial of the British Colonies in the West Indies*, 2 vols. (London: John Stockdale, 1807), vol. 2, 470–474.

48. Burns, *West Indies*, p. 567.

49. B. H. Easter, *St. Lucia and the French Revolution* (Castries: The Voice Publishing Co., 1965), pp. 10, 11.

50. Alec Waugh, *A Family of Islands* (New York: Doubleday, 1964), p. 205.

51. Burns, *West Indies*, p. 568; Waugh, *Family of Islands*, p. 211.

52. Rev. Charles Jesse, *Outlines of St. Lucia's History* (Castries: St. Lucia Archaeological and Historical Society, 1964), p. 24.

53. Henry H. Breen, *St. Lucia: Historical, Statistical and Descriptive* (London: Cass, 1970), p. 74. (Original printing, 1844.)

54. Ibid., p. 78.

55. Hilford Deterville, "The Liberation of Black St. Lucians," *The Crusader* (Castries), May 24, 1970, p. 11.

56. Sociologically, Jamaica is not a two-category racial system. This consideration, however, is beside the point of the characterization elaborated here since all that has been written of color-class continua and "social color" frequently glosses the fact that in Jamaica most black people are poor and most poor people are black.

57. This biblical imagery appears not only in the characterization of Jamaican society by Rastafarians or by vote-seeking politicians but in the popular realm as well. In *New Day*, V. S. Reid depicts George William Gordon exhorting a congregation with lines from the 137th Psalm, the "Rivers of Babylon" Psalm (p. 27).

58. This section is compiled primarily from accounts by Orlando Patterson, *The Sociology of Slavery* (London: MacGibbon and Kee, 1967), pp. 272–282; Mary Reckord, "The Jamaican Slave Rebellion of 1831," in R. Frucht, ed., *Black Society in the New World* (New York: Random House, 1971), pp. 50–66; and Philip Curtin, *Two Jamaicas* (Cambridge, Mass.: Harvard University Press, 1955), pp. 82–89.

59. Curtin, *Two Jamaicas*, pp. 83–84.

60. Patterson, *Sociology of Slavery*, pp. 211–212.

61. Ibid., p. 213.

62. Eric Williams, *British Historians*, pp. 87–88.

63. Quoted in ibid., pp. 102–105.

64. The events of Morant Bay are variously reported in a number of sources, including Williams, *British Historians*, pp. 117–126; Curtin, *Two Jamaicas*, pp. 195–197; and Douglas Hall, *Free Jamaica 1838–1865* (New Haven: Yale University Press, 1959), pp. 245–248.

65. An example of indifference at the highest level is the "Queen's Advice," quoted in Hall, *Free Jamaica*, pp. 244–245.

66. Garvey's career, his writings, and his political philosophy have been the subject of numerous studies. The interested reader is particularly urged to consult Amy Jacques-

Garvey, *Garvey and Garveyism* (London: Collier-Macmillan, 1970) and John Henrik Clarke, *Marcus Garvey and the Vision of Africa* (New York: Vintage, 1974). Much of the material in this section is drawn from these sources.

67. E. Ethelred Brown, "Labor Conditions in Jamaica Prior to 1917," *Journal of Negro History* 4 (1919):351.

68. Clarke, *Marcus Garvey,* pp. 49–70.

69. Ibid., pp. 259–264, 276–283.

70. K. W. J. Post, "The Politics of Protest in Jamaica, 1938: Some Problems of Analysis and Conceptualization," *Social and Economic Studies* 18 (1969):375.

71. For more elaboration of this period and the politics and political organizations of Bustamante and Manley, see Post, "Politics of Protest"; Trevor Munroe, *The Politics of Constitutional Decolonization* (Mona, Jamaica: Institute of Social and Economic Research, University of the West Indies, 1972); and Rex Nettleford, ed., *Manley and the New Jamaica* (New York: Africana Publishing Corp., 1971).

72. Lewis, *The Growth,* pp. 177–178. The suggestion that Garvey may have had the political success of Bustamante confuses tactics with programs. I have already indicated that Garvey's problems in Jamaica after 1927 resulted from the implications of his proposed programs for profound changes in that society. It is therefore questionable how much success he might have been able to achieve at a later time.

73. Nettleford, *Manley and Jamaica,* pp. lxxxii–xciv.

74. Munroe, *Constitutional Decolonization.*

75. Ibid., p. 190.

76. Thomas Balogh, *The Economics of Poverty* (New York: Macmillan, 1966), pp. 293–294.

77. See, for example, the account of "Mitchell Town" in L. Alan Eyre, *Geographic Aspects of Population Dynamics in Jamaica* (Boca Raton, Fla.: Florida Atlantic University Press, 1972), pp. 101–119.

78. An examination of the "Symposium on Sugar and Change in the Caribbean" is instructive in this regard. See *New World Quarterly* 5 (1969):32–57.

79. Electioneering in the 1972 campaign provides a current example. See W. Richard Jacobs, "Appeals by Jamaican Political Parties: A Study of Newspaper Advertisements in the 1972 Jamaican General Election Campaign," *Caribbean Studies* 13 (1973):19–50.

80. A rather dramatic example is the success of Michael Manley's 1972 election campaign. The use of Rasta-tinged rhetoric, the identification with the "sufferers," and the employment of reggae music and other cultural aspects particularly associated with Kingston's urban poor cast Manley's campaign in sharp contrast to that of his opponent. See also Rex Nettleford, *Mirror, Mirror: Identity, Race and Protest in Jamaica* (Kingston: W. Collins and Sangster, 1970), pp. 39–111.

81. Mazrui, *Cultural Engineering,* pp. 36–37.

82. Ibid., pp. 277–293.

83. Ibid., p. 277.

References

Alleyne, Mervin. 1961. "Language and Society in St. Lucia," Caribbean Studies 1:1–10.
Anthony, Michael. 1965. The Year in San Fernando. London: Andre Deutsch.

————. 1967. Green Days by the River. London: Andre Deutsch.

Balogh, Thomas. 1966. The Economics of Poverty. New York: Macmillan.

Brathwaite, Edward. 1967. Rights of Passage. London: Oxford University Press.

————. 1968. Masks. London: Oxford University Press.

————. 1969. Islands. London: Oxford University Press.

————. 1974. "The African Presence in Caribbean Literature," Daedelus 103, no. 2: 73–109.

Breen, Henry H. 1970. St. Lucia: Historical, Statistical and Descriptive. London: Cass. (Original edition, 1844.)

Brown, E. Ethelred. 1919. "Labor Conditions in Jamaica Prior to 1917," Journal of Negro History 4:349–360.

Burns, Sir Alan. 1954. History of the British West Indies. London: Allen & Unwin.

Carty, Wilfred. 1970. Black Images. New York: Teachers College Press.

Clarke, John Henrik. 1974. Marcus Garvey and the Vision of Africa. New York: Vintage.

Curtin, Philip. 1955. Two Jamaicas. Cambridge, Mass.: Harvard University Press.

Deterville, Hilford. 1970. "The Liberation of Black St. Lucians," The Crusader, May 24.

Easter, B. H. 1965. St. Lucia and the French Revolution. Castries: The Voice Publishing Co.

Edwards, Brian. 1807. The History, Civil and Commercial of the British Colonies in the West Indies. Vol. 2. London: John Stockdale.

Eyre, L. Alan. 1972. Geographic Aspects of Population Dynamics in Jamaica. Boca Raton, Fla.: Florida Atlantic University Press.

Hall, Douglas. 1959. Free Jamaica 1838–1865. New Haven: Yale University Press.

Jacobs, W. Richard. 1973. "Appeals by Jamaican Political Parties: A Study of Newspaper Advertisements in the 1972 Jamaican General Election Campaign," Caribbean Studies 13:19–50.

Jacques-Garvey, Amy. 1970. Garvey and Garveyism. London: Collier-Macmillan.

James, Louis (ed.). 1968. The Islands in Between. London: Oxford University Press.

Jesse, Rev. Charles. 1964. Outlines of St. Lucia's History. Castries: St. Lucia Archaeological and Historical Society.

Kent, George. 1973. "A Conversation with George Lamming," Black World 22, no. 5: 4–15, 88–97.

Lamming, George. 1953. In the Castle of My Skin. London: Michael Joseph.

————. 1960. Season of Adventure. London: Michael Joseph.

La Rose, John (ed.). 1968. New Beacon Reviews Collection One. London: New Beacon Books.

Lewis, Gordon K. 1968. The Growth of the Modern West Indies. London: MacGibbon and Kee.

Lowenthal, David. 1972. West Indian Societies. London: Oxford University Press.

Mais, Roger. 1953. The Hills Were Joyful Together. London: Jonathan Cape.

————. 1954. Brother Man. London: Jonathan Cape.

————. 1966. Three Novels. London: Jonathan Cape.

Mazrui, Ali A. 1972. Cultural Engineering and Nation-Building in East Africa. Evanston, Ill.: Northwestern University Press.

Midgett, Douglas. 1970. "Bilingualism and Linguistic Change in St. Lucia," Anthropological Linguistics 12:158–170.

Moore, Gerald. 1969. The Chosen Tongue. London: Longmans.

Munroe, Trevor. 1972. The Politics of Constitutional Decolonization. Mona, Jamaica:
    Institute of Social and Economic Research, University of the West Indies.
Naipaul, V. S. 1962. The Middle Passage. London: Andre Deutsch.
——. 1967. The Mimic Men. London: Andre Deutsch.
——. 1972. The Overcrowded Barracoon. London: Andre Deutsch.
Nettleford, Rex. 1970. Mirror, Mirror: Identity, Race and Protest in Jamaica. Kingston:
    W. Collins and Sangster.
Nettleford, Rex (ed.). 1971. Manley and the New Jamaica. New York: Africana Publish-
    ing Corp.
New World Quarterly. 1969. "Symposium on Sugar and Change in the Caribbean,"
    vol. 5:32–57.
Patterson, Orlando. 1964. The Children of Sisyphus. London: New Authors.
——. 1967. The Sociology of Slavery. London: MacGibbon and Kee.
Post, K. W. J. 1969. "The Politics of Protest in Jamaica, 1938: Some Problems of Analy-
    sis and Conceptualization," Social and Economic Studies 18:374–390.
Ramchand, Kenneth. 1970. The West Indian Novel and Its Background. London:
    Faber and Faber.
Reckord, Mary. 1971. "The Jamaican Slave Rebellion of 1831," in R. Frucht, ed., Black
    Society in the New World. New York: Random House.
Reid, V. S. 1949. New Day. New York: Knopf.
Roberts, W. Adolph. 1942. The French in the West Indies. New York: Bobbs Merrill.
St. Omer, Garth. 1964. "Syrop," in Introduction 2: Stories by New Writers. London:
    Faber and Faber.
——. 1969. Nor Any Country. London: Faber and Faber.
Salkey, Andrew. 1968. The Late Emancipation of Jerry Stover. London: Hutchinson.
Salkey, Andrew (ed.). 1973. Breaklight. Garden City, N.Y.: Anchor/Doubleday.
Savacou. 1970/1971. Special issue, no. 3/4.
Scott, Dennis. 1973. Uncle Time. Pittsburgh: University of Pittsburgh Press.
Stewart, John. 1970. Last Cool Days. London: Andre Deutsch.
Walcott, Derek. 1953. Ione. Mona, Jamaica: Extra-mural Department, University Col-
    lege of the West Indies.
——. 1958. The Sea at Dauphin. Mona, Jamaica: Extra-mural Department, Univer-
    sity College of the West Indies.
——. 1962. In a Green Night. London: Jonathan Cape.
——. 1969. The Gulf. London: Jonathan Cape.
——. 1970. Dream on Monkey Mountain and Other Plays. New York: Farrar, Straus,
    and Giroux.
——. 1973. Another Life. New York: Farrar, Straus, and Giroux.
——. 1974. "The Caribbean: Culture or Mimicry?" Journal of Interamerican Studies
    and World Affairs 16:3–13.
Waugh, Alec. 1964. A Family of Islands. New York: Doubleday.
Williams, Eric. 1966. British Historians and the West Indies. New York: Scribner's.
Wynter, Sylvia. 1972. "One Love—Rhetoric or Reality?—Aspects of Afro-Jamaicanism,"
    Caribbean Studies 12:64–97.

12. STICK SONG

John Stewart

The early swarm of fireflies was over: only a few darting stragglers were still abroad, winking the solid darkness that stretched and rolled away behind the houses. At a dip in the road they could hear dogs barking from the village on the next hill over. Then drums and voices.

The drums were thick, low, a distant rumble across the quiet valley. The voices were not sweet, yet even at a distance the stick-song chorus made Daaga's skin shiver. For a moment it was like being in a dome with only the drums and naked voices reflecting, and in Daaga an elemental stir to dance erupted despite his nagging fear of dancing: his fear of the feelings stirred and their potential power over him.

He had not heard such music in eight years. He had learned to thrive on the subtleties of Miles Davis, Max Roach; had been many times over stirred by Coltrane and Elvin Jones, but not this way. He had thrown rocks at armed policemen; and armed himself with a new name, a new awareness of his historic enormity he had returned to teach, to awaken the peasant mind from which he had once sought deliverance. Awaken it to its own dormant power.

But did he really know better than them the dimensions of that power? Could economic theory, political awareness, a revised history—could any of these overpower a drum beat?

"Them boys beating good keg," Stone said, "but they can't touch we. . . ,"

As the road inclined they could hear the sounds of their village once again, and soon they walked into the tent yard where the men were practicing for carnival. A general noise and bustle blocked out George Village, blocked out the night. Another dome, this one hearty and self-contained, without echo.

"Ah ah, so you come!" the carpenter shuffled forward short and supple, big veins cording his arms and forehead, his face gleaming an enormous smile. So you come! As if some subtle travail by which Daaga was innocently directed had at last succeeded. The carpenter took him by the hand and led him through the thicket of coarse arms, sweat-drenched bodies pressed and humidifying in the electric glare of a naked bulb. Leading him aggressively through the thickened clamor of village men who an hour ago were humble johns or work-wrestled lashleys back-sore and spirit-weary from the unceasing peasant days.

But now!

Originally published in John Stewart, *Curving Road* (Urbana: University of Illinois Press, 1962), pp. 116–28. Reprinted by permission of the author.

Now, as if something had dissolved the cagedness around their reserve, it is exuberance, mettle in their voices, an expansive flash to their eyes. As though they not only knew how heart first came to beat, but were the acknowledged substance of its magic. Who under the glare of this one bulb light fluttered by moths and other forage of the night were boasting, arguing, challenging each other, all the while sharing ritual flasks of mountain dew strong still with the vapor of molasses. Homage to king cane. Which with the scent of herbs crushed down where dancing feet had tramped the yard joined an odor that reached away for Daaga. Faint yet persistent, an odor he must have known in the past, pleasantly.

"Aie, aie," the carpenter was gleeful. "Come, come," he said, tugging Daaga through the crowd. "Aie, Conga Man!" the carpenter called as they burst through to a circular space ringed in by the clamor but itself vacant except for one man.

"Aie, Conga Man!"

And from the center of the ring Conga Man watched them approach without replying. In khaki pants and long white shirt untucked, a cricket cap on backwards over a white headband, he hulked at the center of the ring with his chin propped on the tip of his stick.

"This we king," the carpenter said. And Conga Man affected it. The same who to Daaga had been more formally Robert of two bends down the road, husband, father of seven, workman at the factory—now king. Silently awaiting their approach, eyes steady in his concave black face, and red.

"Look Conga Man, look. Is mi boy. Mi boy come!" the carpenter said.

Then Conga Man pulled himself straight, and smiled. "Well Mr. Daaga, you come to play a little stick?"

Daaga wanted to stop himself from grinning but could not. "Just to watch," he said.

"Well we not having much right now, as you could see," Conga Man said.

"I see," Daaga said, looking around.

There were three drums abandoned on the ground, and though several of the men held sticks, the weave of intercourse was syncopal except for a shouting match or two within clusters for the most part engaged in drinking.

"I tell you he woulda come," the carpenter said. Conga Man smiled, his face nevertheless losing no sense of presence. Like a serpent. "I tell all you," the carpenter continued, "from the first day I see him that he was a gentleman, but that he was one a we. You taking a drink Mr. Daaga?"

"But how you mean if he taking a drink?" Conga Man said, accepting the already proferred flask from the beaming carpenter. He took a little to wash his mouth and spray, then a medium swallow. Daaga accepted the flask and did likewise to the carpenter's glee.

"You drink like one a we, man," the carpenter said . . . "Make my heart feel glad." As he completed the triad.

One drummer had returned and now he rattled his skin a little to call the others.

"So you come back from America," Conga Man said. "They does have stick over there?"

"Naah . . . " Daaga replied.

"This the place where stick born!" the carpenter said, doing a quick kalinda step. "You ever hear of Congo Barra? He born right here. This his grandson." Which Conga Man did not deign to acknowledge.

"They used to have stick in my village too," Daaga said.

"Where that?"

"St. Madeleine."

"Yeah. When I was a little boy we used to have stick there too . . . "

"Yes, I know," the carpenter suddenly becoming wise.

The drum rattled, and someone sang—"When ah dead bury mi clothes . . ." Conga Man, leaning once more on his stick rocked back, closed his eyes and smiled.

"I know," the carpenter said. "I used to have a ladyfriend over there, long time before you born. I know they used to have stick. Your own grandfather brother, he was a tiger. But you 'ent know him. He dead before you born. I know they did have stick there, but that before your time."

"I remember carnival days, and the stick-men singing . . ."

"Bois!" an unexpected voice exploded behind Daaga, and he turned to see tall Mr. Gray dancing before Conga Man, his empty fingers rigid, circling the air like some wrestler's. "Bois!" Mr. Gray lunged at Conga Man, who ducked and came up in time to catch the older man in his arms. The two men embraced and laughed full in each other's faces.

"Gray," the carpenter called, "look Mr. Daaga."

And Gray turned slowly to survey, an unsmiling scrutiny but not unkind. "So. Mr. Daaga you come to pass some time with the boys," he said.

"A little bit."

"I just telling him," the carpenter said. "I just telling him this the place where stick born." And old Gray nodded his head in concurrence, without taking his eyes off Daaga.

"But his grandfather village had one or two good stick-men too, you know."

"Oh yes? Who his grandfather?" Mr. Gray asked.

"Old man Grant, used to pastor that Baptist church outside Usine."

Mr. Gray's eyes narrowed, then his frown relaxed as though he had just solved a problem. "Is so? Boy," he said to Daaga, "you a Grant?"

Daaga smiled. "The old man was my grandfather."

"Who you for—one of his daughters or his son?"

"His son."

"And how you 'ent carrying the name?"

Daaga smiled.

"I've been saying to myself all this time," Mr. Gray announced at large, "I know this man's blood." And back to Daaga, "I used to court one of your tanties, boy."

"He 'ent know 'bout that," the carpenter said. "That before he born." And turning to Daaga asked, "When you went to America Mr. Daaga? What time it was when you leave Trinidad?"

"Nineteen-fifty-eight."

"And you 'ent come back till this year?"

"That's right."

Again the drums rattled, and someone raised "Sergeant Brown calling mi name . . ." but he did not get a chorus. As Mr. Gray returned to scrutinizing.

"Young fella," he finally asked with force, "you know where you get that name?"

To which Daaga smiled, "Sure." Never forgetting how he had self-consciously selected it from the dusty shelves of a North American library, at a time when many like himself had begun to renew, reaffirm, reconstitute the black African in their person. "Sure."

"Hmm," Gray grunted. "Daaga was a hell of a man, you know. Where the bottle?"

"Yes," Daaga said. Wondering however did old unlettered Gray, back villager that he was had come to know anything about the first Daaga.

They drank and Gray went on. "How you get the name, somebody give you or you pick it up yourself?"

"I picked it out," Daaga said. And it should have been pleasant encountering another who knew of and obviously respected the first Daaga, but it wasn't.

"That's what I'm saying," Gray's voice was almost amused, "Because only few people in Trinidad know anything about Daaga. Where you get it, in America?"

"Yes."

"You see!" cried Gray, announcing once more to the crowd at large, "America 'ent only for making money—you getting history there too, man. History."

And how did the history of that first Daaga ever come to old Gray's attention?

"When you know, you know." Gray spoke like one privy to a mystery, and Daaga offered him a smile, hoping to ignite some feeling of kinship, comradeship, some contact beyond the mere breath of their voices. But the old man's eyes would not let him in.

"You ever hear about Daaga?" Gray said pompously to the carpenter.

"No. But the name sound like a stick-man to me."

"Stick-man! Daaga was a warrior! In the eighteenth century when the Spanish still keeping slaves, Daaga turned on them. Man, look! Right there in St. Joseph, oui! And if it wasn't for a kiss-mi-ass traitor he woulda take over this whole island. Yes! The whole island. But the traitor betray him. And when they bring him out to shoot him, he turn his backside gi them, man. They want to see him look sorry and hang-dog, but he turn his back gi them as if to say 'Kiss my ass!' You think they know what to do with that?"

"He must've been a bold man."

"He was a tough man."

"Anybody with a name like that bound to be dangerous. You going up?"

They drank and the flask was empty.

"Kiss mi ass, he tell them," Gray said, pursuing the story or history of that first Daaga with emphasis, as if at one time he might have taken such a name himself, handled such deeds himself.

"Where you get all that Gray?" the carpenter asked.

"The priest."

"What priest, that maracon at the Presbyterian?"

"I'm telling you, man," Gray spoke with forbearance, "these Americans 'ent stupid like all you think."

"What that priest know about Daaga or anything in Trinidad?"

"Them Americans know everything, man. They smart too bad. You 'ent hear this Mr. Daaga here say that where he get his name?"

"That priest only have a lot of books."

"That's knowledge!" Gray's voice rose like a drum clout. "Knowledge!"

Then the drummers were reassembled, and the heavy keg picked up a heartbeat. A strong, steady, muffled beat.

"Book knowledge ain't no kind of knowledge," someone said.

"How about the lost books of the Bible," Gray came back vigorously. "You imagine what is in them?"

The light drum cut into the deep-toned keg, and soon the third drum picked up a second off-rhythm, until together they were sounding memories which caused Daaga to rock with a smile on his face.

All talk trailed to an end.

Conga Man, eyes closed, aloof, slowly raised his arms above his head, stick pointing to the sky. Daaga, Gray, the carpenter, they all moved back leaving Conga alone in the circle. A voice raised—

"My mama gon' pay the bail

Don' let me sleep in the royal jail . . ."

and several immediately chorused—

"Tell the sergeant

Mi mamma gon' pay the bail . . ."

Conga Man began his dance. He leaped in the air, arms outstretched, to land softly on his toes and stalk the circle like a panther wrathfully in search of prey. The cutting drum saluted. Conga weaved, flicking his stick to a defensive position, then abruptly he stood rock still, a challenge to any who dared attack. An agony in his stance, but forever belligerent. Vulnerable he may be, but fearless, and with a price for whoever would find out.

In between the drums a singer chanted his call again, and the chorus answered. Like liquid memory the vibrating beat quivered Daaga's belly and arms, his feet. Aroused to an anciently imbedded dance, he wanted to leap like Conga, stomp the earth, bend the sky. A tremor of fearlessness electrified him.

"You want to play?" the carpenter shouted in his ear above the drums and singing. And Gray was still looking at him, an intensely neutral scrutiny.

Daaga only smiled. When uneasiness, when fear is conquered, man carries out the eternal with nothing but ease. Daaga only smiled.

All the men singing, their voices came sweet. Several danced, though taking care not to confront Conga where he was planted shimmying, his stick crossed and ready. They danced around him, beside him, in complement to his contained power, but never confronting him. The drums rumbled and clapped like sweet thunder, and when Daaga closed his eyes they pounded right in deep beneath his skin and massaged his viscera, so that a power steamed from his head distinct as the smell of sweat, fresh earth, crushed leaves, and something didn't have a name but was bright and blue in color. Deepening to black in moments. A discovery of peace in terror. Demon, benevolent, brave martyr, but above all fearless; at work, peace, or play, fearless; divided, conquered, fearlessly emerging, reassembling, dominating; fearless. Daaga sang with the chorus, rocked his head and bounced where he stood; but waited for himself to calm down.

Then with a flourish the drums came down and the song ended. The men went back to palaver and drinking, several thrusting flasks towards Conga, who, once more pleasant and benign, shook the sweat from around his eyes, joined in the laughter, and drank.

"How you like the boys?" Stone asked, materializing before Daaga. "They good?"

"Yes, yes . . ."

"I did tell you so. I see they make you hot too," Stone grinned, "little bit again and you would've jumped in, right?"

To which Daaga could smile and say, "This music is sweeter than anything I've heard in a long time."

"I tell you though," Stone confided, "if you get hot and want to jump in, don't take on Conga Man. He's very dangerous . . ."

To which Daaga smiled. "Who should I take on, you?"

"Who, me. I don't play stick. I don't want nobody busting my head open." Stone lifting his hat to stroke his head. "This coconut good just as it is and it gon' stay that way till I get to New York. Only way I get mi head buss is if a New York police hit me in a riot . . ."

To which Daaga smiled, relaxed now. Maybe one day Stone would find a library—perhaps the very one Daaga had known—and reemerge with a new name. Then his cultivating Daaga would have been worth it. But again, he might just get lost on Brooklyn Avenue. There was no way Daaga could prepare him for all he would encounter even living the way they did as brothers before his departure. Maybe one day he would come back with something more than the bravado of a big city street corner. To this same village, and be just the finite dream of his ancestors incarnate.

The rum was new and a little bit smoky, but it drank well. The men praised the hand that made it. They talked . . . the babble of men in good spirits because of knowing that weakness and fear would sometime before the gathering broke be exorcised, and they would live sharing the vision. They talked, until the talk divided itself between just two and the others listened. Old Gray's voice shrieked to make a lion pause. "Daaga is a wicked name, oui!"

The other fell like frozen sand on the ear—"I don't believe none of that stupidness . . ." And Crazy Desmond's eyes looked harp with contempt.

"Is a wicked name ah telling you . . ."

"So what it got in that—my name ent wicked too?"

"You? Go on! You ever start a revolution? You ever tell white man kiss your ass? You gon stand up like a man when they point the gun at you? A chicken like you . . ."

"So ah is chicken: a chicken fowl-cock! Well buss mi head, nuh! Look it dey—buss it. Ah is chicken. Well get a stick—ah want to see you buss chicken head . . . "

"Damn Trinidadian so blasted stupid, you can't tell them nothing. Where a stick . . . ?"

A waiting voice raised the song again—

"Mi mamma gon' pay the bail
Mi mamma gon' pay the bail
Tell the sergeant
Mi mamma gon' pay the bail . . ."

and the drums overtook the melody—

Buh gu duk/Buh gu duk . . .

And Daaga, Mr. Daaga, relaxed now. Another rum: the drums. And uncontrollably out of context the memory of himself on a toilet seat in Idylwild. It is a mountain resort in Southern California U.S.A., flat board cabins between the rustic redwood trees, and the company of a brown woman. It is the summer season, with a blue sky, golden sun, high in the desert atmosphere, and bronze-blonde teenagers everywhere eager for experiments to exploit the vulnerabilities ordinarily buttoned down below. It is a porthole toilet: the "closet" of an earlier childhood. With the sun striated through waving fir branches in a sky blue, deep and eternal. What is it? What is it being sucked into a solitude above the world, becoming pure?

What is it—being sucked into the solitude of ephemeral darkness which yet echoes a voice, a warmth, arms clasping.

On the barren ground of an idle hilltop it is the lover embracing his mate beneath the silhouette of empty avocado trees and many unmoved stars in the distance, saying Call my name I want to hear you call my name I want to hear you call my name. And even farther than the stars across the treetops, the ocean washes languidly alike for lovers, dead fish or the melancholy seaman laying down his seine.

All women were one. For a fleeting uncontrollable moment he missed Woman, mermaid of the liquid night. And in a moment resolved to the excruciating sweetness of their future embrace.

Another rum: the drums.

And Daaga, Mr. Daaga, dancing like an ancient warrior before his totem. With a stick in his hand, and the dance coming easily. So that his nostrils burned, and the bones of his face could feel the atmosphere. Daaga dancing in the one-bulb electric light, and the men making room for him, backing off into the traditional circle where it is the drummers, himself, and in a corner the hole where the blood for each night is collected. Daaga dancing. Leaping as lithe as Conga Man on his toes, and the drums filled on dew from the mount following him everywhere, commenting, instructing, sometimes compelling his motion.

The drums tell you what to do.

"Aie, but look, the American dancing!"

"He ent no American: he's a born Trinidadian."

"Aie, but he dancing sweet, man."

"Bound to. No Yankee could dance this dance. Besides, he Daaga."

"Who that?"

"The fella what did kill all the Spanish and them before your grandfather time."

"He come back? He spirit come back?"

"Spirit like that don't bury, you know . . ."

Buh gu duk/Buh gu duk . . .

"Aie ah aie! Ah go buss a head tonight! Tonight, tonight!"

It is Crazy Desmond: in his ten-dollar shirt with the cuffs rolled back, sharkskin pants, alligator shoes, and a brims-up felt hat on his head. Dancing left foot, right foot, marking the ground with his stick. For a second, Daaga would have melted into the night, flowed on back to being idle and wild. But Desmond's scent enveloped him like a woman's perfume edged with a touch of rawness, and behind his back the drums rained thunder from a peak. In his right eye Conga Man stood judiciously, his stick grounded like a staff between his legs; and before him Desmond played his stick like an obeah-man jabbing spirits, then prepared a carré.

Daaga heard the drums inside his head. He danced. Before him Desmond stretched and retracted like a cobra, his stick cocked above his head. Daaga danced: then planted his feet and took a stance. Immediately there came a blur between his eyes and a knocking dullness. In a single voice the men roared. They broke the circle, and several rushed by him to hug Desmond. The blood was warm coming down his face, as Conga Man led him over to the hole and forced him to bend his head over it. Stone's voice said, "But all you wicked, oui! All you let Desmond cut the man?"

The rum bath brought a sting to his forehead. His vision came instantly sharper, as did his ears, so that all around him slowed down, and from the core of an impenetrable calm he waited while they worked on stopping the blood.

"He ent cut bad," said Conga Man.

"But he coulda get his eye dig out!" Stone said. "The man come quite from New York, and all you let him jump in here to get his head buss!"

"Well why you didn't get a stick and stand up then, eh?"

"Me ent tell nobody I is stick-man. But all you let Desmond take advantage man."

"Take advantage, what? When time come, jackass have to bray. Besides, Daaga or whoever his name is ain't from New York. He from right here."

"Yes. And I believe he gon cut Desmond good, good," Conga Man said. "You'll see. If Desmond didn't swinging sideways stick he done cut already!"

"You ent see the way Daaga measure him with his eye?"

"I tell you, Desmond done cut already."

"He gon take him on again."

And in the old days it was terrifying to watch the grown men play. Terrifying to hear their challenges, then see the fierceness on one face turn to blood. Chilling, the vision of dominance and humility in a dance that always ended the same; chilling, the odor of fear when a man knew he was going to be bled, the lust in the eyes of the bleeder. As a child Daaga had cried for weeks on the vision of losers struck down. But tonight he was quite calm.

It would have been better if there were a song of his own. He was going to cut Desmond tonight, and it would have been nice if he had a song to which this verse could be added. Daaga made a mental note to compose one. The cut between his eyes was dressed, and someone had put a petit-quart of the clear rum in his hand. He raised stick and rum above his head and a few men cheered. He did not turn immediately to look for Desmond.

Not too deep in his past it is daylight saving time in Los Angeles, and the town is on fire. Black men women and children on rampage in the streets, harvesting their due from foreign businesses, dancing a bloody ballet to the rat-a-tat of National Guard fire. And at curtain call nobody knows how many dead, God alone how many left wounded, but no mourning. No applause, no mourning, only an argument left between the wrong and the wronged, into which she could not but induct him, falling back into his life suddenly after all the cha cha chas and bossa novas he had spent in quest of a true lady companion asking What are you going to do about it? As if that were indeed a question! Challenging him on the mount in Griffith Park, Haven't you thought about it? Two brown legs smooth, unyielding, resolved to the honey arms of Lady Satin Bellamy from Baton Rouge—never mind the weekends as companion in Beverly Hills—breathing in his ear the native promise everyone knows is but a dream; which nevertheless bears him away promising, promising, promising. What are you going to do? she had asked, Aren't you scared? From the mount in Griffith Park, looking down on a pastel world one corner of which billowed black smoke.

The drums began again, and a chantrèlle raised the lavwé—

"Mamma look ah 'fraid

Mamma look ah 'fraid the demon . . ."

and got an immediate chorus

"Mamma look ah 'fraid

No stick-man don't 'fraid no demon . . ."

Daaga swallowed and handed back the empty petit-quart. He wiped his stick, burnishing the metal cap on its end, then he prepared to pit. The drums rumbled, the circle re-formed. The drums climbed; he started a slow dance. And there was Desmond: leaping tall already, swaying, and retracting. Daaga watched him steadily. They circled. Desmond feinted once, twice. They circled again, then Desmond charged, Daaga saw all clearly: and although Desmond was swift Daaga gave ground evading the blow, then brought his own heavily down upon Desmond's skull a split second before their two bodies crashed together.

It was a mighty roar from the men, someone screaming distinctly, "Oh God! He kill him!" But Desmond was not dead. On the ground his eyes were glazed, and before friends could remove his hat blood ran from beneath it freely down his left temple. They lifted him and without any help from his legs dragged him to the blood hole. The drums played sweet thunder, then broke, and Daaga found himself lifted in the air by many hands.

The men, elated, Conga Man among them, leaped and shouted. They talked aloud in each other's faces and in short time reached consensus Daaga was too rare a phenomenon. When last did anyone see stick play like that? When last did anyone see balance, brains, and fearlessness like that? It was too much for the village to contain that night, and like a compulsive fire going forward they commandeered the four cars resident in the village, crammed into them singing fresh songs, and set out to show, to share this rare phenomenon in George Village across the hills, or any other where men may leave the safety of their homes and come out in the night to see, to challenge this new hero—Daaga. Behind they left Crazy Desmond sitting under the one bulb light still dazed, with a friend or two feeding him rum, shaving the hair from around his wound to lay a patch on it.

13. THE CONTEMPORARY MIGRATION
CULTURES OF ST. KITTS AND NEVIS

Bonham C. Richardson

St. Kitts and Nevis together comprise the British Caribbean's sole remaining Associated State, a political arrangement that calls for internal political autonomy with foreign relations controlled by London. Although only two miles apart, the two islands offer dramatic geographic contrasts, microcosms of the landscape extremes found today in the Commonwealth Caribbean. At first glance, St. Kitts (formally "St. Christopher") appears more "modern" than Nevis—the larger island's ongoing sugar-cane industry creating a protoindustrial atmosphere that is entirely lacking on the smaller island. In terms of Caribbean landscape evolution, however, Nevis is farther along than St. Kitts. Nevis has passed through a sugar-cane plantation period, its lands given over to small producer crops and livestock decades ago. On Nevis, where a local saying has it that "if you buy land, you someone,"[1] there is an almost sentimental attachment to the land. There is little reason for such an outlook on St. Kitts. Land-use contrasts between the two islands are therefore reflected by cultural differences between Kittitians and Nevisians. The islanders themselves recognize these differences, interpreting them as culminating in a St. Kitts–Nevis political rivalry.

In spite of their differences, the people of St. Kitts and Nevis have much in common. Perhaps most important is a heavy reliance upon human migration. As a visitor to St. Kitts and Nevis becomes more familiar with the two neighboring islands, he or she begins to realize that migration provides the very basis for their contemporary cultures.

The Outsider's View: Arriving on St. Kitts and Nevis

St. Kitts and Nevis offer few gaudy tourist trappings for vacationing North Americans. Neither has the tinsel facade of the duty-free emporium of the American Virgin Islands or the casino atmosphere of St. Martin. St. Kitts has a new jetport and golf resort, and Nevis stresses its tranquility in travel advertisements. But neither island has undergone a major transformation to attract North Ameri-

Originally published in Bonham C. Richardson, *Caribbean Migrants: Environment and Human Survival on St. Kitts and Nevis* (Knoxville: University of Tennessee Press, 1983), pp. 32–55. Copyright © 1983 by University of Tennessee Press. Reprinted by permission of Bonham C. Richardson and University of Tennessee Press.

cans to visit in droves. A few small boutiques and craft shops have appeared on both islands in the last few years as concessions to the two islands' incipient tourist industries.

Some visitors even stay for a while, despite a dearth of beach parties and limbo contests. A two-hour taxi ride around St. Kitts affords views of the canelands covering the alluvial aprons beneath volcanic Mt. Misery, the evenly spaced villages of wooden houses along the perimeter road, and Brimstone Hill, a spectacular eighteenth-century colonial fortress in the northwestern corner of the island. In direct contrast to the trim neatness of St. Kitts's canelands, Nevis's landscape of coconut palms, open range, and provision farms, scattered around Nevis Peak (the volcanic centerpiece of the island) gives the smaller island an even slower and sleepier appearance. Nevis boasts Alexander Hamilton's birthplace in Charlestown and the ruins of an old bathhouse, formerly a vacation spa for the planter class of the early Caribbean. A small but influential and highly visible colony of Americans and Canadians have built homes and taken up residence on Nevis in the last fifteen years. They employ a few local maids, gardeners, and construction workers.

Although there are flights between St. Kitts and Nevis, normal passenger travel between the two islands is by boat. A new shallow-draft, diesel-powered vessel, the *Caribe Queen*, covers the twelve miles between Basseterre and Charlestown in about 45 minutes. A limited amount of cargo can be carried on board as well. Other cargo vessels, both motor- as well as sailpowered, carry food, lumber, hardware, automobiles, and appliances from St. Kitts to Nevis. Stevedores offload cargo at the pier with winch and slings, an operation invariably accompanied by a great deal of pushing, shouting, and cursing.

Census takers in 1970 counted 33,737 residents on St. Kitts and 11,147 on Nevis. The population is overwhelmingly of African descent. A tiny white elite — bank managers, retail outlet managers, and government advisers from abroad — live in the Basseterre district. A handful of cloth merchants of Mediterranean origin resides in Basseterre. Middle-level economic positions in the capital town are occupied by lighter-skinned persons of mixed blood as are shopkeeper positions in Basseterre and some villages of the St. Kitts countryside. St. Kitts is otherwise populated exclusively by dark-skinned blacks. With a few exceptions, Nevis has been given over entirely to a black population, and "class" there is based on occupational status rather than skin color. The shopkeepers and merchants on Nevis are landowners as well, the special people of the island, all of whom recollect their grandfathers migrating to work abroad, usually to the Venezuela goldfields before the turn of the century.

With a population of 12,000, Basseterre is the unquestioned metropolis of St. Kitts and Nevis. Basseterre, St. Kitts, is a sun-bleached, tired-looking town of stone, stucco, and wood. Vehicular traffic is slight except for the Saturday morning market along the waterfront. Basseterre is the seat of local government, the site of the cable and wireless office, several modern grocery stores, and dry goods and specialty stores. The main hospital is immediately to the west, and east of town is the island's central sugar mill and refinery next to the electricity generating plant. Basseterre's residents are well to do in a relative sense, although there are pockets of "lower-class" housing in the town.

The trip from Basseterre, St. Kitts, to Charlestown, Nevis, seems to involve a passage back in time. The many land rovers and jeeps give Charlestown an almost frontier look at first glance. Charlestown (population about 2,000) offers little in the way of shopping, recreational, and educational amenities. Walking ashore from the town's (and island's) pier, one passes the cotton gin and goes on to Charlestown's single main street. The courthouse building, post office, and small grocery stores surround a tiny square. In the house yards and streets that intersect Charlestown's main thoroughfare, an extraordinarily large number of dogs, cats, chickens, sheep, and goats wander about under varying degrees of control.

Rural dwellings and settlements of St. Kitts and Nevis are typical of the Commonwealth Caribbean. The houses are neither "primitive" thatch or mud nor do they approach North American opulence. Yet is it less helpful to locate St. Kitts and Nevis houses along a theoretical primitive-to-modern continuum than it is to suggest that houses on the two islands reflect local livelihood strategies: dwellings are adapted to the local environment yet they are built with imported materials. Rural dwellings are constructed of wooden planks and consist of two or three rooms with a wooden cooking structure outside. Bamboo fences often surround house yards, especially in St. Kitts. Even the poorest houses contain some kind of manufactured furniture. Sofas and plastic curtains indicate a certain prosperity or at least the regular receipt of remittances from abroad. Almost every house has a glass-fronted case containing souvenirs, curios, and family photographs. A number of rural houses now have small refrigerators, since electricity has recently been extended to all of the settled areas of both islands.

Few village households have running water. Each community is served by communal waterpipes and faucets served by gravity-powered water systems emanating from catchment areas or springs in nearby mountain areas. On Nevis the spring-fed water reservoirs are only seasonally reliable owing to periodic drought, and the more elaborate dwellings in rural Nevis have their own water cisterns. There are usually community showers in the village areas of both islands, and most houses have private latrine pits. Tenure arrangements for house plots differ from one village to the other. In general, Nevisians own their own houseplots, and Kittitians, whose village communities are often technically on estate land, are renters, paying a nominal fee to nearby plantations.

Both islands are precariously dependent upon imported food, fuel, clothing, and building materials. And although no one seems to know the quantitative extent of the two islands' dependence on outside food, everyone agrees that food imports are vital to daily subsistence. Upper- and middle-class groups of both islands are particularly dependent on food imports. On Nevis there is a generally greater subsistence element in the local diet than on St. Kitts, although everyone on both islands depends heavily upon imported flour from Canada and imported rice from Guyana and the United States. In a descending order of monetary value, the most important imported commodities are flour, milk, poultry, and fish.[2] Imported clothing is popular for special occasions, although children's shirts, trousers, and dresses are usually sewn by village tailors and seamstresses. Shoes and hats are imported and store bought. Small transistor radios are within the means of most local families. Automobiles are owned by foreigners, the most affluent local residents, or persons involved in transportation. While village shops normally carry small items for daily use—soap, kerosene, cooking oil, powdered milk, crackers, cigarettes, and rum—any more important purchases call for a trip by taxi bus into Basseterre or Charlestown. The economies of both islands are based strictly on cash; although some food is cultivated locally and some very rudimentary processing and manufacturing goes on within each household, few economic transactions on either island occur without money changing hands.

The monetary character of the local economy reinforces its precarious, outward-focused, and externally controlled nature. The Eastern Caribbean dollar lost 35 percent of its value relative to the United States dollar from mid-1975 to mid-1976, and St. Kitts and Nevis depend upon Puerto Rico, the U.S. Virgin Islands, the United States, and Canada for more than 20 percent of imported goods.[3] By June 1976, rural shopkeepers were no longer able to stock certain canned goods and powdered milk that had traditionally been imported from the United States and Canada. Local savings also have been seriously eroded by a combination of inflation and a decline in emigration possibilities. In 1965, when emigration possibilities were brighter, local bank accounts showed a collective balance of E. C. $1,337,000. In 1973, the collective balance of local depositors had dwindled to E. C. $505,000.[4]

A visitor to St. Kitts and Nevis sees little evidence of ill health among the populace, although relatively high incidences of malnutrition afflict the very young and very old. Among 2,094 children who were taken to government sponsored "child welfare" clinics on the two islands in 1972, 536 showed signs of some kind of malnutrition. A number of adults suffer from a combination of poor nutrition and gastrointestinal disease. The infant mortality rate in 1972 was 86 per 1,000 live births.[5] There is one hospital on each island and three smaller infirmaries on St. Kitts and one on Nevis. Child innoculation campaigns are carried out by the government with the aid of international organizations. Once an individual passes the critical first year of life, assuming adequate diet, longevity is quite common on the two islands, many older men and women living into their 80s and 90s.

The extremely high percentage of children in the local population is perhaps most apparent at the end of a school day in a rural area of either island, when throngs of uniformed schoolchildren are walking home. There are thirty-five primary and secondary schools on St. Kitts and Nevis with a combined enrollment of 13,551. Despite limited educational resources and crowded classrooms, students of both islands are particularly interested in education, and there is a modicum of literacy among all the families of the two islands. Successful completion of secondary school qualifies one for the few local civil servant or clerical positions available or, very rarely, university training abroad. The teachers and principals on the two islands hold some of the few positions of locally based prestige and are looked upon for leadership and wisdom by both students and adults, especially in the rural communities.

Contrasts in Land Use and Livelihood

A mild earthquake startled St. Kitts in early 1975, causing slight damage to the Anglican churches in Basseterre and Middle Island and to a few other buildings in the capital town. Although actual damage was minimal, the quake was strong enough to remind residents of St. Kitts and Nevis of past tremors and of the earthquake on Nevis during slavery that sent an entire plantation and its village sliding into the ocean, an event unconfirmed by historical records but real enough in Nevisian folklore to help shape attitudes about living in the countryside there. Prior to the passage of Hurricane David in the autumn of 1979, the only serious hurricanes in living memory were those of August 1899 and August 1924, although everyone is quite aware of the hurricane vulnerability of the two islands every year from July to October. Rainfall is unpredictable. Annual averages are from 40 inches in the settled lowlands of Nevis to 100 inches at the highest points on Nevis Peak and from about 50 inches in the St. Kitts coastal villages to 150 inches at its highest elevations.[6] High rainfall variability is so typical of both islands that "average" precipitation totals become meaningless, especially during the frequent periods of drought. The windward sides of both islands suffer from wind desiccation and salt spray, and Nevis's conical peak deflects rain-bearing winds unpredictably so that one part of the island may have a downpour while another area remains dry. Environmental uncertainty is therefore part and parcel of the physical underpinning for the two islands.

Although both are volcanic in origin, St. Kitts (67 square miles) and Nevis (36 square miles) are quite different in general topography and soil types. The smaller island is steeper and stonier with a considerable clay component in the soil. These conditions have always inhibited agricultural activities, especially those calling for mechanization, and fields in Nevis are often separated from one another by stonewalls built with the rocks taken from the fields during cultivation. The Nevis clays are less permeable to water infiltration than are the loamy soils of St. Kitts, helping to explain why Nevis has experienced more soil erosion than the larger island, whose fine-grained volcanic soils have been remarked upon for their fertility since earliest plantation days. St. Kitts has sustained sugar-cane crops continuously for more than three centuries, and soil depletion is becoming a serious problem; thousands of tons of chemical fertilizers are now imported

annually from the United States and Trinidad to enrich the fields. "Natural" vege-
tation on the two islands is confined to the areas just below the highest peaks,
Nevis Peak (3,232 feet) and Mt. Misery (3,792 feet) on St. Kitts. The early colonial forest clearance and more recent cutting for firewood and charcoal has modified the forest cover at all but the highest elevations.

Unlike Nevis, where sugar cane is no longer grown commercially, St. Kitts's
arable land has been in cane since earliest colonial days. During the twentieth
century, the estates all have shipped their cane to the one central mill near Basseterre so that the island essentially has been one large agro-industrial production
unit with the resident black labor force, their efforts coordinated and mediated
by a handful of planters, producing canes for the single sugar factory. St. Kitts is
one of the sole remaining sugar-cane monocultures in the Commonwealth Caribbean, almost all other islands now actively seeking major land-use diversification. Even the locations of most St. Kitts village communities are explained more
because of their lack of potential for cane rather than their suitability as settlement sites. On the eastern side of the island, villages are located in the dank
drainage channels, or "ghauts," that intersect the gently sloping canelands.
Where the land is suitable for cane but where houses are needed for fieldworkers,
the dwellings are packed tightly along the roadside.

On St. Kitts the sugar-cane cuttings are planted by hand after tractors prepare
the soil. Five principal cane varieties are planted on the island in order to guard
against possible pest or disease attack focused on a single genotype. Hand weed-
ing of the cane fields is a job often performed by women and children. Harvesting, lasting from February to June, is accomplished by hand, by male cane-cut-
ting gangs and single cutters and now occasionally by female cutting gangs.[7]
Usually three or four ratoon crops will be cut from a single planting. After the
crop is harvested it is loaded aboard the cane cars of the narrow-gauge railway
that circles the island. The cut cane is thereby delivered to the central sugar factory east of Basseterre, where it is processed into semirefined sugar and then trans-
ported via ocean-going vessels to England for final refining.

The typically seasonal sugar-cane industry of St. Kitts is the island's main business. Cane workers, truck and tractor drivers, and factory hands are active during
the first half of the year, and underemployment characterizes the island during
the other half, although the estates have generally maintained agricultural practices to give sporadic rural employment during the "out-of-crop" season.[8] Individual productivity varies widely: a typical cane-cutter harvests two and one-half to
three tons of cane daily and is paid E. C. $3.50 (about U.S. $1.30) for each ton.
The relatively low average output for Kittitian harvesters is because the cane is
not burned before harvest. Burning reduces sharp foliage and makes cutting easier, but the cane leaves are preserved in St. Kitts in order to retain soil moisture
and retard soil erosion.

Major structural change has occurred recently in the management of the Kittitian sugar industry. The state took control of all of the canelands in December

1975. In late 1976 the government assumed control of the central sugar factory. All phases of St. Kitts sugar production have thus come under full local control. One of the avowed aims of the government's "rescue" operations for the sugar-cane industry is to begin to diversify St. Kitts's agriculture. In 1976 an estimated 10,000 acres of sugar cane were reaped. But nearly 600 acres more were grown in peanuts, carrots, potatoes, root crops, peas, and corn.[9]

Provision farming on St. Kitts, heretofore extremely limited in acreage and tightly controlled by the lowland estates, traditionally has been restricted to the hills above the cane. Highland plots have been tilled by the estate workers, who have rented the land from the individual estates, since the latter have controlled all of the island's land up to the mountain crests. In 1975 there were 2,466 highland farms in St. Kitts, 1,968 of which were less than one acre in size.[10] The cultivation of a highland plot traditionally has been contingent upon work on the adjoining sugar-cane estate. Even then, the estate owner has usually taken one-third of the plot's produce as rent, selling the confiscated food locally. Highland garden plots are sometimes rented for E. C. $10–15 per year, although cash renting is rare. The hillside farming itself is almost invariably accomplished with a heavy hoe, although plots above some of the windward settlements can be reached by rented tractors. Women tend plots in the cool of the morning, and older men often spend weekend days at these gardens. Each plot is characterized by variety. Potatoes, beans, eggplant, pumpkins, peppers, pineapples, and bananas are all cultivated for home consumption with a little extra for cash sale. Drought, soil erosion from highland rainshowers, and crop theft by both neighbors and monkeys pose recurring hazards to provision farming on St. Kitts.

Highland garden farming on St. Kitts is strictly a livelihood necessity rather than a commitment to the land. Villagers say that highland agriculture on the island is a throwback to plantation days when mountain plots were allocated for slave farming, and some old men still refer to the estate-owned plots as "the nigger grounds." The Kittitian villager is relieved of the necessity to work the provision lands when cash is available from abroad to purchase food. During the 1960s when many young people were working in the Virgin Islands and sending money home, some highland provision areas were almost abandoned.

Less noticeable livelihood activities within Kittitian villages supplement the more visible cash-earning jobs and supplementary provision farming. Chickens are kept in many house yards and fed table scraps. Grazing animals are often tethered alongside cane fields where they can eat weeds and grass. Pigs are commonly kept, and several of the more prosperous pig farmers on St. Kitts import feed from the Virgin Islands. Village breadfruit, coconut, citrus, and mango trees, although normally considered the property of a single individual or family, are often picked clean by village children and may constitute an important nutritional supplement for them.[11]

Fishing has never occupied large numbers of men from either St. Kitts or Nevis, although it is an occupation to which many aspire, possibly because of its relative prestige as much as the financial rewards. On St. Kitts, fishermen are found in Dieppe Bay, Sandy Point, Old Road Town, and Basseterre, and they are also in the Charlestown area of Nevis. Small fishing boats and an occasional sailing schooner are constructed locally on the beaches. The smaller boats, powered by outboard motors, take fishermen as far north as the Saba banks and occasionally south to Montserrat. Fishing is potentially profitable and always risky. A man can earn up to E. C. $300 per week or catch nothing. The catch is sold to local villagers at the beach or market, and recent inflation (E. C. $2,000 for an outboard motor) has raised prices for most locally caught fish to E. C. $1.50 per pound.

Although the St. Kitts economy is centered around sugar cane, Basseterre provides enough work for stevedores and for those working in manufacturing and service jobs to generate a light but steady stream of vehicular traffic to and from the capital town during the morning and late afternoon. This is not the case on Nevis because livelihood on the smaller island is focused on village agriculture and livestock husbandry. Nevis was originally a sugar-cane island, but its last muscovado sugar mill closed in 1958. Canes from Nevis were thereafter sent to the St. Kitts sugar factory by sail-powered barge, and the canes often soured or deteriorated from pest attack before they arrived. The last such shipment to St. Kitts was in 1969. Nevis was producing only patches of sugar cane by the late 1970s, for home use and animal feed.

Nevis is an island of small landholders. During this century many of the former estate lands have been broken up into large to medium-sized land parcels, which have become available to individual farmers. The most recent agricultural census of the Commonwealth Caribbean showed 1,690 individuals on Nevis who either owned (904) a plot of land of less than five acres or who controlled such a plot under conditions of "mixed tenure" (786).[12] Land is also rented out by individuals and by officials who administer fifteen different government estates. In 1976 there were 364 different tenants on the government lands, using it mainly for grazing animals.[13] On Nevis, ownership of a piece of land, however small, is a measure of prestige. On St. Kitts, little land is available for purchase by would-be smallholders.

The symmetry and homogeneity of the St. Kitts canelands are in direct contrast to the ragged, unmanaged, and overgrown appearance of Nevis. On closer inspection the land appears overgrown because individual small holdings are characterized by variety. It is not uncommon on Nevis to see yams, pigeon peas, corn, and a few stalks of cane growing in the same small plot, interspersed with banana plants and citrus trees. This is, of course, a typical subsistence adaptation that provides crop variety for family use and some extras for sale, as well as insurance against pest attack, plant disease, and market insecurity.

Sea-island cotton is Nevis's principal cash crop, accounting for more acreage than any other crop on the island. It is cultivated exclusively on small land plots, either by the owners or through sharecropping or hired hand arrangements if owners are absent or too old to work the land. In August 1975, 450 acres on Nevis were planted in cotton. By the following May, 117,662 pounds of sea-island cotton lint had been sold to the Nevis Agricultural Department, the island's sole buyer. In 1976 there were 501 producers of cotton on Nevis, 298 of them women, whose output ranged from 1,415 pounds down to 5 pounds.[14] Cotton is generally cultivated in the gender sloping lands of Nevis, below the 600-foot contour but above the drier coastal zones. It is usually planted in August, but when cane was still a cash crop on Nevis, cotton was planted in May and harvested in the fall so that harvest periods did not overlap.[15] Cotton is hand-harvested, and then the stalks are burned to rid the following crop of the pink bollworm, a pest that has ravaged sea-island cotton on the island for half a century.

No one on Nevis denies that cotton cultivation is ultimately harmful to the island's soil. Older farmers recall that soil erosion became much more serious as cotton began to take over from cane in the first decade of this century. Younger cultivators remark about the problems of sheet erosion of the unprotected, exposed soil between the rows of cotton. The annual burning reduces ground moisture and is detrimental over a long period of time. Burning also disturbs hundreds of flying insects, which then move on to other fields.

As on St. Kitts, the main food crops on Nevis are starchy tubers—yams, sweet potatoes, and cassava. It would appear economically ideal for a two-island state to have one island specializing in a cash crop and the other in food. Provision farmers on Nevis, however, suggest that their relationship with St. Kitts inhibits rather than encourage their food production. Almost all foodstuffs, to be sold in bulk, must be sold to the government's Central Marketing Corporation in Basseterre. Nevisian farmers say that their yams, for instance, could be sold for much higher prices in St. Martin and the U.S. Virgin Islands. They also suggest that government buyers of foodstuffs are incompetent and lazy, often delaying buying trips to Nevis that leave delivered goods rotting at the Charlestown pier.

Nevis's most striking feature is its ubiquitous livestock population. Cattle, and especially the smaller grazing animals—sheep and goats—appear everywhere, but they are most heavily concentrated in the drier parts of the island. There were an estimated 3,700 cattle, 10,000 sheep, and 6,000 goats on the island in 1971, roughly twice the numbers for 1946.[16] The livestock, owned by every rural farmer, are tethered in pasture areas during the day and then brought back to the owner's house at night to feed upon grasses or weeds that have earlier been cut for them along the roadsides. Animals are readily sold to butchers on both islands, and they are also shipped to Guadeloupe and Martinique. Beef export to the French islands is monitored and controlled by the government. Cattle are commonly stolen and butchered in the Nevis countryside.

The high livestock density in the southern and eastern parts of Nevis has led to a complete loss of topsoil through the elimination of all but the most hardy foliage in these drier zones of the island. The landholding system of hundreds of tiny plots has been the setting for inevitable disputes over marauding animals that occasionally roam at will through neighboring garden plots. Nevisians who own rural acreage and who return after a lengthy sojourn abroad sometimes find their land denuded by their neighbors' voracious animals. Small herds of goats clamber over the island's garbage dumps, and sheep commonly outnumber children in the schoolyard of the Charlestown secondary school. Cattle feed is now imported to Nevis for herds used by the small tourist hotels. But this is only a tiny fraction of the island's animal population. The livestock carrying capacity of parts of Nevis has already been exceeded, and routinely now, several animals die whenever drought reoccurs.

The contrasts in land use between St. Kitts and Nevis are inevitably reflected in human livelihood activities, personal financial strategies, and the images or stereotypes that the islanders maintain of themselves and of each other. Everyone on St. Kitts and Nevis acknowledges that the Nevisian is more "rooted in the land" and has greater command over his own economic destiny than the Kittitian, who is typically a wage earner, although everyone is quick to point out that individual farming is very risky. Most Kittitians and Nevisians sharply disagree, however, about the relative virtue and vice associated with island stereotypes. Generally, most Kittitians consider themselves outgoing, generous, articulate, and fashionable as opposed to most Nevisians, who, they feel, are clannish, grasping, secretive, and old-fashioned; most Nevisians, on the other hand, find that they are prudent, family-oriented, trustworthy, and hardworking, in contrast to most Kittitians, whose principal interests they see as centered around drinking, dancing, boasting, and fighting.

Insular stereotypes notwithstanding, distinctions between the two islands and their residents are blurred because of the many family ties between St. Kitts and Nevis and also because many Nevisians have "crossed over" to reside permanently on St. Kitts. A considerable though unknown number of the adult population along St. Kitts's windward coast, for instance, were originally from Nevis and are now regarded as "cane cutters" and "no longer real Nevisians" by those who have stayed on the smaller island.

Financial Strategies and Migration

Residents of both St. Kitts and Nevis depend heavily on the cash earned or sent from abroad. Many families maintain passbook savings accounts of several hundred dollars, often kept in the mother's name. The account balance becomes larger when remittances are received and is often drawn down to almost nothing when little money is coming in. This usually does not lead to the development of even modest financial estates through incremental saving, but it does help avoid chronic indebtedness, a rare phenomenon on the two islands. A traditional savings medium on St. Kitts and Nevis has also been membership in quasi-religious burial groups or "friendly societies." They are open to adults of both sexes, who pay a few cents per week in return for either modest benefits in time of sickness or financial help with family burial costs. In the last twenty-five years the membership of and participation in local friendly societies has declined substantially owing to large-scale migration to England and the Virgin Islands, campaigns by both private insurance companies and a government-sponsored provident fund, and political differences among members of the societies.

Both similarities and differences exist in the investment of savings and earnings on St. Kitts and Nevis. House construction is by far the most common financial obligation a household head faces after the purchase of basic foodstuffs. Construction costs are high, since essentially all building materials are imported — cement from Puerto Rico and lumber from Belize, Guyana, and the Virgin Islands. In both places in 1976 a simple wooden plank house cost about E. C. $1,500 for materials and labor, while a spacious, more modern home with water connections and utilities, a great deal of imported cement, and corrugated iron roofing cost tens of thousands of dollars. In early 1976, the overwhelming majority of the latter houses that had been recently built or were under construction in the housing developments outside Basseterre were financed by Kittitians who were abroad or recently returned.[17] Similarly, modern houses in the Charlestown area are, more often than not, financed by "outside" money.

The money to buy taxis, rum shops, trucks, and fishing equipment can also be traced, almost invariably, to an original extraisland money source, and some small shops and stores have by now been passed on to the next generation. The case of a sixty-year-old shopkeeper from Old Road Town in St. Kitts is typical. He was a gardener and part-time estate worker in St. Kitts until he traveled to Trinidad in 1942 and worked as a cook for the U.S. Army. From there he went to the Shell refinery on Curaçao and stayed until 1958. During his absence he sent "everything" to his mother and then used these savings to establish his small grocery store. He has helped two daughters and a son to "get started" in England and hopes his youngest son will stay to inherit his shop.

The most obvious investment difference between the islands is that Nevisians purchase land plots, whereas land is generally not available on St. Kitts. Moreover, an intermediate class of landholders has emerged on Nevis, but there is little scope for the development of a similar class on the larger island: there are 118 private landholdings of five or more acres on Nevis compared with 36 on St. Kitts, and Nevis has 74 "specified farms" of an average 196 acres, whereas St. Kitts has few of comparable size.[18] Among black Nevisians, there has thus emerged a stratum of small landowners who have attained prestige, not in legal status or life style, but in the amount of property held. Their special status, coming from the investment in land of migration money from abroad, is possibly a continuation of a "migration elite" formed in the Leewards immediately after slave emancipation. In more recent years this group has parlayed migration savings into positions of respect and financial profit on Nevis. According to Richard Frucht,

Many of the returnees have bought large amounts of land, sell smaller plots to
local buyers who are less affluent returnees, or laboring class people now receiving remittances from England. One estate, for example, was sold in 1953 to a
Nevisian just returned from the Dutch islands, where he had spent the previous
ten years. Between 1954 and 1962, he sold not less than 34 plots of various sizes
to as many buyers. He used part of this capital to establish local businesses.[19]

Farm machinery, the effectiveness of which is severely limited by Nevis's rocky
environment, is not a major capital investment there. Simple hand tools—forks,
hoes, and spades—constitute the only cultivating equipment, although more
prosperous cultivators own or rent trucks and vans to haul produce. Livestock
on Nevis is a major form of investment, regardless of the amount of land held or
the availability of grazing acreage. Investing migration money in animals on the
smaller island is a means of beating currency inflation as well as an adaptation
to Nevis's deteriorated environment.

The development of a landed "migration elite" has been impossible on St.
Kitts, since land has never been available. There are nonetheless noticeable differences between those who have successfully migrated away from St. Kitts and
returned in comparison with those who have not. The man who has returned
with enough money saved to become a shopkeeper, taxi driver, truck owner, or
fisherman on St. Kitts has freed himself from field labor, while the man who has
not "works on the estate and belongs to the estate." The admired return migrant
of St. Kitts also has more cash to spend than others, and he is not reticent to share
with family and friends. He occasionally purchases a bottle of rum and shares it
with friends and acquaintances, who are, in turn, expected to listen in awe to
stories of personal experiences set in London, New York, or Aruba. Admiration
on St. Kitts is therefore partly associated with the man who is willing to "spree
out" and share the money that he has earned abroad.

Migrants returning to St. Kitts have maintained a special status on the island
through their political activities. They have been the driving force behind the St.
Kitts Labour party. Party policies and programs have represented an organized
response to plantation domination, which has traditionally inhibited the development of a class of small landholders. St. Kitts plantations have, however, provided
a common foe against which workers' groups and, more recently, labor unions
have organized. In each Kittitian village one finds the Labour party's key supporters—the old-line "labor men" of St. Kitts—who began their working careers in
the cane fields of the Dominican Republic. They have always supported the Labour party with money contributions and, more important, their vocal support in
the villages and towns of the island.

Besides the more tangible manifestations of prestige associated with migration
on St. Kitts and Nevis, it is commonly acknowledged on both islands that more
esteem or respect is accorded the return migrant than the person who has remained behind. The young men of St. Kitts who stay to cut cane are considered

by many to be less intelligent than those who go abroad, and the advice of men and women who have worked away is commonly sought by village children. In a psychological comparison of crew cutters and fishermen of Dieppe Bay, St. Kitts, Joel Aronoff suggests that parents' migration from the island and leaving children behind under the care of relatives are detrimental to a child's psychological development, since it disrupts family structure.[20] This point is not totally convincing, since Aronoff makes no distinction between permanent and temporary emigration. His study emphasizes differences between the dependence and lack of confidence of local cane cutters and the independent, self-assured fishermen of Dieppe Bay. Aronoff analyzes these differences on the basis of local livelihood pursuits, although in his discussion he points out that village fishermen have had backgrounds of more varied work experience and began fishing as relatively older men, suggesting strongly that he is really contrasting those who have "made it" abroad and those who have stayed at home.

Migration, Remittances, and Family

Table 1 reflects the relative population imbalance in sex and age usual in the Commonwealth Caribbean and typically related to emigration. But static population figures do not begin to show the mobile nature of the populace of St. Kitts and Nevis. In 1975, for instance, residents of the two islands generated 17,309 separate trips abroad (7,253 to the U.S. Virgin Islands), almost exclusively by air, and 17,328 returns (7,461 from the U.S. Virgin Islands).[21] These data do not include the heavy back-and-forth travel between the two islands themselves.

A recent United Nations report, using data collected before the tightening of immigration laws in the U.S. Virgin Islands, indicates that the migration rate from St. Kitts and Nevis (17,572 from the two islands from 1960 to 1970) is almost twice as high as the rate for the Commonwealth Caribbean in general. The report also states that no longer do only the young men of the two islands migrate away in order to achieve local success. Young women now have an almost equal propensity to emigrate.[22]

Young people who go away are expected to provide financial support for family and friends left behind, and almost everyone left on the two islands depends, at least in part, upon the success of those, old and young, who have emigrated. Local land use and livelihood in the two islands therefore provide a very incomplete picture of the means by which individuals are sustained economically. In 1960 a local newspaper, the *Labour Spokesman*, reported, "It is not uncommon to hear people say: I don't have to depend on anybody here; I have me father—or mother, sister or brother, son or daughter as the case may be, in America, Curaçao, Aruba or the United Kingdom who is supporting me: It ain't St. Kitts or Nevis money that me eating."[23]

The amount of money sent from abroad is the best measure of the importance of migrants' support, although no data are available to show all of the money sent

Table 1. Population of St. Kitts and Nevis, 1970

Age	St. Kitts				Nevis			
	M	%	F	%	M	%	F	%
0–9	5,510	50.1	5,478	49.9	1,757	50.4	1,731	49.6
10–19	4,453	49.6	4,530	50.4	1,536	48.1	1,656	51.9
20–29	1,298	45.6	1,549	54.4	360	44.6	448	55.4
30–39	890	42.7	1,193	57.3	230	41.4	326	58.6
40–49	1,149	43.9	1,468	56.1	284	39.8	429	60.2
50–59	1,265	46.6	1,450	53.4	402	42.7	540	57.3
60–69	950	42.9	1,265	57.1	361	42.5	488	57.5
70–79	329	35.6	594	64.4	136	34.3	260	65.7
80 and over	73	19.9	293	80.1	61	30.0	142	70.0
Total	15,917	47.2	17,820	52.8	5,127	46.0	6,020	54.0

Source: 1970 Population Census of the Commonwealth Caribbean, III, 146–53.

to the two islands. Postal remittances (see Table 1), almost all from the United Kingdom, during 1975 totaled more than E. C. $1,000,000 to persons on St. Kitts and E. C. $550,000 to those in Nevis.[24] Personal bank checks are sent mainly from the United States and the Virgin Islands. Migrants also send cash through the mail and take money home personally or send it with a friend. It is common for a Kittitian or Nevisian working in the Virgin Islands to wait at the airport on St. Thomas or St. Croix until he finds an acquaintance flying home with whom he can entrust cash for his family.

Some local residents of St. Kitts and Nevis speculate that outside remittances account for more disposable income on the two islands than any other source, including the St. Kitts sugar industry. Money sent home is sometimes considered more valuable than that earned locally. It enables residents to purchase imported frozen meat, gifts for children, a bright square of linoleum, or even a bicycle — items over and above subsistence needs. Merchandise, too, is sent home to the two islands. During each Christmas season, the Basseterre roadstead takes on a carnival atmosphere as "the boats" bring shipments of furniture, used kitchen appliances, and clothing sent from family members working abroad. The relatives themselves often return to spend Christmas, bringing money and swelling the local population, which appears to triple.

Inevitably, a long tradition of labor emigration his led islanders to expect, not simply to hope, that persons leaving will periodically send back money and gifts. In earlier days it was generally a case of male migrants supporting those left behind, who were mainly female. Today it is not uncommon for a father to use his savings to help a daughter go abroad and then for the daughter to send money home. Parents expect their sons and daughters, and children their mothers and fathers, to send money home, and siblings also expect gifts from abroad. Family members make no pretense about relative favor and disfavor of kin abroad in terms of remittances received. One old woman in Basseterre remarked, "I have five children away, but I really have only four—one never sends anything." Similar comments are heard time and again on the two islands. Commitments to kinsmen left behind are usually weakened when obligations are assumed abroad: a typical interview response in this regard is, "My daughter is in the Bronx, but she got married, so we hear from her only once or twice a year."

Male migrants from St. Kitts and Nevis have traditionally sent remittances home to mothers, wives, or girlfriends for their personal expenses, for safekeeping, and for supporting children. This reinforces the mother-centered family, widespread among the "lower-class" black families of the Commonwealth Caribbean. High "illegitimacy" rates on both islands and traditional male absenteeism help lead to matrifocal family types on St. Kitts and Nevis. Formal marriage is most common among, but not confined to, the small middle class on both islands. Marriage never has been regarded as a necessary precondition for poor couples of St. Kitts and Nevis to live together and raise a family. Of 916 live births on St. Kitts in 1974, 774 were from unwed parents; on Nevis 172 of 227 babies were born out of wedlock.[25] On St. Kitts, the birth of a child to an unwed mother results in only slight and temporary disapproval or embarrassment. Often the infant's maternal grandmother immediately assumes responsibility for care of the child, especially if the young mother emigrates.[26]

It is not uncommon among the poorer folk on both islands for a woman to have children by several males, and each successive male may be a temporary resident in the woman's house, which she owns or rents. This therefore provides a temporarily "stable," though not legalized, mother-father arrangement. The women know who the children's fathers are, use the father's surname for his children, and make a rough allocation of funds received from the father for each child, even though the father may be absent. The mother's child-rearing responsibilities are financed from what she earns and from the money her husband or mates furnish. On St. Kitts and Nevis, and throughout the Caribbean, the mother will return to her parents' or mother's household if her mate or mates do not regularly provide money.[27] Later she will most likely come to depend upon money that her children send from overseas. The mating and family system on St. Kitts and Nevis is complex and difficult to categorize. The system whereby the mother comes to depend upon several different sources of cash should be considered more flexible and functional than promiscuous.

Child care is the sole responsibility of the mother if the father is absent, and if both parents emigrate, the job of rearing children falls to the grandparents (usually the grandmother) or to other relatives or friends, with remittances coming from the child's parents. It is often difficult for grandparents to "keep up" with their grandchildren, and much of the school misbehavior on both islands is attributed to the aggressiveness of children who are being raised by mothers alone or by grandparents. Moreover, the lack of "intact families" has been deemed the cause of deep-seated anxiety among young Kittitians whose parents work abroad.[28] In terms of sentiment or obligation, an aunt or grandmother who rears a child on St. Kitts or Nevis may eventually be favored over the child's biological parents and will often be the eventual recipient of remittances from overseas.

Traditionally, many young fathers of "illegitimate" children on the two islands have ignored their offspring until they were one or two years old, then the young father and mother have often established a household together. This, however, may be changing. Young fathers now regularly accompany mothers to government health clinics and care for their babies in public. In fact, the importance of the father in "lower-class" Caribbean families may have been seriously underestimated if information from St. Kitts and Nevis is representative of the area as a whole. The father, though absent out of necessity, has often set an example for his sons by working away. Many of the older men on the two islands recall first meeting their fathers in Cuba or the Dominican Republic when they themselves migrated. More recently, many fathers from the two islands have arranged jobs for their sons in Aruba, Curaçao, or the Virgin Islands.

Household and family in St. Kitts and Nevis cannot be assessed except in the context in which these institutions have evolved. Since slave emancipation, the personal prestige, success, and survival of the common people of the two islands have depended upon emigration to short-lived jobs and the ability to cope with periods when jobs were in short supply. The accumulation of cash, to satisfy survival or subsistence needs, has been a primary goal for an individual, male or female, on both islands. A typical adult male has therefore held some kind of local job while being flexible enough to respond to calls for laborers from abroad, knowing that he will probably return eventually. A typical female, in order to maximize her cash-receiving position in the light of economic uncertainty, has depended on herself, on a male mate—sometimes more than one—and eventually on children working abroad. Individual needs have been fulfilled more often than not by establishing male-female "family" alliances. These flexible alliances, supported by children and other relatives, have seen family members geographically dispersed beyond St. Kitts and Nevis. This dispersal further enhances a cash receipt position for individuals and might be considered an adaptation to the economic circumstances surrounding the common people of the two islands. "Family" on St. Kitts and Nevis is an elusive and ever-changing structure and a social adaptation to change and uncertainty.

A geographic dispersal of family members over a wide area calls for periodic reuniting of the family unit. In many cultures, the celebrations of birth and marriage call family members together. In St. Kitts and Nevis, however, birth is not widely celebrated and marriage is uncommon among members of the "lower-class" black population. This leaves death as the milestone in life celebrated by all Kittitians, Nevisians, and their kin abroad, regardless of their social status or family form. The local funerals on the two islands are not only religious ceremo-

Table 2. Locations of Relatives Abroad of Persons Dying in St. Kitts and Nevis, March 20 to July 19, 1976

		Locations of Relatives Abroad					
	Deaths[a]	United Kingdom	United States	Canada	St. Thomas	St. Croix	Tortola	Netherlands Antilles
St. Kitts								
Males	38	37	23	8	36	8	1	9
Females	60	45	18	16	31	13	5	13
Nevis								
Males	9	10	13	5	16	7	2	1
Females	13	5	11	4	9	6	3	1
Total	120	97	65	33	92	34	11	24

Note: Other locations mentioned where relatives of deceased lived: Anguilla, Antigua, Bahamas, Barbados, Belize, Bermuda, Brazil, Cuba, Dominican Republic, Jamaica, Montserrat, Netherlands, Puerto Rico, Spain, Surinam, Trinidad.
[a]Eighteen of the deceased persons had no relatives abroad specified.
Source: "Death Announcements," Radio Station ZIZ, Springlands, Basseterre, St. Kitts. With permission of the Journal of Cultural Geography.

nies where grief is ritualized but also important socioeconomic events that reunite members of spatially dispersed families and thereby bring considerable sums of money back to the two islands.

Migration and Death Ceremonies

Three times each day on radio ZIZ, the only local commercial radio station on St. Kitts and Nevis, death announcements, accompanied by mournful organ music, inform listeners of local deaths and enumerate grieving relatives (and their locations) left behind.[29] When the death announcements are aired, everyone—whether in houses, rum shops, or markets—stops to listen. The broadcast obituaries are so much a part of daily life that many Kittitians and Nevisians believe they are legally bound to report the death of a family member to officials of ZIZ. Table 2 shows the geographic distribution of relatives abroad of 120 people who died on St. Kitts and Nevis during a four-month period in 1976. All the relatives were enumerated in the particular death announcement, often including aunts, uncles, and cousins as well as members of the nuclear family.

The death announcements usually specify details about funeral arrangements to listeners on St. Kitts, Nevis, and nearby islands. Although the listening range of ZIZ is limited, the station is usually audible at higher elevations in St. Thomas. Listeners there notify friends, and the news travels quickly through the Kittitian-Nevisian population in the Virgin Islands. It is not unusual for relatives from St.

Thomas or St. Croix to arrive on St. Kitts by airplane on the same day that a family member's death has been announced. Relatives in the Virgin Islands and those residing in the United States, Canada, or the United Kingdom are most often notified by telephone or telegram within hours after a death. Air travel from these places allows a return for a funeral within two or three days.

Attendance at a family member's funeral, especially a funeral of a parent, on St. Kitts and Nevis is expected of those residing abroad, an expectation as strong or stronger than the expectation of remittances. Young people abroad will "sacrifice anything" to return for a funeral, since they will be "scorned" if they do not come. Local social pressures are thereby brought to bear on all distant kin to return when relatives die. The funeral is only one part of a wider social event. As in other cultures, family funerals also involve the telling of stories, the renewal of friendships, the incurring and payment of debts, and the discussion of business. Not incidentally, family members returning for funerals usually bring money and gifts. Their appearance at the funeral solidifies their places in the local society. This is especially important for young people working temporarily in the Virgin Islands. If they are eventually forced to return, their welcome will be warm if they have returned for funerals in the interim.

The funerals themselves are Christian rites, religious affiliations on the two islands being legacies of missionary activity that began before emancipation; Methodists predominate in Basseterre, and Anglicans are the most numerous Christian group in rural St. Kitts and Nevis. Fundamentalist sects have gained adherents from both islands over the past four decades. Almost every funeral is coordinated by one of three undertakers, two on St. Kitts and one on Nevis. The recent innovation of corpse refrigeration (since 1961 on St. Kitts and since 1973 on Nevis) leads to considerable expense. More often than not returning migrants pay for the funeral of a family member. The undertakers on the two islands, in fact, often reckon funeral expenses according to where the deceased's kin are located. A "Virgin Islands" funeral costs roughly E. C. $600, while a "U.K." funeral can cost the bereaved as much as E. C. $2,000. Not arbitrary, these costs reflect refrigeration expenses associated with the time and distance involved in traveling from, for instance, England or North America to the Caribbean.

Before the days of high speed international air travel and corpse refrigeration, relatives working away from St. Kitts and Nevis returned home for periods of mourning; the actual funeral was almost always on the same day as the death. Now, as means of travel and funeral technology have become more sophisticated and as workers' incomes have increased, the death ceremonies on the two islands have become more elaborate and more highly attended. The mortuary aspect of religious ceremony, often regarded as a "traditional" element of symbolic culture, appears closely related to the ongoing migration tradition on the two islands. It therefore seems safe to assert that the contemporary importance of local funerals in St. Kitts and Nevis has as much to do with a migration tradition as it does with fulfilling religious and psychological needs.

The Insider's View: A Talk with Isaac Caines

Death ceremonies, family relationships, and the other elements of the contemporary migration cultures of St. Kitts and Nevis are the cumulative products of the activities and experiences of individual Kittitians and Nevisians for more than three centuries. Men and women from the two islands always have had to cope with a host of uncertainties and hostilities at home and abroad. Interviews with older people on the two islands therefore reveal remarkable life histories. One such individual is Isaac Caines, now sixty-seven years old, who lives in a village settlement north of Basseterre. Seated on the side of an antique flatbed truck in his yard, Caines recalled a life of adversity, travel, and hard work.[30]

Isaac Caines was born in 1914 in St. Peter parish, northeast of Basseterre. Before he was born his father went to the Dominican Republic to cut cane and never returned. Caines lived with his mother and his older brothers and sister until he was old enough to leave for the Dominican Republic: "It was the only place to go if you had no money." This was in 1929 when he was fifteen. He traveled to Anguilla via sailing schooner, then on to Santo Domingo via steamer with a larger group of men. In the Dominican Republic he cut cane at the La Romana estate near San Pedro de Macorís in the southeastern part of Hispaniola. Unlike most, Caines "disappeared into the interior" of the Dominican Republic during the off-season and worked there rather than returning to St. Kitts each year after the cane harvest. He came back to St. Kitts in 1932. For the next ten years Caines was a crew member aboard a cargo vessel between St. Kitts and Trinidad. Although he visited all of the intervening islands briefly, he rarely stayed, except for one four-month period when he worked at the cotton gin on Carriacou. During World War II he made U.S. $45 per week for three years as a messenger boy for the U.S. Army's air base at Coolidge Field in Antigua. After returning to St. Kitts, he was imprisoned for six months for drawing a pistol on a local policeman in the midst of a dispute for the attention of a young woman. He then worked for a while on St. Kitts as a fisherman and stevedore, although his local prison record made finding work difficult. In 1955 he traveled to England where he first stayed at a boardinghouse in Ipswich. Then a friend found him work as a mason's assistant in London. Caines, "a man for the money," held a number of laboring jobs in various places in the United Kingdom, always changing jobs if another offered more pay. Every two to three months he sent money home (up to £60 each time) to his mother for safekeeping for his eventual return. While a dock worker in Cardiff, Caines became involved in a gambling dispute with a fellow West Indian and stabbed him (the wound took seventy-eight stitches to repair), an incident that led to his imprisonment for three years. After his release Caines married a woman from St. Kitts in England, but they soon separated. He eventually returned to St. Kitts as he was suffering from arthritis and "wasn't getting any younger." His mother had spent the remitted money in his absence, although he had brought enough home with him to purchase a small boat *(Return)*, outboard motor, and fishpot equipment. Caines now lives with another woman and her children. He has traded his boat and fishing equipment for a truck, which he cannot afford to have repaired, and he obtains occasional laboring jobs through the government. He has always been a steadfast supporter of the St. Kitts Labour party, as have most of the older men who have traveled away and returned. Men who migrate away are more "politically minded" than those who stay.

Isaac Caines (a fictitious name, although one that is recognizably Kittitian) is a real person, and to point out gratuitously that his case is "typical" detracts from the individual tenacity, resilience, and aggressiveness that he his shown throughout his life. Caines has been in trouble with the law more often than most, but this seems more a source of pride than remorse. The Kittitian policeman "had never been anywhere" and was ridiculing Caine's tailored khakis that he had purchased in Antigua. The knifing incident in Wales happened because the other fellow was cheating, and the seventy-eight stitch stab wound is clear evidence that Caines has always been able to resolve his own problems in the face of a host of uncertainties and hostilities.

Since slave emancipation in 1838, men and women, like Caines, of these two small Caribbean islands have traveled away and returned and have remained underspecialized in light of the many changes and hazards in their paths. Mobility, underspecialization, resilience have thus become traits of the migration cultures of St. Kitts and Nevis—cultures that represent these peoples' historical experiences beginning with the establishment of English plantations on the two islands in the early seventeenth century.

Notes

1. Frucht, "Community and Context," 179.
2. "Digest of Statistics no. 9," table 5; Gussler, "Nutritional Implications."
3. "Digest of Statistics no. 9," table 2. E. C. (Eastern Caribbean) $2.70 equals U.S. $1, as of July 1976.
4. Ibid., table 10.
5. "Annual Report of the Chief Medical Officer," 16, 41.
6. Lang and Carroll, *Soil and Land-Use.*
7. Aronoff, "The Cane Cutters."
8. *A Technical Survey of the Sugar Estates of St. Kitts*, I, 13.
9. Data courtesy of William F. Dore.
10. Edwards, "The Agricultural Census 1975," 14.
11. Gussler, "Nutritional Implications," 107.
12. Fernyhough, "The Agro-socio-economic Factors," 13.
13. Figures courtesy of Johnny Clarke, Superintendent of Agriculture, Nevis.
14. "Vendors of Cotton 1975/76."
15. Frucht, "Community and Context," 114.
16. Fernyhough, "The Agro-socio-economic Factors," 35.
17. Figures courtesy of Tom Molyneaux, Central Housing Authority, Basseterre.

18. Edwards, "The Agricultural Census 1975," 14–15, 43–44.
19. Frucht, "Emigration, Remittances, and Social Change," 200.
20. Aronoff, *Psychological Needs*, 31.
21. Data from the Immigration Department, Basseterre police station.
22. *St. Kitts/Nevis Territorial Plan T1*, 20–21.
23. "The Invisibles," *Labour Spokesman*, May 17, 1960.
24. Data from postal remittance records, Basseterre post office. During 1975 the E. C. dollar was worth U.S. $0.47.
25. Data from the Statistical Unit, Government Health Department, Basseterre, St. Kitts.
26. Gussler, "Nutritional Implications," 98.
27. González, "Family Organization," 1273.
28. Aronoff, "The Cane Cutters," 55.
29. Richardson, "Migration and Death Ceremonies."
30. Personal interview by the author, April 12, 1976.

References

"Annual Report of the Chief Medical Officer and Registrar General for the Year Ending 31st December 1972," St. Kitts-Nevis-Anguilla. Mimeographed.

Aronoff, Joel. "The Cane Cutters of St. Kitts," *Psychology Today* 4 (1971):53–55.

———. *Psychological Needs and Cultural Systems: A Case Study*. Princeton, N.J.: Van Nostrand, 1967.

"Digest of Statistics no. 9, January-December, 1973." St. Kitts: Statistical Dept. Mimeographed.

Edwards, Cecil H. R. "The Agricultural Census, 1975, St. Kitts-Nevis-Anguilla." Basseterre: Dept. Agriculture, 1976. Mimeographed.

Fernyhough, D. "The Agro-socio-economic Factors Influencing the Planning of Change in Agriculture in St. Kitts-Nevis: The Effects of History and Prospects for the Future." M.S. thesis, Univ. of Reading, England, 1974.

Frucht, Richard. "Community and Context in a Colonial Society: Social and Economic Change in Nevis, West Indies." Ph.D. diss., Brandeis Univ., 1966.

González, Nancie L. Solien. "Family Organization in Five Types of Migratory Wage Labor." *American Anthropologist* 63 (1961): 1264–80.

Gussler, Judith D. "Nutritional Implications of Food Distribution Networks in St. Kitts." Ph.D. diss., Ohio State Univ., 1975.

Lang, D. M., and D. M. Carroll. *Soil and Land-Use Surveys no. 16, St. Kitts and Nevis*. Trinidad: University of the West Indies, Imperial College of Tropical Agriculture, 1966.

Richardson, Bonham C. "Migration and Death Ceremonies on St. Kitts and Nevis." *Journal of Cultural Geography* 1 (Spring/Summer 1981: 1–11.

St. Kitts/Nevis Territorial Plan T1. Antigua: United Nations Development Program, Physical Planning Project, 1975.

A Technical Survey of the Sugar Estates of St. Kitts. London: Bookers Agricultural and Technical Services, Ltd., 1968.

"Vendors of Cotton 1975/76 as at May 19, 1976," Nevis: Dept. Agriculture. Mimeographed.

14. GENDER AND ETHNICITY AT
WORK IN A TRINIDADIAN FACTORY

Kevin A. Yelvington

Learn that the world is waiting to drag you down. "Woman luck de a dungle
heap," they say, "fowl come scratch it up." But you save yourself lest you
turn woman before your time, before the wrong fowl scratch your luck.

—Erna Brodber,
Jane and Louisa Will Soon Come Home

The conjunction of ethnicity, class and gender is a part of everyday life in Trinidad. It permeates every social situation and depends on day-to-day activity for its
social existence and meaning.[1] In this chapter I focus on three aspects of gender
and ethnicity in social relations in a factory in Trinidad. These are the composition and structural positions of the members of the workforce; the role and forms
of supervision supporting the organization's economic imperatives; and social relations between the workers. Sociological analyses of female workplace behaviour
have often failed to consider the nature and implications of sexual divisions in
industry (Brown 1976: 39). Here I intend to redress that imbalance by suggesting
the existence of an interplay between structural and symbolic properties.

The Factory and its Setting

This chapter is based on a year's participant observation in Trinidad, from July
1986 to July 1987.[2] During that period I worked (without pay) alongside the factory workers described below and generally tried to immerse myself in their
extra-factory lives. I thus studied not only their workplace behavior, but also their
various "survival strategies."

Essential Utensils Ltd (EUL)[3] was established in 1972 by Nigel Tiexiera, a
white Portuguese Creole with a master's degree from a Canadian university
and his wife Jane, who comes from a well-known and wealthy French Creole
family. Since the introduction of the Aid to Pioneer Industries Ordinance in
1950, industrialization in Trinidad and Tobago has been mainly the province of

Originally published in Janet Momsen (ed.), *Women and Change in the Caribbean* (London: James
Currey, 1993), pp. 263–77. Copyright © by James Currey Publishers. Reprinted with permission.

the Industrial Development Corporation (IDC). The Tiexieras applied to the IDC for a factory building and were allocated one on the Diego Martin Industrial Estate.

When a subcontracting agreement with a US multinational ended, Essential began to produce similar items under its own brand name. At that time (1980) it was one of the few locally owned firms to be exporting its products and, in the early 1980s, it won the Prime Minister's Export Award. The firm began by exporting to the Caribbean Economic Community (CARICOM), but during the 1980s expanded into Central and South America. By 1986 it was exporting its products to 24 countries.

Diego Martin is a district northwest of the capital, Port of Spain, and its boundaries extend from Four Roads to the north coast. The area can now be considered a suburb of Port of Spain: every working day commuters into "town" must leave by 6.30 a.m. to avoid the rush hour traffic jam, which is reminiscent of major North American cities. It is an area of wide income disparities, with modern air-conditioned houses with high fences and guard dogs existing alongside "board houses" (dwellings built on wooden stilts and made from plywood, two-by-fours or pine planks). A Caribbean Conference of Churches report (1986: 81) identified "pockets of poverty" in the area. Ethnically, the area has been predominantly Creole (see Table 1), but the proportion of East Indians is increasing. It includes several churches of various denominations, including Spiritual Baptist and Orisha places of worship, one or two mosques and, in recent years, a Hindu temple has been built.

Table 1: Ethnic Breakdown for Diego Martin and Trinidad and Tobago

Ethnic Group	Diego Martin	Trinidad & Tobago
Black	53.0%	40.8%
East Indian	11.6	40.7
Mixed	27.5	16.3
White	4.5	1.0
Chinese	1.4	.5
Other/not stated	1.6	.6
Syrian/Lebanese	.4	.1
	100.0	100.0

Source: Compiled from the 1980 census report

The industrial estate is the site of the area's only manufacturing industry. Besides Essential there are factories manufacturing car batteries, nylon stockings, kitchen appliances, plastic signs and ice cream cones. In addition, there are three garment manufacturers. These factories are similar to Essential in that most of the workforce is female and lives nearby.

Workforce Characteristics

Until it began to break down at the turn of the century, Trinidad had a long history of an ethnic division of labor (Yelvington 1985). The ethnic composition of the workforce at Essential is anachronistic and somewhat reminiscent of Edgar Mittelholzer's (1950) *A Morning at the Office*. The owners are white, most of the office workers are white, Chinese or "high brown," the accountant is East Indian, most of the floor supervisors are white and the line workers are black or East Indian.

There is, of course, a sexual division of labor. The majority of Essential's line workers are female. As can be seen in Table 2, 52 of the 63 line workers (or 82.5 per cent) are females with ages ranging from late teens to mid-forties. The remainder are young men in their late teens and early twenties. There is one 35-year-old male toolmaker with a 20-year-old male assistant, who are both East Indian. The floor supervisors are all males aged between about 30 and 50. Among the female workers, 71 per cent are black and 25 per cent are East Indian. There are five East Indian and six black male line workers. Three of the eight floor supervisors are East Indian, the rest are white. One supervisor is Dutch and one is a white Jamaican, the rest were born in Trinidad.

Table 2: Age, Sex and Ethnicity of Factory Line Workers

Age	Sex	Black	East Indian	Mixed	Totals
16–25	M	6	4	0	10
	F	17	9	2	28
26–35	M	0	1	0	1
	F	6	2	0	7
36–50	M	0	0	0	0
	F	15	2	0	17
Totals	M	6	5	0	11
	F	37	13	2	52

The workers all come from urban working backgrounds, but differ in their "life situations" and personal circumstances. Only a few of the supervisors have had any formal technical training. Ruud, for instance, who trained as an engineer in the Dutch Navy, is responsible for keeping complex machinery in working order. And Vishnu, the toolmaker, can be described as a highly skilled worker. The others merely seem to have acquired general mechanical skills from having worked on cars, which they apply to some of the less complex, relatively antiquated machinery in the factory. All the male line workers, except one, live in households with a parent and other extended kin. These young men have completed at least some secondary schooling, but only Terry, a 20-year-old, has any "O" levels. A few are taking night courses at the John Donaldson technical training college in Port of Spain, including Ben, the assistant toolmaker.

The women's educational and skill backgrounds am different from those of their supervisors. Only two of the female workers over 26 have any secondary school education. None have any technical training as such, but several have completed courses in crafts such as dressmaking and cake-icing. It should be said, though, that some of the more experienced female workers are expected to maintain and know how to repair the machines with which they work and in this area they tend to be more skilled than their supervisors.

Of the younger women, more than half have some secondary school experience. A few have taken craft courses, while others are involved in technical and commercial training. For example, during the period of my fieldwork, Imogen, 19, was completing an electrician's course in Laventille at a Catholic organization, Servol, which specializes in vocational training. Many of these workers were far better placed than their mothers, who were often domestic servants and, in having continuous employment, some had even improved on the positions their fathers had held at corresponding periods of their lives.

Most of the women over 30 are in residential mating relationships, i.e. consensual cohabitation or legal marriage. About 95 per cent of the female workers over 25 have children. Some of the female workers are the main breadwinners of the household, as some of their menfolk have been retrenched recently due to the wider economic crisis in the country, the 'recession', as Trinidadians call it: the country was 20 per cent poorer in 1986 than in 1982. The pattern is for younger women, even if they have children, to live in the same household as their older kin. Table 3 shows the position of the labour force in 1986. Between 1970 and 1984, female participation in the labour force increased by 3.5 per cent, compared to a 1 per cent decrease for men during the same period (Trinidad & Tobago 1987: 49), although by 1977 women's median monthly income was only 65 per cent of men's (Hyacinth 1979:16–17).[4]

It is difficult to say what will happen as the recession deepens. The government, which directly employs between 40 and 50 per cent of the country's workforce, is beginning to reduce the number of its employees. If this is done on the basis of seniority, we can assume that most of those affected will be women. On the other hand, during the later years of the 1980s the government enacted policies which seemed to favour the more traditional of the industrial employers of women. While overall unemployment in garment, textile and footwear production went from 8 to 25 per cent between 1985 and 1986, local garment manufacturers increased their workforce from 2500 in November 1987 to 5000 in November 1988. This was due to new duty-free concessions, a ban on foreign clothes and a task force created to clamp down on the illegal import of goods. One manu-

Table 3: Population, Labor Force & Employment Estimates, 1986

| | (Thousands) | | |
	Both Sexes	Male	Female
Total population	1199.2	600.2	599.0
Non-institutional population	1195.2	598.0	597.5
Population under 15 years	398.5	202.6	195.9
Population 65 years and over	66.8	30.4	36.4
Dependency ratio (%)	63.0		
Non-institutional population 15 years and over	795.2	394.6	400.6
Labor force	471.2	316.3	154.9
Labor force participation (%)	59.0	80.0	39.0
Employment	393.2	265.9	127.3
Unemployed	78.0	50.3	27.7
Unemployment rate (%)	16.6	15.9	17.9

Source: Trinidad & Tobago 1987b (Review of the Economy 1986 and appendix 16)

facturer is quoted as saying (*Trinidad Guardian*, 21 December 1988: 3): "This is a phenomenal turn around in an industry once considered dead. It is probably the most vibrant industry in the economy today."

Gender at Work

To understand why this particular workforce is employed we need to look not only at structural factors, but also at the average worker's options. Unemployment among young women is the highest of any group: there are few options open to young women who have left school without educational qualifications, so employment in a factory that favors their group seems relatively attractive. In practice, marriage is not seen as an alternative to wage labor.

New workers are often the kin of people already working in the factory and almost all had heard about the vacancy from a friend on the inside. Tiexiera said he preferred younger female workers. "The older girls with families aren't as dependable. They're late, they're always having babies, they have to take time off when their children are sick. Nah. I definitely prefer to hire young girls." Apart from the obviously offensive way in which he refers to women as "older girls," he has no real grounds for assuming that women with family responsibilities who depend on their salaries for their children's as well as their own survival, should be less valuable to the firm. For a start, as I discuss later, because "respectable" behavior at work enhances prestige, the older women do not participate in the horseplay and flirting engaged in by the younger workers.

What Tiexiera does not say is that the younger workers are more docile and can be paid less. New workers are categorized as "temporary" and required to

Table 4: Examples of 1986 Wages for EUL Line Workers, in TT$

Temporary		1 Year's Service	
Weekly wage	110.00	Weekly wage	160.00
Hourly rate	($2.75)	Hourly rate	($4.00)
NIS*	3.50	NIS*	4.50
Health Charge	8.25	Health Charge	8.25
Take Home Pay	98.25	Take Home Pay	147.25

Permanent		2 Years' Service	
Weekly wage	130.00	Weekly wage	180.00
Hourly wage	($3.25)	Hourly wage	($4.50)
NIS*	3.50	NIS*	5.75
Health Charge	8.25	Health Charge	8.25
Take Home Pay	118.25	PAYE**	3.00
		Take Home Pay	163.00

* National Insurance Scheme; **Pay as You Earn income tax scheme. *Note*: At the time of the fieldwork, the exchange rate was as follows: TT$3.60=US$1.00, TT$5.28=£1.00

serve a six-month probationary period during which they can be fired without warning and are paid at a lower rate. This cannot justifiably be called a training period because almost all the jobs can be learned in less than half an hour and a new worker with average ability can become as productive as experienced ones in a matter of days. If their performance is satisfactory at the end of the six-month probationary period, the workers are made "permanent" and receive a small pay rise. Sometimes this is withheld as a disciplinary procedure. Wages at Essential are lower than at other similar firms. Figures compiled for November 1986 within the industry group, not differentiated by sex, indicate that the average minimum wage was TT$10.34 an hour for an assembler, $7.99 an hour for a machine operator and $9.72 an hour for a laborer (Trinidad & Tobago 1987a: 35). The examples of wages given in Table 4 show that wages at Essential lag far behind. The wages at Essential are similar to those in the garment industry, the traditional employer of female manufacturing workers, which averaged $214.82 a week in 1986 (Trinidad & Tobago 1987a: 41).

Jobs in the factory are allocated by gender. The women are involved in jobs like soldering wires, testing electrical components, glueing labels and other tedious tasks that require patience and concentration. They are machine operators and they are sedentary. On the other hand, the men are given jobs that require and allow time for mobility within the factory. In fact they seem to take much pleasure in taking the risks associated with leaving their posts and walking around the factory. Some operate machines, but they are mainly responsible for assist-

Table 5: Educational Attainment for Trinidad & Tobago 1980, (Ages 15+)

Level	Male (%)	Female (%)
No education	3.4	6.4
Primary	60.8	56.6
Secondary	31.1	33.8
University	2.9	1.5
Other/unstated	1.8	1.7
Totals	100.0	100.0

Source: Trinidad & Tobago 1980 Census report

ing the supervisors by moving boxes of finished products and retrieving materials from the storeroom. On the whole, they are not in jobs where it could be said that a male was necessary because of the physical strength needed. The workers have an idea about what are appropriate women's and men's jobs. Vishnu teased Jeremy, who was temporarily assigned to operate a machine all day, in the following manner: "I didn't know it didn't have enough girls to work here."

Female workers are seen as less likely to want to join a union and Tiexiera often said that if a union came to Essential he would close the factory down. Two years before my fieldwork he had apparently fired 20 workers who were secretly trying to gain union recognition. In addition, Tiexiera was constantly reminding the workers about the state of the country's economy. "He using this recession as a excuse," said Cheryl, who then *steupsed* (sucked her teeth loudly in disapproval— called *churi* in Suriname and *chups* in other parts of the Caribbean).

Actual recruitment practices seem to contradict the "dual market" theory of female labor, which holds that women are excluded from the productivity-enhancing jobs that would enable them to increase their wages and, hence, their status. However, this view assumes that the market operates impersonally. As Humphrey (1985: 219) shows from studies of Brazilian industry, "the supposedly objective economic laws of market competition work through and within gendered structures. The market does not value male and female labour independently of gender." Likewise, from her studies of women's work in Morocco, Joekes (1985: 189) inverts the presumed causation and argues that women's lower pay is not mainly a reflection of their relative lack of education: "If it is a fact that women can be paid less than men, then by the same token women will be placed in jobs with a low grade rating." In fact, Table 5 illustrates that in Trinidad and Tobago a higher percentage of women than men have secondary education. Table 6 provides information on the enrolment in some selected courses in the country's technical and vocational institutions. What this points out is the extent to which young women and men are still channelled into "traditional" (though not necessarily so for Trinidad and Tobago) occupations.

Trinidadians saw food prices and the general cost of living double during the

Table 6: Enrollment in Technical and Vocational Schools, Final Term 1983/4

	No. of Students (full and part-time)	
Course	Male	Female
Accounting technicians	47	125
Auto and diesel mechanics	115	7
Business management	86	152
Construction carpentry	53	4
Commercial art	24	11
Computer programming	81	64
Domestic electronics service	92	1
Dressmaking and design	-	54
Electrical/electronics engineering	88	7
Electrical installation	171	6
Mechanical engineering	138	5
Plumbing	45	7
Practical cafeteria management	3	12
Shorthand/typing	-	96
Welding	106	5

Source: Compiled from Trinidad & Tobago 1987c (Annual Statistical Digest 1985, Tables 66a and 66b)

1980s.[5] Typical responses to such pressures are to find additional sources of income and to develop "support networks" (Gussler 1980). Comitas (1973) points out the prevalence of occupational multiplicity in the rural Caribbean, but I see this pattern as applying fairly generally to the working class. Many (supervisors included) have supplementary ways of earning money, such as growing and selling fruit and vegetables, dressmaking, minding children, making stuffed animals, installing car stereos and catering for parties and weddings. Some engage in unpaid work on tracts of land owned by kin in the rural areas (cf. Momsen 1987).

The informal internal economy at Essential is almost identical to the one Cuales (1980: 81–3) describes in her study of female workers in a factory in Curaçao. Brian, 21, is training to be a Spiritual Baptist pastor and he sells sweet bread, *aloo* pies and soft drinks at the factory. His godmother makes the sweet bread and he makes the pies; he gives her some of the profits. He is part of a fairly extensive internal informal economy. Myra, who bakes sweet bread and cakes for sale, is Brian's friendly competitor and her profits are reported to be around $40 a week. Denise roasts peanuts, puts them in bags and brings them to work to sell. Tia's aunt, who works in a garment factory on the same estate, often goes to Margarita, a free port island off Venezuela, and brings back items of clothing, which Tia sells at the factory. Trinidadians are known for their preference for foreign goods and the items usually attract attention. However, when their quality is judged to be poor, the customers charge that the aunt is merely supplying goods that are produced in the factory where she works. All entrepreneurs grant credit to other workers and usually there is a scramble to collect what is owed after pay packets are passed out on Friday.

The emphasis on entrepreneurship is indicative of an individualistic ethos, which is found throughout the Caribbean. When asked about the types of jobs they would like, almost all the workers indicated that they would like to open up their own businesses.

Supervision and Resistance

In Trinidad there is much talk of the presence of a so-called "Carnival mentality" and its effect on industrial productivity. The notion derives from a local stereotype of blacks as unserious, fun loving and lazy. East Indians, on the other hand, are considered more industrious. But, despite numerous meetings and government and academic inquiries into productivity in the recent past, no clear-cut solutions to the problem have emerged (cf. Nunes 1987; Williams 1987; Ryan 1982). Some scholars have recently started to explain worker apathy and lack of productivity in terms of management practices, particularly the "driver style" of supervision which is seen as a legacy of slavery. Tiexiera and the supervisors basically adhere to McGregor's (1960) "theory X," which holds that people naturally dislike working and so have to be forced to do so. But the theory of a "Carnival mentality" is, in my view, invalidated by the fact that so many of the workers are engaged in multiple occupations and generally exhibit a strong desire for material possessions.

There is no doubt, however, that a powerful workplace norm operates against being seen to be working hard. At Essential workers of all ages are adept at go-slows and other such delaying tactics, though the older workers are less obvious about it. For example, one of the groups assigned to making a particular product, in which all the workers were under 25, had its daily quota calculated at 200 products. The workers said they did not feel they could make that many and every day made 150. The workers kept a close count on the number produced and, usually, would have almost reached their targets at about 4:00 p.m. Between 4:00 and 4:30 p.m., which was when work stopped, only about three items would be produced. They reasoned, correctly, that if Tiexiera knew they were capable of making 200, he would set the quota at 225. Instead, through their collective action, they were able to alter the formal production schedule. If someone was thought to be working too hard, the usual barb was "Tiexiera your father or what?"

There was a different atmosphere when Tiexiera came out of his office onto the adjacent factory floor. All pretence of not working hard was forgotten and managers and workers alike put their heads down and concentrated on their work: Tiexiera has a bad temper and the supervisors were often insulted (*buffed up*) in front of the workers. On a few occasions during my fieldwork year, Tiexiera caught workers idling and suspended them right then and there. Temporary workers were occasionally fired on the spot.

Though some interpreted Tiexiera's behavior as "racial," others put it down to bad temper and greed. But, since there was always a danger that Tiexiera would walk out of his office door, the workers were taking a considerable risk in being idle. Because of short-staffing, the line supervisors were expected to fill in and therefore could not always keep a watchful eye on the workers. At around 4:00 p.m. the supervisors would often go down into the stores office on the factory floor. The workers would then ease up. I do not believe this is collusion between the supervisors and workers against the owners; I see it rather as the supervisors' acceptance of a situation.

On Fridays work stopped at 4:00 p.m. and the workers would crowd around the stores office to wait for the personnel manager to hand out their pay packets. Though notices are posted on the bulletin board telling workers to go back to work after having been paid, these are always ignored. On pay day, besides paying off accounts for food purchased during the week, the *sou-sou* "captains" take their deposits. (*Sou-sou* is based on a West African rotating credit system: such groups are called *meeting turns* in Jamaica, *partners* in the Eastern Caribbean and *sam* in Curaçao.) In a group of say five people, individuals may put in $50 a week. Each week it would be someone's turn to get his or her "hand" of $250 until the cycle was complete. The captains are the people who run the *sou-sou* and in Trinidad they are almost always women. Women, it was explained to me, could be trusted with money, whereas men could not.

Social distance between supervisors and workforce along ethnic and gender lines seems to have been cultivated by Tiexiera as a factor in the production process. He once told me that "there was a time when we used to look at race, . . . race was important in hiring, but not any more." By this he meant not only the hiring of supervisors, but also that East Indians were preferred as line workers. This conformed to old Trinidadian stereotypes. Though Tiexiera claimed to have abandoned this approach, during the period of my fieldwork a Portuguese Creole supervisor was replaced first by a white man and later by an East Indian man. So, to echo Humphrey (1985), the market does not value labor independently of gender *and* ethnicity.

Older workers told me that there had once been a black supervisor who "stood up" to Tiexiera and argued for more money for them, but that he eventually became disillusioned and left. Some felt that ethnicity had something to do with the supervisor taking up the workers' complaints. But what the workers call selective hiring is not confined to a particular ethnic group. As Martha put it: "Everybody want to push he race to the top. If you go to a Indian place, it only have Indians working there. Negroes, we would do the same. It *natural* to help you own people." This, I think, is evidence of the "culture of ethnicity" in Trinidad.

The day-to-day activities of the supervisors seem to have immediate effects on the workers. What one notices is the amount of sexual horseplay and the way the supervisors flirt with the workers. This was encouraged by the spatial situation at the factory where men and women spend eight hours a day in close proximity. Outside the factory, they operate in relatively separate domains. This horseplay and flirting only occurred among the younger workers. Once, during a break, Lloyd was standing at the front of the factory when Patricia walked by. Patricia, an East Indian, had only been working there for about three months, but from the beginning Lloyd had started to flirt with her in an increasingly licentious way, to which she often responded in kind. It was known that Lloyd, who was divorced, had several outside economic activities and a cabin cruiser moored at the Trinidad Yacht Club, so it is possible that Patricia was trying to use her flirting instrumentally. Henry and Wilson (1975: 178) note that the exploitative nature of Caribbean male-female relationships had necessitated women's "employment of certain manipulative techniques and rationalizations in order to attain, or convince themselves they have attained, it would seem, the kind of relationship they desire."

On this occasion, after commenting to another supervisor about her propensity to wear tight jeans, he said in an audible voice as she turned the corner, walking past, "Ooh, I would love to fuck she." This was a version of the "dropping words" technique,[6] used here by Lloyd to make his intentions explicit. Weeks later they came to the wedding of one of the workers together, but Lloyd got drunk and they apparently had an argument. Back at the factory Lloyd was rather tentative in his subsequent forays and if any sexual relationship ever developed I was unaware of it. I was not aware of any sexual activities within the factory of the kind Roy (1974) documents in his study of an American factory.

Whitehead (1976: 177–9) shows how joking abuse is used by men to control women. Likewise, at Essential, we can say that flirting has the unintended consequence of controlling the workers. Their resultant alienation may explain their apparent lack of interest in trade unions, which they may see as primarily benefiting men.[7] Sexual harassment in Trinidad and Tobago is a much talked-about problem, and I consider the supervisor-worker relationships described above to be examples. In 1987, Singing Sandra won the Calypso Queen title with a song called "Die With My Dignity":

> Yuh want to help to mind you family
> Yuh want to help yuh man financially
> But nowadays it really very hard
> To get a job as a girl in Trinidad
> Yuh looking now to find something to do
> Yuh meet a bossman who promise to help you
> But when the man lay down the condition
> Is nothing else but humiliation

They want to see yuh whole anatomy
They want to see what yuh doctor never see
They want to do what yuh husband never do
Still don't know if the scamps will hire you
Well if is all this humiliation
To get ah job these days as a woman
They will keep their money
I will keep my honey
And die with my dignity

—*Trinidad Express,*
19 February 1987:19

Factory Social Relations

Social relationships in the factory fell into four groups. Women over 30 tended to establish peer group relationships among themselves while younger women formed separate social links. Young male peer groups were differentiated along ethnic lines while supervisors rarely associated with workers. Although I share some of Besson's reservations about Wilson's "reputation and respectability" model in accounting for female behavior, in the factory older women are accorded prestige for acting "respectable." "Proper" behavior for an older woman is constrained in its scope.

Those who do not conform often pay the price in moral sanctions. For example, 45-year-old Vera had never married and had no children. She was seen by the workers as spreading gossip and was ostracized by many of the older women. She was also ridiculed behind her back for spending most of her time in conversation with the two youngest women in her department. One 26-year-old worker, herself the mother of three children, said "no wonder she crazy. It not natural to have no child. If I was she, I'd be crazy too." In Vera's case, I could not tell whether she had resorted to associating with younger workers because she was isolated, or whether she was being ridiculed as a result of spending time with younger workers. Either way, it seems she had little control over her failure to live up to the other workers' expectations.

Denise, 35, was a somewhat different example. She had two teenage children and was divorced. She worked in a department away from the main shop floor and was also regarded by most of the workers as a gossip. Her network consisted almost wholly of younger workers. She often went to parties with the younger workers and flirted with the men. "I find for a big woman she fast [bold and wild]," said Terry, a young man with whom she did not flirt.

The shop floor culture reflects these divisions. The peer groups of the younger female workers are pervaded by an emphasis on romance: they bring to work and share magazines named *Photoromance* and *Kiss*, which are produced in Italy and contain pictures of glamorous white models. Pollert (1981: 137) writes about similar behavior among the younger workers in an English factory and puts it down to the fact that they are cushioned from domestic responsibilities. The workers at Essential, however, are not exempted from domestic duties: indeed, 12 of the 28 females under 25 have children of their own. The workers' responsibilities include contributing to the household income. Some hand over up to half their weekly pay to elder kin. Irene, for example, was 24 and the mother of twin boys, aged 7. Her starting take-home pay was $98 a week and after the six-month probationary period she was made "permanent" and her take-home pay increased to $118. She lived with her mother, step-father, step-sister, step-brother and her two children. She contributed $20 to the household and undertook various household chores, mainly child care.

While the older women workers talk about home and church, as well as their work, male peer groups are generally cut off from each other by ethnicity and their conversation focuses on women, soccer, cars and music. Meeting points between the younger men and women workers mainly consist of flirting. In these relationships, the flirting is initiated by both sides and is part of a general pattern of constant horseplay among the younger women workers, who are mostly confined to one particular department. The men use their mobility within the factory to play the so-called "sex-fame game," the essential element of which is to "sweet-talk" a woman in order to make a sexual conquest. This raises the question of whether flirting relationships may be regarded as joking relationships. Radcliffe-Brown (1952: 100) points out that joking relationships obtain between those who may marry and avoidance between those who may not. In a study of joking relationships in a Glasgow factory, however, Sykes (1966:192–3) shows that relations between younger workers, who were potential sexual partners, were characterized by modesty, while gross obscenity prevailed between those older workers who were not potential sex partners.

At Essential, while black men flirt with black and East Indian young women, East Indian men generally only flirt with East Indian women. This was explained to me by Carla, an East Indian, who said: "You kidding? A black man would love to marry a Indian woman. She will cook for he and keep he house clean and look after the chirren. A black woman, he couldn't keep she at home." This statement is further illuminating on at least two counts: first, while there are few instances of long-term domestic relationships between blacks and East Indians, when they do occur they seem to be between black men and East Indian women. Secondly it suggests that women see themselves through the eyes of men and at times define themselves in terms of what is useful to men. The flirting relationships, then, seem to conform to Radcliffe-Brown's usage, and the ones between supervisors and workers tend to reproduce a system whereby white men had sexual access to black and East Indian women under slavery and indenture.

However, it is a mistake to assume that, in themselves, factory relationships can fully explain factory behavior. I therefore also examined the "networks of support" (cf. Wellman 1981) of a selected group of workers. In this context "support" is taken to mean the exchange of emotional, financial and informational assistance to help each other "mek do." It was noticeable that goods and services were exchanged across ethnic lines much more frequently among women than men, among whom this sort of activity was almost non-existent. Bourdieu (1977: 62) suggests that women are less sensitive to "symbolic profits" and that lending between women is the antithesis of the exchange of honor among men: "The urge to calculate, repressed in men, finds more overt expression in women, who are structurally predisposed to be less concerned with symbolic profits accruing from political unity, and to devote themselves more readily to strictly economic practices." Similarly, I would not want to explain this sort of activity by saying that women are "naturally" less ethnocentric than men, but by pointing out that the women in the factory did not lose status through exchange with others beyond their ethnic group and that, given their structural position and their familial responsibilities, they realized that they would have access to a wider range of resources if they were to initiate exchanges beyond their own group.

Conclusion

In this chapter I have tried to set the patterns of social behavior in the factory in their historical context and to discuss the cognitive aspects of this behavior. I have also shown the responses of the workers to the exercise of power and authority and their creative efforts to better their economic circumstances. I want to conclude with two points: one relates to the future of female workers in Trinidad and Tobago and the other concerns the theoretical contributions of the concepts of gender and ethnicity.

First, as oil revenues decline the government will increasingly look to the opportunities offered by the expansion of foreign capital investment. This move is encouraged by trade agreements with the United States and Canada and by the introduction of free trade zones, both of which tend to foster higher rates of female employment. Success in attracting such employers will depend on keeping local wages down relative to those in other countries (Table 7).[8]

As Table 7 suggests, while comparing favorably with some countries where "off-shore" production is located, the wage structures of CARICOM countries and of the Caribbean area in general place these countries at a distinct disadvantage in comparison with the low wage economies of Asia. Therefore, to attract US investment CARICOM governments must be willing to offer additional "advantages," one of which is cheap female labor.

Secondly, the study suggests that gender and ethnicity are constructed in relation to each other. This argument has also been suggested by Parmar (1982: 258), who has studied women in Britain. She writes that "Women are defined differently according to their 'race'." In addition, I would further argue that gender, ethnicity and class are socially constructed with reference to each other and that

Table 7: Monthly Wages in Manufacturing in 1985

Country		Monthly Pay (in 1985 US$)
Canada		1429.92
Rep. of Korea	(male)	398.67
	(female)	187.01
Singapore	(male)	345.25
	(female)	218.98
Costa Rica		179.13
St Lucia		146.64
Trinidad & Tobago		144.44
Philippines	(skilled)	77.18
	(unskilled)	60.99
Sri Lanka	(male)	36.88
	(female)	25.93

Note: These wages are based on an eight-hour working day and a 20 working-day month. Source: Compiled from the International Labour Office, Yearbook of Statistics 1987 and International Monetary Fund, International Statistics Yearbook 1987, various pages

a multi-dimensional view must be adopted if one is to understand the complexities of power relations in the factory context.

Notes

1. Ethnicity is a particular "involuntary" social identity seen in relation to a socially constructed ultimate ancestral link between an individual and a named group, which have shared an ancestor and a common culture. This subjective identification is not arbitrary nor purely imaginary and is characterized by what Ching (1985), writing on Trinidad, called the "social construction of primordiality." It is here that "practice" approaches to ethnicity, in their current form or with modifications, are useful (Yelvington 1991). I define gender as a particular sense of the self which is socially constructed in relation to perceived and non-perceptable biological criteria. Since perception here is social in origin, and dependent upon the way individual/society relationships may be interpreted in various contexts, we can say that gender is culturally specific.

2. An earlier version was presented as a paper to the Society for Caribbean Studies 12th Annual Conference, Hoddesdon, Hertfordshire, England, 12–14 July 1988. I would like to thank a number of people for their comments on earlier versions of this paper, including Clemen Aquino, Nuraddin Auwal, Bridget Brereton, R. W. Connell, Maria Patricia Fernandez-Kelly, John French, Ralph Grillo, David Harrison, Aisha Khan, Janet Momsen, June Nash, Sheila Smith, Steve Vertovec, and Faustina Ward-Osborne. In addition, I have benefited from conversations, correspondence and encouragement from several people in the Caribbean, UK and US, including John Humphrey, Anthony Maingot, Joycelin Massiah, Patricia Mohammed, Ruth Pearson, Dorian Powell, Ann Whitehead, Donald Wood and Annette Ching, to whom I owe a special debt. I would especially like to thank the workers, managers and owners of Essential Utensils Ltd, who must remain anonymous.

3. The specific characteristics of the factory and the individual owners, supervisors and workers have been fictionalized to protect the anonymity of those concerned.

4. Still, this seems an improvement over the recent past. In 1965, the median monthly income of female workers was TT$83.50, while men's income was $146.50. In 1971, the comparison was $93.00 for females, $167.50 for males. In 1977, the comparison was $293.00 for females, $449.50 for males. However, throughout the period, the median monthly income of female government employees approximated that of male government employees.

5. After running in double figures, inflation in 1985 was 7.6 per cent, the lowest since 1971. But subsidies were withdrawn from certain food imports after the preferential exchange rate was changed in February 1987. There followed two rounds of price increases at the end of March 1987, affecting government-controlled basic food items: evaporated milk (up 41 per cent), powdered baby milk (up 29 per cent), cheese (up 32 per cent), potatoes, onions, garlic and tinned sardines. The Economist Intelligence Unit (1987/8: 11) predicted that inflation in 1987 would run at between 20 and 30 per cent.

6. "Dropping words" is a technique used in Trinidad when someone wants to shame someone else. For example, when the victim is walking by the aggressor might utter some sensitive secret about the victim in an audible voice, but without looking at the victim and without apparently referring specifically to them. To gain status, the victim must remain "cool-cool" and pretend not to hear, for if they are provoked their response is taken as proof by the audience that the accusations were in fact true. In Trinidad, a premium is put on decorum in social exchanges.

7. As part of my research I had several conversations with female union officials about female workers. They told me not only of the general unwillingness of male union officials to incorporate females into the power structure, but of how the husband and boyfriends of female members would occasionally disrupt meetings that were held at night and demand that their womenfolk return home.

8. Protests in Trinidad were started in early 1988 by the pressure group, Women Against Free Trade Zones. This was a joint project of women's groups, the Oilfields Workers' Trade Union, which vociferously opposed the zones (cf. *Vanguard*, 26 March 1988: 3–4) and the Women's Studies Unit at the University of the West Indies.

References

Bourdieu, Pierre (1977) Outline of a Theory of Practice. Translated by Richard Nice, Cambridge: Cambridge University Press

Brodber, Erna (1980) Jane and Louisa Will Soon Come Home. London: New Beacon Books

Brown, Richard (1976) "Women as Employees: Some Comments on Research in Industrial Sociology." In Diana L. Barker and Sheila Allen (eds), Dependence and Exploitation in Work and Marriage, London: Longman, 21–46

Caribbean Conference of Churches (1986) A Social Survey of the Poverty Situation in Trinidad. Port of Spain: Caribbean Conference of Churches

Ching, Annette M. T. (1985) "Ethnicity Reconsidered, with Reference to Sugar and Society in Trinidad." Unpublished D.Phil. thesis, University of Sussex

Comitas, Lambros (1973) "Occupational Multiplicity in Rural Jamaica." In Lambros

Comitas and David Lowenthal (eds) Work and Family Life: West Indian Perspectives, Garden City: Anchor Books, 156–73

Cuales, Sonia (1980) "Women, Reproduction and Foreign Capital in Curaçao," Caraibisch Forum, 1 (2) 75–86

Economist Intelligence Unit (1987/8) Country Profile: Trinidad and Tobago. London: Economist Intelligence Unit

Gussler, Judith D. (1980) "Adaptive Strategies and Social Networks of Women in St Kitts." In Erida Bourguignon (ed.) A World of Women, New York: Praeger, 185–209

Henry, Frances and Pamela Wilson (1975) "The Status of Women in the Caribbean: An Overview of their Social, Economic and Sexual Roles." Social and Economic Studies, 24 (2) 165–98

Humphrey, John (1985) "Gender, Pay and Skill: Manual Workers in Brazilian Industry." In Haleh Afshar (ed.) Women, Work and Ideology in the Third World, London: Tavistock, 214–31

Hyacinth, S. (1979) Changes in the Status of Women 1900–1977. Trinidad & Tobago: Central Statistical Office, (mimeo, restricted circulation)

International Labour Office (1987) Yearbook of Statistics 1987. Geneva: ILO

International Monetary Fund (1987) International Statistics Yearbook 1987. Washington DC: IMF

Joekes, Susan (1985) "Working for Lipstick? Male and Female in the Clothing Industry in Morocco." In Haleh Afshar (ed.) Women, Work and Ideology in the Third World, London: Tavistock, 183–213

McGregor, Douglas (1960) The Human Side of Enterprise. New York: McGraw-Hill

Mittelholzer, Edgar (1950) A Morning at the Office. London: Hogarth

Momsen, Janet Henshall (1987) "The Feminization of Agriculture in the Caribbean." In Janet H. Momsen and Janet Townsend (eds) Geography of Gender in the Third World, London: Hutchinson, 344–7

Nunes, Frederick E. (1987) "Culture, Motivation and Organizational Performance." Asset, 5 (2) 3–16

Parmar, Pratiba (1982) "Gender, Race and Class: Asian Women in Resistance." In Centre for Contemporary Cultural Studies, University of Birmingham, The Empire Strikes Back, London: Hutchinson, 237–75

Pollert, Anna (1981) Girls, Wives, Factory Lives. London: Macmillan

Radcliffe-Brown A. R. (1952) Structure and Function in Primitive Society. London: Cohen & West

Roy, Donald (1974) "Sex in the Factory: Informal Heterosexual Relations Between Supervisors and Work Groups." In Clifton Bryant (ed.) Deviant Behaviour, Chicago: Rand McNally, 44–66

Ryan, Selwyn (1982) "The Role of Management in Productivity." In Trinidad & Tobago, National Consultation on Productivity Report, Ministry of Labour, Social Security and Cooperatives, 41–6

Sykes, A. J. M. (1966) "Joking Relationships in an Industrial Setting." American Anthropologist, 68 (1) 188–93

Trinidad & Tobago (1980) Population and Housing Census, Port of Spain: Government Printing

—— (1987) Social Indicators Report. Port of Spain: Central Statistical Office

—— (1987a) Economic Indicators: October-December 1986, Port of Spain: Central Statistical Office

—— (1987b) Review of the Economy 1986. Port of Spain: Government Printing

—— (1987c) Annual Statistical Digest 1985. Port of Spain: Central Statistical Office

Trinidad Express, 19 February 1987:19

Trinidad Guardian, 21 December 1988: 3

Vanguard. 26 March 1988: 3–4

Wellman, Barry (1981) "Applying Network Analysis to the Study of Support." Resource Paper No. 3, Toronto: Centre for Urban and Community Studies, University of Toronto

Whitehead, Ann (1976) "Sexual Antagonism in Hertfordshire." In Diana L. Barker and Sheila Allen (eds) Dependence and Exploitation in Work and Marriage, London: Longman, 169–203

Williams, Gwendoline A. (1987) "Management and Development in the Business/Industrial Environment of Trinidad and Tobago: A Focus on Major Socio-Cultural Issues." Asset, 4 (1) 17–33

Yelvington, Kevin A. (1985) "The Context of Acculturation: The Modernization Process and Occupational Diversification in Trinidad and Tobago 1891–1980." Unpublished MA thesis, Florida International University

—— (1991) "Ethnicity as Practice? A Comment on Bentley." Comparative Studies in Society and History, 33 (1) 158–68

15. WOMEN IN JAMAICA'S
URBAN INFORMAL ECONOMY

Insights from a Kingston Slum

Faye V. Harrison

Introduction

The West Indian legacy of colonialism and imperialism is the world's oldest and possibly the world's harshest.[1] The work, adaptations, and struggles of Caribbean women, particularly poor Afro-Creole[2] women, warrant scholarly attention, for these experiences can reveal much about the part that gender inequality, especially in its intersection with race and class oppression, plays in colonial and post-colonial domination and in dependent forms of national development.

Much of the material that exists on gender and on women in Caribbean societies can be found embedded in the many studies of lower-class family structure and in the works on internal marketing among peasants.[3] However, over the past decade or so, increasing attention has been more directly focused on the socio-cultural, political, and economic underpinnings of women's lives.[4] The purpose of this paper is not to provide a general framework for analyzing the varying statuses of women across class boundaries in West Indian societies, but to offer a perspective on the positions occupied and roles played by women within what is sometimes called the "informal economy" of urban Jamaica, specifically the Kingston Metropolitan Area.[5] Drawing upon ethnographic data from "Oceanview," a slum in downtown Kingston, the ensuing discussion attempts to elucidate and provide a context for understanding important facets of the everyday lives and struggles of those women who occupy the lowest strata of the Jamaican class structure: women who represent some of the most marginal segments of the working class and the petty bourgeoisie; and who, together with their young and aged dependents, constitute the largest proportion of their nation's poor.

A basic premise of this essay is that the problem of sexual inequality as it obtains in Jamaica today is integrally related to the broader processes of uneven development within the Caribbean periphery of the world capitalist system. That

Originally published in *New West Indian Guide* 62:3/4 (1988), pp. 103–28. Copyright © by KITLV Press. Reprinted by permission of KITLV Press.

is, sexual oppression must be viewed in the national and international contexts of class and regional disparities which condition the specificity of women's everyday lives (Nash and Safa 1980:x–xi). The world capitalist system embodies a structure of labor market segmentation wherein workers in peripheral countries receive no more than one-sixth of the wages received by their counterparts in the advanced industrial center (Amin 1980). Since female workers receive considerably less than their male counterparts, Third World women represent a *cheaper than cheap* segment of the international workforce (Lim 1983:80; Nash 1983:3). Capital accumulation and transfer on a world scale is based upon relations of superexploitation, the brunt of which Third World women bear. The interplay of class and gender is, therefore, integral to capitalist development at both national and international levels.

Patterns of Uneven Development in Jamaica

Jamaica, formally independent since 1962, has historically been one of the most important countries, politically and economically, in the Commonwealth Caribbean. Its current population is approximately 2.2 million, one-half of which is urban and one-third of which is situated in the primary city, Kingston (Department of Statistics 1978b:3). The Jamaican economy is marked by uneven development or "underdevelopment," i.e., historically constituted processes that distort and subordinate domestic production and exchange to the accumulation interests of metropolitan capital (Mamdani 1976:6). Based largely on the production of sugar and bananas, the mining and partial refining of bauxite, tourism, and manufacturing, Jamaica's economic structure is extroverted in that its dominant enterprises and sectors are largely foreign owned or controlled and oriented toward an export market. The economy is internally disjointed, for there are few organic links between domestic sectors (Beckford and Witter 1980:66,81). Instead, the major linkages are vertical; that is, agriculture, bauxite, tourism, and branch-plant manufacturing are integrated into North American (and largely American) corporations. Accordingly, all inputs—raw materials, services, technology, and skilled personnel—are imported, and virtually all outputs from these industries are exported.

However, all of the economy is not directly controlled by corporate capital. Jamaica's peripheral capitalism encompasses variant forms of production and exchange which are subordinate to the dominant capitalist pattern. Some of these subordinate economic forms, e.g., subsistence agriculture, have their origins in earlier non-capitalist modes of production/exchange that have been absorbed into the domestic capitalist system due to the consolidation and widespread penetration of large-scale and primarily foreign capital (cf. Post 1978). Other patterns, such as many of those found within the small-scale, unlicensed sphere of the urban economy, have developed out of contradictions and complexities endemic to peripheral capitalism itself (cf. Kowarick 1979:83).

CRISIS OF THE 70'S AND 80'S

During the 50's and 60's, foreign investment, principally American, propelled a rapid and sustained growth in the economy (Jefferson 1972). This capital-intensive growth benefitted the national bourgeoisie and middle class while it engendered a rise in unemployment and a decline in the poor's share in national income (Girvan and Bernal 1982:37). In sharp contrast to the boom period, the 1970's brought two world recessions, quadrupled oil prices, sharp price increases for manufactured imports, and acute price and demand instability for Third World exports (National Planning Agency 1978:6). The People's National Party (PNP), the ruling party of the 1972–80 period, instituted various reforms to redistribute national income and to secure greater "Jamaicanization" or sovereignty over the economy. One of the most dramatic actions the government took in response to international conditions and pressures from segments of the national bourgeoisie was the imposition of a production levy on the bauxite companies in 1974. Following the levy and Jamaica's part in the formation of the International Bauxite Association, the PNP announced its commitment to democratic socialism and to liberating itself from imperialism.

Fearing that Jamaica would move further leftward and expropriate investments, foreign and domestic capitalists, largely through the agency of the Jamaica Labour Party (JLP) opposition, mobilized a destabilization campaign to undermine the legitimacy of the PNP administration and oust it from office (Keith and Girling 1978:29). Bauxite companies cut back production and filed a litigation suit; the American press discouraged tourism, Jamaica's second largest foreign exchange earner; local capitalists cut back production and, in many cases, closed down business and fled the island with their capital; and international commercial banks ceased making loans to Jamaica.

Facing an economic collapse, in 1977 the country was compelled to seek foreign exchange from the International Monetary Fund (IMF), whose restrictive policies exacerbated the island's economic slump as well as its volatile political climate (Girvan and Bernal 1982:39, 40). In order to gain eligibility for IMF loans, the government had to undertake a number of drastic readjustments, among them cuts in real wages and retrenchment in the public sector. Initially the administration resisted the IMF strategy, but a severe credit squeeze forced it to re-open negotiations. Adhering to the terms of a standby loan, in April, 1977 the government was forced to devalue its currency by almost fifty percent, impose indirect taxes, lift price controls, and limit wages increases. These measures resulted in a thirty-five percent decline in real wages and a fifty percent rise in the price level (Girvan and Bernal 1982:43). After failing fiscal performance tests for two consecutive years, in early 1980 the government called for general elections in order to determine the nation's economic path. A month later the negotiations with the IMF were discontinued. The continuous shortages of basic commodities (even food staples), the rising unemployment (thirty-five percent in 1980) especially affecting young adults and women, the constant currency devaluations and sharp price increases, and the unprecedented wave of political violence accompanying the campaign demoralized the population and eroded its confidence in the PNP government. Within several months the opposition party had electorally ousted the PNP as the country's ruling party and returned the economy to the orbit of Western banks, transnationals, and the IMF.

In spite of massive support from the United States government and international institutions, principally the IMF, the Jamaican economy has deteriorated since the JLP's rise to power. Following stringent IMF directions, the administration de-nationalized public-owned businesses, drastically cut back in public employment, abolished price regulations and food subsidies, imposed restraints on wages, and devalued the national currency several times. The IMF strategy for economic recovery has increased the balance of payments deficit and imposed a degree of austerity on living conditions more severe than the hardships that prevailed during the PNP administration (Headley 1985).

The Urban Informal Economic Sector

Since the consolidation of the capitalist mode at the turn of the century, Jamaica, like many Third World countries, has been unable to offer secure and stable employment opportunities for most of its working-age population. The chronic problem of "surplus" population, severely aggravated by the balance of payments crisis, is manifest in high rates of unemployment, immeasurably rampant underemployment, and successive waves of emigration; and is the consequence of the displacement of labor from both subsistence and modern sectors of the national economy. Much of the surplus working population—the dislocated peasants, displaced and landless wage-workers, and the marginally self-employed—is absorbed into the urban informal economic sector, which encompasses income-producing activities outside formal sector wages, pensions, and gratuities (Portes 1981:87).[6]

Within the urban informal economic sphere are myriad productive, marketing, and service activities and enterprises, most of which are unlicensed, untaxed, and able to circumvent the expenses imposed by State safety and sanitary regulations. This petty-scale sector of the economy is dependent upon large-scale and capital-intensive industry and complements it by taking on tasks that the latter generally neglects because of unprofitability (Roberts 1978) or illegality. Because of the export orientation of capitalist production in most of the Third World, the dominant economic spheres are not organized to satisfy all market demands. Whereas the formal, corporate sector meets the demands of the export market, the informal sector caters to many of the requirements of the domestic market. For example, due to the gravity of economic conditions during the latter years of the PNP administration (when I collected most of my field data), the importation of a wide range of consumer and capital goods virtually ceased. A premium was, therefore, placed on items that had become scarce or unobtainable in the formal domestic market. The informal economy, particularly its illegal segments, became a major source of many goods and services, including such staple foodstuffs as rice, milk, flour, and cheese.

An integral and fairly stable component of Jamaica's illegitimate economic sphere is the production of and trade in ganja or marijuana. While the local and national trade is important, the international distribution of "herb" is even more economically significant (Lacey 1977). In fact, at the height of the balance of payments crisis of the 70's, ganja production and trade was "the only healthy [sector] of the Jamaican economy. The 1.1 billion dollar business [was] the economic lifeline of Jamaica . . . after traditional segments of the economy failed" (*Newsweek* 1980). This starkly illustrates how integral informal sector activities often are in peripheral capitalist economies.

While it may be clear that informal economic processes are subordinate to and dependent upon formally recognized economic sectors, it is also important to realize that capitalist accumulation itself is dependent upon the subsistence-oriented and other petty-scale activities of the informal sphere. The largely unlicensed and unregulated small-scale domain plays a critical role in subsidizing part of the costs of transnational corporations operating in Third World nations, enabling these firms to enforce comparatively low wages on their labor (Portes 1978:37). Moreover, by lowering the costs of reproduction, informal economic activities indirectly subsidize workers in core nations, e.g., the United States, and, thereby, help maintain the rate and transfer of profit (Portes 1981:106). The urban informal sector helps reduce labor costs for corporations in two major ways: first, by providing relatively cheap and/or accessible goods and services and, hence, reducing some of the costs of subsistence for the urban population, particularly wage-workers; and, second, by decreasing the relative size of the formal labor force with its abundant labor available for casual and disguised forms of wage-work.

"Self-employment" or "own-account" work represents a pattern of concealed wage-work which permits capital to extract surplus labor from petty producers and traders. Several scholars, e.g. Portes (1981), Birkbeck (1979), and Scott (1979), have shown that much informal sector activity is actually work done for the benefit of formal sector firms. For example, the informal marketing of formal sector goods constitutes a well organized business ultimately controlled by capitalist firms. Rather than invest in retail chains, distributing firms utilize "independent" traders. In this case, informal trading represents an efficient and profitable means of circulating both national and imported goods in the domestic market. The character of this inter-sectoral linkage is concealed, because capital does not intervene directly in the informal labor process, which is generally organized around personalized, often familial relationships. The informal labor process, therefore, should be distinguished from the underlying social relations of production and appropriation which permit capital to superexploit informal labor (cf. Amin 1980:25).[7]

Informal economic relations, which are typically embedded in kinship and peer networks, permit the use of free or nominally paid labor and, consequently, "an output of goods and services at prices lower than those which could be offered under formal productive arrangements" (Portes 1981:86). While these conditions reduce the costs of reproduction for the petty-scale sphere and, therefore, permit its viability, ultimately, these very conditions maximize surplus extraction by reducing the costs that the dominant sector must pay to reproduce labor power.

THE "FEMINIZATION" OF THE INFORMAL ECONOMY

The part the informal sector plays in lowering the general costs of reproducing labor power for formal sector capital is also the role attributed to a reserve army of labor.[8] Saffioti (1978) bases her theoretical discourse on women in class societies upon the premise that intrinsic to capitalism is the existence of a reserve resulting from the exclusion of considerable segments of the working populations from a secure position in the labor market. Under capitalist social conditions, a large proportion of women, particularly housewives who have been displaced from what are socially defined as productive economic roles, constitute a reserve labor force, whose surplus labor power is absorbed into the domestic domain of the social economy.

While women as housewives, working to reproduce their mates' labor power without the benefit of wages, may indeed represent an important and, in analytic terms, neglected component of the labor reserve, the quintessential reserve in peripheral societies such as Jamaica, where women constitute a sizeable component (47%) of the workforce as well as of the displaced workforce (i.e., informal workers),[9] includes those women who, as breadwinners and quite often as heads of households, must operate within the context of an insecure and informal opportunity structure to eke out a livelihood for themselves and for their young and aged dependents. From these segments of the reserve, middle- and upper-class housewives recruit and hire their domestic helpers, who for pitiably low wages perform most of the functions necessary for maintaining privileged households. From this informal labor force also come many of the female street vendors, called "higglers," who are responsible for distributing staple foodstuffs throughout the urban population, particularly to the poor.

The rate of formal unemployment for Jamaican women (39%) is more than twice as high as that for men (16%), resulting in more than twice as many women (167,900) being unemployed as compared to men (79,200) (Department of Statistics 1978b:26). The relative feminization of unemployment and poverty is manifested in the informal economy wherein females participate in survival and subsistence activities in comparatively larger numbers and proportions. More-over, in view of the pivotal position women occupy within familial and domestic configurations,[10] they tend to play principal mobilizational roles in "scuffling" ventures, i.e., small-scale income-generating processes.

The Sexual Division of Labor in the Informal Sphere

The urban informal economy consists of an expansive, competitive tertiary sec-tor, a small sphere of secondary production or petty manufacture, and, in light of the physical constraints of the urban economy, a restricted sector of primary pro-duction, e.g., gardening and animal husbandry. The principal focus of informal sector activity in the Kingston Metropolitan Area, therefore, tends to be that of commodity circulation and services rather than that of production. The latter process is concentrated largely within the formal sphere of the urban economy. That is to say that petty producers have been substantially displaced by large-scale capital, and this displacement has affected women more drastically than men.

According to government data for the late 1970s and early 1980s, approxi-mately 70% of all female workers in Jamaica were employed in the tertiary sector (i.e., commerce and services), while only about 32–33% of all male workers were active in this sector (Department of Statistics 1978b:27; 1984:308; Statistical In-stitute of Jamaica 1984:10). Only 7–8% of the female work was in manufacture, whereas on average 14% of the male workforce was concentrated there.

The respective distributions of female and male workers in the informal sector of one neighborhood's economic structure (that of Oceanview) indicate that both women and men shared exceedingly large concentrations in the tertiary sector of the locality and metropolitan economy. Still, the percentage of women workers in this sector exceeded that of men by about 11%.[11] Moreover, while a substan-tial percentage of men worked as producers (35%), a much lesser percentage of women (20%) was engaged in productive labor. It seems, therefore, that although most informal sector participants were involved in commercial and service activi-ties, the concentration of women's work in this particular domain was especially high (88%). This evidence suggests that compared with women, men tended to have access to income opportunities across a wider range of occupations, activi-ties, and sectors. Furthermore, the income opportunities accessible to men, e.g., those in construction, provided higher levels of remuneration than female-spe-cific jobs. Many of the higher paying jobs available to males, however, tended to be insecure, or available only on a temporary, casual basis.

Nelson (1979) shows that within the informal economic sector of Nairobi, Kenya, women by and large are restricted to marketing skills (e.g., preparing bev-erages, cooking, caring for children, and washing clothes) practiced in the home, whereas men market a much wider range of skills and services.[12] Evidence from Oceanview confirms this kind of sexual division of labor. For instance, close to 33% of the working women in my sample were engaged in some sort of domestic service, while about 26% were employed in general services (e.g., casual street-cleaning, hairstyling, and spiritual healing). In contrast, 40% of the men in the sample were engaged in general services (e.g., taxi-driving, vehicle repair, and photography).

Approximately 46% of all of the women sampled were involved in either or both the marketing of domestic services (33%) and the marketing of domestic or household consumer goods (24%), e.g., foodstuffs, cooking utensils, and clothing. Few (i.e., 3%) of the men were engaged in services (e.g., baking and cooking) that could be classified as domestic; nonetheless, approximately 18% were involved in marketing domestic commodities—food, durable domestic goods, and clothing. It is important to realize that the majority (78%) of these female marketers were "higglers," i.e., street vendors selling fresh, and, therefore, perishable vegetables and fruits, and only about 22% of the female retailers were shopkeepers.[13] Conversely, 64% of the male retailers were proprietors of small grocery shops, stores, or restaurants while only about 36% were street vendors. Male retailers were more likely to manage larger-scale interprises. Furthermore, whereas these male proprietors generally benefitted from the labor of their spouses and/or kinswoman, their female counterparts were less inclined to have adult males as regular sources of labor.

Although perhaps the large higgler category may evince salient management and organizational skills among women as instrumental actors, these abilities and achievements were not widely channelled into other important areas. Men were more likely to hold supervisory positions and to market leadership skills and services, for example, as foremen of construction and public works crews and as informal labor recruiters and political party brokers. Further, a larger proportion of men than women was engaged in productive and service activities (e.g., vehicle repair, electrical work, plumbing, carpentry, masonry, welding, etc.) which demanded some readily recognized degree of technical expertise.

It is also noteworthy that male and female informants had different patterns of participation in the small urban primary sector. Women, for instance, tended to raise fowl and tree fruits for household and domestic subsistence, while men were more inclined to produce for commodity exchange. Half of the men involved in primary production were engaged in raising pigs or goats for the market. Women's involvement in secondary production, viz., petty manufacture, was largely restricted to the production of children's and women's clothing, while men produced men's clothing, shoes, furniture, woodcarvings, and were involved in building construction. Women's work across all sectors was linked largely to domestic needs and functions.

Another discernible category of informal economic activity is that related to entertainment or recreation.[14] Approximately 22% of the males in my sample admittedly participated in this sphere as barkeepers (5%), ganja traders (14%), and gambling vendors/brokers (3%). Approximately 31% of the women were involved in often multiple and interrelated occupations within this sphere as barkeepers (13%), ganja traders (7%), gambling vendors and housemistresses (11%), and "sportin gals" or prostitutes (5%). Of course, these percentages, which represent only what informants were willing to divulge, grossly underestimate the extent of involvement in illegal activities, particularly in the ganja trade and prostitution. These two illegal spheres seem to reflect a division of labor by gender, in that although women are indeed active in the production and exchange of ganja, the trade is a domain in which males predominate. On the other hand, prostitution at the local-level is largely organized by women, who tend not to have pimps or male superiors. This relative autonomy, however, is absent in the major tourist zones, where commoditized sexual exchanges are typically mediated by male brokers.

Nelson (1979) treats prostitution as well as those serial mating practices in which an economic motive or dimension is apparent as instances of the marketing of services that women practice and perform within the domestic domain.[15] Although she places prostitution and those mating practices which, for all intents and purposes, represent an economic survival strategy into the same category, the two behaviors should not be equated. The sexual services embodied in mating behavior are not commodities, as are the services prostitutes market, but use-values.

In view of this conceptual distinction between commodities and use-values, it is necessary to underscore the fact that the informal economy is not limited to the production and exchange of petty commodities. Of great significance is the production and non-market exchange—what Lomnitz (1977) calls "reciprocal exchange"—of such resources as information and any good and service which contribute in some way to subsistence and economic viability. Non-market exchange is especially crucial for the subsistence of a considerable proportion of ghetto (i.e., slum and shantytown) populations that cannot regularly engage in monetary transactions.

The Social Organization and Construction of Gender

Social networks—or very fluid and diffusely structured social relationships organized primarily around kinship, co-residential, and/or peer ties—constitute the basis for much of the socioeconomic activity within the informal economy. Kinship groupings extend beyond individual residential units, and the embeddedness of these households in broader domestic configurations is critical given the absence of State aid or welfare benefits for the formally unemployed or the non-wage working poor.

The primacy of extended consanguineal ties characterizes the situations of both women and men; however, ghetto women tend to be comparatively more reliant on or committed to kin and domestic groupings for salient and sustained social relationships. Women informants (particularly those in the 18–30 year range) tended to express distrust for friendship and marriage,[16] suggesting that investments in such non-kin relationships would lead to additional demands on limited resource, "trouble" and "war" over gossip and men, and, in the case of legal marriage, constraints on female independence and autonomy. "Me naa keep friends" was the claim of several women who restricted most of their intimate, reciprocal interactions to relatives. Women who were higglers with relatively stable retail enterprises, officers in local-level political party associations or mutual aid societies, or "bankers" in rotating credit networks called "partners" tended to have more intense relationships outside the domestic sphere. For these women peer relationships were often significant; nonetheless, kin ties were viewed as much more reliable and valuable.

While the idiom and organization of kinship are key in the everyday lives of poor urban women, among ghetto men peer bonds are highly valued and play a central role on the street corners where male networks are based (cf. Brana-Shute 1976; Lieber 1976; Wilson 1971). The peer networks of men between the ages of 15 and 35 often assume the form of gangs which may combine to form gang hierarchies extending over the territory of an entire neighborhood or an even more inclusive district or zone. Street corners and their associated gangs provide the context within which subsistence-related information is exchanged, material resources are redistributed, casual labor is recruited for government-sector employment, and legitimate and illegitimate hustling strategies are devised and carried out.

Interestingly, in the way that both women and men talked about their lives and survival struggles, women seemed to place greater emphasis on independence and autonomy than did men. Despite their actual dependence on the "baby-fathers" (i.e., consensual mates), mothers, sisters, and special neighbors of their active networks, women underscored the importance and necessity of independent action in surviving Kingston's slums and shantytowns. They viewed their participation in familial networks, which extend and contract according to need and circumstance, as the outcome of their individual strategies and negotiations rather than as the result of group obligations and duties. "Networking," even among kinspeople, was described as voluntary and instrumental, and it involved no fixed, long-term commitments to a clearly defined social unit.

The assertion of female independence is not at all controverted by kin alignments. In fact, the extended organization of kinship and domesticity, with its internal division of labor and forms of cooperation, frees some women for work and other activities outside the home. Those women remaining at home and in the immediate neighborhood supervise and care for the children, while also carrying out other household-based tasks, some of which generate income. Independence does not, therefore, imply "a shedding of social attachments . . [but] is linked to a strong sense of interpersonal connectedness . . ." (Sutton and Makiesky-Barrow 1981:496).

Manifestations of female autonomy, particularly in the economic domain as evinced by the high rate of female participation in the labor force, have sometimes been taken by the public and by scholars to mean that women enjoy sexual equality (cf. Mintz 1981; Sutton and Makiesky-Barrow 1981). However, evidence indicating that women indeed suffer from underemployment, unemployment, low-paying jobs, and de facto disenfranchisement more disproportionately than their male counter parts serves to dispel this conception. Sexual inequality is also reflected in the incidence of wife-battering and sexual violence as well as in ideological representations in, for instance, mass media advertisements and popular music (Antrobus and Gordon 1984:120; Henry and Wilson 1975:193–94). Male resentment against female competence and assertiveness is expressed in song lyrics which often encourage men to control or dominate women lest the latter's alleged cleverness, deviousness, and promiscuity endanger men's standing in the home and community (cf. Henry and Wilson 1975: 193).

Despite the ambivalence men may feel toward women's presence outside the home, women's work is expected and tolerated. The tolerance for female independence and for individual independence regardless of gender originated during the slavery era when both sexes were equally involved and exploited in the "public" domain of plantation work (Sutton and Makiesky-Barrow 1981). Mintz (1981) hypothesizes that since enslaved men could not assert "paterfamilial" domination over female slaves, and since slave masters relegated both male and female Africans to the status of chattel property, respect for individual rights and prerogatives for both men and women was strong among Afro-Jamaicans.

Historically, the masses of Jamaican women have been conspicuous as workers not (wholly) dependent on their kinsmen and mates for their sustenance and security. During the post-emancipation period, peasant women complemented the work of male producers through a system of internal marketing controlled largely by the market women themselves. However, with the expansion and consolidation of capitalist social relations at the turn of the century, the autonomy of Afro-Jamaican women—and that of peasants, artisans, and traders on a whole—diminished. Owing to the entrenchment of colonial state power over the hitherto independent peasantry,[17] male dominance gained further legitimacy and was imposed on the society by established churches, schools, laws, and a system of job segregation and wage differentials.[18]

Gender and Politics

In the mid-1970s, a government redevelopment agency charged with upgrading housing, utilities, and social services in the Oceanview vicinity conducted a survey in order to identify the neighborhood's leadership on the basis of reputation. These "area leaders" were then to comprise an advisory committee that would aid in implementing the government program's objectives. Out of the 23 persons identified, only one was a woman. In a locality where women are quite visible in the economic arena and where their membership and work keep alive and active local-level political party groups and branches, why were women underrepresented as area leaders?

The term "leader" tends to connote authority and official status and is typically applied to middle-class political party functionaries. In this sense, Oceanview respondents would claim that there are no leaders among the locality's residents. With a qualified, expanded definition of leader as one with the respectability, personal influence, mobilizational skills, and resources to determine and implement local or factional goals (Swartz 1968: 1), respondents would generate a list of persons strategically situated in grassroots sociopolitical fields. The redevelopment program sought to identify the latter persons; yet the survey results yielded a predominantly male pool.

Contrary to the impression the neighborhood survey may have given, and although females may be denied legitimate recognition, it is not at all unusual for women to be principal political agents, i.e., de facto protagonists, catalysts, directors, and sustainers of sociopolitical action at the local level. Beckford and Witter (1980:99) confirm this observation by pointing out that women are the main party workers in groups and branches. They maintain the party machinery during terms of government office, and they are the most committed campaigners during electoral contests. Their activism is manifested not only in association membership, but also in the leadership of neighborhood party organs, for they often appear as secretaries, vice-presidents, and presidents. Nonetheless, by and large, despite various exceptions, women's power is largely confined to the lowest levels of political party structure and the inclusive State apparatus; they are not highly visible in the decision-making echelons. Even at the local level, the power and leadership of party women may be preempted by gang brokers who are often more strategically placed in the party machine.

In view of the constraints on their political role and participation, women are inclined and, in some respects, encouraged to assert their unevenly formed power by manipulating and influencing those men who are authorized or empowered actors in parties, government, street gangs, and mainstream churches.[19] For example, a former female group president recounted how she was pressured to become "friendly" with higher level party brokers in order to gain access to important information and job opportunities for her local area. Another woman, one who never joined a party association, used her acquaintance and intimacy with a party broker and a police officer to acquire favors which were crucial in securing and expanding her ganja trade business. In another case, a former group leader resigned from party activism because of the sexual harassment she encountered. She claimed that sexual services were often expected of women in exchange for party patronage. While women may sometimes gain power, influence, and control over resources through their relationships with male brokers, this dependent access to political capital leaves women vulnerable to manipulation and abuse.

The greatest proportions of women are found in informal fields of power, e.g., revival churches, school associations, and markets, wherein there arise opportunities for women as individuals and as groups to define and implement strategic local goals—Swartz's definition of politics (1968:1). Generally, this sphere of activity is not perceived or designated as political, despite its intrinsic political dimensions and its articulation or interpenetration with formal political domains. Henry and Wilson suggest that because of the subservient role women play in society, they predominate in lower-class religious cults or sects (1975:190). They claim that

> religion is one of the few areas . . . where women find some measure of equality with significant others. It is also an area where women have free access and the fact that they can hold positions of office gives them a measure of status outside the religious group which they might not otherwise be able to achieve (1975:190).

In localities like Oceanview, where inter-party rivalry often attains volatile and life-threatening proportions, a large percentage of residents tends to retreat from "politricks" and are distrustful of partisan activities and activists. Parent Teacher Associations, mutual aid societies, and churches are more likely to be perceived as non-partisan and therefore potentially more reflective of the interests and needs of a broader cross-section of the neighborhood. It is in such extra-domestic situations that many women are able to mobilize their limited resources for the survival of their families and neighborhoods as well as for a sense of collective defense and autonomy.

Through their involvement in these often predominantly female spheres of action, women produce an emergent praxis of sisterhood marked by ambiguity and contradiction. The sisterhood engendered in certain informal fields can be seen as a constructive reaction to the constraints women confront as single-parents, formal and informal workers, and political constituents. For example, many of the members of Oceanview's PTA consider that organization an alternative to the local party associations that have been unable to promote community development, peace, and unity. The PTA (whose agenda encompasses much more than educational objectives) represents a non-partisan vehicle for actively resisting the various forms of victimization and oppression its members experience in their everyday lives.

Nonetheless, sisterhood may also comprise elements of collusion (cf. Westwood 1985) and escapism. Some Oceanview women believe that politics is intrinsically "wicked" and not a righteous means of meaningful change. The recurring statement "Me naa deal in politics; only God can save Jamaica" reflects this view. For these women any politician or political activist, leftist or rightist, sincere or opportunist, is suspect and unworthy of support; and churches, friendly societies, or other associations provide a refuge. Whereas the informal sphere may provide women with alternative outlets for constructive political expression, it can also offer a means of retreat, suppressing effective opposition and resistance.

An informally organized sector of Oceanview's social organization not readily open to women's mobilization and empowerment is that of the Rastafari. Local followers of Rastafari, particularly the more senior and devoted "true Rastas," organize their religious worship, economic activities, and domestic life along clear lines of male dominance.[20] Rastafari represents one of the most significant mass movements, culturally and politically, in contemporary Jamaica.[21] Its ideology and idiom of protest and rebellion have permeated the slums and shantytowns, where displaced wage-workers and the marginally self-employed dwell. In Rastafarian views and practices, women are essentially spiritual and political dependents (Kitzinger 1969:260, 1971:583; Rowe 1980). Men must guide women in order for the latter to achieve spiritual wholeness and "sight," the "I/eye."[22] I broach this issue of patriarchy among Rastafari simply to highlight the sexist character of important elements in Jamaican culture and to suggest some of the contradictions within sociocultural forces that exert considerable influence on the uneven and often contradictory patterns of opposition, protest, and accomodation within some of the most alienated segments of Jamaican society.

The sexism that shapes and inhibits the political behavior of women active in the informal economy impedes the political development of the entire informal and casual workforce. While this relationship between the social construction of gender and political underdevelopment holds also for the organized working class as well as for any class, it is especially critical for informal workers, because women are disproportionately represented among them.

I raise this question of the political character of informal labor, because anthropologists and other social scientists have questioned whether the urban informal sector functions as a safety valve reinforcing the status quo or whether it represents a potential source of pre-revolutionary rebellion (McGee 1971; Worsley 1972). Roberts (1978:135) claims that the fragmented organization of small-scale socioeconomic enterprises, combined with the present-day survival orientation of the actors themselves, give rise to sporadic and inhibited patterns of political action. Elsewhere I have argued that supralocal or State-level political processes also contribute to the containment of rebellion. Patronage-clientelism undermines solidarity among grassroots constituents; police and army repression thwarts efforts to disrupt or challenge the social order; and by labelling many forms of protest and rebellion as crime, the State delegitimates certain political behaviors and isolates rebels from potential allies in, for instance, the formal working class (Harrison 1982:326–335).

An additional factor that contributes to the underdeveloped political character of the informal labor force, and one that has not been pinpointed, let alone accentuated, is the suppression of women's participation in politics, particularly in those fields most strategically aligned to or embedded in national- (and international-) level political structures. These most strategic fields, arenas, and institutions are male dominated and conditioned largely by middle- and upper-class interests.

Conclusions

Sexual or gender inequality represents an essential and integral feature of social relations and cultural construction in Jamaica, where for the past four hundred years colonial and imperialist exploitation have governed the development
of economic, political, and sociocultural patterns and structures. Although the
focus of this paper has been on women and, more generally, on gender differentials within the urban petty-scale sphere of the Jamaican economy, it is extremely
important to further contextualize the subordination and oppression characteriz-
ing these women's position by taking into account the pervasive impact of racism.
During the course of Jamaica's history, the exploitation of the masses has been
legitimated and rationalized by a system of ideas and symbols which has elaborated the allegedly inherent and functional inferiority of Africans as a distinct
racial grouping and as bearers of a peculiar, "cultureless" culture. Racist ideology
and institutional arrangements have historically supported and permitted the superexploitation of Afro-Jamaicans as a labor force, the violation of black and
brown women as objects of sexual indulgence, and the political alienation and
repression of the island's majority.

The many segments of the working-age population which, to varying extents,
are absorbed into the urban informal economy may represent a surplus labor
force from the point of view of their surface relationship to corporate capitalist
spheres; however, the casual workers, scufflers, hustlers, and the petty producers
and traders who fill the streets, lanes, and yards (i.e., communal residences) with
their daily survival struggles are vertically integrated into peripheral capitalist
structures that depend upon the articulation and interpenetration of variant socioeconomic patterns, the asymmetrical conjuncture of which constitutes a socioeconomic formation specific to the complexities and contradictions of Jamaica's historical development within a world system.

In a central way, the feminization of the informal sphere contributes to the
reproduction of a cheap, casual, and concealed workforce accessible to capital
for performing its temporary and largely unskilled tasks. Although responsible for
supporting appreciable proportions of the nation's dependents and for organizing their non-wage-compensated work into minimally lucrative household-based
ventures, women have the most limited access to income and capitalization opportunities. Despite the undisputable existence of substantial numbers of higglers, visible with the results of their mobilization of petty capital, the informal
sector is not ruled by matriarchs. The economic status higglers have rests upon
the marketing of domestic and household use goods and, therefore, on a sexually
segregated system of economic opportunities which confines women to spheres
related to domestic consumption. Moreover, whatever status and power individual higglers and other female retailers may in fact have within their communities,
associations, and their primary networks of kinspeople, friends, and clients, this

power and status cannot be generalized to depict the situation of the majority of women in the slums and shantytowns of urban Jamaica. These latter women scuffle under fluctuating and unpredictable circumstances to eke out minimal subsistence for themselves and their "pickney" (children), either with or without sustained support from their "babyfathers," and under diffuse and ambiguous contracts of support and alliance with kin and fictive kin.

The mass of Jamaican women, who in some form or another operate as informally organized workers, have a legacy to inform their lives and struggles. On one hand, that legacy is long with the pain and blood of "sufferation" and "downpression," but, on the other hand, that legacy is also marked by the integrity of a people at some levels conscious of its potential power as resisters, rebels, and rulers of its own destiny. Despite obstacles and constraints, Afro-Jamaican women have historically made their footprints in paths of struggle on both economic and political planes. In light of the critical current state of affairs in Jamaica, it is becoming increasingly obvious that for "deliverance"[23] and change to come, Jamaica has to mobilize all of its people, men and women. How exactly this proposisition will be translated into political discourse and applied to organization and praxis is a question for which only the unfolding of social history can provide answers.

Notes

1. Williams (1944) and Knight (1978) have written on political and economic aspects of Caribbean history. For studies of underdevelopment and dependency, see Beckford (1972; 1975), Beckford and Witter (1989), Girvan (1973; 1976), Mintz (1977), and Thomas (1974).

2. The term *Creole* refers to the Caribbean-born descendants of the Africans and Europeans who peopled the West Indies during the colonization and slavery era. The category is not applied to post-emancipation immigrants such as the Chinese and East Indians.

3. For examples of classic family studies, see Blake (1961), Clarke (1957), and Gonzalez (1969). See Bolles (1983) for a more current analysis of urban working-class households in crisis-torn Jamaica. For work on internal marketing, see Mintz (1959; 1964; 1981).

4. Henry and Wilson (1975) have addressed the general status of Caribbean women; Moses (1981) treats women's status in Montserrat, and Sutton and Makiesky-Barrow (1981) focus on Barbadian women. Bolles (1983) deals with women's family and work responsibilities in the context of the economic austerity exacerbated by the International Monetary Fund.

5. My perspective is based largely on fieldwork done on political and economic processes in a locality in the Kingston Metropolitan Area in 1978–79. This research was made possible by a Fulbright-Hays Predoctoral Fellowship. The period of data-analysis was supported by a grant-in-aid from the Wenner-Gren Foundation for Anthropological Research and a Danforth-Compton Fellowship from the Danforth Foundation. Comments and support from Louise Lamphere, Deborah D'Amico-Samuels, and Chandra Talpade Mohanty were invaluable in the re-writing of this paper.

6. It is impossible to directly measure the actual extent of participation in the informal

sphere of an economy, because informal activities and enterprises tend, for the most part, not to be recorded or registered. We can assume, however, that this sector absorbs the unemployed (defined as those actually seeking wage-work or those willing to do wage-work) and those segments of the population which have never sought formal wage-employment. It is also important to note that, to varying extents, formal workers—even members of the established middle-class—are involved in informal economic activities as a means of supplementing their income. While the informal economy acts as a buffer against unemployment, it also provides capitalization opportunities for petty entrepreneurs and petty capitalists. In fact, Stone (1977) claims that an indeterminant number of businesspeople from the most precarious segments of Jamaica's petty bourgeoisie commonly engage in informal and sometimes in illegal means of capitalization and appropriation (e.g., gambling and ganja ventures) in order to maintain and expand their legitimate enterprises.

7. This distinction between labor process and social relations of production is pertinent in light of the argument that the informal sector represents a distinct mode of production (cf. Davies 1979).

8. The reserve, surviving under tenuous and insecure social and economic circumstances, consists of unemployed workers, casual workers moving from job to job, displaced peasants and agroproletarians forced into cities, and long-term "scufflers" and the marginally self-employed. See Braverman (1974:388) for a discussion of Marx's formulation of surplus population.

9. In 1978 women represented approximately 47% of Jamaica's total recorded labor force (Department of Statistics 1978b:26). Over 65% of all women above the age of 14 were part of this force. In light of the factor that in 1978 38% of the female labor force was formally unemployed, and an even larger percentage underemployed, it appears that women are dislocated and excluded from normal labor market opportunities at a higher rate than men, who suffered a 16% rate of unemployment in 1978.

There is a history of relatively high rates of both formal and informal employment among women in former plantation slave societies such as Jamaica. During the slavery era, both men and women were fully employed as slave labor. Scholars (e.g., Patterson 1967; Mintz and Price 1976) have suggested that at this juncture the sexual division of labor was slight; however, women experienced a double drudgery in that they were responsible for both field and household tasks (Davis 1981). Women also played pivotal roles in the "proto-peasant" sphere of the slave economy, and were partly responsible for marketing their agricultural surplus. The peasant economy of the post-emancipation period was organized around a clear sexual division of labor in which men were primarily responsible for cultivation while women were largely responsible for marketing.

10. One-third of all households in Jamaica are headed by women (Department of Statistics 1978a:10).

11. The data for this discussion were collected from a small sample of 45 women and 56 men. These data were gathered as part of a broader investigation of the organization of socioeconomic and political life in Oceanview. Although the sample is limited, the data it yielded are consistent with the results of government surveys (e.g., those done by the Urban Development Corporation) conducted in the 1970's.

12. This pattern of sexual segregation in work (domestic vs. non-domestic) has been noted by anthropologists such as Rosaldo (1974) who underscore the relevance of the domestic vs. public dichotomy in a wide variety of sociocultural cases.

13. Of all the women sampled, 16% were higglers and 5% shopkeepers (e.g., grocers). Among the men, 7% were street vendors and 12% grocers and restaurateurs. Interestingly, outside of this domestic goods realm, female proprietors outnumbered their male counterparts. For instance, whereas 13% of the women in the sample were barkeepers, only 5% of the men were proprietors of bars. Most of the regular clientele of neighborhood bars are men and their guests. I am suggesting that women play an important role in entertaining men, for whom public drinking and, perhaps, less open gambling, are regular features of peer-related socializing and recreation.

14. This category which Nelson uses in her Kenya study is misleading in the sense that ganja traders may also be seen as providing a product necessary for religious rituals and healing, and gamblers may consider their activity hard work rather than mere recreation.

15. Nelson's conception of prostitution as domestic activity is consistent with the generally held definition of domesticity or domestic functions: all those activities involved in the production or preparation of food, in childrearing, in consumption, and in sexual reproduction or mating (Yanagisako 1979).

16. Most women in the sample as well as in the population at large were not legally married but involved in common-law unions and visiting relationships.

17. In the aftermath of emancipation, a reconstituted peasantry arose in opposition to the declining plantation system. This peasantry emerged before the formation of a capitalist mode of production and the consolidation of a class of agrarian capitalists. At this juncture peasants were in a strong position relative to large landholders. The former usually owned their own plots and paid little or nothing in taxes to the State. Furthermore, they were able to circumvent the expropriation of some part of the product of their labor by controlling exchange relations through networks of higglers—the mothers, wives, sisters, and daughters of peasant households (Post 1978).

18. See Henry (1983:100–107) for a discussion of the post-emancipation cultural colonization of Afro-Jamaicans, and Post (1978:34–35) for a treatment of the role of colonial State policies in thwarting the development of a free peasantry and enhancing the power of an emergent capitalist class. I have extended this line of argument to the realm of gender.

19. Henry and Wilson (1975) bring out that in the popular view women are often depicted as devious, manipulative, and conniving. It is also noteworthy that these stereotypes also apply to perceptions of lumpenproletarians who also commonly activate strategies of manipulation when dealing with politicians.

20. Whereas a large number of "youths" (i.e., male adolescents and adult males under 35) wear their hair in dreadlocks and claim to be Rastafarian, I am concerned with that minority of males who are committed to Rastafari religious beliefs and lifestyle, and who are designated as "true Rastas" within the locality. This segment exerts considerable influence over the secular "dreads."

21. See Smith, Augier, and Nettleford (1960), Nettleford (1970), Barrett (1977), Chevannes (1981), and Campbell (1987) for analyses of the Rastafari in Jamaica. See Austin (1983:236) for comments on the routinization of the movement during the past two decades.

22. Within the past decade, however, women have become more visible and vocal within the Rastafari movement. For instance, in 1980 three women's organizations were established. While "daughters" claim not to challenge the patriarchal tenets and structure

of the movement, their very mobilization and "reasonings" (i.e., consciousness-raising rituals) seem to be generating new perspectives on women and on Rastafari itself.

The concept of "sight" refers to spiritual vision and knowledge of truth. That of the "I" also refers to vision, but "I" also signifies the collective Rastafari, the "I and I," whose shared "reasonings" and sacramental rituals (ganja smoking and Nyabingi) lead to heightened transcendence.

23. "Deliverance" is a religious concept applied to popular political discourse in Jamaica. During the 1980 electoral campaign against Michael Manley and the PNP, Edward Seaga, the present Prime Minister, promised deliverance to Jamaica. Politicians commonly manipulate popular religious symbols when mobilizing the electorate. The PNP made use of Rastafarian and revivalist (i.e., syncretist Christian) symbols in earlier campaigns.

References

Amin, Samir, 1980. The class structure of the contemporary imperialist system. Monthly
    Review 31 (8): 9–26.
Antrobus, Peggy and Lorna Gordon, 1984. The English-Speaking Caribbean: A journey
    in the making. In Robin Morgan (ed.), Sisterhood is global: The international
    women's movement anthology. Garden City, Anchor Books/Doubleday, 118–126.
Austin, Diane J., 1983. Culture and ideology in the English-speaking Caribbean: A view
    from Jamaica. American Ethnologist 10: 223–40.
Barrett, Leonard, 1977. The Rastafarians: Sounds of cultural dissonance. Boston: Beacon
    Press.
Beckford, George L., 1972. Persistent poverty: Underdevelopment in plantation econo-
    mies of the third world. New York, Oxford University Press.
———— (ed.), 1975. Caribbean economy: Dependence and backwardness. Mona, Institute
    of Social and Economic Research, University of the West Indies.
Beckford, George and Michael Witter, 1980. Small garden . . . bitter weed: The political
    economy of struggle and change in Jamaica. London, Zed Press.
Birkbeck, Chris, 1979. Garbage, industry, and the "vultures" of Cali, Colombia. In Ray
    Bromley and Chris Gerry (eds.), Casual work and poverty in third world cities. Chi-
    chester, John Wiley and Sons, 161–184.
Blake, Judith, 1961. Family structure in Jamaica: The social context of reproduction. Glen-
    coe, Free Press.
Bolles, A. Lynn, 1983. Kitchens hit by priorities: Employed working-class Jamaican
    women confront the IMF. In June Nash and Maria Fernandez-Kelly (eds.), Women,
    men, and the international division of labor. Albany, State University of New York
    Press, 138–160.
Brana Shute, Gary, 1976. Drinking shops and social structure: Some ideas on lower-class
    male behavior. Urban Anthropology 5: 53–68.
Braverman, Henry, 1974. Labor and monopoly capital: The denigration of work in the
    twentieth century. New York, Monthly Review Press.
Campbell, Horace, 1987. Rasta and resistance: From Marcus Garvey to Walter Rodney.
    Trenton, Africa World Press, Inc.
Chevannes, Barry, 1981. The Rastafari and urban youth. In Carl Stone and Aggrey Brown

(eds.), Perspectives on Jamaica in the seventies. Kingston, Jamaica Publishing House, 392–422.

Clarke, Edith, 1957. My mother who fathered me. London, George Allen and Unwin, Ltd.

Davies, Rob, 1979. Informal sector or subordinate mode of production? In Ray Bromly and Chris Gerry (eds.), Casual work and poverty in third world cities. Chichester, John Wiley and Sons, 87–104.

Davis, Angela, 1981. Women, race, and class. New York, Random House.

Department of Statistics, Jamaica, 1978a. The labour force. Kingston.

——— 1978b. Statistical abstract. Kingston.

——— 1984. Statistical Yearbook of Jamaica, 1982. Kingston.

Girvan, Norman, 1973. The development of dependency economics in the Caribbean and Latin America: Review and comparison. Social and Economic Studies 22: 1–33.

——— 1976. Corporate imperialism: Conflict and expropriation. Transnational corporations and economic nationalism in the third world. New York, Monthly Review Press.

Girvan, Norman and Richard Bernal, 1982. The IMF and the foreclosure of development options: The case of Jamaica. Monthly Review 33 (9): 34–48.

Gonzalez, Nancie L. Solien, 1969. Black Carib household structure: A study of migration and modernization. Seattle, University of Washington Press.

Harrison, Faye V., 1982. Semiproletarianization and the structure of socioeconomic and political relations in a Jamaican slum. Unpublished doctoral dissertation. Stanford University.

Headley, Bernard D., 1985. Mr. Seaga's Jamaica: An inside look. Monthly Review 37 (4): 35–42.

Henry, Frances and Pamela Wilson, 1975. The status of women in Caribbean societies: An overview of their social, economic and sexual roles. Social and Economic Studies 24: 165–198.

Henry, Paget, 1983. Decolonization and cultural underdevelopment in the Commonwealth Caribbean. In Paget Henry and Carl Stone (eds.), The newer Caribbean: Decolonization, democracy, and development. Philadelphia, Institute for the Study of Human Issues, 95–120.

Jefferson, Owen, 1972. The post-war economic development of Jamaica. Mona, Institute of Social and Economic Research, University of the West Indies.

Keith, Sherry and Robert Girling, 1978. Caribbean conflict: Jamaica and the United States. NACLA Report on the Americas 12 (3): 3–36.

Kitzinger, Sheila, 1969. Protest and mysticism: The Rastafari cult of Jamaica. Journal for the Scientific Study of Religion 8:240–262.

——— 1971. The Rastafarian brethern of Jamaica. In Michael Horowitz (ed.), Peoples and cultures of the Caribbean. New York Natural History Press, 580–588.

Knight, Franklin W., 1978. The Caribbean: The genesis of a fragmented nationalism. New York, Oxford University Press.

Kowarick, Lucio, 1979. Capitalism and urban marginality in Brazil. In Ray Bromley and Chris Gerry (eds.). Casual work and poverty in third world cities. Chichester, John Wiley and Sons, 69–85.

Lacey, Terry, 1977. Violence and politics in Jamaica, 1960–1970. Manchester, Manchester University Press.

Lieber, Michael, 1976. "Liming" and other concerns: The style of street embedments in Port-of-Spain, Trinidad. Urban Anthropology 5: 319–334.

Lim, Linda Y. C., 1983. Capitalism, imperialism, and patriarchy: The dilemma of Third World women workers in multinational factories. In June Nash and Maria Fernandez-Kelly (eds.), Women, men and the international division of labor. Albany, State University of New York Press, 70–91.

Lomnitz, Larissa Adler, 1977. Networks and marginality: Life in a Mexican shantytown. New York, Academic Press.

Mamdani, Mahmood, 1976. Politics and class formation in Uganda. New York, Monthly Review Press.

McGee, T. G., 1971. Revolutionary change and the third world city. In McGee, The urbanization process in the third world. London, G. Bell and Sons, Ltd., 64–93.

Mintz, Sidney W., 1955. The Jamaican internal marketing pattern. Social and Economic Studies 4: 95–103.

——— 1964. The employment of capital by market women in Haiti. In Firth and Yarney (eds.), Capital, savings and credit in peasant societies. Chicago, Aldine Publishing Company, 256–286.

——— 1977. The so-called world system: Local initiative and local response. Dialectical Anthropology 2: 253–270.

——— 1981. Economic role and cultural tradition. In Filomina Chioma Steady (ed.), The black woman cross-culturally. Cambridge, Schenkman Publishing Company, 515–534.

Mintz, Sidney W. and Richard Price, 1976. An anthropological approach to the Afro-American past: A Caribbean perspective. Philadelphia: ISHI.

Moses, Yolanda T., 1981. Female status, the family, and male dominance in a West Indian community. In Filomina Chioma Steady (ed.), The block woman cross-culturally. Cambridge, Schenkman Publishing Company, 499–514.

Nash, June, 1983. The impact of the changing international division of labor on different sectors of the labor force. In June Nash and Maria Fernandez-Kelly (eds.), Women, men, and the international division of labor. Albany, State University of New York Press, 3–38.

Nash, June and Helen I. Safa., 1980. Sex and class in Latin America: Women's perspectives on politics, economics and the family in the third world. South Hadley, Bergin & Garvey Publishers.

National Planning Agency, 1978. Five year development plan, 1978–82. Kingston, Ministry of Finance and Planning, Jamaica.

Nelson, Nici, 1979. How women and men get by: The sexual division of labor in the informal sector of a Nairobi squatter settlement. In Ray Bromley and Chris Gerry (eds.), Casual work and poverty in third world cities. Chichester, John Wiley and Sons, 283–302.

Nettleford, Rex, 1970. Mirror, mirror: Identity, race and protest in Jamaica. Kingston, William Collins and Sangster (Jamaica) Ltd.

Newsweek, 1980. Jamaica: Back in business. December 15, 86.

Patterson, Orlando, 1967. The sociology of slavery, an analysis of the origins, development and structure of Negro slave society in Jamaica. Rutherford, Fairleigh Dickinson University Press.

Portes, Alejandro, 1978. The informal sector and the world economy: Notes on the struc-
    ture of subsidized labor. Institute of Development Studies Bulletin 9: 35–40.
—— 1981. Unequal exchange and the urban informal sector. In Portes and John
    Walton. Labor, class, and the international system. New York, Academic Press, 67–
    106.
Post, Ken, 1978. Arise ye starvelings: The Jamaican labour rebellion of 1938 and its after-
    math. The Hague, Martinus Nijhoff.
Roberts, Bryan, 1978. Cities of peasants: The political economy of urbanization in the
    third world. Beverly Hills, Sage Publications.
Rosaldo, Michelle, 1974. A theoretical overview. In Michele Rosaldo and Louise Lam-
    phere (eds.), Women, culture, and society. Stanford, Stanford University Press, 17–42.
Rowe, Maureen, 1980. The woman in Rastafari. Caribbean Quarterly 26 (4): 13–21.
Saffioti, Heleieth I. B., 1978. Women in class society. New York Monthly Review Press.
Scott, Alison MacEwen, 1979. Who are the self-employed? In Ray Bromley and Chris
    Gerry (eds.), Casual work and poverty in third world cities. Chichester, John Wiley
    and Sons, 105–129.
Smith, M. G., F. R. Augier, and Rex Nettleford, 1960. The Ras Tafari movement in Kings-
    ton, Jamaica. Mona, Institute of Social and Economic Research, University College
    of the West Indies.
Statistical Institute of Jamaica, 1984. The labour force, 1983 preliminary report. Kingston.
Stone, Carl, 1977. The political economy of gambling in a neo-colonial economy. In
    Stone and Aggrey Brown (eds.), Essays on power and change in Jamaica. Kingston,
    Jamaica Publishing House, 58–64.
Sutton, Constance and Susan Makiesky-Barrow, 1981. Social inequality and sexual status
    in Barbados. In Filomina Chioma Steady (ed.), The black woman cross-culturally.
    Cambridge, Schenkman Publishing Company, 469–499.
Swartz, Marc J., 1968. Introduction. In Swartz (ed.), Local-level politics: Social and cul-
    tural perspectives. Chicago, Aldine Publishing Company, 1–52.
Thomas, Clive Y., 1974. Dependence and transformation: The economics of the transi-
    tion to socialism. New York, Monthly Review Press.
Westwood, Sallie, 1985. All day, every day: Factory and family in the making of women's
    lives. Urbana, University of Illinois Press.
Williams, Eric, 1944. Capitalism and slavery. Chapel Hill, University of North Carolina
    Press.
Wilson, Peter, 1971. Caribbean crews: Peer groups and male society. Caribbean Studies
    10 (4): 18–34.
Worsley, Peter, 1972. Frantz Fanon and the lumpenproletariat. In Ralph Miliband and
    John Saville (eds.), The Socialist Register. London, The Merlin Press, 193–230.
Yanagisako, Sylvia J., 1979. Family and household: The analysis of domestic groups. An-
    nual Review of Anthropology 8: 161–205.

16. CULTURE AND IDEOLOGY IN THE ENGLISH-SPEAKING CARIBBEAN

A View from Jamaica

Diane J. Austin

Anthropology in the English-speaking Caribbean is marked by an analytical antinomy that reflects the great historical ambiguity of Caribbean societies. The antinomy is that these societies tend to have been interpreted either as arenas of conflict or cultural opposition (Mintz 1974; Herskovits 1969; M. G. Smith 1965a; Manning 1973; Wilson 1973), or as paradigms of metropolitan dominance or the dominance of a local elite (Levitt and Best 1975; Cross 1979; Braithwaite 1975; Henriques 1976; R. T. Smith 1967). The historical ambiguity is that though these societies have been marked by radical social inequalities, they have nevertheless been relatively stable since the time of emancipation and have certainly been without the upheavals of Chile or Cuba. This stability in the English-speaking Caribbean reflects a situation of *conflict contained by domination*, a theme that should be central in Caribbean anthropology.

The dichotomy I draw between types of anthropology in the Caribbean does some violence to the work of those concerned. If Sidney Mintz stresses opposition in Caribbean life, he does not neglect to emphasize the power of the plantation. By contrast, if Raymond T. Smith (1956) stresses the value integration of creole society, certainly his ethnography demonstrates that he is well aware of class-specific behavior. These writers are involved in a juggling of apparently opposing themes, without a consistent language for both. This juggling reaches its epitome in the work of Peter Wilson (1973). His opposition between respectability and reputation, which he ascribes in turn to metropolitan and indigenous sources, echoes some of the themes of Mintz's work. At the very same time, Wilson seeks to constitute a cultural system of this value opposition which encompasses whole societies and embodies the different perspectives of male and female gender.

Wilson's resolution of the antinomy, which involves reinterpreting an opposition as a sytem, is unsatisfactory in that it neglects the crucial issue of power. I have in mind not only the power to dominate others politically and economically but also to constrain ideas and to intervene in attempts to construct alternative

Originally published in *American Ethnologist* 10:2 (May 1983), pp. 223–40. Reproduced by permission of the American Anthropological Association. Not for further reproduction.

models of society. Certainly, theories of plantation dependency (Best 1968; Beckford 1972; Cross 1979) offer an analysis of the economic and political domination that has pervaded Caribbean societies for much of their history. However, there has been no concerted attempt to translate the phenomenon of conflict in the midst of domination into an interpretation of the dynamics of Caribbean culture. Such a translation requires that we make a distinction between the notion of culture and the notion of ideology. This is certainly not a new distinction in anthropology but one that has been used haphazardly in the Caribbean literature. Although subordinate classes in the Caribbean (and elsewhere) generate their own culture or "collective practice," this does not preclude degrees of ideological domination.[1] Consequently, domination and cultural opposition as they are interpreted in the Caribbean literature are not mutually exclusive; they exist concurrently. Divergent cultural practices within the midst of domination manifest a situation of conflict contained, and it is this notion of conflict contained that may resolve the antinomy of Caribbean anthropology.

Elsewhere I have written of constraints found in working-class conceptualizations of class relations in Jamaica (Austin 1979). Although my informants often argued that inequalities of wealth placed them where they were, they were nevertheless inclined to accept a view of themselves as outside a qualified Jamaican society. As a consequence, they tended to demand equal opportunity rather than a reordering of society. They placed the onus on themselves to prove their capacity for human achievement. In this fashion, I suggested that their ideas and thereby their critique of Jamaican society were constrained. At the same time, working-class behavior and belief were not simply blueprints of procedures in other classes. These people had a range of institutions through which they maintained their own systems of prestige and their own ideology. Manning (1973), Wilson (1973), and Brana-Shute (1979) pursue this aspect of Caribbean life first analyzed by Jayawardena (1963, 1968) when he described the drinking groups of Indian laborers and their ideology of equality. Working-class cultures exist, even thrive, in the Caribbean. The issue posed here is the degree to which working-class cultures combat or mitigate the legitimating ideologies of the powerful, as these ideologies shape workplace activities and political life.

There is no uniform answer to the questions raised by this issue for the Caribbean or for other societies. I suggest that, at least in Jamaica, the capacity of working-class people to generate their own institutions in the form of bar groups, domino clubs, inspirational religion, Rastafarianism, and household forms, is constrained by the pervasive power of major institutions that are largely controlled by other classes. Forms of production involving wage labor, the education system, and in Jamaica a political system that operates to render many in the working class as clients of middle-class brokers (Stone 1980) are salient examples of this pervasive power that penetrates workers' lives. Although working-class people in Jamaica may be successful in welding together a set of daily practices that manifests certain values and even their own ideology, this does not exclude the fact that part of this culture involves participation in institutions controlled elsewhere in the society. It is reasonable to expect that the practice of these institutions will involve propagation of legitimating ideologies that constrain to a greater or lesser degree any critiques of the social order.

To clarify this view, I consider three different aspects of the issue. First, I offer a reinterpretation of a debate in Caribbean anthropology known as the "plural society debate." Although the literature of this debate is often declared to be out of date, we still have much to learn from the two major protagonists, Raymond T. Smith and Michael G. Smith. Both anthropologists grapple with the antinomy outlined without quite resolving it. If today their work is judged unsatisfactory, it is not simply because it addresses colonial rather than postcolonial society but because of the inadequate notions of society, culture, and ideology employed (see, e.g., Stone 1980:21–22). A parallel difficulty is present in Caribbean literature that is in, or closer to, a Marxist tradition—literature that very often does address postcolonial society. In the second section of the essay I turn to my own fieldwork in two neighborhoods of Kingston, Jamaica, one working class and the other middle class. I illustrate briefly how life in these neighborhoods can exhibit both institutional divergence and institutional domination. In the third section of the essay I discuss the dominant ideology of the neighborhoods. I offer reasons why this ideology, which for the middle class may be seen as a legitimating one, has become pervasive in working-class life due to the institutional intervention of middle-class political and cultural brokers in the lives of working-class people.[2] In the conclusion I discuss an opposing view of contemporary Jamaican society in order, ultimately, to recommend my own view that divergent cultures can persist within larger ideological schemata and do not necessarily signal the end of domination.

The Plural Society Debate Reinterpreted[3]

R. T. Smith's analysis of Caribbean society was part of a larger response to interpretations of New World societies in terms of African and European cultures in contact (Herskovits 1969). These new writers argued that Caribbean culture could only be interpreted in terms of the social process of Caribbean life (R. T. Smith 1967; Henriques 1976; Braithwaite 1975). To this end, Smith (1967:234) gave a particular meaning to the term "creole society" as a form of colonial society in which all members acknowledged "the moral and cultural superiority of things English." His point was that English, African, and Indian sectors of creole society were not simply so many groups loosely connected but were in fact arranged in a hierarchy of privilege reinforced by a set of legitimating values. Smith (1967:235) observed,

> Force was a very important element in the stabilisation of post-emancipation society, but it was not the only element. . . . there was also a deliberate attempt to create a set of common values or an ideology, for the whole society. These values

stressed the importance of christianity or education, respect of the law. . . . the need for moral upliftment and . . . proper language; all factors which emphasised not only the de facto power of the Europeans but also the superiority of English culture.

Smith described this rise during this colonial period of an indigenous creole elite who, rather than distinguishing themselves from the working class simply by means of color shade, also propagated a view that they were the "intelligensia" of their society. Consequently, they forged a new qualitative ideology. The view Smith described was that though they were not different at birth from working-class people, they became so over time because of their socialization and cultural milieu. He wrote of the colonial middle class, "Its members came to believe themselves to be *qualitatively* different from other non-Europeans by virtue of their 'refinement' " (Smith 1967:257).

In addition to this theme, R. T. Smith (1956) is best known for his analysis of matrifocality in working-class households. Here he addressed the issue of cultural divergence among working-class people in order to show that institutional forms often judged as nonnormative or deviant were in fact a practical and reasonable response to male marginality in the work force. As I would like to describe it, matrifocality is part of the collective practice of working-class people. Smith's position was undone by his insistence, in light of strong evidence to the contrary, that Guyana, as well as other English-speaking Caribbean societies, was value integrated. M. G. Smith's (1966) critique of this position is very well known. The interesting issue for reflection is why, when R. T. Smith's work shows a ready awareness of the process whereby elites propagate an ideology to legitimate their position, and working people generate their own institutional forms in order to cope with their position, he maintained that these societies were value integrated. Surely the issue of conflicting class interests could not be conceptually distant.

The issue is resolved by reference to the type of theory of society embraced by R. T. Smith. The Parsonian theory he shares with Braithwaite has as a fundamental tenet that societies are value integrated. There is little room in the framework to acknowledge the differential power that might accrue to conflicting interests. Thus, the phenomenon Smith describes correctly as an elite ideology becomes reinterpreted as universal integrative values, the property of the whole society. It is interesting to note, however, that the two sides of the Caribbean antinomy are definitely present in his work: the issue of domination and the issue of a creative cultural capacity among a subordinate class. Missing is the language by which to acknowledge these factors as part of a single process.

M. G. Smith (1965a), with his model of the plural society, provides the counterpoint to the integrated culture of the Parsonian position. Influenced by the writings of J. S. Furnivall (1956), Smith contrasts societies such as the United States and Brazil with another type of society within which he places Jamaica. These latter are, by and large, neo-colonial societies ruled by a dominant minority with a culture foreign to the masses. In such societies, maintenance of the colonial status quo demands that institutional integration be kept at a very elementary level to justify exclusion of the majority populace from major economic and political decision making. A corollary of this position is that these plural societies are held together not by shared values but by the sheer force of political domination (M. G. Smith 1960). Political domination is central to Smith's (1960:765) model, for he chooses to define societies simply in terms of territoriality and discrete governmental institutions.

Having excluded from his definition of society the notion of a social structure and especially a class structure based on a particular form, or forms, of economy, culture becomes Smith's major concept. Cultures consist of sets of institutions forming a "mutually supporting" complex. In fact, the import of Smith's analyses in the Caribbean area is that these institutional complexes are *mutually exclusive*. Thus, different forms of economic or political activity are interpreted not as different modes of participation in one institutional complex but as different institutions per se. With this theoretical orientation, M. G. Smith (1965b:163) could describe Jamaican society of the 1950s as comprising "three *distinctive* cultural sections" (my emphasis). Added to this description of white, brown, and black cultural sections is an account of values in marked contrast to the interpretation offered by the Parsonians. While the most powerful section of Jamaican society embraces the value of materialism, the middle section is concerned with color and the lowest section "with values of immediate physical gratification" (1965b:174). More revealing, Smith (1965b:174) continues, "the coexistence of these divergent value-systems within a single society involves continuous ideological conflict. . . . interpretations of events by reference to one or another of these competing moral systems is the principal mode of thought that characterises Jamaican society." For Smith there are no universal values in Jamaica; it is only the power of the dominant group that holds the society together.

M. G. Smith's account of Caribbean society continues to make fascinating reading both for its insights and for its radical failings. Furnivall (e.g., 1956), from whose work Smith draws his basic concepts, was writing in the dual-economy tradition whereby colonial societies were interpreted as political units encompassing separate modern and traditional economic sectors. This dual-economy notion stands at the root of Smith's ideas of separate cultural sections in society. The feature that both notions share is that they could only represent a brief period of colonial life beyond which we would expect to find some forms of cultural domination, as well as economic and political domination, extending from the elite group into the traditional sectors of society (cf. R. T. Smith 1961; Hoogvelt 1976:97–98). M. G. Smith is simply ambiguous concerning whether or not this political structure transforms the lives of subordinate sectors. Certainly he does not see particular political institutions as transforming the values of other cultural sections. Thus, his account of domination becomes simply an account of coercion, and he thereby commits himself to two untenable positions. First, he assumes that domination can proceed over long periods of time simply through the use of force. As noted earlier, R. T. Smith argues that it is most unlikely that such a situation can exist without the development of legitimating ideologies at least in part internalized by those so dominated. Second, M. G. Smith implies that because there are divergent value systems in society they thereby compete on equal terms. Yet, if domination is ideological as well as economic and political, then it is most unlikely that the ideologies of classes or cultural sections will so compete.

This brings us to the issue of a distinction between culture and ideology. It is clear that both parties to this debate have a very acute sense of subordinate classes involved in their own practical activity, yet constrained by superior power. R. T. Smith's view of their position is unduly pessimistic—value integration means lack of dissent, and certainly there has been plenty of dissent in Caribbean society. However, M. G. Smith's position is rather too optimistic—value divergence does not mean cognitive independence. If a subordinate group has particular ends or values in life that are different from other groups, this does not thereby ensure that they also think these values should be the primary ones for an entire society. Degrees of domination and constraint are still possible in the interpretation and realization of these values.

It is quite noticeable that both M. G. Smith and R. T. Smith treat "values" and "ideology" as interchangeable terms. When discussing the ideology of the creole elites, R. T. Smith (1967:235) expressly refers to the "set of common values or . . . ideology." M. G. Smith (1965b:174) speaks of "divergent value-systems" constituting "ideological conflict." Where ideology is taken to mean simply a system of ideas, the substitution would seem legitimate, though misleading. We do not normally think in terms of cultures being more or less powerful or more or less convincing, but we do think of ideologies in these terms. A shared set of beliefs spontaneously generated is quite a different phenomenon from a set of beliefs propagated through powerful institutions that constrain the experience of the people subject to them. In this latter sense of "ideology," an elite ideology is quite different from the shared values of society. It is not an instrument of integration but one of domination. Again, if by divergent value systems we mean simply the different ideas and ends of different groups, then there is no reason to think of these systems in terms of more or less efficacy. However, if these systems are in fact the sets of beliefs by which groups with vastly different resources and institutional power attempt to defend or improve their position, then it does make sense to ask which will be more efficacious, the ideology of the powerful or the ideology of the weak.

By conflation of the notions of cultural values and ideology, both protagonists in this debate fail to tie their respective emphases on institutional convergence and institutional divergence to issues of economic interest and political power. Institutional convergence becomes value integration rather than ideological domination; institutional divergence becomes cultural pluralism rather than conflict in the midst of domination. Both sides of the debate fail to grasp the idea that, though all classes have their distinctive forms of practical activity (which we may call "culture"), these forms of activity, like the ideologies that legitimate them, will be more or less pervasive depending on the power and interests of those concerned. Indeed, this principle extends even to those cases where institutions and beliefs of subordinate groups that have proved especially effective in defining a political cause are co-opted by the powerful and transformed from the property of a class into the property of "a nation." This process, which has engulfed Rastafarianism, black identity, and reggae music in contemporary Jamaica, has undermined these themes as potential foci for an exclusive working-class movement.

The notion of ideology employed in this discussion is fundamentally a Marxist one (see Marx 1970; Drucker 1974). The notion of culture as collective practice or practical activity also has a basis in Marx, though it can be found as well in anthropologists of a materialist persuasion such as Malinowski, Julian H. Steward, and, certainly, Sidney Mintz. This is not to say, however, that those in or closer to a Marxist tradition have necessarily avoided the analytical antinomy of Caribbean anthropology.

Three positions stand out in Caribbean sociology as emphasizing class or a notion of political economy. Gordon K. Lewis (1968:44) described the plural society debate (after the words of G. K. Chesterton) as "the argument of the suppressed alternative." Caribbean societies, he observed, were class societies wherein "class oppression and paternalism" prevailed. Lewis rejected M. G. Smith's pluralism, which ultimately attributed variable behavior and belief to ethnicity rather than to class. However, he also rejected the view that Caribbean societies, with their gross inequalities, possibly could be value integrated or consensual societies, as the Parsonians suggested. Lewis's (1968:44) description of Caribbean societies was made of sterner stuff:

> Social bullying and economic intimidation are pretty much the order of the day in the life of the masses. . . . Nor does the political fact of independence . . . necessarily change the social system. It merely transfers its control from the metropolitan masters to the local ruling groups. And because these groups understand the majority better than did the expatriate officials they might be able, indeed, to tighten up the psychological screws that hold the majority in their prison.

Lewis, a historical sociologist, here focuses on the political and ideological structures of colonial and postcolonial society. His interpretation emphasizes the subordination and ideological dependence of the less powerful classes, a theme continued in the work of those economists and sociologists who generated the theory of plantation dependency (see Beckford 1972; Best 1968; Cross 1979).

Central to the thesis of plantation dependency is the view that plantations are simply the first among a succession of metropolitan ventures that render Caribbean economies as extensions of the metropole (see Amin 1970). Plantation sectors not only inhibit local capital accumulation but also limit the land available to peasantries that develop following the period of forced labor. As populations grow, peasant land becomes increasingly divided, and peasants become involved in largely subsistence activity bolstered by periods of wage labor on plantations or elsewhere (Best 1968; Marshall 1968). Rural poverty fosters mass migration to the cities, but this migration does not create an industrial proletariat. Employment in manufacturing is limited, and a large proportion of the urban labor force is unemployed or involved in service activities not unionized and often underemployed (Cross 1979:26–30). Levitt and Best (1975:45) sum up this position when they observe that "the key to an understanding of plantation economy lies precisely in the fact that it is, from its inception, an extension of the metropolitan capitalist economy. The quasi-proletariat, the quasi-peasantry and the quasi-bourgeoisie are creatures of the plantation sector."

The focus of this account of Caribbean societies is on the relation between these societies and their international trading partners. The message is that irrespective of formal political relations, the terms of international trade and investment facilitate a continuing structure of domination. This view tends to collapse the position of different classes within the Caribbean. Just as Lewis plays down working-class resistance in order to emphasize elite domination, so do these Caribbean economists play down relations of domination within Caribbean society in order to emphasize the larger patterns of domination created by external economic relations.

This approach may be contrasted with that of Mintz, who has made class conflict within the Caribbean the hallmark of his analyses. Adopting and developing, particularly in his explorations of history, the cultural ecology of Julian Steward (Steward, Manners, Wolf, Padilla, Mintz, and Scheele 1956), Mintz was also inspired by Fernando Ortiz (1947) in his accounts of the opposition between peasant and plantation economies and culture. In his studies of Puerto Rican plantation workers (Mintz 1956, 1960), and his accounts of the Jamaican peasantry (Mintz 1974), Mintz depicts a faceless plantation and a very human peasantry and rural proletariat who pick and choose their values and practice them in the village, field, and work place. The very generation of culture is for Mintz a form of class action, and his emphasis on the material aspect of Caribbean peasant life makes plausible the cognitive independence he attributes to them. They are practical problem solvers, a "reconstituted" peasantry (in opposition to the capitalized plantation; Bolland 1981).

Mintz grasps admirably the process of class conflict in Caribbean societies and emphasizes the unequal power of the classes, but nowhere does he make explicit that relations between classes therefore must reflect a degree of domination. As Eugene Genovese (1975:77) has commented, in an appreciation of Mintz's work, ruling classes when they are not in their death throes and relying on naked force, rule by mediating [cultural] differences within the context of a hegemonic ideology—"hegemonic" because it compels the lower classes to define themselves within the ruling system even while resisting its aggression with enormous courage and resourcefulness. The main difficulty with Mintz's brilliant work in the relationship between class and culture lies in his skirting of the problem of hegemony.

Mintz's work skirts the problem of hegemony because he is concerned with the process of conflict and the genesis of culture rather than with the structure of domination. Genovese points out, however, that we must be concerned with both.[4]

There is a parallel between these latter writings and the plural society debate which I believe has not been previously identified. Both exhibit the dilemma involved in attempts to describe domination and conflict in tandem. When R. T. Smith argued that ideology rather than mere force helps to secure the position of an elite, he simply voiced in rather different terms the same observation made by Genovese with regard to Mintz's work. I suggest that the resolution of this antinomy in a language useful for anthropologists and sociologists requires that a distinction be made between culture as practical activity and the ideology or interpretation of that culture in the form of beliefs that promote an economic interest more or less powerful. This distinction allows us to acknowledge that subordinate classes do forge their own cultural practices, not simply in response to a material environment but also to provide identity and prestige in a milieu often denigrated by the rest of society. At the same time it is optimistic, even romantic, to suggest that these forms of creative response to a subordinate position can exist in the majority of cases unaffected by the ideologies of the powerful as propagated in the very institutions in which working-class people experience their subordination. The key to this perspective is that we understand that institutions are not class exclusive. Especially in the case of the powerful, institutions primarily in their control can and do penetrate working-class culture. Thus, although workers in a Kingston neighborhood may have divergent religious and leisure institutions, at the same time they are constrained and dominated in political life and in the formal socialization of the schools.

Institutional Divergence and Domination in the Neighborhood

The two neighborhoods in which I worked are predominantly working class (Selton Town) and predominantly middle class (Vermount), though residents rank neither among the poorest nor among the wealthiest of their respective classes.[5] Residents of Selton Town are primarily manual workers, while the majority of residents in Vermount hold clerical and lesser professional positions. Selton Town was once middle class and prestigious, but since the 1940s the area has experienced an influx of urban workers. Most houses have been subdivided into rental apartments, and up to 20 adults and children can reside in one of these tenements. Vermount is a suburb of more recent origin. It is a privately financed housing development that opened to occupants in the early 1960s. Sewerage, sealed sidewalks, and family homes mark it as a residential area superior to Selton Town, yet since its initial construction many homeowners have left. Houses have been reoccupied by tenants rather than prospective owners, and there has been some deterioration of properties. Vermount has become a modest middle-class area, while Selton Town is much superior to the nearby shanty town in the Wareika Hills. I emphasize that these two neighborhoods (Selton Town and Vermount) do not represent the extremes of class inequality in Kingston. Nevertheless, they do serve to show some fundamental cultural differences between people of different classes. I propose to mention here only the play life of men and the religious life that in these areas is more the domain of women.

The Vermount shopping center is arranged around a circular courtyard and accommodates just two bars. Although dominoes is played there and men gather to discuss the best bets in future race meetings, these are fairly muted gatherings, with the bars mostly deserted by 9:00 or 10:00 in the evening. Indeed, with a population of over 8000 in Vermount, it is obvious that the vast majority of male residents never visit these bars. The reasons are clear. Most Vermount men drive to work in privately owned cars. Their bar life is meshed with their work life downtown; they may adjourn to a bar after work and before the trek home. Those who do not gather downtown often entertain in the evening on their own verandas. The wife or household help bring the men some beer or a flask of rum and a jug of water to be drunk from chilled glasses kept in the refrigerator. The men dominate the veranda for the duration of the evening; the women of the household most often retire inside to watch television. These intimate little groups are the most common form of male socializing in Vermount, complemented by bar activity downtown, by attendance at service clubs such as Rotary and Kiwanis, and perhaps by participation as a social member in a cricket club frequented by old school friends. Neighborhood socializing is privatized, and socializing beyond the neighborhood is closely connected with career interests and the maintenance of useful contacts through the manipulation of various middle-class institutions.

The milieu of Selton Town is quite different. There, the major commercial street houses six bars, another five can be found on the main road bordering the area, and at least five or six more can be found on various street corners. Although not even this number of bars could accommodate all the males in Selton Town's population of around 9000, certainly the proliferation of bars indicates that men in Selton Town perceive play life as being neighborhood based and a public concern. Once again, the reason is not difficult to discern. Apart from the fact that many houses do not have a refrigerator, bar life provides for Selton Town working-class men a system of achievement, prestige, and respect independent of their work life. The way a man "carries" himself in the bar is a matter of personal performance and display, rather than a matter of wealth. For this reason the ritual of bar life, though it shares its basic components with the bars of Vermount, is more elaborate, more boisterous, and more important in the eyes of participants. Moreover, though particular bars become the precinct of particular industrial groups, politics and bar life are the foci of attention rather than the demands of a career path which most workers do not have.

Local bars in Selton Town are places in which a man proves his character as a man over and above the level of his income or his competence at his job. At least three factors are involved: First, a man must be controlled in his social habits. Although he should not drink too sparingly, he should be able to hold his liquor and at the evening's end "carry himself home." Second, a man ought to have his domestic affairs in control. What this means varies according to age group. For young men it means primarily that they are popular with girls and can recount a number of conquests that have precipitated no major "fuss" in the neighborhood. The welfare of dependents becomes more important as a man ages, and gossip reveals that above all a man must command the loyalty and fidelity of his spouse. Because the man has bought furniture for his household, has "made his investment," infidelity on the part of his woman is seen to "mek him a fool." This concern with sexuality is reflected in drink preferences: stout and Irish Moss are favored by older men because they are believed to increase potency.

Finally, a man can display excellence in one of two major areas. First, he may be a good conversationalist, which itself involves a number of talents. He should be humorous and able to tell a tale, generally of someone's misfortune and perhaps involving a woman, and very often the misfortune of "country people." The tale should terminate with a bawdy joke or with an illustration of someone's "foolishness." As the tale is told, the man will remain quite calm, speaking very rapidly. He will reveal only the merest flicker of a smile, but after the tale is told he will vent his mirth along with his friends, who have been laughing and slapping their sides all the while. To say of someone that he "is joke" is to recommend his storytelling, and men with this skill are much "appreciated."

Second, a man may be accepted among his peers if he excels at some game. Within the context of bar life, the major games are dominoes, cards, and race tipping. Dominoes is by far the most important of these games and in fact produces a contrasting type to the good conversationalist. The champion domino player is generally a quiet and sometimes older man. He reaches a pitch of voluble excitement only occasionally. Perhaps a major contender has beaten him and his partner a number of times and a match or rubber is in danger. Then, if the man wins a series of games to save the situation in the very last game, he will slam his dominoes down on the table, cry out, and tease the opposing pair to illustrate that he, afterall, is the master. Although the crowd around a domino game may be noisy, serious players revere their concentration and seldom make extreme claims for their prowess.

The gamesmanship of Selton Town bar life, whether in discussing women, politics, or sports, in drinking, storytelling, or dominoes, constitutes a source of prestige independent of work life. The bars of Vermount present only an embryonic form of the same institutions because Vermount men regularly derive acknowledged prestige from their work roles and can look forward to further advancement. Thus, Vermount bars do not constitute a proving ground for men, but simply a location for relaxation away from home and office. The values of egalitarianism and gamesmanship in the "Anancy" tradition, which are ever present in the Selton Town bars, are simply not at issue for middle-class Vermount men who are embued with notions of achievement and hierarchy in their social, sporting, and service clubs.

Hierarchy, as opposed to egalitarianism, and cooperation are also the different values we may use to distinguish religious activity in the two neighborhoods. Although not all of Selton Town's practicing Christians attend Fundamentalist churches, many do; in Vermount this form of religion is virtually unknown (see Austin 1981). The independent Pentecostal churches of Selton Town are subject to frequent fission. Given that anyone may be called to the evangelical enterprise, it is common for young deacons or evangelists to break away from their parent church and form new congregations. Although this process is testimony to an element of egalitarianism in the churches, it also results in a proliferation of small groups in financially precarious positions. If a significant proportion of a congregation is unemployed, and this is often the case, the position of these churches can become precarious. Consequently, the independent Pentecostal churches attempt to cooperate, and churches exchange preachers regularly. A group of "saints" (born-again Christians) at one church will be delegated to attend Sunday services at another, and churches will be asked to pray for each other. These cooperative efforts culminate in a series of rallies that are part religious service, part entertainment, and part fund raiser. In Selton Town, a network of six Pentecostal churches participate in these joint rallies, which are publicized widely among the churches. Members are reminded that if they do not supplement the funds of others, they cannot hope for similar returns. These rallies very seldom raise large amounts of money, but they are important nonetheless, for without them many of these churches would not survive. During the period of my fieldwork, a church that was deliberately excluded from the network failed and disappeared from the area, while another only survived by virtue of a benefactress who channeled finances into it from her modest business.

Vermount religious life is dominated by the "established" or "denominational" churches, as they are described in Kingston. These include the Anglican, Methodist, Roman Catholic, and Moravian churches. In addition, Vermount harbors a Church of God, with a home base in Indiana, which has rejected inspirational religion for a more subdued version of the born-again experience. Although the differences in doctrine between these churches can be marked, they share complex forms of organization that are absent in the small backyard churches of Selton Town. The churches with branches in Vermount generally were founded in

Jamaica as missionary enterprises. Moreover, these churches almost uniformly began as European initiatives catering to black and brown Jamaicans. The Anglicans, who acknowledge their lack of missionary zeal at the outset, now emphasize their ministry to the poor and the black. The frequent visits to Vermount churches by representatives based in the United States and Britain underscore a continuing close association with the metropolitan world. The churches share the organizational structure of their parent bodies whether they are constituted as branches or churches in Jamaica. The sophistication of their organization makes for rapid accumulation of funds to be expended not only in the local church but also passed back to the metropole, and in some cases distributed to missions. The practice of these churches, as any Fundamentalist will argue, is dominated by notions of training, learning, membership, and levels of authority from layman, to cleric, to major administrator in the parent church.

Institutional Mechanisms of Ideological Domination

These two examples of institutional divergence are sufficient to illustrate how classes forge different forms of practical activity and different values. Moreover, in the case of the subordinate class there is no doubt that those involved regard their activities as valid, viable forms from which they derive personal satisfaction. This is not the entire picture of cultural relations among classes in Kingston or elsewhere in the Caribbean. Certainly, many of the middle-class residents with whom I spoke regarded Pentecostalism as a form of "uneducated" religion, indicative of the undisciplined, superstitious, and inferior life of the working class. Bar life was seen as raucous, irresponsible, and also further evidence of the lack of both education and discipline in working-class life. Moreover, "respectable" working-class women denigrated Pentecostalism and turned either to the neighborhood Roman Catholic church or to a more subdued Orthodox Baptist church downtown. A working-class informant, one among many, spoke disparagingly of workmates grown too fond of bar life:

> I have a lot of chaps where I work and they earn good salaries, and yet they put it to no use. . . . I stop and have a few drinks with them you see, and well, they just don't have one drink. The one drink turn out to be three, four drinks and then they invite their friends, and so right there now, he is actually spending his week's pay entertaining the crowd. And he goes home poor. . . . Then he cries out that life is hard. But who makes it hard? He makes it hard. So these fellows now, I can't understand what at the back of their brain. . . .

There is, then, an alternative interpretation of these working-class institutions that judges them inferior and, furthermore, explicable in terms of individual failings. A young Catholic working-class woman commented on Pentecostalism: "It shows a really bad dark side in men. . . . This getting in the spirits is just people degrading themselves and acting like animals." A working-class man, referring to his friends, wondered what was wrong with their "brains." Both comments suggest that working-class people who are engaged in these activities are slightly deficient in intelligence and socialization. Moreover, this is not a view heard simply among the middle class, or even a minority of the working class; these are sentiments that all working-class people I met would articulate during one or another period of frustration.

If we are to look to the institutional bases for the propagation of this ideology in working-class life, then we must look first to Jamaica's education system which, since 1973, has held out hope to working-class children that they may enter secondary high schools, gain academic qualifications, and move out of the working class. The battery of examinations children must take to enter these schools makes life between the ages of 11 and 15 a difficult time. Moreover, despite the fact that the high schools can accommodate only a tiny minority of working-class children, the pressure from parents to attend is great (Kuper 1976; Manley 1963). Institutional endorsement of the view that inequality is due to differential ability or "brains" is not peculiar to Jamaica (Bowles and Gintis 1976; Willis 1978; Connell, Ashenden, Kessler, and Dowsett 1982; Foster 1980). However, in a society with a tradition of ascriptive ideology, this form of legitimation has particular force. Black working-class people, even today, can quietly ponder the idea that perhaps being "uneducated" or "dumb" is related to being black. The common use of the abusive term "nigger" by working-class Jamaicans to describe working-class people seen to be ill-mannered, vicious, or stupid shows that ascriptive ideology is still alive and well.

The effect of this situation on the lives and attitudes of working-class people is illustrated by an incident I observed during fieldwork. Selwyn, the son of a waterside worker, left school at the age of 15 without any major certificates. The only job he could obtain was as a roustabout in a supermarket. However, his mother was a member of the Catholic church and the local priest visited one evening to announce that a prestigious Catholic lawyer had a vacancy in his office for a young man. Selwyn was offered the job. The family was jubilant and his father was beside himself with pride. On his first morning in the new job the young man left his parents' apartment wearing a white shirt and collar, a tie rather loosely tied, and a suit borrowed from relatives. A week passed and the priest came again to tell the mother that the lawyer had complained about Selwyn's shoddy work. An elder sister decided to help Selwyn with his spelling, only to discover that the lad was functionally illiterate. Within another week Selwyn was fired. The father cursed his son and then did not speak to him for weeks, so embarrassed was he among his work mates. The mother refused the suggestion of a friend that the lad should go to literacy classes, maintaining that the family had been shamed enough already. Selwyn remained unemployed for a year and has had only intermittent laboring work since. I do not know how Selwyn himself interpreted this series of events. However, the "shame" of illiteracy is something many spoke of in Selton Town, despite an active adult literacy campaign. It seems unlikely that Selwyn's parents' response did not have some impact on him.

One course taken by young men like Selwyn, and also by women who are household heads, is to join a political party in the hope of a patronage job when the party is in power. Both Selton Town and Vermount had active PNP (People's National Party) groups during my period of fieldwork, which coincided with a PNP period in power. The major vehicle for patronage was the Impact Programme, a program of public employment as street cleaners for party members who otherwise would be unemployed. This patronage program was mainly for women and predominated in Vermount where group members were recruited not from the neighborhood itself but from an impoverished rural village nearby. In Selton Town this type of patronage for women was supplemented by the distribution of council construction contracts for men. This latter area of patronage was a turbulent one, with severe competition for work among both contractors and laborers. Work sites were often guarded by armed men, while those who had managed to gain employment sometimes attempted to sneak friends onto the site.

In a society such as Jamaica, where shortages of goods and resources affect all classes, patronage, graft, and favoritism are experiences that are not peculiar to working-class life. However, only among the working class are so many dependent entirely on political patronage for a livelihood. Moreover, even though group leaders are often recruited from the working class, councilors and members of parliament who distribute the patronage jobs are usually middle class. This situation emphasizes to working-class participants the clientage nature of their positions. From an institutional point of view, large numbers of working-class people in areas such as Selton Town pass from a school system in which they have failed under teachers invariably identified as "middle class" to a dependent position in political and economic life as clients of the same class. These are the institutional mechanisms through which ideological domination is perpetuated in those areas of Kingston with which I am familiar. Stone's (1980) study of clientage in Jamaica offers evidence that this is a common pattern both in the neighborhood and in industrial life. The process of rendering one class as clients of another ensures that the bases of conflict are contained and that expressions of conflict are constrained. Working-class culture is elaborated most in those social spheres having marginal relevance to the distribution of power.

I have suggested that the ideology accompanying this intervention is concerned with superior education, socialization, and role competence of a middle class. It would be a mistake to assume, however, that this ideology is merely a product of Jamaica's postwar industrialization. This is an ideology, in my view, that has its roots in the historically peculiar position of a brown middle class in a color-stratified society.

Jamaica's Middle Class and the Ideology of Education

During the slavery period, Jamaica's "free people of color" could hardly be regarded as a middle class, for legal freedom alone could not confer economic well-being. In a society dominated by slave labor, no one would purchase the skills of free men unless those skills were rare and highly accomplished. In addition, a harsh system of taxation discriminated against small landholders who were free coloreds (M. G. Smith 1965c; Brathwaite 1972: 169–175; D. Hall 1972).

For some of Jamaica's free coloreds there was a solution. Those who inherited substantial wealth, property, or both from their fathers could and did apply to the Jamaican Assembly for the privileges of a white man (cf. N. A. T. Hall 1975). Privileges were granted on the condition that petitioners were baptized members of the Anglican church, as well as educated; it was all the better if this education had been received abroad. Without question, a free colored in preemancipation Jamaica could not obtain an education unless a parent had considerable wealth, but the ideology of the situation was such that education and a moral life made one equal to a white man. A section of a petition for privileges, presented in 1783, is illustrative.

> That the petitioner has caused all his . . . natural children to be *baptised, educated and instructed, in the principles of the Christian religion* and intends bringing them up in a respectable manner. . . . That, by the unfortunate circumstances of their births, they are subject . . . to the same pains and penalties as free negroes and mulattoes are, *who have no education.* . . . The petitioner therefore humbly prays that the house will be pleased to give leave to bring in a bill, for the granting unto . . . the before-mentioned children, the like privileges as has been hitherto granted to persons under the same circumstances (quoted in Brathwaite 1972:171; my emphasis).

Here, perhaps, were the beginnings of a middle-class ideology of education that incorporated the notion of socialization as well as qualifications.

After emancipation, the embryonic middle class was gradually expanded by freed men from the plantations (Mintz 1974:146–179; Brathwaite 1972:155; Eisner 1961:210–235; Paget 1955). The small farmers who were to form Jamaica's rural middle class produced pimento, ginger, and coffee for export, in addition to sugarcane (D. Hall 1976). Later, the same category of farmers became contract growers for the banana industry (D. Hall 1964). During the early years of the banana industry, which took the place of sugar as the major export earner, the expansion of small- to middle-scale farms was marked. However, plantations effectively blocked further expansion of this rural middle class. After 1902, farms of less than 2 hectares began to proliferate as land under profitable cultivation was increasingly subdivided (Eisner 1961:220).

Commerce was an area already dominated by European and European Jewish minorities, the latter resident in Jamaica since Spanish times. Consequently, Jamaica's rural, brown middle class turned from agriculture to meet the colonial government's demand for professionals in the public service. There was no universal free secondary education in Jamaica before 1973; this path was open only to those whose parents could afford to pay. These were Jamaica's successful middle-range export farmers. Eisner (1961:315) comments on the "conspicuous success" of these Jamaicans in the professions:

> At first there were positive restrictions on their opportunities. To remove these it was necessary to demonstrate equality through the attainment of education and living standards. Removal of civil disabilities, however, still did not bring acceptance by the whites and the need to prove equality remained. This need was met by acquiring advanced educational qualifications and entering the professions, and especially by the prestige and power conferred by public office.

Education became the salvation for a rural middle class unable to expand due to lack of land. Medicine, law, teaching, and nursing became the hallmark of Jamaica's middle class. During the colonial period they were the civil service class, the class that molded and guided contemporary nationalist politics. It was not intellectual ability and right values alone that provided the basis for Jamaica's new middle class, but inheritance and some success in export farming. It is the ideology of this class that presents the legitimating elements alone, and yet this ideology of education is not without its puzzles.

Due to the very late provision of free public secondary education, educational achievement is a less convincing explanation of the middle class's position in Jamaica than it would be in many other industrialized and semiindustrialized societies. Why, then, was this the meaning the middle-class Jamaicans gave to their position? To begin with, their intermediary position in a color-stratified society meant that they could not use an ideology of color alone to differentiate themselves from a black working class. Such an ideology would ultimately condemn them to a secondary position in relation to whites; and whatever the social mores of the period, the nationalist movement of the 1920s and 1930s made it clear that many did not believe themselves to be inferior to whites (Post 1979:205–237; Nettleford 1970). What was required was an ideology that established them as qualitatively different from the poor, but without reference to color. This is the role that the qualitative or ascriptive notion of education played in Jamaican society, and this is why the concept of education in Jamaica has dual connotations. The view has been that the middle class gained and deserved their access to higher education and the professions because their socialization and Christian ways have made them superior to the uneducated, indeed uncivilized, working class (Kuper 1976:88).

This brief history of Jamaica's middle class leaves no doubt that the values of education and Christian morality had their source as a legitimating ideology in the dynamics of upward mobility of this class. Moreover, in the form of a legitimating ideology, these values have served this class more profitably than other sectors of Jamaican society. The prevalence of these values among members of different classes reflects the influential position of the middle class in Jamaican society rather than a spontaneous consensus on the worthy things of life. This is not surprising when we understand that the Jamaican middle class has dominated the teaching profession and acts as broker in the politics of the working class. Despite the creation of their own institutions and an alternative ideology, working-class Jamaicans cannot entirely escape this domination.

Conclusion

The analysis of culture and consciousness offered here is directly contrary to that provided by Stone (1980:21) in his recent study:

> Most analyses of the Jamaican social structure . . . prior to independence centered around the dominance of European values and the white bias. . . . These analyses . . . have lost contemporary relevance in the face of the growth of black racial consciousness . . . the aggressive assertion of lower-class culture through popular music and the growing acceptance and popularity of Rastafarianism as it penetrates all levels of the ethno-class structure.

I rest my case with the observation that while Rastafarianism in the 1940s and 1950s, and even into the 1960s, did provide a focus for a form of working-class politics (Nettleford 1970:41–111), this is no longer the case. Rasta and reggae have become marketable national commodities co-opted by a middle-class intellectual elite and by Jamaica's entrepreneurs (Chevannes 1977). In the meantime, this elite has shifted its ideological emphasis from color to education, from birth to socialization, from "manners" to social competence, retaining all the while a qualitative component designed to maintain their privileged class position. Certainly, the middle-class emphasis on manners has been strongly resisted by working-class youth and rejected in part or in toto by some segments of the middle class in favor of an ideology of black identity. However, the projection of cultural symbols and ideology is a constantly contested area and my fieldwork leads to the conclusion that Jamaica's middle class retains a very definite power to co-opt and reformulate ideology and turn it back as a new means of domination, even in the face of resistance. The recent landslide election of a party reputed to be antagonistic toward the black power cause and its support for competitive achievement in economic life supports this conclusion.[6]

Stone (1980) denies the importance of an ideology of education in working-class consciousness, as noted by myself, by Foner (1973), and by Kuper (1976) in fieldwork throughout the 1970s. Nevertheless, Stone's data show that an overwhelming majority of his respondents in six major classes designate "teacher" as the preferred occupation for their children. He rejects the implications of these data by focusing on the fact that respondents themselves prefer independent small business as an occupation. Stone (1980:42–43) describes these as the "ideal" and "realistic" hopes of his informants. Yet, given Jamaica's chronically depressed economy, surely working-class aspirations to private ownership in business are no more realistic than aspirations for children to enter the teaching profession. Stone misses the point that large numbers of Jamaica's working class conceptualize a better future for their children in terms of an education simply not available to the vast majority. Beyond success in private enterprise, this is the only alternative they see. This fact seems to me to be ready evidence of criticism constrained by hegemony. It may be the case that analyses of the "white bias" in Jamaica are out of date, but Stone has not shown that analyses of ideological domination are thereby out of date. This is a form of analysis I advocate, in conjunction with accounts of class culture, as a means of addressing the main issues of Caribbean society today. In particular, it seems to me that the role of middle-class intellectuals as political and ideological brokers in Caribbean society needs attention, for they must continually refurbish their "plausibility base" if domination is to continue. Even given the enormous economic power of the metropole, it is this local process of conflict and domination that will decide whether or not the ambiguity of Caribbean history continues.

As for the antinomy of anthropology in the English-speaking Caribbean, let me make the following observations. All of the societies involved are faced with situations of scarce resources and inequalities of power that tend to generate two conditions: radically different contexts for everyday life and radical conflicts of interest. The former condition tends to produce different values and institutional complexes on the part of different classes, regional groups, and ethnic groups. The latter condition (of conflict) tends to produce competing ideologies of legitimation propagating the interests of these different cultures. Only the most ill-informed anthropologist would argue that all classes in the Caribbean live the same type of life, and only the most naïve anthropologist would suggest that each group's belief system has equal political influence and efficacy. Again, I emphasize that analyses of these societies that stress simply conflict and cultural opposition, or simply domination or value integration, must misrepresent the situation. However, if we understand that divergent practices, particularly in institutions peripheral to the centers of power, do not necessarily signify autonomy in social life, the antinomy can be resolved. The practice of a divergent culture does not necessarily free a group from economic, political, and ideological domination. Conflict can be culturally manifest and yet constrained within the bounds of a stable institutional and ideological situation. This, I believe, is the case in Jamaica.

Notes

The late Chandra Jayawardena, and Dr. Jeremy Beckett of the University of Sydney, made helpful comments on earlier drafts of this paper. My debt to Raymond T. Smith of the University of Chicago is both diffuse and enduring.

1. I am indebted to R. W. Connell et al. (1982) for the term "collective practice."

2. The theoretical sources of my position within anthropology are Asad (1979) and Bourdieu (1977: 159–171). Beyond anthropology I have been influenced by Gramsci (1957:28–51; 1971). Singham and Singham (1973) are suggestive for the Caribbean area itself.

3. Two major discussions of the plural society debate at its height are found in Braithwaite (1960) and Cross (1968).

4. Whitten (1974), in the adjacent area of Latin America, presents a more satisfactory amalgamation of the elements to which Genovese refers.

5. I made four field trips of varying durations to Kingston between 1971 and 1977. A more detailed account of life in these neighborhoods is given in Austin (1983).

6. I refer here to the election of the Jamaica Labour Party in November 1980. The party's antagonism toward black power, and particularly toward those intellectuals who supported its cause, is documented in Nettleford (1970:116–117) and Post (1979:vii).

References

Amin, Samir
   1970   Accumulation on a World Scale. New York: Monthly Review Press.

Asad, Talal
   1979   Anthropology and the Analysis of Ideology. Man (NS) 14:607–627.

Austin, Diane J.
   1979   History and Symbols in Ideology: A Jamaican Example. Man (NS) 14:497–514.
   1981   Born Again . . . and Again and Again: Routinised Communities among Jamaican Pentecostals. Journal of Anthropological Research 37(4):226–246.
   1983   Culture, Class and Ideology: A Study of Two Neighbourhoods in Kingston, Jamaica. New York: Gordon and Breach.

Beckford, George
   1972   Persistent Poverty: Underdevelopment in the Plantation Economies of the Third World. London: Oxford University Press.

Best, Lloyd
   1968   Outlines of a Model of Pure Plantation Economy. Social and Economic Studies 17:283–299.

Bolland, O. Nigel
   1981   Systems of Domination after Slavery. Comparative Studies in Society and History 23:591–619.

Bowles, S., and H. Gintis
   1976   Schooling in Capitalist America. New York: Basic Books.

Bourdieu, P.
    1977   Outline of a Theory of Practice. Cambridge: Cambridge University Press.
Braithwaite, Lloyd
    1960   Social Stratification and Cultural Pluralism. In Social and Cultural Plural-
            ism in the Caribbean. Vera Rubin, ed. Annals of the New York Academy
            of Sciences 83:816–836.
    1975   Social Stratification in Trinidad. Mona: Institute of Social and Economic
            Studies.
Brana-Shute, G.
    1979   On the Corner: Male Social Life in a Paramaribo Creole Neighbourhood.
            Assen: Van Gorcum.
Brathwaite, Edward
    1972   The Development of Creole Society in Jamaica 1770–1820. Cambridge:
            Cambridge University Press.
Chevannes, Barry
    1977   The Literature of Rastafari. Social and Economic Studies 26:239–262.
Connell, R. W., D. J. Ashenden, S. Kessler, and G. Dowsett
    1982   Making the Difference: Schools, Families and Social Divisions. Sydney:
            George Allen and Unwin.
Cross, Malcolm
    1968   Cultural Pluralism and Sociological Theory. Social and Economic Studies
            17:381–397.
    1979   Urbanization and Urban Growth in the Caribbean. Cambridge: Cam-
            bridge University Press.
Drucker, H. M.
    1974   The Political Uses of Ideology. London: Macmillan.
Eisner, Giselle
    1961   Jamaica 1830–1930: A Study in Economic Growth. Manchester: Manches-
            ter University Press.
Foner, N.
    1973   Status and Power in Rural Jamaica. New York: Teachers' College Press.
Foster, P.
    1980   Education and Social Inequality in Sub-Saharan Africa. Journal of Mod-
            ern African Studies 18:201–236.
Furnivall, J. S.
    1956   Colonial Policy and Practice. New York: New York University Press.
Genovese, Eugene
    1975   Class, Culture and Historical Process. Dialectical Anthropology 1:71–79.
Gramsci, A.
    1957   The Southern Question. In The Modern Prince. pp. 28–51. New York: In-
            ternational Publishers.
    1971   Selections from the Prison Notebooks. Quentin Hoare and G. Nowell
            Smith, eds. and transls. London: Laurence and Wishart.

Hall, Douglas
  1964   The Early Banana Trade from Jamaica, 1868–1905: A Descriptive Account. In Ideas and Illustration in Economic History. pp. 56–80. New York: Holt, Rinehart and Winston.
  1972   Jamaica. In Neither Slave nor Free. D. W. Cohen and J. P. Greene, eds. pp. 193–213. Baltimore: Johns Hopkins University Press.
  1976   Free Jamaica. Kingston: Caribbean Universities Press.

Hall, N. A. T.
  1975   Some Aspects of the "Deficiency" Question in Jamaica in the Eighteenth Century. Caribbean Studies 15:5–19.

Henriques, Fernando
  1976   Family and Colour in Jamaica. London: Granada.

Herskovits, Melville
  1969   Problem, Method and Theory in Afroamerican Studies. In The New World Negro. pp. 43–61. New York: Minerva Press.

Hoogvelt, A. M. M.
  1976   The Sociology of Developing Societies. London: Macmillan.

Jayawardena, Chandra
  1963   Conflict and Solidarity on a Guianese Plantation. London: Athlone Press.
  1968   Ideology and Conflict in Lower Class Communities. Comparative Studies in Society and History 10:413–446.

Kuper, Adam
  1976   Changing Jamaica. London: Routledge and Kegan Paul.

Levitt, K., and L. Best
  1975   The Character of Caribbean Economy. In Caribbean Economy. George Beckford, ed. pp. 34–60. Mona: Institute of Social and Economic Studies.

Lewis, G. K.
  1968   The Growth of the Modern West Indies. New York: Monthly Review Press.

Manley, D.
  1963   Mental Ability in Jamaica. Social and Economic Studies 12:51–71.

Manning, F. E.
  1973   Black Clubs in Bermuda: Ethnography of a Play World. Ithaca: Cornell University Press.

Marshall, W. K.
  1968   Peasant Development in the West Indies Since 1850. Social and Economic Studies 17:252–263.

Marx, K.
  1964   The Economic and Philosophical Manuscripts. New York: International Publishers.
  1970   The German Ideology, Part 1. C. J. Arthur, ed. New York: International Publishers.

Mintz, Sidney
  1956   Cañamelar: The Culture of a Rural Puerto Rican Proletariat. In The

People of Puerto Rico. J. Steward, R. A. Manners, E. R. Wolf, E. Padilla, S. W. Mintz, and R. C. Scheele. pp. 314–417. Urbana: University of Illinois Press.

1960   Worker in the Cane. New Haven: Yale University Press.

1974   Caribbean Transformations. Chicago: Aldine.

Nettleford, Rex
1970   Mirror Mirror. Identity, Race and Protest in Jamaica. Kingston: William Collins and Sangster (Jamaica).

1971   General Introduction. In Manley and the New Jamaica. pp. xi–xciv. Trinidad: Longman Caribbean.

Ortiz, Fernando
1947   Cuban Counterpoint: Tobacco and Sugar. New York: Knopf.

Paget, H.
1955   The Free Village System in Jamaica. Caribbean Quarterly 1(4):7–19.

Post, Ken
1979   Arise Ye Starvelings: The Jamaican Labour Rebellion of 1938 and Its Aftermath. The Hague: Mouton.

Singham, A. W., and N. L. Singham
1973   Cultural Domination and Political Subordination: Notes Towards a Theory of the Caribbean Political System. Comparative Studies in Society and History 15:258–288.

Smith, M. G.
1960   Social and Cultural Pluralism. In Social and Cultural Pluralism in the Caribbean. Vera Rubin, ed. Annals of the New York Academy of Sciences 83:763–785.

1965a   A Framework for Caribbean Studies. In The Plural Society in the British West Indies. pp. 18–72. Berkeley: University of California Press.

1965b   The Plural Framework of Jamaican Society. In The Plural Society in the British West Indies. pp. 162–175. Berkeley: University of California Press.

1965c   Some Aspects of Social Structure in the British Caribbean about 1820. In The Plural Society in the British West Indies. pp. 92–115. Berkeley: University of California Press.

1966   Introduction. In My Mother Who Fathered Me. E. Clarke. pp. i–xxxviii. London: George Allen and Unwin.

Smith, Raymond T.
1956   The Negro Family in British Guiana. London: Routledge and Kegan Paul.

1961   People and Change. New World Quarterly. Guyana Independence Issue. pp. 49–54.

1967   Social Stratification, Cultural Pluralism and Integration in West Indian Societies. In Caribbean Integration: Papers on Social, Political and Economic Integration, pp. 226–258. Rio Pedras: Institute of Caribbean Studies.

Steward, Julian, R. A. Manners, E. R. Wolf, E. Padilla, S. W. Mintz and R. C. Scheele
1956   The People of Puerto Rico. Urbana: University of Illinois Press.

Stone, Carl
    1980   Democracy and Clientalism in Jamaica. New Brunswick, NJ: Transaction Books.
Whitten, N. E., Jr.
    1974   Black Frontiersmen: A South American Case. Cambridge, MA: Schenkman.
Willis, P. E.
    1978   Learning to Labour. Hampshire, UK: Gower.
Wilson, Peter
    1973   Crab Antics: A Social Anthropology of English-speaking Negro Societies of the Caribbean. New Haven: Yale University Press.

17. CELEBRATING CRICKET

The Symbolic Construction of Caribbean Politics

Frank E. Manning

Cricket has suffered, but not only cricket. The aestheticians have scorned to take
notice of popular sports and games—to their own detriment. The aridity and
confusion of which they so mournfully complain will continue until they include
organized games *and the people who watch them* as an integral part of their data.

—C. L. R. James 1963:191–192; emphasis in original

The failure of art critics to appreciate the aesthetics of popular sport has been no
less myopic than the failure of anthropologists to grasp its social importance. Although folklorists and protoethnologists of the previous century showed an interest in games—much of it inspired by E. B. Tylor's evolutionary and diffusionist
speculations—the anthropology of play did not advance appreciably until the late
1950s (Schwartzman 1978:5). A great deal of the recent attention, however, has
been directed at either children's play or at relatively small-scale games—a corpus
pioneered by the early collaborative studies of Roberts and Sutton-Smith (1962,
1966). A significant literature on mass ludic spectacles such as popular sports
events and public celebrations is only now emerging, much of it inspired by the
interest of Gluckman and Turner in "secular ritual" (Moore and Myerhoff 1977)
and by Geertz's (1972) paper on the Balinese cockfight.

The seminal work of these latter figures converges on a conceptual approach
to the relationship between symbolic and social phenomena. For Turner (1977),
"liminoid" performative genres such as festivals and carnivals are "proto-" or "me-
tastructural," generating cultural comprehension by abstracting and recombin-
ing—often in novel, metaphorical ways—a social structure's basic principles. For
Gluckman (see Gluckman and Gluckman 1977), whose views were articulated
in the last article published before his death, symbolic events such as sports at-
tractions and theatrical productions differ from traditional religious rites in being
an imaginative "presentation" of society rather than a "re-presentation" or copy
of it. For Geertz (1972), the cockfight is a fictive story about its social context, a

Originally published in *American Ethnologist* 8:3 (August 1981), pp. 616–32. Reproduced by permission of the American Anthropological Association. Not for further reproduction.

"metasocial commentary" on it that is analogous to a literary text in using the devices of aesthetic license to disarrange conventional semantic contexts and re-arrange them in unconventional ways. Geertz also underscores a point that is less forcefully made by Gluckman and Turner: that symbolic forms are not only a reflexive interpretation of social life, but also a means through which people discover and learn their culture. The lesson for anthropology is that symbolic inquiry, besides laying bare a social system, can also tell us a great deal about the epistemological processes whereby that system is revealed to those whose lives it shapes.

Drawing from these positions, as well as other perspectives that have thrown light on public play and mass performance, this paper examines Bermudian cricket festivals. I focus on the social history of these festivals, on the manner in which they are celebrated, and on a highly significant side activity, gambling. My contention is that the total genre dramatizes a fundamental, racially oriented conflict between cultural identity and economic interest—a conflict that is generalizable to the Caribbean (and perhaps other decolonizing areas) and that underlies the region's political situation. Consistent with Cohen's (1979:87) observation that anthropology's chief contribution to the study of politics has been the analysis of nonpolitical symbols that have political implications and functions, I propose that celebration can provide a unique understanding of the conceptual parameters in which political awareness is developed and expressed.

Blacks in Whites

In the West Indies the game of cricket is played with elegant skill, studied with scholarly intensity, argued with passionate conviction, and revered with patriotic pride. Young boys with makeshift bats and balls play spiritedly in yards, fields, and beaches, learning the skills that in the past century have made West Indians among the world's outstanding cricketers. Organized competition begins in school and continues—often through middle age—in amateur sports clubs. Island-wide teams drawn from the clubs provide the Caribbean's premier sports attraction when they play annually in a touring series known as the Shell Shield. There is also a pan-West Indian team that represents the region in "test" (international) matches and that has been the outstanding exception to a catalog of failed attempts at West Indian unification.

One gleans the historical significance of the game in *Beyond a Boundary*, C. L. R. James's (1963) autobiography cum cricket analysis. A Trinidadian journalist, teacher, historian, political critic, and, above all, cricket devotee, James contends that in the West Indies cricket was traditionally seen as embodying the qualities of the classic British character ideal: fair play, restraint, perseverance, responsibility, and the moral inflections of Victorian Puritanism. Paradoxically, Afro–West Indians were taught to esteem those standards but were denied the means of achieving and demonstrating them. Cricket organizations—clubs, leagues, selection committees, governing bodies—conformed to the wider system of color-class stratification, and when the races occasionally played together, it was customary for whites to bat and blacks to bowl (St. Pierre 1973:7–12).

The phrase "put on your whites" is instructive. Literally, it means to don the several items—white or cream-colored—that make up a cricket uniform: shoes, pants, shirt, sweater, protective gloves, knee pads. Figuratively, it is a metonym of the black struggle in cricket, itself a metonym as well as an instrument of the more general black struggle under British colonialism. In cricket there were a succession of black goals: to get to bat, to gain places on island-wide teams and regional tours, and, as recently as the 1960s, to be named vice-captains and captains of test teams, positions reserved for whites even after racial criteria had been virtually eliminated from selection procedures. Cricket successes brought recognition to Afro–West Indians both internationally and, more begrudgingly, in the upper strata of local society, gradually transforming the sport into a powerful symbol of black ability, achievement, and aspiration.

Bermudian cricket is a variation on these themes, but one that, like Bermuda itself, caricatures and often strikingly illuminates the Caribbean pattern. Lying a thousand miles and a climatic zone north of the West Indies, Bermuda has a five-month summer cricket season and therefore does not participate in most major West Indian tournaments, which are held during the winter. Nor do Bermudians take the game as seriously or as professionally as West Indians do. In the Caribbean, for example, festival games—occasions when a cricket match takes place in a setting of festive sociability—are relatively informal, localized, and of little general interest (James 1963:20–21).[1] In Bermuda, however, festival games are both the highlights of the cricket season and, aside from Christmas, the calendar's most significant holidays. Bermudian festival cricket is the counterpart of Caribbean carnivals, but it enriches the spirit of celebration with the drama of a popular sporting classic.

The racial division of Bermudian cricket was shaped by an apartheidlike form of segregation, rather than by the West Indian system of color-class stratification. Introduced by British military personnel in the 19th century, the game was originally played in white sporting clubs. Blacks responded by forming neighborhood cricket clubs that have since evolved into the country's major centers of sport, entertainment, and sociability (Manning 1973). Through the clubs, blacks gained unquestioned superiority in cricket; when racial integration was nominally introduced in the 1960s, whites virtually withdrew from the game.

Two of the oldest black clubs, Somerset and St. George's, were begun primarily to promote an informal cricket contest held each August 1st in commemoration of the 1834 emancipation of slaves in British territories—an occasion marked by varied festivities throughout the Commonwealth Caribbean. Under club sponsorship the event developed into Cup Match, the oldest and most prominent cricket festival. Now held on the Thursday and Friday closest to August 1st, the game's historical identification with blacks is maintained by the white practice of observing the first day of Cup Match as Somers's Day, named after the British Admiral Sir George Somers who discovered Bermuda in 1609.

Besides Cup Match there are the Eastern, Western, and Central County Games, each involving four clubs in a series of three matches staggered between June and September. As these series progress there is a buildup of festivity and sporting interest, so that the final games—in effect, sequels to Cup Match—are like Cup Match as occasions of mass celebration. In white society the County Games are paralleled by summer yachting competitions, notably the renowned Newport-Bermuda race. Nowhere in the Caribbean is there a more striking example of the pluralistic segmentation that Smith (1965) attributed to British West Indian societies.

While Cup Match commemorates emancipation from slavery, the County Games celebrate diffuse aspects of the black tradition and life-style. The Eastern and Western series, the two most popular, reflect variants in the black situation that figure in the deeper-level meaning of festival cricket. Begun in 1904, the Eastern Games involve clubs that draw from old, demographically stable neighborhoods. In each neighborhood there is a core of black extended families, typically small property owners deriving modest incomes from family stores, trades, service jobs, and, in earlier generations more than now, part-time farming and fishing. The principle of family-neighborhood integrity is the basis of Eastern County selection rules. Eligibility is based on having been born in the club's neighborhood—the usual and preferred criterion—or having been a resident of it for at least two years. Although in a number of cases current players have moved away from their ancestral neighborhoods and play for other clubs in league games, their return for the County Games makes each club roster a roll call of familiar surnames, re-creating the networks and reviving the sentiments of traditional social organization.

The Western County Games, begun in 1962, are a product of newer social influences. The Western parishes have grown appreciably since the time when the series started, as new luxury hotels have created employment and as the demand for housing among blacks short of middle age has been met by the conversion of large estates into fashionable residential subdivisions (Newman 1972:3). Reflecting these trends, the Western Games are touted not as neighborhood rivalries, but as slick, highly competitive all-star games. Clubs vie intensely for Bermuda's best cricketers, offering lucrative incentives that lure players from outside the Western parishes and that encourage opportunistic switching between clubs from one year to the next. The clubs have even extended recruitment into the Caribbean, scouting the region for prospects and arranging their immigration. In the mid-1970s, the final game of the Western series was extended from one day to two, a move aimed at raising the caliber of play, generating wider public interest, and boosting gate receipts. The emphasis on aggressive commercialism is also seen in other areas of club activity, notably entertainment. Two of the clubs involved in the series (as well as other clubs in the Western parishes) have built elegant lounges which remain open as late as 5 a.m., offering formidable competition to the area's hotels.

Underlying the varying inflections of the Eastern and Western County Games are changes in the terms of clientage, the basis of the black Bermudian socioeconomic condition. Traditionally, Bermuda was run by a white aristocracy whose relations to blacks were paternal in both a biological and social sense. Descendants of the original 17th-century British settlers, the aristocracy were seafarers until the 1870s, agricultural exporters from then until the 1920s, and more recently an interlocking establishment of merchants, bankers, and corporate lawyers. Functioning as a ruling class in an almost feudal sense (Lewis 1968:323), they used the instruments of patronage—jobs, loans, credit, mortgages, charity—to maintain the allegiance and even the endearment of blacks, who make up three-fifths of the population, as well as a white underclass consisting of old "poor cousin" families, newer immigrants from Commonwealth countries, and Azorean Portuguese imported as indentured agricultural laborers. Patron-client relations were typically transacted within neighborhoods and parishes and between extended families, reinforcing residential identity and producing alliances between black and white kin groups that crosscut the system of institutionalized racial segregation. The common Caribbean metaphor of island society as a single large family (Wilson 1973:47) was powerfully resonant in Bermuda, yielding a meaningful context in which patronage took the social form of a relationship between benevolent, although demanding, white patriarchs and filial black dependents.

Since the early 1960s, however, the power and prestige of the aristocracy have been substantially eroded. The tourist boom has made foreign-owned hotels the major employers and, along with the development of an offshore corporate business sector, brought to Bermuda a class of expatriate managers who wield an appreciable influence in local affairs. In addition, the buoyancy and expansion of the economy has allowed the aggressive rise of underclass whites, notably Bermuda-born Portuguese, and a handful of black professionals and entrepreneurs. Tellingly, many of the aristocracy's merchant houses on Front Street, the commercial frontispiece of Hamilton, are now dominated by whites whose rise to economic prominence has come about within the past two decades.

What these changes have done to the patronage system is alter its character and style while maintaining, and perhaps strengthening, its grip on the overwhelming majority of blacks. The benevolent paternalism of the aristocracy has been replaced by the bureaucratic orientation of the new elite, and largess has been escalated to include company directorships, investment opportunities, business partnerships, and well-paid managerial positions. Blacks enjoy the life-style provided by an affluent economy, but at the cost of remaining in a position of clientage and subordination.

"We black Bermudians," an old man cautioned, "can easily fool you. We're laughing on the outside, but crying on the inside." This commonplace statement derives its impact from oxymoron, the figure of speech that combines conceptual and emotional antitheses. Viewed as a collectively enacted "text," festival cricket is also built on oxymoron. Overtly and purposefully, these games articulate the meaning of freedom, family, community, club, and, above all, cricket itself—symbols that manifest to blacks their identity, their solidarity, their survival. But the games also reflect, implicitly but no less significantly, the field of socioeconomic relations in which blacks are dependent on a white power structure that has lost its traditional character but preserved its oppressive force. In this juxtaposition—this dramatic oxymoron—lies the basis of both the political system and the political imagination.

Food, Liquor, Clothing, and Money

Soliciting a description of festival cricket early in my first Bermudian fieldwork, I was told it was the time "when we eat everything in Bermuda, drink everything in Bermuda, wear everything in Bermuda, and spend everything in Bermuda." Although popular interest in the game runs unusually high, festival cricket is an occasion of participation, not spectatorship. The festival ethos is one of hedonistic indulgence, gregarious sociability, histrionic exhibitionism, lavish hospitality, conspicuous consumption—behaviors that epitomize and celebrate the black Bermudian self-image. In Singer's (1955) terms, festival cricket is a cultural performance, a dramatic spectacle in which a people proclaim and demonstrate their sense of who they are.

Like Carnival, festival cricket involves a period of preparation that is considered nearly as much fun as the event itself. For weeks before Cup Match there is intense speculation about the selection of teams. Pundits offer their personal choices in letters to the editor, and the subject is heatedly discussed in bars, in buses, and on street corners. The principal centers of activity are the black clubs, where people go, in the words of one informant, "just to hear the arguments." The arguments peak a week before the game, when the club selection committees announce their picks to the membership at a meeting in which dramatic suspense, flamboyant and often fiery oratory, and uproarious entertainment combine ritualistically to induct chosen players into the club tradition. In the final days before the game there is a general buildup of festive sociability, a flurry of shopping activity for food, liquor, and clothing, and extended expressions of team loyalty through the display of club colors on cars and items of apparel. For County Games the scenario is similar, but on a smaller scale.

Game days begin early, as fans laden with coolers, umbrellas, collapsible chairs, and briefcase-sized portable radios arrive at the grounds several hours before the first ball is bowled at 10 a.m. Locations around the periphery of the field are carefully staked out, mostly by groups of friends who have made arrangements to contribute to a common supply of food and liquor. A more enviable location is in makeshift pavilions erected at the edge of the field or on surrounding hillsides. Wooden frames covered with canvas or thatch, the pavilions bear colorful names such as "Honey Bee Lounge" and often fly flags made of liquor banners or team insignia. Organized by club-based peer groups, the pavilions accommodate 10–20 couples who pay a set fee — as much as $100[2] for the two days of Cup Match — for food, liquor, and other amenities. Most pavilions are wired to the clubhouse, enabling the use of lights, appliances, and stereos that typically have auditorium-sized electronic speakers.

In all groups there is emphasis on extravagance, sophistication, ostentation. Bottles of brand-name liquor ranging from the 40-ounce to the 1-gallon size are set out on coolers and tables, flanked by cherries, lemons, limes, angostura bitters, and more specialized garnishes and liqueurs for concoctions that gain popularity during a particular festival season (Scotch, milk, and grenadine was the favorite one year). Food is plentiful and of two kinds: the cherished "soul" dishes built around chicken, fish, and "hoppin' john" (black-eyed peas and rice); and festive specialties, notably cassava pie and a chicken and pork filling baked pastry made from shredded cassava. At the Eastern County Games one is also likely to see a number of festive seafood dishes, including mussel pie, conch stew, and hash shark. For those without enough food or liquor, there are at least 2 bars in the clubhouse and 2 or more bar concessions, along with 20 or more food concessions, on the grounds.

Liquor is a basis of hospitality patterns that link individuals and groups with the larger audience. People generously offer drinks to passing friends, whose visit is enlivened by joking, teasing, insult swapping, and other forms of verbal performance characteristic of Afro-Caribbean and Afro-American culture (Abrahams 1970; Kochman 1970). The visitor invariably extends an offer of reciprocal hospitality, creating an opportunity, and something of a social obligation, for the hosts to return the visit later in the day. In the pavilions persons are allowed to entertain two guests at a time, an informal rule that balances the importance of hospitality with a check against overcrowding.

The continuous traffic around the field is known as the "fashion show." Celebrants sport outfits acquired for the festival cricket season, occasionally handmade but more often purchased during the advertising campaigns that retail merchants mount in the weeks before Cup Match. Drawn from black American and West Indian trends, styles are valued for combining smartness with sexuality. A decade ago, for example, the style known in Bermuda as "black mod" was dominant. Women paraded in arousing "hot pants" outfits, suggestive two-piece ensembles, bell-bottom and two-tone slacks, close-fitting pants suits, wool knit skirts and jerseys, low-slung chain belts, bubble blouses, leather collars, suede fringed handbags, large round earrings, ostentatious bracelets and necklaces, pink and yellow tinted sunglasses, and "natural" coiffures. In the same period, men wore jump suits, silk shirts slit open to expose the chest, two-tone and wide-cuffed flair pants, bolero and ruffled shirts with dog-ear collars, and suede vests over the bare skin. More recent styles have been varied, ranging from "black disco" to "unisex chic." Women have adopted pleated balloon pants, terry cloth outfits, and "corn-row" coiffures elaborated with beads and braids—a style that can cost upwards of $100 in Bermudian hairdressing salons. Men have taken to West Indian styles, notably shirt-jacs, kareba suits, and among youth, Rastafarian dreadlocks. The jewelry portfolios of both sexes center on a half-dozen necklaces of various sizes and designs. Designer jean outfits are in vogue, as are athletic shorts that are worn by women with halter tops, by men with athletic shirts, and by both sexes with inscribed T-shirts.

The popularity of T-shirts warrants special comment. The leading black dealer in the field estimates selling 1,000 to 1,500 shirts for Cup Match alone, many of them at the cricket grounds in a concession stand that he equips with his printing and dyeing machines. His most popular line is what he calls his "black" shirts—motifs about festival cricket, pan-African identity, racial solidarity, and black entertainment genres. Next in popularity, and sometimes combined with racial motifs, are sexual themes, most of them using slang double entendres for genitalia and copulation in conjunction with humorous inscriptions of invitation, challenge, and braggadocio. The manufacture of T-shirts at the game epitomizes the rapid popularization of new styles and the ready satisfaction of customer demand for them, central values in black Bermudian fashion culture.

Performative and provocative, the fashion show is closely observed by radio commentators, who mix accounts of the cricket game with animated descriptions of fashion plates. Indeed, one of the major reasons fans bring radios to the game is to hear these accounts of themselves and their fellow celebrants. Like liquor, fashion is a medium of exchange that integrates an aggregate audience into a cultural community. It is also, again like liquor, what Sapir (1934) termed a symbol of condensation: it exemplifies what it signifies, namely an ethos of affluence, hedonism, sophistication, and display. An observable result of this symbolism is that fashion evokes the black conversational mode known as "rapping," a lewd and lively exchange between men and women aimed both at entertainment and at the initiation or enhancement of sexual partnerships. Like Carnival, festival cricket has a rich lore as a period of license and sexual hyperactivity.

Other modes of performance compete with fashion for public attention. Steel, brass, and rock bands play on the sidelines, stimulating impromptu dancing. Also present are Gombey Dancers, masked mummers who render a Bermudian version of the John Canoe dance to the rhythm of drums, fifes, snares, and whistles. High on surrounding hillsides are groups of Rastafarians, who smoke *ganja*, translate the festival ambience into poetry, and orate philosophically about a black millennium. A profane version of that millennium is enacted on adjacent waterways, where "boojee" (black bourgeois) yachtsmen display their boats and hold swank deck parties.

The cricket match concludes at 6:30 p.m., but festivities continue well into the night. The clubhouse is jammed with revellers who fraternize with the cricketers, replay and comically argue every detail of the game, and get very drunk as the

evening wears on. Other fans extend their merriment onto the field and may remain there all night. Several clubs run evening events ranging from dances and
parties to outdoor concerts featuring black American and Caribbean performers.

A final ancillary activity warrants separate discussion for both ethnographic and
analytic purposes. That activity is gambling, which takes place during the cricket
game on the periphery of the field in a large tent known as the "stock market."
As festival cricket amplifies a mode of behavior that is manifest in less spectacular
ways on a day-to-day basis, stock market gambling caricatures a general style
of acquisition premised on calculated opportunism (Manning 1973:87–114), as
well as a particular fondness for gambling that has put soccer pool agencies and
off-track betting parlors among Bermuda's lucrative businesses and has, within
the club milieu, given rise to regular bingo nights, organized card games, raffles,
lotteries, and so on. The significance of gambling here is twofold: first, it explicitly
symbolizes a relationship between culture and money that is represented more
implicitly in other phases and spheres of festival cricket; second, at a deeper level,
it dramatizes the culture-money relationship in a manner that qualifies and questions the meaningful thrust of the total festival. Juxtaposed to its own context,
gambling illustrates the tension that pervades black political life.

The Stock Market

Framed with wood or tubular steel and covered with canvas or sheet plastic,
the stock market is a makeshift casino for a dice game known as "crown and anchor." Played on boards set atop wooden horses, the game involves betting on
one or more of six choices: the four suits of cards, a red crown, or a black anchor.
Three dice are rolled, their sides corresponding to the choices on the board. Win-
ners are paid the amount of their bet times the number of dice on which it is
shown, while losers have their money taken by the board. If a croupier rolls a
crown and two spades, for example, he collects the money on the four losing
choices, pays those who bet on the crown, and pays double those who bet on the
spade.

Like cricket, crown and anchor is a game of British origin that has gained immense popularity in the Caribbean, particularly at festivals. I have personally
watched it being played by Antiguans at Carnival and by Jamaican Maroons at
the celebration of Captain Cudjoe's birthday in the remote mountain village of
Accompong.[3] In Bermuda the game is distinguished by the amount of money that
is displayed and bet. Croupiers hold thousands of dollars in their hands, and players are likely to hold several hundred. The minimum bet is one dollar, but only
novices and casual players, mostly women, bet that little. Regular players tend to
bet between $10 and $50 each time, although much higher bets are common.
Some boards place a ceiling of $100 on bets, but the larger boards—i.e., those
with bigger cash floats—generally have no ceiling. An informant lighted on the
ostentatious display of cash as the chief difference between festival cricket and

Christmas, the calendar's two major holidays. At Christmas, he observed, money is spent; at festival cricket, it is both spent and shown.

Crown and anchor is marked by a peculiar paradox. Although the odds marginally favor the board, regular players say that an effective strategy is to bet on choices that have not come up for two or three rolls of the dice and are therefore "due" simply by the laws of probability. A more defensive tactic, and one that is easily combined with the above, is simply to double bets on the same item until it eventually comes up and all losses, as well as the initial bet, are recouped. The only limitation is lack of ready cash, but this is minimized by the substantial sums that players carry and by the ready willingness of the boards to accept personal checks and even to loan money.

In practice, however, players tend to bet erratically and lose, often substantially. In the parlance of the stock market, they succumb to "greed" and "lose their heads" in a futile attempt to "break the board." What is potentially a game of strategy—the type associated with mastering the environment—is in effect a game of chance, the type associated with divining an uncontrollable environment (Roberts, Arth, and Bush 1959). The following example from my field notes is representative of a pattern evidenced by the stock market's "high rollers":

> Placing $10 and $20 bets unsystematically, a man lost his own money—about $60—as well as $50 that he borrowed from the board. He then borrowed another $50 and increased it to about $85 by winning a few small bets. He next bet $70 on the club, which came up on three dice to add $210 to his money. But although he owed the board $100, he kept playing rather than pay back the debt and quit with a net winning. Within a half hour he had lost all his money, as well as a third loan of $50. As he left the board he quietly told the croupier: "I owe you $150. I'll see you Monday morning."

The familiar experience of losing is offset by the claim that gambling money is expendable. As one man put it after losing $100, "If I have money to spend, I spend it. If I lose it, I don't give a fuck. I'll go back to work next week and get some more."

Although the overwhelming majority of bettors are black, the running of boards—the profitable side of the stock market—has been dominated by the Portuguese. In the 1930s, Manuel de Souza (a pseudonym), the teenage son of an Azorean-born farm laborer, watched crown and anchor being played in the segregated white section of the racetrack. Surmising the game's appeal to blacks, he started going to festival cricket matches with a dice cup, a small table, and a tarpaulin that he stretched between some trees to make a crude tent. De Souza's winnings put him on the road to acquiring a modest complex of businesses: a fleet of taxi cabs, several small farms, and a restaurant. "You can say that I owe what I have to crown and anchor," he acknowledged. "It gave me my start in life."

As de Souza's business and gambling profits grew, he began running more boards in partnership with other Portuguese. In the 1960s he was challenged by the clubs, which successfully pressed the claim that the stock market should be under their control. De Souza countered with patronage, supporting club build- ing projects and occasionally contributing a share of his winnings. In return he was given first option on buying the entire gambling concession, an arrangement that gave the clubs a substantial cash flow to stock their bars for festivals and that made de Souza something of a "czar" or, better perhaps, "godfather," of the stock market. With his partners he ran a half-dozen tables and reports that his share of their net profits averaged $30,000 per season. He made a further profit by selling the remainder of the space in the stock market, chiefly to a growing group of Portuguese who had acquired gambling reputations in private house parties.

Although de Souza and other Portuguese board operators were generally astute enough to hire black assistants, black gamblers gradually pushed the clubs for a bigger stake in the stock market, and ultimately for control of it. Their efforts have been partially successful; for several years the concession of Cup Match and the Western County Games has been sold to a syndicate of black businessmen, while in the Eastern County series one club continues to favor de Souza and the others run the stock market themselves. The change has resulted in more blacks and fewer Portuguese, although the new concession holders sell choice space (near the outside and sheltered from the afternoon sun) to the remaining Portuguese, including de Souza, who are respected in gambling circles and known to attract heavy bettors.

Yet the racial change in the stock market is less radical than it may appear. Many of the black-run boards, and a clear majority of those which have no ceil- ing on bets, are backed financially by whites, including Portuguese, or by racially mixed investment syndicates. The backers provide the cash float—as much as $15,000 at some boards—in return for a 40 to 60 percent share of the winnings. The parallel between the stock market and the wider economic system is fre- quently observed: blacks are in visible positions and appear to be making money, but whites are behind them and in control. Reflecting on the situation, one black gambler observed: "You know, come to think of it, I don't know a single black person in this country who has made money without having a white sponsor."

Another parallel between the stock market and the broader Bermudian situa- tion is observed in connection with mid-1970s legislation requiring the host club to pay $500 for a one-day gambling permit and preventing the boards from taking bets later than one hour after the scheduled end of the cricket game. The cost of the permit has been passed on to the concession holders and, in turn, to individ- ual board operators, while the time regulation has stopped boards from stay- ing open to increase winnings, recoup earlier losses, or simply capitalize on late betting action—a restriction that has hurt mainly the smaller, black-run boards, which are on the inside and therefore wait longer for bettors. For blacks, these new statutes typify a pattern of reaction against black economic gain. As one black board operator put it, "When the stock market was run by the Portuguese, it was wide open. As soon as we boys started to get a little piece of the action, Government stepped in. That's the general trend in Bermuda."

Whatever the economic position of blacks in the stock market, their cultural presence there is highly visible and clearly dominant over whites—another correspondence, of course, to the larger society. The Portuguese play quietly and dress plainly, almost dourly. Their boards are about six feet long and staffed by two, or at most three, croupiers. They keep a supply of cold beer but do not offer it until a player has begun betting. They rarely socialize with bettors or other operators, viewing the gambling relationship as an exclusively economic transaction. As de Souza explained, "People don't play at my board because they like me. They play because they want to break me." The Portuguese leave unobtrusively after the game and abstain from the evening festivities. I once went looking for de Souza after an Eastern County Game and found him working soberly in his restaurant. He said that he cleared $1,800 from his three tables—"a day's pay"—but volunteered that his lack of emotion made it impossible for most people to tell whether he had won or lost.

The image of black gamblers, by contrast, is an ideal type of the highly performative, black-oriented expressive style that Wilson (1973:227–228) terms "reputation"—the ethos that pervades the entire festival. Croupiers dress and behave flamboyantly, standing on platforms to increase their visibility, spreading their bills like a fan, throwing their dice cups high in the air, handing out one dollar bills to passersby to engage them in the game, and barking stock invitations to bet: "Get some money for your honey. . . . Come in here on a bike, go home in a Rolls Royce. . . . Take your hands out of your pocket and put your money on the table. . . . Wall Street slumps, but this stock market pays double. . . ." The black tables average eight to ten feet, with sets of betting squares on each end and often with added decorations such as the signs of the zodiac. At the larger tables there may be a staff of six, typically a "house man" who shakes the dice and holds the $50 bills, two or three assistants who collect and pay the bets, and one or two others who serve as bartenders and greeters. Both liquor and beer are freely offered to onlookers as well as bettors, and when a person's drink is half empty it will be wantonly thrown on the ground and replaced with a fresh drink.

Black gamblers extend and exploit the festival's sexual license. At least two black operators have reportedly imported prostitutes, a commodity virtually absent from Bermuda, from the United States. The more common practice is to give gambling money to well-endowed women in return for their appearing at the board in plunging necklines, loosely crocheted blouses, diaphanous T-shirts, tight shorts, and similar fashions aimed at attracting—and distracting—male gamblers. As a sequel to this gimmick, a few black operators have begun hiring female croupiers and even forming gambling partnerships with women. Conversely, women have increasingly become regular and sometimes heavy bettors, a trend that is particularly noticeable in the western parishes where a good number of well-paid hotel positions are held by women. The effort to attract—and hold—women bettors enlivens the barking calls with colorful exchanges.

> A middle-aged woman was about to bet on heart, but withdrew the money. The operator countered: "Don't blame me if three hearts come up, lady. 'Cause you and I—I've been looking at you for a long time—I figure our hearts could get together. We don't need no crown and anchor, honey. Our hearts could really do something."
>
> A woman was betting, and winning, on the black choices (spades, clubs, the anchor), which are all on the bottom of the board. The operator tried to persuade her to diversify her betting: "You gotta go topside. No woman in the world is satisfied on the bottom side."
>
> A woman in her early thirties had been breaking even on small bets and drinking heavily. Towards the end of the day she put a double entendre to the operator. "All I want is a piece of you." He took up the challenge and carried on a series of lewd but playful insults that drew raucous laughter from those at the table. But she got the last word: "Knobby, you wouldn't know what to do if you tripped and fell on top of me."

Black operators indicate that their gambling success depends on establishing their reputations within a broader context of public sociability. One prominent operator spends several hours per day outside the bar that he owns in partnership with another black and two whites, engaging passersby in brief conversation, waving at pedestrians on the other side of the street, and shouting at passing cars. This strategy, he explains, provides the exposure that is needed to attract people to his crown and anchor board (as well as to his bar and to a nightclub that he owns with his partners).

A modern Bermudian proverb is at this point appropriate: "Black is black and white is white, but money is green." Culturally different and socially divided, the races nonetheless come together for a common goal: the acquisition of money. There is no better illustration of this proverb than stock market gambling, which magnifies the unique black cultural identity that is celebrated in festival cricket at the same time that it brings the races together in a staged encounter aimed at fast and easy wealth. That scenario is a dramatic rendition of what Bermudian politics, at bottom, is all about.

Festival and Politics

Racial inversion underlies the dramatic form of festival cricket. Blacks dress up in "whites" to play a white game that they have transformed into a celebration of black culture. Blacks take a white gambling game and make it the setting for a hyperbolic performance of their social personality. Whites enter a black milieu and baldly demonstrate their superordinate position. Such inversion exemplifies the carnivalesque, a genre in which the characteristic multiplexity of symbolic expression is extended by the tendency for symbols to be used playfully and for primarily aesthetic effect. This tendency creates what Babcock (1973) calls a "surplus of signifiers," a Rabelaisian profusion of images and condensed metaphors framed in a mode of liminality.

While the range of significance is vast, fragmented, and often highly individualized, the exegete can take clues from recurrent and centrally placed symbols. A major, meaningful thrust of festival cricket, manifest in the tradition and style of celebration, is the relation of a reflexive version of black identity to hedonism, high style, and money. Turner's (1964:29–31) contention, that dominant clusters of symbols interchange social and sensory-material themes, is appropriate. Like similar symbolic formulations in the club milieu, festival cricket contributes to the multifaceted process whereby black Bermudians are rejecting a stance of social inferiority in favor of a positive and assertive sense of self-awareness (Manning 1973:149–183).

There is also an antithetical thrust of meaning, reminding blacks of their economic subordination and dependency on whites. The reminder is implicit in the overall emphasis on fashion and indulgence, for Bermudian blacks are acutely aware, even in festival, that consumerism keeps them in clientage. In the stock market, however, the message is explicit: big money and effective power are still in white hands. Blacks can commemorate their traditions and exhibit their ethos, but they must also deal with whites, who have the odds—mathematical and psychological—in their favor. If festival cricket is viewed as a dramatic form, the black gamblers are both heroes and clowns. In the former role they glamorize a social vision of black culture, while in the latter they enact an economic relationship in which the vision is transparently irrelevant. Like the ludic inversion of racial categories, this sense of juxtaposition and self-parody is characteristic of the carnivalesque.

As a formative feature of the black Bermudian experience, the culture-economics interplay has a variety of demonstrable references. The most clear and currently paramount, however, is the system of party politics. An arena of intense interest and extraordinarily high participation, Bermudian politics bears both a striking conceptual similarity and an uncanny ethnographic correspondence to festival cricket. Let us briefly consider this double relationship.

Party politics came to Bermuda in 1963 with the formation of the Progressive Labour Party (PLP) by black groups who had previously been active in the successful universal suffrage movement.[4] In the election of that year, the party contested 9 of 36 parliamentary seats, winning 6 of them and clearly demonstrating the practical benefits of party organization. The aristocracy responded to the challenge a year later by forming the United Bermuda Party (UBP), which was initially joined by 24 of the 30 independents in the House of Assembly, all but 1 of them white. For the remainder of the decade the UBP sought to co-opt the issues pressed by the PLP, espousing, at least nominally, constitutional reform and the bread-and-butter issues of universal free education, health and welfare benefits, and the Bermudianization of the labor force. The UBP's trump card, however, was the promise of a thoroughgoing "partnership"—the term used in campaign slogans—between blacks and whites in the running of Bermuda. The partnership was demonstrated politically by strenuous efforts to recruit black candidates in the 1968 and subsequent elections, a general tactic of putting blacks in highly visible positions in both the party organization and the Cabinet; the naming of a black premier between 1971 and 1975; the appeasement of a black-dominated parliamentary "reform" group which forced the resignation of that premier's white successor in 1977; and, from the late 1970s onward, the gradual implementation of demands put forth by an internal black caucus seeking greater leverage in both the party and the national economy.

Rhetorically, the UBP presents the partnership as a guarantee of security as well as an opportunity for gain. Only through the visible demonstration of racial integration, it is claimed, can Bermuda continue to attract tourists and international companies, the sources of prosperity. The UBP couples this appeal with an emphasis on its traditional role as manager of the economy. In the 1980 election campaign, for example, Premier David Gibbons, a white who also holds the finance portfolio and whose family controls Bermuda's largest conglomerate, told an audience:

> This election is not about personalities. It is about the conditions of people's lives. Day in and day out. People's jobs, income, housing. And, above all, the strength and stability of our economy, upon which all else depends.
>
> Look to the United Bermuda Party's management of our economy. At a time when so many nations in the West are struggling and losing ground, Bermuda maintains one of the highest rates of per capita income in the world. . . . Stability, security. These are facts. And they've come to pass because of experience and prudent, efficient management.

The UBP gave its economic theme a dimension of grave urgency in a full-page newspaper advertisement published on polling day:

> Today is the day when you vote . . . either to maintain Bermuda's economic growth and your own financial security and stability or . . . take a chance on the PLP. Think carefully and vote UBP.

The UBP's accommodations to black interests and its emphasis on economic security have given it an unbroken winning record at the polls, albeit by successively reduced majorities. The PLP's reaction, moderated in tone as its political position has improved, has been to emphasize its "true" blackness and therefore its legitimate and logical claim to black voter support. For the first decade of its existence, the PLP projected a posture of militant racial chauvinism, articulated through American and Caribbean "Black Power" rhetoric. In the middle 1970s, the PLP embraced the idiom of revivalist religion, a move aimed at making inroads among black church groups and, more generally, at appealing to racial consciousness implicitly rather than explicitly by stirring the powerful and pregnant association between revivalism and black culture. In the 1980 campaign, the PLP balanced the emphasis on religion with a more secular appeal to racial identity. The campaign slogan was "Xpress yourself," a black Bermudian colloquialism borrowed jointly from American soul music and Jamaican reggae lyrics and combining an allusion to the marking of a ballot paper with a slang encouragement for self-assertion. One television commercial showed a group of blacks, dancing funky style, while a singer chanted "express yourself" and an announcer extolled the merits of the PLP.

Whatever their stated differences on issues—and these have converged considerably in recent years as both parties have sought a center ground—the essential partisan distinction is racial. Recent surveys indicate that whites vote almost unanimously for the UBP, and that four-fifths of the black votes go to the PLP—a division that crosscuts and overrides class, age, sex, ideological disposition, and other pertinent social factors (Manning 1978a:199–209). The choice for blacks remains what it has always been: cultural attachment or economic security, loyalty and commitment to blacks, or strategic alignment with whites.

The distinction between the parties is manifest ethnographically in the festival setting. Hodgson (1967:311), a black Bermudian historian and PLP polemicist, describes Cup Match as "the one and only true symbol and celebration of the black man's emancipation." Her enthusiasm, however, is offset by a skepticism that blacks will forsake such symbols in order to participate in white festivities that have now dropped the color barrier. This concern, while lacking empirical foundation, has prompted PLP politicians to present a high profile at cricket festivals, making the general environment one in which PLP supporters are familiar and welcome and UBP supporters are somewhat isolated and uncomfortable. The festival's partisan association is extended by the PLP's considerable efforts to court the club constituency (Manning 1973:210–249), a tactic exemplified by party leader Lois Browne-Evans's speech at a club dinner in 1978.

> Your long and illustrious history . . . needs to be told. Essays ought to be held for your children to write what they think Daddy's club is all about . . .
> Let not economic strangulation be the cause of your enslavement. For I am convinced that you have a part to play in the Bermuda of the future, just as your forbears played a vital role in the Bermuda of the past.

You must continue working until your country is free from paternalism and patronage, free from all the shackles that we know. Do not remove one form of
chains for another. You must avoid the tendency to be dependent. . . .

The stock market, however, presents a striking contrast to the overall festival
milieu. The black table operators, like their Portuguese counterparts and white
backers, are primarily UBP supporters. The coterie is informally led by a black
UBP member of the House of Assembly, who is also renowned, on a few occasions scandalously, for the organization of invitational crown and anchor parties in private homes. At least two prominent backers also hold UBP seats in Parliament, and it is widely known that several black board operators are being
groomed as future UBP candidates. Talking to me on the street, one of the blacks
who operates a table on which there is no betting limit explained his support for
the UBP as follows: "There is not one black person in Bermuda with any money
who is PLP. Not one. . . . If the [white] man looks after you, then you've got to
protect him. . . ." When a PLP member within earshot began to challenge him,
the gambler yelled: "Shut the fuck up. It's niggers like you that are holding back
motherfuckers like me."

PLP activists, on the other hand, tend to eschew the stock market, or at most
to congregate outside or walk through without betting. Observing the action at a
crown and anchor board, one PLP politician told me with a wink: "I only watch
the stock market. I never invest." This avoidance is encouraged by the PLP's oft-
stated position that gambling is functionally supportive of the status quo and by
its general desire to adhere, publicly at least, to the strong moral condemnation
of gambling made by the black churches.

Festival cricket, then, is a metapolitical commentary. It is a carnivalesque
rendition of the semantic context in which Bermudian politics is conceived, institutionalized, and transacted. Through celebration, black Bermudians dramatize—and, indeed, define and discover—a fundamental aspect of their social
position and its relationship, conceptual and ethnographic, to their political options. (Logically, of course, the argument is reversible; politics could be con-
strued as a concordance for festival cricket. From a Bermudian standpoint, however, it is politics, not festival, that requires comprehension, choice, and
commitment. Festival is merely for enjoyment, and perhaps profit.)

It is here that the relationship of symbolic to social phenomena, of festival to
politics, is crucial, and that the convergent positions of Turner (1977), Gluckman
and Gluckman (1977), and Geertz (1972), attributing creative autonomy to ludic
symbolic forms, are useful. Although festival cricket evidences myriad correspondences to the political system, it is no more a mere reflection of politics than it
is a functional appendage of it. The festival version of black culture is not the
ideological and instrumental type of racial awareness propounded by the PLP,
but a comical caricature of the black life-style and a joyous fantasy that links racial identity to the material wealth and glamor promised by a white-dominated,

consumer-oriented economy. Likewise, the festival version of biracial partnership is not the liberal and pragmatic plea for partnership advanced by the UBP, but a naked dramatization of white control that lays bare both the crass acquisitiveness of blacks and their continuing subordination to whites, and that further plays on these meanings in a burlesque of the whole patronage system that transforms money from an object of need to one of show.

In Durkheimian terms—which are the ancestry of much symbolic theory—festival cricket is a "transfiguration" of Bermudian political society (cf. Nisbet 1965:74). The semantic essence of festival cricket is that it throws the realm of politics into relief by disassembling its parts and reordering them in patterns consistent with the aesthetics of celebration, fun, and performance. Festival cricket *reveals* politics in the way that only an extended metaphor can—by creatively connecting disparate realms of experience in a manner that highlights the definitive features (in this case, the interplay of cultural identity and economic interest) on which the connection is predicated. To borrow Bateson's (1972:177–193) classic model of cognition, festival cricket is a map for the territory of politics—not a literal, drawn-to-scale map that merely replicates its referent, but a metaphorical map, an interpretive guide, that figuratively situates its referent and conveys social knowledge about it. It is this knowledge that makes Bermudian politics a comprehensible phenomenon.

Conclusion

Like any venture into the analysis of symbolic forms as texts, the interpretation offered here rests ultimately on the anthropologist, who "strains to read over the shoulders of those to whom they [the texts] properly belong" (Geertz 1972:29). In part, the validity and value of such an interpretation depends on whether it can be generalized, as a theoretical construct and heuristic device, to other cultures. Limitations of space and scope make it impractical to address that consideration here, but a few condensed examples from the West Indies may suggest the basis of a comparative approach.

The major festival genre of the eastern Caribbean is Carnival, which evolved in Trinidad but has diffused throughout the Windward and Leeward islands with minor changes in format.[5] Like Bermuda's Cup Match, the historical referent of Carnival, for blacks, is emancipation from slavery. The festival's major performative symbols—from the canboulay parade, ritualized stickfighting, and gang warfare in earlier times, to calypso and steel bands in recent generations—make it unequivocally black. Naipaul (1973:364), one of the Caribbean's leading literary figures, describes Carnival as "a version of the lunacy that kept the slave alive . . . the original dream of black power, style, and prettiness . . . a vision of the black millenium." Calypsonians put it more simply, toasting Carnival as the "Creole bacchanal."

But the blackness of the Carnival ethos is confronted by a strong nonblack influence in the festival's economic organization. East Indian, Chinese, and Lebanese bandleaders predominate, as do white and mulatto choreographers, and, of course, the government-controlled Carnival Development Committee — all of these groups striving, rather successfully in recent years, to make the event an international tourist attraction. Celebrants are exposed to the poignant contrast between the revelry of "jump-up" on the streets and the ribaldry of the calypso tent, on the one hand, and a variety of scenarios that demonstrate the racially based socioeconomic class system, on the other hand: the judges' stand, the paid grandstand, the commercial nightclub scene, the maze of bureaucratic rules imposed by organizers and censors, and the presence of local elites, and even metropolitan tourists, in the privileged sections of masquerade bands.

Jamaica lacks a Carnival tradition but has the entertainment idiom of reggae music, a symbol system replete with religious and political significance (Barrett 1977; de Albuquerque 1979). One of the best indigenous artistic commentaries on the reggae milieu is Perry Henzell's (1973) film *The Harder They Come*. Its protagonist is a country boy who comes to Kingston to learn the fast side of Jamaican life. The voyage of discovery is twofold. He becomes a reggae star and a "rudie" (rude boy), mastering expressive styles that are quintessentially black, often in a militant, even revolutionary sense. But he also learns that the music industry is controlled by Chinese, mulattoes, and other groups deemed white from the black cultural viewpoint, and that the authorities — police, government, and international economic interests — are geared to crushing the challenge that he represents. Ultimately, he is shot down by their guns.

Are such symbolic forms a metacommentary on West Indian politics? Correspondences are harder to draw than in the Bermudian case, partly because, in the Caribbean, race is a figurative more than a phenotypical category. Virtually all local political actors are generically black, and whiteness is associated less with a visible local elite than with the abstractions of foreign ownership and imperial influence. In short, a racial analysis is a more complex and problematic task in the West Indies than it is in Bermuda.

Still, it is notable that, ever since the "Black Power" wave of the early 1970s, the most dynamic and ideologically intense political conflict in most of the West Indies has come from the challenge made to established political parties by radical movements, most of them extraparliamentary. These radical movements revive indigenous linguistic terms (Morris 1973), stress cultural affinity and social solidarity with Africa, and associate themselves with Afro-Caribbean religions, notably Rastafarianism, which has spread from Jamaica throughout the Caribbean and has become a cultural rallying ground and pervasive symbol for revolutionary politics (de Albuquerque 1980). Contrastingly, established politicians are villified as "Afro-Saxons" (Lowenthal 1972:278), imitators of white values who court foreign investment, sell out to multinational corporations, embrace the image promoted by mass tourism, and compact unholy alliances with metropolitan countries.

A litany of citations from academic, popular, and polemical literature could be introduced here, most of them familiar (and indeed, redundant), to scholars of the Caribbean. For present purposes, however, it is better to make two broad and general assertions. First, economic interest and cultural identity are often perceived in the West Indies as conflicting concerns. Second, the conflict is focused in racial symbolism, dramatized in festivity and other artistic productions, and current to political discourse. If these assertions are granted, they suggest an agenda aimed at integrating symbolic and political analyses of Caribbean societies, and perhaps of other areas that have undergone comparable historical experiences. The discussion of Bermudian cricket festivals offered here shows one direction in which such an agenda can proceed.

Notes

I am grateful to the late Max Gluckman, cricket aficionado and analyst par excellence, whose conversations with me were an inspiration to develop this paper. Jeanne Cannizzo and Jim Freedman offered helpful comments on a draft. For fieldwork support I am grateful to the National Science Foundation (GS-2549) and to the Institute of Social and Economic Research, Memorial University of Newfoundland; grants from these bodies enabled me to witness Cup Match in 1970,1976, and 1978, and to see 20-odd County Games since 1969. Earlier versions of this paper were presented to the Canadian Ethnology Society, in 1979, and to the Association for the Anthropological Study of Play, in 1980. Part of the present version was delivered as a guest lecture at the University of Michigan, in 1980.

1. I know of no other written sources on West Indian festival cricket, but am informed by a Jamaican student that "bush cricket" in Jamaica has the same general characteristics as James's example from Trinidad.

2. The Bermuda dollar is at parity with the U.S. dollar.

3. I am told by Jeanne Cannizzo (1979: personal communication) that a version of crown and anchor is played at festivals in Sierra Leone. I have also seen it played at a number of fairs and amusement exhibitions in Canada, usually in booths where a wheel is spun, rather than dice thrown, to determine winning bets.

4. For a fuller discussion of Bermuda's recent political history, see Hodgson (1967), Manning (1973, 1978a), and Ryan (1973).

5. The most accessible general overviews of the Trinidad Carnival are those of Hill (1972) and Pearse (1956). Literature on other Caribbean Carnivals includes Abrahams (1970) on Tobago, Abrahams and Bauman (1978) on St. Vincent, Crowley (1956) on St. Lucia, and Manning (1978b) on Antigua.

References

Abrahams, Roger
    1970   Patterns of Performance in the British West Indies. In Afro-American Anthropology: Contemporary Perspectives. Norman E. Whitten, Jr. and John Szwed, eds. pp. 163–179. New York. Free Press.

Abrahams, Roger, and Richard Bauman
    1978   Ranges of Festival Behavior. In The Reversible World: Symbolic Inversion
            in Art and Society. Barbara Babcock, ed. pp. 193–208. Ithaca: Cornell Uni-
            versity Press.
Babcock, Barbara
    1973   The Carnivalization of the Novel and the High Spirituality of Dressing
            Up. Paper presented at Burg Wartenstein Symposium No. 59, Ritual:
            Reconciliation in Change. Gloggnitz, Austria.
Barrett, Leonard
    1977   The Rastafarians: Sounds of Cultural Dissonance. Boston: Beacon Press.
Bateson, Gregory
    1972   Steps to an Ecology of Mind. New York: Ballantine.
Cohen, Abner
    1979   Political Symbolism. Annual Review of Anthropology 8:87–113.
Crowley, Daniel
    1956   Festivals of the Calendar in St. Lucia. Caribbean Quarterly 4:99–121.
de Albuquerque, Klaus
    1979   The Future of the Rastafarian Movement. Caribbean Review 8(4):22–25,
            44–46.
    1980   Rastafarianism and Cultural Identity in the Caribbean. Paper presented at
            the Caribbean Studies Association meeting, Willemstad, Curacao.
Geertz, Clifford
    1972   Deep Play: Notes on the Balinese Cockfight. Daedalus 101(1):1–38.
Gluckman, Max, and Mary Gluckman
    1977   On Drama, and Games, and Athletic Contests. In Secular Ritual. Sally F.
            Moore and Barbara Myerhoff, eds. pp. 227–243. Assen/Amsterdam: Van
            Gorcum.
Henzell, Perry
    1973   The Harder They Come. Kingston, Jamaica: New World Films.
Hill, Errol
    1972   The Trinidad Carnival: Mandate for a National Theatre. Austin: University
            of Texas Press.
Hodgson, Eva
    1967   Second-Class Citizens, First-Class Men. Hamilton, Bermuda: Published
            by the author.
James, C. L. R.
    1963   Beyond a Boundary. London: Hutchinson.
Kochman, Thomas
    1970   Toward an Ethnography of Black American Speech Behavior. In Afro-
            American Anthropology: Contemporary Perspectives. Norman E. Whitten,
            Jr. and John Szwed, eds. pp. 145–162. New York: Free Press.
Lewis, Gordon
    1968   The Growth of the Modern West Indies. New York: Monthly Review Press.

Lowenthal, David
1972   West Indian Societies. New York: Oxford University Press.

Manning, Frank
1973   Black Clubs in Bermuda: Ethnography of a Play World. Ithaca: Cornell
          University Press.
1978a   Bermudian Politics in Transition: Race, Voting, and Public Opinion.
          Hamilton, Bermuda: Island Press.
1978b   Carnival in Antigua: An Indigenous Festival in a Tourist Economy. Anthro-
          pos 73:191–204.

Moore, Sally F., and Barbara Myerhoff
1977   Secular Ritual. Assen/Amsterdam: Van Gorcum.

Morris, Desmond
1973   On Afro-West Indian Thinking. In The Aftermath of Sovereignty: West In-
          dian Perspectives. David Lowenthal and Lambros Comitas, eds. pp. 277–
          282. Garden City, NY: Doubleday Anchor.

Naipaul, V. S.
1973   Power to the Caribbean People. In The Aftermath of Sovereignty: West In-
          dian Perspectives. David Lowenthal and Lambros Comitas, eds. pp. 363–
          371. Garden City, NY: Doubleday Anchor.

Newman, Dorothy
1972   The Population Dynamics of Bermuda. Hamilton, Bermuda: Bermuda
          Government, Department of Statistics.

Nisbet, Robert
1965   Emile Durkheim. Englewood Cliffs, NJ: Prentice-Hall.

Pearse, Andrew
1956   Carnival in Nineteenth Century Trinidad. Caribbean Quarterly 4:176–193.

Roberts, John, Malcolm Arth, and Robert Bush
1959   Games in Culture. American Anthropologist 61:597–605.

Roberts, John, and Brian Sutton-Smith
1962   Child Training and Game Involvement. Ethnology 2:166–185.
1966   Cross-Cultural Correlates of Games of Chance. Behavior Science Notes
          1:131–144.

Ryan, Selwyn
1973   Politics in an Artificial Society: The Case of Bermuda. In Ethnicity in the
          Americas. Frances Henry, ed. pp. 159–192. The Hague: Mouton.

St. Pierre, Maurice
1973   West Indian Cricket: A Sociohistorical Appraisal. Caribbean Quarterly
          19:7–27.

Sapir, Edward
1934   Symbolism Encyclopaedia of the Social Sciences 14:492–495.

Schwartzman, Helen
1978   Transformations: The Anthropology of Children's Play. New York: Plenum
          Press.

Singer, Milton
    1955   The Cultural Pattern of Indian Civilization. Far Eastern Quarterly 15:23–
                36.
Smith, Michael G.
    1965   The Plural Society in the British West Indies. Berkeley: University of Cali-
                fornia Press.
Turner, Victor
    1964   Symbols in Ndembu Ritual. In Closed Systems and Open Minds: The
                Limits of Naivety in Social Anthropology. Max Gluckman, ed. pp. 20–51.
                Chicago: Aldine.
    1977   Variations on a Theme of Liminality. In Secular Ritual. Sally F. Moore
                and Barbara Myerhoff, eds. pp. 36–52. Assen/Amsterdam: Van Gorcum.
Wilson, Peter
    1973   Crab Antics: The Social Anthropology of English-Speaking Negro Socie-
                ties of the Caribbean. New Haven: Yale University Press.

18. RUMBA

Social and Aesthetic Change in Cuba

Yvonne Daniel

Organic Change in Dance

Because dance involves the body as the tool of the art as well as the art product itself and because the body is part of a constantly shifting process of physical change, each performance of dance, each enactment of special movement, is subject to minuscule, incremental, or drastic change. While artistic directors, choreographers, and dancers at all levels of proficiency may strive to retain specific movements, replicate designs and an organization, or recreate feelings, the dance is constantly influenced, reinterpreted, and reformulated. As performers continuously embroider, emphasize, miniaturize, augment, crystallize, or spontaneously create nuances and embellishments, even while dancing within set sequences, slight changes occur that eventually develop and shape the dance as a whole. The dance product changes in the eyes of viewers, who have different understandings depending on their historical backgrounds, contemporary trends, and the immediate environment of the performance. Change, as a result, is a significant part of tradition, but it is a constant in dance.

Traditional dance is not static, therefore, but part of a dynamic process. This process is an ongoing one of selection, presentation, elimination, augmentation, and manipulation. Specific esteemed elements of movement, which are recognized within a given group from a given location and which characterize a style, complex, or tradition, are identified and given social value. In many ways, traditional dancers and performers of other traditional arts must work carefully to safeguard a particular style or form of the past. Aesthetic preferences and dance qualities evolve slowly (although sometimes "traditions" are not so old; see Hobsbawm and Ranger, 1983, and Horner, 1990, chap. 1). They are selected from many available cultural items; they come into being as "traditional dance," both through the molding of separate aesthetic elements into a structured form and through the incorporation of gradual change. Immediate or severe change is seen

Originally published as "Social and Aesthetic Change in Cuba," in Yvonne Daniel, *Rumba: Dance and Social Change in Contemporary Cuba* (Bloomington: Indiana University Press, 1995), pp. 138–49. Reprinted by permission of Indiana University Press.

and felt as a violation of consensus, precepts, or rules. Traditional dance defines, traces, captures, projects, and enlivens a particular set of images and symbolizes ideas and attitudes that are culturally understood and generally agreed upon.

Cuban traditional dances negotiate delicately between the prescribed repetition of set music/dance sequences and necessary, natural, organic change. Cuban dance traditions that are performed daily as part of professional company rehearsals display the peculiar play between the unchanging and the changes of tradition. Cuban dancers and dance administrators limit and channel movement because of organic tendencies to vary and change. Daily repetition of esteemed dance patterns safeguards the dance structures but places the content, substance, or essence of dance in jeopardy of performance death.

Without change, performance can become deadly, dry, lacking in excitement. Lifelessness in dancing or music making often occurs when the performance is separated from the original purpose of the tradition. (Consequently, for the musical theater dancer, lifelessness due to repetition is not so serious a problem, since the dance purpose is intimately involved in its repeated performance.) If the dance is routinized by repeated practice away from its significant context, its vitality can dissolve; performance death can occur.

Professional Cuban dance companies alternate the performance of dance traditions to present dynamic entertainment and didactic artistry; however, they are still subject to the dangers of routinization and performance death. Even the use of informantes—the living archives of traditional dance—cannot always ignite the vivifying essence of dance in its original setting, nor always sustain freshness and vitality in performance (Martinez-Furé, 1986). While musicians and dancers remain the experiential librarians of varying traditions, it should be remembered that it is through their ever-changing bodies that scores are stored. Efforts to conserve dance traditions must acknowledge and incorporate change as an organic and vital component of dance.

Change in Rumba

As with other ethnic dance material, that is, dance that is connected in important ways to national or ethnic identity, such as the Mexican hat dance, Hawaiian hula, and Haitian Vodun dances, rumba's African and Spanish movement sequences connect powerful physicality and aesthetic stimulation to feelings regarding the Cuban nation and its people. Like other African-derived dance traditions, rumba incorporates other arts (music, drama, storytelling) and makes reference to aspects of social life within movement (see Primus, 1969; Wilson, 1981; and Nketia, 1965). The "consummate vitality" of African sculpture, according to Robert Farris Thompson (1974:1–48), and the "dynamism" of Surinamese carving, according to Sally and Richard Price (1980:166–87), are compounded and accentuated when applied to dance performance. Thompson identifies the characteristics that shape African performance, including its "get-down" quality, coolness, swing, flexibility, and ephebism. The Prices refer to performance among the Surinamers of African descent in terms of spontaneous expressions that are enculturated early and result in dynamic essence. Rumba has the same force or surge of physical energy. Its dynamism, or consummate vitality, is embodied in performers through the exertion of specified movement and is kinesthetically transferred to viewers. The physical demand on the body culminates in fatigue, but the body is deeply relaxed as a result of such a demand in dancing. The aesthetic force of rumba in combination with the physical release of tension govern its potency. Rumba focuses a multiplicity of stimulating elements; it overlaps phrasing and moments of emphasis and thereby creates suspension and dynamic interest within physical action. Such physical power and illocutionary force are the reasons for the continuity of Cuban rumba despite its mixed messages and political-economic appropriation.

Although few Cubans dance rumba well and those who do tend to be black or dark-skinned Cubans, rumba generates particular interest and draws special attention: it is treated like no other dance in Cuba. No other dance is accorded a one-two week festival in its honor. No other dance punctuates the calendar of events in casas de cultura programming. No other dance form within balletic, modern, or folkloric styles is exposed as much to international visitors. It is used strategically to display Cuban culture and to promote deep, fundamental change in values. Within non-Cuban contexts, it portrays a new Cuba in an artistic manner and encourages gradual change.

Rumba could be designated the Cuban national dance of the twentieth century, yet it competes with conga and son (see Daniel 1995, and Evleshin, 1989). Of the three dances, conga is most easily performed by all ages and both sexes; thus it can be argued that conga is more communal. It is a group dance; everyone dances at the same time. Rumba, on the other hand, is the dance of a single couple or male soloist, dancing alone most of the time. Rumba is communal performance, while conga is communal participation. Even though conga is easier and more communal, rumba has received more official support.

Neither was the most popular, social, and historic dance, son (which continues as salsa in current North American terminology and as casino in contemporary Cuba), appropriated as the national dance of the twentieth century (Orozco, 1984:382–85). In light of its tremendous popularity as the most performed social or popular dance in Cuba, it is conceivable that most Cubans would select casino as the national dance. Apparently casino lacks something seminal to national objectives, as conga does also.

Rumba's prominence apparently was based on criteria other than ease, popularity, and communal participation. In a structured form, within specific spaces, and at particular times, rumba fulfills strategic goals. Analysis points to the fact that Cuban society has a preference for performance within a mass as opposed to mass performance. Rather than the mass participation of casino or the unstructured abandon in conga, rumba gives prepared culture to the masses; it provides education and values. Rather than a focus on the individualistic passing, turning, and designing of patterns in casino or a focus on the improvisational and unstructured activity of conga, rumba has emerged as a dance structure that coincides with socialist perspectives, a cultural symbol of social relations.

Meaning in rumba has varied consequences in terms of the dance and its performers. In the dance, there is a search for the vacunao, for possession of the female and community prestige. Dancers work at the search through the call and response acknowledged between dancers and drummers and through the exchange of movements between dancers (exchange of vibrating shoulder motifs, the series of responsorial actions in vacunao, turns, fake vacunaos, implosive holds). The meanings of rumba are not only possession of the female or winning the competition between males or between drummer and dancer but also prestige and status among rumberos, Cubans, and foreigners (see Graburn, 1976:49–51).

A more problematic meaning of rumba manipulation and appropriation, which is shared by other Cuban artists, is concern for artistic freedom, a parallel issue with routinization of performances but now in terms of performers. The dark-skinned or black rumbero still sings of liberation and is concerned with social dignity and personal artistic self-worth; however, where is artistic freedom in rumba as it is officially and most frequently presented? In Cuba there are few presentations of new ideas, new performance modes, or new creative dances and, until very recently, little social criticism. Artistic freedom is limited—that which would permit rumba to develop in the spontaneity of the moment and would be congruent with its original form. How will rumberos receive artistic stimulation to invent or fashion something new other than redundant prescribed messages, if rumba is always prepared? Routinization develops technique but stifles, if not suffocates, creativity in all artists.

Regard for artists entails more than providing a means for their personal welfare and performance or maintenance of techniques and performance technologies. It encompasses an ambiance of artistic freedom that generates creativity and requires attention to their notions of self-worth and dignity. Such an environment permits and encourages experimentation, growth, and acceptance or rejection of all sorts of ideas. In a striking manner, Sally Ness uses the image of a basketball that is held loosely but possessively as she analyzes *sinulog* dance and Filipino society in terms of looseness within a possessive relationship. She states that "basketball is a game about possession and control. However, its most important object, the ball itself, cannot be clutched firmly. It has to be released continually from any possessor's grasp" (1992:124). Cuban artists, particularly rumberos, need and deserve such a loose hold.

Rumberos represent not only Afro-Cubans but also fellow Cuban artists in the development of creativity and artistic freedom. Rumba signals a need for rectification of injustice to artists, certainly to rumberos and folkloric dancers. In this manner, rumba echoes human universals and basic aesthetic needs (Langer, 1953; Blacking, 1973; Hanna, 1979; Lewis, 1984).

Although artists were hesitant to discuss this point with me in 1986 and 1987, an article by Coco Fusco in the *Nation* suggests that conditions are changing:

> In contrast to tense moments in the past, when the official response was to redouble control, the current interest in and tacit approval of the younger generation are signs of the foresight and sensitivity of many in power. . . . Stylistically heterogeneous, this generation of artists has an unabashed interest in information about art outside Cuba. What unifies them even more than their artwork is their strong opposition to any reductive or repressive definition of revolutionary culture. (1988:399)

Change in Cuba

Although dance is not a specific priority within national objectives, it assists Cuba's commitment to self-determination, social equality, and collective solidarity as a small, independent nation. In Cuba, dance and all forms of expressive culture are used to support socialist ideology and egalitarian behavior. Within domestic organization and the international arena as well, national ideology emphasizes values that rectify historical hierarchy and dance can express such changes.

Cuban artists and expressive culture are exciting and powerful aids to political struggle and economic development. Throughout Cuba, the arts are celebrated; ample and active participation of the public in close dialogue with artists (painters, sculptors, and writers as well as dancers and choreographers) has been encouraged as part of governmental directives specific to the arts. Artists are a vital component of education programs via the casa de cultura system. In other words, the artistic community has been accessible to national efforts that inform the public of contemporary events, increase awareness, and develop consciousness of national goals. Through performance of national dance traditions, the construction of a new value base has been underlined; the use of the arts has been developed as a means of educating and reeducating the public toward government objectives and as a means of indoctrinating new values.

What rumba dance/music does irrespective of what people say or believe and irrespective of what the government intends is revealed both in the social currents and conditions of contemporary Cuba and in the dancing body, that is, in changing values and attitudes. A reformation is in process: of economic, political, and social circumstances on one hand and of sentiment, attitudes, ideology, and values on the other. By means of a well-established dance and the important sentiments and feelings that are generated within, around, and because of it, the gap between ideals and reality is perceivable and change can be initiated.

Rumba is well-established, identifiable, and successful over other dance forms in evoking elevated feelings that are necessary for symbols of national consequence. Rumba has emerged in postrevolutionary Cuba by means of three sociopolitical processes: politicization, commoditization, and secularization.

Through the examination of Rumba within these differing milieux, a model that investigates social change is established; rumba becomes an indicator or a test of change in Cuba.

While there are artistic reasons for promoting rumba (it makes a great finale, it can involve audience participation, it contains play, interest, and suspense), other reasons have instigated the special position of rumba in contemporary Cuba. One current comes from the top, within the Ministry of Culture and from arts administrators. As discussed, the ministry broadly organizes and outlines cultural activities toward the goals of the Revolution. Fidel Castro's framework for the arts has been the mission of the ministry, given succinctly in June 1961: "Inside the Revolution, everything; against it, nothing" (Matas, 1971:432–36). By means of financial, organizational, and ideological support, the ministry and arts administrators have been instrumental in the promotion of rumba and have determined its prominence among dance professionals and within the public.

Apart from the forceful persuasion of governmental support at the top, another current comes from the bottom, among sincere folkloric performers and the public at large. Folkloric dancers and musicians have enjoyed the new elevated status of folklore and have been eager to integrate the goals of the Revolution into their artistic lives. Dancers have put material into their choreographies and dance events that have been ignored previously and material that they consider relevant to their future. In 1980, Teresa Gonzalez and Rogelio Martinez-Furé received consensus among company members in the *asamblea* to support Rumba Saturday as a peak event. Folkloric and artistic contribution to contemporary Cuban history was validated and, from the bottom up, artists were instrumental in the emergence of rumba as a nationally promoted dance. The enthusiastic support of the public was important as well, and as a result of Cuba's cultural education programs, the general public accepted and echoed the elevation of rumba officially.

A third current of national concern comes from the international dance community (see Graburn, 1984:393, and 1986). The aesthetic power of rumba is that which mesmerizes the international dance community. Even though international dancers do not share the exact meanings of rumba with Cubans, they become involved through the reputation of rumba and are affected by the experience of rumba, the dance/music complex and Rumba, the dance event. International students and artists have seen and heard rumba as it has been promoted and professionalized lately, but also they have experienced Rumba throughout the world. Rumba Saturday's success did not go unnoticed.

Within Cuba before the Revolution, rumba had been widespread, spontaneous, and popular among dark-skinned or black Cubans. Rumba was not taken from these Cubans; they were not paid to perform a meaningless symbol. Instead the government paid Cubans within one segment of the population, who formerly danced rumba frequently yet intermittently, to perform it more frequently for the entire nation. There is little resentment from those who formerly enjoyed rumba because rumba is still accessible to them—even more than before. Now it is prepared more frequently than ever and is showing small signs of growth in terms of popularity beyond the Afro-Cuban segment of society.

The larger segment of the population, which did not share the dancing, has been slow to take on new and previously lower-class values (cf., on the crisis of meaning, Hintzen, 1978:1–47). But the larger sector is learning how to dance rumba through its youth. Young persons of all colors are learning rumba in schools and casas de cultura all over Cuba. These young dancers and dance teachers participate in Rumba from time to time and teach the dance form to others. They are the white or lighter-skinned Cubans who join in the competition of columbia or who know how to deflect the vacunao in guaguancó. While there is still reluctance, the force of multivocalic rumba that has official support and ideological references yields its important position and demonstrates its potential.

Clifford Geertz (1973) says that art is interpretive, a story that participants tell themselves about themselves. In this case, rumba announces the class equality that the Revolution has sought to implement by featuring the former lower-class representatives; rumba is no longer confined to the barrio but is representative of the nation in community centers and theaters. Its illocutionary force projects and persuades its audience as well as its performers, so that the images, messages, or statements presented are usually unquestionable and inarguable and cannot be rejected. Rumba's overiding statements are concerned with social equality, national identity, and communitas.

The data presented show evidence of promotion, manipulation, and appropriation of rumba in order to elevate and conserve it as a cultural symbol. Professionalization of the form through dance company organization and proliferation of dance performances through casas de cultura organization have institutionalized rumba throughout the country. Meanings previously associated solely with the choreography are transformed to national interests and international demands. Racial and gender stratification that are discovered with analysis are subordinated under current issues of Cuban identity and women's liberation. Stimulated by national interests and international demands (including tourist demands and dance specialists' interests), the symbols within rumba are immersed in a reformation process. Rumba is the nexus of sensuality, solidarity, attraction, unity, and well-being, and ultimately it expresses the essence of postrevolutionary Cuba and its efforts toward egalitarian organization.

Toward Change

When people experience bodily the dynamics of a dance/music event as it builds climactic segments and speeds toward a rhythmic and harmonic apex, they also experience sensations of well-being, pleasure, joy, fun, sex, spontaneity, tension, opposition, musicality, or simply human physicality. Cubans and non-

Cubans associate pleasurable feelings and sentiments with Rumba, and Rumba is capable of transforming their reality.

Among rumberos, social interconnectedness increases, diverse worldviews are meshed if not suspended, and differing degrees of social stratification unite in the liminal world created by the Rumba event. Rumba dancing provides what the Turners call "the structured, highly valued *route* [my emphasis] to a liminal world where the ideal is felt to be real, where the tainted social persona may be cleansed and renewed" (1978:30). Cubans and non-Cubans repeatedly acquaint themselves with the equality and social justice that the Rumba event suggests and primarily promotes. Equanimity is real, experienced bodily, in the liminal world of Rumba, and its extension into the social world seems possible. Rumba persists by means of its power to generate communitas and because of the fundamental, dynamic, and contagious nature of dance.

The occurrence, popularity, and understanding of Rumba are increasing and ever thriving among rumberos, Afro-Cubans, and international art market patrons; these attributes also are increasing gradually within the general Cuban population. There is continuity of meaning in the communitas no matter how the form changes or the timing shifts. Whether the form is yambú, guaguancó, columbia, or batarumba, Rumba means heightened sensitivity and communal fun. When the speed increases or decreases or when the duration is expanded or reduced, Rumba still focuses mainly on attraction, seduction, competition, and play. Even when the space changes from barrio to theater, the potential to generate communitas is intrinsic and ever present.

The intrinsic quality associated with communitas is within the nature and essence of dance. Not only does the eye or the ear bring excitement and ultimately understanding, but the entire human body, with all of its sensory receivers, does so too. The many sensory channels of dance mediate multiple meanings simultaneously. Meanings come from its origins in the nineteenth-century Cuban experience: a dance of lower-class Afro-Cubans expressing male and female attractiveness in rhythmic form. Simultaneously, other meanings are imposed from the social conditions of twentieth century Cuba: a dance of all Cubans expressing egalitarian goals. All meanings are embodied in the dance and are exposed fully only by means of detailed analysis.

The Cuban Ministry of Culture and folkloric *empresas* change the time and space of Rumba, but they count on the intensification of energy in rumba as the ultimate expression of communitas. The formal setting is transcended and often even unconcerned, disinterested, detached attitudes of musicians, dancers, or spectators are transformed and involved. Rumberos transform themselves and others as they create a sustained stream of pleasurable feelings or an explosion of pure emotion.

Organizers in postrevolutionary Cuba seek ways to develop a new orientation from the hierarchical past, ways that encourage communal interest and collective involvement. Educators and managers of the arts attempt to attach the consistent and repeatable dance/music elements of Rumba to egalitarian meanings. Dance, and Rumba in particular, afford the exceptional possibility of a nexus between communitas and ideology, between feelings and goals. To the extent that white or mulatto Cubans participate in Rumba fully and enthusiastically with black or darker-skinned Cubans, that women dance columbia and dance less defensively in guaguancó, that Rumba Saturdays in Cuba and rumba workshops elsewhere generate foreign currency and prestige, that Rumba continues to embrace religious dance material, the complex process of changing values in Cuba can be identified and measured.

Rumba analysis reveals the contrasts and contradictions that exist in contemporary Cuban society. Rumba articulates social conditions: it illustrates socialist ideals as well as social control, machismo as well as women's liberation, sociological race as well as national identity. Rumba performance mediates contradictory issues: spontaneity, freedom, sensuality, and, simultaneously, structured form and set order. Cubans must evaluate all that rumba does and weigh the benefits to determine if it is sufficiently and effectively strategic as it now operates within Cuban society.

Rumba can and does assist ideology, but it can do more. Rumba has a potential for change that is intrinsically present. The potential is the communitas that it is capable of generating: a combination of dance—music elements that encourages a liminal state and consequent equanimous feelings. This potential makes rumba essential, not simply in reflecting social change but also in effecting social change.

Even though it is exceedingly difficult to change values and attitudes, it is not impossible. Rumba, in its prepared form, ignites communitas, but in its extended, spontaneous forms it sustains and maintains communitas even more. The encouragement of spontaneous Rumba events and the proliferation of spontaneity in prepared and extended Rumba would permit the organic development of a fundamental Cuban expression and would allow the resultant communitas to grow, to increase in intensity and in scale. More Cubans would potentially be susceptible to its liminal world of equality and equanimity and more Cubans and non-Cubans might be subject to attitude and value change. The organic emergence or resurgence of batarumba offers the possibility of more significant rumba performance and thus an increase in the efficacy of rumba as a national symbol.

A Rumba Portrait for the Future

The Rumba that is awaited is the congregational fiesta of Cuba and the United States. The clave has been sounded since independence came to the Americas — the insistent, persistent, resistant call of the people, the clave of Americans who speak Navajo, Cherokee, and Seminole languages, Spanish, French, Patois,

Papimiento, Taketake, English, Dutch, German, Chinese, Japanese, Korean, Vietnamese, Arabic, Hebrew, Farcsi. Their rhythm is rumba clave since they dance to a syncopated rhythm, suspending the "and" of beat four and tending to vibrate their shoulders adeptly, often on that beat alone. Cuba's conga has voiced its decorated ostinato in concepts of solidarity and sovereignty, followed by the seis por ocho of diplomatic maneuvers over three decades in order to generate equality as a founding principle of their social organization and of global relations. Castro's indefatigable efforts to fight against the inhumane principle of profit, the enunciating brass capitalist call around the world, have been heard as the virtuoso, improvisational quinto that smacks harshly and irregularly but ingeniously and with the ultimate of philosophic integrity. A small chorus in the United States has held a solitary madruga pulse as a democratic refrain, "liberty, freedom, equality," for the rhythmic preparation of new U.S. leadership. The guagua is the quick, busy, fleeting, but interested voice of young Cubans in Cuba who want the values of their homeland and relatives, but who also want experiences and discoveries afar. Their voice in the polyrhythmic layering, "ahora, rectificación," gives the rumba gas to progress and intensify on both sides. The displaced Cubans from south Florida and northern New Jersey to San Francisco are eligible estrofa singers who are daily creating verses of longing for their childhood homes and families, real *congrí nativo*, and radical change. The main personages, the Cuban and United States government officials, are the long-awaited rumberos. The rumba circle is prepared; why don't they dance the rumba of respect and interdependency together? It is only through cooperation that we will experience a less unfair and more equitable world.

In light of this study's conclusions, dance reveals its potency. It is because rumba is multivocalic, multisensory, multilayered, dynamic, lively, and full of spirit that it is able to effect all its meanings. More specialized neuropsychological data may give a tangible form to the route of rumba's communitas and articulate the elements that form its essense or determine which combinations permit a heightened, humane state to emerge.

Dance, as part of an aesthetic system, offers intangible but indelible results. The non-native may not share the same meaning of the dances with native performers, but with willingness to be aware and especially to dance, cultural understandings become more evident. In dancing rumba, Cubans and groups of unrelated, culturally plural people are drawn together in their distinctiveness.

I hope that Cubans will continue to conserve their folkloric dance forms and document and publish the resulting analyses.[1] I hope that the information contained here will be of assistance in that effort as an outside perspective on rumba and that this study has communicated the concern I have for rumba, Cuban dance, and Cuba. I expect that the essence of rumba will resonate within its diverse audiences and that the communitas it generates will facilitate substantial change, hopefully from inequality to equality.

Note

1. The Cuban dances chart outlines many dances that I researched, but there are several others that I did not find adequately examined, e.g., the dances of Haitian-Cubans (*babul, yuba, cate, tacona* or *mason*), the Arará tradition (*sollí, afrekete, gebioso,* etc.), the dance of female societies (*bríkamo*), the dance of spiritists (*de Cordon*), etc. As elsewhere, Cuba has a rich repository of dance information that can yield a deeper understanding of dance as universal and particular behavior.

References

Blacking, John
    1973   How Musical Is Man? Seattle: University of Washington Press.

Fusco, Coco
    1988   Drawing New Lines. In Nation, October 24, pp. 397–400.

Geertz, Clifford
    1973   Deep Play: Notes on the Balinese Cockfight. In The Interpretation of Cultures. New York: Basic Books.

Graburn, Nelson (editor)
    1976   Ethnic and Tourist Arts: Cultural Expressions from the Fourth World. Berkeley: University of California Press.
    1984   The Evolution of Tourist Arts. In Annals of Tourism Research, vol. 14, no. 1, pp. 393–340.
    1986   Cultural Preservation: An Anthropologist's View. In P. Brown et al. (editors). Problems in Cultural Heritage Conservation. Honolulu: Hawaii Heritage Center, pp. 39–46.

Hanna, Judith
    1979   To Dance Is Human. Austin: University of Texas Press.

Hintzen, Percy
    1978   Myth, Ideology and Crisis in Plantation Society: The Guyanese Example. In Working Papers in Caribbean Society, Skrikia, no. 4, October-November.

Hobsbawm, Eric and Terence Ranger (editors)
    1983   The Invention of Tradition. Cambridge: Cambridge University Press.

Horner, Alice
    1990   Conceptualized Tradition: Intellectual Approaches in Assumptions of Tradition: Creating, Collecting, and Conserving Artifacts in Cameroon Grassfields (West Africa). Ph.D. Dissertation, University of California, Berkeley.

Langer, Susanne K.
    1953   Feeling and Form. New York: Scribner.

Lewis, Gordon K.
    1983   Main Currents in Caribbean Thought. Baltimore: Johns Hopkins University Press.
Martinez-Furé, Rogelio
    1986   La rumba. Havana: Conjunto Folklórico Nacional de Cuba, pp. 1–3.
Matas, Julio
    1971   Theater and Cinematography. In Carmelo Mesa-Lago (editor). Revolutionary Change in Cuba. Pittsburgh: University of Pittsburgh Press, pp. 427–446.
Ness, Sally
    1992   Body, Movement, Culture: Kinesthetic and Visual Symbolism in a Philippine Community. Philadelphia: University of Pennsylvania Press.
Nketia, J. H. Kwabena
    1965   The Interrelations of African Music and Dance. Studia Musicologica 7: 91–101.
Orozco, Danilo
    1984   El son: Ritmo, baile o reflejo de la personalidad cultural cubana? In Zoila Gómez García (editor). Musicología en Latinoamérica. Havana: Editorial Arte y Literatura, pp. 363–389.
Price, Sally and Richard Price
    1980   Afro-American Arts of the Surinamese Rain Forest. Los Angeles: Museum of Cultural History and University of California Press.
Primus, Pearl
    1969   Life Crises: Dance from Birth to Death. In American Dance Therapy Association, Proceedings from the Fourth Annual Conference, Philadelphia, pp. 1–13.
Thompson, Robert Farris
    1974   African Art in Motion. Berkeley: University of California Press.
Turner, Victor and Edith Turner
    1978   Image and Pilgrimages in Christian Culture: Anthropological Perspectives. New York: Columbia University Press.
Wilson, Olly
    1981   Association of Movement and Music as a Manifestation of a Black Conceptual Approach to Music Making. In Irene V. Jackson (editor). Essays on Afro-American Music and Musicians. Westport, Conn.: Greenwood Press, pp. 1–23.

19. THE VOODOOIZATION OF POLITICS IN HAITI

Michel S. Laguerre

Pilgrimage, Voodoo, and Politics

The study of pilgrimage as a socio-religious phenomenon can be carried out at three different levels: (1) the study of shrines as sacred places, (2) the pilgrims themselves, and (3) the goals, motivations and reasons why pilgrims journey to specific shrines in an attempt to gain material and spiritual reward (Raphael 1974: 11; Turner 1974, Turner and Turner, 1978). Pilgrimage as an individual and collective march to a sacred place can be a mechanism for social integration in the same way that Durkheim (1915) perceives the function of religion in society. But religion has also been shown sometimes to play a disruptive role in society, as in the case of nativistic and revitalization movements (Lanternari 1963; Wallace 1956).

In this chapter, pilgrimage as a social system will be interpreted in terms of a center-periphery framework. A center becomes a center when it is in dialectical relation with a periphery (Galtung 1972; Shils 1974). It is postulated here that because they live in a peripheral situation (not necessarily a geographical, but a spiritual periphery), pilgrims initiate their journeys to shrines to be a part of a spiritual center. This might be done as a rite of re-affirmation of their faith and purification (Turner 1973). The shrine where Haitian pilgrims congregate will be considered a center, a "sacred place," a focus of spiritual energy, a place of "hierophany," where the manifestation of a saint—in this case, the Holy Virgin— has been recorded. In other words, a shrine is a center in the sense that the "sacred" is somehow "located" there and because the pilgrims believe that to be so. Their recognition of a shrine as a spiritual centre is based on their faith and their acceptance of physical healing occurring within and outside the shrine as a gesture of a divine manifestation. Moreover, a shrine as a center might also be a national symbol, capable of lending force to a nationalist ideology that political activists can at times use for political purposes, as in the case of the Nuestra Señora de Guadalupe shrine in Mexico (Wolf 1958).

In order to describe and explain the social function of the Haitian pilgrimage to the shrine of Notre Dame de Saut D'Eau, I will focus on the one hand on the

Originally published as "Pilgrimage, Voodoo and Politics" and "Public Policies and National Prospects," in Michel Laguerre, *Voodoo Politics in Haiti* (New York: St. Martin's Press, 1989), pp. 82–128. Copyright © by Michel Laguerre. Reprinted with permission of St. Martin's Press, Incorporated and Macmillan Press Ltd.

shrine itself, on the pilgrims before and during their pilgrimage, and on syncre-
tistic processes embracing folk Christianity and Voodoo practices. On the other
hand, I will discuss how Haitian politicians have twice exploited the apparitions
of the Holy Virgin in Saut D'Eau in times of national political crisis to make
peasants fight against foreign enemies, and also how the pilgrimage plays an integrative role in maintaining the status quo in contemporary Haiti.

The study of pilgrimage is in the process of becoming a specialized field of
investigation amongst social scientists researching Latin American societies and
cultures. Indeed, a growing body of literature on pilgrimage as a sociological
phenomenon is now available (Mair 1959; Gottlieb 1970, Macklin 1973). Religious pilgrimages cannot be considered isolated facts in the national life of Latin
American peasants; they are in the very center of some Latin American religious
traditions. Most Latin American countries have their own national and regional
shrines, and pilgrimages have special social functions among the peasant population. In these countries every year at certain periods, pilgrims travel to shrines—
often far from their homes—to fulfill vows or accomplish other objectives. For example, many Mexicans make their pilgrimage annually to the shrine of Nuestra
Señora de Guadalupe, Chileans to Nuestra Señora de Andacallo, Colombians
journey to Virgen de Las Lajas, Ecuadorians to the Virgen del Quinche and Virgen del Cisne and Bolivians to Nuestra Señora de Copacabana. Peruvians make
their pilgrimage to the Nuestra Señora del Pachacamac shrine, Brazilians journey to the Bom Jesus da Lapa and Dominicans go to Nuestra Señora de Altagracia del Higuey. In Haiti, at the Notre Dame du Mont Carmel or Vierge de Saut
D'Eau shrine, the celebration of the feast is on 16 July, the day of the first apparition of the Holy Virgin in Saut D'Eau, a village in western Haiti. On this day
the shrine attracts people from the entire island.

There are few ethnographic descriptions of Saut D'Eau pilgrims. Writing early
this century, Antoine Innocent (1906: 60–105) gave a good account of the social
and religious atmosphere of Saut D'Eau during the month preceding the feast of
Our Lady of Mount Carmel. During this month, peasants from all over Haiti
converged on Saut D'Eau, travelling by donkey, mule and horse, praying during the journey for their inward conversion and transformation. During this
same period, Aubin (1910: 53) was struck by the number of pilgrims who wore
sac collet (penitential uniforms).

Later, Price-Mars (1928: 168–77) collected from oral traditions the history of
the apparitions and of the pilgrimage and provides a description of the Saut
D'Eau milieu in July 1926, when he attended the pilgrimage. According to Price-
Mars, among the pilgrims there were peasants, Voodooists, prostitutes, beggars,
gamblers and penitents. Like Price-Mars, Herskovits (1971: 285–289) recorded
his observations on Saut D'Eau while he was there in 1934 and witnessed spirit
possession among Voodoo pilgrims.

Alfred Métraux (1957: 92–5) pointed out the continuing Voodooization of
the pilgrimage center and the huge number of Voodoo priests and pilgrims who
visited Saut D'Eau annually. More recently, Hérold Désil—a native of Saut

D'Eau—wrote his MA thesis on the ethno-sociology of the Saudolese community. Although his thesis lacks a theoretical framework, Désil gave some original
information from his own observations on the economy and the demographic
balance of Saut D'Eau and also mentioned the total disappearance of the *feux de
la Saint Jean*, which used to take place on the eve of Our Lady of Mount Carmel
feast (Désil 1967: 32).

THE VILLAGE

Saut D'Eau, a small village in the *Département* of the west, is situated in
the western portion of the Chaine-des-Matheux between Mirebalais and Saint
Marc.[1] The village is geographically limited according to a presidential decree of
26 January 1911, as follows: to the east by the *Habitation Louisia*, to the north by
the *Habitation Tibreuil*, to the west by the *Habitation Rinville*, and to the south
by the *Habitation Lavoute* (Moniteur du 26 janvier 1911). The sergeant commanding the military post, the tax collector, the Catholic priest and a few Voodoo
priests are the most influential people in the village.

According to the census of 1950, the village then had a population of about
150 households, that is, about 1314 inhabitants. A more recent census (1971)
gave the following figures for Saut D'Eau: 775 houses, 442 families, and 1886
inhabitants. Saudolese villagers—artisans included—hold small farms in nearby
Saut D'Eau, where some grow crops for local consumption. As a consequence of
the division of the land among inheritors, no large plantations exist in the area.
Since the first agrarian reform initiated in 1805 by Jean Jacques Dessalines, the
land has been fragmented into small portions and distributed amongst peasants.
The Saudolese people are involved mainly in agriculture and live on a subsistence economy base. There are no industries and no factories in Saut D'Eau;
foreign business has no investments there.

The public market is held twice a week in the village. Saudolese attend this
market to sell the produce from their small farms and to buy what they are in
need of. Middlemen buy from market sellers at low prices the goods they can
then resell to export companies in Port-au-Prince. The presence of pilgrims in
Saut D'Eau during the time of the pilgrimage means that the local market is attended by greater numbers of people, and the village economy improves slightly.

When the annual pilgrimage is over, Saut D'Eau becomes again a quiet place
not much different from other Haitian villages. Parents in Saut D'Eau, as elsewhere in Haiti, make great sacrifices to send their children to finish their high
school education in Port-au-Prince, the economic centre or the nation. Generally, after graduation, these students do not return to live in the village, looking
instead, for jobs in the capital or moving to New York to join relatives. Since
the 1960s, owing to harassment by Duvalier's secret police, the emigration of
Saudolese to New York has been increasing—furthermore the village faces the
problem of the emigration of its active and educated population. With a growing
number of emigrants leaving Saut D'Eau, the subsistence economy of the re-

maining villagers depends more and more upon the money sent by relatives working in Canada and the US.

A few pilgrims also visit Saut D'Eau during Holy Week and for the feast of Notre Dame de la Merci on 24 September. These two feasts do not generate a national migration to the village; rather, the pilgrims come from neighbouring villages. They are few in number and stay in Saut D'Eau for only one or two days—their presence during those times affects the economy and the social life of the village very little.

In Saut D'Eau, as in most of the other Haitian villages, there are neither hotels nor motels. From June onwards, the Saudolese build a few temporary shacks to rent to pilgrims, mainly to vendors. During this period, the cost of renting single rooms increases and it is difficult to find a place to stay if one does not have friends and relatives there. Most of the Saudolese rent a room or two of their homes to pilgrims. Patios and porches are also transformed into rented accommodation.

During the pilgrimage, the pilgrims circulate not only on the two main unpaved village streets but also make several visits to Nan Palm, Saint Jean and Le Saut, all located less than half a mile from the village. Pilgrims go to those places because the Holy Virgin is supposed to have appeared at each one—and Damballah and Aidda Oueddo, two Voodoo spirits, are believed to live there permanently.

The Catholic church and the Voodoo temples are the two major religious institutions in the village. Protestants in Saut D'Eau number about 175, including Baptists and Seventh Day Adventists, and are mainly found in rural areas adjacent to Saut D'Eau. The major Protestant denomination, the Baptist church, is of recent origin in the village. It was introduced there by an American Baptist missionary minister, Lee Karoll, in 1948, almost a century after the apparitions of the Holy Virgin in Saut D'Eau.

THE DEVELOPMENT OF SAUT D'EAU AS A PILGRIMAGE CENTER

The development of Saut D'Eau as a pilgrimage center—that is, as an alternative shrine—was a reaction against the satellite or periphery status and the dependency character of Haitian pilgrims *vis-à-vis* the Nuestra Señora del Altagracia shrine in the Dominican Republic, where Haitians once flocked annually. The history of the village is linked with the history of its shrine, which attracts thousands of pilgrims from all over the country every year. Before the earthquake of 7 May 1842, which devastated Cap-Haitien—the second largest city in Haiti—and caused the formation of a majestic waterfall in Saut D'Eau, Saut D'Eau was simply a small district of the rural section of the Canot River (Rouzier 1891: 262).

It was only during the reign of Faustin Soulouque, president and then emperor of Haiti (1847–1859), that Saut D'Eau began to become a place of pilgrimage.

The political as well as the economic situation of Haiti was deteriorating when Soulouque took office: Jean-Pierre Boyer, a former president for life (1818–1843), had succeeded in politically unifying the island—both Haiti and the Dominican Republic—during his regime, but after Boyer's fall, *"présidents de doublure"* (puppet presidents) were elected who spent only a few months in office. They were chosen by ambitious politicians and generals who took advantage of the office for promoting their own interests. In fact, Soulouque, a Voodoo practitioner, was named to serve his term as a puppet president, but he did not allow himself to be dominated by his political advisors.

In the early years of his reign, Soulouque faced three major political problems (Léger 1907: 197). First, he could not recapture easily the eastern portion of the island because the Dominican Republic, having been separated from Haiti in 1844, proclaimed its independence the same year. The new Republic had placed its army in a state of alert to prevent Haitian troops from invading once more its territory. The Haitians were suddenly cut off from their traditional pilgrimage center of the island at Nuestra Señora de Altagracia del Higuey—Haitian pilgrims had been accustomed to crossing the border and journeying to this shrine every year. Second, the peasants of the south, namely the Piquets, revolted against their lack of land and their neglect by corrupt politicians. Third, Soulouque, uneducated and known for his repressive policies, had to crack down and find ways of solving problems raised by the presence of black and mulatto political factions in his government.

After the defeat of his military attempt to recover the Dominican portion of the island (6 March–6 May 1849), Soulouque decided to strengthen his authority at home. Searching for excuses to name himself emperor, Soulouque found an opportunity when a rumour that the Holy Virgin had appeared in a palm tree on the property of one Debarine in the Champ-de-Mars began circulating in Port-au-Prince (Cabon 1933: 45). Those who had seen the apparition declared that the Holy Virgin was covered with a mantle and a crown—and Soulouque interpreted the event as God's approbation for his coronation. This took place early in July, 1849.

Later, on 16 July of the same year, apparitions were reported in Saut D'Eau. Soulouque interpreted these events for the Haitian masses as a sign from God that he should become emperor.[2]

On Monday, 23 November 1849, with another rumor circulating that the Holy Virgin had again appeared in the Champ-de-Mars, the emperor's wife went to see the event. Her visit strengthened popular and national beliefs in the veracity of the apparitions.

The question of apparitions preoccupied Soulouque's government, and members of the legislative cabinet were appointed to study the phenomena of Saut D'Eau. Among the top officials appointed were Louis Dufresne (general of the army and minister of war, the navy and foreign relations), Jean-Baptiste Francisque (minister of justice, worship and public education) and Lysius Félicité Salomon (minister of finance). Upon receiving the report of this committee, Sou-louque ordered that a chapel be built in Saut D'Eau in honor of the Holy Virgin. From then on, Saut D'Eau has become the national pilgrimage center of the Republic of Haiti (Jolibois 1970b). The French missionary clergy were circum-spect about the apparitions; Father Sapini, the pastor of Mirebalais who was in charge of conducting an inquiry on Saut D'Eau, showed some doubt about the authenticity of the apparitions (Jolibois 1970a). Other members of the missionary clergy, however, accepted the apparitions as genuine—Father Pisano for exam-ple, at that time pastor of Petionville, proclaimed the authenticity of the appari-tions (Cabon 1933: 407).

When Saut D'Eau started to attract pilgrims, Faustin Soulouque changed the region's status from that of rural section of the River Canot to a military post (*poste militaire*). On 3 September 1885, President Lysius Félicité Salomon made Saut D'Eau a *quartier* and appointed a courtroom judge and a county officer to record births, marriages and deaths (Jolibois 1970c). Before this, the people of Saut D'Eau had depended on the county officer of Mirebalais. In 1904, on the order of President Nord Alexis (1902–1908), Saut D'Eau became a parish, and Julien Conan, then archbishop of Port-au-Prince, appointed a priest there on a permanent basis. On 28 January, 1911, President Antoine Simon (1908–1911) changed the status of Saut D'Eau again and made it a *commune*.[3]

Saudolese describe with emotion the miraculous apparitions of the Holy Vir-gin and remember from oral traditions the major dates in the history of the pil-grimage. The following narrative was collected from an 83-year-old Saudolese villager. This same story was recounted to me again and again by others, with some minor modifications.

During the regime of Faustin Soulouque, in 1849, a young man, Fortuné Morose, looked one morning for his horse which had left his garden the night before. In search of this animal, he penetrated a bush area not too far from the place where the village of Saut D'Eau is now located. Once he pushed his way in, a strange noise made by the rubbing of leaves attracted his attention. Great was his surprise to see a young lady inviting him to look at her. Despite the solicitations of this beautiful young lady, Morose was taken by fear and went to report the event to the nearest police station. A policeman was delegated to accompany Morose to be a witness to the event. Unhappily, the unknown lady did not show up when they arrived or they did not see her. A little bit later, they were still looking for her everywhere when the policeman turned his look toward a palm tree. Surprise. He saw a great and beautiful animated picture on a palm leaf. He invited Morose to look at the picture. Morose identified it as the picture of the lady that he had seen previously. Immediately they went out and announced the news to anyone that they could meet in the region.

From this time on, the people of the surrounding area came from time to time to see if the picture was still there and waited patiently until the leaf fell to observe it more closely. After about a month, the leaf fell and the picture was not on it.

But the same picture was reproduced on another leaf. The news of the apparitions of the Holy Virgin in Saut D'Eau raced throughout the country. The place where the palm trees on which the Holy Virgin appeared is known as Nan Palm. It has become since then a holy place, and every 16 July, pilgrims make a trip to Saut D'Eau.

In the proximity of the well-known palm tree, a spring still flows. This source has miraculous power. For example, a young blind lady, Mme. Dorvilus Etiène, had heard about the apparitions. She asked somebody to drive her from Jacmel to Saut D'Eau. In Saut D'Eau, she washed her eyes with water taken from this spring, and after repeating this three days, she began to see again. To accomplish her vows to the Holy Virgin, she brought all of her children to Saut D'Eau, and every 16 July, her grandsons and granddaughters come in pilgrimage to Notre Dame du Mont Carmel shrine.

The Saudolese keep fresh in their memories the sad history of two priests who cut down the trees where the Holy Virgin had appeared. In 1891, under the administration of President Florvil Hyppolite, a French missionary named Father Lenouvel considered the tree of the first apparitions the locus for superstitious practices and cut it down. Having done so, he went to the church, lost consciousness, and died the same day—the faithful believe that he was thus punished for his sacrilegious act (Haïti Littéraire et Sociale, 1905). The pilgrims continued to venerate another palm tree in the vicinity of the original one. Driven by his missionary zeal to get rid of Voodooists in Saut D'Eau, another priest named Father Cessens cut down this second palm tree—strangely enough, this priest suffered a paralytic stroke and died a few months later. This occurrence strengthened the pilgrims' faith in the apparitions and was interpreted as the revenge of both the Holy Virgin and Voodoo spirits. The blessing of various Haitian governments of Saut D'Eau as the national pilgrimage center and the faith of the Saudolese and the pilgrims have to some extent forced the Catholic clergy to accept this situation as a fact of life.

The miracles that seem to occur yearly in Saut D'Eau, the need to have a national shrine after the independence of the Dominican Republic, the waterfall (the residence of Voodoo spirits) and the crowds that continue to come to Saut D'Eau every year are some of the elements accounting for the development of Saut D'Eau as the national pilgrimage center.

THE PILGRIMS

Pilgrims start arriving one month before the day of the feast of Our Lady of Mount Carmel. They come from every corner of Haiti by foot, on horseback, and in trucks—very few arrive in private cars. A week before the feast, the *tap-taps* (small buses painted in loud colours) that normally travel between Carrefour and Port-au-Prince or Petionville and Port-au-Prince change their routes for Port-au-Prince to Saut D'Eau. On the morning of 16 July, chartered buses bring various groups of pilgrims to Saut D'Eau. Throughout the entire journey, pilgrims recite rosaries together and sing Christian songs to the Holy Virgin.

A large number of pilgrims come from the central plateau. They usually rent horses for eight days or so, bring their own luggage as well as feed for their animals, form groups of two, three, four, or five people and sing songs to encourage each other on the route to Saut D'Eau. These groups are organized on the basis of kinship, friendship and neighborhood ties. When they arrive in Saut D'Eau, pilgrims stay together and may help each other financially if there is any need.

I have witnessed in Lascahobas, a village in the central plateau, how chartered buses are organized for the pilgrimage. At the beginning of July, a lady well known in the village told friends and neighbors that there would be a bus for Saut D'Eau and invited them to write their names on a list. When she had enough persons interested in the project, she went to make arrangements with a bus driver. On the day of the pilgrimage the bus was full (pilgrims did not have to pay for children who accompanied them). These village people all knew each other, and upon arriving in Saut D'Eau they decided where and when they would have to pick up the bus to go back home. They stayed together in groups of two or three and knew where the members of the other subgroups were in case of need.

In addition, also one month before the feast, mendicants and physically handicapped persons arrive in Saut D'Eau. Most of them come by foot, sometimes from the farthest corners of the island. They come in the hope of a miracle, and in the belief that the Holy Virgin will better their lives. In this sense, they are also pilgrims—but they have other reasons for coming to Saut D'Eau. They know that they might obtain money and food from the wealthy Voodoo pilgrims who come there to distribute to the needy. These better-off pilgrims do so partly to fulfill vows to the Holy Virgin but, more important, to carry out the order of their local Voodoo priests.

At the front door of the Catholic church, in Saint Jean, Le Saut and Nan Palm, mendicants sit and wait in line, asking for charity in the name of God. They have a *coui* (plate) that they present to people who pass by. Upon receiving something, they bless the giver (*"moin mandé bon Dié poul béni ou"*) and thank the Holy Virgin for sending someone to them (*"mèsi manman la Vièg"*). One of the most common street scenes is that of pilgrims distributing food to the needy. For example, when coffee is being distributed, every mendicant stands around the giver and shows his *coui*. The giver must be careful to give something to everyone. Mendicant pilgrims sleep everywhere—on the doorsteps of the church, in the marketplace and on unoccupied porches.

Voodoo penitents circulate the streets of Saut D'Eau in every direction. They are people who are or have been sick, who have had bad luck or who simply believe that spirits are bothering them. Voodoo priests ask them to wear penitential clothes. Before their journey to Saut D'Eau, they are requested to attend Catholic mass every Sunday during the Lenten period and are invited to remain at the back of the church. Until their penance is over, they are not allowed to wash their penitential clothes. This custom was very popular before the anti-superstition campaign organized in the 1940s by French Catholic missionaries. Although Voodoo penitents still wear penitential clothes, they are allowed to wash them from time to time! Some women simply prefer to cover their *robe sac* with another clean dress. The *robe sac* is now disappearing more and more, even among peasants; instead, women wear blue or white clothing with white girdles around their waists and medals and scapulars around their necks.

The *"madan-sara"* (vendors) are everywhere in the village, selling everything from candies to clothes. They flood the Saut D'Eau public market with produce from Port-au-Prince or from surrounding villages. In front of the church, as well as in Nan Palm, Saint Jean, and Le Saut, they sell candies, medals, girdles, rosaries, chromolithographs of Catholic saints, candies and bread, as well as Voodoo paraphernalia. In Saut D'Eau, the church keeps no shop where pilgrims may buy religious articles, and this function is taken on by *madan-sara*.

Prostitutes from Port-au-Prince and from other cities, as well as gamblers, arrive in Saut D'Eau one week before the feast. These prostitutes and the *madan-sara* consider themselves pilgrims and attend church services. The prostitutes come often to the church to ask the Holy Virgin a favor—that of sending them good clients. They pray that the Holy Virgin intercede so that they may gain financial profit from their trip to Saut D'Eau, and they make donations to the church and vow to donate even more if the Holy Virgin does send them clients! Their job, as they perceive it, does not serve as a barrier to good relations with the Holy Virgin; instead, it allows them to bargain with her.

Gamblers bring various kinds of gambling tables into Saut D'Eau. Their tactics are to allow peasants to win once, and after that to empty their pockets. During the day, gamblers gather around small gambling tables that are placed in proximity to the public market. At night, they assemble in the vicinity of the Catholic church, waiting for pilgrims who have attended the novena. Because there is no electricity in Saut D'Eau, they use *lampes-têtes-gridappes* (peasant lamps) at night.

A few days before the feast, nearby Catholic priests arrive to help the pastor of Saut D'Eau. During this period, more donations for masses are recorded than during the rest of the year altogether. Pilgrims who have received special favors from the Holy Virgin fill the pastor's office to pay for masses. Voodooists who have collected money for the Holy Virgin and Damballah from other peasants in their home villages bring it at this time to the priest in charge of the shrine.

In the streets, some pilgrims sing songs to the Holy Virgin while others may gather around someone who is possessed by a spirit. There is an air of gaiety in the village—the pilgrims have fulfilled their vows and feel renewed.

Pilgrims come to Saut D'Eau for many reasons: to make a promise or to accomplish a vow, to give thanks, to acquire good luck in order to make money, to follow the orders of Voodoo priests, to get married or to beget a child. For both Catholics and Voodooists, Saut D'Eau is a spiritual centre, a place to renew good relationships with the supernatural world.

The pilgrims pass through sequential phases that can be seen in terms of rites of passage (Van Gennep 1960). In this process, there are ways of identifying instances of separation (with the departure from home to start the journey), instances of transition (the journey is a kind of rebirth, a rite of purification; the pilgrims are aware that the journey is not a permanent venture and that they must go back home after the feast or after they have paid a visit to the shrine), and finally re-incorporation (the rite of returning to their familial milieu and their original community).

Pilgrims make their journeys to a shrine in order to reduce structural distances between themselves and a spiritual center, a center of energy. The journey represents for them a symbolic passage from periphery to center—one marches them from a satellite position to a specific center. Pilgrimage is thus the process of separating oneself from a peripheral situation to move—not permanently—to a center position in order to reaffirm and strengthen one's faith. In the Muslim tradition the Koran prescribes that one should make a pilgrimage at least once in one's life, but in the Christian tradition, pilgrimage is an act of free piety (Fahd 1973: 68). Pilgrimage is a process of affirmation of faith through a symbolic death for a spiritual rejuvenation.

FOLK CHRISTIANITY AND VOODOO PRACTICES

Before the pilgrimage begins, relatives and friends remaining at home ask the pilgrims to pray for them and to bring back medals of the Holy Virgin. It is not important for everyone to go there, but someone in the family should make the trip. As soon as they arrive in Saut D'Eau, pilgrims buy medals and scapulars and ask a priest to bless them. They then wear some of them and take the others home to their children and relatives.

The pilgrims' religion is one of vows and promises (Marzal 1967; Gross 1971; Turner 1974; Laguerre 1969)—they come to Saut D'Eau to make or accomplish a vow. This interchange with the Holy Virgin is strict—she gives something, but it is important to fulfill the vow in order to avoid failing ill or having bad luck. The harmony will not be broken if one does what one has promised to do.

Nine days before the feast, there is a novena in honor of the Holy Virgin. This is an evening worship from 7 to 10 pm and interspersed with the recitation of the rosary are songs to the Holy Mary. The church is crowded, and one must be there by about 6 pm to secure a seat—in the aisles, as well as outside the church, those without seats remain standing. During the entire week the pastor comments on the role of Mary in the church and the history of the Holy Virgin's apparitions throughout the world. Candles burn throughout the service and during the collection pilgrims offer money or candles. Each night toward the end of the service, the pastor admonishes the pilgrims not to attend Voodoo services or to organise and participate in public dances; instead, he invites the assembly to meditate and to pray.

On the day of the feast, the crowd assemble in the church for the procession through the village. Altar boys with a cross lead the procession, followed by the children in two lines, the women, the priests in front of the float on the top of which the statue of the Holy Virgin stands and finally the group of men. The float is elaborately decorated with flowers and oriflammes, and the procession passes through the main streets of the village while the pilgrims recite rosaries and, at intervals, sing.

Most of the houses on the main streets are decorated with plants and flowers. Mass is celebrated and an invited priest delivers the homily. In the church, the statue of the Holy Virgin attracts the attention of the pilgrims, who pray with their hands open during the consecration, imploring the mercy of God. After mass, everyone wants to kiss or at least to touch the statue.

A crucifixion scene, placed at the entry to the village, also attracts pilgrims who light candles and talk aloud to the "suffering" Christ. Staying on their knees, they open their arms while they gaze fixedly at the crucifix—they also touch and kiss the base of the crucifix three times. Before leaving, they put candles and flowers on the altar of the calvary, and at the front door of the calvary, as well as in front of the church, pilgrims burn candles—not for the Holy Virgin, but for the *loa* (spirit) Legba, guardian of all entrances.

Other elements of folk Christianity can also be perceived among prostitutes and Voodooists in their dealings with the church. According to the church, extra-marital sexual relations are sinful. The prostitutes themselves do not see anything wrong in prostituting themselves to better their lives economically; they see prostitution rather as a survival strategy and they ask the Holy Virgin to intercede for them. Although they feel rejected by the church, they still believe in belonging to some kind of spiritual or Christian community. They also believe that what the community of men cannot understand, the Holy Virgin does. Someone who is not aware of the situation may find it strange that the same ladies who were in the brothels the night before come to participate in the church services early in the morning. Voodooist prostitutes make several visits to Le Saut and wash themselves in the water where Damballah and Aidda Oueddo are believed to live.

About one month before the feast, Voodooists collect money from door to door in their own villages to offer to the Holy Virgin. People who will not be able to go to Saut D'Eau give some money in the belief that these Voodooists will bring it to Our Lady of Mount Carmel. In the streets of Saut D'Eau these same Voodooists again go from door to door asking for money for the Holy Virgin. If someone asks them why they are making this collection, they give the name of the *loas* (spirits) who have asked for this kind of penance—the money is then given to

Saut D'Eau's pastor to say a solemn mass for them. This is a penitential act, and a Voodoo priest may ask any penitent to perform it in order to restore good relations with the *loa* that has been offended.

Voodoo pilgrims gather in Le Saut, Nan Palm and Saint Jean because these places are loci of previous apparitions of the Holy Virgin, but followers of two aquatic Voodoo spirits called Damballah and Aidda Oueddo also make the journey to Saut D'Eau to venerate them. In Le Saut, people toss money into the water, light candles, bathe for good luck, become possessed and make predictions. In the proximity of the spirits, pilgrims feel themselves to be in another world.

In Saint Jean, Nan Palm, and Le Saut, pilgrims not only wash themselves in the spring, but they also hang ribbons around trees, believing that most of the trees in this area are inhabited by spirits.[4] Before leaving, they take some water with them to be poured into the basins of Voodoo temples sacred to Damballah and Aidda Oueddo.

Nan Palm is the place where the Virgin Mary first appeared, according to the oral tradition started by the Saudolese. The original tree has been cut down, but pilgrims still believe that *loas* inhabit the neighboring trees. These trees are choked with votive girdles. Soil taken from the base of the palm trees is mixed with other ingredients and used as an unguent in Voodoo temples. Lighted candles, girdles, food, and money are presented to Damballah and Aidda, while pilgrims repeat prayers that *mambo* (Voodoo priestesses) and *houngan* (Voodoo priests) recite, and *houngans* talk to the *loas* and ask them special favors for sick Voodooists.

Voodoo pilgrims do not go alone to Nan Palm, Le Saut, and Saint Jean — they are accompanied by relatives, friends, or quite often by Voodoo priests and *mambo*. This is a technical precaution to avoid being drowned, for by the time they become possessed someone needs to take care of them. Other people gather round them while they are possessed to salute the *loas* and to listen to their predictions. Voodoo and bush priests officiate as folk physicians in Nan Palm, Le Saut and Saint Jean. The penitents who accompany them distribute food to the mendicants in response to the demand of *loas* protectors — on their knees, they pray to the *loas* who inhabit the trees and kiss the soil three times before leaving.

In the streets of Saut D'Eau, Voodooists become possessed and are surrounded by other pilgrims. They speak for their *loa* protectors and make predictions in a jargon that is difficult to understand. Their eyes are wide open, their limbs are well stretched and they are out of themselves — possessed. Scenes of this kind provoke spontaneous gatherings from time to time in the streets of Saut D'Eau.

In Le Saut, Nan Palm and Saint Jean, I witnessed Voodoo priests sitting under trees with large containers of Voodoo concoction in front of them. They used it for curing and healing purposes when a Voodoo devotee came to them. Passing Voodoo priests came to shake hands with them and to find out which degree they had reached in the Voodoo hierarchy — instances of spirit possession were also

observed in these circumstances. In the evenings, more devotees gathered round
the priests and they participated in Voodoo dances.

Saut D'Eau is a Christian as well as a Voodoo center. The distinction between
folk Christianity and Voodoo practices is not made by Voodooists because one
needs to be a Christian in order to belong to a Voodoo congregation—there is
such a mixture in the pilgrims' religious practices that it is difficult to see where
folk Christianity ends and Voodoo starts. Voodoo priests commonly order devotees to make a pilgrimage to Saut D'Eau during their initiation to the *hounsi
canzo* degree (first degree in the Voodoo hierarchy) and before their ordination
to the Voodoo priesthood. In this sense, one can understand why some mendicants are accomplishing a religious obligation when they beg for money that they
later give to the Catholic priest in Saut D'Eau. Saut D'Eau is the only place
during the feast of Our Lady of Mount Carmel where one can find in the same
niche all the varieties of Voodoo tradition on the island. By coming to Saut
D'Eau, Voodoo priests try to attract national attention and to gain national recognition for the Voodoo church, which has a peripheral status in contrast to the
Catholic church—the state church—which has a central status.

USE OF THE HOLY VIRGIN'S APPARITIONS IN HAITIAN POLITICS

The first apparitions were interpreted by Faustin Soulouque as a national
event. Initially, he made people believe that the apparitions were a sign of God's
approbation for his accession to the throne as emperor of Haiti,[5] but eventually,
by recognizing the authenticity of the apparitions of Saut D'Eau, he encouraged
soldiers as well as peasants to believe that the Holy Virgin was with him and on
the side of the Haitian army in their efforts to recapture the Dominican Republic
(Aubin 1910: 93).

During the occupation of Haiti by US marines (1915–1934), Haitian guerrillas
used the name of the Holy Virgin of Saut D'Eau to incite peasants to struggle
against them. These political guerrilla leaders interpreted US presence in their
country as being against the will of the Holy Virgin and the heroes of the struggle
for independence. Thus, peasant resistance to liberate the country was animated
by their patriotic feeling and sustained by this religious ideology.

Wearing around their necks the Holy Virgin scapulars and medals blessed
in Saut D'Eau, many peasants engaged in guerrilla warfare in the mountains of
Pensez-y-Bien, Crochus and Morne-à-Cabrit and strengthened their solidarity
with other bands under the leadership of Charlemagne Péralte and Benoît Batraville, who struggled in the regions of Lascahobas, Belladère and Mirebalais.
Despite their lack of weapons—trusting only in the scapulars they wore—they
were able to attack successfully the US military station in Croix-des-Bouquets,
and with the help of General Codio by May 1916 they had occupied Croix-des-
Bouquets. Against these peasants, the US placed 800 soldiers on the *Habitation*

Leroux, 400 in Montet, three kilometres north of Carrefour-de-Beaurepos and another regiment in Terre-Rouge (Jolibois, 1970d).

The US was aware of the political use made of the apparitions by the guerrillas—this was one of the reasons why a marine posted in Mirebalais ordered one of the palm trees of Saut D'Eau cut down, for this palm tree was an object of veneration to the peasants. A few days later the marine became sick and was sent back to the US, thus reinforcing the peasant belief that the Holy Virgin was against the US occupation of Haiti.

Haitian politicians are aware of how the apparitions have been used against foreign enemies, although no movement has yet been initiated from Saut D'Eau by any group of pilgrims or others using the Holy Virgin's name to incite the masses to overthrow any Haitian government. Nevertheless, the possibility seems to be latent. This was clearly understood when the Haitian government prohibited students from taking part in the pilgrimage of 1964. It was believed that the political situation was at such a climax that any movement initiated under the Holy Virgin's name could overthrow the Haitian government.

Since the reign of Soulouque, the Haitian government has had *manu militari* as well as symbolic control over the national pilgrimage centre. During the period of the feast, detectives and policemen are sent there so that the government may have absolute control over the situation. Every year the president sends his financial contribution to Saut D'Eau's pastor, who in turn announces it to the congregation—like any other pilgrim, the president in this way fulfills his vows. He is believed to be a pilgrim even without coming to Saut D'Eau, and because of his financial contribution to the Holy Virgin many pilgrims feel sympathetic toward him.

PILGRIMAGE AND THE MAINTENANCE OF SOCIAL ORDER

This pilgrimage is in various ways functional to the system. It plays an integrative role at village level by opening channels of communications among villagers. Groups of villagers make the trip together and get to know and are bound up with one another—making new friends is a positive element as far as village cohesiveness and unity are concerned. The case of Voodooists who pass from door to door to collect money for the Holy Virgin is a good example of how social integration occurs at village level. One collects the money this year; someone else will do so next year. This simple act reinforces solidarity and friendship among people of the same village.

For the Saudolese the pilgrimage generates a periodic cash flow. Besides being able to sell their products at good prices (some store rice, beans and corn, waiting for the coming of pilgrims to sell them), they also make a little money by renting rooms in their homes. The pilgrimage relieves the monotony of village life as the Saudolese participate in the "pilgrimage cycle." They live and adapt themselves to the "in-between pilgrimage" situation, but after the feast is over, the Saudolese look forward to the next one—this gives them a sense of hope.

For the mendicants, the pilgrimage plays the role of a non-existent Haitian welfare bureau. For at least a month, the mendicant is provided with food and some
money. The trip to Saut D'Eau also has a minimal effect on the distribution of
the population of Haiti. After the feast of Our Lady of Saut D'Eau, a few of the
mendicants move to Port-au-Prince, thereby increasing the population of the
slum areas of the capital.

Supposedly, the pilgrimage—by bringing people from different clan statuses
together—should help break down class barriers among the pilgrims. However,
class barriers remain. Mulattoes do not mingle with peasants, and in fact, the
mulattoes and educated blacks look down upon the peasant Voodooists. Equally,
those who come with their private cars, speak French and are well mannered can
be distinguished from the crowd of peasants. The pilgrimage therefore provides
a microscopic view of class structure in Haitian society.

Pilgrims of the same village manifest solidarity amongst themselves and also
toward others, but they experience the feeling of brotherhood more deeply with
people of their own groups and with friends. They may refrain from becoming
involved with other people because of the fear and rivalry that exists among Voodooists. Thus, the pilgrims experience a certain communal harmony in their respective subgroups, but also, more or less, a *cassure* or disharmony with the community of pilgrims taken as a whole.

Peasant pilgrims do not come to Saut D'Eau for practical political purposes;
they come to accomplish private vows, to visit the shrine and to communicate
their problems to the Holy Virgin. They come for personal reasons, hoping that
their situation will change for the better in the near future. Even when a trip
to the shrine is organized for a group, each individual has his own projects and
vows—there are definitely no common projects. It is not that the villagers nourish a cult of fatalism and resignation; rather, they look for individual alleviation.
They are more motivated to change their spiritual and economic situation than
to struggle for change at either a local or national level.

The pilgrimage promotes the development of continuous religious syncretism
among the peasants less in terms of "material acculturation" (Bastide 1970: 144)
than in terms of *weltanschauung*. Voodoo *loas* and Catholic saints are in proximity to each other. By invoking the Holy Virgin and/or Damballah Oueddo, pilgrims strengthen their ties with the supernatural world and gain enough spiritual
force to live by until the next pilgrimage. The pilgrims leave their problems in
the hands of the Holy Virgin and/or Damballah and hope that these sources of
spiritual help will solve their problems at their earliest convenience.

CONCLUSION [TO THIS SECTION]

Although there are several pilgrimage centers in Haiti, Saut D'Eau remains
the main one and stands as a national symbol for the whole country. In the past,
Haitian politicians have used the apparitions of the Holy Virgin in Saut D'Eau
to make peasants fight against Dominican guerrillas and against US marines—

however, the apparitions have not historically been exploited to overthrow any Haitian regime.

The pilgrimage makes it possible for pilgrims to renew good relations both with the Holy Virgin and the Voodoo *loas*. In Saut D'Eau, *loas* and saints maintain good relations and are symbolic of the harmony—so the Voodoo peasants believe—that must exist among Haitians. The pilgrims feel fulfilled by accomplishing their vows or *promesa*. All the pilgrims—the penitents, the voodooists, the mendicants, the *madan-sara*, the prostitutes, and the gamblers—gain spiritually, psychologically or economically by going to Saut D'Eau.

The fact that pilgrims come to Saut D'Eau in search of individual alleviation, with the consequent lack of a common political project; their belief in the Holy Virgin and/or Voodoo spirits as solely capable of solving their problems; the effect of the pilgrimage on the social cohesiveness of other villages; the harmonious marriage between folk Christianity and Voodoo in Saut D'Eau, and government control to avoid having the Voodoo priests in their trance make predictions against the elected president of the Republic. These are the variables which explain why apart from any period of crisis during which the Haitian regime faces foreign enemies, the pilgrimage is functional to the maintenance of the social system.

Politics and Voodoo during the Duvalier Era

One of the most intriguing aspects of Haitian governmental politics during the Duvalier era was its pervasive ramifications and far-reaching influence on the Voodoo belief system and its co-optation of local Voodoo leaders (Manigat 1964). It is not possible to fully understand the functioning of local Haitian politics over the past two decades without paying attention to the pivotal role played by some Tontons Macoutes (militiamen), who were also influential Voodoo priests in their communities (Diederich and Burt 1969; Laguerre 1982a). During the administrations of François "Papa Doc" [1957–71] and Jean-Claude "Baby Doc" [1971–86] Duvalier, Voodoo became so central in the organization of the Haitian political system that its political content deserves further analysis.[6]

The politicization of Voodoo was first discussed by Jean Price-Mars (1928), who linked the success of the Haitian Revolution to the commanding role played by Voodooist insurrectionist leaders. Jean Price-Mars went as far as to say that, had it not been for Voodooist participation in the revolutionary movement, Haiti would not have become an independent nation in 1804. François Duvalier and Lorimer Denis in their celebrated essay "L'Evolution Stadiale du Vodou," published in 1944, reached a similar conclusion. They also suggested that the events of the Haitian Revolution have had a tremendous influence on Voodoo ethno-theology in that a few of the heroic leaders were thereafter canonized Voodoo spirits (Duvalier 1968a: 178). One had to wait until 1958 to see a full historical documentation and analysis of Voodoo during the wars of independence (Mennesson-Rigaud 1958).

The use of Voodoo by the Duvalier regime has been the subject of several studies. For example, Manigat (1964) has suggested that Papa Doc had a few Voodoo priests who served as his special assistants, and that with their help he was able to reach and control a section of Haitian society. Montilus (1972) notes that in contrast to the repressive measures against Voodoo taken by previous administrations, the Duvalier regime was most sympathetic to Voodooists. The historical evolution of the interplay between Voodoo and politics was taken up by Rotberg (1976), who saw Papa Doc as the Voodoo priest *par excellence* who used Voodoo to mystify the masses. David Nicholls's (1970) analysis of religion and politics in Haiti touches only tangentially on Voodoo and more substantially on the Catholic and Episcopal churches. On a more speculative level, Hurbon (1979a) discusses Papa Doc's manipulation of the negritude and Voodoo ideology in order to legitimise his power over the masses. In a more recent study of local level politics in an urban slum in downtown Port-au-Prince, the participation of the Voodoo priests in the affairs of the state and their community was brought into light and substantiated (Laguerre 1982).

It was the late Rémy Bastien (1966) who painstakingly analyzed the relationship between Duvalierist politics and the Voodoo church. Living in exile, he was unable to substantiate some of his pronouncements, but he was the first to pinpoint the need to analyse "the relationship between Duvalier and *vodoun* . . . from the standpoint of the relations between church and state" (Bastien 1966: 56). This implies a recognition of the state and Voodoo as two separate and distinct entities and furthermore suggests that the Voodoo church maintains its own autonomy *vis-à-vis* the rest of society.

I propose to look at Voodoo and politics as two poles of the same continuum. This approach reflects my way of dissecting Haitian national culture as comprising, on the one hand, the dominant Western-oriented culture and, on the other, the mass-based popular culture, both of them meshed together as each integrates selected elements from the other. The relationship between elite culture and popular culture must be seen as an expression of asymmetrical relationships between the dominant sector of society and the exploited masses.

To understand the interplay between Duvalierist politics and Voodoo, one must bear in mind that François Duvalier integrated into his regime the political aspect of Voodoo, the one that accounts for the independence of the island according to Duvalier's own interpretation and that perpetuates the mark of African civilization on the matrix of Haitian society and culture.[7] Thus, it is less the Voodoo ritual that was retained than the political significance of the Voodoo church and the structure of relationships that it generates. The two Duvalier administrations appropriated the political aspect of Voodoo and consequently made the church an ideological symbol, part of the national political culture.

The root of the use of Voodoo in Duvalierist politics must be sought in François Duvalier's own writings before he even entered the field of politics.[8] One is forced to turn the clock back to the period between the two World Wars. Duvalier and his collaborator, Lorimer Denis—both of them disciples of Price-

Mars—set for themselves the task of validating the culture of the masses as a reaction to the humiliation of the US occupation (1915–1934) and the cultural
"*bovarysme*" (ambivalence) of the pro-Western mulatto elite.

FRANÇOIS DUVALIER AND THE GRIOTS GROUP

In any dependency context, the elite play the role of brokers linking the center
to the periphery. Although they are more often political and economic middlemen, they also play an ideological role because any system of domination, subjugation and exploitation tends to develop its own ideological apparatus to justify itself (Santos 1968). With their nationalist philosophy and criticisms of the
ideological practices of the traditional bourgeoisie, the members of the Griots
group—among them François Duvalier—aspired to become the new brokers of
the nation. They purported to accomplish their goal by taking into account local
customs and ways of life.

François Duvalier was one of the founders of the journal *Les Griots*, which, on
23 June 1938, published its declaration of intent. According to the editorial, the
journal was to serve as a vehicle "to formulate the literary and scientific doctrine"
of the Griots group (Duvalier 1968a: 35). The October–December 1938 issue
presented the essential points of the group's philosophy. They wrote that "all our
'effort from independence to this day has consisted of a systematic repression of
our African heritage. . . . Our goal now is to recognise and accept our racial background" (Duvalier 1968a: 38).

With the goal of validating the folk culture of the masses, Duvalier began to
study Voodoo with the intent of showing not only its African roots, but also its
influence on national politics during the period of the wars of independence
(Denis and Duvalier 1944). He came to the conclusion that a religion that served
a a catalyst for national unity and that was part of Haiti's folk culture should not
be denigrated, but maintained.[9] It did not take him long to realize that the people
loved their Voodoo and it was the elite who despised it (Denis and Duvalier
1955).

At the time Duvalier formulated his Voodoo heritage statement, the Catholic
church fervently opposed the practice of Voodoo in rural and urban Haiti.[10] The
general policy of the Catholic church was to campaign against superstition (Roumain 1937). The campaign, which went on until the late 1950s, forced Voodooists to present their cultic objects and paraphernalia to their parish priest to
be burned. It also forced them to take an oath of loyalty to the Catholic church,
swearing that they would miraculously die if they ever practiced Voodoo again.

The battle of some middle-class intellectuals—including François Duvalier—
against church practice was opposed in Port-au-Prince by, among others, the
priests of the Catholic newspaper *La Phalange*. One proponent of the anti-Voodoo policy of the Catholic church, Father Joseph Foisset, became the focus of
attention of these young writers, among them François Duvalier and Lorimer

Denis (Duvalier 1968a: 403–408). The latent animosity between Duvalier and the French clergy developed during those years.

For Duvalier, Voodoo had to be preserved at all costs because it represented the authentic soul of the Haitian people (Duvalier 1968a: 277–285). The rehabilitation of Voodoo meant that the struggle would have to be fought against the ideology of the pro-Western elite and the European clergy who had tried to dismiss things African and co-opt the Haitian people into Western civilization. No doubt, to be successful, such a battle needed to be fought in the political arena. And the various studies that Duvalier wrote or co-authored had only one goal: to show that the Voodooists were the authentic Haitians, making up the majority of the population, and that they had fought for the independence of the republic and had been kept in poverty and out of mainstream politics. It was time to bring them into the mainstream of Haitian politics and to liberate them from their position of subordination *vis-à-vis* the French Catholic church and the pro-Western mulatto elite (Duvalier 1967). We will see that once Duvalier became president, he delivered a fatal blow to these two groups. At the same time, he nominated certain influential Voodoo priests to serve as his advisors and permitted Voodoo people to practice their religion openly with state protection.

VOODOO AND ELECTORAL POLITICS

The success of national brokers in maintaining their position depends a great deal on the support they received from local brokers. Electoral politics provides a situational context for understanding these structural links of dependency between both center and periphery. This is one facet of the articulation of imperialism at national and local levels.

Before the Duvalier era, during the electoral campaigns, one could especially observe how the politicians manipulated Voodoo people in order to enhance their own popularity. Bastien (1966: 56) wrote, "candidates to an elective office . . . cultivate the friendship of the key *houngans* [Voodoo priests] of their district, make donations to their temples, offer ceremonies and in addition, go to mass every Sunday." He adds that they depend on "the support and the favourable influence the *houngan* will exercise upon the electorate" (Bastien 1966: 56). Manigat (1964: 29) has made a similar observation: "as for the *houngans*, they are frequently flattered by politicians, eager to use for their own career and influence the moral authority these Voodoo priests exert upon the masses. . . . the politicians know how to form their own circles of *houngans* in order to control the local population and insure popularity."

In the late 1940s, the Haitian Parliament passed a bill making it obligatory for the president to be elected by popular vote and not solely by the senators and the chamber of representatives (Weil *et al.* 1973: 109). During the elections of 1950, presidential and legislative candidates began to flirt more openly with influential Voodoo priests (and Catholic priests as well) to enlist their collaboration and their votes and the support of their followers. It was probably with the elections of 1957 that the ability of Voodoo priests to deliver votes was taken more seriously and was also proven to be effective (Laguerre 1982a: 97–126).

During the presidential campaign in 1957, François Duvalier enlisted the aid of a number of Voodoo priests. They were mostly men from Port-au-Prince who had served as informants when he wrote his analyses of Haitian Voodoo (Laguerre 1982a; Duvalier 1968a). Some of them—quite influential in the slums of Port-au-Prince—were familiar faces at the Institute of Ethnology. Through these priests and supporters, Duvalier was also able to enlist the help of other priests in the countryside (Laguerre 1982). One of the strategies of the Duvalier campaign at the local level was to formally request the help of these politically conscious Voodoo priests. In fact, some of them used their temples as local headquarters of the Duvalier campaign.

The sympathy that Duvalier displayed toward the Voodooists made him less acceptable to the Catholic clergy and consequently unsuitable, in the minds of the elite, for the highest office in the land. The fact that Catholic clergy were preaching during the electoral campaign to vote Catholic and not Voodoo not only turned the proindigenist native clergy pro-Duvalier, but also strengthened the Catholic vote for the light-skinned mulatto presidential candidate Louis Déjoie.

Voodooists were easily able to distinguish their candidate from that of the Catholic clergy, however. The equation Duvalier = Voodoo was established by the Catholic church itself; Duvalier did not present himself as a Voodoo candidate. In fact, he even complained about it. He wrote in a speech delivered in Port-de-Paix on 19 March 1957, that "because my humble contribution to the study of some social phenomena deals with aspects of Haitian folklore, some people less informed in the domain of cultural anthropology have attempted to establish an insidious confusion between these phenomena which have been the subject of my studies and my religious convictions" (Duvalier 1968b: 172).

Duvalier also complained more generally about the negative image that the French clergy were projecting of him. He later spoke of "the campaign of denigration" that Jean Robert, Bishop of Gonaives, had organised against him during the course of the presidential campaign (Duvalier 1968b: 90). At the peak of the electoral campaign he went to present his political platform to the editorial staff of the Catholic newspaper *La Phalange*, and afterwards complained that "they preferred to present in an unfavourable way the future President of Haiti" (Duvalier 1968b: 140).

One must remember that throughout the electoral campaign the Catholic church's anti-superstition crusade was still going strong. It was evidently to most Voodooists' advantage to vote for François Duvalier as a way of protecting their church. After the two other black presidential candidates—Daniel Fignolé in exile in New York and Clément Jumelle—had withdrawn from the race, Duvalier became the natural leader of the masses. The Voodooists' sympathy toward the presidential candidate strongly benefited him at the polls and contributed in no insignificant way to his victory. That Voodoo priests could muster a significant number of votes on behalf of a presidential candidate became an unquestionable political reality during the elections of 1957.

THE VOODOOIZATION OF HAITIAN POLITICS

From the standpoint of national politics, the dependency process conveys the idea of two poles involved in an asymmetrical type of relationship. In such a structure, the national brokers exert their political domination over the masses through the complicity of local leaders who serve as peripheral brokers. Starting in 1957, the Voodooization of Haitian politics became a means to control the local institutions of the masses and to maintain that structure of inequality. We will see later exactly how the Duvalier administration was able to exploit local centers of power such as the Voodoo church.

After Duvalier had been elected president, the Catholic church, and especially its Breton clergy, headed on a collision course with his administration. The end result was that several priests were expelled or removed from their lucrative posts in Port-au-Prince (Pierre-Charles 1973: 76–78).

Here we have described a battle of ideologies in which François Duvalier was a participant. He identified himself with the masses and promoted their dreams and religious aspirations in reaction against a dominant ideology. More precisely, Duvalier's support of Voodoo became a battle for the control of the national religious space which was totally dominated by the Catholic church and its ideological apparatus. The marginal religious space used by the Voodoo church was fragile because it did not have any legal status. It survived only at the mercy of those who held political office at national and local levels. The presidency of François Duvalier had the curative effect of giving some form of legitimacy to the Voodoo church (Rotberg 1976). The politicization of Voodoo was made possible because of the open support it gained from the administrations of François and Jean-Claude Duvalier.

Among all the twentieth century presidents of Haiti or Haitian administrations, the Duvaliers were the only ones who openly supported Voodooists in their attempt at national recognition. One of the innovative moves of François Duvalier's administration was to bring Voodoo into the open in the political process by co-opting Voodoo priests as brokers and Tontons Macoutes in their respective communities and by openly sponsoring Voodoo liturgies on behalf of his government (Diederich and Burt 1969).

I see the Voodooization of Haitian politics in two distinct ways: in the use of Voodoo by national political leaders and in the participation of Voodoo priests in national and local level politics. The fact that politicians have sometimes been Voodoo believers is not a new phenomenon—what is new is public recognition of it. Some influential people in the Duvalier administrations have been known to be Voodooists—they were chosen not only because of their support for Duvalier during the electoral campaign, but also because they enabled him to tip the balance of power in certain regions. For example, in the Département of Artibonite, the most important authority was a Voodoo priest Tonton Macoute. His position as special representative of the president in the region was created as a way of neutralizing the power of the local bishop, who happened to be one of the staunchest anti-Voodooists and anti-Duvalierists of the Catholic clergy (Duvalier 1969). Later the dismissal of the bishop and the nomination of one of his native priests to head the Ministry of Education was part of the general trend or the "Duvalierisation" of both the Catholic and Voodoo churches.

One cabinet minister during the Papa Doc administration saw fit to build his own Voodoo temple in the Carrefour area. Evidently, he was not the only top-ranking government official involved (Diederich and Burt 1969). Throughout the country there were also individual Voodoo practitioners who held key government positions, but the Voodoo apparatus of the government became known through the participation of the palace personnel in Voodoo ceremonies on the eve of the celebrations of 22nd May, the day of national renewal (Laguerre 1982). It was known that, on the eve of these celebrations, advisors to the president and other government officials came to the countryside to participate in Voodoo thanksgiving ceremonies on behalf of the permanent regime. The point I am making here is not that François Duvalier believed or paid for these ceremonies, but that they seem to have received his blessings—at least, he did not care to stop them.

One of Papa Doc's boldest moves was to have incorporated Voodoo priests in his government, especially at the local level. Voodoo priests served as informants, spying on members of their congregation, and as Tontons Macoutes within the boundaries of their communities and neighborhoods (Laguerre 1982). Through the network of Voodoo priests, it was possible to reach the masses and also to control them. Their temples were used for the diffusion of the Duvalierist ideology.

Several writers have stated erroneously that Voodoo temples are isolated from each other and that a clever politician needs to deal with them on a one-to-one basis (Bastien 1966; Métraux 1958). This is evidently not true and is the result of a misunderstanding of the structure of relationships generated by the Voodoo churches.

The majority of Voodoo churches are part of a network controlled by a single temple that functions as the primary node of that network. Satellite or associate temples that are attached to the node belong either to the priest, his common-law wife or individuals who have obtained their training through the central temple. They continue to maintain their kinship and ritual ties to the primal core.

In one of the Upper Belair temples that I studied, the priest owned two temples: one in Port-au-Prince and the other in Cayes. The Port-au-Prince temple was connected to two other satellite temples, one in Carrefour and the other in Cité St Martin (each is a district in the Port-au-Prince metropolitan area). In

Cayes, his temple was connected to a satellite temple in the periphery of the city and to another one in a southern village.

These connections were made possible because the priests in the satellite temples had been trained through the owner of the central temple in Port-au-Prince and Cayes. They remained loyal to him, maintained contact with his temples and sometimes sent complicated cases of illness to him for cure. In addition, they all belonged to the same secret society.

A network of Voodoo churches can be established for several different reasons. For example, the priests of satellite temples may train through the central church — in such a situation, the relationship between the central church and the peripheral temples ends up being asymmetrical. One can also think of a network of churches based on consanguineal relationships. In Upper Belair, for example, a Voodoo priest married a woman from Croix-des-Bouquets whose father had a temple there. Over the years, there was a blending of Voodoo traditions in both temples — although each kept its own autonomy. These temples developed a *modus vivendi* that allowed them to collaborate and complement each other.

In a universe of n temples $(A_1 \ldots A_n)$, each temple can influence only its own members. If, in Model I, $n=9$, then one has nine independent temples with no interconnection. Anyone wanting to influence the voting patterns of all the temples must contact each one separately. In this case, $x(\text{contacts})=9$.

The first model presents a situation where each temple is autonomous but may be part of a *lakou* (extended family compound) arrangement. By and large Voodoo temples that are isolated and autonomous units are geared toward domestic cults and do not attract the general public.

In Model II, there are three independent temples (A2, A3, and A9) and three sets of temples with symmetrical relationships (A1A4, A5A6, and A7A8). Anyone wanting to influence the nine temples need only contact each one of the three independent temples and one in each set of temples; $x=6$.

The second model presents a case where two temples previously separated and isolated from each other have become connected through the marriage of one of the priests to someone in the other temple. No temple here is in any position of structural superiority in relation to the other. In fact, their link is maintained through a restrained symmetrical relationship.

In Model III, there are three independent temples (A3, A7, and A9) and two sets of temples (A1A2, A1A4, A4A2 and A5A6, A5A8, A8A6), each temple in a set headed by the same Voodoo priest. To influence all the congregations in this universe, one needs to contact the three independent temples and one temple in each of the two sets; $x=5$.

The third model presents a situation where the owner of the central temple also has additional temples elsewhere. Because he owns all of them, the congregation of each one is naturally connected to the others.

In Model IV, there are three sets of temples (A1A4, A2A3, A2A6, and A5A7, A5A8) and an independent temple (A9). To influence all the temples, one needs

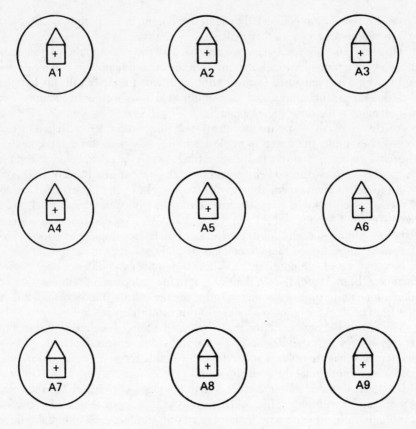

Model I: Independent Temples

to contact the independent temple and the central church in each set (A1, A2, and A5); x=4.

The fourth model presents a situation where the central temple is connected to satellite temples owned by individuals who have been trained through the same patriarch-priest. They remain *pitit-kay* (devotees), and their congregations are an extension of the central temple. Their associate temples continue to request the help of the patriarch-priest whenever they need it.

In Model V, there are two independent temples (A3, A9) and two sets of temples (A1A4, A4A2, and A5A6, A5A8, A8A7). To influence all the temples, one needs to contact the two independent churches and the central unit in each set (A4 and A5); x=4.

The fifth model is the situation where the central temple has its associates who have in turn their own associates. The second row of associates have received their training from the first associates, who have received theirs from the central tem-

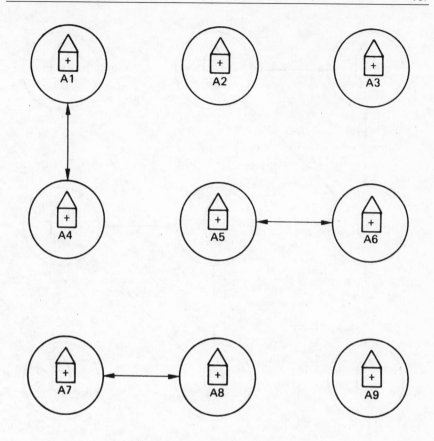

Model II: Temples with Symmetrical Relationships

ple. In other words, these satellite centres may also generate relations with dependent churches without losing their ties with the central church. They play a central role in relation to the satellite churches and a satellite role in relation to the central church.

It is postulated here that the flow of communication goes from the central church to the periphery and *vice versa*. By co-opting the central figure, it is possible to have access to his congregation, the associate-priests and the congregations of his associates. However, there is no guarantee that all associates in the network will follow the political will of the central figure, although his moral authority may make it a little easier to convince others.

In the beginning of the Duvalier era, Voodoo priests who were members of the opposition did not enjoy the same privilege as pro-Duvalier priests who resented maintaining their affiliation with opposition temples because they could be said to be dealing with enemies of the regime. As a result, the pro-Duvalier priests put

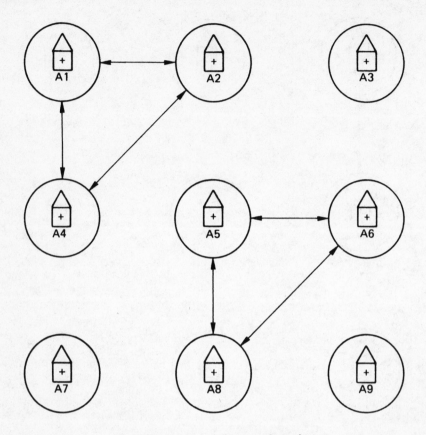

Model III: Temples with Common Ownership

pressure on each participating church in the network to support Duvalier so that
they could operate in relative security.

The political exploitation of the Voodoo priests by the Duvalier regime was
accomplished through the use of an ideological ritual. For example, Duvalier
arranged to make his public announcements on the 22nd of the month because
22 was known to be the Duvalier family's lucky number.[11]

One of the aspects that has been overlooked in the analysis of the interplay between Voodoo and politics is the political use of Voodoo secret societies (Laguerre
1980b: 147–160). My research in Upper Belair indicates that the secret societies
are a paramilitary group connected to the Voodoo temples and that the most powerful bands of Mardi Gras and Rara are owned and operated by the leadership of
the secret societies. The co-optation of these local leaders as Tontons Macoutes
deeply grounded the political regime in the populace. For example, during the
carnival season, these bands used political songs in which they portrayed François

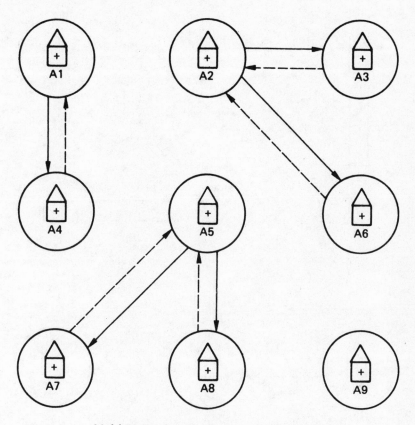

Model IV: Temples with Asymmetrical Relationships

Duvalier as a good papa, a benefactor of the new Haiti. Also, these bands were allowed to circulate in the streets of Port-au-Prince on the eve of 22 May to show popular support for the administration of Jean-Claude Duvalier.

The Voodooization of Haitian politics is partly due to the fact that there are individual politicians who have become Voodoo practitioners to protect them-selves from the malevolent intent of others—in fact, Voodoo accusation is part of Haitian daily political life. The rumor that a prominent politician uses Voodoo to ensure his success is likely to make an opponent seek help from Voodoo. In my judgment, several politicians have become Voodooists precisely because they seek political office—a sharp contrast to the majority of the Haitian masses who practice Voodoo because they are ill or have illness in the family.

François Duvalier made no attempt to make the Voodoo church into a state church; to do so would have given fuel to his critics because he maintained that he was not a Voodooist. He also understood the possible international implica-

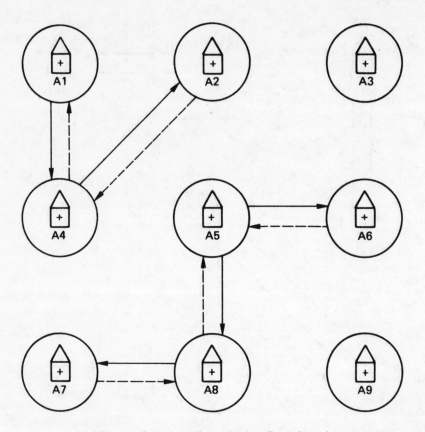

Model V: Temples with Satellite and Subsatellite Relationships

tions of such a move. Nor did it seem to have been part of his cultural renaissance program. For their part, neither have Voodoo people exerted any sustained pressure on either François or Jean-Claude Duvalier to change their status.

THE POLITICIZATION OF HAITIAN VOODOO

Political brokers, whether they function at the national or local level, tend to exploit the system to their own advantage because of their strategic position. This means that political dependency is not unidirectional. While the Voodoo church depends on the national elite for recognition, the elite are also dependent on Voodoo people for support. The politicization of Voodoo basically means the recognition of the Voodoo church as a center of power in the local community and of the Voodoo priest as a broker on behalf of his congregation.

The politicization of Voodoo goes hand in hand with the political status of the Voodoo priest. At times, it has been a question of survival for the church (Deren 1953: 160). From the Haitian Revolution onwards the Voodoo temple has been used to plot political maneuvers and the Voodoo priest has participated along with his congregation in creating political turmoil (Laguerre 1974a). To understand the politicization of Haitian Voodoo during the Duvalier era one must focus on the Voodoo priest's status as a local politician, the identification of the Voodoo temple as a Duvalierist institution, and the incorporation of the late François Duvalier in the pantheon of Voodoo spirits.

Before the Duvalier era, the Voodoo priest was from time to time incorporated into the national political structure by astute politicians to combat or advance a specific cause (Rigaud 1953). Their presence was needed and their help sought for the success of ephemeral revolts in the mid-nineteenth century or even during the US occupation. Until 1950, Voodoo priests played a minor role in the election of the head of state because the president was elected by the Haitian congress and not by popular vote. However, they were more active during the period that preceded the end of an administration. Strikes by university students and the business community were always backed up by the proletariat of Port-au-Prince, most of them connected with a Voodoo temple and some of them members of secret societies. And once an administration had been pushed out of office, Voodoo priests were the first to parade and dance in the streets of Port-au-Prince and organize nightly *peristyle* (patio) parties for the residential community surrounding their Voodoo temples to celebrate their victory.

The Voodoo priest's political role can be appreciated when one understands how territorial and mystical space is divided in Haiti. Each priest or network of priests has control over a certain territorial domain granted to him because of his affiliation with a specific spirit or a central temple (Laguerre 1980a). This domain cannot be crossed over by another Voodoo group. That situation is made clearer when one looks at a Bizango passport, for example. On that passport are written the names of persons and villages who welcomed and honor it.

Duvalier used this network of Voodoo temples to control the residential communities that surround them—controlling one central temple gains one access to all the others. However, a satellite temple in a network may also have an autonomous stance on specific political issues. It is here that one may see the tension between the political options of the center *vis-à-vis* those of the periphery. A local leader may decide for both personal and strategic reasons to further his own interests. More often, however, the priest in the central temple will influence those on the periphery.

During the administrations of both Duvaliers, many Voodoo priests joined the Tonton Macoute force for the following reasons: to be able to operate their temple freely without any harassment from the state, to maintain control over their own domain, to compete with neighboring priests, to provide security for their own congregations, to serve as a broker with the government on behalf of their brethren, to become a prominent figure of authority in the community, to ensure a monthly salary from their job as a Tonton Macoute—or simply because they did not have any alternative.

Here we find a *modus vivendi* between the government and the Voodoo community and its priest. The government allowed the priest–Tonton Macoute to strengthen his leadership role and to practice his religion freely, but at the same time, the priest provided information on the community to the government—which gave the government an opportunity to maintain its grip on the neighborhood. In this dialectical relationship, the Voodoo church became an extension of the government function in the community. There was here a symbiotic relationship between the government and the Voodoo church that helped maintain the ecological balance of power. This evidently rooted the regime very deeply in the local community.

Before François Duvalier became president, the Voodoo temple functioned mainly as a religious and medical center. During his administration, one more ingredient was added to it. Political meetings were held there as well as ceremonies, intended to propagandize the regime. The *loas* were manipulated to speak in praise of the regime and extol its accomplishments. The spirits were also under government control. In Port-au-Prince, the term "Tonton Macoute" and "Voodoo priest" became synonymous in some districts. It was almost impossible for one to be an influential Voodoo priest without being a Tonton Macoute or for a Voodoo church to be successful without being headed by a priest–Tonton Macoute.

As a result, the temple became the place where people sometimes came to seek help, not necessarily from the Voodoo priest as priest but from the priest as Tonton Macoute. If he happened to be the most influential Tonton Macoute in the district, his influence extended well beyond his congregation. Non-Voodooists as well as Voodooists came to see him and depended on him for protection against police and Tonton Macoute brutality.

The politicization of the Voodoo church went beyond the priest's participation in national and local level politics; it penetrated the internal structure of the Voodoo ritual itself. The Duvalierist flag was used when the priest presided over a ceremony. It was also common to see the priest carry a Tonton Macoute revolver on his waist while invoking a spirit and to see other Tontons Macoutes in uniform performing with him. The most profound penetration of national politics in the church was through the canonization of François Duvalier who is now venerated as a Voodoo spirit.

In the summer of 1976, while I was attending a Voodoo ceremony in Upper Belair, I was surprised to see the priest dressed up to resemble François Duvalier—in a dark suit and black hat, wearing heavy reading glasses and holding a pistol in his right hand. He spoke with a nasal voice, imitating François Duvalier's speech. I asked another Voodoo priest who was sitting next to me to identify the spirit for me. He replied that he was *"loa 22 os."* I later found out that, in the Voodoo pantheon, François Duvalier is known as *loa 22 os.* The magical number 22 that he had so often used during his administration seems to follow him even after his death.

The canonization of a government official as a Voodoo spirit is not new in the political history of Voodoo (Rigaud 1953). Throughout the history of Haiti, political leaders have been canonized and venerated as Voodoo spirits.[12] For example, Toussaint Louverture and Jean Jacques Dessalines figure prominently in the pantheon of Voodoo spirits (Duvalier 1968a: 178). For the Voodooists, Duvalier is one such national political hero.

CONCLUSION [TO THIS SECTION]

The Duvalier administration's contribution to our understanding of the structural organization of the Voodoo church is invaluable. By systematically co-opting the Voodoo priests, it has brought the Voodoo church openly into the political process and enabled us to see a series of linkages and ramifications from the nucleization of Voodoo temples.

A Voodoo priest may exert some influence on other priests' political behavior and is often part of a network of contacts. In fact, the urban Voodoo centers with which I am familiar maintain links with peripheral temples. These contacts may or may not be frequent. For example, the rural priest may visit his urban homologue in search of a new cure or may send a patient to him. Rural centers are sometimes an extension of an urban center. In addition, there are in certain Voodoo centers other Voodoo priests who do not own a temple but serve as associates. Thus, a Voodoo priest in Port-au-Prince can influence other priests' decisions, and a clever politician may not have to deal with Voodoo priests on a one-to-one basis, but can rather enlist the help of the most influential ones, as Duvalier did.

One element that became evident in the Duvalierization of the Haitian Voodoo church was that some temples emerged as nuclei of a network, not as isolated although autonomous units. Although the Voodoo church is not as hierarchically centralized as the Catholic church, most Voodoo churches are part of a network.

Voodoo church leaders who do not belong to the same temple tend to compete among themselves. A politician can exploit their weaknesses by co-opting them so as to control their organization. By elevating the status of the Voodoo priest to that of a Tonton Macoute and by enabling them to operate in the open rather than underground the government could better monitor their activities and exploit them politically.

One must recognize here the ability of the François Duvalier administration — not necessarily the president himself, but his entourage — to circulate Voodoo-related gossip in the local communities. This served to enhance the regime's power.

In a country like Haiti, what is important is not the veracity of these stories but whether they effectively project a certain image and perception of the government.

Two exogenous factors also made possible the Duvalier dynasty's manipulation of the Voodoo church. The regime's sympathy toward Voodoo was eased by the insistence of the Second Council of the Vatican for tolerance of local religious customs and the desire of the elite for a slow "Haitianisation" of the local Catholic church. Without this social context, the Duvalierization of the Voodoo church would have met more resistance from the larger Catholic community.

The Duvalierization of Voodoo made the church more acceptable to a large segment of Haitian society—before François Duvalier's administration people were ashamed to speak of their Voodoo affiliation. During the administrations of both Duvaliers, even the bourgeoisie gave Voodoo names to their children as a form of cultural renaissance.

A mutation in the political use of Voodoo occurred from François to Jean-Claude Duvalier. François Duvalier ruled the masses through the use of local centers of power, among them the Voodoo churches. Jean-Claude Duvalier went one step further by integrating these centers into the rural development process. The Voodoo priests and their cohorts were also members of local community councils. Sometimes they played a leadership role within these structures or at least motivated their flock to join this governmental effort (Laguerre 1976b). They evidently continued to use their church as a power base.

One of the major consequences of the Duvalierization of Voodoo is that it is a force to be reckoned with in the post-Duvalier era. The Voodoo church will continue to be a power base in the local community, and the Voodoo priest will maintain his role of broker or middleman to enhance his prestige, power and popularity. Thus, every constitutional president of Haiti will need a functional knowledge of Voodoo if he wishes to become a popular and successful leader.

This analysis of Voodoo and politics confirms the idea that religion can be used in a functional way to politically dominate a sector of society and, in return, that religious leaders can serve as political brokers. It allows us to understand a multiplicity of arrangements of the local churches and their links to the central political system. It also tells us that, in a situation of asymmetrical relationships, both poles are able to take advantage of each other, even though one definitely has the upper hand. Here is an instance where religious ideology was recuperated by the mainstream political system and used strategically to maintain a system of domination and inequality.

Public Policies and National Prospects

The analysis of the relationship between Voodoo and politics reveals the ramifications of Voodoo in both local and national level politics throughout the history of Haiti. During the colonial era, the slave and maroon leaders used the church to give impetus to the liberation movement that was crucial in their attempt to overthrow the colonial regime; more recently, the Duvalier administrations co-opted church leaders in an effort to control their organization and the surrounding neighborhood communities they served. If one may argue that Haitian politicians have always exploited the church to their advantage, it is also accurate to say that Voodoo has used in its hierarchical and regional organization the imagery of the administrative structure of the Haitian governmental system. This is why I consider it important to look at how the state's politico-military structure is reflected in the church's organization. Here is one focal point whereby the intersection between Voodoo and politics can be fruitfully analyzed.

Voodoo today uses various political and military titles that are similar to those that have been used by either the military or civilian government ever since the colonial period—although the government was no longer using some of the titles when the status of the nation changed from kingdom to republic. Voodooists have continued to use them in their church. Once a government title is appropriated by Voodoo it tends to remain functional longer there than in the secular structure or the state—the linguistic categories in Voodoo are more culturally resilient than similar ones found in government. For example, the title of queen does not correspond to any governmental function in Haiti today, but it is still used in the hierarchical structure of the Voodoo church. Although government titles are used in the context of a specific form of administration, Voodoo, in contrast, tends to accumulate both old and new political and military titles. For example, one finds next to the president in the Voodoo church a queen, even when the leader is not using the title king. However, not all past and present government titles are used in Voodoo—some are and others are not.

The early description of Voodoo provided by Moreau de Saint-Méry (1958) points to the existence of a king and a queen as the two leaders of the local church. No doubt this was a remnant of past African practices. Although the existence of the king of France was known by some slaves, he was not considered to be a high priest—a title that African kings held. If during the colonial period the title of Voodoo king was derived from a recent African past, after independence, a syncretism of functions occurred, probably due to the Voodooists' exposure to the reality of the kingdom of Henri Christophe (King of Haiti, 1807–1820). As the old slaves died, the referents to the king's secular functions were likely to be Haitian ones, but those to the king's religious functions were probably still mythic African king figures. This interpretation is based on the fact that the king of Haiti was never the religious head of a particular church so he was not a religious leader but, like the king of France, a political leader with religious responsibilities. Following the change in the political status of the country from kingdom to republic there was also a change in the title, though not necessarily in the functions, of the Voodoo priest from king to president. Even today, the high priest of a Voodoo temple may hold both a political function—as head of a secret society—and a religious one, as head of a church.

Identification of the head of government as a religious leader is not unique to Voodoo. In Palestine, we find Jesus referring to himself as a king or as the lord. For that matter, an entire doctoral dissertation has been written on the political, religious and biblical titles of Jesus (Sabourin 1961). There is even today a Sunday set apart in the Catholic church to celebrate the believed reality of Jesus the King.

Political and military symbolism can be found in the ritual itself, the division of the Voodoo territory, the titles of the spirits and the hierarchy of the church. It is my contention that the history of the Haitian people can also be unveiled through decoding the political and military symbolism of the Voodoo church.

THE GOVERNMENT OF GOD

Since the colonial era, Voodooists have developed their own theological view of the supernatural world, which they see in terms of a complex politico-military structure that operates on a spiritual as well as a human level. The major spirits are known to have a specific function in this government, and each one has a military or political title. For example, General Clermeil is believed to be in charge of springs and rivers, General Brisé is supposed to protect the trees of Chardette, Baron Samedi is a senator and diplomat. Zaka is minister of agriculture and Loko is minister of public health while Danbala is minister of finance. Agoué is a navy officer, the highest ranking member of the Coast Guards. *Loa 22 os*, a Voodoo spirit embodying François Papa Doc Duvalier, is president for life. Ogou is a brigadier general, Sobo is a captain of the armed forces, Jean Baptiste is a lieutenant general. Carrefour is president (Herskovits 1971: 228). Legba is minister of the interior. In Baron Cimetière, one finds the Haitian imperial title of "Baron"—there are several spirits in the Guédé family who hold that title.

In this government, as well as in any military or civilian one, there is a compilation of titles and functions and one does not necessarily contradict the other. It is important to note here that there was an adaptation of roles in the case of the ancestral African spirits; that is, they continued in Haiti the functions they had performed in Africa. In the case of the Creole spirits, they tend to hold the same functions they had while living on earth. For example, Jean Jacques Dessalines, the first emperor of independent Haiti, is now a Voodoo spirit called Empereur Dessalines—he is an emperor in the government of God.

The Voodoo clergy have also borrowed titles and functions from the civilian government.[13] During the colonial era, the priest was known as the king of the group; now he has the title of president. He receives all the honors of a head of state from other Voodooists, and he has an army of both spirits and men to protect the territory under his supervision. One finds also a *honsi* with the function and title of Queen Silence (*Reine Silence*). The *ogénikon* is known as *Reine Chanterelle* (Singing Queen). Probably the most common title in any Voodoo society is the "*Laplas*." This is a post-colonial government title, a contraction that stands for "*Commandant de la Place.*" In the nineteenth-century politico-administrative vocabulary, he was the military head of a region and the government's official representative. The same titles one finds among the spirits are acted out by Voodooists when they are possessed. For example, when Baron Samedi possesses an individual, his "host" dresses up like a diplomat.

The site of the ritual provides a niche where the politico-military symbolism of Voodoo can be decoded. The temple is the place where ritual, mystical and territorial spaces meet and where territorial divisions are structurally reduced under the same roof. The large territory under the charge of the priest and the regional territory under the command of the *Laplas* are here physically and symbolically represented. In other words, inside the temple, the political functions of the state are represented in the persons of various degree holders. Territorial and administrative distances between the priest (president); and the *Laplas* (military head of a region) are reduced and coalesced in the same ritual site. The territorial divisions that make up the political geography of Voodoo are represented by the spirits (or those who are possessed by them), whose respective domain of governance is the sea, the crossroad, the forest, the cemetery and so on.

The paraphernalia used in the temple probably best symbolizes the military imagery in Voodoo. The flag is that of the "society," which is an army unit. The machete used by the *Laplas* represents the sabre used in the nineteenth century by the *Commandant de la Place*. Ogou's stick represents the rifle used during the post-independence era by the *général de Division* or the brigadier General. They symbolize the strength of the government of God to vanquish all enemies.

Spirits and degree holders occupy functions similar to those found in the various forms the Haitian government has experienced: empire, kingdom, presidency for life, military junta, council of government, term presidency and the various branches of government including the executive, the judiciary, the legislative and the army. Voodoo provides us in a very compact way with the political history of Haiti—which can be decoded through an analysis of titles used in the church. We find layers of historical sequences compacted in the titles and paraphernalia used by Voodooists within the realm of their church.

VOODOO SPACE

Before one can start looking into the policy options of the state, one must have an idea of the territorial organization of the Voodoo church. The appropriation of territorial space by the Voodooists is an indication of the peripheral political status of the Voodoo church. However, one must distinguish between ritual, mystical and territorial space. Ritual space can easily be localized, is known by both Voodooists and non-Voodooists, and can serve a private or a public function. As a public space, it can be used by the congregation as well as by the public. As a private space, it can be used only by the spirits, the priest, his assistants, and Voodooists who are invited to do so.

Voodooists construct their mystical space through mental mapping. It is seen as a sacred space with its topography and the places where the spirits live. This mystical space encompasses both ritual and territorial space.

Unlike the Catholic church or state church, whose dioceses coincide with departmental boundaries, Voodoo territorial space intersects but does not coincide with the departmental divisions of the territory.[14] It comprises a set of spatial units that may intersect with one another and that are under the mystical control of Voodoo spirits, the religious control of one or more priests and the military control of a secret society.

PUBLIC POLICY

Throughout the history of Haiti, the state has developed five different strategies to deal officially with Voodoo: (1) outlaw it, (2) physically persecute it, (3) ignore it, (4) recognize it as genuine national folklore and (5) politically exploit the church. None of these policies—or the lack of them—has dealt in any appropriate manner with the issue.[15] I think that we now understand the parameters of the church and are better informed about its structural features to develop a policy that, on the one hand, recognizes and protects the civil rights of the Voodoo practitioners and, on the other, reflects the general sentiment of the nation.

The Voodoo church has always been outlawed in Haiti, a policy inherited from the French colonial regime. President Jean Pierre Boyer officially outlawed the church in his rural code, although this policy was more to embellish the image of the country abroad than to forcefully eradicate or uproot the church. President Salomon, who was himself a Voodoo believer and who used to consult a Voodoo priestess named Reine Ti Bonne (Jean 1938: 30), had opted to officially ignore it. President Vincent outlawed the church and persecuted it with the help of the Catholic church. President François Duvalier—who had the means to officially recognize the church—did not do so. However, he invited Voodoo priests to participate in his government and allowed them to practice Voodoo openly.

State policies *vis-à-vis* the church have never been appropriate because they have not been based on an understanding of the issue but were, instead, responses to external and internal pressures. The views of Voodoo people have never been sought and consequently they have never upheld the state's negative policies toward their church.

Historically, church persecution has always been felt where the secret societies are not well organized. In the Artibonite Département, where they have an underground network of cells, they have been able to protect their temples and memberships—this may explain why the Voodoo church is stronger there than in the south, for example.

Before one can hope to understand church organization and how its functioning relates to state policies, two epistemological questions need to be clarified.

First, one must distinguish the church from its paramilitary organizations—the secret societies—and this is where the "problem" lies. Second, it is unrealistic to believe that there is a Voodoo "problem" in Haiti or that the state can eliminate the church. Voodoo is not a problem, but a reaction to unremitting national problems. Voodoo has developed its paramilitary organizations to "save" the independence of Haiti. Even today they still remain in the eyes of rural folk a main avenue for the preservation of national security against any foreign invasions. They provide safeguards against the appropriation of peasant land by military officers, prominent politicians and the bourgeoisie. They provide the kind of justice that they believe the state cannot provide. Until these problems are solved the secret societies will continue to function as an underground police force and judicial body, although their judicial codes and moral values do not coincide with those of the state. Evidently one is dealing here with a dual system of government: one above ground and one underground. What is the way out of this dilemma? Our goal here is only to clarify some aspects of the issue and not necessarily to provide a set of recommendations.

There are in Voodoo two separate organizations that one must distinguish from each other: one is the church, and the other is the paramilitary government with its judicial body, its army and its network of spies. The church performs its ceremony in the open, and its membership is known to the public. The secret society is an underground organization, and like all secret organizations, its membership, rules and policies cannot be revealed to outsiders. The church fills a religious, medical and recreational function in the neighbourhood, while the secret society has mainly a judicial and police function.

If the state decides to give official recognition or status to the Voodoo church, the latter has to be structurally separated from the secret society. Although there may be good ideological reasons to propose that Voodoo be made a church with a legal right to existence, the same cannot be said of secret societies—unless they were to change their *modus operandi*. However, they will not fade away until the state is able to provide the following safeguards to the Voodooists that the secret societies provide: protection of their land against spoliators, protection from rival Voodoo groups, protection of the community against outsiders' abuses and punishment of citizens who violate the law and general moral rules of the community. One cannot eliminate the secret societies as an underground organization without also eliminating the reasons for their existence.

The state may want to continue to exercise surveillance over the secret societies because they hold the potential to engage in illegal or unlawful activities. Their organizations must be registered with the state: permission must be required if they want to continue to hold evening marches. Of course, to curtail possible fights and retaliation among members of competing groups, these evening rallies must be under state control and the local police must be able to protect those on whom the secret societies prey. Furthermore, they should not be allowed to pass judgment in their underground courts, not even in cases of witchcraft accusation. Finally, people should be encouraged to report without fear for their lives any unlawful activities or threats by members of secret societies.

Official recognition of Voodoo could be beneficial to both state and church. It may lead the Voodoo church to participate in the ecumenical dialogue with the other churches. It may also either trivialize the church by eliminating the shroud of mystery that surrounds it or eventually transform it into a competitive political institution. At the same time, it will allow the state to know more about the day-to-day activities of the Voodoo church. Because the Voodoo church is also a provider of medicine, its medical practices must be under state surveillance: the Voodoo priest currently practices medicine without a licence.

However, official recognition of the church may not necessarily solve the dilemma because there is no guarantee that the church can be separated from the secret societies. For that to happen, the state must be able to provide the local communities with the previously listed protective measures. If the state fails, regional branches of the existing secret societies will probably proliferate. This could eventually lead to chaos and internecine wars and weaken the regular army's ability to protect the citizens of the republic.

So far, effective persecution of the secret societies has been carried out by the US marines, the Catholic and Protestant clergy and zealous members of those churches—but not by the army. In an interview with a soldier-informant in a village on the central plateau, I found to my surprise that the majority of the armed forces there—who serve basically as a police force—hold membership in the Bizango secret society. I was told that this is a common practice throughout the country because at night the soldiers are forced to patrol alone the streets of the village or the city where they reside. They join the secret societies out of fear because they believe that their lives would otherwise be endangered. Furthermore, some members of the army are too dependent on Voodoo for promotion and are much too afraid of the malevolent intent of Voodooist fellow officers to engage in any aggressive activities against these secret organizations. By and large, the army has so far been unable to protect the peasantry against the nightly and sometimes unlawful activities of the secret societies. Since the independence of Haiti in 1804 the peasantry has not yet experienced one single evening without a curfew or a night during which they could circulate freely inside or outside their hamlets or villages without having to carry a secret society's passport in their pockets or purses for protection. The state must liberate peasants from this kind of burden of fear and interference in their private lives.

The Voodoo question is an issue of national importance, for after the fall of the dynastic Duvalier regime many Voodoo priests were killed and their temples destroyed. This is the second time in less than 50 years that their churches have been vandalized and they have been physically abused. Disagreement with the practices of Voodoo is not a valid reason for the persecution of practitioners. Although Voodooists are numerically a majority, they hold a minority status as a religious group. There is an urgent need, I believe, to seek a solution to this dilemma. However, there are so many aspects in regard to the development of appropriate state policies toward Voodoo in Haiti that it seems legitimate for the government to create a commission with the task of further studying the question and providing applicable recommendations.

Notes

1. Data for this chapter were gathered while I was in Saut D'Eau during the summers of 1962 and 1963. A field trip sponsored and financed by the University of Illinois Research Board allowed me to do further research on Saut D'Eau during the winter of 1974. I am grateful to the villagers and particularly to Rev. Freud Jean and M Victor Jean, two Saudolese, for the comments on an earlier French draft of this chapter. I am also grateful to Dr Jean Baptiste Romain, Dean of the Faculty of Ethnology of the State University of Haiti, to Dr Norman E. Whitten, Jr of the University of Illinois, and to the late Dr Vera Rubin of the Research Institute for the Study of Man for their encouragement to write this chapter.

2. On the use of the apparitions in Champs-de-Mars for Soulouque's political purposes, Justin Bouzon writes: "Vers le commencement du mois de juillet 1849, sur une propriété du champs-de-Mars de Port-au-Prince, la crédulité publique, habilement exploitée, voyait des signes manifestes de faits miraculeux qui se produisaient sur un palmier dominant la place. La Sainte Vierge, ayant le divin enfant dans ses bras, faisait de fréquentes apparitions, mais elle ne se faisait voir qu'à des élus. Un jour il fut permis à tout le monde de voir la Vierge. Une feuille sèche se détache de l'arbre et sur la tache qui en tomba, les plus incrédules pouvaient voir le portrait de la Mère de Dieu. On ramassa la feuille fort respectueusement et on l'apporta au palais. Un premier peintre appelé pour tracer les contours de l'image déclara ne rien distinguer; un second, un mystificateur, qui n'entendait nullement se mettre mal avec le Chef de l'Etat, en suivant les marques de l'eau imprimées sur la tache, montra les formes générales de la Vierge, destinées par la nature, puis le manteau et enfin une couronne formée sur la tête . . . Voilà comment le ciel lui-même avait destiné une couronne à Soulouque" (Cabon 1933: 406).

3. Haiti is divided into nine *départements*, 27 *arrondissements*, 118 *communes*, and 558 *sections rurales*. The *commune* is administered by a communal council (*Conseil Communal*), which is presided over by a mayor.

4. In July 1924, Emmanuel Jeannot published a short pamphlet containing useful information on the curative waters of Saut D'Eau.

5. Religion has always been strongly linked with and manipulated by politicians in Haiti. During the Haitian Revolution (1791–1803), ringleaders and maroons used Voodoo as a religious and political ideology to get rid of the French (Laguerre 1973a, 1974a, 1974b). Since independence in 1804, politicians have never neglected to have some prominent Voodooists on their side to maintain political control over the masses (Laguerre 1973b, 1976a, 1980a).

Under the Duvalier regime, Voodoo ceremonies were under government control and Voodoo priest activities were watched over (Laguerre 1976b). The Catholic church itself is not free of government control. Since the concordat of 1860, archbishop and bishops, on the very day of their episcopal consecration, need to take an oath of faithfulness to the

Haitian government. Church rectors need to have presidential approval to be appointed to their new functions. This is precisely to prevent the church from becoming a state within the state (Courlander and Bastien 1966).

6. The Voodoo priest is not simply a religious or medicine man, he is also a political person. He is the locus of "personal power" because he serves as a middleman between his congregation and the Voodoo spirits and of "institutional power" because he is a mediator between the political establishment and his community. While in the former case he plays an intermediary role because of his religious power, in the latter he does so because of his influential position.

7. For a useful essay on the "phenomenon of the appropriation of the cultural manifestations of certain social groups by others in society and their transformation into national symbols," see Oliven (1984).

8. A collection of Duvalier's writings on Voodoo was published in *Les Oeuvres Essentielles* (Duvalier 1968a). See also Laguerre (1982).

9. Lorimer Denis and François Duvalier published studies of Voodoo rituals in 1938, 1939 and 1940 as they were establishing the foundations of the indigenous movement in Haiti.

10. For an account of the anti-Voodoo policy and practice of the Catholic Church, see Robert (1965).

11. For an explanation of the content of that ritual, see Laguerre (1982: 106).

12. Duvalier (1968a: 178) wrote, "Je tressaillis de stupéfaction quand, ce soir du 24 décembre au cours d'un service en l'honneur du tout-puissant Pétro, le dynamisme émotionnel parvenu à son paroxysme, la personnalité du houngan chavira dans l'hypnose et que surgit des profondeurs de sa conscience: Dessalines l'empérator. C'était vraiment lui, le visage farouche, la physionomie fanatique, et tout le corps sculpté en un geste de vengeur."

13. Voodoo is not the only folk institution that borrows the titles of its dignitaries from the government, others have used the same strategy. For example Rara, Mardi Gras bands, secret societies, co-operative labor groups and so on are all organized hierarchically using government titles. Titles such as king, queen, president, general, minister and senator are employed in these Haitian folk instructions.

14. The secret societies are multi-departmental organizations and protect all the Voodoo temples and congregations under their aegis. The territorial division of Voodoo is made up of networks of sites, each network being under the surveillance of a secret society.

15. The following texts against the practice of Voodoo were issued by the Haitian government in the nineteenth and twentieth centuries. In Jean Pierre Boyer's *Pénal Code* of 1826, one reads: "Art. 405. Tons faiseurs de ouangas, caprélatas, vaudoux, Donpèdre, macandals et autres Sortilèges seront punis de trois mois à six mois d'emprisonnement et d'une amende de soixante gourdes à cent cinquante par le tribunal de simple police; et en cas de récidive, d'un emprisonnement de six mois à deux ans et d'une amende de trois cents gourdes à mille gourdes, par le tribunal correctionel, sans préjudice des peines plus fortes qu'ils encourraient à raison des délits ou crimes par eux commis pour préparer ou accomplir leurs maléfices.

Toutes danses et autres pratiques quelconques qui seront de nature à entretenir dans la population l'esprit de fétichisme et de superstition seront considérées comme sortilèges et punies des mêmes peines.

Art. 406. Les gens qui font métier de dire la bonne aventure ou de deviner ou de pronostiquer, d'expliquer les songes ou de tirer les cartes seront punis d'un emprisonnement de deux mois au moins et de six mois au plus et d'une amende de cent gourdes à cinq cents gourdes.

Tous individus condamnés pour les délits prévus au présent article et en l'article 405 subiront leur peine dans les prisons maritimes et seront employés aux travaux de la marine.

Ils seront, en outre, à l'expiation de leur peine, placés sous la surveillance de la haute police de l'Etat, pendant deux ans, par le fait seul de leur condamnation.

Art. 407. Les instruments, ustensiles et costumes servant ou destinés à servir aux faits prévus aux deux articles précédents seront de plus saisis et confisqués, pour être brulés et détruits" (cited in Simpson 1970: 254).

In the article 12 of Président Riché's *Loi sur la Police des Campagnes*, one reads "Tous les individus condamnés par un tribunal compétent pour sortilèges, tels que vaudou, macandats, dompèdres, ouanga, tires-de-cartes, etc. subiront leurs peines dans les prisons maritimes et seront occupés aux travaux de la marine" (cited in Montilus 1972: 299).

President Geffrard in the "Circulaire No. 4034 Aux Commandants D'Arrondissement" ordered them to act "avec fermeté à faire disparaître de notre sol ces derniers vestiges de l'esclavage et de la barbarie et à remplacer ces pratiques superstitieuses par le culte du vrai Dieu" (cited in Montilus 1972: 300).

On 5 September, 1935, during President Stenio Vincent's term in office, a decree against the practice of Voodoo was issued: "Art. 1. Sont considérés comme pratiques superstitieuses: 1) les cérémonies, rites, danses et réunions au cours desquels se pratiquent en offrande à des prétendues divinités, des sacrifices de bétail ou de volailles; 2) le fait d'exploiter le public en faisant accroire, par des moyens occultes, qu'il est possible d'arriver soit à changer la situation de fortune d'un individu, soit à le guérir d'un mal quelconque, par des procédés ignorés de la science médicale; 3) le fait d'avoir en sa demeure des objets cabalistiques servant à exploiter la crédulité ou la naïveté du public.

Art. 2. Tout individu, convaincu des dites pratiques superstitieuses, sera condamné à un emprisonnement de six mois et une amende de quatre cents gourdes, le tout à prononcer par le tribunal de simple police.

Art. 3. Dans les cas ci-dessus prévus, le jugement rendu sera exécutoire, nonobstant appel ou pourvoi en cassation.

Art. 4. Les objets ayant servi à la perpétuation de l'infraction prévue dans l'article 3 seront confisqués" (cited in Simpson 1970: 255).

References

Aubin, Eugène
    1910   En Haïti. Planteurs d'Autrefois, Nègres d'Aujourd'hui. Paris: Armand Colin.
Bastide, Roger
    1970   Le Prochain et le Lointain. Paris: Cujas.
Bastien, Rémy
    1966   Vodoun and Politics in Haiti. In Harold Courlander and Rémy Bastien (editors). Religion and Politics in Haiti. Washington, D.C.: Institute for Cross-Cultural Research, pp. 39–68.

Cabon, Adolphe
    1933   Notes sur l'Histoire Religieuse d'Haïti. De la Révolution au Concordat
            (1789–1860). Port-au-Prince: Petit Séminaire Collège Saint-Martial.

Denis, Lorimer and François Duvalier
    1944   L'Evolution Stadiale du Vodou. Bulletin du Bureau d'Ethnologie serie II,
            no. 12.
    1955   La Culture Populaire de la Poésie, du Chant et des Danses dans l'Es-
            thétique Vodouesque. Bulletin du Bureau d'Ethnologie serie III, no. 21.

Deren, Maya
    1953   Divine Horseman. The Living Gods of Haiti. New York: Thames and
            Hudson.

Désil, Hérold Clothes
    1967   Une Esquisse Ethnosociologique de la Communauté de Ville-Bonheur
            Considérée dans ses Rapports avec Certains Phénomènes d'Ordre Reli-
            gieux. Thèse de Licence. Faculté d'Ethnologie, Université d'Etat d'Haïti.

Diederich, Bernard and Al Burt
    1969   Papa Doc: The Truth about Haiti Today. New York: McGraw-Hill.

Durkheim, Emile
    1915   The Elementary Forms of the Religious Life. London: Allen and Unwin.

Duvalier, François
    1967   Bréviare d'une Révolution, 40 Ans de Doctrine, 10 Ans de Révolution.
            Port-au-Prince: Imprimerie de l'Etat.
    1968a   Oeuvres Essentielles. Eléments d'une Doctrine. Port-au-Prince: Presses Na-
            tionales d'Haïti, vol. 1.
    1968b   Oeuvres Essentielles. La Marche à la Présidence. Port-au-Prince: Presses
            Nationales d'Haïti, vol. 2.
    1969   Mémoire d'un Leader du Tiers-Monde. Mes Négociations avec le Saint
            Siège on une Tranche d'Histoire. Paris: Hachette.

Fahd, Tonfic
    1973   Le Pèlerinage à la Mekke. In Les Pèlerinages. De l'Antiquité Biblique et
            Classique à l'Occident Médiéval. Paris: Geuthner.

Galtung, Johan
    1972   A Structural Theory of Imperialism. Journal of Peace Research 2 (3): 81–117.

Gottlieb, Eric
    1970   Chalma Pilgrimage Pattern. Ph.D. Dissertation, Columbia University.

Gross, Daniel R.
    1971   Ritual and Conformity. A Religious Pilgrimage to North Eastern Brazil.
            Ethnology 10 (2): 129–148.

Herskovits, Melville J.
    1971   Life in a Haitian Valley. New York: Anchor.

Hurbon, Laënnec
    1979a   Culture et Dictature en Haïti: L'Imaginaire sous Contrôle. Paris:
            L'Harmattan.

Innocent, Antoine
1906   Mimola on l'Historique d'une Cassette. Petit Tableau de Moeurs Locales. Port-au-Prince: E. Malval.

Jean, Alfred
1938   L'Election de Monsieur Louis Etienne Félicité Lysius Salomon à la Présidence de la République: Une Séance de Nuit, de l'Assemblée Nationale (23 Octobre 1879). Port-au-Prince: Imprimerie Nemours Télhomme.

Jolibois, Gérard
1970a   Notre Principal Pèlerinage Marial. Le Nouveau Monde, no 1288, jeudi 30 juillet 1970.
1970b   Notre Premier Pèlerinage Marial. Le Nouveau Monde, no. 1290, 1er août 1970.
1970c   Notre Pèlerinage Marial. Le Nouveau Monde, no. 1296, 8 août 1970.
1970d   Notre Pèlerinage Marial. Le Nouveau Monde, no. 1303, 18 août 1970.

Laguerre, Michel S.
1969   Le Sous-Développement Latino Américain. Perspectives Sociales 24 (5): 130–134.
1974a   Voodoo as Religious and Political Ideology. Freeing the Spirit 3 (1): 23–28.
1976b   The Black Ghetto as an Internal Colony: Socio Economic Adaptations of a Haitian Urban Community. Ph.D. Dissertation, University of Illinois.
1980a   Voodoo Heritage. London: Sage Publications (Sage Library of Social Research, vol. 98).
1980b   Bizango: A Voodoo Secret Society in Haiti. In S. K. Tefft (editor). Secrecy: A Cross-Cultural Perspective. New York: Human Sciences Press, pp. 147–160.
1982   Urban Life in the Caribbean: A Study of a Haitian Urban Community. Cambridge: Schenkman.

Lanternari, Vittorio
1963   The Religions of the Oppressed. New York: Knopf.

Léger, J. N.
1907   Haiti, Her History and Her Detractors. New York: Neale Publishing.

Macklin, June
1973   Three North Mexican Golf Saint Movements. Comparative Studies in Society and History 15 (1): 89–105.

Mair, Lucy
1959   Independent Religious Movements in Three Continents. Comparative Studies in Society and History 1: 113–136.

Manigat, Leslie F.
1964   Haiti of the Sixties, Object of International Concern: A Tentative Global Analysis of the Potentially Explosive Situation of a Crisis Country in the Caribbean. Washington, D.C.: Washington Center of Foreign Policy Research.

Marzal, M. M.
1967   La Religiosité du Sous-Développement. Parole et Mission 39: 663–672.

Métraux, Alfred
    1957   Haiti, La Terre, les Hommes et les Dieux. Neuchatel: LaBaconnière.
    1958   La Vaudou Haïtien. Paris: Gallimard.

Montilus, Guérin
    1972   Haïti: Un Cas Témoin de la Vivacité des Religions Africaines en Améri-
            que et Pourquoi. In Les Religions Africaines comme Source de Valeurs de
            Civilisation. Paris: Présence Africaine, pp. 287–309.

Moreau de Saint-Méry, Médéric Louis Elie
    1958   Description Topographique, Physique, Civile, Politique, et Historique de
            la Partie Française de l'Ile de Saint-Domingue. Paris: Société de l'Histoire
            des Colonies, 3 vols.

Nicholls, David
    1970   Religion and Politics in Haiti. Canadian Journal of Political Science 3 (3):
            400–414.

Pierre-Charles, Gérard
    1973   Radiographie d'une Dictature. Haïti et Duvalier. Montréal: Les Editions
            Nouvelle Optique.

Price-Mars, Jean
    1928   Ainsi Parla l'Oncle. Paris: Imprimerie de Compiègne.

Raphaël, Freddy
    1973   Le Pèlerinage. Approche Sociologique. In Les Pèlerinages. De l'Antiquité
            Biblique et Classique à l'Occident Médiéval. Paris: Geuthner, pp. 11–30.

Rigaud, Milo
    1953   La Tradition Vaudou et le Vaudou Haïtien. Paris: Niclaus.

Rotberg, Robert I.
    1976   Vodun and the Politics of Haiti. In Robert I. Rotberg (editor). African Dias-
            pora. Cambridge: Harvard University Press, pp. 342–365.

Roumain, Jacques
    1937   A Propos de la Campagne Anti-Superstitieuse. Port-au-Prince: Imprimerie
            de l'Etat.

Rouzier, Sémexan
    1891   Dictionnaire Géographique d'Haïti. Paris: Charles Blot.

Sabourin, Léopold
    1961   Les Noms et les Titres de Jésus. Paris: Desclée de Brouwer.

Santos, Theotonio Dos
    1968   El Nuevo Caracter de la Dependencia. Santiago: Cuadernos de Estudios
            Socio-Economicos 10, Centro de Estudios Economicos, Universidad de
            Chile.

Shils, E.
    1974   Essays in Center and Periphery in Macrosociology. Chicago: University of
            Chicago Press.

Turner, Victor
    1974   Dramas, Fields and Metaphors. Ithaca: Cornell University Press.

Turner, Victor and Edith Turner
1978 Image and Pilgrimage in Christian Culture. Anthropological Perspectives. New York: Columbia University Press.

Van Gennep, Arnold
1960 The Rites of Passage. Chicago: University of Chicago Press.

Wallace, Anthony F.
1956 Revitalization Movements. American Anthropologist 58: 264–281.

Weil, Thomas E., et al.
1973 Area Handbook for Haiti. Washington, D.C.: U.S. Government Printing Office.

Wolf, Eric R.
1958 The Virgin of Guadalupe: A Mexican National Symbol. Journal of American Folklore 71: 34–39.

CONTRIBUTORS TO VOLUME II

DIANE J. AUSTIN, Radcliffe Brown Professor of Anthropology at the University of Sydney, Australia, has written extensively on class and race and on religion and gender in the Caribbean, with special emphasis on Jamaica. More recently, she has taken up an interest in religion and race in Central Australia.

YVONNE DANIEL, Associate Professor of Dance and Anthropology at Smith College and the Five College Consortium in Massachusetts, specializes in dance and cultural performance in the Caribbean and mainland South America. She has published the results of her original research on dance from Suriname, Haiti, and Cuba.

LEO A. DESPRES, Professor of Anthropology at the University of Notre Dame, is one of the few social scientists to have conducted extensive field research in Guyana and in Brazil. His primary foci are ethnicity, political economy, and the structure of plural societies.

LEE DRUMMOND, Director of the Center for Peripheral Studies, Palm Beach, California, undertook extensive ethnographic research in the Caribbean and mainland South America before turning his attention to the application of anthropological concepts and complexity theory to sectors of American society and culture. His current research includes sports, movies, and belief in extraterrestrials.

FLORESTAN FERNANDES, late Professor of Sociology at the Universidade do São Paulo, Brazil, specialized in the fields of social structure, race relations, and ethnohistory. His pioneering work included extended research with Afro-Brazilian peoples and indigenous Tupi-speaking peoples of that nation.

RALPH C. GOMES, Professor of Sociology and Director of the Ph.D. Program in Sociology of Howard University, specializes in the Caribbean and Eastern South America. He has published scholarly articles about Caribbean society, especially about his native Guyana, in numerous journals and books.

FAYE V. HARRISON, Professor of Women's Studies at the University of South Carolina, specializes in the Caribbean and African-diaspora ethnography; she is also a social and political-economic theorist.

MICHEL S. LAGUERRE, Professor of Afro-American Studies and Religion at the University of California at Berkeley, specializes in his native Haiti and the Haitian diaspora (including New York and San Francisco) and in the francophone Caribbean. He is a widely published author on a number of subjects of Haitiana.

The late FRANK E. MANNING taught at the University of Alberta, Canada. In addition to his ethnographic field research on play, ritual, and festival in Bermuda, he published extensively on these subjects cross-culturally.

DOUGLAS MIDGETT, Associate Professor of Anthropology and Associate Director of International Studies at the University of Iowa, specializes in the Caribbean. His long-term ethnographic research in Grenada and St. Lucia is complemented by a systematic study of black St. Lucians in London.

MICHAEL MITCHELL, Associate Professor of Political Science at Arizona State University, has authored several articles on Afro-Brazilian politics and society. He continues his active field research on subjects associated with blackness in Brazil.

B. EDWARD PIERCE, Associate Professor of Anthropology at the State University of New York at New Paltz, specializes in the Caribbean and in Suriname on the mainland of South America. His focal topics include kinship, religion, and cultural change.

SALLY PRICE, Dittman Professor of Anthropology and American Studies at the College of William and Mary, has conducted (with her husband, Richard Price) extensive field research among the Saramaka nation in Suriname and in Guyane (French Guiana), focusing especially on arts in the African diaspora.

BONHAM C. RICHARDSON, Professor of Geography at the Virginia Polytechnic Institute and State University, has extensive experience in the Caribbean, Central America, and Middle America. He specializes in economy, social conflict, and regional systems analysis.

The late M. G. SMITH taught anthropology at University College, Jamaica, the University of California at Los Angeles, and Yale University. A principal founder of the theory of the plural societies, Smith applied his theory through extensive field research in Africa and in the Caribbean.

JOHN STEWART, Director of the African and African-American Center and Professor of English at the University of California at Davis, specializes in the United States, the Caribbean, and Africa. In addition to his anthropological, ethnohistorical, and literary skills, Stewart is an accomplished writer of short stories and novels.

MARGARET THOMPSON DREWAL, Associate Professor of Performance Studies at Northwestern University, specializes in African Yoruba culture and the descendants of Yoruba culture in Brazil. Her publications deal with the arts in ritual performance.

ARLENE TORRES, Assistant Professor of Anthropology and African American Studies at the University of Illinois at Urbana-Champaign, specializes in Afro-American and Latino/a Studies in the Caribbean and in the United States. She has conducted long-term ethnography in Puerto Rico and Barbados.

NORMAN E. WHITTEN, JR., Professor of Anthropology and Latin American Studies, Affiliate of Afro-American Studies, and Senior University Scholar at the University of Illinois at Urbana-Champaign, has conducted extensive research in African American and Native American settings, principally in northern South America, since the early 1960s.

KEVIN A. YELVINGTON, Associate Professor of Anthropology at the University of South Florida, specializes in the Caribbean. He has undertaken ethnographic research in Trinidad. His research interests include ethnic, class, and gender relations.

INDEX

Abertura Democrática (Brazil), 77–93
Aboikono, Songo, 35
Abraham, R. C., 277n.8
Abreu, Hugo, 82, 95n.14, 95–96n.23
Afonso Arinos Law (Brazil), 116–17, 123
Africa and Africans: Cuban nationalism, 12;
  language and concepts of power, 33; and
  early history of Puerto Rican, 44; cosmology
  of Nengre of Suriname, 221, 233n.9; cultural engineering in East Africa, 338–39,
  357; creative literature and historiography in
  West Indies, 341–43; performance of rumba
  in Cuba, 484–85; Voodoo and culture of
  Haiti, 511, 527, 528. *See also* African diaspora; Ashanti; Kenya, women and informal
  economy of; Maasai; Yoruba
African diaspora, and blackness in Latin America, 15–22
African Society for Cultural Relations with In-
  dependent Africa (ASCRIA), 172–74, 180,
  184n.10
Afro–Latin American Research Association
  (ALARA), 34, 37
Agriculture: economy of Guyana, 164, 169;
  economy of St. Kitts and Nevis, 379–84, 386
Aid to Pioneer Industries Ordinance (Trinidad,
  1950), 396
Aidda Oueddo (Voodoo spirit), 498, 505, 506,
  509
Ajiaco methaphor, and national identity in
  Puerto Rico and Cuba, 285–86
Alegría, Ricardo, 41, 300
Alexander, Jack, 212n.12
Alexis, Nord, 500
Alonso, Manuel A., 294–95
Alvarez Nazario, Manuel, 41
American Revolution, 349
Anthony, Michael, 341
Anthropology: theoretical orientations and eth-
  nogenesis, 181–83; plural society debate in
  Caribbean, 438; analyses of play and sports,
  460–61
Anti-Discrimination Movement (ADM), 174,
  180

Arango, Sancho de, 42
Arawak: slavery in Caribbean, 19; wedding
  practices in Guyana, 201. *See also* Taíno
Arens, William, 31, 33
Aronoff, Joel, 387
Art: gender roles in Maroon society of Suri-
  name, 236, 237–38, 239–44, 250–52,
  253nn.4,7; spirit mediumship in Yoruba
  sculpture, 263–64; Cuban nationalism, 487.
  See also Dance; Literature; Music
Asad, Talal, 455n.2
Ashanti, and cosmology of Nengre of Suri-
  name, 221, 233n.9
Asians, socioeconomic status of in Brazil of
  1950s, 102. *See also* East Indians
Aubin, Eugène, 496
Austin, Diane J., 49, 431n.21, 455n.5
Authenticity, and Black-Soul movement of
  Brazil, 88
Authoritarianism, and pro-democracy move-
  ment in Brazil, 75–76, 84, 85, 90, 93
Autodeterminación indígena, 9–10
Ayoade, J. A. A., 256

Babalola, S. A., 259
Babcock, Barbara, 473
Baptist War (Jamaica, 1831), 351–52
Barbados, and elite of Grenada, 320
Barnes, Sandra T., 261
Barreto, Plinio, 117
Bartenieff, Irmgard, 276
Barth, Fredrik, 160, 162, 181, 183n.3, 211n.2
Bastide, Roger, 6, 273–74
Bastien, Rémy, 511, 513
Bateson, Gregory, 477
Batraville, Benoît, 507
Bauxite industry, 169, 184nn.7,8, 230
Beckford, George, 425
Bedoya, Preciado, 5
Behague, Gerhard H., 278n.28
Beier, Ulli, 259
Bennett, Lerone, Jr., 15
Bentes Monteiro, Eular, 95n.22
Bermuda, race and cricket festivals, 460–79